# LATE ROMAN GLASSWARE AND POTTERY FROM AMARNA AND RELATED STUDIES

ONE HUNDRED AND SECOND EXCAVATION MEMOIR
EDITED BY PAUL NICHOLSON

# LATE ROMAN GLASSWARE AND POTTERY FROM AMARNA AND RELATED STUDIES

BY

JANE FAIERS

with contributions by

Gillian Pyke and Wendy Smith

EGYPT EXPLORATION SOCIETY
3 DOUGHTY MEWS, LONDON WC1N 2PG
2013

LONDON
SOLD AT
THE OFFICES OF THE EGYPT EXPLORATION SOCIETY
3 Doughty Mews, London WC1N 2PG
www.ees-shop.com



British Library Cataloguing-in-Publication Data
A catalogue for this book is available from the British Library
ISBN: 978-0-85698-212-5

PRINTED IN GREAT BRITAIN
*Typeset by Julia Thorne, www.tetisheri.co.uk*
*Printed by Short Run Press, 25 Bittern Road, Sowton Industrial Estate, Exeter, Devon, EX2 7LW*

# Contents

# Acknowledgements

Barry Kemp for preparing plans and a map of the site and surrounding area, and for introducing me to Amarna. Donald Bailey for his support and advice, and for sharing his unpublished work on the glass from the Rathbone-Polemon survey and for the lamp identifications. Gillian Pyke for her invaluable assistance in the field, cataloguing and drawings. Alison Gascoigne for her drawings. Gwil Owen for photographing pottery and glass. Rosemary Luff for information on fish remains. Richard Reece for kindly reading the draft of the last chapter and his useful suggestions. Eva Panagiotakopulu for her comments concerning the last chapter. John Hemmer for advice on the construction of compartmented dishes. Elizabeth O'Connell and Julie Anderson of the British Museum for discussing monastic sites with me. Duncan Schlee for ensuring the careful excavation and recording of the pot slot feature in Room C. The Museum of Romain-en-Gal (Vienne), France, for their photographs of the amphora floor and permission to reproduce these. Michael Faiers for his help and patience during the time it has taken to produce this volume. The Egypt Exploration Society for funding the research at Kom el-Nana and permission to use maps and photographs from Faiers 2005 and Smith 2003. All involved owe a great debt to the Supreme Council of Antiquities of Egypt and its officials, both in Cairo and in the regional inspectorate of el-Minia, for permission to work at Amarna and for innumerable acts of help and co-operation.

Wendy Smith's research on the archaeobotanical assemblage from Kom el-Nana was funded by the Natural Environmental Research Council (award no.GT/94/7/B) and the Egypt Exploration Society.

# Abbreviations and conventions

Cross referencing in the corpora and elsewhere uses abbreviations, some of which are constructed around site names. The explanations for these abbreviations are given below.

**Akoris** H. Kawanishi, *Akoris. Report of the excavations at Akoris in Middle Egypt* (Kyoto, 1995)
**Alexandrie** M. Rodziewicz, *Alexandrie 1: La céramique tardive* (Warsaw, 1976)
**Antinoe** L. Guerrini, 'Materiali ceramici', in S.Donadoni et al., *Antinoe (1965–68)* (Rome, 1974)
**Apa Jeremias** J. E. Quibell, *Excavations at Saqqara (IV) (1908–9), (1909–10): The Monastery of Apa Jeremias* (Cairo, 1912)
**ARS** African Red Slipware
**Ashmunein, 1998** D. M. Bailey, *Excavations at El-Ashmunein V: Pottery, lamps and glass of the Late Roman and Early Arab Periods* (London, 1998)
**Carthage, Salammbo** M. G. Fulford and D. P. S. Peacock, *Excavations at Carthage: The British Mission, 1 (2): The pottery and other ceramic objects from the site* (Sheffield, 1984)
**D** Diameter
**Elephantine X** R. D. Gempeler, *Elephantine X: Die Keramik römischer bis früharabischer Zeit* (Mainz, 1992)
**ERS** Egyptian Red Slipware
**Esna** H. Jacquet-Gordon, *Céramique et objets: Les ermitages chrétien du désert d'Esna III* (Cairo, 1972)
**Gurna** K. Mysliwiec, *Keramik und Kleinfunde aus der Grabung im Tempel Sethos 1 in Gurna* (AVDAIK 57, Mainz, 1987)
**Kellia** M. Egloff, *Kellia III: La poterie copte* (Geneva, 1977)
**LRP** J. Hayes, *Late Roman Pottery* (London, 1972)
**LRP Supplement** J. Hayes, *Supplement to Late Roman Pottery* (London, 1982)
***MDAIK*** *Mitteilungen des Deutschen Archäologischen Instituts, Abteilung Kairo*
**Monastery of Epiphanius** H. Winlock and W. Crum, *The Monastery of Epiphanius at Thebes I* (New York, 1926)
**Nazlet Tuna** J. A. Tyldesley and S. R. Snape, *Nazlet Tuna* (BAR IS 414, Oxford, 1988)
**RBH** Rims, bases and handles
**Sidi Khrebish** J. A. Riley, 'The classification and quantification of the pottery', in A. J. Lloyd (ed.), *Excavations at Sidi Khrebish, Bengazi (Berenice), 2* (Tripoli, 1979)
**Syene** H. Jaritz and M. Rodziewicz, 'Syene – Investigation of the Urban Remains in the Vicinity of the Temple of Isis (II)' (*MDAIK* 52, 1996)
**Wadi Sarga** W. E. Crum, H. E. Bell and R. Campbell Thompson, *Wadi Sarga. Coptic and Greek Texts* (Hauniae, 1922)

A separate set of abbreviations is used for both the glass and pottery. These are explained in Chapters 1 and 2.

A separate set of abbreviations is used for the pottery fabrics. These are explained in Chapter 2.

# Introduction

This is the second volume dealing with the site of Kom el-Nana at Amarna (figs a and b). Archaeological investigation at Kom el-Nana commenced in 1989 when a programme of excavations at the site was specifically undertaken in order to explore the remains of a New Kingdom (fourteenth century BC) temple complex dedicated to Nefertiti by Akhenaten. As excavations moved to the northern area of the site in the 1989, 1993–1994 and 1999–2000 excavation seasons, remains of a settlement dating to a much later period (AD 400–650) were discovered (Kemp, 1993; 1995a; 1995b). Although it may have been tempting to refocus excavations elsewhere at Amarna, Kemp continued to excavate the Late Roman remains at Kom el-Nana.

Initially, the Kom el-Nana area of Amarna was identified as a Roman camp by both Petrie (1894) and Frankfort and Pendlebury (1933). This interpretation of the site was primarily based on the recovery of 'Roman' pottery on site and the identification of a sizeable tower-like structure. Although a recent papyrological study of the Roman military in Egypt still claims that a tower found in the 'Main City' at Amarna (area T34.3) and the settlement at Kom el-Nana are forts (Alston, 1995, 33), excavation results do not obviously support the conclusion that the 'Roman' settlement at Kom el-Nana was military in character. However, Clackson has shown through her work on the ostraca from Kom el-Nana that there was a link between what we now believe to be the monastery and a Roman army camp nearby (Clackson in Faiers, 2005, 248, Ostraca 2).

According to the information available from ostraca, pottery and coins in volume one, Kom el-Nana was a desert-edge monastery named Teclooce, which was in existence for around two hundred years from approximately AD 425 to AD 650.

The recovery and analysis of Late Roman pottery was a major research priority during excavation and Faiers, assisted by Gillian Pyke, was on-site during excavations. Establishing a pottery catalogue of the forms and fabrics was a key objective of the pottery analysis programme. The pottery already published in the first volume was mainly from unstratified deposits, but the present volume contains the stratified pottery excavated from 1992 to 2000 and all the glass available in store from both these excavations and previous unstratified deposits.

Excavations only ceased at Kom el-Nana once evidence for a church on the site was discovered in 2000 (Kemp, 2000, 13 and plate 11, 1; Kemp, 2005). The discovery of the church provided compelling supportive evidence for the religious character of the settlement and brought fieldwork at Kom el-Nana to a close. It is hoped that in the future funding may be available to continue work at the site since about two thirds remain unexcavated.

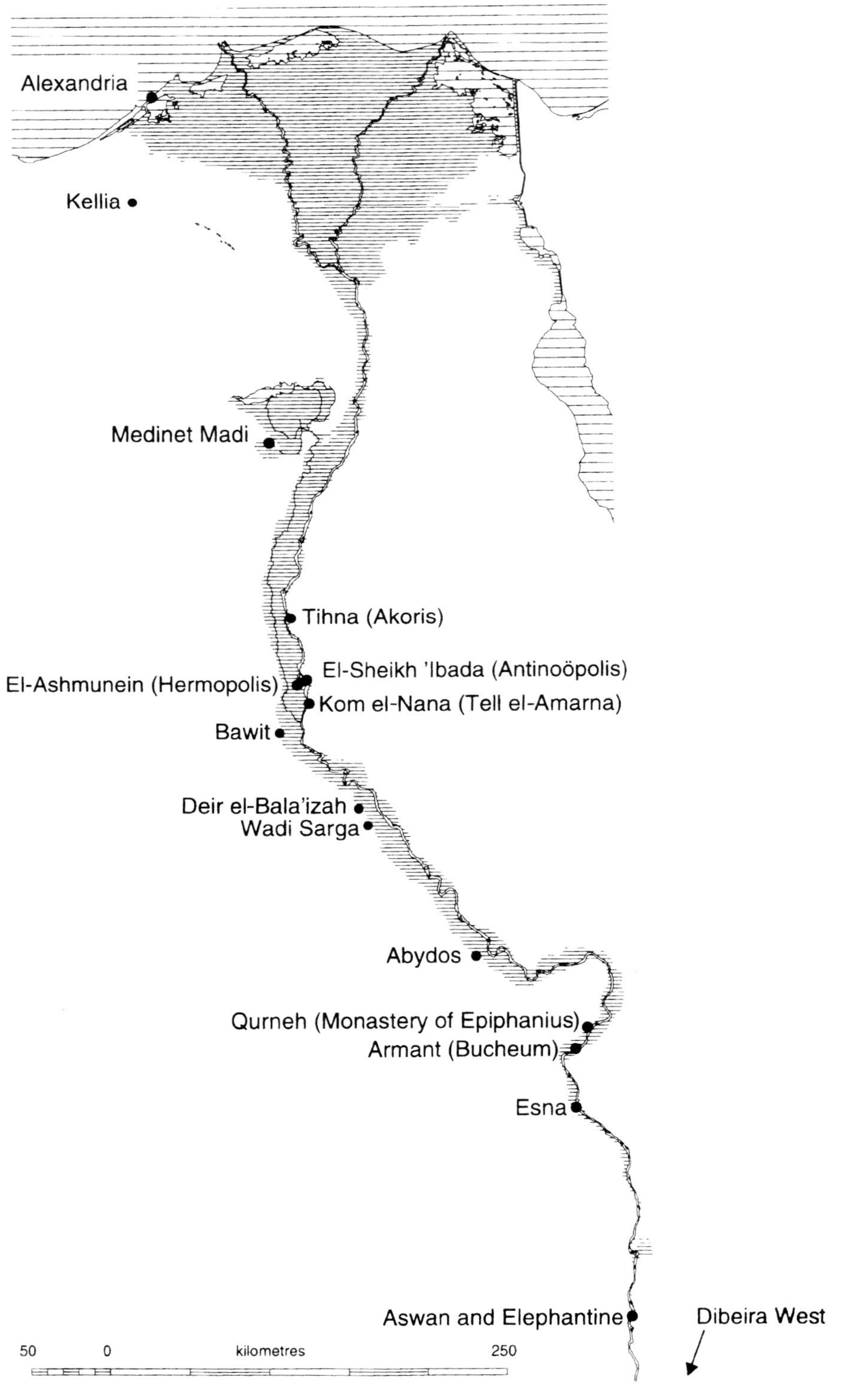


*Figure a Map to show sites mentioned in text*

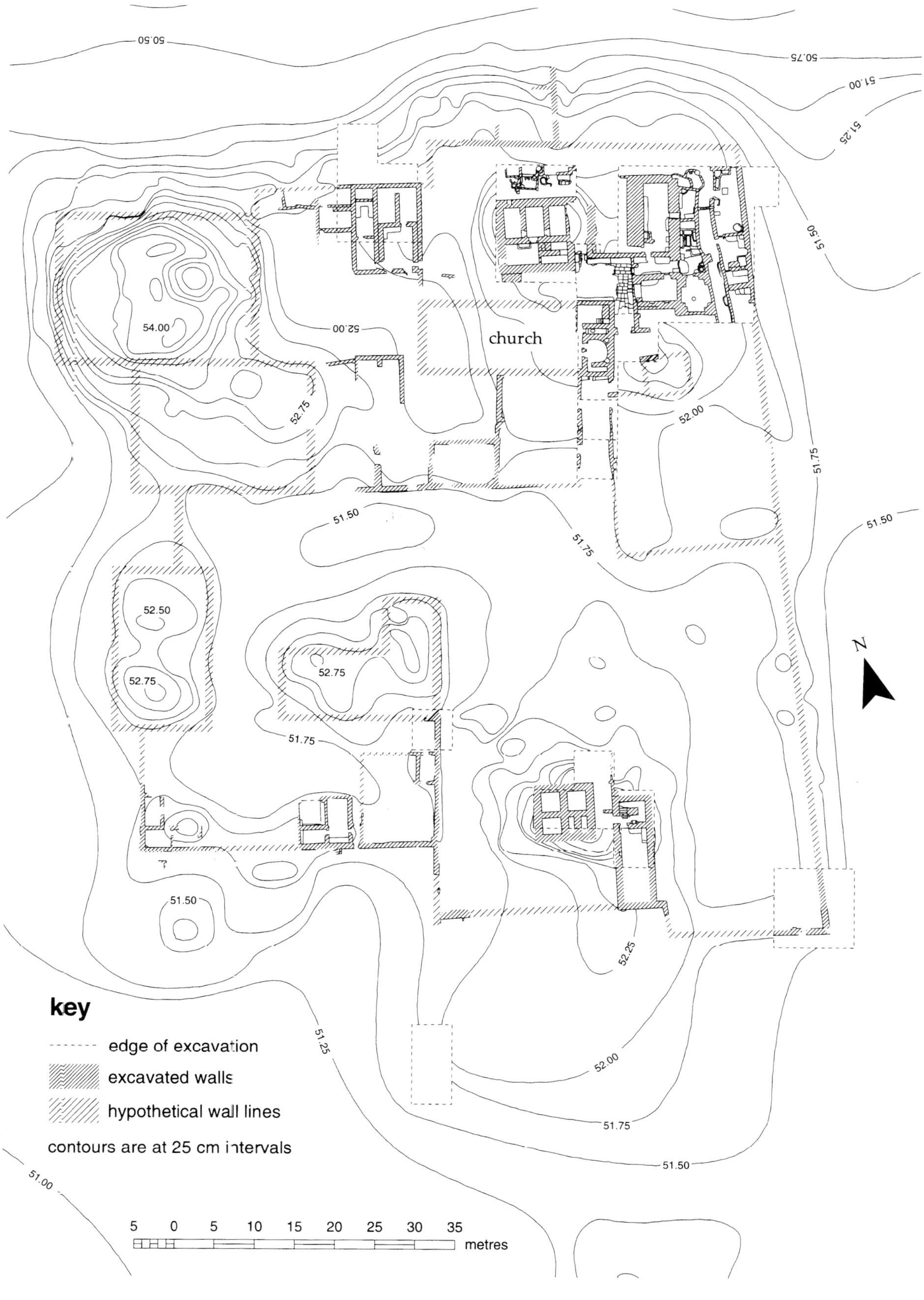


*Figure b Site plan of Kom el-Nana*

# Chapter 1

# The Glass from Kom el-Nana

by Jane Faiers

The glass in the main part of this chapter is the sum total of glass found at Kom el-Nana during the years 1990–2004 and, although 2,219 glass sherds were catalogued, only 657 could be identified by form, and in the case of approximately 10 per cent of the latter there were queries as to the exact form represented. The total was, therefore, was reduced to 592 items, of which 529 were rims, bases and handles (RBH). Altogether, 229 items of these 592 are illustrated here.

The colour of the glass given is that as seen in light transmitted through the sherd.

The predominant colour of glass found at Kom el-Nana (approximately 60 per cent) was of various shades of bluish-green, which is probably the most common colour found during this period, due to impurities in the sand used in manufacture. Colourless glass was produced by the addition of manganese or alternatively by the use of very clean, fine sand. Other colours included yellow (14 per cent), green (11 per cent), colourless (eight per cent) and brown (four per cent), with very small amounts of dark blue, red and black decorative trailing. Two bracelets of Islamic date were of brightly coloured glass, one in ruby red and the other yellow, orange and black. The thickness of the glass dictated the darker colour of some bases although there are vessels whose base is of a different colour to its body, e.g. nos 144, 145 and 157.

Isings notes (Isings, 1957, 26) that, "in the fourth century AD, although some glass of good quality was made, the ordinary household ware as well as table glass was badly made". This is borne out in the fifth and sixth centuries here by the misshapen appearance of some of the vessels from Kom el-Nana, e.g. nos 52, 53 and 78, the goblets in general seeming to be either badly made, hastily made or both. In any case, it is probable that misshapen vessels were used or sold cheaply in the vicinity of their place of manufacture. This begs the question as to where the glass at Kom el-Nana was made and at present there is no evidence for manufacturing at the site during this period, although certain glass sherds in the collection appear to be the dross of glass making. In general, the glass was very thin indeed, more like present day light-bulb thickness, or in some cases even thinner. There was a mixture of mould-cast and blown vessels.

Although these vessels were presumably for use in the monastery itself, decoration or decorative techniques were, surprisingly, fairly common and included: two sherds (not illustrated) of mould-blown colourless glass with small bulges which may belong to a small bottle in the shape of a bunch of grapes (Isings, 1957, 78e); indents, as nos 33, 34 and 206; trails in either colourless, as nos 91–93 and 223, or an opaque colour, as nos 27, 45, 124 and 125; blobs, as no. 29; a mixture of trails and blobs in an opaque colour, as nos 98 and 116; pattern moulding, as nos 89 and 91–93; impressed design, as nos 189–199; opaque coils around the base of a flagon (?), as nos 210 and 211; and a scratched design on the inside base of a platter, as nos 214–216.

Impurities in the glass such as black specks and bubbles were common, but only those more markedly visible are mentioned. The condition of the majority of the glass sherds was good, probably due to the arid conditions, but weathering and decomposition was evident in certain sherds showing iridescence, and others having a hard surface of white or black 'enamel'. Others were flaking. The rate of decomposition may be due to the chemical composition of the glass.

Dating of vessels via parallels can be rather vague as these may rely on site dates only, i.e. in the case of Amorium, the term Byzantine can stretch from the mid fifth century AD to AD 1071 (Gill, 2002, 3: Late Roman–Early Byzantine, mid fifth century AD to early seventh century AD; Byzantine Dark Ages, early seventh century AD to mid ninth century AD and Middle Byzantine, mid ninth century AD to *c.* AD 1071 (the Battle of Manzikert)). However, it is useful to note similar vessels appearing elsewhere, as this gives an idea of the spread of glass forms over a geographical area.

Dating of pottery and coins where they occur in the same context at Kom el-Nana is given with the entry, before any parallels and listed as either Vol. 1 (Faiers 2005) or Vol. 2 (this volume), see Chapter 2.

- Key to catalogue entries: (example, AD [1900]) AD = five-metre-square number on the site; [1900] = unit context number; JF/G/100, JF Drawn by Jane Faiers; G = Glass drawing; 100 = number of drawings. Scale: 1:2

A comparison between the rims, bases and handles of the pottery corpus and the glass corpus provides an insight into the use of the two different commodities on site.

| | **Pottery Forms RBH 1990–92, 1993–4 & 2000** | % | **Glass Forms RBH 1990–2, 1993–4 & 2000** | % |
|---|---|---|---|---|
| Jars | 2,374 | 13.0 | 35 | 6.6 |
| Bowls/basins | 3,688 | 21.0 | 31 | 5.8 |
| Dishes | 860 | 4.8 | 14 | 2.6 |
| Platters | 0 | 0 | 81 | 15.2 |
| *Qadus* | 1,827 | 10.5 | 0 | 0.0 |
| Pitchers/jugs | 84 | 0.4 | 4 | 0.7 |
| Cooking pots/ casseroles | 1,816 | 10.5 | 0 | 0.0 |
| Lids | 318 | 1.7 | 0 | 0.0 |
| Lamps | 24 | 0.1 | 35 | 7.0 |
| Colanders | 170 | 0.9 | 0 | 0.0 |
| Flagons & flasks | 663 | 3.8 | 46 | 8.6 |
| Cups/beakers/ goblets | 97 | 0.5 | 275 | 52.0 |
| ? | 18 | 0.1 | 0 | 0.0 |
| Ladles | 34 | 0.2 | 0 | 0.0 |
| Storage vessels | 78 | 0.4 | 0 | 0.0 |
| Buckets | 17 | 0.1 | 0 | 0.0 |
| Amphorae | 5,188 | 30.0 | 0 | 0.0 |
| Miscellaneous | 36 | 2.0 | 8 | 1.5 |
| | | | | |
| **Totals** | **17,292** | **100** | **529** | **100** |

*Table 1.1 Comparison between Pottery RBH and Glass RBH*

Table 1.1 clearly illustrates the importance of glass in the use of drinking vessels on site. As can be seen, cups, beakers and goblets in glass outnumber those in pottery by nearly three to one. These forms only accounted for 0.5 per cent of the pottery RBH, but 52 per cent of the glass. Flagons and flasks are also well represented in glass, while platters are non-existent in pottery, but are 15.2 per cent of the glass RBH.

## Glass Catalogue

### Platters and shallow dishes

Those found were usually in pale yellow glass. Eighty-one of the platter or shallow dish rim form were identified, i.e. 15.2 per cent, with 23 illustrated here. Interestingly, dishes only made up 4.8 per cent of the total pottery RBH, and evidently glass platters/ shallow dishes replaced pottery dishes where needed (Table 1.1). Two glass sherds (not illustrated due to their very small size), are worth mentioning due to the coin evidence in the same layer; these were:

Platter with looped rim. Olive green. D = 29 cm.
AB51 [7648]. JF/G/172.
Coins: AD 425–50 (one), fifth century (five).

Platter with ledged, looped rim. Pale yellow.
D = 24 cm.
AD49 [8146]. JF/G/198.
Coins: Roman copies, fourth to seventh century AD.

This form, as with many glass forms, remains current for perhaps hundreds of years. The two platters mentioned above, dated by coins to AD 425–450 and the fourth to seventh centuries AD, are virtually the same as no. 1 in this catalogue, which is compared to a platter or shallow bowl from Quseir al-Qadim dated to probably no later than AD 200 (Meyer, 1992, 13), and one from Esna (Jacquet-Gordon, 1972, pl. CCXXXIII, 7), which is dated AD 500–640. The latter date would seem to fit the Kom el-Nana example.

1. Platter with looped rim. Pale yellow. Small bubbles and black/blue flecks on surface. D = 24 cm.
AA47 [9853]. JF/G/1.
Vol. 2, no. 6, African Red Slipware (ARS), AD 300–375 or AD 400–550 (the latter date is more likely).
Meyer, 1992, pl. 7, 124, from Quseir al-Qadim.
Jacquet-Gordon, 1972, pl. CCXXXIII, 7 from Esna.

2. Platter with looped rim. Pale yellow. Very small bubbles visible. D = 26 cm.
AA47 [9853]. Another at AA46 [9837]. JF/G/2.
Vol. 2, no. 6, ARS, AD 300–375 or AD 400–550 (the latter date is more likely).

3. Platter with looped rim. Pale yellow. D = 16 cm.
AB49 [9834]. JF/G/52.

4. Platter with looped rim. Pale yellow. D = 16.5 cm.
AA52 [7649]. JF/G/28.

5. Platter with looped rim. Very pale yellow. Line in rim. D = 32 cm.
AC52 [7645]. JF/G/73.

6. Platter with ledged, looped rim. Pale olive green. D = 28 cm.
AG34 [8844]. JFG/193.

7. Dish with looped rim. Pale yellow. D = 29 cm.
AD52 [7519]. JF/G/250.
Vol. 2, no. 20, AD 400–500/525
Harden, 1936, Class 1, no. 1 or 17 from Karanis, context fourth to fifth century AD.
Kawanishi, 1995, fig. 163, 3, from Akoris, dated fourth to the fifth century AD.

8. Dish with looped rim. Pale green. D = 23 cm.
Y39 [5653]. JF/G/224.

9. Dish with looped rim. Pale green. D = 26 cm.
AC11 [6157]. JF/G/195.
Parallels as no. 7.

10. Dish with ledged, looped rim. Bubbles.
D = 16 cm.
AB49 [8334]. JF/G/177.

11. Dish with looped rim. Pale yellow. D = 18 cm.
AD54 [7402]. JF/G/243A.

12. Dish with folded rim. Pale olive green. D = 26 cm.
AE50 [8393]. JF/G/152.
Harden, 1936, Class II, no. 117.

13. Platter. Pale yellow. D = 20 cm.
AD53 [7502]. JF/G/239A.

14. Platter. Pale brown. D = 20 cm.
Y39 [5702]. JF/G/225.

15. Dish. Pale yellow. D = 24 cm.
Z36 [7432]. The same shape also occurs in Z36 [7559] and Z36 [7460]. JF/G/232.
Vol. 1, no. 76, mainly first half of the sixth century AD; [7559] Vol. 2, not illustrated, AD 425–475; Vol. 2, no. 24, AD 600–700; Vol. 2, no. 25, AD 500–700 or AD 325–525.

16. Dish with knobbed rim. Pale yellow. Black specks and elongated bubbles. D = 28 cm.
AD49 [8452]. JF/G/155.

17. Dish with knobbed rim. Pale brown. D = 20 cm.
AB/AC/AD [8148]. JF/G/206.
Coins: fourth to sixth century AD (four).

18. Dish. Pale brown with red-tinged lines in the glass. Black specks visible. D = 32 cm.
X38 [5126]. JF/G/88.

19. Platter with ledged rim. Pale yellow. D = 24 cm.
AD49 [8336]. JF/G/161.
Coins: fourth to sixth century AD (three).
Vol. 2, no. 30, AD 400–500.
Harden, 1936, Class I, no. 74 from Karanis.

20. Dish. Pale green. Fire-finished rim. D = 16 cm.
X39 [5135]. JF/G/93.

21. Shallow dish with flattened rim. Colourless, but pitted and worn. Inner surface opaque. D = 30 cm.
AB52 [7653]. JF/G/31.
Harden, 1936, Class I, no. 74 from Karanis.

22. Dish. Pale green. Fire-finished rim. D = 24 cm.
AB50 [7790]. JF/G/48.
Jaquet-Gordon, 1972, pl. CCXXXIII, 11, from Esna, site date AD 500–640.

23. Dish. Pale yellow. Fire-finished rim. Very small black flecks and bubbles. D = 16 cm.
AA50 [9807]. JF/G/3.

**Bowls**

Bowls and basins amounted to 21 per cent of the total pottery RBH count, which is more than the 5.8 per cent provided by the glass catalogue. It would seem that fewer bowls were needed in glass, which would have been more breakable.

24. Bowl. Pale green with bubbles. Moulded with a fire-smoothed rim. D = 20 cm.
AA45 [9816]. JF/G/12.
Possibly to be compared to Harden, 1936, Class II, 128 from Karanis, but the Kom el-Nana version is much more clumsy.

25. Bowl or dish. Hooked rim. Olive green with visible black specks. D = 27 cm.
AB50 [7790]. JF/G/49.
Meyer, 1992, 142, 40, from Quseir el-Qadim, before AD 200.

26. Bowl or dish. Pale brown. Moulded. D = 28 cm.
AB46 [9800]. JF/G/55.
Meyer, 1992, 146, 73, from Quseir el-Qadim, before AD 200. Bailey (forthcoming) no. 1260, from Medinet Guran (this vessel had blue spots under the rim). Probable site date fifth to eighth century AD.

27. Small bowl. Pale blue-green with red horizontal trailed stripes. D = 10 cm.
AC52 [8211]. JF/G/82.
Bailey (forthcoming) no. 1299 from Deir el-Banat, probable site date fifth to tenth century AD, but given parallels from Tebtunis which also have red trails (Foy, 2001, 484, 57–8), seventh to eighth century AD and first half of the seventh century AD.

28. Small bowl (possibly a cup or beaker) with inward-curving folded rim. Pale green. D = 10 cm.
Z36 [7432] and Z36 [7457]. JF/G/230.
[7432] Vol. 1, no. 76, mainly first half of the sixth century AD.

29. Bowl. Body sherd only, rim missing. Olive green with dark-blue blob.
AA34 [7670]. JF/G/178.
Vol. 2, ARS, not illustrated, AD 530–570.

30. Bowl with fire-finished rim. Possible lip for pouring. Pale yellow. D = 13 cm.
Y39 [5702]. JF/G/223.

31. Small bowl with rounded, fire-finished rim. Pale green. D = 10 cm.
AB46 [9800]. JF/G/54.
Bailey (forthcoming) no. 1264 from Magdola, probable site date sixth to eighth century AD.

32. Small bowl with out-folded, fire-finished rim. Pale blue-green. D = 10 cm.
AD50 [8781]. JF/G/164.

**Jars**

There were not many jars in the glass assemblage, i.e. 6.6 per cent (Table 1.1), and their function was probably fulfilled by other pottery vessels. Jar RBH amounted to nearly 13 per cent of the total pottery forms (third highest).

33. Jar with cracked off, incurving rim. Pale olive green. Moulded with fluting/ribbing. D = 14 cm.
AC52 [7712]. JF/G/67.

34. Jar with cracked-off rim. Moulded with fluting. Pale green. D = 8 cm.
AF33 [8359]. JF/G/201.

35. Jar with handle(s), possibly a jug. Fire-finished rim. Pale blue-green. Virtually opaque. Ribbed. Folded handle. D = 6 cm.
AA49 [9836]. JF/G/23.
Vol. 2, no. 14, AD 395–640

36. Jar neck. Broken off under rim. Pale green. Bubbles. Approx. D = 12 cm.
AB52 [7653]. JF/G/39.
Gill, 2002, fig. 1/13, 179 and 180, from Amorium.

37. Jar neck. Broken off under rim. Brown.
AB52 [7649]. JF/G/40.
See parallel for no. 36.

38. Jar neck. Broken off under rim. Pale brown. Approx. D = 14 cm.
W30 [5593]. JF/G/101.
See parallel for no. 36.

39. Small jar. Yellow. Tiny black flecks. D = 4 cm.
AA50 [9807]. JF/G/4.

40. Jar with out-turned, fire-finished rim. Pale yellow. D = 8 cm.
AC52 [8383]. JF/G/158.
Coins: AD 527–565 (three), fourth to sixth century AD (21).

41. Jar with out-turned, fire-finished rim. Pale green with black specks. D = 8 cm.
AD49 [8311]. JF/G/150.
Bailey forthcoming; 1,291 from Kom Tifeh; site date *c.* fifth to twelfth century AD.

42. Jar. Very pale yellow. Many bubbles in the glass. D = 8 cm.
AC52 [7652]. JF/G/77.
Gill 2002, fig. 1/13, 164, from Amorium. See also Bailey, 2007, 92 from Mons Porphyrites.

43. Jar. Rounded rim. Very pale yellow. Black specks in the glass. D = 8 cm.
AA45 [9816]. JF/G/24.

44. Jar. Folded rim. Pale olive green shading to yellow on body. D = 8 cm.
AC52 [7712]. JF/G/68.

45. Globular jar. Mid blue horizontal slip trails on colourless body. D = 8 cm.
V51 [8293]. JF/G/119.
Vol. 1, no. 42, AD 500–600. Also found at the North Tombs site about two miles from Kom el-Nana as a surface find. Seen by the author in March 2010.

46. Narrow-mouthed jar with inward-curving looped rim. Pale yellow. D = 5 cm.

Z52 [8518]. JF/G/115.

47. Jar with out-turned, fire-finished rim. Pale green. D = 6 cm.
AF33 [8489]. JF/G/162.

48. Long necked jar (?) with badly finished rim. Pale blue-green. D = 6 cm.
AC52 [7645]. JF/G/70.

49. Jar, possibly a beaker. Badly finished rim. Pale blue-green. D = 10 cm.
AD51 [7570]. JF/G/252.
Coin: AD 538–565.

50. Jar with short, upright, fire-finished rim. Pale blue-green. D = 6 cm.
AC49 [8146]. JF/G/184.
Coins: Roman copies (?), fourth to seventh century AD (two).
Vol. 2, no. 41, first half of the sixth century to the seventh century AD, no. 47, AD 550–700+.

51. Jar with rounded, fire-finished rim. Pale blue. D = 12 cm.
AB50 [8608]. JF/G/163.

### Drinking vessels

It is evident from the lack of drinking vessels in the pottery corpus (only 0.5 per cent), that the majority of these vessels were of glass, as drinking vessels formed 52 per cent of the total RBH glass sherds. Admittedly, some of the smaller pottery jars and bowls could have been used for drinking, but it appears that the preference was for glass. The thinness of the glass would also seem to indicate that the drink they contained was cold, rather than hot. It is also very probable that wine (watered or otherwise) was consumed on a reasonably large scale due, in part, to the questionable quality of the water available. The pottery corpus contained 30 per cent amphorae, of which the majority were Egyptian wine amphorae.

*Goblets*

These goblets of fifth to seventh century AD type appear on many other Late Roman sites in the Near East apart from Egypt, e.g. Amorium in Turkey (Gill, 2002, figs 2/3, 2/4 and 2/5), at Sabratha in Libya (Hayes, 1985, fig. 121, 54–60) and Palestine (Harper, 1995, figs 22, 24, 25 and 26). In Egypt they have been found at Karanis (Harden, 1936, pl. XVI, Class V), Akoris (Kawanishi, 1995, fig. 162, 8, 9, 12 and 14) and Esna (Jaquet-Gordon, 1962, pl. CCXXXIII, 3, 12 and 13). On the other hand, Winlock and Crum in their publication of the Monastery of Epiphanius at Thebes in 1926 do not mention goblets (p85). The British Museum has a collection from Wadi Sarga, about 40 miles away from Kom el-Nana, near Assyut in Middle Egypt (the collection from Wadi Sarga was made by Campbell-Thompson for the Byzantine Research and Publication Fund in 1913–14). Wadi Sarga is of approximately the same date as the one suggested for Kom el-Nana, i.e. AD 425/50–650, but could be a little later, i.e. well into the seventh century AD.

The goblets from Kom el-Nana have solid stems and fire-finished bases. There were no looped bases or hollow stems in the collection. This contrasts with goblets from Amorium, which had both of these characteristics (Gill, 2002, pl. 1/4, 1/5, 1/6 and 1/7). Perhaps this may provide a means of dating these vessels as those with looped bases and hollow stems may be later in date?

Goblets nos 52, 53 and 54 have a parallel at Akoris (Kawanishi, 1995, fig. 62, 12). The Akoris example was greenish-yellow and given a date of sixth to the first half of the seventh century AD.

52. Long stem and large part of goblet bowl with rounded, fire-finished rim. Misshapen. Pale blue-green. D = 7 cm.
AC52 [8410]. JF/G/127.

53. Long stem and part-bowl of goblet. Pale blue-green.
AC52 [8402]. JF/G/129.

54. Part-bowl of goblet with slightly in-turned, fire-finished rim. Probably of the long stemmed variety. Pale blue-green. D = 6 cm.
AC52 [8402]. JF/G/128.

55. Part-bowl of goblet (or beaker) with rounded, fire-finished rim. Pale blue-green. D = 7 cm.
AC52 [8410]. JF/G/127A.

56. Part-bowl of goblet with in-folded, fire-finished rim. Pale blue-green. Slight iridescence. Bubbles. D = 6 cm.
AD/AC50 [8783]. JF/G/159.

57. Rim and part of the bowl of a goblet. Pale yellow, fading to colourless. D = 6 cm.
AB50 [7790]. JF/G/50.

58. Part-bowl of goblet with rounded, fire-finished rim. Pale blue-green. Some white weathering and iridescence. D = 9 cm.

AD50 [8407]. JF/G/134.

59. Goblet with rounded, fire-finished rim. Pale blue-green. Weathered. D = 9 cm.
AD50 [8469]. JF/G/188.

60. Part-bowl of goblet with rounded, fire-finished rim. Pale blue-green. D = 8 cm.
AB49 [8177]. JF/G/176.

61. Stem and base of goblet. Pale yellow stem and base, blue bowl. Joined stem and bowl. Pontil mark. Base D = 3.2 cm.
AB35 [7658] (bowl) and AB35 [7662] (stem and base). JF/G/42.

62. Stem, base and part-bowl of goblet. Pale blue-green. White weathering. Bubbles. Pontil mark. Base D = 3 cm.
AC50 [8325]. JF/G/124.

63. Stem, base and part-bowl of goblet. Pale blue-green. Bubbles. Black blob of glass on base. Pontil mark. D = 3.2 cm.
AA49 [9838]. JF/G/26.
Vol. 2, no. 46, sixth to seventh/eighth century AD.

64. Stem and part-base of goblet. Pale blue-green. Bubbles. Black specks. Base D = 3.5 cm.
Y52, unstratified. JF/G/137.

65. Stem, base and part-bowl of goblet. Pale green base. Pale blue bowl with white weathering and iridescence. Bubbles. Pontil mark. Base D = 4 cm.
AE51 [8395]. JF/G/138.
Vol. 2, no. 75, fifth to sixth century AD.

66. Stem, base and part-bowl of goblet. Pale blue-green. Pontil mark. Base D = 4 cm.
AC49 [8146]. JF/G/112.
Coins: Roman copies (?), fourth to seventh century AD (two).
Vol. 2, no. 41, first half of the sixth to the seventh century AD. Vol. 2, no. 47, AD 550–700+

67. Stem, base and part-bowl of goblet. Pale blue-green. Pontil mark. Base D = 3 cm.
AD52 [7519]. JF/G/247.
Vol. 2, no. 20. AD 400–500/525.

68. Stem, base and part-bowl of goblet. Pale blue-green. Pontil mark. Base D = 4 cm.
Y52 [8512]. JF/G/219.
Vol. 1, no. 59, after AD 500.

69. Stem, part-base and part-bowl of small goblet. Green. Pontil mark.
Z51 [7423]. JF/G/256.
Vol. 2, no. 52, second quarter of the fifth century AD to the last quarter of the sixth century AD.

70. Stem, part-base and part-bowl of goblet. Pontil mark.
AD51 [7631]. JF/G/255.
Vol. 2, no. 45, AD 600–700 or AD 500–600/700.
Hayes, 1986, fig. 121, B57 from Sabratha, given a date of mid fifth century AD at the earliest.

71. Stem, part-base and part-bowl of goblet. Pale blue-green. Pontil mark. Base D = 5 cm.
AD49 [8168]. JF/G/114.

72. Stem and part-bowl of goblet. Pale green.
AB52 [7406]. JF/G/46.
Jacquet-Gordon, 1972, CCXXXIII, 12 and 13 from Esna. Also, Isings, 1957, Form 111.

73. Stem, part-base and part-bowl of goblet. Sea-green-blue. Pontil mark.
AD49 [8308]. JF/G/240.

74. Stem and part-base of goblet. Pale blue-green. Opaque.
Y51 [7418]. JF/G/214.

75. Stem, part-base and part-bowl of goblet. Pale green. Weathered. Iridescent. Pontil mark.
AI52 [8114]. JF/G/203.

76. Long stem and part-base of goblet. Pale green.
AC51 [8400]. JF/G/71.
Ashmunein, 1998, pl. 93, Y66 *bis*, given a date of sixth to seventh century AD.
Possibly to be equated with Bailey, forthcoming, from Kom Tifeh, pl. 4, no. 1252, site date fifth to twelfth century AD. Also near Jaquet-Gordon, 1972, CCXXXIII, 12 and 13 from Esna.

77. Stem and part-bowl of goblet. Pale yellow stem and pale blue-green bowl. Pontil mark. Stem opaque. Bowl clear.
AB27 [5132]. JF/G/59.
Jaquet-Gordon, CCXXXIII, 12 and 13, from Esna.

78. Stem of goblet. Blue-green.
AA45 [9807]. JF/G/25.

79. Stem of goblet. Pale blue-green.
AB52 [7649]. JF/G/29.

X39 [5135]. JF/G/92.

121. Flask with rounded, fire-finished rim. Pale blue-green with pale blue diamond-shaped trailing on body and four horizontal trails under rim. Bubbles in glass. D = 7 cm.
AB51 [7630] JF/G/64.
Coin: fifth to sixth century AD.
Vol. 2, no. 73, AD 500–600 or AD 450–650

122. Flask with rounded, fire-finished rim. Pale blue-green with black horizontal trailing. D = 5 cm.
AC50 [8324], AC49 [8146] and AC49 [8149] JF/G/148.
Coins: Roman copies, fourth to seventh century AD, AD 49 [8146] (two).
AC50 [8324]. Vol. 2, no. 17, second quarter of the fifth to the third quarter of the sixth century AD.
AC49 [8146], Vol. 2, no. 41, first half of the sixth century to the seventh century AD.
AC49 [8149], Vol. 2, no. 42, sixth to seventh/eighth century AD or AD 375–450, the latter context given a validity 'A'.

123. Flask with rounded, in-turned, fire-finished rim. Uneven. Pale blue-green. D = 4 cm.
AD51 [7547]. JF/G/254.
Vol. 2, no. 2, sixth century AD.

124. Flask with knobbed rim. Pale blue-green with black trailed lines. Bubbles visible in glass. D = 5 cm.
Z36 Surface. JF/G/211.
Foy, Picon, Vichy, Thirion-Merle, 2003, fig. 20, VRR 272 found in Beirut. Seventh century AD.

125. Flask with rounded, fire-finished rim. Pale blue-green with black trailed lines. D = 5 cm.
Z52 [7614]. JF/G/212.

### Lamps and bottles

Glass lamps and possible lamp bases in the collection (seven per cent), compared with the very small number of pottery lamps or small bowls being used as lamps (0.1 per cent), seem to indicate a preference for glass over pottery in this form, although the lack of numbers in both pottery and glass indicate that there would also have been forms of lighting other than pottery oil lamps and glass lamps—such as rush lights—available.

Glass lamps were usually hung from a *polycandelon*, which was often made of metal in a round shape with cut-outs in which the lamps hung (British Museum Guide, 1921, pl. 62, 103). There is also evidence from Karanis that a small wooden tripod was used to hold a single lamp, perhaps on a table (Gazda, 2004, p25). The diameter sizes of vessels at Kom el-Nana vary from 6 to10 cm.

Rims of lamps seem to differ from those of beakers, being cracked-off rather than fire-finished, making a cracked-off rim more likely to be from a lamp rather than from a drinking vessel. However, the declining quality of glass and its manufacture during the fifth and sixth centuries (which appears to have started in the fourth century according to Isings, 126) makes it possible that even items meant to be drinking vessels may have had cracked off rims and been carelessly finished. In support of this premise, the same form as nos 2, 3, 5 and 6 in this catalogue is included as a conical beaker at Salammbo (Tatton-Brown, 1984, fig. 66, no. 35, 199).

There were no decorated lamps in the Kom el-Nana collection, although two sherds similar in form to nos 127 and 128 (but with blue blobs on the sides, nos 4 and 5 below) were found by Barry Kemp at South Sector Site S1, El-Arbe'in/El-Hawata. This may well be another monastic site similar to Kom el-Nana, but with an earlier start date of around AD 350–360 (Faiers, 2005, 270).

Some of the small coiled or ring-off pontil bases may well be small bottles, as indeed these can be manufactured in the same way. Not having a complete profile makes it difficult to be certain as to whether the item with this sort of base is a bottle or a lamp. This is the reason for including bottles in this section of the catalogue. Possibly the way to differentiate between bases of lamps and bottles is whether the pontil mark on the base is very pronounced, thus stopping a bottle from standing upright and therefore probably belonging to a lamp which stood in, or was hung from, a holder. It was, therefore, decided to count these as lamp bases. Some of the stable bases are counted as small bottles with the proviso that some of these too could be lamp bases. Differing colours in base and body were found at Akoris and it is probable that a vessel having these characteristics is a bottle, with more care having been taken in the making.

The numbers of these vessels in the collection (figs 1.9 and 1.10) point to their use as lamps rather than bottles due to the large numbers which may have been involved in breakage and replacement during refilling with oil.

126. Lamp. Out-curving, cracked-off rim. Olive green. D = 10 cm.
AC51 [7411]. JF/G/75.

127. Lamp. Out-curving, cracked-off rim. Yellow. D = 10 cm.

AB51 [7407]. JF/G/47.

128. Lamp. Out-curving, cracked-off rim. Colourless with black flecks and pitting. D = 7 cm.
AA48 [9848]. JF/G/8.

129. Lamp. Out-curving, cracked-off rim. Pale yellow. Small bubbles and black specks in glass. D = 8 cm.
AD50 [8158]. JF/G/242A.
Coin: fifth to sixth century AD.
This form was also found at the North Tombs site about two miles upstream. Seen by the author March 2010. Also near Spencer, 1996, pl. 88, 15, from Diaspolis Inferior (Tell el-Balamun). A surface find, probably not much later than the fifth century AD. Foy, Picon, Vichy and Thirion-Merle, 2003, fig. 3, VRR 55 and fig. 4a, of fifth century AD date from Port Vendre, France.

130. Lamp. Out-curving, cracked-off rim. Pale green. D = 6 cm.
Z30 [5523]. JF/G/215.
Also found at the North Tombs site as above.

131. Base of a lamp. Colourless.
AB35 [7309]. JF/G/58
Amorium, fig. 1/2, 63, lamp type 6, no. 24. Isings, 106a.

132. Body sherd nearing the base of a lamp or small bottle. Pale yellow with brown deposit inside.
X39 [5135]. JF/G/95.

133. Body sherd nearing the base of a lamp. Pale green. Base D = 1.5 cm.
AB35 [7309]. JF/G/57.

The following are probably the bases of conical lamps.

134. Coiled (or ring-off pontil) base of lamp. Pale green opaque base and colourless body. Pronounced pontil mark. Base D = 2.4 cm.
W38 [5654]. JF/G/132.

135. Coiled (or ring-off pontil) base of lamp. Pale green opaque base with brown body. Pronounced pontil mark. Base D = 1.5 cm.
W29 [5521]. JF/G/109.

136. Coiled (or ring-off pontil) base of lamp. Pale blue-green opaque base with pale blue-green body. Pronounced pontil mark. Base D = 2.5 cm.
AC50 [8313]. JF/G/120.

137. Coiled (or ring-off pontil) base of lamp. Pale blue opaque base with pale blue body. Pontil mark. Base D = 1.8 cm.
AD49/50 [8452]. JF/G/156.

138. Coiled (or ring-off pontil) base of lamp. Green opaque base with green body becoming opaque with weathering. Pontil mark. Base D = 2.1 cm.
AD49 [8317]. JF/G/123.

139. Coiled (or ring-off pontil) base of lamp. Opaque green base. Pontil mark. Base D = 2 cm.
Z36 [7459]. JF/G/237.
Vol. 2, no. 55, AD 500–600.

140. Coiled (or ring-off pontil) base of conical lamp or bottle. Green opaque base and pale green body. Pontil mark. Base D = 2 cm.
Z36 [7559]. JF/G/235.
Not illustrated, ARS, AD 425–475. Vol. 2, no. 24, AD 600–700. Vol. 2, no. 25, AD 500–700 or AD 325–525. Vol. 2, no. 53, AD 400–500.

141. Coiled (or ring-off pontil) base of bottle or conical lamp. Sea-green-blue opaque base and sea-green-blue body. Pontil mark. Base D = 1.8 cm.
AE52, unstratified.

142. Coiled (or ring-off pontil) base of bottle or conical lamp. Pale blue-green opaque base. Pale yellow body. Pontil mark. Bubbles. Base D = 2.1 cm.
X39 [5135]. JF/G/94.
Ashmunein 98, pl. 93, Y64, small bottle. Sabratha (Hayes in Kenrick), fig. 121, B53, lamp.

143. Coiled (or ring-off pontil) base of bottle or conical lamp. Pale blue opaque base. Colourless body. Pontil mark. Base D = 2.1 cm.
Surface. JF/G/99.
Parallels, see no. 142.

144. Coiled (or ring-off pontil) base of bottle or conical lamp. Pale blue-green opaque base. Yellowish-green body. Pontil mark. Base D = 1.8 cm.
AB29 [5132]. JF/G/62.
Parallels, see no. 142.

145. Coiled (or ring-off pontil) base of bottle or conical lamp. Pale blue-green opaque base. Colourless body. Pontil mark. Base D = 1.8 cm.
AB21 [5441]. JF/G/61.
Parallels, see no. 142.

146. Coiled (or ring-off pontil) base of bottle or conical lamp. Pale blue-green opaque base. Pale yellow body. Pontil mark. Bubbles. Base D = 2.2 cm.

X39 [5135]. JF/G/94.

147. Coiled (or ring-off pontil) base of bottle or conical lamp. Pale green opaque base. Colourless body. Pontil mark. Base D = 2 cm.
AB52 [7406]. JF/G/69.

148. Coiled (or ring-off pontil) base of bottle or conical lamp. Pale brown opaque base. Pale brown body. Pontil mark. Base D = 2 cm.
AC49 [8312]. JF/G/117.
Similar to Bailey 2007, 183 from Mons Porphyrites.

149. Coiled (or ring-off pontil) base of bottle or conical lamp. Pale blue-green base. Pale blue-green body. Pontil mark. Base D = 1.8 cm.
AC49 [8146]. JF/G/118.
Coins: Roman copies (?), fourth to seventh century AD (two).
Vol. 2, no. 41, first half of the sixth to the seventh century AD. Vol. 2, no. 47, AD 550–700.

150. Coiled (or ring-off pontil) base of bottle or conical lamp. Pale blue-green base. Yellow-green body. Pontil mark. Base D = 1.8 cm.
AB29 [5132]. JF/G/62.

151. Coiled (or ring-off pontil) base of bottle or conical lamp. Pale blue-green opaque base. Pale blue-green body. Pontil mark. Base D = 1.8 cm.
AB21 [5441]. JF/G/61.

152. Coiled (or ring-off pontil) base of bottle or conical lamp. Pale green opaque base. Pale olive-green body. Pontil mark. Base D = 2.5 cm.
AB35 [7309] JF/G/169.

153. Coiled (or ring-off pontil) base of bottle or conical lamp. Pale green opaque base. Pale brown body, weathered. Pontil mark. Base D = 2 cm.
AE52 [8185] JF/G/208.

154. Coiled (or ring-off pontil) base of bottle or conical lamp. Pale blue-green opaque base. Pale blue-green body. Pontil mark. Base D = 2 cm.
AB29 [5132]. JF/G/168.

155. Coiled (or ring-off pontil) base of bottle. Pale blue-green opaque base. Colourless body. Pontil mark. Base D = 2.2 cm.
AA48 [9848]. JF/G/7.

156. Coiled (or ring-off pontil) base of bottle. Pale green opaque base. Pale yellow body. Pontil mark. Bubbles. Base D = 2.4 cm.
AA48 [9832]. JF/G/9.

157. Coiled (or ring-off pontil) base of bottle. Pale blue-green opaque base. Pale blue-green body. Pontil mark. Base D = 1.5 cm.
AD49 [8311]. JF/G/243.
Coins: fourth to sixth century AD, fifth to sixth century AD (two).

158. Coiled (or ring-off pontil) base of bottle. Blue opaque base. Colourless body. Pontil mark. Base D = 1.4 cm.
AB49 [8793]. JF/G/121.

159. Coiled (or ring-off pontil) base of bottle or conical lamp. Pale green opaque base. Pale brown body. Traces of sediment inside. Pronounced pontil mark. Base D = 2.2 cm.
Z36 [7459]. JF/G/239.
Vol. 2, no. 55, AD 500–600.

**Miscellaneous Rims**

160. Rim of cup (?) with rounded, fire-finished rim. Pale blue-green. D = 6 cm.
AA47 [9800]. JF/G/13.
Ashmunein 98, 1261. Vol. 2, no. 29, AD 365–640.

161. Rim of bowl or cup (?) with rounded, fire-finished rim. Colourless. D = 8 cm.
AA37 [7348]. JF/G/14.

162. Rim of dish (?) with rounded, fire-finished rim. Pale yellow. Black specks and very small bubbles. D = 8 cm.
X38 [5126]. JF/G/108.

163. Rim of dish (?) with wavy rim in dark blue, superimposed on colourless out-looped rim. D = 16 cm.
AD50 [8145]. JF/G/154.
Not illustrated, ARS, *c.* AD 510–540.

164. Rim of beaker (?) with rounded, fire-finished rim. Pale green. D = 8 cm.
W30 [5598]. JF/G/105.

165. Rim of jar (?) with rounded, fire-finished rim. Blue-green. Very small bubbles. D = 14 cm.
U52 [8693]. JF/G/160.

166. Rim of beaker (?) with rounded, fire-finished rim in dark blue on colourless body. D = 6 cm.

Surface find 1993. JF/G/140.

167. Rim of goblet with rounded, fire-finished rim in pale brown. Brown deposit inside. D = 6 cm.
W29 [5521]. JF/G/145.

168. Rim of beaker or goblet with rounded, in-turned, fire-finished rim. Pale yellow, weathered white with iridescence in patches. D = 7 cm.
AE51 [8395]. JF/G/139.
Vol. 2, no. 75, fifth to sixth century AD.

169. Rim of goblet (?). Pale yellow. D = 7 cm.
Z36 [7432]. JF/G/231.
Vol. 2, no. 76, mainly first half of the sixth century AD.

170. Rim of beaker. Pale blue-green. D = 6 cm.
AC50 [8324]. JF/G/76.
Vol. 2, no. 17, second quarter of the fifth to the third quarter of the sixth century AD.

171. Rim of beaker (?). Pale blue-green. D = 7 cm.
AC49 [8146]. JF/G/66.
Coins: Roman copies (?), fourth to seventh century AD (two).
Vol. 2, no. 41, first half of the sixth to the seventh century AD. Vol. 2, no. 47, AD 550–700+.

172. Rim of cup or jar. Pale blue-green. D = 6 cm.
AB50 [7790]. JF/G/51.

173. Rim of beaker (?). Sea-green-blue. D = 8 cm.
W30 [5523]. JF/G/98.
This vessel was found in an unstratified context. The same form was also found as a surface find at the North Tombs about two miles upstream from Kom el-Nana.

174. Rim of goblet (?). Pale blue-green. D = 8 cm.
AD50 [8781]. JF/G/190A.

175. Rim of beaker (?). Colourless. Black specks.
D = 6.5 cm.
AA36 [7317]. JF/G/19.

176. Rim of beaker (?). Pale olive green. D = 8 cm.
AB/AC50 [7784]. JF/G/173.

177. Rim of cup or jar. Pale blue-green. D = 7 cm.
AA37 [7348]. JF/G/16.
Vol. 2, no. 78, AD 400–550.

178. Rim of beaker (?). Pale blue-green. Very small bubbles. D = 8 cm.
AB52 [7783]. JF/G/35.

179. Rim of beaker or flagon. Pale blue-green with dark blue-green rim and two dark blue-green lines in the glass under the rim. D = 6 cm.
AD52 [7516]. JF/G/246.

180. Rim of beaker (?). Pale blue-green. D = 8 cm.
AC51 [8588]. JF/G/186.

181. Rim of flask (?). Colourless, but blackened.
D = 4 cm.
Z30 [5523]. JF/G/217.

182. Rim of flask (?) with small handle. Blue.
D = 6 cm.
AD49 [8319]. JF/G/242.

183. Rim of goblet. Pale yellow. D = 6 cm.
AB52 [7649]. JF/G/36.

184. Rim of beaker (?) with out-turned bead rim. Fire-finished. Colourless. Iridescent and opaque.
D = 7 cm.
Z52 [7693]. JF/G/222.

185. Rim of beaker (?) with rounded, fire-finished rim. Pale yellow. Black specks. D = 6 cm.
AA34 [7670]. JF/G/21.
Not illustrated, ARS, AD 530–570.

186. Rim of beaker (?) with rounded, fire-finished rim. Pale yellow. Black specks. D = 5 cm.
Z30 [5523]. JF/G/216.

187. Jar (possibly a bowl) with outward-curving, knobbed rim. Olive green. Small bubbles. D = 16 cm.
AC10 [6154]. JF/G/81.

188. Flagon (?) with outward-curving, knobbed rim. Pale green. D = 14 cm.
AD49 [8450]. JF/G/149.

**Miscellaneous bases**

The criss-cross moulded decoration on the bases of nos 189–199 appears for a comparatively short period in the fifth and sixth centuries AD (Bailey, forthcoming, from the Fayum, commenting on pl. 4, 1,242–1,247, all of which have these impressed bases. See also Harden, 1936, pl. XII, 90 and 107). Other similar bases of drinking cups appear in Kawanishi, 1995, fig. 161, 22, dated to the fourth to fifth centuries AD and fig. 162, 14 dated to the sixth to the first half of the seventh centuries AD.

189. Base of bowl. Pale brown. Criss-cross lines impressed/moulded around foot. Base D = 10 cm.
AA34 [7670]. JF/G/22.
Not illustrated, ARS, AD 530–570.

190. Base of bowl. Pale brown. Criss-cross lines badly impressed/moulded on foot. Base D = 10 cm.
AC10 [6154]. JF/G/86.
Bailey 98, forthcoming, from the Fayum, pl. 3, 1,232.

191. Base of bowl. Pale brown. Criss-cross lines badly impressed/moulded on foot. Base D = 12 cm.
AD49 [8168] JF/G/122.

192. Base of bowl. Pale brown. Criss-cross lines impressed/moulded around foot. Base D = 5.5 cm.
AA30 [5132]. JF/G/18.
Bailey 98, forthcoming, from the Fayum, pl. 3, 1,235.

193. Base of bowl. Brown. Criss-cross lines impressed/moulded around foot. Pontil mark. Base D = 5 cm.
AD52 [8599]. JF/G/111.

194. Base of bowl. Pale green. Criss-cross lines impressed/moulded on foot. Pontil mark. Base D = 4.5 cm.
AB35 [7658]. JF/G/44.
Bailey 98, forthcoming, from the Fayum, pl. 3, 1233 or 1234.

195. Base of bowl. Pale olive green. Criss-cross lines impressed/moulded on foot. Pontil mark.
Base D = 5 cm.
Z52 [8518]. JF/G/221.

196. Base of bowl. Pale green. Criss-cross lines impressed/moulded on foot. Pontil mark.
Base D = 8 cm.
AB49/50 [8343]. JF/G/174.
Not illustrated, ARS, part stamp *c*. AD 400–450.

197. Base of bowl. Pale green. Criss-cross lines impressed on foot. Pontil mark. Base D = 5 cm.
X36 [5126]. JF/G/238.

198. Base and stem of pedestal bowl or goblet. Olive green. Criss-cross lines impressed on foot. Pontil mark. Base D = 5 cm.
T/U35/36 [7556]. JF/G/87.
Harden, 1936, pl. XVI, 479. See also Frankfort and Pendlebury, 1933, pl. XLVIII, 4: a goblet from Area T33.4 at Tell el-Amarna. This may be a more complete version of the base given above. Bailey, 1998, pl. 4, 1,242–1,247.

199. Stem and part-base of pedestal bowl or goblet. Olive green. Criss-cross lines impressed on base.
AE52 [8193]. JF/G/256.

200. Base of bowl. Yellow. Base D = 6 cm.
X38 [5126]. JF/G/89.

201. Base of bowl. Colourless. Base D = 12 cm.
AA50 [9800]. JF/G/5.

202. Base of bowl (?). Olive green. Base D = 14 cm.
AB49 [9834]. JF/G/53.
Hurst and Roskams, 1994, fig. 65, 23, no date given.

203. Base of bowl. Folded, looped foot. Colourless. Base D = 12 cm.
Y52 [8512]. JF/G/153.
Vol. 1, no. 29, after AD 500.

204. Base of bottle or flask. Pale blue-green. Small bubbles. Base D = 4.5 cm.
AA37 [7429]. JF/G/15.
Esna, pl. CCXXXIII, 4.

205. Base of bottle or jar. Colourless. Base D = approx 5 cm.
W30 [5697]. JF/G/166.

206. Base of bottle or flask. Colourless. Indentations visible on body. Pontil mark. Base D = 3 cm.
AC50 [8314]. JF/G/157.
Coin: fourth to fifth century AD.
Bailey, 2007, fig. 8.10, 83, no date given.

207. Base of beaker or jar (?). Rounded. Pale blue-green. D = approx. 4 cm.
AD51 [7547]. JF/G/79.
Vol. 2, no. 2, sixth century AD.

208. Base of bottle or flask. Pale green. Base D = 4 cm.
AC51 [7403]. JF/G/72.

209. Base of bottle. Pale yellow. Base D = 6 cm.
Y30 [5523]. JF/G/102.

210. Base of flagon (?). Blue-green. Spiral of glass trailed around base. Base D = 5 cm.
W30 [5523]. JF/G/97.

211. Base of flagon. Pale green. Spiral of glass trailed around base. Base D = 7 cm.
AD52 [7787]. JF/G/248.
Vol. 2, no. 26, AD 500–600.

212. Base of platter (?). Pale blue-green.
Base D = 15 cm.
AB52 [7782]. JF/G/33.

213. Base of bottle (?). Sea-green-blue. Raised pontil mark. Base D = 3 cm.
AD51 [7547]. JF/G/251.
Vol. 2, no. 2, sixth century AD.

214. Body sherd of base of platter (?). Pale green. Etching on inner surface of glass.
Z36 [7459]. JF/G/257.
Vol. 2, no. 55, AD 500–600.

215. Body sherd of base of platter (?). Pale blue-green. Etching on inner surface of glass.
U52 [8684]. JF/G/205.

**Miscellaneous**

216. Body sherds (two joining). Pale green. Incised or scratched design.
AD49 [8311]. JF/G/189.
Coins: fourth to sixth century AD, fifth to sixth century AD (two).
Parallel as no. 217.

217. Body sherds (four joining). Brown. Incised or scratched design. Possibly part of the base of a platter as 214 and 215 above.
AB51 [8604], AC51 [7514], AC51 [8207] and AD51 [7547]. JF/G/74.
Apa Jeremias, pl. LII, no. 4, second from left.

218. Body sherd. Pale yellow. Circular indentations.
AD49 [8320]. JF/G/190.
Coins: fourth to fifth century AD, fourth to sixth century AD (two).

219. Body sherd. Pale blue-green with red trailed design.
AD51 [7567]. JF/G/253.

220. Body sherd. Pale blue-green with pale blue trailed design. Possibly part of a flagon as no. 121, Flagons and Flasks, JF/G/64.
AB52 [7309]. JF/G/170.

221. Rim of small vessel. Pale blue-green. Uneven.
D = 3 cm.
AD49 [8168]. JF/G/191.

222. Neck and part-body of bottle/flask (?). Pale green.
AD50 [8169]. JF/G/116.
Coin: fourth to sixth century AD (one fragment).

223. Neck of bottle or flask. Pale green. Applied horizontal trails.
AB49 [8175]. JF/G/183.

224. Base of a lamp (?). Pale green. Opaque.
W50 Surface. JF/G/131.
Foy, Picon, Vichy, Thirion-Merle, 66, VRR269.

225. Handle. Pale green. Opaque.
U51 [8196]. JF/G/207.

226. Handle joined to Body sherd. Pale olive green. Fluted body. Possibly a bowl.
AC52 (7712). JF/G/67A

227. Part handle (?). Pale green. Opaque.
AB29 [5132]. JF/G/167.

228. Bead. Dark blue. Opaque. Twisted. Approx. 2 cm.
AC51 [8400]. JF/G/113.
This bead appears to be similar to the three found at the Monastery of Epiphanius at Thebes (Winlock and Crum, 1926, 95, which were also 2 cm in size).

229. Bracelet in moulded glass with faceting. Ruby red. Opaque. D = approx. 7 cm.
AA28 [5133]. JF/G/17.
Islamic.

230. Bracelet. Dark yellow centre with twisted coil, yellow and orange on either side and black on outer edges. All opaque. D = 7 cm.
V51 [8691]. JF/G/133.
Islamic. See Meyer, 1992, pl. 20, 570–571.

## The Glass from El-Arbe'in/El Hawata

The glass in this section was collected and drawn in 1977 by Barry Kemp. This site may be another monastic site and is situated approximately 4 km away from Kom el-Nana (Faiers, 2005, Site 1).

**Goblets**

1. Stem and part-bowl of goblet.
As no. 77 in catalogue of glass from Kom el-Nana.
Jacquet-Gordon, 1972, CCXXXIII, 12 and 13 from Esna.

2. Part-stem and base of bowl of goblet.

As no. 73 in above catalogue of glass from Kom el-Nana.

**Flagons**

3. Flagon rim, folded and fire-finished (?)
See nos 104 and 111 in above catalogue of glass from Kom el-Nana.

**Lamps**

4. Rim of lamp glass or beaker, fire-finished with decoration of blue (?) glass blobs.
Ashmunein 98,Y38, pl. 93, sixth to eighth century AD. Foy, Picon, Vichy, Thirion-Merle, 2003, fig. 3, VRR5 and fig. 4, of fifth century AD date. Kawanishi, 1995, fig. 161, 21 from Akoris. No date given. Harden, 1936, pl. XVI, Class 6.

5. Rim of lamp glass or beaker, fire-finished with decoration of blue (?) glass blobs in the glass.
Parallels as no. 4.

6. Rim of lamp glass or beaker, cracked off (?) with decoration of blue (?) glass blobs in the glass.
Parallels as no. 4.

7. Rim of lamp glass or beaker. Fire-finished.
Harden, 1936, pl. XVI, Class 6.

For nos 8, 9 and 10 see comments before section on lamps in preceding Kom el-Nana Glass Catalogue. Also bases of lamps or bottles in that catalogue.

8. Coiled (or ring-off pontil) base of lamp or small bottle. Probably a small bottle as the base is very level.

9. Coiled(or ring-off pontil) base of lamp or small bottle. Probably a lamp base.

10. Coiled (or ring-off pontil) base of lamp.

**Miscellaneous**

11. Base of bottle or flask.

12. Base of bowl with rolled foot.
The same form was also found as a surface find at the North Tombs site about two miles upstream from Kom el-Nana. See Harden, 1936, 215ff, which shows coil bases for flasks and jugs of the fourth century AD, and later, found in Egypt. Isings, 1957, 149f, 120a. See also Tatton-Brown, 1985, fig. 68, 100–102 from Carthage, Salambo. No date given.

13. Base of small bowl. Impressed on foot.
See comments before Miscellaneous bases in the Kom el-Nana Glass Catalogue above.

14. Body sherd towards the base of a small bottle.

15. Body sherd with decoration.

16. Body sherd with decoration.

17. Body sherd with decoration.

18. Body sherd with decoration.

19. Body sherd with trailed decoration (?). Very similar to the decoration on nos 98 and 121 in the Kom el-Nana Glass Catalogue above.

20. Body sherd with trailed decoration.

21. Body sherd with trailed decoration.

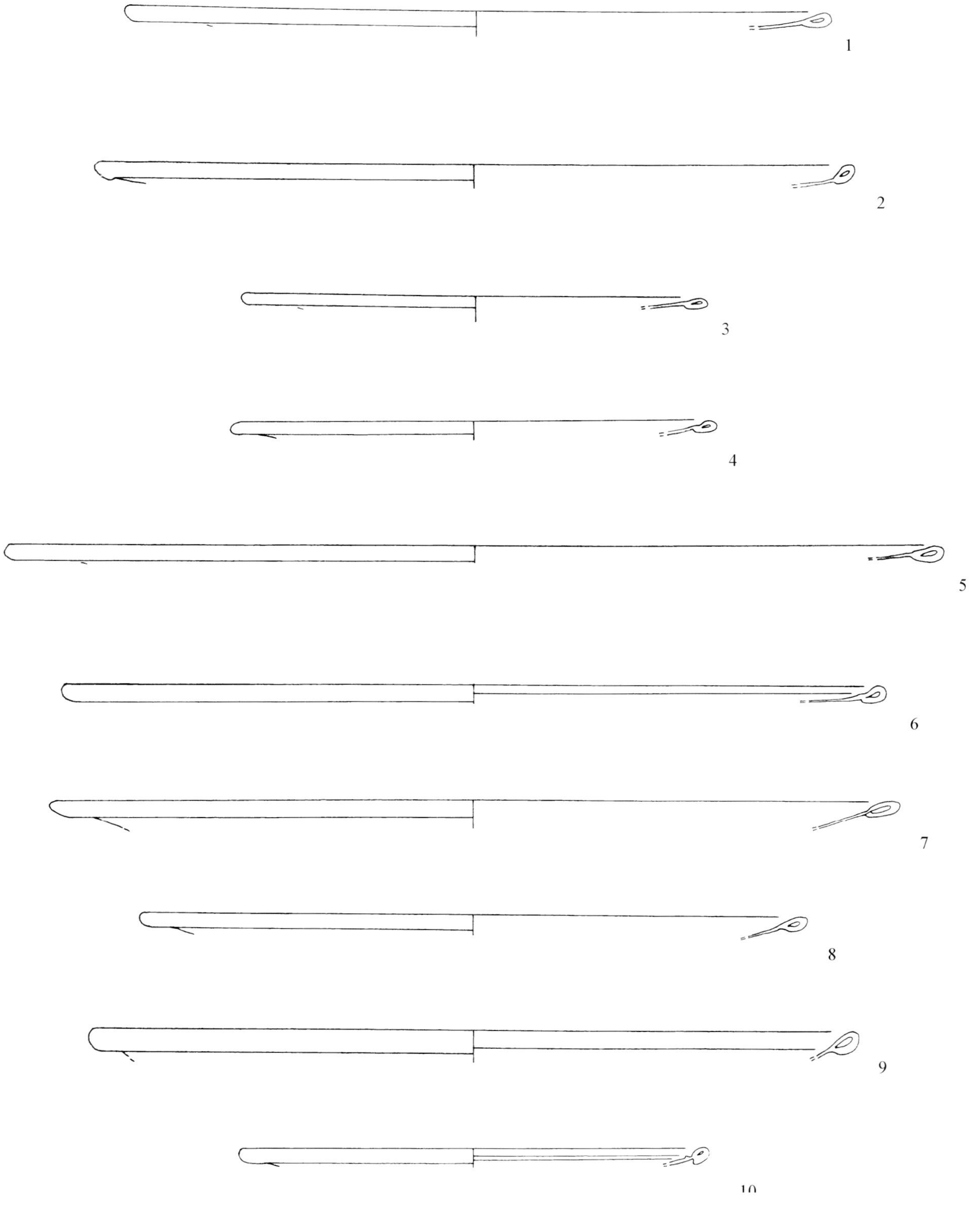


*Figure 1.1 Glass platters and dishes, nos 1–10. Scale 1:2*

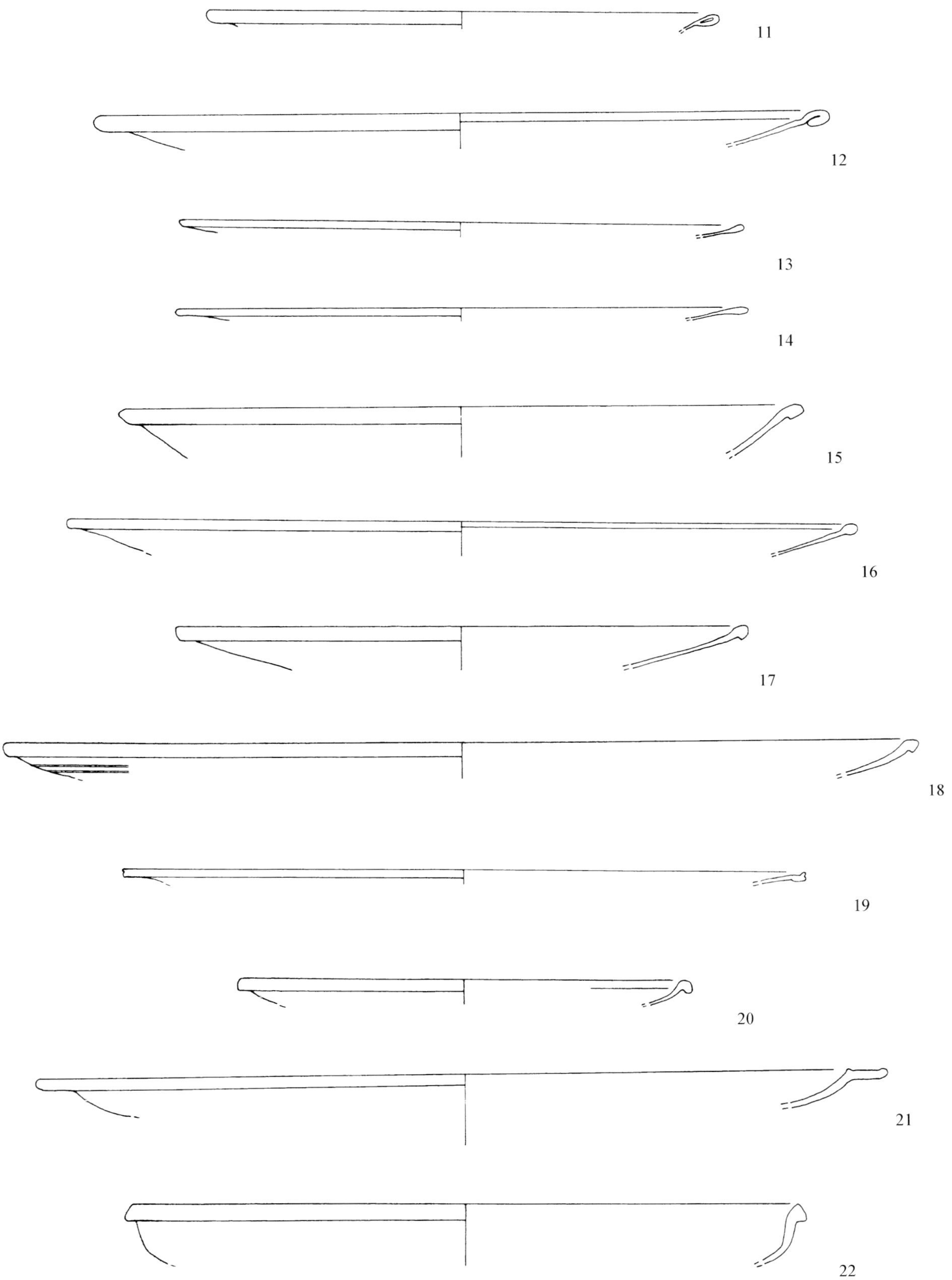


*Figure 1.2 Glass platters and dishes, nos 11–22. Scale 1:2*

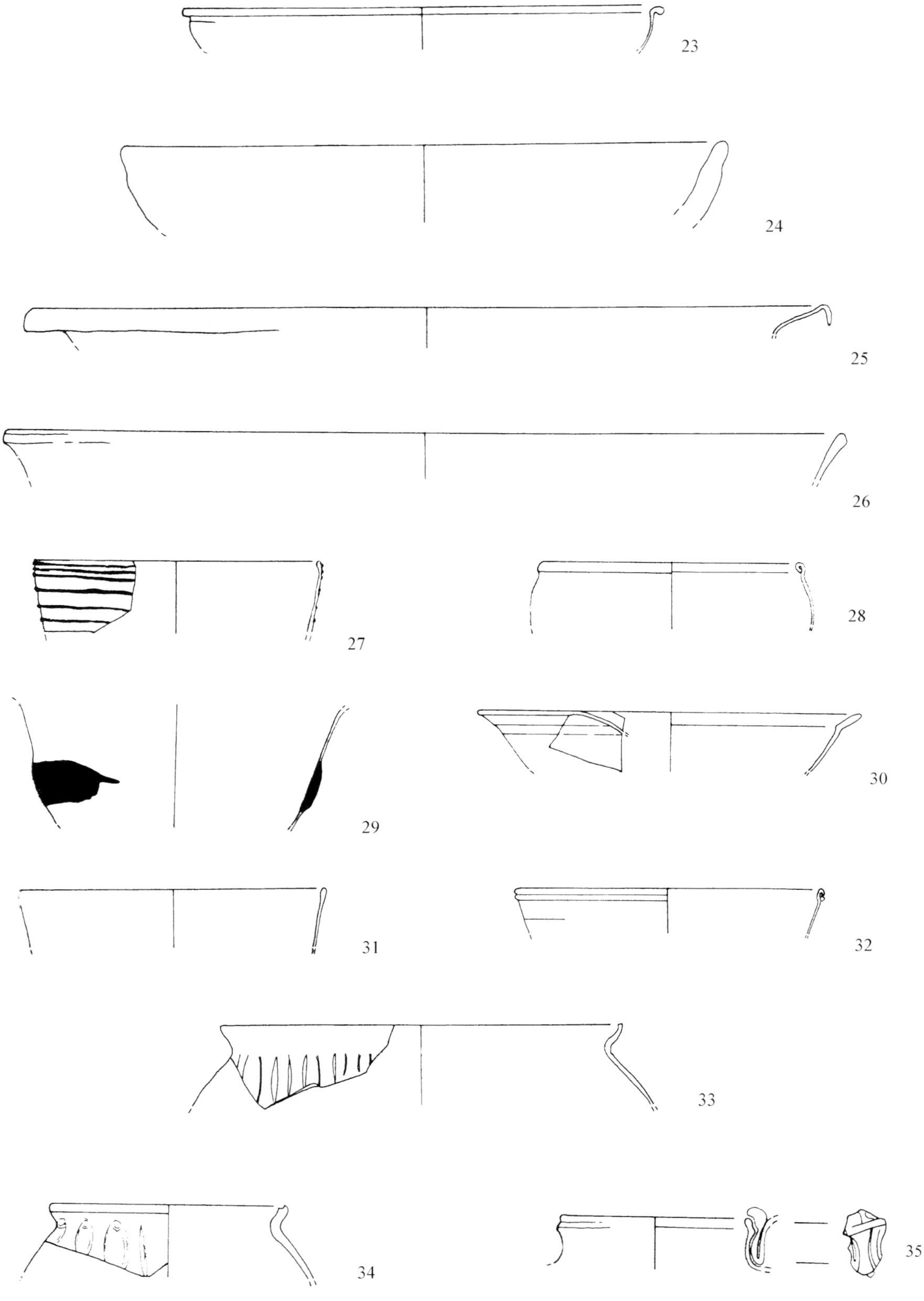


*Figure 1.3 Glass dishes and bowls, nos 23–32, and jars, nos 33–35. Scale 1:2*

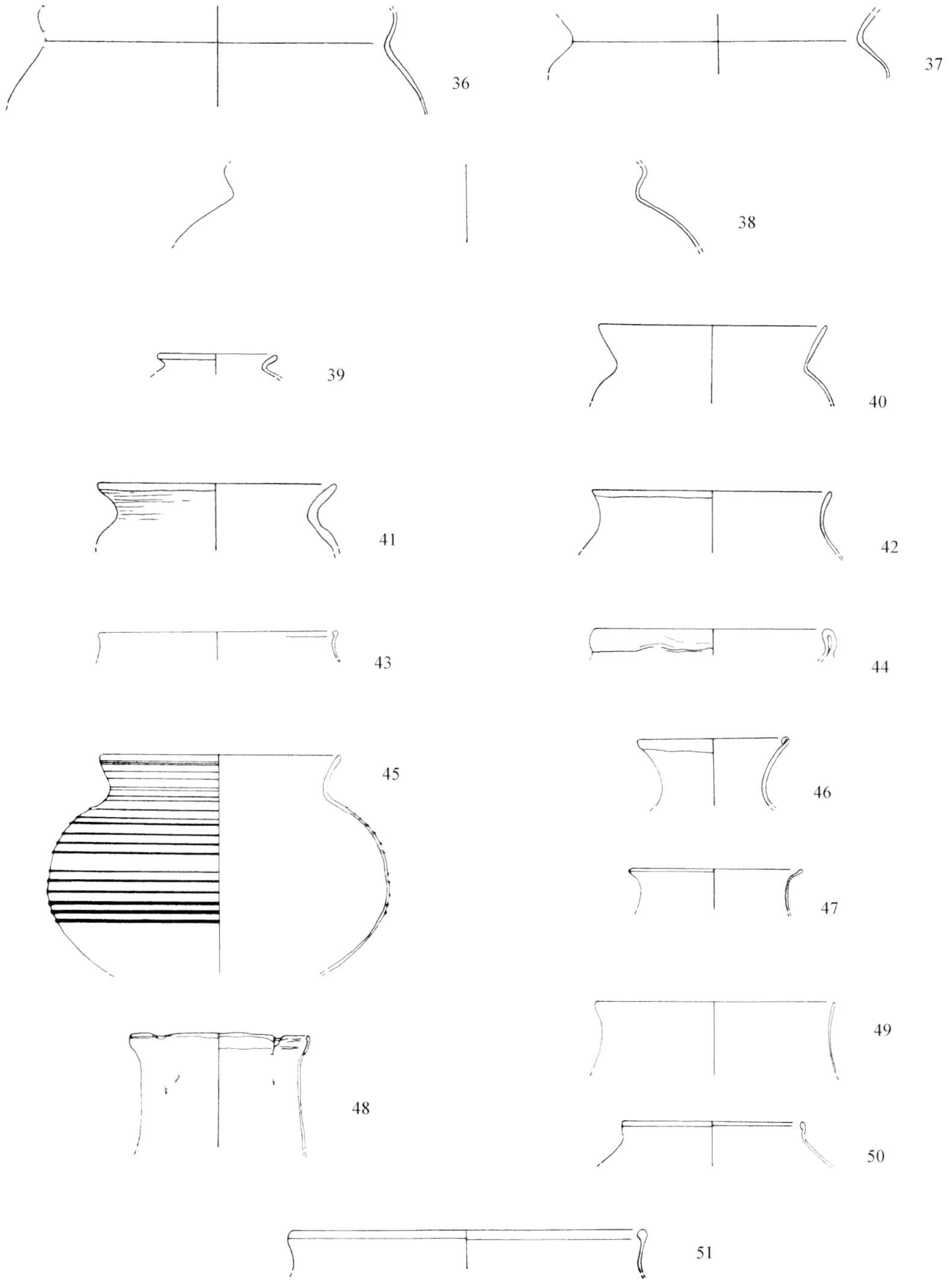


*Figure 1.4 Glass jars, nos 36–51. Scale 1:2*

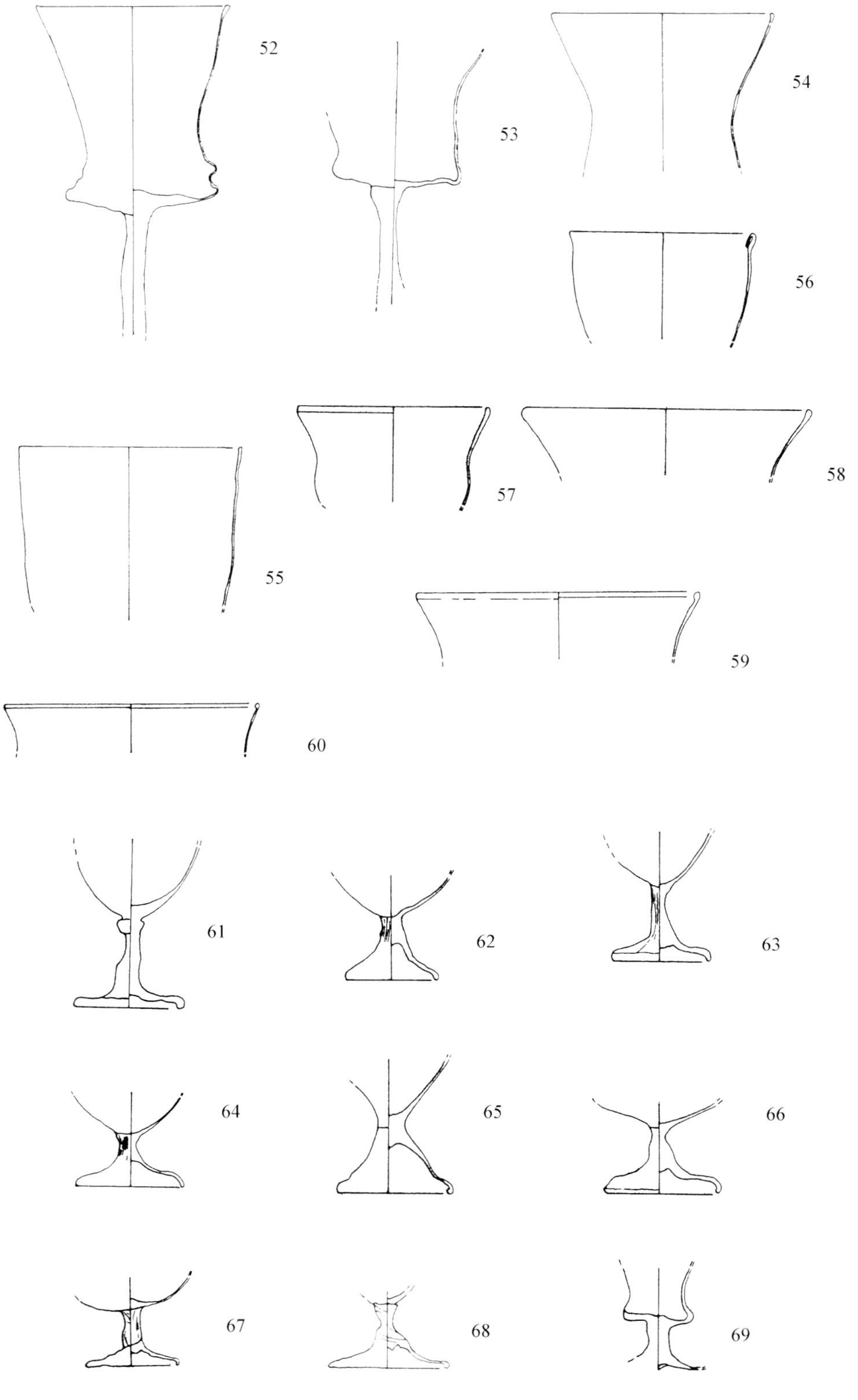


*Figure 1.5 Glass goblets, nos 52–69. Scale 1:2*

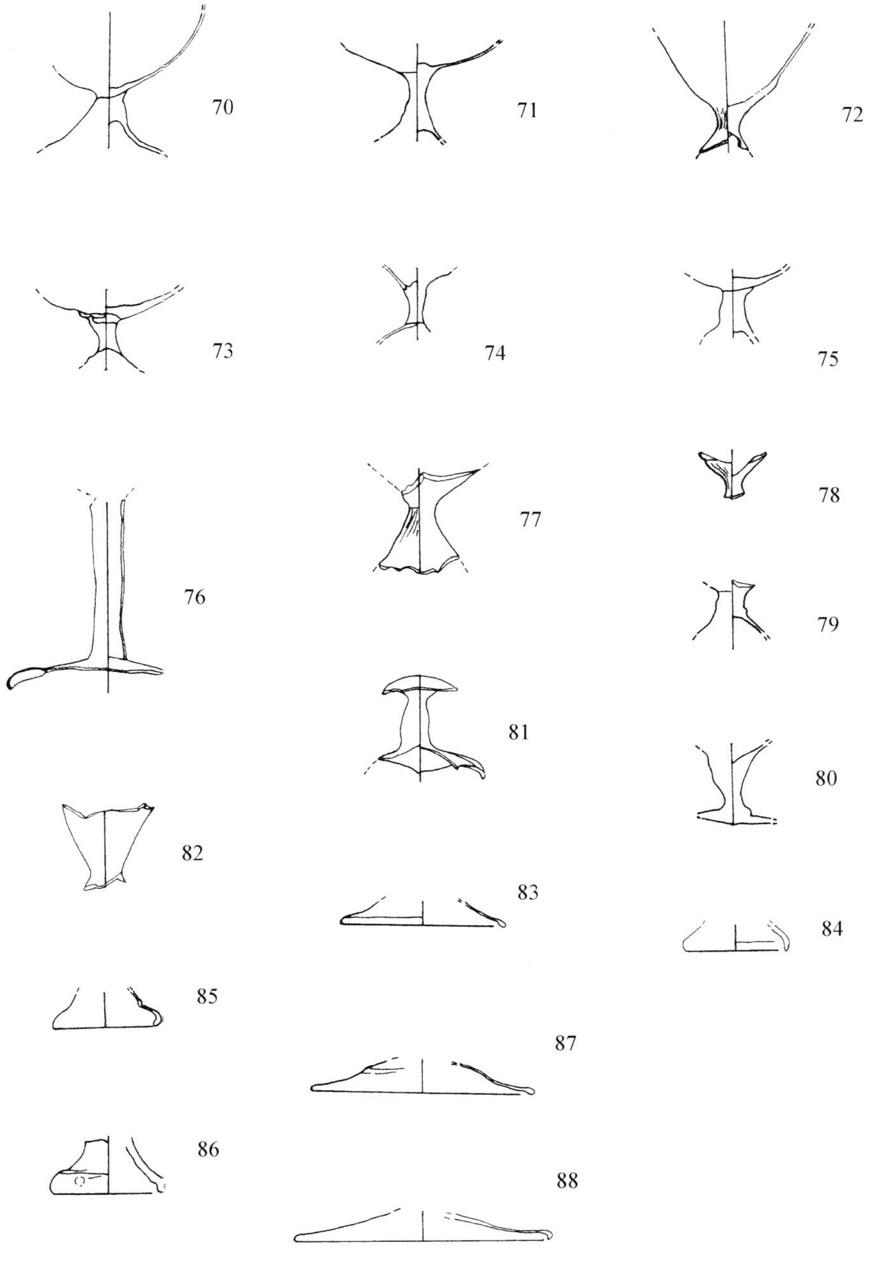


*Figure 1.6 Glass goblets, nos 70–88. Scale 1:2*

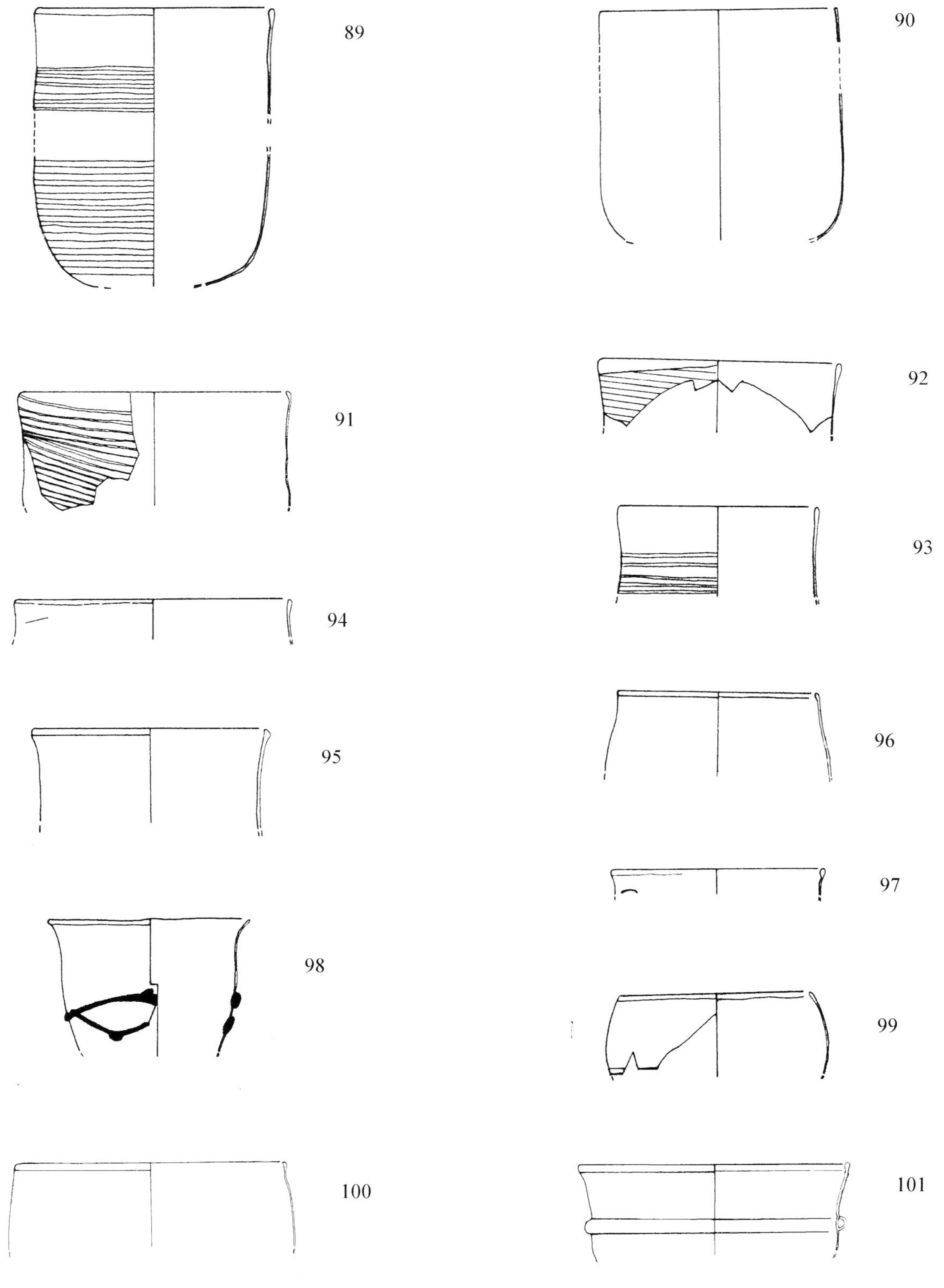


*Figure 1.7 Glass beakers, nos 89–101. Scale 1:2*

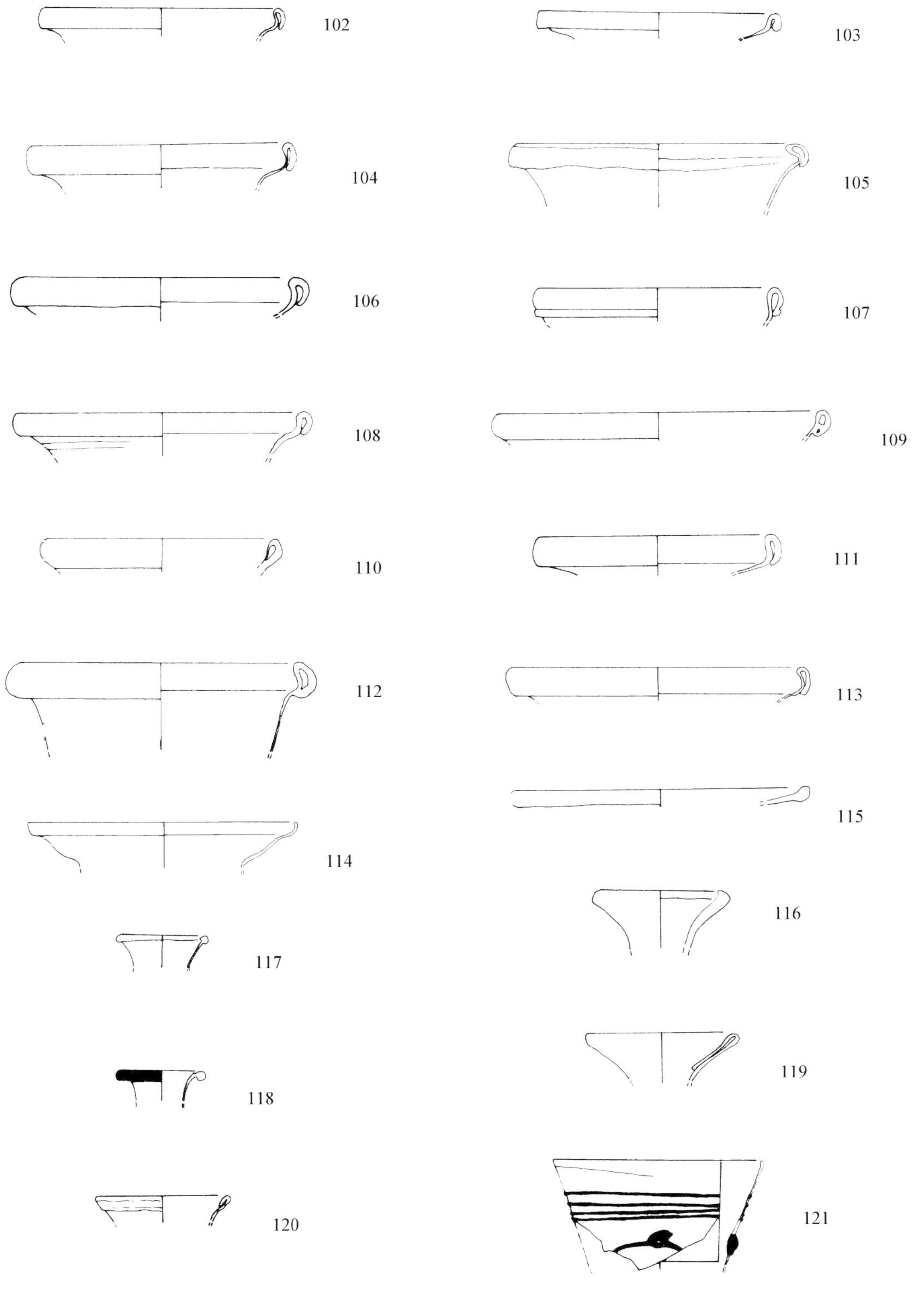


*Figure 1.8 Glass flagons and flasks, nos 102–121. Scale 1:2*

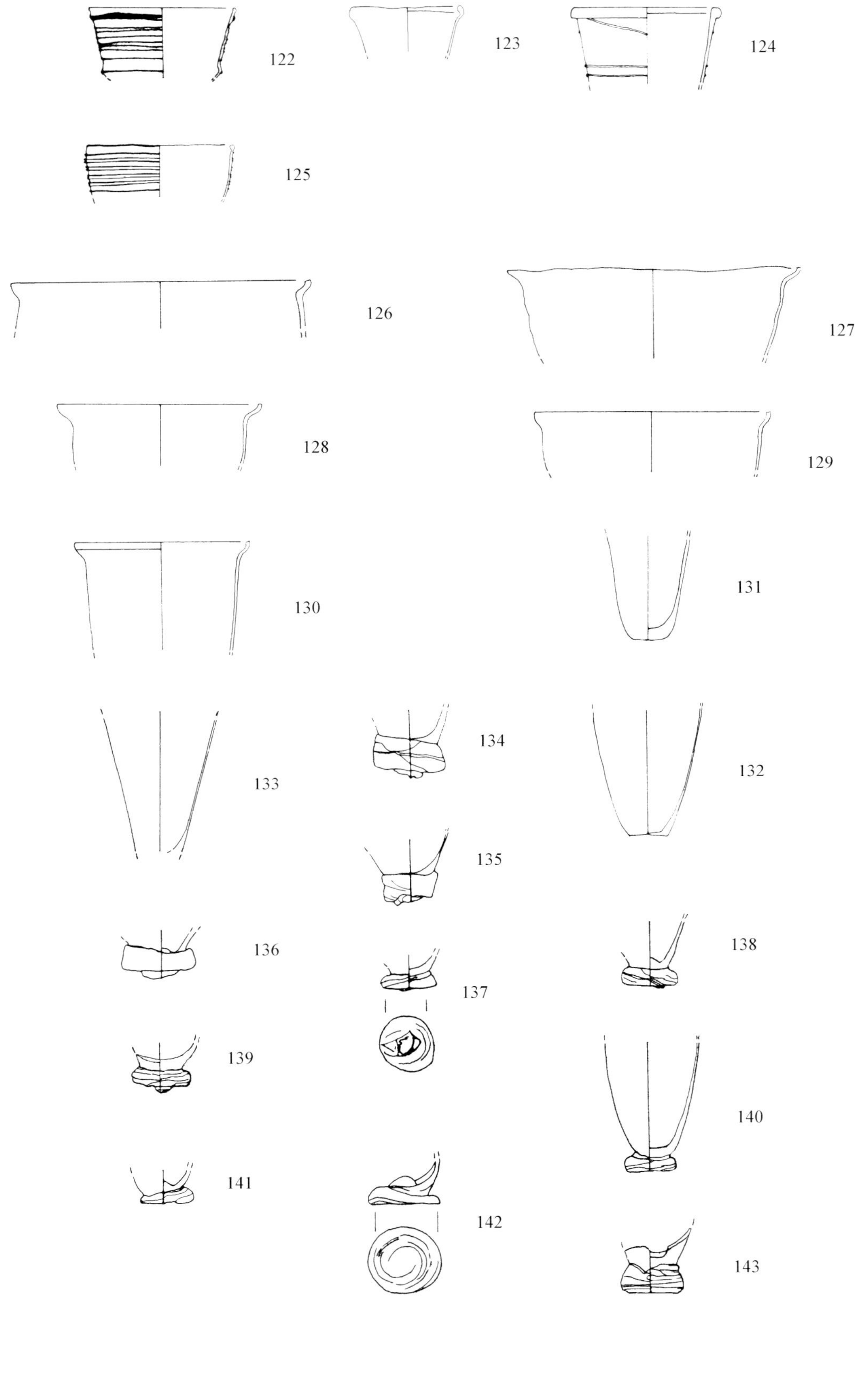


*Figure 1.9 Glass flagons and flasks, nos 122–125, and lamps, nos 126–143. Scale 1:2*

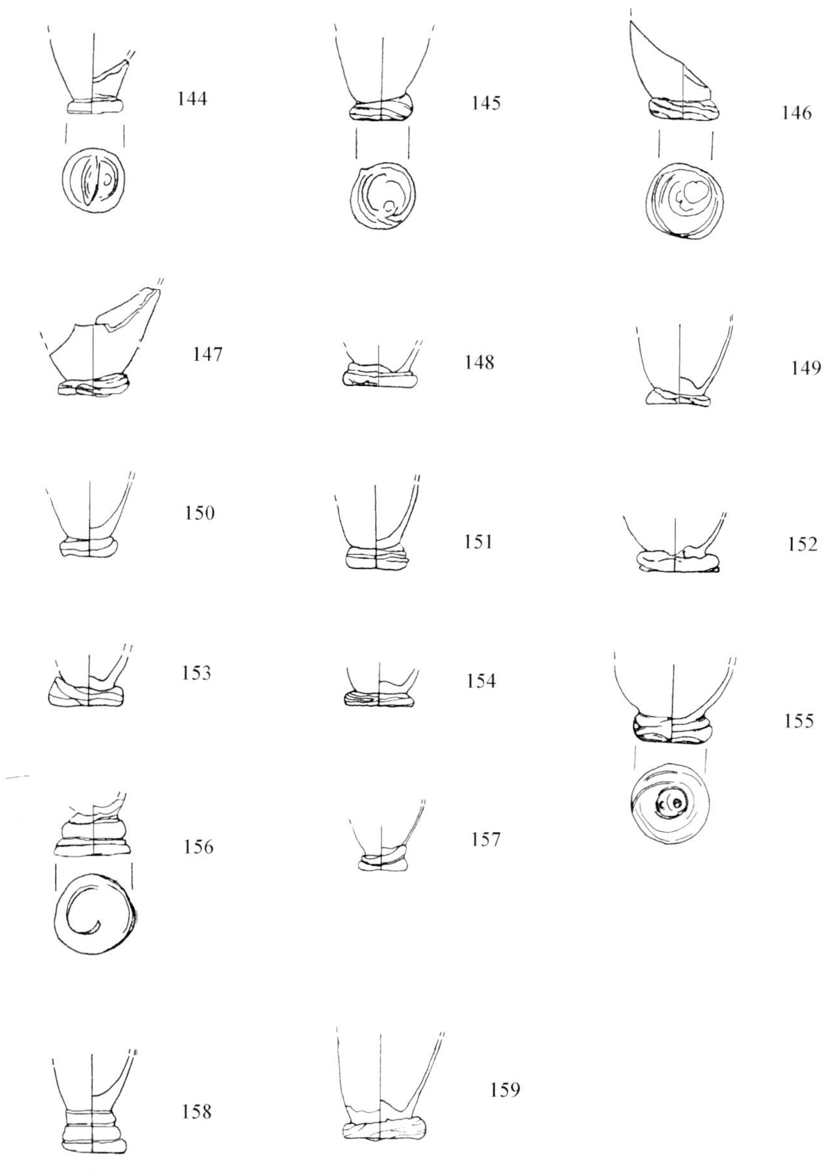


*Figure 1.10 Glass lamps and bottles, nos 144–159. Scale 1:2*

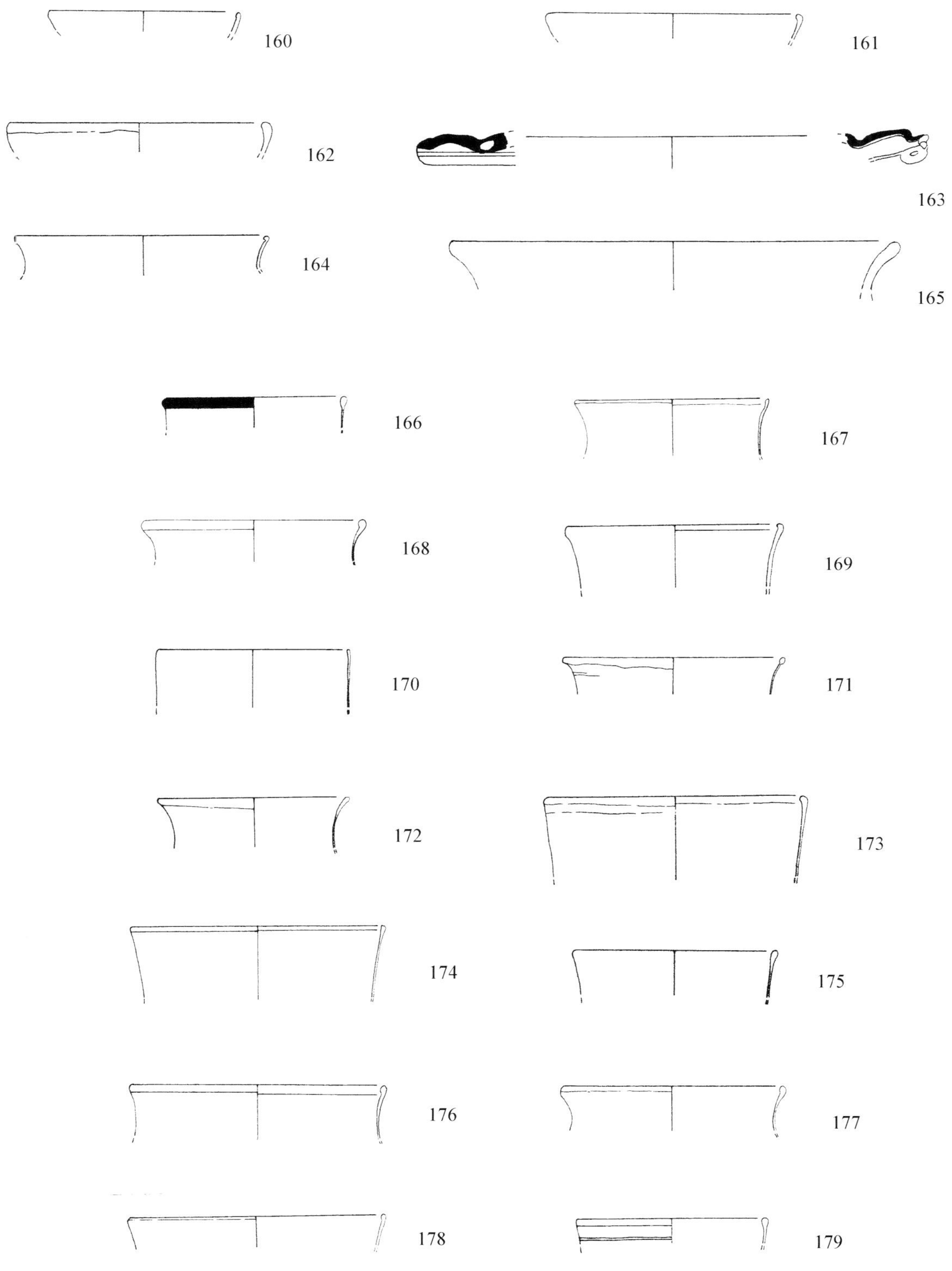


*Figure 1.11 Miscellaneous glass rims, nos 160–179. Scale 1:2*

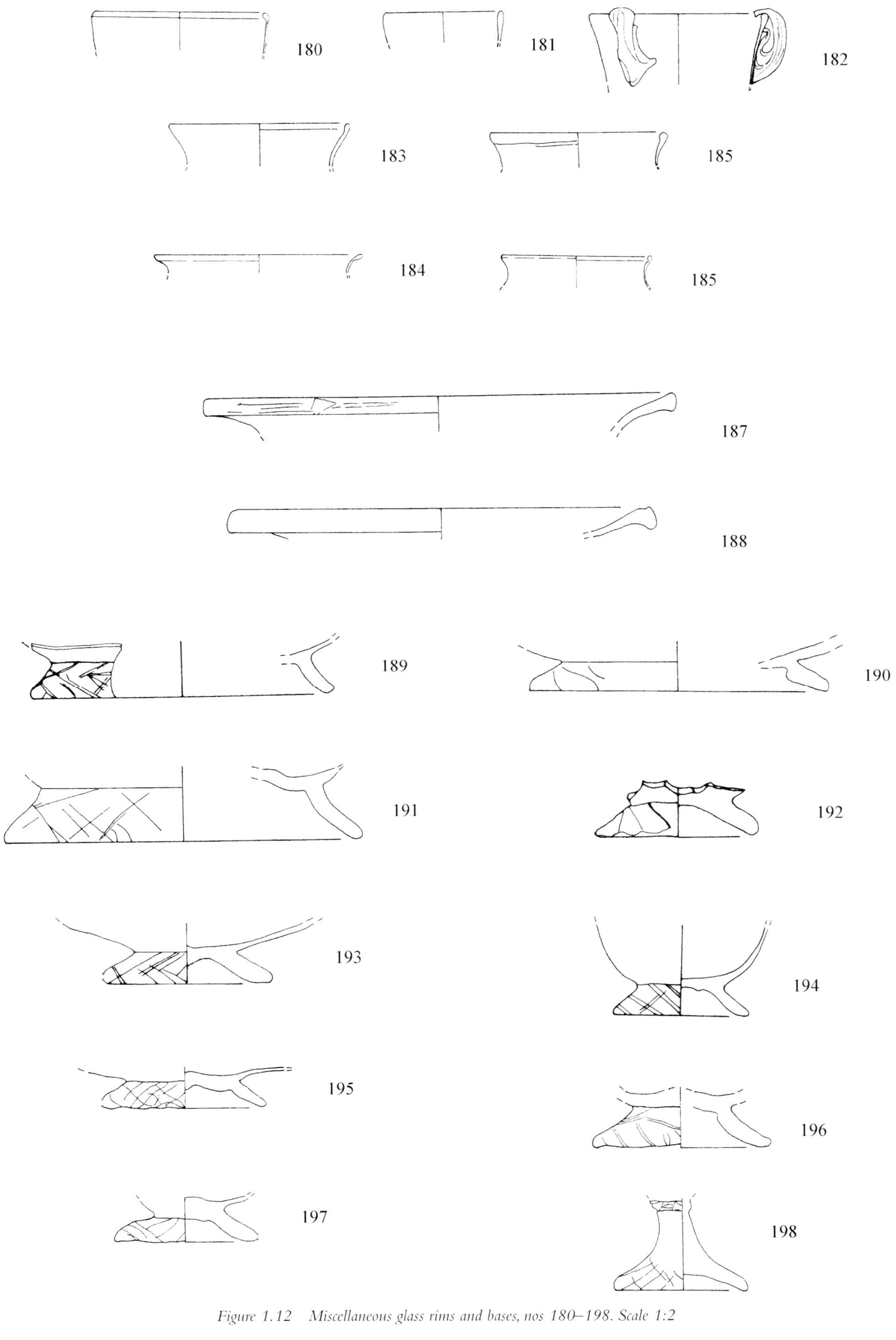


*Figure 1.12 Miscellaneous glass rims and bases, nos 180–198. Scale 1:2*

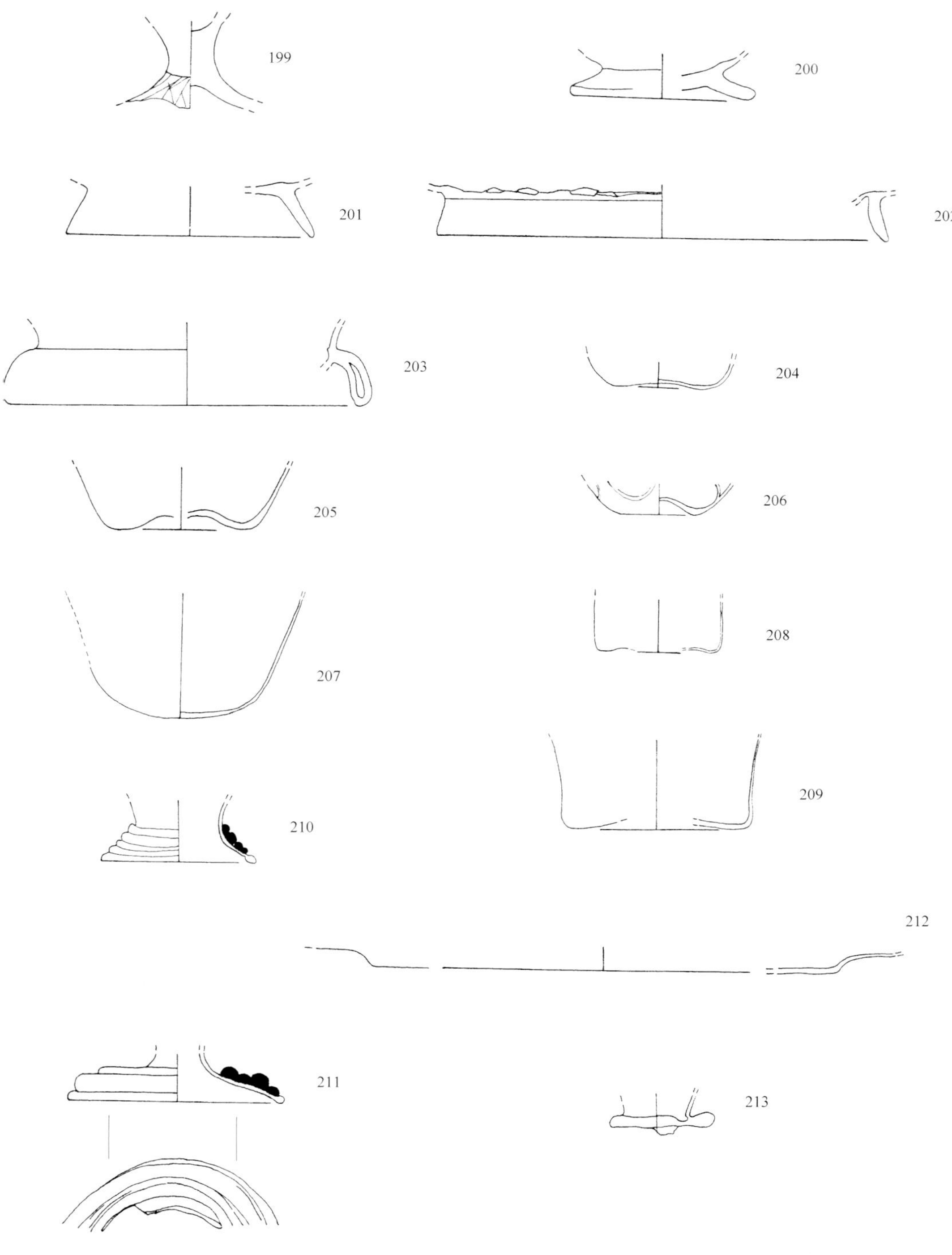


*Figure 1.13 Miscellaneous glass bases, nos 199–213. Scale 1:2*

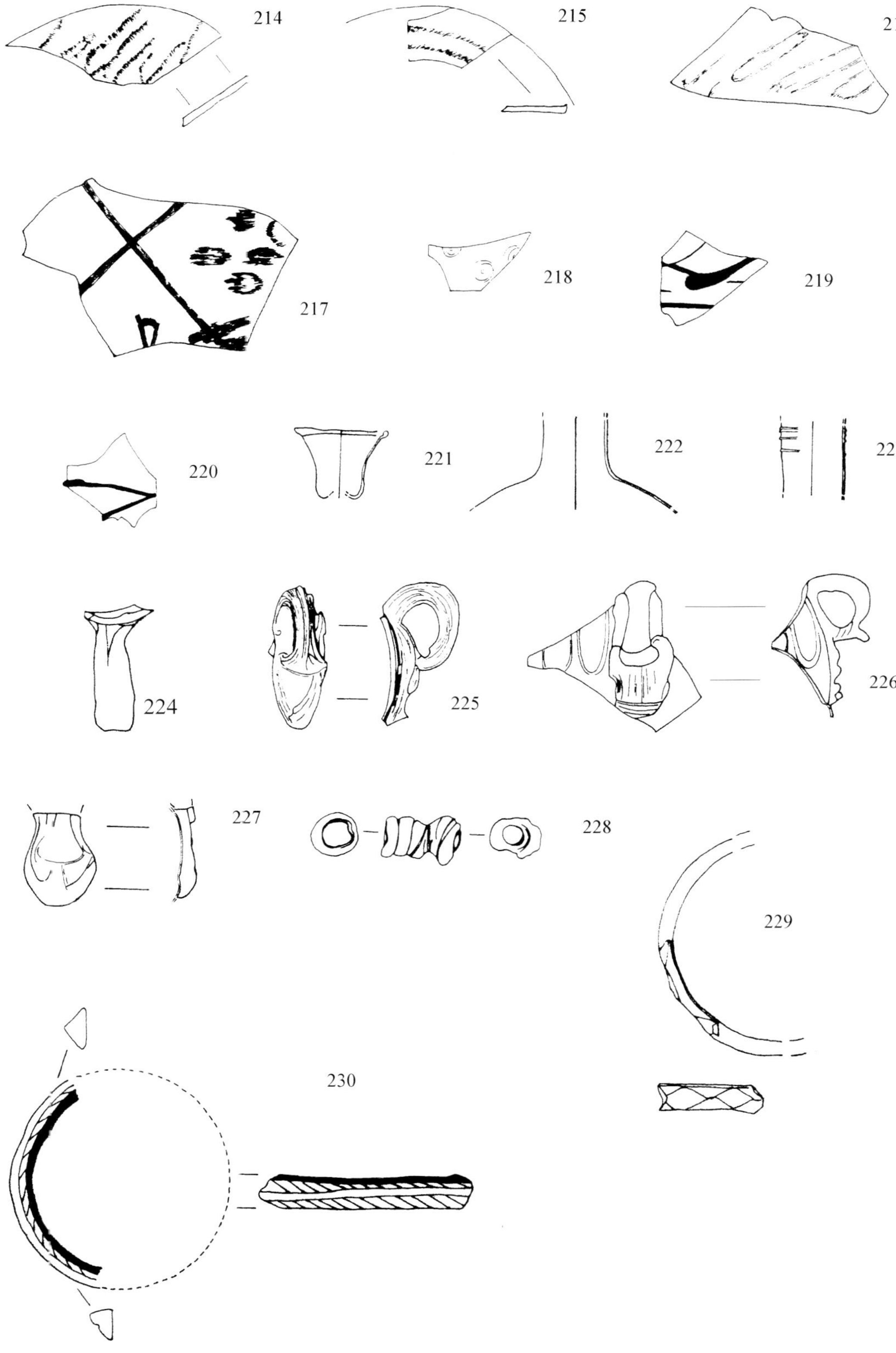


*Figure 1.14 Miscellaneous glass, nos 214–230. Scale 1:2*

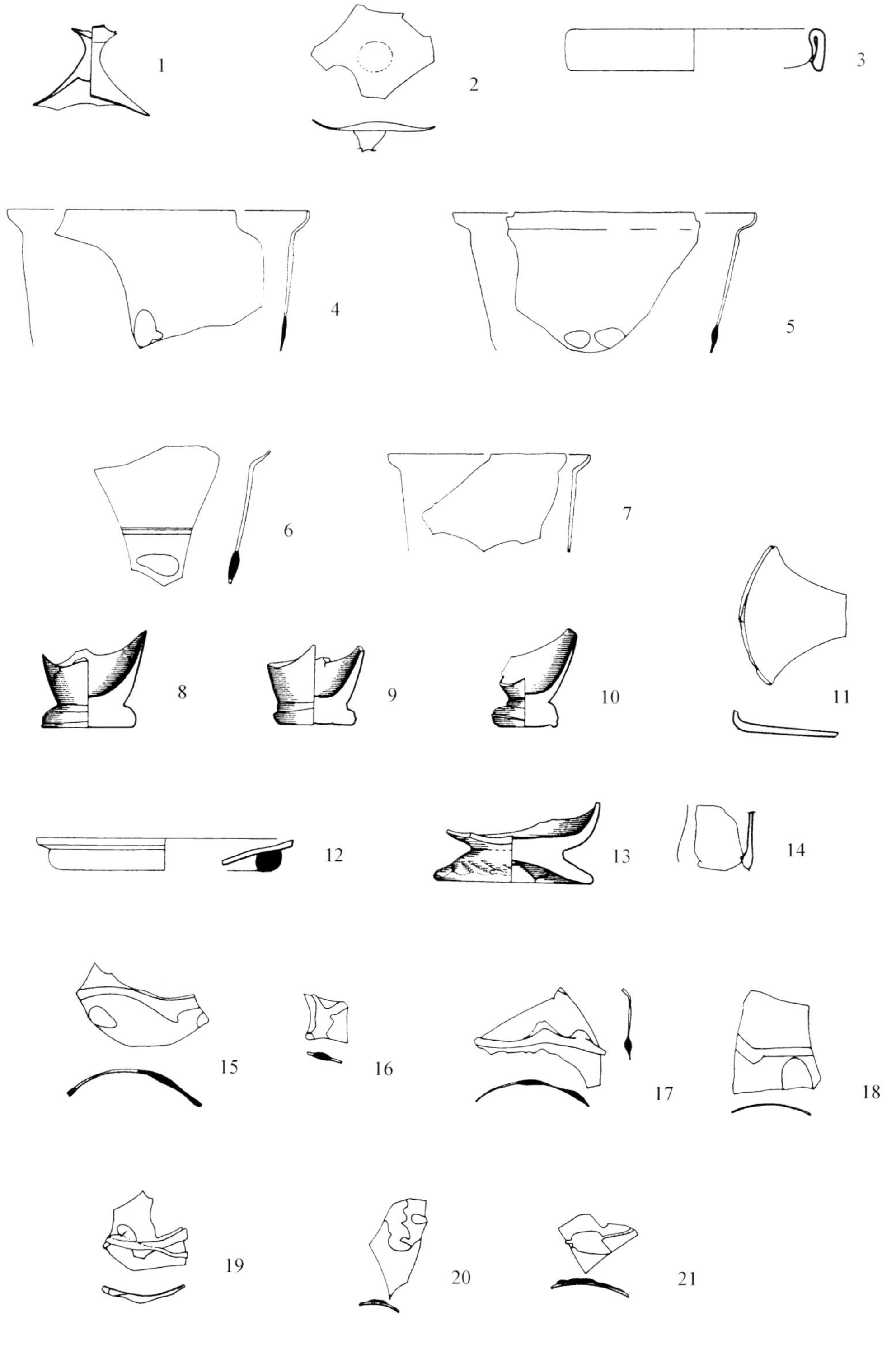


*Figure 1.15 Miscellaneous glass from el-Hawata, nos 1–21. Scale 1:2*

# CHAPTER 2

# A second corpus of Late Roman pottery from Kom el-Nana

by Jane Faiers

## Methodology

This second corpus of pottery from Kom el-Nana contains the stratified material from excavations carried out in the years 1993, 1994 and 2000. The first volume contained 103 drawings of stratified vessels from the 1993–94 excavations.

Quantification of the pottery was as described in Volume 1 and is repeated below.

Rims, bases and handles were separated out, counted, recorded and retained, and the total number of sherds noted. All sherds were inspected for marks, stamps or decoration and those found were kept. Any unusual sherds were noted and kept. Body sherds were discarded unless able to be joined or unless they belonged to a stratigraphically important level, in which case all pottery was kept for more detailed study. Some types of pottery not already included in the corpus were marked, drawn and recorded. Any pot which was whole, or nearly so, was retained.

Division of the catalogue into finewares and coarsewares has been made on the basis of the fabric of any given vessel, and comments on the various wares or forms have been incorporated into the catalogue before the relevant items.

Where found, parallels for various wares or forms on other sites are given, together with a suggested date where appropriate. Sometimes there are conflicting dates given by excavators for the same vessel form and it is left to the reader to decide which date to accept. As in Volume 1 the author has relied heavily on the published material from el-Ashmunein, as this site is close to Kom el-Nana and much of its pottery is of the same period.

The fineware category includes African Red Slipware (ARS), imported wares and Egyptian finewares, namely Egyptian Red Slip (ERS) 'A' Ware, from the Aswan region; Egyptian Red Slip 'B' Ware from Middle Egypt, the Delta or Fayoum (this is listed under Long-Distance Traded Wares, as the place of manufacture of the ware found at Kom el-Nana is at present not known), and Egyptian Red Slip 'H' Ware, probably from the region of Hermopolis Magna (el-Ashmunein) or Antinoopolis (Antinoe), which here is considered as a short-distance traded ware. The fabric of the ERS 'H' ware at Kom el-Nana corresponds to that of the ERS 'H' found at el-Ashmunein, and therefore, although similar red slipwares are found in other parts of Egypt (see Bailey, 1990, 4–5), it seems probable that this fabric comes from within this region.

All illustrations of the pottery are at one-third scale, except where otherwise stated. For painted wares the following conventions are used:

Black = black or dark brown
Diagonal lines right to left = red
Diagonal lines left to right = pink
Vertical lines = orange or yellow
Dots = cream or white slip

All paints and slips are fired-on ceramic colours. Diameters are the outside rim measurement in centimetres.

JF = drawn by Jane Faiers
GP = drawn by Gillian Pyke
AG = drawn by Alison Gascoigne

Site numbering system: in the example W30 [5523], W30 is the five-metre-square number on the site (see the overall site plan, fig. b) and the number in square brackets [5523] is the unit (context number).

## Wares

Codes and descriptions of the distinguishing characteristics of the wares illustrated in this catalogue are given in the following sections:

**Finewares**

ARS
(LRP, 1972, 13–14, ARS.) Hard, coarse, rather granular appearance. Orange-red to brick red. Conspicuous white and black particles, occasional mica. Slip a shade or two deeper in tone than the body clay.

O1
Red or pink slipped (LRP, 1972, 387–388, ERS 'A'). Equivalent to Rodziewicz Group O.

O1W
Cream or yellow slipped (LRP Supplement, 531). Equivalent to Rodziewicz Group W. Generally loose textured and flaky. Occasionally, when it has been carefully produced and hard fired it approaches African Red Slipware in quality. Pink, sometimes orange-red. Matrix contains fine black and quartz particles, gold mica flakes and some larger red particles.

O2
(LRP, 397, Egyptian Red Slipware.) Fabric description as above, fired to yellowish-cream colour. Polished.

M5
(LRP, 397–398, ERS 'B'.) Soft and crumbly, very fine and dense. Uniform brown on surface and in section. Matrix includes mica, sand, fine chaff and limestone inclusions. Red slipped. Clumsy technique with thick walls and carelessly applied decoration.

M6
(Ashmunein, 1982, 27, ERS 'H'.) Dense, hard fabric containing some mica in small particles. Dark-pink core with a thin outer layer, orange in colour but the surface, where unslipped, has a reddish-brown appearance. The slip is of an Indian-red colour, fairly matt; more often than not, applied to the inside of the vessel and the outside of the rim only.

**Coarsewares**

VCM1
Hard, very porous and 'corky', very coarse Nile-silt fabric. Quantities of straw, large particles of limestone and other inclusions visible. Usually showing a wide carbon streak in section and confined to very large hand-made vessels.

M1
Hard, very porous and 'corky', coarse Nile-silt fabric. Quantities of straw, large particles of limestone and other inclusions visible. Usually showing a wide carbon streak in section.

M2
Hard, medium-to-fine Nile-silt fabric. Usually well and evenly fired. Red-brown with a thin red, rarely black, core in section. Vessel walls vary from 0.4–1.0 cm in thickness.

M4
Hard, if not brittle, due to repeated heating during cooking. Very fine, Nile-silt fabric, containing sand, mica and small particles of charcoal (?) and black and white particles. Yellowish-brown 10YR 5/4 to 2.5YR 4/6, commonly ribbed and stained black/sooted, with a red or violet (never black) core. Pottery in this fabric often has very thin walls.

P22
Hard, sandy with flecks of mica. Fine pink surface with light-orange core. Possible mixture of Nile silt and desert marl, but could occur naturally.

P23
Hard, sandy, pink-beige fabric often with a dirty cream surface.

W1
Fairly hard, coarse white/cream, sometimes with a greenish tinge. Evenly textured, but with numerous voids. Black and red inclusions giving a speckled appearance. Fabric so far restricted to flagons.

W2
Fine version of W1.

**Lamp wares**

L1
Fine, red-brown, micaceous fabric. Sometimes red-brown slipped.

L2
Fine, red-brown, micaceous fabric with black inner core. Red-brown slipped.

L3
Fine, brown, micaceous fabric. Sometimes red-brown slipped.

L4
Fine, light-pink/brown fabric with a buff surface.

| Fabric | Rims | Bases | Handles | Total RBH | Weight in grams | % |
|---|---|---|---|---|---|---|
| ARS | 19 | 14 | 0 | 33 | 844 | 0.30 |
| O1 | 561 | 296 | 0 | 857 | 22,846 | 7.00 |
| O2 | 3 | 2 | 0 | 5 | 87 | 0.04 |
| O1W | 15 | 6 | 0 | 21 | 249 | 0.20 |
| M5 | 268 | 163 | 0 | 431 | 13,051 | 3.60 |
| M6 | 394 | 213 | 1 | 608 | 26,573 | 5.02 |
| VCM1 | 232 | 77 | 11 | 320 | 108,182 | 2.65 |
| M1 | 1,977 | 504 | 227 | 2,708 | 167,988 | 22.45 |
| M2 | 1,512 | 398 | 69 | 1,979 | 71,234 | 16.41 |
| M4 | 795 | 300 | 36 | 1,131 | 30,515 | 9.40 |
| W1 | 22 | 9 | 9 | 40 | 673 | 0.40 |
| P23 | 5 | 5 | 0 | 10 | 255 | 0.10 |
| L1 | 1 | 0 | 0 | 1 | 53 | 0.00 |
| L2 | 2 | 0 | 0 | 2 | 15 | 0.01 |
| L3 | 1 | 1 | 1 | 3 | 72 | 0.02 |
| L4 | 1 | 0 | 0 | 1 | 50 | 0.00 |
| L5 | 3 | 1 | 0 | 4 | 65 | 0.03 |
| **Amphorae** | **Rims** | **Bases** | **Handles** | **Total RBH** | **Weight in grams** | **%** |
| M3 | 826 | 818 | 2,003 | 3,647 | 360,927 | 30.24 |
| N1 | 87 | 11 | 74 | 172 | 32,023 | 1.40 |
| N7 | 7 | 2 | 2 | 11 | 289 | 0.10 |
| N8 | 1 | 0 | 0 | 10 | 155 | 0.01 |
| N9 | 32 | 14 | 17 | 63 | 12,290 | 0.52 |
| N10 | 5 | 0 | 0 | 5 | 357 | 0.04 |
| N11 | 0 | 0 | 2 | 2 | 280 | 0.01 |
| O1 | 1 | 0 | 1 | 2 | 93 | 0.01 |
| ? | 4 | 1 | 1 | 6 | 250 | 0.04 |
| **TOTAL** | | | | **12,063** | **849,456** | **100%** |

*Table 2.1 Total numbers of rims, bases and handles in the various fabrics, 1992–1994 and 2000 combined*

## Amphorae

M3
Egypt (Late Roman 7 = Riley, 1979; Egloff 177 = Egloff 1977; Peacock and Williams Class 52 = Peacock and Williams, 1986). A soft, fairly rough, sandy, micaceous fabric, dull brown (10YR 4/4) in colour.

N1
Borders of the Black Sea: south coast of Turkey; Cyprus; Rhodes (Late Roman Amphora 1a and 1b = Riley, 1979; British Bii = Thomas, 1959; Ballana 6 = Emery and Kirwan, 1938; Peacock and Williams Class 44 = Peacock and Williams, 1986). Hard, sandy fabric with limestone inclusions, ranging in colour from pinkish-cream (7YR 8/2–4) to reddish-yellow (5YR 7/6). LR1a is the smaller version of LR1b.

N7
Eastern Mediterranean region (?). Hard, rough, dense, slightly micaceous fabric. Strong dark red in colour. Sometimes has a worn cream surface caused by the addition of seawater or salt to the preparation of a red firing clay.

N8
Egypt (R Tomber and D Williams (forthcoming), *Egyptian amphorae in Britain and the western provinces*). Rough, sandy, slightly micaceous fabric. Light reddish-brown in colour 2.5YR 6/4 and 6/6. Frequent grains of quartz, flecks of mica, a little limestone and opaque iron oxide. A number of organic voids.

N9
(Late Roman Amphora 4 = Riley, 1979, 'Gaza jar'; Peacock and Williams Class 49 = Peacock and Williams, 1986.) Hard, thick, sandy fabric with a little white limestone scattered throughout. Drab brown (5YR 5/6) in colour sometimes with a greyish core.

N10
North African (Peacock and Williams Class 51 = Peacock and Williams, 1986). Hard, pinkish-orange with frequent inclusions of quartz and limestone.

N11
(Late Roman Amphora 5 = Riley, 1979. 'Palestinian'; Peacock and Williams Class 46 = Peacock and Williams, 1986.) Soft, very sandy, beige to reddish-orange fabric.

Total estimated vessel equivalent numbers for the forms present will be found in the various sectors of the site discussed in Chapter 3.

It was decided not to give dishes a specific part of the catalogue in this volume as they appear in various other categories such as ARS, O1 and cooking wares.

Percentages of the various wares are given before the respective entry in the catalogue together with the comparison between these and figures in Faiers 2005.

| Form | RBH | % | 1990–2 % |
|---|---|---|---|
| Jars | 1,646 | 13.65 | 13.91 |
| Bowls/basins | 2,538 | 22.00 | 21.97 |
| Dishes | 551 | 4.56 | 5.90 |
| Qadus | 783 | 6.50 | 19.94 |
| Pitchers/jugs | 53 | 0.43 | 0.59 |
| Cooking pots/ casseroles | 1,424 | 12.00 | 7.49 |
| Lids | 251 | 2.08 | 1.28 |
| Lamps | 18 | 0.14 | 0.11 |
| Colanders | 144 | 1.20 | 0.50 |
| Flagons | 392 | 3.25 | 2.90 |
| Flasks | 103 | 0.84 | 0.31 |
| Cups | 74 | 0.60 | 0.44 |
| ? | 11 | 0.10 | 0.13 |
| Ladles | 33 | 0.30 | 0.02 |
| Storage vessels | 77 | 0.62 | 0.06 |
| Buckets | 16 | 0.13 | 0.00 |
| Amphorae | 3,908 | 32.00 | 24.41 |
| Miscellaneous | 33 | 0.30 | 0.10 |
| Totals | 12,055 | 100% | 100% |

*Table 2.2 Rims, bases and handles in the various forms and percentages for the years 1993–4 and 2000 combined. Percentages only for 1990–92 for comparison*

## Finewares, imported: African Red Slipware (ARS)

This ware, made in what is now Tunisia and imported into Kom el-Nana, provided a total of 33 diagnostic sherds in 1993–1994 and 2000 combined, approximately 0.3 per cent of the total RBH (Table 2.1). Dates given range from AD 300 to AD 625, the earliest being for no. 6, given a date of AD 300–375 in Hayes, LRP, but later in context at Ashmunein (Bailey, 1998, A7, AD 400–550), which is more in keeping with the date range established for Kom el-Nana in Volume 1, i.e. AD 425/450–650. Apart from the early date of no. 6, the other sherds of ARS cover the period AD 400–625.

The number of ARS rim, base and handle sherds in Volume 1 amounted to approximately one per cent (45 RBH) of the 5,235 counted from the 1990–92 excavation and 2.2 per cent (11 RBH) of the 509 from the Midden; a total of approximately 3.2 per cent out of 5,744 RBH. These were from unstratified deposits and would therefore be reasonably expected to amount to more than those found in stratified deposits, which is indeed the case here, there being only 33 ARS RBH out of 12,062 counted, i.e. 0.3 per cent. This, therefore, may strengthen the case for ARS vessels being rather special or valued as a luxury item at the monastery, being more difficult to obtain or possibly accepted as gifts from grateful guests. On the other hand, perhaps the more easily obtained, and presumably cheaper, pottery from Aswan or even nearer at hand, as at Hermopolis (el-Ashmunein) was the preferred choice. Bailey suggests that perhaps ARS was probably not that expensive as some vessels at Ashmunein had been used as frying pans (Bailey, 1998, 2). It may, however, be the case that where they were not easily obtainable, as in a monastery and not in a town such as Hermopolis, their value as a special tableware increased, or that certain forms were more expensive than others, and that these were the vessels regarded as fine tableware.

1. Bowl. D = 34 cm.
AC52 [7655]. JF 781.
LRP Form 104, C29, AD 550–625.

2. Dish with bead rim. Two shallow grooves below rim. D = 16 cm.
AD51 [7547]. JF 872.
This form is related to LRP Form 63, of mid fourth century AD to *c.*AD 400–500, but correlates more readily with a vessel at Carthage (Fulford and Peacock,

1984, V1, 2, p.50, fig. 11, form 2.9), which seems to belong to the sixth century AD.

3. Dish with straight sloping wall. D = 22 cm.
AA50 [8252]. JF 873.
LRP Form 5C, B. *c.*AD 350–400+.
Ashmunein, 1998, pl. 2, A16, conjectural date AD 400–550.

4. Bowl with high-placed, prominent flange with a down-turned edge. Vessel sides slope quite steeply.
D = 20 cm.
AA50 [9834]. GP 481.
Elephantine X, Abb.2, 8. LRP Form 91A, dated mid-to-late fifth century AD. The dating of this form appears to be the subject of ongoing discussion (Hayes, Supplement, xlix). Timby in Fulford and Tomber, (1994, 100) dates the whole of Form 91 to the fourth to seventh century AD with no sub-divisions.

5. Bowl with flat-topped flange rim, the edge of which is lost. Possibly a dish as the sides of the vessel are quite steeply sloped with a slight curve. D = *c.*36 cm.
AA47 [9853]. GP 637.
Possibly LRP Form 58A, AD 300–375.
See also Ashmunein, 1998, A7, given a date of AD 400–550.

6. Bowl with flat-topped flange rim and curved sides.
D = 16 cm.
AA49 [9838]. GP 603.
Possibly LRP Form 93, which is larger and of late fifth to early sixth century AD date. Also similar to Fulford and Tomber, 1994, fig. 20, 104 in ARS, unclassified there, but listed under sixth to seventh century AD bowls and dishes.

7. Base of bowl.
AA50 [8260] JF 848. Another in AH52 (8112).
LRP Form 104B, *c.* AD 570–600.

8. Base of bowl.
AA34 [7570]. GP 421.
LRP Form 103, 10, *c.* AD 500 to the third quarter of the sixth century AD.

9. Base sherd of bowl with flute lentoid and cross stamp.
Y51 [7425]. JF852.
LRP fig. 54, 259g, with fig. 44, 125t. Also Gurna, 988.
Close to AD 500.

10. Base sherd of flanged bowl with feather rouletting.
Z50 [8247]. JF 846.
LRP Form 91 or 92, A or B, mid-to-late fifth century AD or *c.* AD 450–530.
Not illustrated:
Small sherd of flange of bowl.
AD51 [7575].
LRP form 76, 3, *c.* AD 425–475.

**Finewares, long-distance traded: Egyptian Red Slipped 'A' Wares; ERS 'A' (O1); ERS 'A' variant with cream/yellow slip (O1W); and ERS 'A' variant fired to yellowish-cream colour and polished (O2)**

These wares formed 7.24 per cent of the total RBH for the combined years 1993–4 and 2000 (Table 2.1); a total of 883 RBH out of 12,062 RBH. This can be compared to the percentages found in the unstratified deposits of 1990–92, and the Midden deposit, i.e. 5.74 per cent and 4.5 per cent respectively, totalling approximately 10 per cent (Faiers, 2005). It is fair to point out, however, that vessels in O1W and O2 amounted to only a very few, with no RBH of either ware having been found in the 1990–2 or Midden groups. This may point to their rarity, because of either supply or expense. Both wares are finely made with comparatively thin walls and must therefore be carefully handled or be easily broken. This may also be due to the differences in supply to town and monastery, i.e. Kom el-Nana has no vessels of types C97 and C110 which are found at el- Ashmunein (Bailey, 2005, pl. 7).

Of those in the group below, the following must be singled out: no. 52, a shallow bowl or dish in O1 fabric, badly warped in firing, which has been used, as evidenced by the wear marks inside the bowl, but could never have been very stable; no. 53, a bowl in O1 fabric which is blackened inside the bowl and has been reused as a lamp; and no. 64, a compartmented dish in O1W, the use of which is disputed.

With regard to no. 64, it is more usually supposed that such compartmented dishes were used as food containers, rather in the form of an hors d'oeuvre dish, to separate various foodstuffs. It has also been suggested that this vessel was used as the carrier of oil lamps (Montserrat, 1995, 443). One of these dishes found at Esna was made of glass (Jacquet-Gordon, 1972, pl. CCXXXIII, no. 9), measuring 28 cm, with possibly six or seven compartments. This would probably be less robust than a pottery model. There are no indications of burning or oil spillage or other damage on the Kom el-Nana vessel, which would seem to make the lamp-carrier suggestion be less likely than a holder for dips or *mezze*.

These vessels were made in a range of sizes with differing numbers of compartments. The vessel cited by Hayes in LRP (Hayes, 1972, fig. 33, F111) from Tocra in African Red Slipware, with a suggested date of late sixth to the first half of the seventh century AD, had an estimated diameter of 55 cm and eight to ten compartments. Other examples are: the Ashmunein vessels (Bailey, 1998, 32), which were 38 cm and 24 cm respectively, with five and six compartments; Elephantine (Gempeler, 1992, Form 241, 80) was 36–41 cm, with six compartments; the vessel from Epiphanius which had a diameter of 35 cm, with five compartments (Winlock and Crum, 1926, pl. 40, 89); two compartmented dishes at Deir el-Naqlun (Godlewski et al., 1993, 244, 18.7) of around 30 cm, one appears to have five compartments around the outside and one in the centre; four compartmented dishes from Tod, measured approximately 28 cm (Pierrat, 1991, fig. 55, i), 25.2 cm with five compartments (Pierrat, 2003, pl. 12, 151), 31.5 cm with seven compartments (Pierrat, 2003, pl. 12, 152) and approximately 38 cm with seven compartments (Pierrat, 2003, pl. 12, 153). These last push the date of these vessels later to around AD 900, as their dates there range from AD 750 to AD 900. There are also three of these vessels in the pottery from Wadi Sarga (a site approximately 40 miles upstream from Kom el-Nana) whose dates venture into the Islamic Period on the basis of pottery, coin and philological evidence. The size of two of these vessels can be estimated at 40 cm and 29 cm; the third is a small body sherd (British Museum nos 1919.0505.422, 423, 424, and 435—these are from the same vessel, but not joining—and 1919.0505.429 and 430).

The dish in this catalogue has a painted pattern which occurs elsewhere: at the Monastery of Epiphanius at Thebes (Winlock and Crum, 1926, pl. XXXIII), Wadi Sarga (British Museum 1919.0505.429), Antinoe (Guidotti and Pesi, 2004, Tavola XXXV, 190) and Tod (Pierrat, 1991, fig. 55, i). Thus the dish is being used at a variety of settlements including monasteries and towns. The dish at Antinoe comes from the North Necropolis and may well have a funerary context, although this hypothesis seems to be discarded by Guidotti and Pesi based on the find spots of the various other vessels of the same form and to the absence of Christian symbols, thus making it more likely that these vessels had a domestic use. A funerary use, for offerings for example, is, however, not ruled out (Guidotti and Pesi, 2004, 55). Julie Anderson has indicated (in a personal communication to the author) that there are graves at her site at Dangeil in Sudan where small vessels are grouped together in a similar manner to the dishes mentioned here.

Manufacture of this vessel was probably by press moulding in part or whole. This is indicated by the very thin bases and walls of the compartments as the clay disk was pressed into the mould and stretched to fit. Another method would be to throw the disc or platter and then cut holes into which small 'pinch pots' were fitted. This would again be mould-made. It would be reasonably easy to see which method had been used by examining the way in which the compartments fitted the dish. So far, the first method appears to have been used for the pots found at Kom el-Nana. The base would be applied at the leather-hard stage.

It seems evident that these are very specialised vessels and perhaps not needed in quantity. However, many other fragments of these dishes were found in the same deposit at Tod (Lecuyat and Pierrat, 2004, pl. 12, 151), so it seems possible that many were used and broken over a long period of time, and that the form could have survived for around three hundred years at least, from around AD 575 to AD 900. Apart from the glass vessel at Esna and the African Red Slipware vessel in LRP, the majority appear to have been manufactured in the region of Aswan.

Dating of the sherds illustrated gave a time scale of AD 100 to 700+, but the main bulk of likely dates for the O1/O1W and O2 group falls between AD 450–650.

11. Bowl with small flange and line of rouletting on outside of rim. O1. D = 22 cm.
U53 [8682]. JF 850.
Esna, E19, *c.*AD 550–630. Elephantine X, Abb.38, T323b, 11–15, second quarter of the fifth to the seventh century AD. Ashmunein, 1998, C354, conjectural date AD 650–800.

12. Bowl with small flange and line of rouletting on outside of rim. Filled with gypsum plaster. O1.
D = 15 cm.
AB35 [7563]. JF 893.
Date as no. 11.

13. Bowl with small flange and line of rouletting on outside of rim. O1. D = 16 cm.
Y52 [8660]. Same vessel in Z36 [7559]. JF 817.
Date as nos 11 and 12.

14. Bowl with flange. Dark red-orange slipped over rim. O1. D = 13 cm.
AA49 [9836]. GP 545.
Gurna, 1089, AD 395–640.

15. Bowl with flange. Orange slipped over flange. O1.
D = 16 cm.
AF34 [8358]. GP 356.

Ashmunein, 1998, C367, AD 400–500. Elephantine X, Abb.34, 19, T312a, second quarter of the fourth to the mid fifth century AD. Gurna, 1200, *c.* AD 395–640.

16. Bowl with flange. Orange slipped. Brown rim. O1. D = 10 cm.
AB46 [9800]. JF 935.
Similar to Ashmunein, 1998, C367, dated AD 400–550. See also Elephantine X, Abb.36, T318b, dated third quarter of the fifth (?) to the middle of the sixth (?) century AD.

17. Bowl with flange. O1. D = 18 cm.
AC50 [8324]. GP 158.
Elephantine X, Abb.37, 1, T319c, second quarter of the fifth century to the third quarter of the sixth century AD.

18. Bowl with flange. O1. D = 16 cm.
AB35 [7662]. GP 372.
Coin: fifth to sixth century AD.
ARS in same layer, LRP Form 104, C23, dated AD 550–625.
Elephantine X, Abb.40, 10, T325, second quarter of the fifth to the middle (?) of the seventh century AD.

19. Bowl with flange. O1. D = 11 cm.
Y52 [8516]. JF 829.
Elephantine X, Abb.36, 1–6, T318a, last quarter of the fourth to the second quarter of the sixth century AD. Ashmunein, 1998, C377, context date AD 675–750. Esna, E36, *c.* AD 550–630.

20. Bowl with flange. Red slipped over rim. Badly shattered and abraded. O1. D = 25 cm.
AD52 [7519]. JF 891.
Gurna, 1201, *c.* AD 395–640. Ashmunein, 1998, *c.* AD 400–500 (?). Close to Elephantine, Abb.36, 6, T318a, second quarter of the sixth century AD.

21. Bowl with flange and high foot. O1. D = 27 cm.
AB36 [7443]. JF 903.
LRP, fig. 85h. AD 500. Based on LRP Form 93, late fifth to early sixth century AD. The same form is to be found at Gurna, no. 1210, but in O1W.

22. Bowl with flange and high foot. Worn red slip inside and out. Flaking badly. Stamped inside at base. O1. D = 30 cm.
AD52 [7502] and AD52 [7504]. JF 871.
Based on LRP Form 95. Elephantine X, Abb.42, 2, T341b, closest, sixth century AD.
Stamp: LRP, 396, Group B, first half of the sixth century AD.

23. Bowl with everted flat rim. Groove near edge of rim and rouletting on body under rim. O1. D = 18 cm.
AD50 [8150]. JF 702.
Close to Ashmunein, 1998, C384, sixth to eighth century AD. Also near to LRP, 391, Type R given as early (?) sixth century AD.

24. Bowl with flange. Line of rouletting under rim and high on body. O1. D = 28 cm.
Z36 [7559]. GP 164.
Ashmunein, 1998, C516, dated AD 600–700. Near Elephantine X, Abb.42, 2, T383, of around seventh to eighth century AD.

25. Bowl with plain, everted rim. O1. D = 22 cm.
Z36 [7559]. GP 223.
Ashmunein, 1998, C525 *bis*, conjectural context date *c.* sixth century to eighth century AD. Elephantine X, Abb.10, T210a, probably second quarter of the fourth to second quarter of the sixth century AD.

26. Bowl with everted rim. O1. D = 16 cm.
AD52 [7787]. GP 303.
Gurna, 1269, sixth to seventh century AD.

27. Bowl with knobbed rim. Three lines of rouletting under rim. O1. D = 20 cm.
V52 [8692]. JF 849.
Elephantine X, Abb.40, 5/6, T325, second quarter of the fifth to the middle (?) of the seventh century AD. LRP, 391, pl. 86, O/N.18.

28. Bowl with knobbed, slightly hooked flange. Single line of rouletting about 1.5 cm below the base of the flange on the exterior. Red slipped. Dark-red rim. O1. D = 26 cm.
AA48 [9800]. GP 631.
Elephantine X, Abb.40, T325b/c, second quarter of the fifth to the mid (?) seventh century AD. Monastery of Epiphanius, pl. 37, O?N, dated to the sixth century AD. Alexandrie, O35, dated sixth and seventh centuries AD.

29. Bowl with knobbed flange. Single line of rouletting about 1 cm below the base of the flange. Orange-red slipped with a dark-red rim. O1. D = 20 cm.
AA47 [9800]. AG 105.
Gurna, 1145 (no rouletting), dated AD 395–640.

30. Small bowl with knobbed rim. Line of rouletting on body. O1. D = 13.5 cm.
AD49 [8336]. JF 782.
Ashmunein, 1998, C126, pl. 7 and 14, fifth to seventh century AD. Also near Elephantine X, Abb.38, T322, date unsafe, but nothing before the fifth century AD.

31. Small bowl with knobbed rim. O1W. Cream-slipped overall. D = 10 cm.
Y52 [8512]. JF 701.
Ashmunein, 1998, C126, but without rouletting, fifth to seventh century AD. Also near Elephantine X, Abb.50, T356, probably sixth century AD.

32. Small bowl with knobbed rim. Orange slipped with red rim. O1. D = 12 cm.
AB48 [9800]. JF 932.

33. Bowl with knobbed rim. Interior and rim top are pink slipped and the exterior is red slipped. O1. D = 20 cm.
AB46 [9800]. JF 934.
Elephantine X, Abb.7, T202, of uncertain date.

34. Bowl with knobbed rim and high foot. Two grooves inside at base of bowl. O1. D = 36.5cm.
AE50 [8408]. JF 930.
Elephantine X, Abb.17, T226b, *c.* second quarter sixth to mid seventh (?) century AD.

35. Bowl with thickened, knobbed rim. Slight internal ledge and a shallow ring base. The exterior has a single row of wide rouletting about 1 cm below the base of the rim. Red-slipped over rim. O1. D = 22 cm.
AA48 [9844]. GP 607.
Similar to Ashmunein, 1998, C139, AD 400–500. See also Gurna, 1070, AD 395–640

36. Bowl with knobbed rim. The exterior has a single line of widely spaced narrow rouletting just below the base of the rim. Dark red-brown slipped over rim. O1. D = 16 cm.
AB48 [9813]. GP 650.
Parallels as no. 35.

37. Bowl with knobbed rim. The interior base is decorated with concentric incised circles, feather rouletting, stamped circles and a fragment of a central cross or chi-rho (?) stamp. Dark-red slipped over rim. O1. D = 33 cm.
AA48 [9842] and AB50 [8608]. GP 573 and GP 86.
Similar to Elephantine X, Abb.18, T228, last quarter of the fifth century to the third quarter of the sixth century AD or later, but said to imitate LRP Form 84, *c.* AD 440–475.

38. Bowl with knobbed rim and internal ledge. Orange-red slipped overall. O1. D = 40 cm.
AA49 [9814]. GP 623. Same vessel at AB48 [9807].
Elephantine X, Abb.19, T230b, first half of the sixth century to the seventh century AD. Gurna, 1002, AD 395–640. See also Ashmunein, 1998, C299, cross referenced to Tod, pl. 8, fig. 111, end of the fifth to the mid seventh century AD.

39. Bowl with knobbed rim. Dark orange slipped over rim. O1. D = 12 cm.
AA48 [9842]. GP 560.
Ashmunein, 1998, C213, AD 550–650. Similar to Gurna, 1155, AD 395–640. See also Elephantine X, Abb.14, T220c, second quarter of the fifth to the early seventh century AD, and perhaps later.

40. Bowl with knobbed rim. Red-slipped over rim. O1. D = 12 cm.
AC50 [8150]. JF 740.
Close to Ashmunein, 1998, C213, in a context dated AD 550–650.

41. Bowl with knobbed rim. O1. D = 18 cm.
AC49 [8146]. JF 705.
Coins: Roman (?) copies, fourth to seventh century AD.
Elephantine X, Abb.39, T324b, 15–17, first half of the sixth to the seventh century AD.

42. Bowl with knobbed rim. Line of wide-spaced rouletting on rim. O1. D = 22.5 cm.
AC49 [8149]. JF 704.
Near Elephantine X, Abb.43, T344, sixth to seventh/eighth century AD. Also Ashmunein, 1998, C253, context date AD 375–450. See also a surface find from Nazlet Tuna, 131, 2.

43. Bowl with knobbed rim and interior ledge. Dark red slipped over rim. O1. D = 23 cm.
AA49 [9839] and AA49 [9814]. GP 602.
Similar to Gurna, 996 (no stamp), dated AD 395–640. Also Elephantine X, Abb.43, T344c, sixth to seventh/eighth century AD. Broadly similar to Ashmunein, 1998, C270–293, but no clear parallel.

44. Bowl with knobbed rim and stepped floor. Low carination. O1. D = 26 cm.
AD51 [7631]. GP 432.
Ashmunein, 1998, C292, conjectural context date AD 600–700. See also Elephantine X, Abb.43, T344b, sixth to seventh/eighth century AD.

45. Bowl with knobbed rim and stepped floor. Low carination. O1. D = 20 cm.
AD51 [7547]. GP 292.
Parallels as no. 44.

46. Bowl with knobbed rim and interior ledge. Dark red slipped rim. O1. D = 24 cm.

AA49 [9838]. GP 601.
Elephantine X, Abb.43, T344b/c, sixth to seventh/eighth century AD. Broadly similar to Ashmunein, 1998, C270–293, but no clear parallel.

47. Bowl with knobbed, grooved rim. Two downward slashes on rim O1. D = 24 cm.
AC49 [8146]. JF 706.
Ashmunein 1984, fig. 33, 2 and 3 AD 550–700+.

48. Bowl with knobbed, grooved rim and stepped floor. O1. D = 26 cm.
AC50 [8150]. JF 743.
Elephantine X, Abb.43, T344b, stated as being very frequent and given a date of sixth to seventh/eighth century AD.

49. Bowl with knobbed, grooved rim and stepped floor. Red-slipped over rim. O1. D = 24cm.
AC49 [7649]. JF 761.
Elephantine X, Abb.13, T219, closest to no. 6 and dated second quarter of the fifth to the last quarter sixth century AD.

50. Small bowl with knobbed rim. O1. D = 15 cm.
AC52 [7635]. JF 778.
Similar to Elephantine X, Abb.13, T219, no. 9. See also Kellia, pl. 40, 13, batiment 1, depot A.

51. Shallow bowl with knobbed, grooved rim. Red-slipped over rim. O1. D = 24 cm.
AE51 [8179]. GP 305.
Elephantine X, Abb.13, 7 or 8, T219. This form was frequent at Elephantine where the date given is the second quarter of the fifth to the last quarter of the sixth century AD.

52. Shallow bowl with knobbed, grooved rim. Badly warped in firing. O1. D = approx 24 cm.
Z51 [7423]. JF 847.
Parallels as no. 51.

53. Bowl with knobbed and grooved rim. Blackened inside, reused as a lamp. O1. D = 16 cm.
Z36 [7559]. GP 211.
Ashmunein, 1998, conjectural date AD 400–500. Near Gurna, 1117, AD 395–640.

54. Small bowl with knobbed and grooved rim. Stamped inside at base. O1. D = 15 cm.
AB49/50 [8343]. AG 92.
The rim is similar to Ashmunein, 1998, C175, AD 600–700. Base as Ashmunein, 1998, C530, AD 650–800+.

55. Small bowl with plain rim. O1. D = 15 cm.
Z36 [7459]. GP 178.
As Ashmunein, 1998, C20. Paralleled at Elephantine X, Abb.20, T233, sixth to seventh century AD.

56. Shallow bowl/dish with thickened rim. Dark-red rim. O1. D = 29 cm.
AB48 [9813]. GP 610.
Gurna, 1014, AD 395–640. Similar to Esna, E16.

57. Bowl with plain, flat rim. Stamped inside at base. O1. D = 29 cm.
Z52 [7610]. JF 816.
Monastery of Epiphanius, Abb.37, Form G, end of the fifth to the beginning of the sixth century AD. At Elephantine X, Abb.19, T231b, the vessel is dated to the first half of the sixth to the seventh century AD. See also Alexandrie I, pl. 28, O38b, 21. Probably sixth century AD at Kom el-Nana.

58. Bowl. Orange slipped with cream and black splodges. O1. D = 30 cm.
AD52 [8452] and AD49/50 [8344]. JF 738.
Close to Ashmunein, 1998, C630, no date given. Elephantine X, Abb.42, T342a, 8–10, second quarter of the sixth to the second half of the sixth century AD. An example was also found by the Wadi Umm Atlee Survey, BEOO/4 (information supplied by Gillian Pyke).

59. Bowl. Dark orange slipped towards rim. O1. D = 14 cm.
AE52 [8199]. JF 888.
Kellia, pl. 41, no. 1, batiment 1, depot L. This type more usually has rouletting on the body.

60. Bowl. Dark orange slipped towards rim. Rouletted. O1.
AB49 [9834]. JF 975.
Alexandrie I, 23, O4a. Elephantine X, Abb.73, T625, 10, fifth (?) to sixth century AD.

61. Bowl with grooved outer rim and rouletting under the two grooves. O1. D = 14 cm.
AD51 [7408]. JF 777.
Elephantine X, Abb.38, T322, 4, in an unsafe context with nothing before the fifth century AD.

62. Dish with curved rim. O1. D = 18 cm.
AD49/50 [8323]. JF 730.
Elephantine X, Abb.19, T231a, 8, first half of the sixth to the seventh century AD.

63. Dish with curved rim. O1. D = 20 cm.

AF51 [8181]. JF 920.
Kellia, pl. 40, surface find. Ashmunein Church Site, AD 390–460, or even AD 420–450. Elephantine X, Abb.19, T231a, 10, first half of the sixth to the seventh century AD.

64. Compartmented dish. O1W. D = 46 cm.
AD50 [8168], AD50 [8170], AD50 [8470], AD51 [7691], AC/AD50 [8460], AG33 [8357]. JF 931.
Monastery of Epiphanius, pl. CCCIII, has the same pattern of flowers and dots but appears to have fewer compartments than the Kom el-Nana example, which has three still remaining in part, being two large and one small, but probably had nine when complete (four large compartments and four small compartments alternately, and one large compartment in the middle of the vessel). This form should be late sixth or first half of the seventh century AD, if in African Red Slipware (see LRP, Form 111). This date is more than likely for this vessel from Kom-el Nana. See comments at the beginning of this section.

65. Bowl with wide, everted, stepped, flanged rim. O1W. D = 34 cm.
AC52 [7646]. GP 368.
Elephantine X, Abb.46, T353a, no. 1 for form and no. 4 for decoration, *c.* second quarter of the sixth century to the first quarter of the seventh century AD, and perhaps later. Base, Ashmunein, 1998, C580.

66. Bowl with wide, everted, stepped, flanged rim. Hole in side of high-footed base possibly to facilitate hanging. O2. D = 32 cm.
AA48 [9857], AB52 [7406], AD49 [8416], AD51 [7404], AD51 [7570]. GP 590.
Similar to Elephantine X, Abb.46, T353a, dated to the second quarter of the sixth century to the first quarter of the seventh century AD, and perhaps later. Gempeler suggests that the form is derived from LRP Form 95, dating to the first half of the sixth century AD. Similar to Ashmunein, 1998, C581–582, but no exact parallel.

67. Very shallow dish with knobbed rim. Groove in the flat base. O1. D = 20 cm.
AD50 [8145]. JF 747.

68. Small bowl or cup. Warped. Two wide-spaced lines of rouletting on body. O1. D = 8 cm.
Y52 [8276]. GP 200.
Similar to Faiers, 2005, no. 44 from Kom el-Nana; Gurna, 1084; Esna, CCXX1, D5 and 6; LRP, 389 D. Dated in LRP to AD 500 from an example from the Monastery of Epiphanius; Alexandrie I, O4; Antinoe, pl. 36, 2. Ashmunein, 1998, C46, sixth to seventh century AD.

69. Cup. Cream slipped with orange rim and two black lines inside. O1W. D = 10 cm.
Y52 [7427]. Another at Z50 [8253]. JF 911.
Bir Umm Fawakhir, 1993, no. 11. Elephantine X, Abb.35, T316a, middle of the fourth century to the sixth century AD.

70. Cup or small bowl. Cream slipped with dark brown firing line over rim. O1W. D = 12 cm.
AF51 [8190]. JF 854.
Elephantine X, Abb.35, T316, 13, mid fourth to sixth century AD. See also Ashmunein South Church Site, pl. IV, fig. 5, 35–36, *c.* AD 390–460. Ashmunein, 1998, C42, given a conjectural date of sixth to eighth century AD.

71. Cup. Orange slipped with cream slip over rim and two painted black lines under rim. O1. D = 9 cm.
AC50 [8150]. JF 742.
Elephantine X, Abb.72, T615a, 7–10, second quarter of the fifth to the first half of the seventh century AD.

72. Cup or small bowl. Orange-brown rim. O1. D = 12 cm.
AA46 [9837]. GP 586.
Close to Ashmunein, 1998, C6, AD 500–650. See also Elephantine X, Abb.40, T326, late fifth to early seventh century AD.

73. Cup or small bowl. Red-slipped over rim. O1. D = 9 cm.
AB51 [7630]. JF 771. Another at U53 [8684], GP 197, reused as a lamp.
Ashmunein, 1998, C310, possibly sixth to seventh century AD. Elephantine X, Abb.72, T615a, 7, second quarter of the fifth to the first half of the seventh century AD.

74. Base of beaker. O1W.
AE50 [8408]. JF 869. Part of same vessel in AE50 [8584].
Elephantine X, Abb.73, T624a, 7–9 (7 closest), mid sixth to seventh century AD.

75. Body of a flagon. Orange-slipped overall with cream band overlaid with black lines towards the bottom of the flagon and black lines on body towards base of neck. O1.
AE51 [8395], AE52 [8396], AC52 [8402]. JF 886.
Elephantine X, Abb.76, T711, 16, fifth/sixth century AD. Esna III, pl. CCXXVI, 5.

76. Flagon top. O1. D = 7.5 cm.
AC50 [7706]. JF 776.
Elephantine X, Abb.77, T714, 6, possibly no earlier than the sixth century AD.

77. Flagon top. O1. D = 7 cm.
AD51 [7632]. GP 429.
Elephantine X, Abb.78, T735, 7, sixth to seventh century AD.

78. Lid. O1. D = 5 cm.
AA37 [7348]. JF 915.
Ashmunein, 1998, C672, conjectural date AD 400–550.

79. Lid. Traces of cream slip. O1W. D = 8cm.
AA48 [9807]. JF 933.
Ashmunein, 1998, C665–667, given a date of *c.* fourth century to *c.* eighth century AD.

80. Base of bowl (?). O1. Orange-slipped overall.
AE52 [8188]. JF 870.
LRP, fig. 86, E, sixth century AD.

81. Base of bowl with high ring. O1W. D = 10 cm.
AA48 [9813]. GP 609.
Elephantine X, Abb.45, T349, probably imitating LRP Form 93B, first half of the sixth century AD, but Gempeler states that many of these bowls were produced later.

82. Base of bowl with blurred double-jewelled cross stamp. O1.
AF33 [8487]. JF 720.
LRP, 396, Stamp 294, Group 'A', with subsidiary motifs. Probably third quarter of the fifth to the early sixth century AD.

83. Stamped sherd. Double-jewelled cross. O1.
AD52 [7573]. JF 905.
Parallels as no. 82.

84. Stamped sherd. Double cross. O1.
AB50 [7784]. GP 407.
LRP, 396, Stamp 299, Group 'A', date as no. 82.

85. Stamped sherd. O1.
AA36 [7808]. JF 864.
Ashmunein, 1998, C526, AD 600–700. Near Elephantine X, Abb.15, T222a, 6, second quarter of the fifth to the early seventh century AD.

86. Stamped sherd. O1.
Y52 [7420]. JF 840.
Close to LRP, fig. 46, style E, 146h, which occurred on African Red Slipware Form 99.7, tending towards type 'B' dated around AD 530–580.

87. Stamped sherd. O1.
U51 [8190]. JF 841.
Elephantine X, Abb.20, T236b, 14, sixth to the first half (?) of the seventh century AD.

88. Amphora. O1. Orange-slipped inside and out. D = 5 cm.
AE 52 [8396], AE 52 [8201]. JF 887.
Elephantine X, Abb.77, T726, 23, undated.

**Finewares, long-distance traded/short-distance traded: Egyptian Red Slipped 'B' Ware (M5)**

This ware amounted to 3.6 per cent of the total RBH (Table 2.1) for the years 1993–4 and 2000 combined, compared to 6.46 per cent in Volume 1. This may well be due to the fact that the pottery in this volume is from excavated contexts and therefore possibly only recently discarded.

As before in Volume 1, it has been decided to separate Egyptian Red Slipped Wares 'B' and 'H' although Donald Bailey has combined these, but with reservations (Bailey, 1998, 38). There are differences in the two fabrics; the fabric of ERS 'B' observed at Kom el-Nana was a uniform brown with no 'sandwich' layer, whilst that of the 'H' fabric exhibited the layer. This may, however, be due to the firing as suggested in the author's Volume 1 and Bailey's discussion in the above reference. Bases of ERS 'H' vessels were not usually slipped as the base appears to have been held in order to dip the vessel into the slip, coating the inside and over the rim. However, the vessels in ERS 'B' and ERS 'H' found at Kom el-Nana are very similar in their disposition of slip coatings. Of the ERS 'B' vessels below on which slip was visible, 14 had slip inside and over the rim, whilst 16 had slip both inside and outside the vessel. Of the following collection of ERS 'H', 19 have slip inside and over the rim and 31 had an overall slip. It must be stated, however, that 13 of the ERS 'H' vessels are carinated bowls, which may have required a complete slip to provide a base for other decoration and this would reduce the number to 18. It would seem, therefore, that the two vessel fabrics are treated in much the same way with regard to slip coating, and this may have a relevance to the provenance of these, in that both may well have come from Middle Egypt, given the proposal on firing above.

This ware can be listed under both long-distance traded or short-distance traded because, although chemical analysis in 1987 on ERS 'B' has shown the fabric to conform to amphora fabrics from Middle Egypt (Ballet and Picon, 1987, 40–41), it is thought there may also be additional sources in the Delta and Fayoum century as originally proposed by Hayes (LRP, 387–401). A fuller discussion on this subject is given by Bailey (Bailey, 1998, 38).

89. Flanged bowl with high, knobbed rim. Red slipped inside and over rim. D = 22 cm.
AB35 [7662]. GP 371.
Coin: fifth to sixth century AD.
Ashmunein, 1998, D328, conjectural context date AD 500–650.

90. Flanged bowl with high, knobbed rim and small flange. Red-slipped inside and over rim. D = 22 cm.
AA48 [9847]. GP 605.
Ashmunein, 1998, D315, AD 400–550.
Also Syene, type 48 is similar, mid fifth to early sixth century AD or earlier, in O1 fabric.

91. Small, flanged bowl with high, knobbed rim and small flange. Burnt areas on interior and exterior. Warped. Red-slipped inside and over rim. D = *c.*13 cm.
AA49 [9838]. GP 600.
Ashmunein, 1998, D336, AD 650–800+ is similar.

92. Flanged bowl with low rim and hooked flange. Red-slipped inside and over rim. D = 18 cm.
AA48 9842. GP 562.
Ashmunein, 1998, D302, AD 400–550.

93. Flanged bowl. Flat rim, grooved. Red-slipped inside and outside. D = 21 cm.
Y50 [8530]. JF 823.
This is a copy of an African Red Slipware bowl, LRP Form 97, AD 490–550. Given the time taken to copy existing, possibly higher-value vessels, this bowl may well be a little later in date than the LRP vessel.

94. Flanged bowl with groove in rim. Red-slipped inside and over rim. D = 12.5 cm.
Z35 [7559]. JF 919.
Similar to Deir el Naqlun 1988–1989, 19.38, seventh to eighth century AD.

95. Flanged bowl. Red-slipped inside and over rim. D = 20 cm.
AD52 [8396]. JF 754.
Ashmunein, 1998, D392, fifth to seventh century AD.

96. Flanged bowl. Red-slipped inside and out. D = 21.5 cm.
Z35 [7559]. JF 917.
Similar to Ashmunein, 1998, D350, AD 650–800+, but without the carination on the Ashmunein version.

97. Deep, flanged bowl with two grooves in rim. Red-slipped inside and outside. D = 34 cm.
AD51 [7547]. GP 290.
Similar to Alexandrie, B12, which has no grooves in the rim. See also Kellia, pl. 7 in the same fabric with only the inner groove.

98. Dish with out-turned rim. Groove under rim. Red-slipped inside and outside. D = 24 cm.
Z51 [7425]. JF 844.
Esna, 17, AD 550–630. See also Gurna, 1372.

99. Deep, flanged bowl or basin with out-turned rim. Red slipped inside and outside. D = 32 cm.
AA36 [7667]. GP 274.
Close to el-Hibeh 1980, 112.

100. Dish or shallow bowl with flattened, knobbed rim. Red-slipped inside and over rim. D = 24 cm.
AE52 [7517]. GP 309.
Ashmunein, 1998, D350, AD 650–800+.

101. Bowl with small out-turned rim and steep sloping sides. Red-slipped inside and over rim. D = 22 cm.
V52 [8692]. GP 177.
Ashmunein, 1998, D341, probably of late fourth or fifth century AD. See also Kellia, pl. 43, 4.

102. Bowl with small, out-turned rim and steep sloping sides. Red-slipped inside and outside. D = 15.5 cm.
Z50 [8247]. GP 214.
See no. 101.

103. Bowl with knobbed rim and internal ledge near base. Red-slipped inside and outside. D = 30 cm.
AE52 [8186] and AE52 [8180]. GP 291.
Gurna, 1151 in O1, AD 395–640.

104. Shallow dish with thickened rim. Red-slipped inside and outside. D = 32 cm.
AA48 [9800]. GP 635.
Ashmunein, 1998, D258, around sixth to eighth century AD.

105. Small, shallow dish or bowl with thickened rim. Red-slipped inside and over rim. D = 18 cm.
AA49 [9834]. GP 591.
Gurna, 1234, AD 395–640.

106. Dish or shallow bowl with knobbed rim. Red-slipped inside and outside. D = 42.5 cm.
AD49/50 [8323]. JF 731.
Coin: Justinian I, IB, AD 527–565
As Ashmunein, 1998, D242, *c.* AD 600–700. Similar to Elephantine X, Abb.13, T218b in ERSA (O1), *c.* second quarter of the fifth century to the early seventh century AD.

107. Dish or shallow bowl with knobbed rim and internal ledge. Red-slipped inside and outside.
D = 30 cm.
AC52 [7409]. GP 455.
Gurna, 1232 or 1233, AD 395–640.

108. Dish or shallow bowl with knobbed, grooved rim. Internal ledge and groove on body approximately 2 cm below rim. Red-slipped inside and outside.
D = 36 cm.
Z36 [7559]. GP 170.
Similar to Gurna, 1250. No direct parallel found.

109. Shallow dish with knobbed, grooved rim. Some blackening on external rim. Red-slipped inside and outside. D = 28 cm.
AA48 [9842]. Same vessel in AA48 [9844] and AA48 [9800], not joining. GP 561.
Ashmunein, 1998, D134, AD 450–500 and Gurna, 1243–1244 are similar.

110. Shallow bowl with knobbed rim. Red-slipped inside and outside. D = 36 cm.
Z36 [7559]. GP 217.
Close to Ashmunein, 1998, D470, conjectural date AD 650–800+. Also Elephantine X: Abb.24, T259, probably second half of the sixth or early seventh century AD. The latter in ERSA (O1).

111. Bowl with knobbed rim. Red-slipped inside and outside. D = 29.5 cm.
AD50 [7515] GP 250.
Ashmunein, 1998, D113, AD 400–550.

112. Bowl with internal ridging. Exterior heavily blackened and encrusted. Badly worn. Interior red slipped. D = 20 cm.
AA48 [9842]. GP 574.
Similar to Gurna, 1377. Ashmunein, 1998, D506, AD 450–500.

113. Lid. Red-slipped inside only. D = 18 cm.
Z36 [7451]. GP 224.
Gurna, 1398, found in contexts dated fifth to eighth centuries AD.

114. Flagon. Encrusted with a black oily deposit. Slip not visible. D = 7 cm.
AD49 [8337]. JF 762.
Close to Esna, N2, pl. CCXXV1, AD 550–630.

115. Base of jar or flagon. Encrusted black deposit on inside. Slip not visible.
AD51 [7647]. JF 929.

116. Base of bowl (?). Red-slipped inside and outside.
AF34 [8358]. GP 355.

117. Stamped base sherd of bowl or dish. Red-slipped inside only.
Y51 [7721]. JF 909.
This stamp is similar to one found at Elephantine X on Form T236b and dated sixth to the first half of the seventh century (?) AD.

118. Stamped base sherd of bowl or dish. Red-slipped inside only.
AE51 [8202]. JF 880.
Close to Ashmunein, 1998, C352, on ERS 'A' dated AD 600–700.

119. Stamped base sherd. Post-firing hole in sherd. Red-slipped inside only.
AA49 [9834]. GP 617.
Similar stamp to Ashmunein, 1998, D179 and D180. Conjectural context date *c.* AD 400–550.

120. Stamped base sherd. Red-slipped inside only.
AA48 [9842]. GP 572.
LRP, fig. 420, Type 75, and p.243, of around the first half of the fifth century AD.

**Finewares, short-distance traded: Egyptian Red Slipped 'H' Ware (M6)**

This ware, probably from the el-Ashmunein area, amounted to 5.02 per cent of the total RBH (Table 2.1). However, if Bailey is correct in his supposition that the ERS 'B' (M5) could have been made in the locality (see discussion at ERS 'B' above), then the two percentages added together total 8.62 per cent—higher than the Aswan wares at 7.34 per cent—which would seem to make sense if the latter had to come from a longer distance. The previously published figure for M6 in Volume 1 (Faiers, 2005) was 5.52 per cent.

121. Bowl with high rim and small flange. Red-slipped inside and outside. D = 22 cm.
AB35 [7561]. GP 443.
Ashmunein, 1998, AD 375–450.

122. Bowl with high rim and small flange. Red-slipped inside and over rim. D = 22 cm.
AA48 [9848]. GP 554.
Ashmunein, 1982, E49.1, probably to be dated AD 400–500.

123. Bowl with high rim and small flange. Red-slipped inside and outside. D = 28 cm.
Z36 [7559]. JF 806.
Nazlet Tuna, 113, 3 or 115, 3, both surface finds.

124. Bowl or basin with high rim and small flange. Red-slipped inside and outside. D = 30 cm.
Z36 [7559]. JF 819.
Ashmunein, 1998, D315, AD 400–550. Also at the South Church at el-Ashmunein dated to around AD 360–460. Nazlet Tuna, 113, 4, surface find.

125. Bowl or basin with high rim and small flange. Four evenly spaced grooves on body below flange. Red-slipped inside and outside. D = 30 cm
AD50 [8778]. GP 91.
Elephantine X, Abb.51, T359c, close in O1. Second half of the sixth to the eighth century AD.

126. Bowl or basin with low rim and flange. Red-slipped inside and outside. D = 37 cm.
Y51 [7425]. AG 57.
Nazlet Tuna. 117, 4, surface find, but with rouletting on body. See also Esna, pl. CCXXII, E36.

127. Bowl with low rim and flange. D = 29 cm.
AA49 [9833]. GP 514.
Esna, pl. CCXXII, E36, about AD 550–630.

128. Bowl with low rim and flange. Red-slipped inside and outside. D = 14 cm.
AA48 [9840]. GP 613.
Elephantine X, Abb.51, T359a, is close, but in O1, *c.* mid sixth to eighth century AD.

129. Bowl with very low rim and flange. Surfaces worn. No slip visible. D = 16 cm.
AA49 [9834]. GP 592.
Berenice, fig. 131, 1017, in a coarseware occurring mainly in the fourth and fifth centuries AD, but also in the sixth century AD.

130. Bowl with low rim and frilled flange. Red-slipped inside and outside. D = 24 cm.
AA46 [9800]. GP 539.

131. Small bowl with flat flange and low foot. Badly burnt. Red slip inside and over rim. D = 20 cm.
AC/AD50 [8196]. JF 892.
LRP, Form 108 is similar and dated early seventh century. This form is said to be derived from Form 98, dated early sixth century AD.

132. Small bowl with flat flange and groove in flange. D = 12 cm.
AE52 [8199]. GP 326.

133. Small bowl with slight flange. One-half burnt, but traces of red slip on the other half. Two holes in the side under the rim. D = 16 cm.
V51 [8586], V51 [8294] and V51 [8689]. JF 866.
Close to Ashmunein, 1998, D359, AD 500–650.

134. Bowl with out-turned rim. Red-slipped inside and over rim. D = 22 cm.
Z36 [7432]. GP 210
Gurna, 1367 for body and 1369 for rim. Sixth to eighth century AD.

135. Shallow bowl or dish. Red-slipped inside and over rim. D = 28 cm.
AF34 [8490]. GP 359.
Similar to Ashmunein, 1998, D350, *c.* AD 650–800+. See also Elephantine X, Abb.58, T377, in ERS 'A' roulette, not before the second half of the sixth or the seventh century AD.

136. Bowl with out-turned, knobbed rim, and low carination. Red-slipped inside and over rim.
D = 26 cm.
AF34 [8489]. AG 16.
See Ashmunein, 1998, D9, of AD 600–700 date and classed as a 'frying pan', but similar to Bailey, CCE 4, 1996, pl.VII, fig. 11, 52, from below the South Church at el-Ashmunein and dated AD 390–460.

137. Bowl with knobbed rim. Groove on top of rim. Red-slipped inside and over rim. D = 30 cm.
AD51 [7650]. GP 450.
Gurna, 1367, but with no groove in the rim of the Gurna example.

138. Dish or shallow bowl with knobbed, slightly hooked rim, internal grooves inside base. Red-slipped inside and over rim. D = 32 cm.
AA36 [7667]. GP 381.
Close to Ashmunein, 1985, H50, AD 600–700.

139. Dish with knobbed, slightly hooked rim. Red-slipped inside and outside. D = 26 cm.
AD52 [7416]. JF 883.
Similar to Ashmunein, 1998, 259D, conjectural

context date AD 600–700.

140. Bowl with thickened, in-turned rim. Grooved internally at the top of rim and approximately 2 cm down from rim top. Red-slipped inside and outside.
D = 25 cm.
AC11 [6157]. JF 811.
Close to Nazlet Tuna, 121, 1. See also Gurna, 1120, 1.

141. Dish with knobbed rim and internal groove in floor. Red-slipped inside and outside. D = 27 cm.
Z36 [7432]. JF 899.
Ashmunein, 1998, D112, from topsoil in a context dated eighth to tenth century AD. Possibly based on LRP, Form 63.1, dating to the last quarter of the fourth century AD. Close to Nazlet Tuna, 111, 5, AD 350–650.

142. Bowl or dish with knobbed rim. Red-slipped inside and outside. D = 28 cm.
AD51 [7631]. AG 51.
Nazlet Tuna, 121, 1, AD 350–650.

143. Dish with knobbed rim. Red-slipped inside and outside. D = 22 cm.
Z36 [7559]. JF 799.
Ashmunein, 1998, D109, sixth to eighth century AD, possibly a 'frying pan'.

144. Dish or bowl with slightly in-turned rim and groove on body above carination. Red-slipped inside and outside. D = 16cm.
AC11 [6157]. JF 814.
Esna, pl. CCXXIV, H9, AD 550–630.

145. Bowl with straight sides and carination. Badly burnt. No slip visible. D = 20 cm.
AD50 [8168]. JF 896.
Esna, pl. CCXIX, A7, AD 550–630.
Kellia, pl. 40, 12.

146. Dish or bowl with handle(s). Burnt outside. Red-slipped inside only. D = 24 cm.
AD50 [8158]. JF 881.
Coin: fifth to sixth century AD.
This appears to be a handled version of vessels such as Esna, pl. CCXIX, A7, or Kellia, pl. 40, 12, which was a surface find.

147. Bowl with straight sides and internal grooving. Red-slipped inside and over rim. D = 22 cm.
AI52 [8124]. GP 454.
'Frying pan' type, similar to Ashmunein, 1998, D8, although the Ashmunein example is late for Kom el-Nana at AD 650–800+. See also Elephantine X, Abb.83, D120c, fifth to seventh century AD.

148. Bowl with slightly out-turned rim and low carination. Red-slipped inside and over rim.
D = 30 cm.
AC51 [8588]. JF 719.
'Frying pan' type, Ashmunein, 1998, D5, late fourth to eighth century AD. Close to Bailey, CCE 4, 1996, pl.VII, figs 11, 51 and 53, AD 360–460.

149. Dish with internal grooves. Red-slipped inside. 'Frying pan' type. D = 26 cm.
AD51 [7632]. AG 52.
Ashmunein, 1998, D5 and 9. This was a common form at Ashmunein dating from the fifth to the seventh century AD.

150. Dish or bowl with thickened rim. Thick red slip inside and outside. D = 26 cm.
AA48 [9842]. GP 578.
Similar to Esna, pl. CCXXII, E25.

151. Dish with thickened rim and slight groove in rim. Red-slipped inside and outside. D = 30 cm.
AA49 [9838]. GP 598.
Ashmunein, 1998, D242, in a conjectural context date of AD 600–700.

152. Dish with thickened rim. Red-slipped inside and outside. D = 18.5 cm.
Z51 [7469]. AG 69.
Ashmunein, 1998, D256, sixth to eighth century AD.

153. Bowl with reeded rim and low-placed carination. Red-slipped inside and outside. D = 24 cm.
AE52 [8201]. JF 890.
Ashmunein, 1998, D222, dated by an example from Tod from the end of the fourth century to the end of the fifth century AD.

154. Bowl with reeded rim and low-placed carination. Red-slipped inside and outside. D = 24 cm.
AE52 [8201]. GP 321.
Imitating LRP, Form 84. Elephantine X, Abb.18, 4, T228, last quarter of the fifth to the third quarter of the sixth century AD.

155. Dish with reeded rim and handle(s). Red-slipped inside and over rim. D = 28.5 cm.
Z51 [7461]. JF 861.
Possibly to be used as a casserole. Gurna, 1452 (which has no handles), is similar, AD 550–630.

156. Dish with upright, thickened rim and low foot. Red-slipped inside and outside. D = 28 cm.
U53 [8682] and U53 [8684]. GP 239.
Elephantine X, Abb.12, 9, T218a in Egyptian Red Slipped 'A' Ware is the nearest, dated to the second quarter of the fifth to the early seventh century AD.

157. Dish or shallow bowl with upright, grooved rim and internal spiral stamp/groove. Red-slipped inside. D = 16 cm.
AB50 [7699]. JF 874.
Ashmunein, 1998, D132, is a larger version of this dish. The internal stamp is as Elephantine X, Abb.12, 13, T218a, or LRP, fig. 40, 27–29. Given a date of mid fourth to mid fifth century AD on African Red Slipware.

158. Small bowl. Red pigment caked on the inside. Red-slipped inside and over rim. D = 11.5 cm.
AC50 [7702]. JF 775.
Elephantine X, Abb.39, 7, T324a, second quarter to the mid of the fifth to the end (?) of the seventh century AD. The Elephantine X vessel is in Aswan ware (01), and the form is listed as frequent during the period given.

159. Bowl with dip in rim, possibly for a lid seating. Red-slipped inside and outside. D = 18 cm.
Z36 [7454]. GP 228. Another D = 26 cm at AB48 [9813].
Ashmunein, 1998, N36 and N38 in a Nile-silt fabric and given a date of AD 375–450. Also in African Red Slipware at Sabratha (V.II, Part 1), figs 19, 84 and 85, unstratified. The form is also present in a coarseware in Berenice, fig. 127, 930 under 'Mid-Roman plain wares'.

160. Dish or shallow bowl with upright thickened rim. Red-slipped inside and over rim with vestigial black painted line on lower rim. D = 22 cm.
AA37 [7436]. JF 882.
Close to Nazlet Tuna, 131, 3. The Kom el-Nana vessel is shallower.

161. Dish with in-curving rim, pink-slipped inside and out with decoration over rim of black uneven line with red spots. Traces of a black line on inside of rim. D = 22 cm.
AF33[8489]. JF 916.
A plain version of this dish can be found at Ashmunein, 1998, D61, AD 400–550.

162. Small bowl or cup with straight sides and carination. Decorated with black and cream blotches above carination. Red-slipped inside and outside.
D = 11 cm.
AE52 [8192]. GP 288. Another at AD51 [7652].
Coin: fourth to sixth century AD at AE52 [8192].
Similar to Elephantine X, Abb.74, T630b, a beaker of late sixth to eighth/ninth century AD.

The following vessels, nos 163–174, are carinated bowls of the type found at el-Ashmunein (Bailey, 2005, pl. 31, p. 55 and pl. 53, 1–6). It is probable that the Kom el-Nana vessels had ring bases, as several of these bases have been found separately, but unfortunately none of the illustrated vessels had a base so this is not a certainty. This form was also made in the local M2 fabric with the same sort of decoration such as arcs, intersecting arcs, blobs and lines in fired-on ceramic colours of black, white and pink. No. 230 in M2 also has a line of what appears to be string impressions at the carination, the string probably held the bowl in shape whilst drying and before firing.

163. Carinated bowl. White dots over black bands on red ground. Interior black. D = 26 cm.
Z51 [7463]. GP 393.
Ashmunein, 1998, D548, AD 400–550. The collection of these vessels found at el-Ashmunein is cited as being mostly of the fifth and sixth centuries AD, but possibly of the sixth and seventh centuries AD. See also Kellia, pl. 45, 8.

164. Carinated bowl. Black decoration on red slip inside and outside. D = 28 cm.
AA47 [9800] and AA47 [9833]. GP 515.
Similar to Gurna, 1588.

165. Carinated bowl. Red-slipped inside and over rim. White blob on inner rim. D = 26 cm.
AG33 [8487]. GP 392.
Nazlet Tuna, 95, 2, or Kellia, pl. 46, 1.

166. Carinated bowl with black line on inner rim and black design on body. Red-slipped inside and outside. D = 24 cm.
AA48 [9855]. GP 634.
Gurna, 1566.

167. Carinated bowl with notched rim and white/cream dots on black line on body. Thin, red slip inside and outside. D = 24 cm.
Z50 [8253]. GP 376.
Nazlet Tuna, 95, 3.

168. Carinated bowl with white/cream dots on black cross design. D = 26 cm.
AA48 [9832], AA48 [9848] and AA49 [9838]. GP 485.

169. Carinated bowl with internal ledge. Red-slipped inside and out with black and white/cream decoration on body. D = 25 cm.
AA50 [8252]. GP 117.

170. Carinated bowl with internal ledge and white/cream decoration on body. D = 21 cm.
AE52 [8200] and AE52 [8201]. GP 329.
Esna, pl. CCXXI, E12, or Kellia, pl. 45, 8.

171. Carinated bowl with black decoration on body. Red-slipped inside and outside. D = 22 cm.
Z50 [8253]. JF 803.
Kellia, pl. 45, 8.

172. Carinated bowl with slightly grooved rim. Red-slipped inside and out with black decoration.
D = 28 cm.
AA49 [9838]. GP 596.
Gurna, 1553 and 1555 for the rim and 1557 for the decoration.

173. Carinated bowl with two grooves in rim and black design on body. Red-slipped inside and over rim. D = 23 cm.
AC49 [8146]. JF 714.
Coins: Roman copies (two), fourth to seventh century AD.
Variation of 172 above.

174. Carinated bowl (?). Red-slipped inside and out with black design on body and inside rim. D = 28 cm.
Z36 [7559]. GP 377.
Kellia, pl. 46, 6.

**Finewares: miscellaneous**

175. Carinated jar with internal ledge. Red-slipped inside and outside with white/cream decoration.
D = 14 cm.
AB52 [7701]. JF 773.
Gurna, 1693 and 1694, found in contexts of fifth to eighth century AD.

176. Base of bowl. Red-slipped inside and outside. Base D = 16 cm.
AA48 [9832] and AA48 [9842]. GP 577.
Possibly the base of a very large, shallow bowl such as Ashmunein, 1998, D476, AD 600–700.

177. Base of bowl. Stamped on inner base. Red slipped inside. D = 12 cm.
Z36 [7459]. GP 203.
This base is similar to Hayes, Form F, LRP, 391, dated sixth to early seventh century AD. The stamp is possibly part of a jewelled cross motif.

178. Stamped sherd. Red slipped inside.
AB48 [9807]. JF 936.

179. Stamped sherd. Red slipped inside and outside.
V50 [8681]. JF 839.

**Coarsewares, short-distance traded: bowls and basins**

This form comprised the second highest figure in the total RBH for 1993–4 and 2000 at 21.05 per cent (Table 2.2). This figure is almost exactly the same as the percentage RBH for bowls and basins in Faiers 2005, which was 21.97 per cent.

Although these vessels can be dated only vaguely to AD 400–700, nine of those below were found with coins dating from AD 300–600, and the most closely dated coin was from the same layer as no. 254, i.e. AD 425–450. Of the other vessels found with coins in the same layer, five were of the fifth to sixth centuries AD.

*Plain bowls and basins*

180. Small bowl with out-turned rim. M1. D = 12 cm.
Y52 [8656]. GP 181.

181. Small bowl, ribbed below flat, inward-slanting rim. P23. D = 14 cm.
V50 [8681]. JF 828.

182. Small bowl. M2. D = 16 cm.
AE51 [8395]. GP 410.

183. Small, carinated bowl with lid seating. W2.
D = 16 cm.
Y52 [8656]. JF 889.

184. Small, flanged bowl. M2. D = 12 cm.
AB51 [7409]. JF 898.
Ashmunein, 1998, C350, nearest, dated fifth to seventh century AD.

185. Small bowl. M4. D = 14 cm.
Z52 [8278]. JF 792.

186. Small bowl. M1. D = 17 cm.
Z50 [8247]. JF 790.
Ashmunein, 1998, N187, fifth to seventh century AD.

187. Bowl, possibly a dish. M1. D = 22 cm.
Z36 [7559]. GP 284.

A derivative of Hayes, LRP, Form 87a, this form appears to be copying an Aswan vessel such as Elephantine X, Abb.14, T220a, 1–3, of second quarter of the fifth to the early seventh century AD, and probably later.

188. Bowl, possibly a dish. M4. D = 22 cm.
Z36 [7559]. JF 800.
Similar to Ashmunein, 1998, C294, in Aswan ware (O1). Also Elephantine X, Abb.43, T344a, *c.* sixth to seventh or eighth century AD. The latter vessel also in O1.

189. Small bowl. M2. D = 14 cm.
AC51 [7567]. GP 363.
Esna, pl. CCXIX, A4.

190. Small bowl. M2. D = 12 cm.
AD50 [8145]. GP 96.
Esna, pl. CCXX, C2.

191. Dish. Interior and exterior red slipped. M2.
D = 25 cm.
AA49 [9834]. GP 593.
Similar to Ashmunein, 1998, C126 *bis*, in ERS 'A'.

192. Carinated bowl/basin with out-turned rim. M1.
D = 30 cm.
V51 [8633], V51 [8689] and V52 [8683]. GP 337.
Close to Nazlet Tuna, 62, fig. 3.17, 2.

193. Bowl. M2. D = 26 cm.
AD51 [7632]. GP 418.

194. Basin with slight externally ribbed flange. M1.
D = 30 cm.
AB52 [7710]. GP 415.
Close to Nazlet Tuna, 58, fig. 3.15, 4. The Nazlet Tuna vessel is decorated.

195. Basin with knobbed, ribbed rim. VCM1.
D = 30 cm.
AB48 [9813]. GP 648.
Possibly a heavy, carinated bowl as Esna, pl. CCXXI, D12.

196. Basin. M1. D = 38 cm.
AD50 [8168]. JF 756.

197. Basin. M1. D = 34 cm.
AE49 [8456], AE50 [8408] and AE50 [8392]. GP 294.

198. Basin. M1. D = 24 cm.
AD50 [8168]. JF 756.

199. Basin with knobbed, grooved rim. M1.
D = 34 cm.
Z36 [7451]. GP 168.

200. Bowl. M1. D = 26 cm.
AA36 [7667]. AG 34.
Similar to Gurna, 1954. See also Elephantine X, Abb.115, 8, K516. Probably fifth to sixth century AD. The Elephantine X example does not have a ribbed body.

201. Basin with knobbed, slightly hooked rim and ribbed body. M1. D = 34 cm.
AA48 [9840]. GP 612.

202. Bowl with lid seating and ribbed body. M2.
D = 26 cm.
AA36 [7313]. GP 272.
Similar to Gurna, 1640–1643.

203. Basin. Lid seating. M1. D = 32 cm.
U51 [8697]. JF 810.

204. Basin with flanged rim. M1. D = 39.5 cm.
AF34 [8489]. AG 17.

205. Bowl with flanged rim. M1. D = 30 cm.
AB36 [7448]. AG 64.
Gurna, 1269.

206. Bowl with flanged rim. M1. D = 24 cm.
AB49 [8339]. GP 143.

207. Basin with out-turned, rounded rim, M1.
D = 31 cm.
Z51 [7490]. AG 77.

208. Bowl with slightly out-turned, squared-off rim.
M1. D = 26 cm.
AB36 [7443]. GP 394.

209. Basin with knobbed rim. M1. D = 39 cm.
AB35 [7662]. GP 474.
Coin: fifth to sixth century AD.
Gurna, 1962a.

210. Basin with knobbed rim. M2. D = 36 cm.
AA48 [9847]. GP 606.
Gurna, 1926a.

211. Bowl. M1. D = 24 cm.
AB51 [7409]. GP 387.

212. Bowl. Rounded rim with ribbing on outside for

2.5 cm downwards from rim. Hanging hole 0.5 cm under rim. M1. D = 22 cm.
Z36 [7460]. JF 784.
Ashmunein, 1998, D131, conjectural context date AD 400–550. This vessel was also 22 cm in diameter.

213. Bowl with two holes in the side for hanging. VCM1. D = 36 cm.
AE52 [8823] and AF33 [8565]. AG 99.
Esna, pl. CCXX, C24.

*Painted bowls and basins*

See the note on carinated bowls in M6. Nos 219–221 and 223 in this collection are the same form.

214. Small bowl with out-turned rim. Very uneven body. Red blob on overall pink slip. M2. D = 12.5 cm.
AC51 [8588]. JF 718.

215. Small bowl with out-turned rim. Orange overall slip and black horizontal bands with cream band between. M1. D = 16 cm.
AB49/50 [8343]. GP 121.

216. Basin with knobbed, grooved rim. Cream-slipped interior. VCM1. D = 42 cm.
AF51 [8190]. AG 18.

217. Small bowl with bead rim. Black blobs on rim. Overall red slip. M2. D = 13 cm.
AB35 [7662]. AG 81.
Coin: fifth to sixth century AD.
The shape of this vessel is the same as an ERS 'A' (O1) form at Elephantine (Elephantine X, Abb.41, 10, 335), given a sixth century AD date.

218. Small bowl with black blobs on rim and black blobs on vertical band on body. M4. D = 12 cm.
Z36 [7559]. GP 215.

219. Carinated bowl with traces of a black arc and cream decoration. M1. D = 28 cm.
AB49 [8334]. GP 109.
Esna, pl. CCXXI, E15.

220. Carinated bowl with black decoration. M2.
D = 23.5 cm.
AE52 [8201]. GP 328.
Esna, pl. CCXXI, E15.

221. Carinated bowl. Cream-slipped rim with cream slip intersecting arcs on body. M2. D = 27 cm.
AB35 [7563]. JF 825.
Ashmunein, 1998, D591, AD 600–700.

222. Large bowl. Black lines on outside of rim and black arc on body. M1. D = 40 cm.
AB52 [7653]. GP 89.

223. Carinated bowl. Black arcs with splashes of black slip on and over rim. Traces of cream slip behind black arcs. Traces of stringing marks at carination. M2.
D = 28 cm.
Z36 [7432]. GP 230.

224. Bowl with sloping sides. Black blobs and cream decoration outside with traces of black and cream decoration inside and around flattened rim. M1.
D = 28 cm.
Z36 [7451]. GP 173.
Gurna, 1548–1550, or Nazlet Tuna, 85, fig. 3, 28.2.

225. Bowl with flat rim and sloping sides. Cream-slipped on flat rim. M1. D = 20 cm.
AE51 [8389]. GP 317.
Gurna, 1954, undecorated.

226. Bowl with knobbed, flattened rim. Traces of cream decoration on interior with black spots on a cream ground on the rim. M1. D = 26 cm.
AA47 [9853]. GP 636.

227. Basin with flat rim. Cream-slipped externally with traces of black and cream and red decoration internally. M1. D = 32 cm.
Y51 [7472]. GP 346.

228. Bowl with 'pie crust' rim. Patches of red slip on exterior. Pink and black decoration internally. M1.
D = 30 cm.
AA47 [9836]. GP 608.

229. Bowl with 'pie crust' rim. Traces of cream slip over rim. M2. D = 26 cm.
AA47 [9857]. GP 640.

230. Bowl with 'pie crust' rim. Pink slipped overall with black and red decoration internally. M4.
D = 28 cm.
AE51 [8385]. JF 895.

231. Bowl with 'pie crust' rim. Internal black, cream/white and red decoration. M1. D = 24 cm.
Z52 [8518]. GP 344.

232. Basin with 'pie crust' rim. Red and cream slip externally. Black grid, wavy line between black lines

with red, and cream slip internally. Black spots, line and arcs on cream slipped rim. M1. D = 40 cm.
V51 [8681,V51 [8294] and V52 [8687]. JF 818.

233. Pedestal bowl with 'pie crust' rim. Pink-slipped internally and externally with black and red decoration internally. M1. D = 24.5 cm.
AC49 [8149]. JF 707.

234. Bowl with ledged, 'pie crust' rim. Pink and black decoration internally and black and orange decoration under rim. M1. D = 36 cm.
Z36 [7562]. GP 543.

235. Bowl with ledged rim. Black dots on red band on rim. Pink-slipped inside and outside. M2. D = 32 cm.
AA49 [9834]. GP 594.

236. Bowl with ledged rim. Black, red and cream decoration on rim and internally. M1. D = 30 cm.
AD49 [8320]. GP 98.
Coin: fourth to fifth century AD.

237. Bowl with ledged rim. Pink-slipped overall with black blobs on rim. M2. D = 30 cm.
AB51 [7793] and AB52 [7679]. GP 320.

238. Bowl with ledged rim. Pink-slipped internally and externally with black blobs on rim. M2. D = 22 cm.
U53 [8684]. GP 198.

239. Bowl with ledged rim. Traces of red and black decoration on inner rim. M2. D = 22 cm.
V52 [8292]. GP 199.

240. Bowl with ledged rim. Black spots on red slip on rim. Black fish decoration on red-slipped interior. M2. D = 36 cm.
AD50 [8158], AD49 [8320] and AC49 [8326]. GP 384.
Coins: fifth to sixth century AD in AD50 [8158], and fourth to sixth century AD in AD49 [8320].

241. Bowl with ledged rim. Worn cream slip externally and internally. Red and black decoration inside and black decoration on rim. M1. D = 30 cm.
AA49 [9838]. GP 599.

242. Bowl with out-turned rim. Black, red and cream decoration internally. M1. D = 30 cm.
Z36 [7559]. GP 541.

243. Basin with out-turned rim. Red-slipped externally. Red, black and cream decoration internally with black, orange and cream decoration on rim. M1. D = 40 cm.
Z36 surface find. GP 542.

244. Bowl with out-turned rim. Black, orange and cream decoration on rim. M1. D = 44 cm.
Y52 [7724], [8501] and [8512], Z52 [8518], AD49 [8450]. GP 349.
Ashmunein, 1998, K22 and K23 are similar, but no date given.

245. Bowl with out-turned rim. Black stripes and arcs with cream and red slip on inner rim. Red-slipped externally. M1. D = 40 cm.
V51 [8683]. GP 345.
Parallel as no. 244.

246. Bowl with out-turned rim. Cream-slipped externally with black blobs towards base of bowl. Red, black and cream decoration on rim and internal surface. M1. D = 32 cm.
Z36 [7451] and Z36 [7559]. JF 928.

247. Basin with knobbed, out-turned rim. Traces of red, cream and black decoration on rim, and red and black traces internally. M2. D = 34 cm.
Z36 [7559]. GP 166.
A selection of similar vessels to nos 247–254 can be found at Gurna, 1526–1539.

248. Basin with out-turned rim. Two bands of cream and black line decoration externally. Black and cream decoration internally. M1. D = 39 cm.
AC51 [8583]. JF 826.

249. Basin with out-turned rim. Cream-slipped internally and over rim. M1. D = 37 cm.
AC49 [8146]. JF 736.
Coins: Roman (?) copies (two), fourth to seventh century AD.

250. Basin with out-turned rim. Red-slipped exterior with cream rim, black horizontal bands enclosing cream band. Traces of black decoration between rim and horizontal band. Red, cream and black decoration on rim, with cream, black and orange decoration internally. M1. D = 37.5 cm.
AD49 [8168] and AD49 [8336]. GP 338.
Coins: fourth to sixth century AD (three), AD49 [8336].

251. Basin with out-turned rim. Cream patches on exterior. M1. D = 32 cm.
AC49 [8146]. GP 104.
Coins: Roman (?) copies (two), fourth to seventh century AD.

252. Basin with out-turned rim with two ridges on inner rim. Red-slipped internally and over rim on exterior. M1. D = 34 cm.
V52 [8683]. GP 333.

253. Basin with flattened rim. Black and red decoration on rim. Red-slipped patches externally and internally. M1. D = 32 cm.
AB52 [7700]. GP 190.

254. Basin with flattened rim. Red slip with black blobs on rim and a dribble of red slip internally. M1. D = 34 cm.
AB51 [7648]. JF 774.
Coin: cross in wreath, AD 425–450.

255. Bowl with knobbed rim. Cream-slipped internally and externally. M1. D = 24 cm.
Z36 [7451]. JF 809.

256. Basin with knobbed rim. Black and cream external decoration in a band at base of rim to approximately 3 cm below. M1. D = 30 cm.
Z36 [7451]. GP 216.

257. Bowl with in-turned, knobbed rim. Cream decoration internally and over rim. M1. D = 26 cm.
AB49 [8334]. AB49/50 [8152] and AB49/50 [8343]. GP 140.

258. Bowl with handle(s). Pink slip decoration externally. Red slip decoration internally. M4. D = 24.5 cm.
AE52 [8192]. JF 901.
Coin: fourth to sixth century AD

259. Bowl with stubby handle(s). Cream-slipped decoration externally and internally. M2. D = 32 cm.
AB52 [7653]. GP 441.

260. Base sherd of bowl (?). Red-slipped overall with red, black and cream decoration in the form of fish.
AD49 [8168] and AD50 [8170]. JF 879.
Ashmunein, 1998, K8 and L18.

*Tubs and Large Basins (vessels over 50 cm)*

261. Tub with flattened rim. VCM1. Handmade. D = 52 cm.
AC51 [8400]. JF 763.

262. Tub with flattened rim. Traces of cream slip. Vertical finger marks and smoothing. VCM1. Handmade. D = 62 cm.
AA48 [9800], AA48 [9842] and AA48 [9844]. GP 575.

263. Basin with flattened rim. Wavy lines incised on outside. VCM1. Handmade. D = 56 cm.
AD52 [7507]. JF 885.

264. Basin with knobbed rim. M1. D = 50 cm.
Z50 [8247]. JF 788.

265. Large basin with sloping sides. Applied 'orange segment' decoration. Traces of cream slip. VCM1. D = *c*.80 cm.
Z36 [7459]. GP 457.
Esna, pl. CCXXVIII, S5.

266. Basin with flattened rim. Traces of cream slip. VCM1. Handmade. D = 52 cm.
AC51 [7576]. GP 473.

267. Basin with flattened rim. Wavy lines on body. Traces of cream slip. VCM1. Handmade. D = 66 cm.
Z52 [7612] and Z52 [7613]. GP 408.
Gurna, 1977.

268. Deep basin with wavy lines under rim on exterior. Cream slip band over wavy lines. VCM1. Handmade. D = 54 cm.
AB35 [7662]. GP 458.
Coin: fifth to sixth century AD.
Kellia, pl. 88 (one).

269. Basin with uneven rim. Traces of red slip on the exterior. Deep finger-marks in base and below rim. VCM1. Handmade. D = 41 cm.
AD51 [7801]. AG 87.

**Cooking wares (including cooking pots, dishes, lids, jars and casseroles)**

These wares constituted 11.8 per cent of the RBH for the years 1993–4 and 2000 (Table 2.2). This was a higher percentage than that found in the 1990–1992 collection, which was 7.49 per cent. It was interesting that, with the higher numbers of RBH catalogued, cooking pots and casseroles in M4 and M2 fabrics were almost equal, with only a small number of RBH in fabric M1. Another difference from Volume 1 figures was the incidence of handles. These were a comparative rarity in the 1990–1992 figures and it was supposed that either only the sides of the pot without handles had been found and illustrated or that the lack of handled cooking pots and casseroles was a regional anomaly, not withstanding that pots with handles had been found in the vicinity at the North Tombs at

Amarna (Jones, 91, figs 2, 4 and 5), at the Great Wadi (Faiers, 2005, 182, fig. 3.2, no. 5) and at South Sector Site 1 (Faiers, 2005, 192, fig. 3.7, no. 480).

There were 80 separate handles listed during the making of the catalogue for this volume, and 18 of the pots with recordable diameters had handles. Of the latter, 10 were attached to M4-fabric cooking pots/casseroles and eight to M2-fabric cooking pots/casseroles. This is a total of 48 cooking pots/casseroles with handles, if the eighty handles are taken as forty pots (although the figure could well be higher). So, it would appear that the first premise — that only the sides of pots without handles had been found — is the correct one and that, although fairly scarce, these pots were by no means missing from the record.

A comparison between the sizes of round-bodied cooking pots in this collection of 625 RBH and that of Volume 1 shows that again, sizes ranged from 8 cm to 32 cm, with the sizes 18 cm, 20 cm and 16 cm being the most popular in the same order as before.

Out of the 45 cooking pots listed, 23 can be paralleled at Ashmunein, which is not surprising as the point of supply was probably close to both.

These vessels probably span the life of the settlement, i.e. AD 425/50–650, other than those dated by coins found in the same layer. This last fact is shown in the entry for the vessel.

270. Cooking pot with upright rim and rilled body. M4. D = 16 cm.
AE50 [8408]. GP 373.
Ashmunein, 1998, E130, fifth to eighth century AD.

271. Cooking pot with upright rim. Plain body except for two lines of rilling near base. Exterior smoke blackened. M2. D = 18 cm.
Z36 [7459]. GP 186.

272. Cooking pot with rilled body and lid seating. M4. D = 16.5 cm.
Z36 [7559]. JF 805.

273. Cooking pot with out-curved rim and lid seating. Exterior blackened. M2. D = 16 cm.
AC49 [8146]. JF 735.
Coins: Roman (?) copies (two), fourth to seventh century AD.

274. Cooking pot with out-curved, grooved rim and rilled body. M2. D = 18.5 cm.
Z36 [7559]. GP 442.

275. Cooking pot with out-curved, grooved rim. M4. D = 18 cm.
AA37 [7445]. GP 351.
Similar to Ashmunein, 1998, E300, *c.* AD 500–650.

276. Cooking pot with out-curved, grooved rim and rilled body. M2. D = 15 cm.
Z36 [7459]. AG 59.
Ashmunein, 1998, E306, *c.* AD 500–650.

277. Cooking pot with out-curved rim and rilled body. Blackened. M4. D = 20 cm.
Z36 [7559]. JF 804.

278. Cooking pot with stubby, out-curved, grooved rim and rilled body. M4. D = 16 cm.
Z51 [7490]. AG 65.
Similar to Ashmunein, 1998, E316, of around seventh century AD.

279. Cooking pot with out-curved, grooved rim and rilled body. M4. D = 16 cm.
V50 [8681]. GP 209.

280. Cooking pot with out-curved rim and rilled body. M2. D = 18 cm.
V51 [8197], V51 [8291] and V51 [8292]. GP 208.
Ashmunein, 1998, E349, *c.* AD 650–800+.

281. Cooking pot with small, upright rim. M4. D = 20 cm.
AD52 [7506]. GP 258.
Coin: Tiberius II, AD 578–582.

282. Cooking pot with short rim, lid seating and rilled body. M4. D = 18 cm.
AD52 [7491]. GP 413.

283. Cooking pot with out-curving rim and rilling on upper part of body. M4. D = 22 cm.
Z36 [7559]. GP 417.
Ashmunein, 1998, E131, fifth to seventh century AD.

284. Cooking pot with out-curving rim and rilled body. Chipped rim with pitch covering the whole of the interior and splashed on the exterior. M2. D = 18 cm.
AC51 [8588]. JF 698.
Pot slot no. 25. See Chapter 4.

285. Cooking pot with short rim and rilled body. M2. D = 26 cm.
AD52 [7506] and AD52 [7507]. GP 295.
Coin: Tiberius II, AD 578–582 in AD52 [7506].

286. Cooking pot with short rim, lid seating and a

rilled body. There is a hole in the neck of the pot, presumably for hanging. M1. D = 21 cm.
Z52 [7694]. AG 31.
Similar to Ashmunein, 1998, E364, *c.* AD 600–700.

287. Cooking pot with stubby rim, lid seating and a rilled body. M4. D = 16 cm.
AF34 [8490]. GP 358.
Similar to Ashmunein, 1998, E364, *c.* AD 600–700.

288. Cooking pot with stubby, grooved rim and rilled body. M4. D = 18 cm.
Z36 [7451]. JF 824.

289. Cooking pot with slightly out-curved, grooved rim and rilled body. M2. D = 24 cm.
V52 [8689]. GP 233.
Ashmunein, 1998, E306, *c.* AD 500–650.

290. Cooking pot with short, upright, grooved rim and rilled body. M4. D = 20 cm.
V51/2 [8677] and V52 [8297]. GP 336.

291. Cooking pot with upright rim and stubby handles. Rilled body. M2. D = 20 cm.
V51 [8196], V52 [8297]. GP 332.
Similar to Ashmunein, 1998, E153, sixth to eighth century AD. The handles are lower down the body on the Kom el-Nana example.

292. Cooking pot with short rim, lid seating and handles. M4. D = 16 cm.
AB50 [8408]. GP 388.
Similar to Ashmunein, 1998, E207, *c.* AD 600–700.

293. Cooking pot with stubby, grooved rim, rilled body and handles. M4. D = 16.5 cm.
AB35 [7662]. AG 85.
Coin: fifth to sixth century AD.
Ashmunein, 1998, E364, *c.* AD 600–700.

294. Cooking pot with stubby, grooved rim, rilled body and handles. M4. D = 16 cm.
U53 [8684]. JF 843.

295. Cooking pot with stubby, grooved rim, rilled body and handles. M2. D = 20 cm.
AD49 [8320]. GP 138.
Coins: fourth to fifth century AD (one), fourth to sixth century AD (two).

296. Cooking pot with stubby rim, rilled body and handles. M4. D = *c.*18 cm.
AD49 [8168]. AG 40.
Coin: fourth to sixth century AD.

297. Cooking pot with stubby, bead rim, rilled body and handles. M4. D = 31 cm.
AB51 [7793]. GP 456.

*Painted cooking pots*

298. Cooking pot with upright rim and rilled body. Cream slip in patches on exterior. M2. D = 21 cm.
AD51 [7631]. AG 44.
Ashmunein, 1998, E143, fifth to eighth century AD.

299. Cooking pot with upright bead rim. Rilled body. Cream swag (?) on exterior. M2. D = 20 cm.
V52 [8292]. JF 842.
Near Ashmunein, 1998, E130, fifth to eighth century AD. The Kom el-Nana example has a bead rim.

300. Cooking pot with out-curved rim. Cream slip swags (?) on body. M2. D = 26 cm.
Z36 [7559]. GP 163.

301. Cooking pot with out-curved, grooved rim and rilled body. Cream slip swags on exterior and over rim. M2. D = 16 cm.
V52 [8689]. GP 232.
Ashmunein, 1998, E312 closest, *c.* AD 600–700.

302. Cooking pot with out-curved, grooved rim and rilled body. Black-slipped on rim and cream slip spots on exterior which was badly blackened. M4. D = 18 cm.
AD50 [8145]. JF 744.
Ashmunein, 1998, E261, *c.* mid fifth century AD or a little later.

303. Cooking pot with out-curved rim and rilled body. Cream slipped over rim. M2. D = 18 cm.
AC52 [7209]. GP 248.

304. Cooking pot with short rim, lid seating and handles. Cream-slipped over rim and traces on body. M2. D = 18 cm.
AD49 [8320]. GP 139.
Coins: fourth to fifth century AD (one), fourth to sixth century AD (two).

305. Cooking pot with short rim and lid seating. Cream-slipped band on body. M4. D = 18 cm.
Z36 [7559]. GP 379.

306. Cooking pot with short rim, internal ledge and rilled body. Cream-slip blotches on exterior. M2.

D = 14 cm.
Z36 [7559]. GP 185.

307. Cooking pot with stubby, grooved rim and rilled body. Cream-slipped over rim. M2. D = 20 cm.
Z36 [7432]. GP 342.
Similar to Ashmunein, 1998, E359, *c.* AD 650–800 AD.

308. Cooking pot with short, flattened rim and rilled body. Cream-slip blob on body. M2. D = 16 cm.
Z51 [7461]. GP 226.

309. Cooking pot with short, grooved rim and rilled body. Cream slip in two broad bands on exterior and over rim. M2. D = 16 cm.
AC49 [8175]. GP 94.

310. Cooking pot with incipient bead rim and rilled body. Cream slip in blotches on exterior. M4. D = 20 cm.
AE52 [8192]. GP 263.
Coin: fourth to sixth century AD.

*Cooking bowls, dishes and lids*

311. Shallow dish with plain rim. M4. D = 20 cm.
V52 [8682]. GP 180.
Gurna, 1401.

312. Shallow dish with plain rim. M4. D = 20 cm.
Z50 [8253]. JF 794.

313. Bowl with plain rim and carination. M2. D = 25 cm.
AD51 [7547]. GP 244.

314. Bowl with plain rim. M2. D = 20 cm.
AB50 [8614]. GP 246.

315. Bowl with plain rim. M4. D = 28 cm.
AD51 [7631]. AG 49.

316. Bowl with plain rim and slight internal ledge. M4. D = 22 cm.
AD51 [7631]. AG 58.

317. Dish with flattened rim and ribbed exterior. M4. D = 21 cm.
AF33 [8500]. AG 21.

318. Dish with flattened rim. M2. D = 26 cm.
Z50 [8253]. GP 219.

319. Dish with bead rim. M4. D = 21 cm.
AC49 [8792]. JF 759.

320. Dish with flattened rim with a groove and ribbed exterior. M4. D = 30 cm.
AB35 [7662]. AG 79.
Coin: fifth to sixth century AD.
Similar to Esna, pl. CCXIX, A10, but without handles, of about AD 550–630.

321. Dish with in-turned, grooved rim, ribbed exterior and handle(s). M2. D = 22 cm.
AB36 [7443]. GP 343.

322. Bowl with grooved rim and a band of ribbing on the exterior. M4. D = 20 cm.
AE49 [8496]. GP 411.
Gurna, 1432, 1433 and 1444 are similar.

323. Dish with bead rim and internal ledge. M2. D = 20 cm.
V52 [8683]. GP 187.

324. Dish with grooved rim. M4. D = 24 cm.
V50 [8681]. JF 827.

325. Dish with small bead rim. M4. D = 20 cm.
Z51 [7479]. JF 833.

326. Bowl/casserole with out-turned rim and handles. Red-slipped interior and exterior. M2. D = 20 cm.
AA46 [9800]. GP 589.

327. Dish with out-turned, grooved rim. M4. D = 26 cm.
AC52 [7566]. AG 9.

328. Bowl/casserole with flattened rim, ribbed body and carination. M4. D = 22 cm.
AB35 [7662]. GP 463.
Coin: fifth to sixth century AD.

329. Bowl/casserole with out-turned rim and carination. M2. D = 22 cm.
AC49/50 [8460] and AC50 [8323]. GP 159.

330. Bowl/casserole with out-turned rim and internal lid seating. M4. D = 16 cm.
AD52 [7506]. GP 428.
Coin: Tiberius II Hahn 63, *c.* AD 578–582.

331. Bowl/casserole with out-turned rim, lid seating and a band of ribbing on the body above carination. M4. D = 23 cm.
ADAD49/50 [8323]. JF 768.

Coin: Justinian II, AD 565–578.

332. Bowl/casserole with 'pie crust' rim and lid seating. Ribbed under rim. Badly sooted and burnt. M4. D = 26 cm.
AE49 [8589]. JF 900.

333. Bowl/casserole with 'pie crust' rim and lid seating. Ribbed under rim. Blackened on the exterior. M4. D = 24 cm.
AD52 [7519]. JF 902.

334. Dish with out-turned rim and lid-seating. M4. D = 22 cm.
AB35 [7662]. GP 467.
Coin: fifth to sixth century AD.

335. Dish with lid seating and pronounced carination. M2. D = 22 cm.
Z50 [8247]. JF 789.

336. Dish with out-turned, grooved rim. M4. D = 18 cm.
AF51 [8182]. AG 20.

337. Dish with cream slip over rim and on body. Possibly a lid. M2. D = 17.5 cm.
AF51 [8190]. Another at Z36 [7432], Z51 [7418] and Z51 [7461]. GP 352.
Similar to Esna, pl. CCXXII, E23.

338. Dish or lid with out-turned rim. M4. D = 14 cm.
V51 [8294]. JF 832.

339. Dish or lid with in-turned rim. M4. D = 12.5 cm.
AE52 [8386]. AG 38.
Coin: fourth to sixth century AD.

340. Dish or lid with flattened, in-turned rim. M2. D = 18 cm.
Y51 [7418]. JF 831.

341. Dish or lid with out-turned rim. M4. D = 22 cm.
U53 [8682]. JF 835.

342. Dish or lid with flanged rim. M2. D = 18 cm.
Z36 [7451]. JF 834.

343. Dish or lid with everted rim. M4. D = 20 cm.
AB48 [9813]. GP 646.

*Miniature cooking pots and jars*

344. Casserole with straight sides and carination near base. M4. D = 10 cm.
Z52 [7423]. GP 406.

345. Cooking pot or jar with ribbed exterior, groove on inner rim. Lip on one side of the rim for pouring. M2. D = 8 cm.
AE51 [8395]. JF 782A.

346. Cooking pot or jar with ribbed exterior. Red pigment inside and over rim. M2. D = 8.5 cm.
AC52 [8402]. JF 865.

347. Cooking pot or jar. M4. D = 9 cm.
AC49/50 [8344]. GP 287.

348. Cooking pot or jar with ribbed exterior. M4. D = 8 cm.
AB48 [9813]. GP 611.

349. Cooking pot or jar. Cordon at base of neck and ribbed at base. M2. D = 9 cm.
AC50 [8150]. JF 748.

*Painted miniature cooking pots and jars*

350. Jar. Cordon at base of neck. Pink slipped with black spots under cordon and black band at base. M2. D = 10 cm.
AD52 [7410]. GP 155.

351. Jar with cordon at base of neck. Band of two black lines with dots between under cordon and same design in swags on body. Pitched internally and over rim. M2. D = 6 cm.
AD51 [7632]. AG 45.

352. Jar with everted rim. Red slipped. M2. D = 8 cm.
Y52 [8512]. GP 154.

353. Jar with wide-spaced ribbing on body. Cream-slipped exterior and over rim inside. M2. D = 9 cm.
AB35 [7662]. AG 83.
Coin: fifth to sixth century AD.

354. Jar with ribbed body and black spot decoration. W2. D = 6 cm.
V52 [8294]. JF 822.

355. Jar with everted rim and cream slip over rim. M1. D = 5 cm.
AD49 [8320]. GP 160.

356. Very small jar with ribbed body. Cream-slipped overall with red spots. M1. D = 3.5 cm.

AC51 [8588]. JF 717.

## Jars

These vessels formed 13.65 per cent of the total RBH (Table 2.2). The figure in Volume 1 was 13.91 per cent. As with the previous category, these vessels are difficult to date accurately as the forms change little over time. Fortunately, some of these vessels had coins found in the same layer. This can, however, prove rather vague as in the case of no. 360 where the coin is dated fourth to seventh century AD. Nos 382 and 399 have a closer dating, i.e. fifth century AD, and fifth to sixth centuries AD plus AD 527–565. The coin evidence, however, merely proves the context was open at the time the coin was dropped.

*Plain jars*

357. Jar with ribbed body under rim. M1. D = 17 cm.
AE49 [8456], AE49 [8459] and AE49 [8589]. GP 282.

358. Jar with carination. M2. D = 18 cm.
AC50 [8334]. GP 382.

359. Jar with everted rim. M2. D = 18.5 cm.
AB52 [7692]. AG 29.

360. Jar with ribbed body. M1. D = 14 cm.
AC49 [8146]. JF 713.
Coins: fourth to seventh century AD, Roman copies or exotic (two).

361. Jar. M2. D = 18 cm.
AD52 [7519]. GP 256.

362. Jar with lid seating and squared rim. Ribbed body. M2. D = 18 cm.
Y51 [7425]. AG 54.

363. Jar with groove in out-turned, rounded rim. Ribbed body. M1. D = 18 cm.
AC51 [8146]. JF 715.

364. Jar with out-turned rim and ribbed body. M2. D = 20 cm.
U51 [8296]. GP 207.

365. Jar with out-turned rim. Slight grooving on body. M1. D = 10 cm.
AB35 [7662]. GP 462.
Coin: fifth to sixth century AD.

366. Jar with high neck and bead rim. M2. D = 12 cm.
AB50 [7699]. GP 422.

367. Jar with two handles. M2. D = 20 cm.
AC49 [8146]. GP 106.
Coins: Roman copies (two), fourth to seventh century AD.

368. Jar with two handles. Slight ribbing on body. M1. D = 16 cm.
AD52 [7507]. AG 4.

369. Storage jar with high neck. M1. D = 42 cm.
AA46 [9800]. GP 538.

*Painted or decorated jars*

Some 103 vessels from the excavated material from 1993–4 were included in Volume 1. Five of these vessels were jars. One was an exceptional vessel with a crowd scene of curly heads in rows, together with fish and parts of standing figures (Faiers, 2005, nos 277, 279, 280 and 282). Two of the other painted jars appear here in Chapter 4 as they were contained in the 'Pot Slots'. Of the other two jars, one, no. 286, is dated by coins: fourth to fifth century AD (one); fourth to sixth century AD (five); fourth to sixth century AD fragments (two); fifth to sixth century AD (?) copy; AD 460–560 (two).

The designs on these pots echo others at various other sites such as Kellia (Kellia, pl. 75, Type 58), whilst Armant (Mond and Myers, 1940, pl. LXXV), Antinoe (Guerrini, 1974, pl. 49, and 2004, 150, no. 329) and el-Ashmunein (Bailey, 1998, pl. 54, K8) all have pots with depictions of fish—a popular Christian symbol. There are also birds, an animal and people depicted on pots from Antinoe (Guidotti and Pesi, 2004, 128, no. 84, 151, no. 336 and 129, nos 92 and 94). As at el-Ashmunein, there are no painted animals on flagons, jars or bowls at Kom el-Nana. Antinoe and el-Ashmunein are quite nearby (map at fig. a) and may well have supplied some of the pots found at Kom el-Nana; the date range given for the above pottery from Antinoe fits well with the dates for Kom el-Nana, i.e. fifth to seventh century AD, other than no. 84 which is given a date of seventh to eighth century AD.

370. Jar with cream slip trails on exterior. M4. D = 14 cm.
Z36 [7559]. GP 535. Also a plain version in M2 at AD49 [8320], GP 103.

371. Jar with flat base and a pouring dip in the rim. Cream-slipped band under rim and cream swag on body. M1. D = 18 cm.

Y50 [8529]. GP 335.

372. Jar with ribbed body under rim and cream slip trails on exterior. M1. D = 17.5 cm.
AB34 [8334]. GP 353.

373. Jar with lid seating. Cream-slipped over and inside rim. M1. D = 22 cm.
Z36 [7559]. GP 188.

374. Jar. Cream-slipped band under rim and possible swag (?) on body. M2. D = 26 cm.
AE49 8589]. GP 380.

375. Jar. Cream-slipped interior and exterior. M1.
D = 28 cm.
AD49 [8311]. GP 375.
Coins: fourth to sixth century AD (one), fifth to sixth century AD (two).

376. Jar. Ribbed body on exterior under cream-slipped rim M2. D = 19 cm.
Z36 [7559]. GP 165.

377. Jar with very irregular rim. Cream slip thickly applied to exterior with a lighter covering on interior. M1. D = 24 cm.
AA48 [9848]. GP 555.

378. Jar with knobbed rim and lid seating. Cream-slipped interior and over rim on exterior. M1.
D = 26 cm.
V51 [8294]. GP 428.

379. Jar with cream-slipped band under rim on exterior and cream-slipped swags on body. M2.
D = 16 cm.
AC50 [8708]. AG 3.

380. Jar with cream-slipped band under rim on exterior and cream-slipped swag on body. Misshapen. M2. D = 19.5 cm.
AC/AD49 [8804]. GP 334.

381. Jar with cordon under rim. Wide, vertical grooving under cordon. Patches of red slip on exterior. Cream-slipped bands on exterior and interior. M1.
D = 18 cm.
AB51 [7409]. GP 88.

382. Jar with cream-slipped band on shoulder. M1.
D = 16 cm.
AD51 [7573]. GP 357.
Coin: fifth century AD.

383. Jar with out-turned rim. Groove in rim. Cream band under rim with dribble on body. M1.
D = 13 cm.
AD51 [7634]. AG 72.

384. Jar with out-turned rim. Groove in rim. Red, black and cream decoration on body. M1. D = 15 cm.
AC/AD50 [8783]. GP 430.

385. Jar with high neck and rounded rim. Ribbed body. Cream swags on body under shoulder. M2.
D = 22 cm.
AA48 [9848] and AA49 [9838]. GP 553.

386. Jar with groove in rim. Ribbed body. Red-slipped interior and exterior. Cream blotches on body. Traces of blackening on rim. M4. D = 20 cm.
AA47 [9845]. GP 584.

387. Jar with high neck and squared rim. Red slip over pink slip with traces of black decoration. M2.
D = 16 cm.
AA48 [9842]. GP 565.

388. Jar with out-turned rim. Red-slipped interior and exterior. Black blobs on rim. Black and white blobs on body. White slip smear on interior. M1.
D = 26 cm.
Y51 [7425] and Y52 [7424]. GP 391.

389. Jar with high neck. Cream slip swags on body. Slight ribbing towards base and at base. Resin on interior and dribbles on exterior. M2. D = 19.5 cm.
AB35 [7455]. AG 76.

390. Jar with slight lid seating and ribbed body. Cream-slipped over rim on exterior and interior. M4.
D = 10 cm.
AA48 [9847]. GP 580.

391. Jar with slight lid seating and traces of cream slip on body and over rim on inside. M2. D = 10 cm.
Z51 [7490]. AG 53.

392. Jar with squared-off rim and notch on inner rim. Rouletting or small slash marks in a band on body about 1.5 cm under rim. M1. D = 12 cm.
AB49 [8334]. GP 108.

393. Jar with high neck and out-turned rim. Cream, red and black decoration on exterior. M1.
D = 27.5 cm.
Z36 [7451/9]. JF 856.

394. Jar with high neck and bead rim. Cream-slipped exterior with black horizontal lines enclosing orange band. M1. D = 28 cm.
AC49 [8146]. GP 100.
Coins: fourth to seventh century AD, Roman copies or exotic (two).

395. Jar with high neck and flattened bead rim. Traces of resin on interior. Black, cream and red decoration on exterior. M1. D = 18 cm.
AC50 [8334]. GP 378.

396. Jar with high neck and flattened rim. Black, cream and red decoration on exterior. M1. D = 12 cm.
AC52 [8412]. JF 855.

397. Jar with high neck. Red-slipped exterior with cream and black band decoration. Resin on interior. M2. D = 12 cm.
AC52 [8402]. JF 732.

398. Jar with high neck. Possibly pink-slipped exterior with a decoration of red and black horizontal lines. M2. D = 16 cm.
AB35 [7662]. GP 464.
Coin: fifth to sixth century AD.

399. Jar with high neck and flattened rim. Orange, cream and black decoration. M1. D = 15 cm.
AC50 [8323], AC50 [8324], AC50 [8350], AC50 [8356], AD49 [8154], AD49/50 [8323], AD50 [8145], AD50 [8170], AD50 [8179] and AD52 [8122]. JF 858.
Coins: fifth to sixth century AD, from AD49 [8154], and a coin of Justinian I IB, of AD 527–565 from AD49/50 [8323].

400. Jar with high neck and flattened bead rim. Orange-slipped exterior with black and red decoration. See no. 328 for similar decoration. M2. D = 10 cm.
AD52 [7519]. GP 339.

401. Neck and rim of jar with flattened rim. Cream slipped with black horizontal line on exterior. Cream, red and black design on inside of neck. M2. D = 10 cm.
AE52 [8200]. GP 348.

402. Jar with high neck and flattened rim. Traces of cream, pink and black decoration on exterior. Resin on interior. M2. D = 14 cm.
AD49 [8336]. JF 687.
Coins: fourth to sixth century AD (three).

403. Rim of very large storage jar. Lid-seating evident. Traces of cream slip over rim and on inside of rim. Wavy line incised on outside of rim. VCM1. D = 56 cm.
AD51 [7631]. GP 402. Another at AA50 [9834], 36 cm, GP 551.
See also Faiers, 2005, no. 254 in Kom el-Nana, Volume 1, a surface find. Kellia, pl. 87, 4, Type 326, Depot E, AD 400–450.

404. Jar, missing most of neck and rim. Red-slipped overall with black painted decoration which includes a fish. M2.
AC50 [8579]. JF 710.
Pot Slot no. 13. See Chapter 4.

405. Jar with knobbed rim and handles (?). Black design of bird, star and spirals on cream ground. Handle scars evident. M1. D = 24 cm.
AB49 [8177], AB49 [8158], AB50 [8176], AD49 [8168], and AD49 [8337]. GP 92.

406. Large storage jar with flattened rim and handles at rim onto shoulder, probably four originally. Base not joining but same fabric, carinated towards base with three rows of stringing below carination. Intricately decorated in cream, black and red. VCM1. D = 38 cm.
AC49 [8192], AC49 [8329], AC50 [8152], AC50 [8312] and AC50 [8334]. JF 859.
Esna, pl. CCXXIV, 2, 3 and 7.

407. Jar with two handles. Cream band under rim with cream swag cross on body and cream spot on handle. M1. D = 19 cm.
AC50 [8707]. AG 7.
Ashmunein, 1998, E196, AD 375–450.

408. Jar with two handles. Cream-slipped over rim with cream swags on body. M1. D = 27 cm.
AC51 [8579]. JF 708.
Pot Slot no. 23. See Chapter 4.

409. Jar with lid seating and two handles. Cream slipped on exterior and dribbled beneath handles. M2. D = 24 cm.
AB52 [7649]. AG 39.

410. Jar with two handles. Cream slipped on body. M2. D = 18 cm.
AC50/51 [8412]. JF 750.
Pot Slot no. 11. See Chapter 4.

411. Jar, handle scars evident. Ribbed body, cream slipped on bottom third of exterior with cream swags above. M1. D = 21 cm.
AC51 [8587]. JF 739.

412. Large jar with handle(s), missing rim. Cream-slipped exterior with red slip in patches and cream dribbles on interior surface. Large burnt patch on exterior and also burnt patches on interior. M1.
AD36 [7448]. GP 459.

*Painted body sherds*

413. Bodysherd of large jar. Red and black decoration including guilloche, flowers and part of a fish. M2.
AD49 [8168]. AG 89.

414. Bodysherd of large jar. Red and black decoration. M2.
AC/AD50 [8698] and AC/AD50 [8895]. GP 471.

415. Neck and shoulder of jar. Red, cream and orange decoration. M2.
AC51 [8402]. JF 721.

416. Bodysherd of large storage jar with carination. Red, cream and black decoration. Lines of stringing visible from carination downwards. VCM1. D = 48 cm, across carination.
Y51 [7425]. AG 41.

**Jugs or pitchers, short-distance traded**

With only 0.43 per cent of the total RBH (Table 2.2), the jug or pitcher is again a relative rarity in the assemblage. As said before in Volume 1, these forms may not be recognised as such as the potters made *qawadiis* and jars with the same rim form, and if the handle or handle scar is missing, then distinguishing the ultimate form is impossible. Alternatively, the 'jar' function may have been performed by flagons in pottery and glass.

417. Jug with one handle. M1. D = 7.5 cm.
Z52 [8518]. GP 536.

418. Jug with one handle. Decoration in black inside rim. M1. D = approx. 5 cm.
AD49 [8158]. JF 876A.

419. Jug with one handle and cordon at base of neck. Cream-slipped swag on neck and body. M2.
D = 12 cm.
AA30 [7808]. GP 461.

**Flagons**

The distance traded was dependant on the fabric. Fabrics W1, W2 and P23 are probably long-distance traded whilst the other fabrics M1, M2 and M4 are short-distance traded.

This form accounted for 3.25 per cent of the total RBH in 1993–4and 2000 (Table 2.2), and slightly less in Volume 1 at 2.9 per cent.

These are difficult to parallel closely as each settlement seems to have had its own local supplier and therefore exhibits differing features in its pots, as the potter may have either painted his own pots or employed a more artistic person to do the job. The shape of the vessels also changes little over the course of time, which is also inconvenient for dating purposes. The flagons at Kom el-Nana were decorated with various fired-on ceramic colours: red, cream, black, orange and pink with designs which include grilles, swags, grapes, wavy lines, bands of colour, swirls/spirals in black, blobs or dots and a bird (the last on no. 450). El-Ashmunein had no animals depicted on flagon sherds (Bailey, 2005, p82).

At other sites the decoration varies, often with the same theme of flowers and geometric patterns, animals, birds and occasionally people (usually of the religious variety), but at Antinoe there seems to be a woman (?) wearing a necklace depicted on a bowl (Guidotti and Pesi, 2004, 129, no. 92). There seems to be no clear connection between sites, but there may possibly be site-specific decoration, for example on the water bottles/flagons found at monastic sites, i.e. from Deir el-Naqlun (Godlewski, Derda and Górecki 1989–93, 259, 22.13), Hawara (Bourriau, 1981, 92, 180) and Wadi Sarga (Faiers, forthcoming, British Museum Accession nos 72947/1919/505/554, 556 and 557).

On the heavily decorated flagons at Kellia in Lower Egypt there are similar dots, bands and grilles, but designs include more flowing patterns of leaves and a horse (?) and lion (?) (Kellia, pl. 68, 2 and 3, pl. 69, 1, 3 and 4 and pl. 65, 1). In Upper Egypt at Epiphanius there is linear decoration, but also the flowing leaf pattern as at Kellia. Antinoe has very similar patterns to el-Ashmunein, as might be expected, as both are close to the likely supplier (Guerinni, 1974, pls 24, 25 and 27). Therefore, although the designs are fairly formalised in the main, the individual potter may have deviated from this to supply a specific establishment or outlet, perhaps with a certain form of vessel decorated in a particular way, as with the water flagons mentioned above or with religious themes. Examples include saints with haloes painted on vessels at Wadi Sarga (British Museum Accession nos AES 73573, 73561 and 73568). Also, the more heavily decorated flagons may well have been more expensive than the plain flagons. There is also the question of what was 'in vogue' or fashionable, what the customer would most likely buy and the final destination of the pot, whether in a market place or for a specific client. It must also be borne in mind that the artistic abilities of those decorating the pots would vary from place to place.

*Plain flagons*

420. Flagon top with sloping sides. Two ridges below rim. W1. D = 9 cm.
AB46 [9800]. GP 526.

421. Flagon with out-turned rim. External surfaces accidentally altered while still wet, or possibly part of upper handle attachment. M2. D = 7 cm.
AB48 [9813]. GP 644.

422. Flagon top with sloping sides and carination approximately 4 cm under rim. Ribbed under rim to start of carination. Resin-coated inside. M4.
D = 8 cm.
Z50 [8246]. JF 793.

423. Flagon with a rounded, rilled body, tall neck and a lid attached by a pottery ring to the handle. The base of the vessel and rilling on the body was soot blackened. M4. D = 7.5 cm.
AC51 [8593]. JF 694.
Similar to Elephantine X, Abb.81.4, T852, which is undated and in O1 fabric. Another flagon from Elephantine X, Abb.124, 5, K725, is in a Nile-silt fabric as M4, but is lacking its lid. The latter is dated fifth to sixth century AD. See also Lecuyot and Pierrat, 2004, pl. 16,225, also in O1 (Aswan ware) and dated around AD 750–900.

424. Flagon top with lid seating. M2. D = 7 cm.
AD51 [7576]. AG 23.

425. Flagon with lid seating. Part of handle attachment evident. P23. D = 6 cm.
AB48 [9813]. GP 625.

*Painted or decorated flagons*

426. Flagon top with sloping sides and carination approximately 2 cm under rim. Cream blobs overlaid with black along carination. M4. D = 8 cm.
AB51 [7793]. GP 316.

427. Flagon top with sloping sides. Pink and cream decoration. M4. D = 10 cm.
AE52 [8186]. AG 61.

428. Flagon top with sloping sides. Cream and red decoration. M1. D = 6 cm.
AF34 [8564]. AG 11.

429. Flagon top with slightly knobbed rim and sloping sides. Decoration in black and cream on the outside, the black line at the rim extending over to the inside. M4. D = 8 cm.
AC50 [8321]. GP 300.

430. Flagon top with sloping sides and pulley rim. Decoration in red and cream bands. M1. D = 9.5 cm.
AD51 [7576]. AG27.
Ashmunein, J56, conjectural date *c.* AD 600–700.

431. Flagon top with lid seating. Cream-slip splashes inside and outside. M2. D = 7 cm.
AC50 [8314]. GP 315.
Coin: fourth to fifth century AD.

432. Flagon top. Ribbed exterior. Cream-slipped inside and outside. W1. D = 7 cm.
AD50 [8150]. JF 741.

433. Large Flagon top. Black blobs on carination under rim on exterior and on rim edge. W1. D = 10 cm.
AA36 [7441] and AA36 [7848]. GP 448.

434. Flagon with hooked rim and ribbed neck. Black and cream bands on rim with a broad black band on the neck. Trace of cream slip under the band on the neck. M4. D = 7 cm.
AB49/50 [8343]. GP 119.

435. Flagon top with out-turned rim and a carination approximately 2 cm below the rim. Black swag on exterior with black splashes on the interior. W1.
D = 6 cm.
Z50 [8247]. JF 791.

436. Flagon body and neck. Base and rim missing. Rim possibly as no. 435. Two stubby handles below neck. Ribbed body. Black painted above carination at the top of the neck. W2.
AD49 [8311], AD49 [8313], AD49 [8320]. JF 851.
Coins: fifth to sixth century AD (two) and fourth to sixth century AD (one) in AD49 [8311]. Fourth to fifth century AD (one) and fourth to sixth century AD (two) in AD49 [8320].

437. Flagon top with ribbed neck, two handles and neck strainer (?). Cream-slipped exterior. M1.
D = 4.5 cm.
AA36 [7684]. GP 446.

438. Flagon top with high, ribbed neck. One handle evident, but the vessel probably had two. Orange-slipped exterior with black blobs over rim. M1.
D = 6.5 cm.
V51 [8586] AG 2.

439. Flagon top and part of body. Two handles. Orange and black decoration on exterior with cream slip on interior. M1. D = 4 cm.
AC51 [8588]. GP196.

440. Flagon top with ribbed neck and part of body. Two handles. Neck strainer. Cream-slipped exterior. M1. D = 4.5 cm.
AB35 [7662]. GP 465.
Coin: fifth to sixth century AD.

441. Flagon with tall, ribbed neck. Cream-slipped exterior and interior with an area of no slip beginning to show inside. M1. D = 4 cm.
AA49 [9814]. GP 620.
Ashmunein, J34, conjectural date *c.* AD 400–550. Also similar to Esna, N21, and Gurna, 1759.

442. Flagon body, with ribbed base and most of the ribbed neck. Neck strainer. No handles evident. Red, black and cream decoration on exterior. M1.
AC51 [8579]. JF 711.
Pot slot no. 14. See Chapter 4.

443. Flagon body and neck. Base and rim missing. Two handles. Cream slipped with a black arc on exterior. Dribbles of cream slip inside neck. M1.
AC51 [8588]. JF 716.
Pot Slot no. 26A. See Chapter 4.

444. Flagon body and base, with foot and part of neck. Two handle scars. Cream-slipped exterior with two black bands enclosing a red band on body and black 'grille' design with central red spot just below the neck. Repeating 'grilles', two between each handle. Neck strainer. M1.
AC51 [8412] JF 709.
Kellia, pl. 103, Type 204, *c.* AD 450–550.
Pot Slot no. 10. See Chapter 4.

445. Flagon body with part of base with foot and part of neck. Two handles. Three black bands on body enclosing red band and black blobs. Painted red on neck with black band. Two 'grille' designs enclosed by two circles, each with three black blobs under neck between handles. Red paint evident under this design. Black figure-of-eight design painted alongside circles. M1.
U53 [8684]. GP 341.
See parallel for no. 444.

446. Flagon body with part of neck and two handles. Base and rim missing. Neck strainer. Cream-slipped exterior with black band enclosing red band on body. Two spiral designs in black on red with black blobs between handles. M1.
U53 [8684]. GP 340.

447. Flagon body. Two handles. Cream-slipped exterior with red band overlaid with five black lines. Black spiral with black blobs and grapes (?). M1.
AC52 [8402]. JF 862.

448. Flagon body and base with foot. Two handles. Cream-slipped exterior with red, orange and black bands. Spirals in black on red. Black painted arcs containing hatching and loops in black. M1.
AD49 [8450] and Y52 [8776]. GP 347.
See parallel for no. 444.

*Flagon body sherds*

449. Flagon body with ribbing. Handle scar. Black grape (?) designs on shoulder. W1.
AE52 [8386]. AG 88.
Coin: fourth to sixth century AD.

450. Flagon body. Cream slipped with bird in black, black squiggles and blobs. Black cross-hatching contained in two circles with blobs. Grapes in black. Black lines containing red band. M1.
AD49 [8320]. GP 354.
Coins: fourth to sixth century AD (two).

451. Flagon shoulder with spout scar and hole. Resin around edge of spout scar but none on interior. M1.
AA48 [9859]. GP 639.

452. Flagon base with foot. Thick black line on base and dribbles of black on exterior. Underside of base is also black painted. P23.
Z36 [7459]. GP 435.

453. Flagon body sherd. Red, cream, pink and black decoration including part of a grille encircled in black. M1.
AB50 [8608]. GP 85.

**Colanders, short-distance traded**

This form constituted 1.2 per cent of the assemblage (Table 2.2), but only 0.5 per cent in Volume 1.

As stated in Volume 1, this form appears to be rare elsewhere, with none at all in the published corpus at el-Ashmunein. There are again various sizes, both of the vessels and the colander holes. Some holes were made before firing (as in no. 465) and some after firing (as in no. 466). No. 465 has very small holes and no. 466 very large holes, whilst no. 456 has only one large hole in the base of the vessel and may well be a flower-pot. It would appear, therefore, that these vessels were being used for a specific purpose, possibly for different commodities or for various stages of one process. It is possible that the potter was using the same form for both colanders and bowls as is the case with some jars and *qawadiis*, so, without a hole or two to distinguish between the forms, some vessels may well be assigned to the wrong category.

*Plain colanders*

454. Colander with flat rim and holes in base. Three grooved bands on body. M1. D = 26 cm.
AD49 [8337]. JF 757.

455. Colander (?). Possibly a bowl. Grooved band on body. Flat rim. M1. D = 22 cm.
AB50 [8608]. GP 144.

456. Colander with one hole in base. Possibly a flower pot. Burnished exterior and interior. M2. D = 24 cm.
AC52 [7643]. AG 71.

457. Colander with holes in base and groove on body approximately 2.5 cm below rim. M2. D = 26 cm.
AD49 [8336] and AD49 [8337]. JF 875.
Coins: fourth to sixth century AD (three) at AD49 [8336].

*Painted colanders*

458. Colander with holes in base. Decorated internally with cream swags. M1. D = 28.5 cm.
Z52 [7610] and Z52 [7611]. AG 6.

459. Colander (?). Possibly a bowl. Grooved band on body under rim. Decorated with black and cream spots internally, with black lines on cream on flat rim. M1. D = 26 cm.
AE52 [8201]. GP 323.

460. Colander with holes in base and on the side above a high foot. Decorated with cream blotch internally and black blobs on cream on a flat rim. M1. D = 28 cm.
AD50 [8168]. JF 755.

461. Colander with holes in base made post firing. Grooved band on body. Decorated with black blobs on red on flat rim. M1. D = 26 cm.
AB50 [8614], AB50 [8793] and AB/AC49 [8335]. GP 265.

462. Colander with holes in base. Concentric ribbed wheel-marks on exterior of base as on bases of cooking pots. Cream band on rim and dribble on exterior. Cream swag or band on interior. M2. D = 36 cm.
AA50 [9834]. GP 549.

463. Base of colander with very small holes in base and on body. M2.
AD51 [7632]. AG 48.

464. Base of colander with part-hole in base and a hole in body above low foot. Interior and exterior red slipped. M4.
AA49 [9834]. GP 616.
Similar to Gurna, 2115.

465. Base of colander with very small holes in base and on body. Holes made before firing. M2.
AC49 [8336]. JF 867.

466. Base of colander with four holes in base made after firing. Traces of red slip inside and outside. M1.
AC49 [8336]. JF 868.

## Water pots/*qawaddiis*, short-distance traded

These vessels formed 6.5 per cent (783 RBH) of the assemblage (Table 2.2), which is in fourth position, as opposed to the third position held by the collection in Volume 1 of mainly unstratified 1990–92 material. There were 1,044 RBH in the latter, i.e. nearly 20 per cent. This probably reflects the numbers of broken water pots dumped over a period of many years, rather than the excavated material in this volume which would (hopefully) be the pots just broken or in use at the time.

Some of these vessels may well have been used for storage rather than water-wheel pots, as the same rim form was used for both.

467. *Qadus*. Rim slightly warped. M1. D = 18 cm.
AA49 [9838]. GP 595.

468. *Qadus*. Finger-mark visible on rim. M1.
D = 20 cm.
AB36 [7448]. AG 66.

469. *Qadus*. M2. D = 19 cm.
V51 [8293] GP 206.

470. *Qadus*. Uneven edge to rim. M1. D = 15 cm.
AB35 [7567]. AG 84.

471. *Qadus*. Warped. M1. D = 17 cm.
AB35 [7662]. AG 86.
Coin: fifth to sixth century AD.

*Painted water pots*/qawadiis

472. *Qadus*. Ribbed rim. Cream band under rim and cream swag decoration. M2. D = 18 cm.
Z52 [7611]. AG 33.

473. *Qadus*. Cream band under rim and cream swag decoration. M1. D = 16 cm.
AB35 [7563]. AG14.

474. *Qadus*. Cream band with dribbles under rim. Cream splashes on body. M1. D = 18 cm.
Y52 [7727]. GP 205.

475. *Qadus*. Base deliberately chipped off. Crude lip for pouring. Cream band under rim with cream swags on body. M1. D = 15 cm.
AB35 [7563] and AB35 [7561].

## Cups and goblets, short-distance traded

Cups and goblets made up 0.61 per cent of the assemblage, i.e. 74 RBH (Table 2 2).

The lack of drinking vessels was rather a mystery in the first volume where there were 23 RBH out of 5,235 RBH (0.44 per cent). However, the small numbers of these vessels in this volume is more than offset by the numbers of such vessels in glassware (Chapter 1). This shows that glass goblets and cups/beakers were being used in greater numbers than the pottery equivalent. There were 657 glass RBH, of which 275 RBH were drinking vessels (41.85 per cent), whereas for the pottery drinking vessels, even if the two assemblages are added together, i.e. the unstratified of 1990–92 and the stratified of 1993–4 and 2000, the figure is 97 RBH out of 17,292, i.e. 0.56 per cent.

*Plain cups*

476. Cup. M1. D = 6 cm.
AD50 [8168]. GP 427.
See Monastery of Epiphanius, fig. 38, 88 where vessels such as this are used as lamps or alternatively as a cup, Ashmunein, 1998, pl. 59, M62.

477. Cup. M2. D = 8 cm.
AD50 [8170]. GP 299.

*Painted cups and goblets*

478. Cup. Cream band over rim with splashes of black resin and cream decoration inside. M1. D = 8 cm.
AB50 [7699]. GP 254.

479. Goblet. Cream slipped with resin on interior and over rim. M1. D = 11 cm.
AC50/51 [8412]. JF 696.
Deir el Naqlun, 247, nos19.12–19.15. The Kom-el Nana vessel is more elaborate.
Pot Slot no. 6. See Chapter 4.

## Miscellaneous bases

*Plain bases*

480. Base of bottle (?). Ribbed on exterior with resin on interior. M4.
AB/AC/AD [8148]. JF 727.

481. Base of small jar or bottle. M2.
AE50 [8408]. GP 279.

482. Base of small jar (?). Ribbed on exterior. M2.
Z36 [7559]. JF797.
Similar to Ashmunein, 1998, pl. 70, O58, *c.* late fourth to eighth century AD.

483. Base of jar (?). M1.
AB35 [7662]. JF 918.
Coin: fifth to sixth century AD.

484. Base of jar. M1.
AC49 [8146]. GP 97.
Coins: Roman copies or exotic (two), fourth to seventh century AD (one).

*Painted bases*

485. Base of ?. Cream slip visible on exterior. Resin on interior. M2.
AB35 [7662]. GP 468.
Ashmunein, 1998, pl. 70, O61, *c.* seventh century AD.
Coin: fifth to sixth century AD.

486. Base of ?. Cream slip band on exterior. Resin on interior. M2.
U53 [8684]. GP 192.
Ashmunein, 1998, pl. 70, O62, *c.* seventh century AD.

487. Base of unguentarium (?). Red-slipped exterior

with cream arc and black blob decoration. Resin on interior. M2.
AD51 [7631]. GP 397.

488. Base of basin with splashes of cream paint on interior. M1.
AE49 [8459]. GP 319.

489. Base of very large jar or basin. Cream slipped on exterior. M1.
Y50 [8254] and Y50 [8259]. GP 202.

*Bases with holes*

490. Base with hole made before firing. M2.
AD51 [7570]. AG 12.
Coin: Justinian Hahn 166, AD 538–565.

491. Base with hole made after firing. Black deposit around base. M1.
U53 [8684]. GP 195.

492. Base with hole made before firing. M1.
AC49 [8152]. JF 765.

493. Base of ?. Ribbed exterior. Resin lump in base, sealing hole made before firing. M2.
Z52 [7610]. JF692.

494. Base of strainer (?). M1.
AB35 [7662]. AG 82.
This is another of the vessels for which there is still no clear use. More complete versions of the same vessel can be found in Faiers, 1993, nos 424, 425 and 426.
Coin: fifth to sixth century AD.

**Lids, short-distance traded**

These formed 2.08 per cent of the total RBH compared to 1.28 per cent in the earlier volume (Table 2.2). This later figure may mean that lids were better looked after and less likely to be broken and therefore in use for longer.

Lids are never very well represented and, as today, one lid could have served more than one vessel. The following types are represented:

**L1** Type 1 with hole in knob
**L1P** as Type 1 but with painted decoration
**L2** Type 2 without hole in knob
**L2P** as Type 2 but with painted decoration
**L4** Type 4 with handle
**L4P** as Type 4 but with painted decoration

Type 3, a stopper-type lid, was not represented in this collection of pottery. See Faiers, 1993, no. 396.

*Plain lids*

495. Lid with two indentations towards the top to facilitate handling. L2. M1. D = 17 cm.
U53 [8682]. JF 834.

496. Lid with ribbed exterior. L2. M1. D = 22 cm.
Z30 [7459]. JF 680.

497. Lid. L2.VCM1. D = 21 cm.
AD51 [7631]. AG 42.

498. Lid. Handmade. L2.VCM1. D = 26 cm.
AI51 [8139]. GP 268.

499. Lid. Blackened rim. L2. M2. D = 26 cm.
Z52 [7423]. GP 389.

500. Lid. L2. M4. D = 22 cm.
AC52 [7655]. JF 780.

501. Lid. Burnt and blackened. L2. M1. D = 18 cm.
AC52 [7209]. GP 318.

502. Lid. L2. M4. D = 24 cm.
AD51 [7576]. AG 26.

503. Lid. Roughly oval in shape. L2. M1. D = 21.5 cm.
AD51 [7570]. AG 10.
Similar to Ashmunein, 1998, P10, fifth to seventh century AD.
Coin: Justinian Hahn 166, AD 538–565.

504. Lid. Interior and exterior blackened. L2. M1. D = 21.5 cm.
AB35 [7563]. AG 74.

505. Lid with hole for steam to escape. L1. M2. D = 17 cm.
Z36 [7459]. AG 56.

506. Lid with hole for steam to escape. Perhaps for a cooking pot? L1. M4. D = 22 cm.
AC49 [8146]. GP 330.
Coin: fourth to seventh century Roman copies or exotic (two).

507. Large lid. Virtually flat. Patches of burning on the interior and exterior. Handmade. L2.VCM1. D = 50 cm.
AD51 [7547]. GP 434.

*Painted or decorated lids*

508. Lid. Red slip over pink slip decoration. L2P. M2. D = 14 cm.
AF34 [8490]. GP 360.

509. Lid. Cream decoration on exterior. Interior and rim blackened. L2P. M2. D = 20 cm.
AA49 [9834]. GP 626.
Ashmunein, 1998, P13, undecorated, *c.* fifth to seventh century AD. Esna, type V5.

510. Lid. Red and cream decoration on exterior. Rim and interior blackened. L2P. M2. D = 22 cm.
AA49 [9814]. GP 621.

511. Large lid. Cream-slipped over rim and in patches on exterior. L2P.VCM1. D = 46 cm.
Z52 [7461]. GP 419.

512. Large lid. Traces of cream slip. Fingerprint dents as a pattern on exterior. Handmade. L2P.VCM1. D = 44 cm.
Y50 [8259]. AG 62. Another at AA50 [8252], D = 56 cm.
Elephantine X, Abb.131, K820, third to fourth century AD. S-1, sixth to seventh century AD and S-2, seventh century AD.

513. Large lid with handle. 'Notch' decoration on top around rim. L4.VCM1. Handmade. D = *c.*43 cm.
Z51 [7463]. GP 390.
See Kellia, pl. 89, 1 and 2, for similar lids.

514. Large lid with handle. Traces of cream slip on exterior. VCM1. L4P. Handmade. D = 46 cm.
AD50 [8490]. JF 753.
Parallel as no. 513.

**Lamps**

This form was represented by 18 RBH, at 0.14 per cent (Table 2.2). This is almost the same percentage as in Volume 1, which was 0.11 per cent.

Although there are very few lamp sherds in this assemblage there are 35 lamp RBH in the glass catalogue (Chapter 1), which seems to indicate the availability of a variety of lighting choices at Kom el-Nana, i.e. the standard Roman oil lamp; small bowls used as lamps; and the reuse of vessels as lamps, as no. 525, and also no. 73 in this catalogue which is paralleled in the un-illustrated GP197 from Area U53 [8684]. There were also glass lamps which either hung from the ceiling in a *polycandelon* (a flat, circular, metal device with holes cut into the surface into which the glass lamps were placed) or were held singly in a wooden holder which could be placed on a table or shelf, as at Karanis (Gazda, 2006, 25). I am grateful to Donald Bailey for his comments on nos 515, 517 and 518.

515. Carinated lamp. Handle broken off. O1W.
AD49 [8337]. GP 396.
Not unlike Petrie, 1904, pl. LXIX, N20 and N22; no provenance. Also compare Bailey, 1988, Q2278; perhaps from the Fayoum, dated sixth or seventh century AD.

516. Carinated lamp. Handle and front section broken off. Red slipped. L2.
AC/AD50 [8699]. GP 399.
Compare perhaps Michelucci, 1975, no. 404, but not very close.

517. Rear part of carinated lamp. Handle intact. L2.
Y52 [8276]. GP 395.
No parallels found.

518. Front of carinated lamp. L1.
AC49 [8313]. GP405
No close parallel, but possible examples are: Hayes, 1980, several near including no. 481 with a fifth/sixth century date suggested; Shier, 1978, no. 422 which is dated too early; Bailey, 1988, lamps *c.*Q2246–2249, some from Hermopolis Magna (el-Ashmunein), with a suggested date of sixth to mid seventh century AD; Guerrini, 1974, pl. 38, 7 and others on the same plate, all from Antinoopolis, with a fifth/sixth century dating; Petrie, 1904, near pl. LXI, L 89, from House E in that city (only those lamps with a House Letter written on them certainly come from Ehnasiya).

519. Lamp. L1
Z31 [7451]. GP 400.

520. Bottle-shaped lamp. Interior blackened. M2.
Z36 [7559]. AG 50.

521. Cup lamp. Blackened patches interior and exterior. L5. D = 8 cm.
AC49 [8310]. AG 46.

522. Cup lamp. Blackened interior and exterior. L5. D = 7.5 cm.
AC49 [8309]. AG 43.

523. Cup lamp. Interior blackened. L2. D = 7 cm.
Z36 [7432]. AG 32.

524. Cup lamp. Interior blackened. M2. D = 6 cm.

AC49 [8146]. GP 398.
Coins: Roman (?) copies (two), fourth to seventh century AD.

525. Base of ? reused as a lamp. M1.
AD51 [7575]. GP 537.

526. Lamp sherd. L1.
AD50 [8168]. JF 910.

**Miscellaneous vessels**

These vessels amounted to 0.3 per cent of the form total in this volume (Table 2.2), and 0.1 per cent in the first volume.

527. Drainpipe (?). Constricted at one end and beginning to be thicker and more flared at the other. M1. D = 9.5 cm.
AB50 [7699]. AG 1.
Ashmunein has a similar pipe (Bailey, 2000, Q77), but this is of first or second century AD date. The Kom el-Nana example is more utilitarian and resembles that found at the Monastery of Epiphanius (Winlock and Crum, 1926, 92, fig. 48, D).

528. Cylindrical vessel. Possibly a pot stand. Red, cream and black decoration. M1.
Z52 [7423], [7471], [7610] and Y52 [7727]. GP 470.
Similar to a decorated vessel at Esna, pl. CCXXX, 1K. See also Guidotti and Pesi, 2004, 139, nos 220–223. Listed as incense burners and given a sixth to seventh century AD date.

529. Cylindrical vessel. Possibly a pot stand. Orange and black decoration. M2.
AD51 [8183]. GP 296.
Similar cylindrical vessels were found at Elephantine X, Abb. 131, 8, Form S-6a, 9, Form S-6b and 10, Form S-6c. Dated sixth century AD. See also Epiphanius, 42, fig. 48 A and B. See also Guidotti and Pesi, 2004, as above no. 528.

530. Pot stand. VCM1. D = 13 cm.
AD51 [7632] and AD52 [7517]. AG 47.

531. Bucket. M1. D = 26.5 cm.
AC49 [8312]. JF 729. Another at AC50 (8324), 21 cm diameter, with a band of cream slip under the rim.

532. Incense burner or *Tazza*. Orange and cream decoration. Badly blackened and sooted on interior with patches of burning on exterior. VCM1.
D = 11 cm.
AA37 [7445]. JF 925.
Kellia, pl. 85, 2. See also a selection at Esna, pl. CCXXVIII, 11–17.

533. Brazier or incense burner. Traces of red slip on exterior. VCM1.
AA37 [7445] and Z36 [7451]. JF 926.

534. Brazier. Cream, red and black painted decoration on exterior and interior. Blackened on interior. Hollow centre to facilitate draught of air. M1.
D = 14 cm.
V52 [8692]. JF 906.
Sidi Khrebish, fig. 114, 700.

**Ladles**

Ladles were well represented in this collection, numbering 33 RBH, 0.3 per cent (Table 2.2), against 0.02 per cent for 1990–1992.

One ladle RBH from the 1993–4 excavation was included in Volume 1: no. 429 (Faiers, 2005). All ladle sherds were found in AC and AD contexts. See Chapter 3 for a discussion on distribution of forms.

535. Ladle. M2.
AD49 [8309]. GP 404.
Coins: fourth to sixth century AD (three); fourth to sixth century AD fragments (two); fifth to sixth century AD (?) copy.

536. Ladle. M2.
AC51 [8588]. GP 403.

537. Ladle. M2.
AC49 [8146] and [8446]. GP 466.
Coins: fourth to seventh century AD, Roman copies or exotic at AC49 [8146].

538. Bottle or small flask. M4. D = 2 cm.
Z50 [8247]. JF 787.

539. Funnel or lid. M2. D = 12 cm.
AC49/50 [8323]. JF 838.
Ashmunein, 1998, N29 (a funnel), fifth to seventh century AD. See also Esna, pl. CCXXIX, V8 and V9, both lids.

540. Very small 'thumb' pot, possibly a beaker as the vessel is meant to hold liquid of some sort. Resin on interior and exterior. Handmade. M4. D = 3.5 cm.
AB 35 [7683]. JF 703.

541. Candlestick (?). W1.

AA37 [7436]. JF 878.
Berenice, fig. 130, 1006. No date given other than mid Roman.

542. Circular pottery disc with hole in the centre. Possibly a spindle whorl or loom weight? VCM1.
AD52 [7519]. GP 366.
Esna, pl. CCXXXIII, 1 and 2.

**Amphorae**

These vessels made up 32.42 per cent of the total forms in this volume (Table 2.2), compared to 24.41 per cent in the first volume, 1990–92.

Most of the amphorae, i.e. 30.24 per cent of the total, were of the Egyptian Kom el-Nana M3 type (Table 2.3). This accords with the findings in Volume 1, where only 2.01 per cent of the amphorae total were of non-Egyptian origin. In this volume the figure is 2.24 per cent (Table 2.3). It was suggested in Volume 1 that the long-distance traded amphorae were perhaps a gift to the monastery, or represented a better class of wine acquired especially for the hierarchy and this seems as good a hypothesis as any.

*Late Roman Amphora 1: Peacock and Williams Class 44, Kom el-Nana N1.*

N1
Origin: shores of the Black Sea; the south coast of Turkey; Cyprus and Rhodes in Greece; northern Syria.

Contents: not known. Possibly oil (Liebeschuetz, 1972, 79–81).

Date: from the early fifth to the seventh century AD. The smaller version, Late Roman 1a, in circulation in the fifth century AD and the larger form, Late Roman 1b, in the sixth century AD.

543. Amphora. Small version of N1. LR1a. Rim, part of neck, shoulder and two handles. N1. D = 9 cm.
AC49 [8152]. JF 857.
Kellia, pl. 57, 6, dated AD 425–550.

544. Amphora. Almost complete. *Dipinto* in red on shoulder. N1. LR1b. D = 10 cm.
AC51 [8588]. JF 764.
Berenice, fig. 91, 337.

*Carthage Late Roman Amphora 4, Sciallano and Sibella Late Roman Amphora 4: Peacock and Williams Class 49, Kom el-Nana N9.*

N9
Origin: Palestine, in the region of Gaza, or Egypt.

Contents: not known, probably wine or oil. Various other contents have been suggested including pickled fish (Grenfell, Hunt and Bell, 1924), fish (Zemer, 1977), beer (Riley, in a personal communication to Bailey in Ashmunein 1982), olive oil and sesame oil (Passi et al., 1981) and wheat (Colt, 1962, no. 85). The last was actually recorded as a secondary use but others in this list may well be refills. A more detailed discussion of these vessels can be found in Bailey, Ashmunein, 1998, 123–124.

545. 'Gaza jar'. Large clods of clay and a pebble adhering to exterior around rim. N9. D = 12 cm.
AA48 [9840] and AA49 [9814]. GP 614.
Ashmunein, T64 cross referenced to Majcherek Form 2, AD 300–450.

546. 'Gaza jar'. N9. D = 10 cm.
AA48 [9800]. GP 632.
Majcherek Form 2, AD 300–450.

547. 'Gaza jar'. Two handles. Resin on interior and over rim. N9. D = 11 cm.
AD51 [7631]. GP 433.
Majcherek Form 3, AD 450–600.

548. 'Gaza jar'. Resin on interior and over rim. N9. D = 11.5 cm.
AB36 [7443]. GP 289.
Majcherek Form 3, AD 450–600.

Spatheion *amphora*

The term *spatheion* refers to a group of amphorae with a long narrow body, long tapering spike and a fairly high neck with everted rim and two short handles (Peacock and Williams, Class 51, p.202). Two forms exist, large and small. One of each variety is listed below.

*Peacock and Williams Class 51, Kom el-Nana N10.*

N10
Origin: North Africa.

Contents: not known, but examples from Cap Dramont contained many olive stones (Joncheray, 1975, 141–146).

Date: fifth to seventh century AD, with the smaller version occurring mainly in the sixth and seventh centuries (Peacock and Williams, 1991, 203).

549. Amphora. Cream coating caused by leaching out of salt deposit. Large spatheion type. N10. D = 15 cm.
AD51 [7570]. JF 724.
Coin: Justinian Hahn 166, AD 538–565.

550. Amphora. Small spatheion type. N10. D = 8 cm.
AC49 [8152]. JF 766.
N8
Origin: Egypt.

One base sherd only from Y50 [8254]. Not illustrated.

*Late Roman Amphora 7: Egloff 177, Peacock and Williams Class 52, Kom el-Nana M3.*

M3
Origin: Egypt.

Contents: Wine.

Date: Late fourth to the sixth and seventh century AD.

For a more detailed discussion of this form see Bailey, 1998, 129–132.

Where the term 'Pot Slot no. *X*' occurs at the end of the entry, this refers to a vessel appearing in Chapter 4.

551. Amphora. M3. D = 8 cm.
AA48 [9842]. GP 559.

552. Amphora. Resin on interior and over rim. M3. D = 8 cm.
AA49 [9814]. GP 618.
Ashmunein, 1998, V13, around fifth to eighth century AD, but poorly dated.

553. Amphora (?). M3. D = 10 cm.
AA47 [9836]. GP 544.

554. Amphora. Resin on interior and over rim. M3. D = 7 cm.
Z36 [7451]. JF 801.

555. Amphora. Resin on interior and over rim. M3. D = 7 cm.
AB36 [7443]. GP 286.

556. Amphora. Resin on interior and over rim. M3. D = 6 cm.
AB52 [7406]. GP 240.

557. Amphora. Resin on interior and over rim. Unusual rim form. M3. D = 8 cm.
Z52 [7477]. GP 369.

558. Amphora. M3. D = 7 cm.
V51 [8680]. JF 785.

559. Amphora. Resin on interior. M3. D = 6 cm.
V52 [8692]. GP 193.

560. Amphora. Resin on interior. M3. D = 6 cm.
V51 [8293]. GP 194.

561. Amphora. *Dipinto* on shoulder. Resin on interior and over rim. M3. D = approx. 8.5 cm.
AD49 [8309] and [8320]. GP 283.
Coins: fourth to sixth century AD (three); fourth to sixth century (two); fifth to sixth century AD copy (?).

562. Amphora. M3. D = 7 cm.
AB36 [7440]. GP 438.

563. Amphora. Neck and shoulder. M3.
AC51 [8579]. JF 712.
Pot Slot no. 18.

564. Amphora. Neck and shoulder. M3.
AC49 [8792]. GP 365.

565. Amphora. Shoulder. Two stubby handles. Traces of resin on interior. Unusual form of M3.
AC51 [8587]. GP 242.

566. Amphora. Shoulder. M3.
AC51 [8579]. GP 151.
Pot Slot no. 26.

567. Amphora. Neck, shoulder, part of body and two handles. M3.
AC51 [8588]. GP 150.
Pot Slot no. 27.

568. Amphora. Part of body. Decoration: crosses and vertical and horizontal bands in dark cream/yellow. M3.
V51 [8292] and V51 [8294]. GP 84.
Shape of body as Ashmunein, 1998, V27, fifth to early sixth century AD.

569. Amphora. Neck and shoulder with two handles. GP Type 3B. Resin on interior. M3.
AB52 [7760]. GP 437.

570. Amphora. Part of neck and shoulder. Part of one handle evident. GP Type 3B. M3.
AB36 [7455]. GP 412.

571. Amphora. Shoulder and part of body. *Dipinto* on shoulder. Part of one handle evident. M3.
AD51 [7647]. GP 364.

572. Amphora. Neck, shoulder, two handles and part of body. Post-firing hole in neck. M3.
AB36 [7455]. GP 460.

573. Amphora. Neck, shoulder, two handles and most of body. GP Type 3B. M3.
AD52 [7304]. GP 475.

574. Amphora. Neck and shoulder with two handles. Rope marks on shoulder. M3.
Y52 [8276]. GP 83.
Ashmunein,V53, dated AD 400–550.

575. Amphora. Toe and rim missing. M3.
AC51 [8579]. GP 135.
Ashmunein, 1998,V28, fifth to early sixth century AD.
Pot Slot no. 22.

576. Amphora. Missing rim. M3.
AC50 [8580]. GP 130.
Pot Slot no. 17.

577. Amphora. Missing neck and handles. Rope marks on shoulder. M3.
AC51 [8579]. GP 136.
Pot Slot no. 24.

578. Amphora. Body and toe, missing neck and handles. Decoration: cream swags. M3.
V51 [8294]. GP 128.

579. Amphora. Body, missing toe, neck and handles. GP Type 3B M3.
V52 [8689]. GP 113.

580. Amphora. Body, missing toe, neck and handles. GP Type 3B M3.
V52 [8689]. GP 114.

581. Amphora. Body and toe, missing neck and handles. GP Type 3A. M3.
U51 [8296]. GP 112.

582. Amphora. Part of body, neck and two handles. M3.
AC51 [8580]. GP 132.
Ashmunein, 1998,V28, fifth to early sixth century AD.
Pot Slot no. 19.

583. Amphora. Neck, toe and handles missing. *Dipinto* on shoulder. M3.
AC51 [8412]. GP153.
Ashmunein, 1998,V28, fifth to early sixth century AD.
Pot Slot no. 5.

584. Amphora. Neck and handles removed or missing. M3.
AC51 [8412]. GP 133.
Pot Slot no. 9.

585. Amphora. Rim missing. M3.
AC51 [8412]. GP 131.
Ashmunein, 1998,V29, AD 500–650.
Pot Slot no. 12.

586. Amphora. Body. Exterior burning and oily residue. M3.
AC51 [8412]. GP 127.
Pot Slot no. 8.

587. Amphora. Body. M3.
AC51 [8412]. GP 126.
Pot Slot no. 4.

*Unidentified amphorae*

588. Base of amphora. Resin-coated interior. M3 (?)
AA48 [9844]. GP 588.
No sign that the vessel is warped in any way. The walls of the vessel are a consistent thickness throughout with no indication that an attachment to a spike base was intended. This resembles more closely the base of an Aswan (O1) amphora of omphalos type.

*Amphora reuse*

Nos 589–595 below have been adapted for reuse.

Nos 589–592 are Egloff 177, Late Roman 7 Egyptian amphorae which were found in the 'Pot Slots' adjacent to the proposed kitchen area, which is discussed in Chapter 4. The rims, necks and handles of these amphorae had been knocked off and the base of the neck smoothed. It would appear that this was to facilitate a secondary use after their original contents (probably wine) had been used. They had then been reused for a second time, together with other pottery as under-floor humidifiers.

There can only be speculation as to the secondary use, but as this sector of the site appears to have been a storage/kitchen area, the amphorae may well have been employed as storage containers. This could have been for pickling or preserving various commodities such as fish or vegetables as at Wadi Sarga, where monk Apa John of the pickle store is mentioned, and also salted fish (Wadi Sarga 87 and 89). At the Monastery of Epiphanius (Winlock and Crum, 1926, 148–149), *garum* is taken to mean pickled herbs and *tarichaeion* is translated as preserved vegetables. The terms are usually taken to mean fish sauce and pickled fish respectively.

Clackson has pointed out that the ostraca found at the Monastery of Baouit (Bawit) can be clearly associated with CPR XX ostraca in which *tarichaeion* is clearly used of fish products (Clackson, 2002, 10–11; Maspero and Drioton, 1931). Dried and salted fish were found at Bawit during the excavation (Maspero and Drioton, 1931, 44, xii).

Luff has identified schall fish bones from Kom el-Nana which are of a much smaller size than in the earlier Pharaonic period, and would appear to be targeted for a specific purpose, which is most likely to have been to be salted and preserved in ceramic vessels such as amphorae (Luff, 2007, 173). Very small schall, impregnated with salt, were identified at the Monastery of Phoebammon, and were thought to be the remains of salted fish (El-Duweini, 1961, 55), and at the Monastery of Kellia five amphorae were excavated which contained small fish (Egloff, 1977, 114, 117).

589. Amphora. Shoulder and most of body. Red spot on slope of shoulder. Rim, neck and handles have been removed down to the base of the neck, which has then been carefully smoothed. M3.
AC50 [8579]. GP 134.
Ashmunein, V28, dated fifth to early sixth century AD.
Pot Slot no. 15.

590. Amphora. Shoulder and most of body. Rim, neck and handles have been removed down to the base of the neck, which has then been carefully smoothed. M3.
AC50/51 [8412]. GP142.
Ashmunein, V28, dated fifth to early sixth century AD.
Pot Slot no. 2.

591. Amphora. Shoulder and most of body. Rim, neck and handles removed down to the base of the neck, which has then been carefully smoothed. M3.
AC50 [8579]. GP 129.
Pot Slot no. 1.

592. Amphora. Shoulder and body. Rim, neck and handles removed down to the base of the neck, which has then been carefully smoothed. M3.
AC51 [8412]. GP 123.
Ashmunein, 1998, V28, dated fifth to early sixth century AD.
Pot Slot no. 3A.

*Part amphorae*

593. Base of 'Gaza jar'. N9.
Z52 [7611]. GP 370.

594. Base of 'Gaza jar'. N9.
AE51 [8395]. JF 877.

595. Part of the toe of an Egyptian M3 amphora. Scored with a wear mark, possibly made by rope?
AD52 [8598]. GP 367.

## Discussion and conclusions

Most comments have been made before the relevant fabric or form and will not be repeated here. However, there are some differences between the 1990–1992 Midden, which were dealt with in Volume 1, and the stratified material in this volume. There is also a full discussion of the distribution of the wares in Chapter 3.

The African Red Slipware percentage is much lower in the stratified deposits of 1993–4 and 2000, together with Egyptian Red Slip 'B' Ware (M5). The Aswan product, Egyptian Red Slip 'A' Ware (01), is higher, together with M4 (usually cooking wares). This could possibly indicate that the African ware is more difficult to obtain or more expensive or that the Aswan wares have replaced them as the fineware of choice, being easily available in the local markets. The decline of Egyptian Red Slip 'B' (M5) could possibly be due to different firing techniques as discussed before the relevant wares earlier in this chapter.

There were no O2 wares (an ERS 'A' variant fired to a yellowish-cream colour and polished), or O1W wares (an ERS 'A' variant with cream/yellow polished slip) in Aswan wares in 1990–92. It was also not well represented in the stratified deposits described in this volume (Table 2.4). This may point to fewer being made and supplied to this particular area and those vessels which were obtained were well looked after. They are thin-walled compared to the other ERS 'A' vessels and could have been expected to break more easily.

There was less VCM1 in the Midden, which is probably due to its thickness, weight and the fact that it was broken less easily and thus lasted longer. There was more in stratified deposits, again due to the previously mentioned factors, and also because the size of some of the vessels would have meant that they remained in one place for long periods, possibly for life. Very large vessels are few, possibly because they would have been difficult to move and so remained in one place for long periods.

Amphorae M3 are about the same in excavated/

stratified deposits as in the Midden. Imported amphorae, which appear only in small amounts, are more or less the same in all contexts.

The Estimated Vessel Equivalents (EVES) for the years 1990–2 was 240 vessels which, as was said in Volume 1, is not likely to represent an accurate indication of the real number present. The assessment of actual vessel numbers included various ways of estimating the number of vessels present: drawn vessels, amphora handles divided by two; actual numbers of vessels and average weight of 10 rims, 10 bases and 10 handles for the more prolific M3 amphora, divided into the total weight for 1990–1992. This produced an overall number of 940 vessels. This was for nearly half the number of sherds present in the stratified group. A number of 782.36 for 1993–4 and 2000 is probably much smaller than the actual number needed to sustain the monastery in its day-to-day activities. Chapter 3 has addressed the distribution of pottery over the site.

Table 2.2 shows the forms represented, and whilst in the 1990–92 unstratified material five vessel forms—*qadus*, bowl, jar, cooking pot and amphora—accounted for nearly 88 per cent of the total RBH, in 1993–4 and 2000 the percentage had reduced to nearly 86 per cent, the difference being the smaller numbers of *qadus* and the larger numbers of amphorae in the stratified group.

From Table 2.4 below it can be seen that the bulk of the assemblage was made in Egypt. Dividing the percentages for fabrics as given in Table 2.4 into short-distance traded wares, long-distance traded wares and imported wares produces the following result together with a comparison between these and figures from Volume 1 (Faiers, 2005, 173).

There is the possibility that ERS 'B' (M5) could be a short-distance traded ware made in Middle Egypt. If so, and transferred to this combined category, this would bring the amount made within the immediate area to 89.83 per cent. The total manufactured in Egypt does not differ significantly between the various years with the only reduction being in the Midden deposit (discussed in Volume 1), containing only 509 sherds. Only 2.37 per cent of the stratified deposits in this volume was imported and the majority of these are amphorae.

The locally produced amphorae Egloff 177 (M3) and their contents appear to have been of great importance to the community, forming just over 30 per cent of the total sherds. These vessels probably originally contained wine, and kiln sites have been found in the vicinity at Antinoopolis, Hermopolis Magna (el-Ashmunein), Zawyet el-Maietin—which appear to have produced both amphorae and other forms (Ballet, Mahmoud, Vichy and Picon, 1991, 134–138)—and Akoris (Ballet and Picon, 1987). Various quantities and conditions of wine are mentioned in the Wadi Sarga texts including new (Wadi Sarga, no. 186), pure (?) (Wadi Sarga, no. 377), unmixed (Wadi Sarga, no. 179) and boiled (Wadi Sarga, no. 210). Wine vinegar could also have been carried by these vessels, as much was needed to preserve or pickle various commodities such as vegetables and fish.

| Fabric | 1990–92 | 1993–4 | Midden |
|---|---|---|---|
| ARS | 0.86 | 0.30 | 2.20 |
| O1 | 4.74 | 7.10 | 4.50 |
| M5 | 6.46 | 3.60 | 5.90 |
| M6 | 5.50 | 5.00 | 4.30 |
| VCM1 | 1.13 | 2.65 | 0.60 |
| M1 | 37.2 | 22.45 | 33.30 |
| M2 | 15.22 | 16.41 | 12.80 |
| M4 | 4.26 | 9.40 | 3.60 |
| W1 | 0.15 | 0.40 | 0.00 |
| L1 | 0.02 | 0.00 | 0.00 |
| L3 | 0.08 | 0.02 | 0.00 |
| L4 | 0.02 | 0.00 | 0.00 |
| **Amphorae** | **1990–92** | **1993–4** | **Midden** |
| M3 | 22.41 | 30.24 | 30.80 |
| N1 | 1.36 | 1.40 | 1.60 |
| N7 | 0.08 | 0.10 | 0.00 |
| N9 | 0.46 | 0.52 | 0.40 |
| N10 | 0.11 | 0.04 | 0.00 |

*Table 2.3 Fabric percentages, rims, bases and handles comparison between the years 1990–2, 1993–4 and 2000, and the midden.*

Many amphorae were reused, sometimes more than once, or may have been sent back to be refilled. As mentioned in the section on M3 amphorae, those under the floor in the kitchen area had been modified once already and this would be their third time of using. One contained Acacia pods, which were possibly stored in the vessel before it was used in the slots under the floor. See Theodore Pena for more instances of reuse (Pena, 2007).

Lamps again were not numerous, and the pottery versions may have been outnumbered by glass lamps. Alternatively, the preference may well have been for small bowls/cups to be used instead, as shown by nos 521–525 in this catalogue. This practice was also noted at the Monastery of Epiphanius (Winlock and Crum, 1926, 88) and at Esna (Jacquet-Gordon, no. 8).

The ? vessels which were discussed in Volume 1 (Faiers, 1995, 162–163), were thought perhaps to be used as strainers (fig. 2.1), may be part of a dovecote as seen in the nearby village of el-Til (fig. 2.2).

Ladles (or parts of ladles) were found in the main

body of the Monastery at Areas AC and AD, apart from three pieces found in AE and AA. There were 144 colander RBH in the assemblage, again many more than appear elsewhere such as at Nazlet Tuna, el-Ashmunein, and Elephantine. The reason may well be that this was an enclosed community catering for a large number of people, which necessitates all the cooking apparatus being in one or two areas.

The corpus of pottery is indicative of a reasonably thriving, but not high status, society mainly concerned with the day-to-day activities which kept the monastery and its monks alive. Although decorative techniques and patterns are reasonably predictable on Coptic sites, one would expect a higher level of religious themes depicted on the pottery. However, this would depend on where the pottery was made, its price, the expertise of the potter or his artist and of course whether the pottery was specifically made for the monastery.

| **Imported** | **% of 12,063 sherds** | **% of Vol. 1 5,235 sherds** | **% Midden Vol. 1 509 sherds** |
|---|---|---|---|
| ARS (N. Africa) | 0.30 | 0.86 | 2.20 |
| N1 (Antioch/Cilicia/Lycia) | 1.40 | 1.36 | 1.60 |
| N7 (E. Mediterranean) | 0.10 | 0.08 | 0.00 |
| N9 (Palestine/Gaza) | 0.52 | 0.46 | 0.40 |
| N10 (N. Africa) | 0.04 | 0.11 | 0.00 |
| N11 (Palestine) | 0.01 | 0.00 | 0.00 |
| **Total Imports** | **2.37** | **2.87** | **4.20** |
| **Long-Distance Traded** | | | |
| M5 | 3.60 | 6.46 | 5.90 |
| O1 | 7.01 | 4.74 | 4.50 |
| O2 | 0.04 | 0.00 | 0.00 |
| O1W | 0.20 | 0.00 | 0.00 |
| W1/P23 | 0.50 | 0.15 | 0.00 |
| **Total of Long-Distance Traded** | **11.35** | **11.37** | **10.40** |
| **Short-Distance Traded** | | | |
| M6 | 5.02 | 5.52 | 4.30 |
| M1 | 22.45 | 37.12 | 33.30 |
| M2 | 16.41 | 15.22 | 12.80 |
| M4 | 9.40 | 4.26 | 3.60 |
| VCM1 | 2.65 | 1.13 | 0.60 |
| M3 Amphora | 30.24 | 22.41 | 30.80 |
| L2,3 & 5 (Lamps) | 0.06 | 0.08 | 0.00 |
| L1 (Lamp) | 0.00 | 0.02 | 0.00 |
| **Total of Short-Distance Traded** | **86.23** | **85.76** | **85.40** |
| **Total manufactured in Egypt** | **97.58** | **97.13** | **95.80** |

*Table 2.4 Percentages of fabrics in 2.2 apportioned as to likely origin*

*Figure 2.2 Dovecote at el-Til, Middle Egypt*

*Figure 2.1 Strainer vessels*

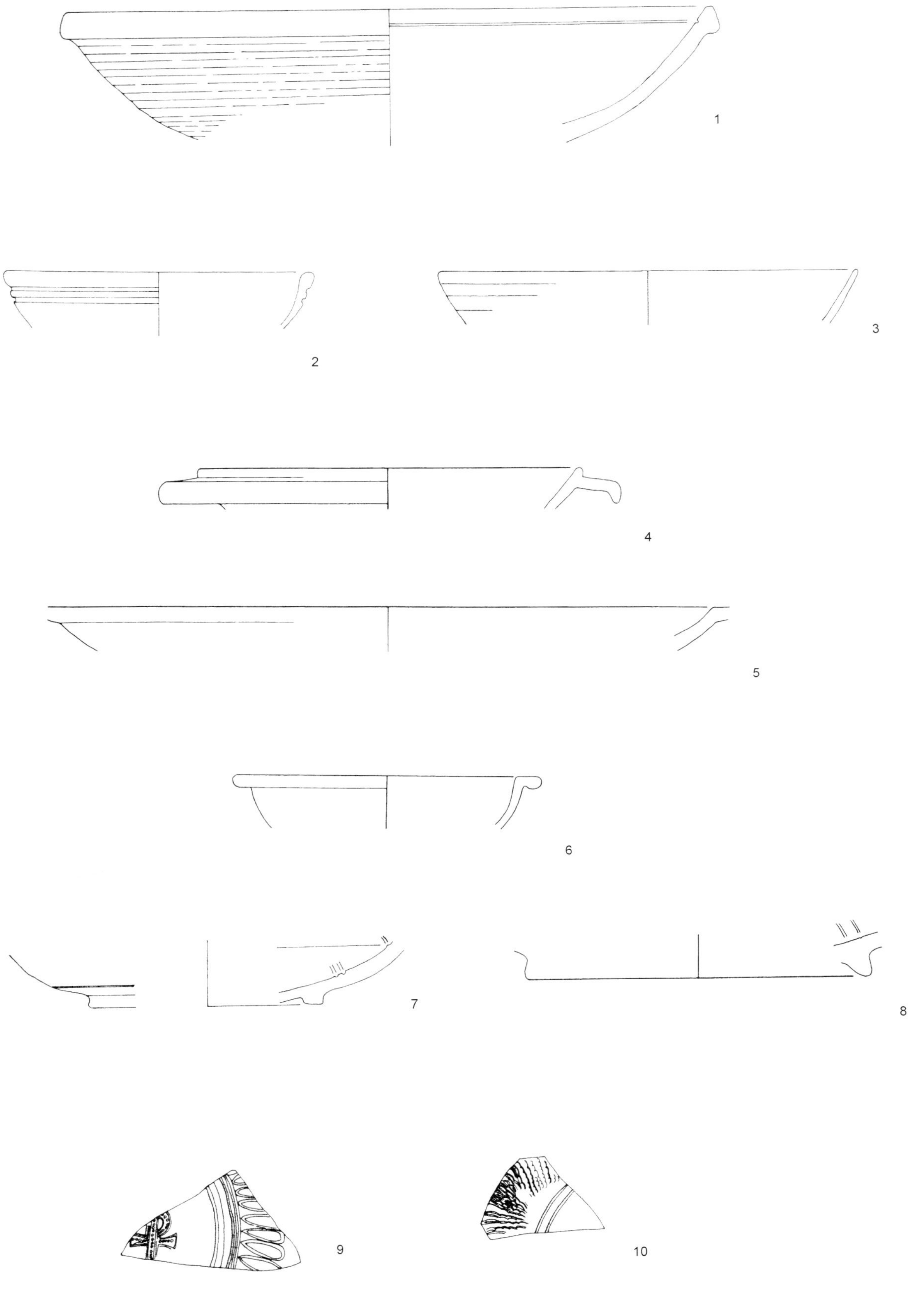


*Figure 2.3 Catalogue 1–10, African Red Slipware. Scale 1:3*

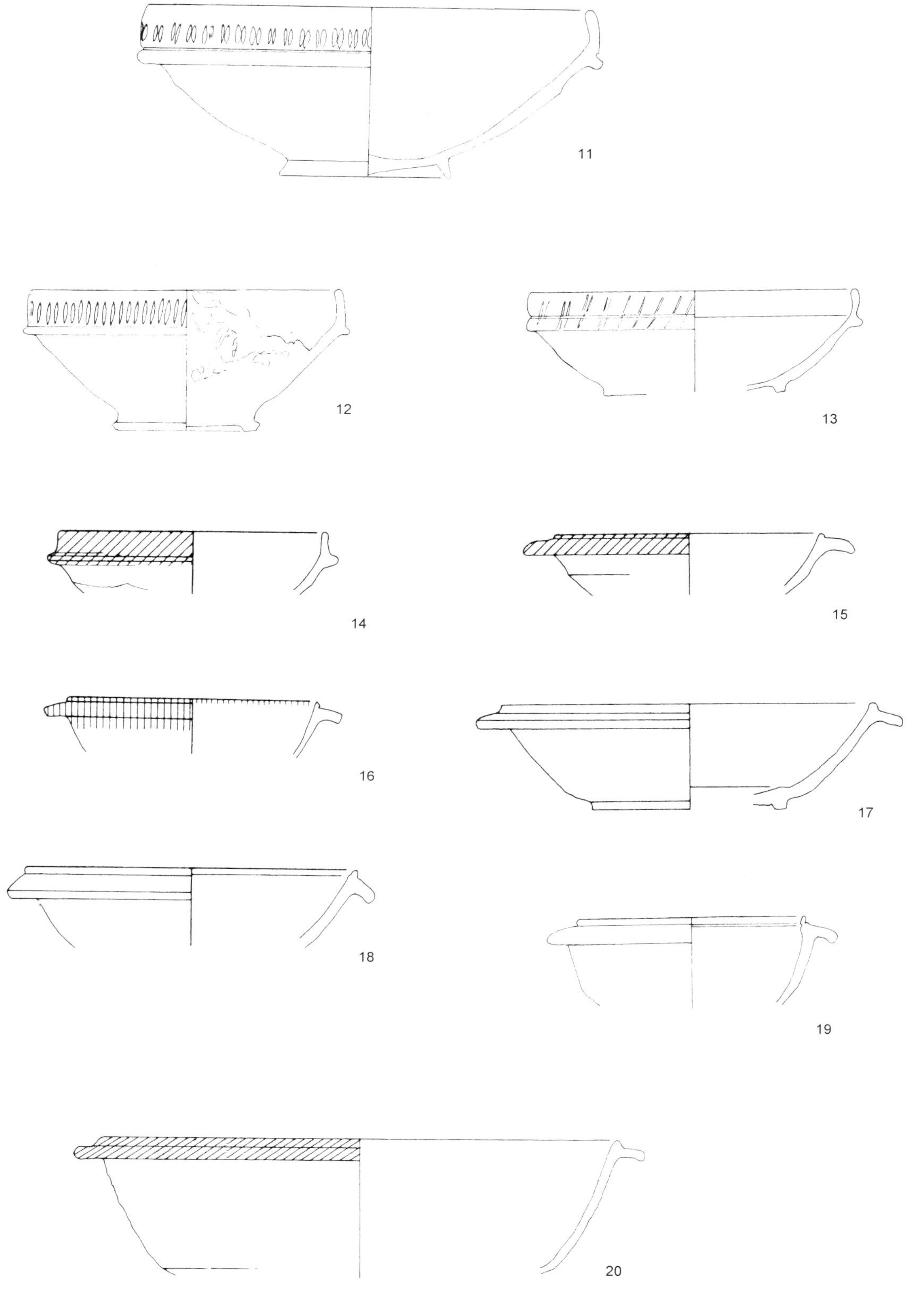


*Figure 2.4 Catalogue 11–20, Egyptian Red Slip 'A' ware. Scale 1:3*

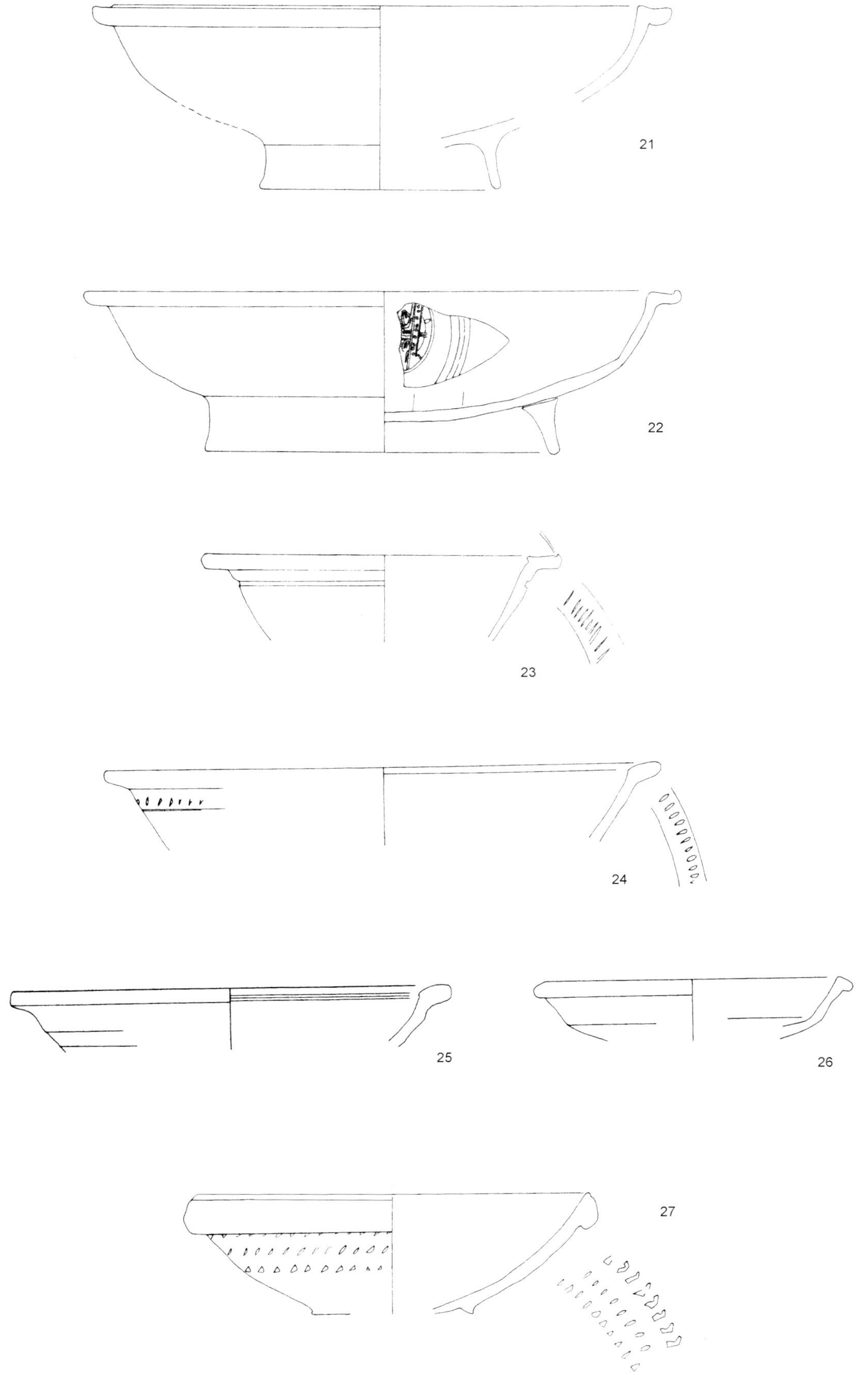


*Figure 2.5 Catalogue 21–27, Egyptian Red Slip 'A' ware. Scale 1:3*

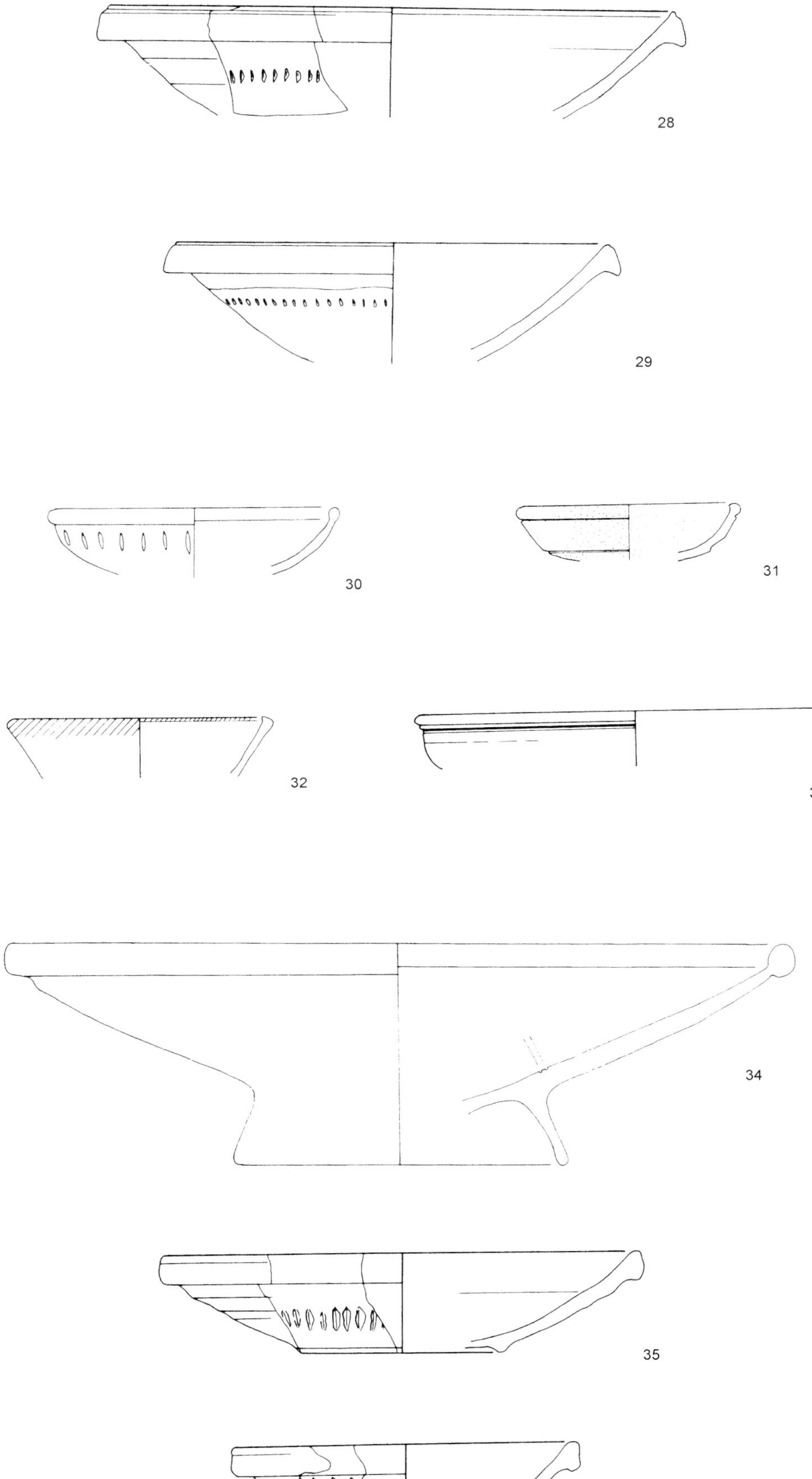


*Figure 2.6 Catalogue 28–36, Egyptian Red Slip 'A' ware. Scale 1:3*

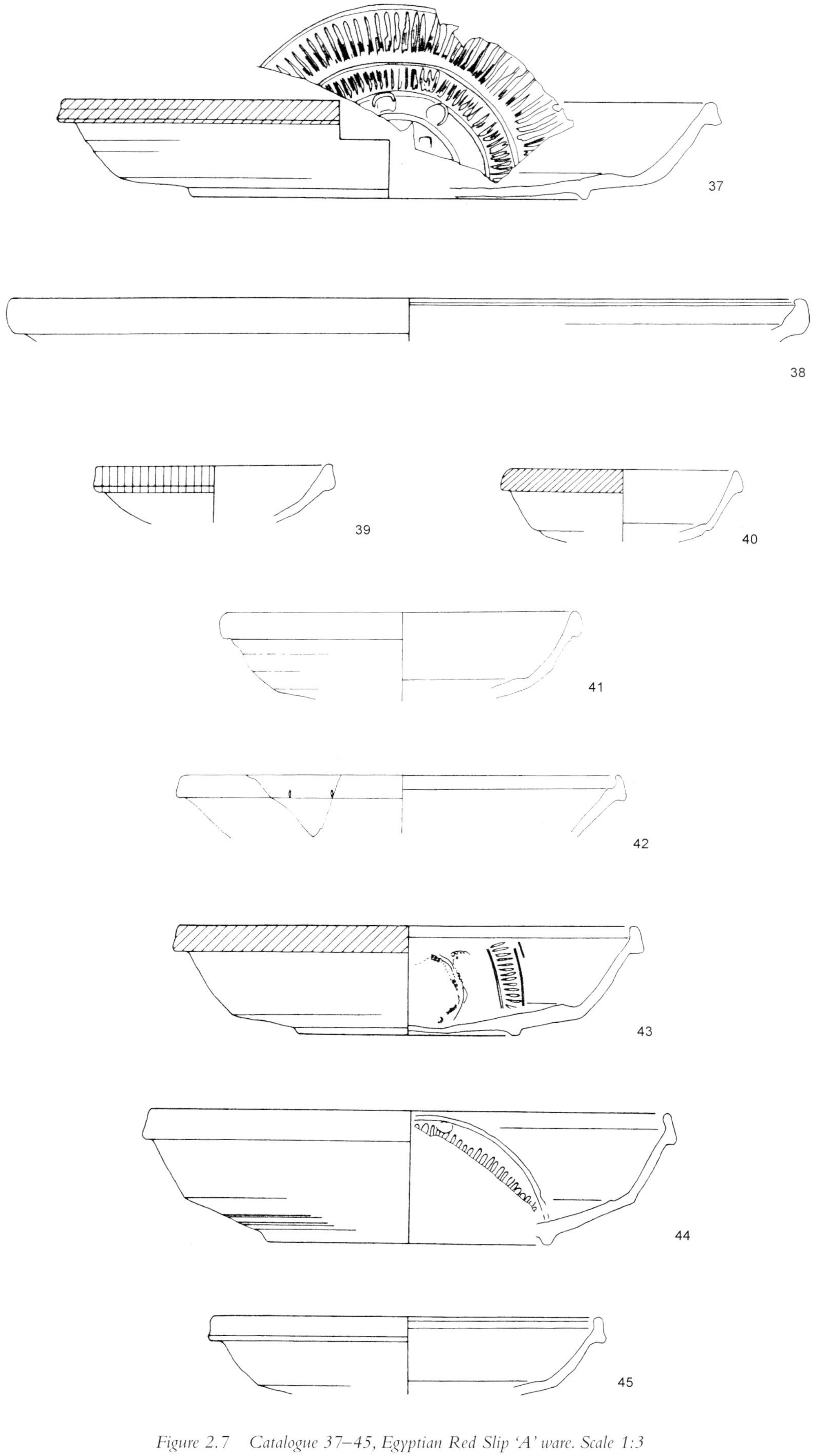


*Figure 2.7 Catalogue 37–45, Egyptian Red Slip 'A' ware. Scale 1:3*

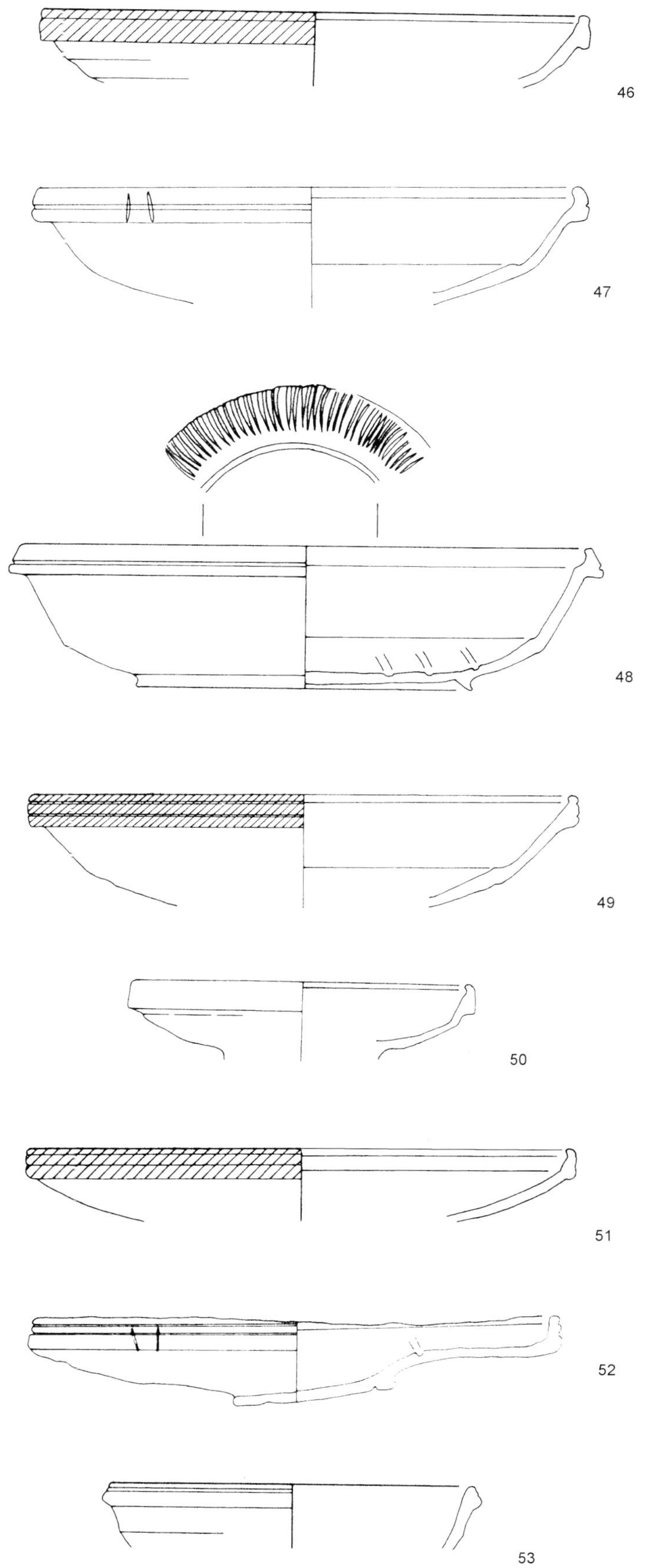


*Figure 2.8 Catalogue 46–53, Egyptian Red Slip 'A' ware. Scale 1:3*

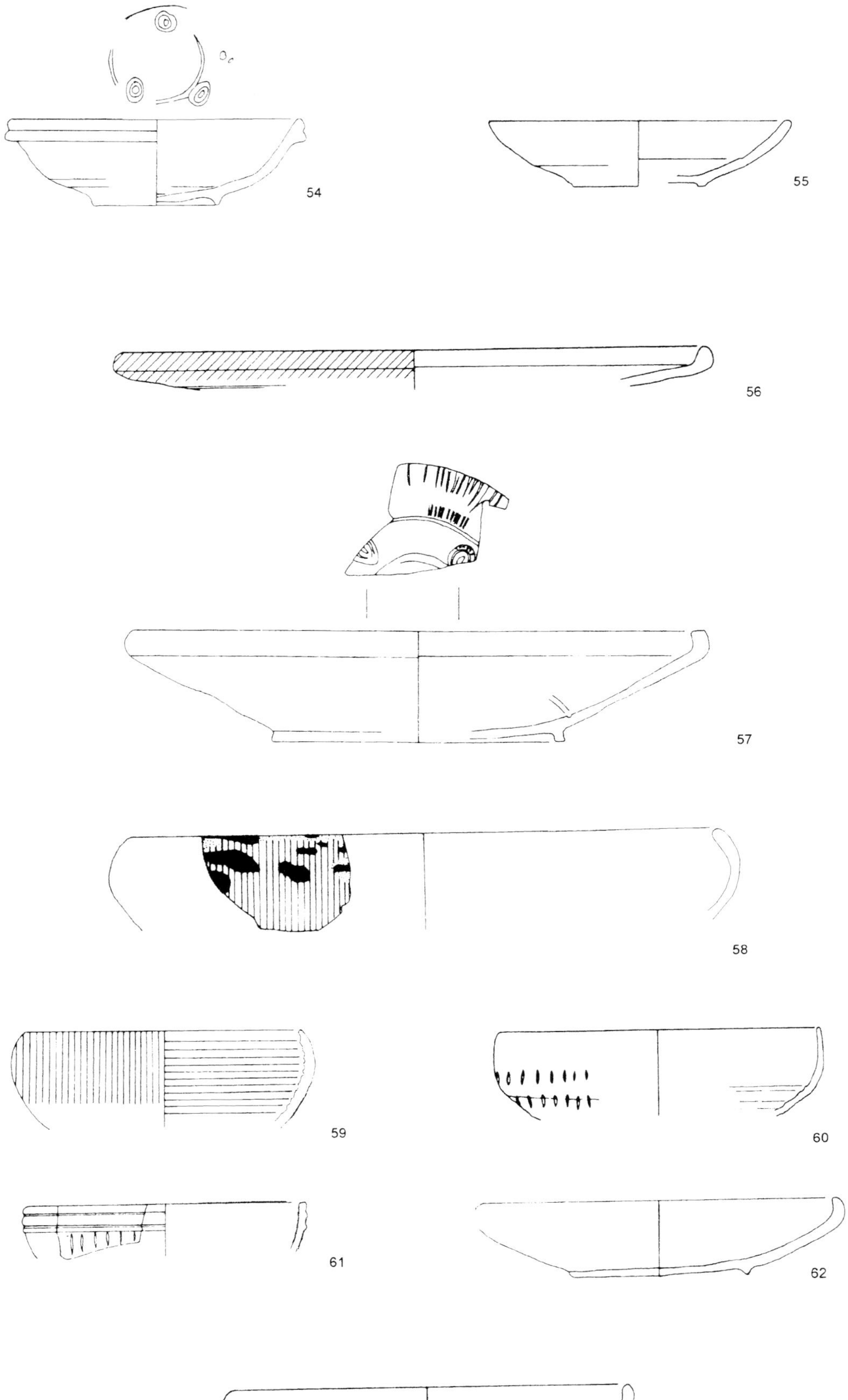


*Figure 2.9 Catalogue 54–63, Egyptian Red Slip 'A' ware. Scale 1:3*

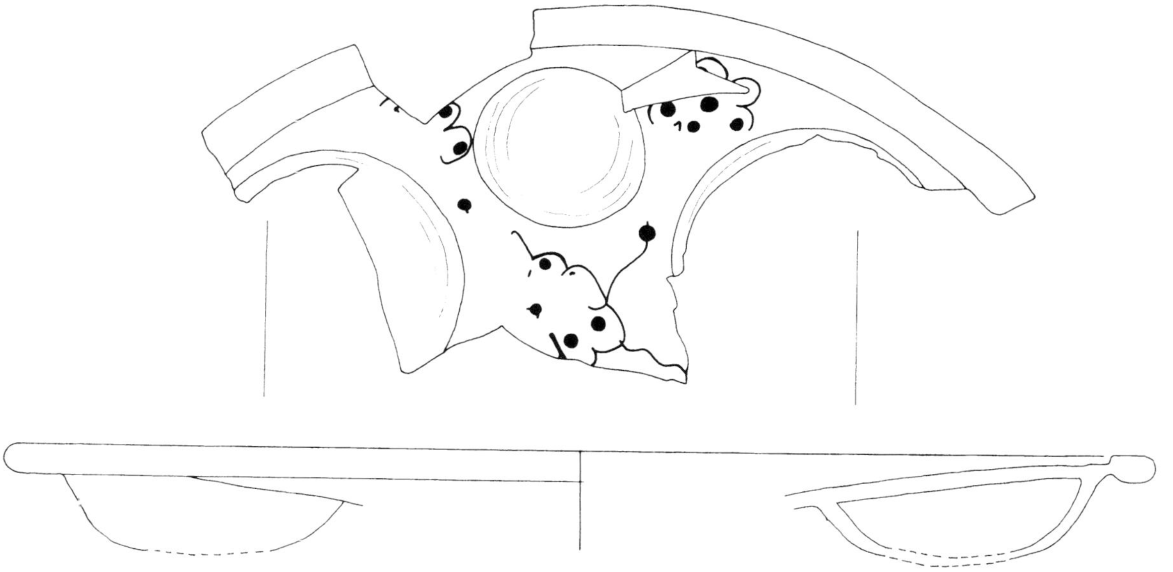

64

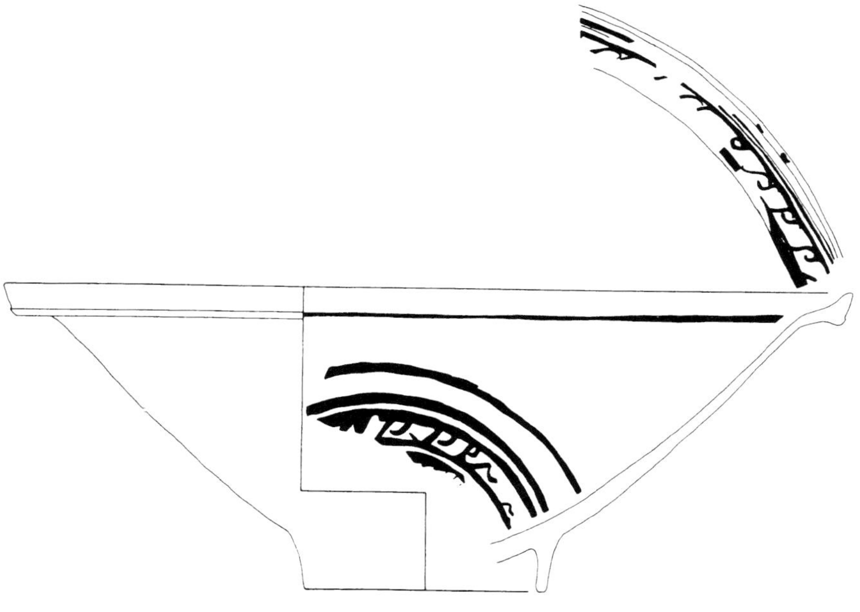

65

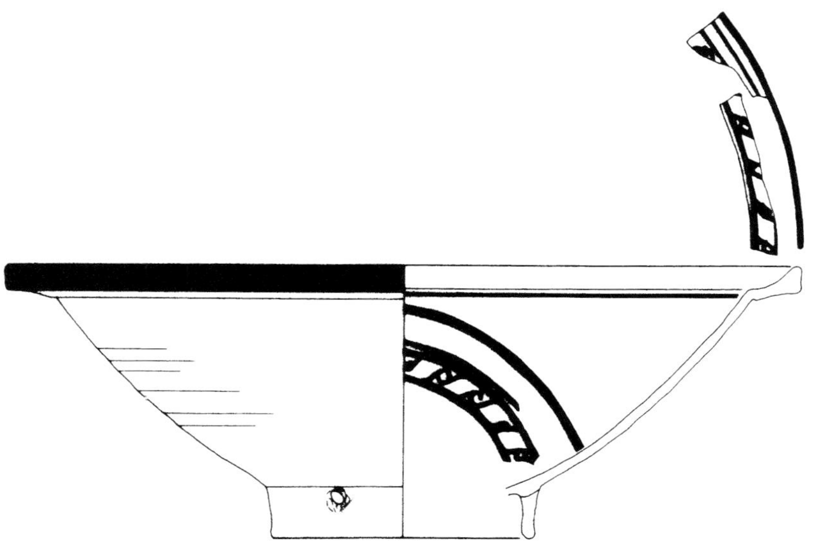

66

*Figure 2.10 Catalogue 64–66, Egyptian Red Slip 'A' ware. Scale 1:3*

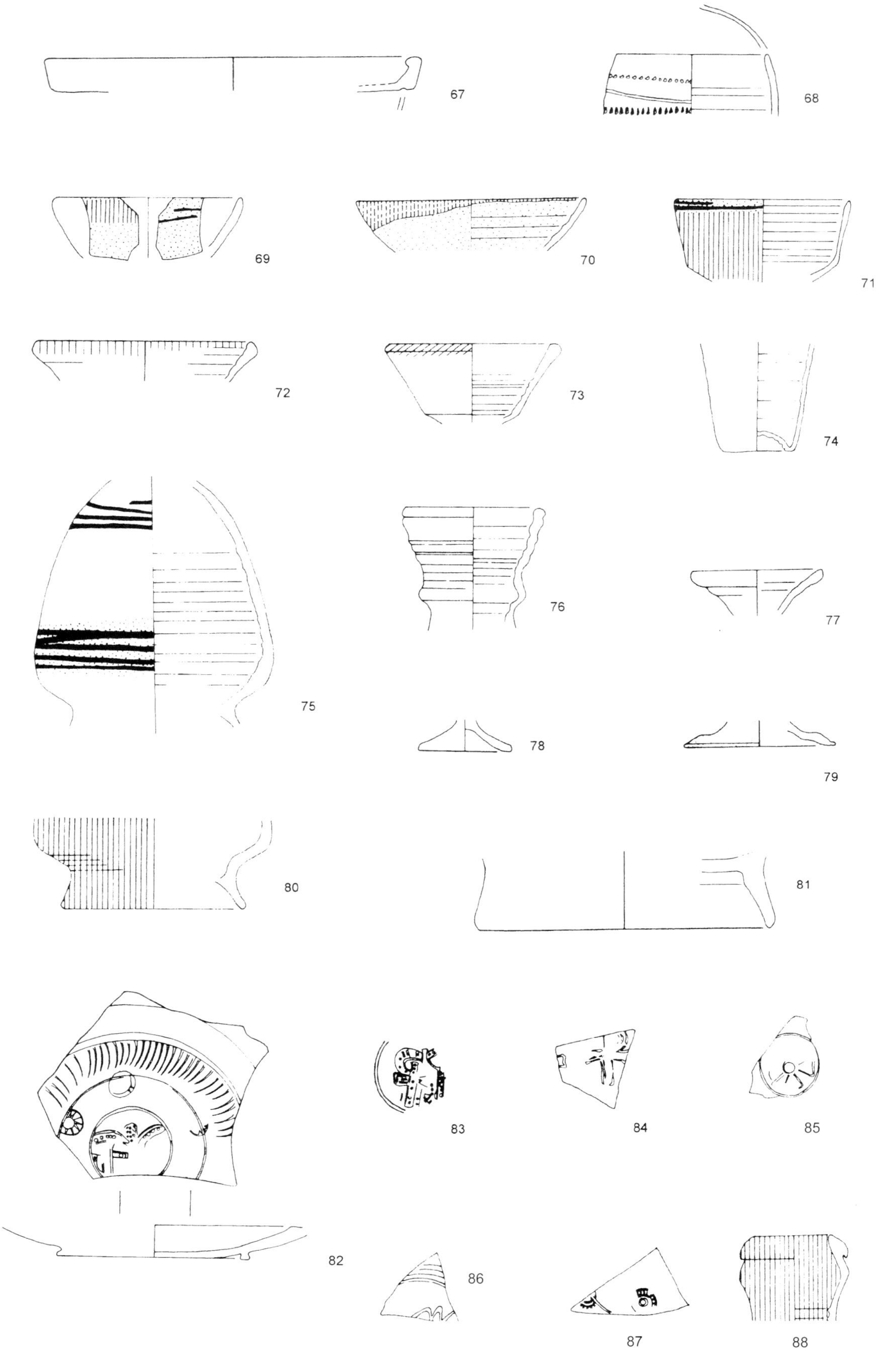


*Figure 2.11 Catalogue 67–88, Egyptian Red Slip 'A' ware. Scale 1:3*

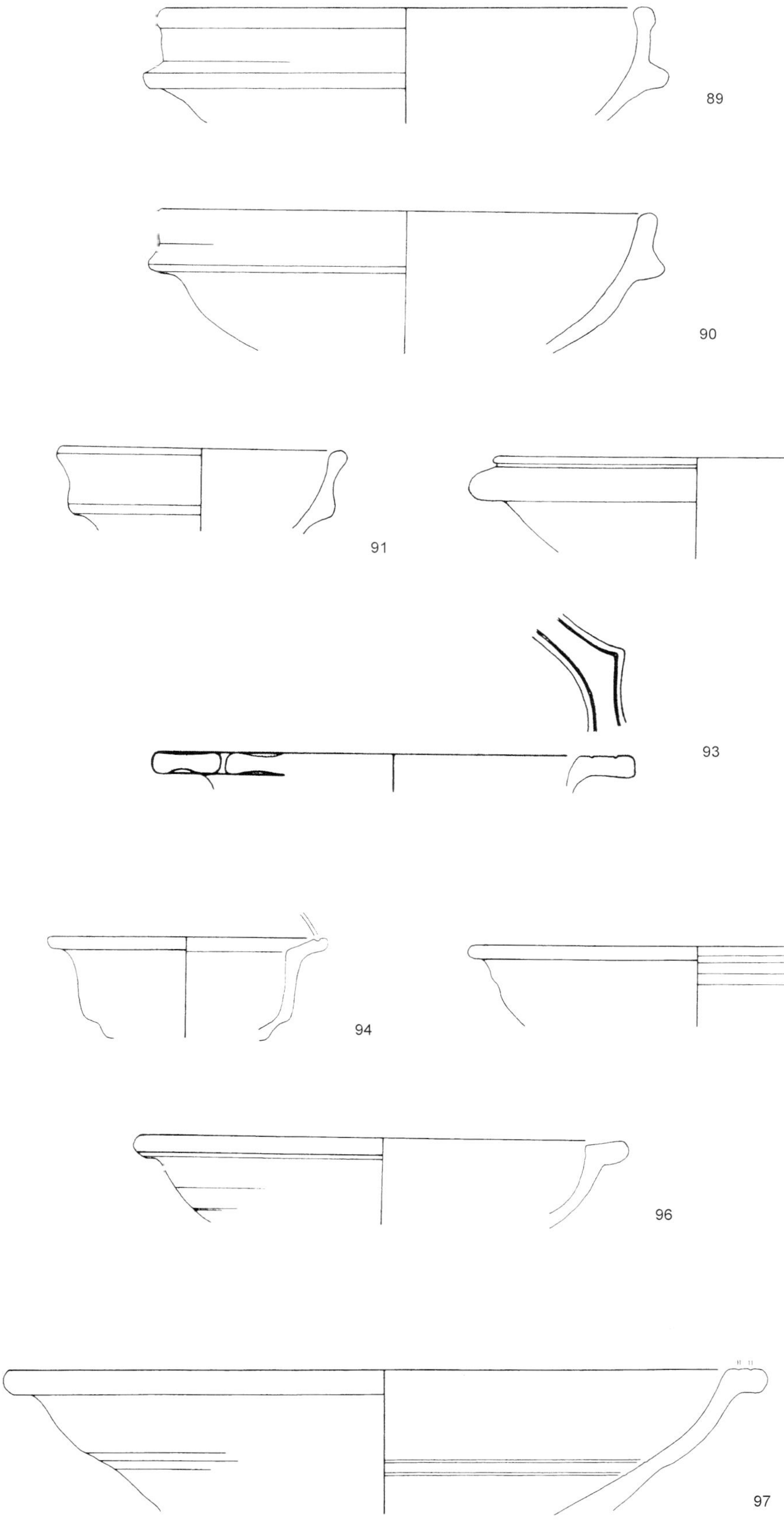


*Figure 2.12 Catalogue 89–97, Egyptian Red Slip 'H' ware. Scale 1:3*

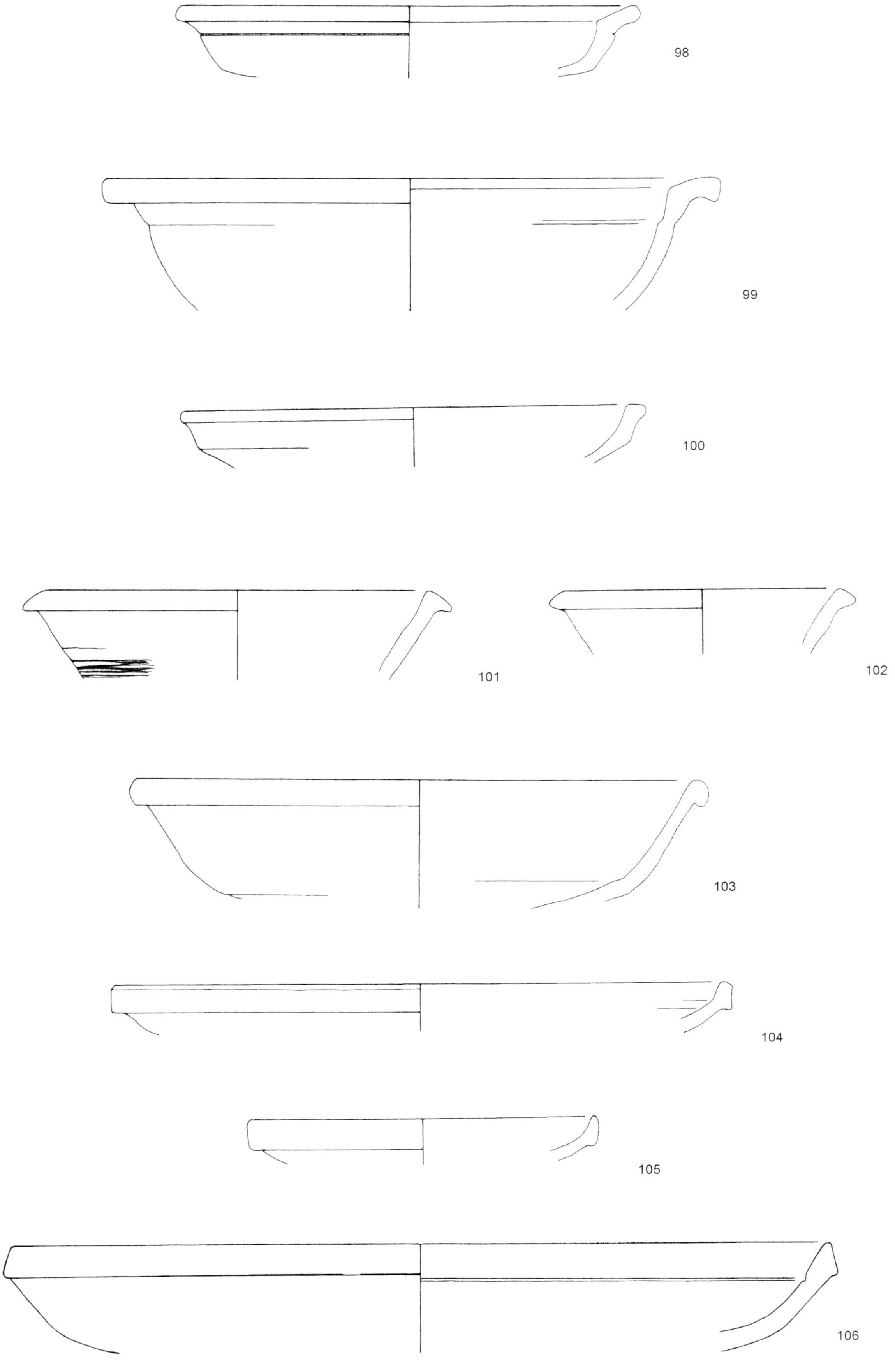


*Figure 2.13 Catalogue 98–106, Egyptian Red Slip 'B' ware. Scale 1:3*

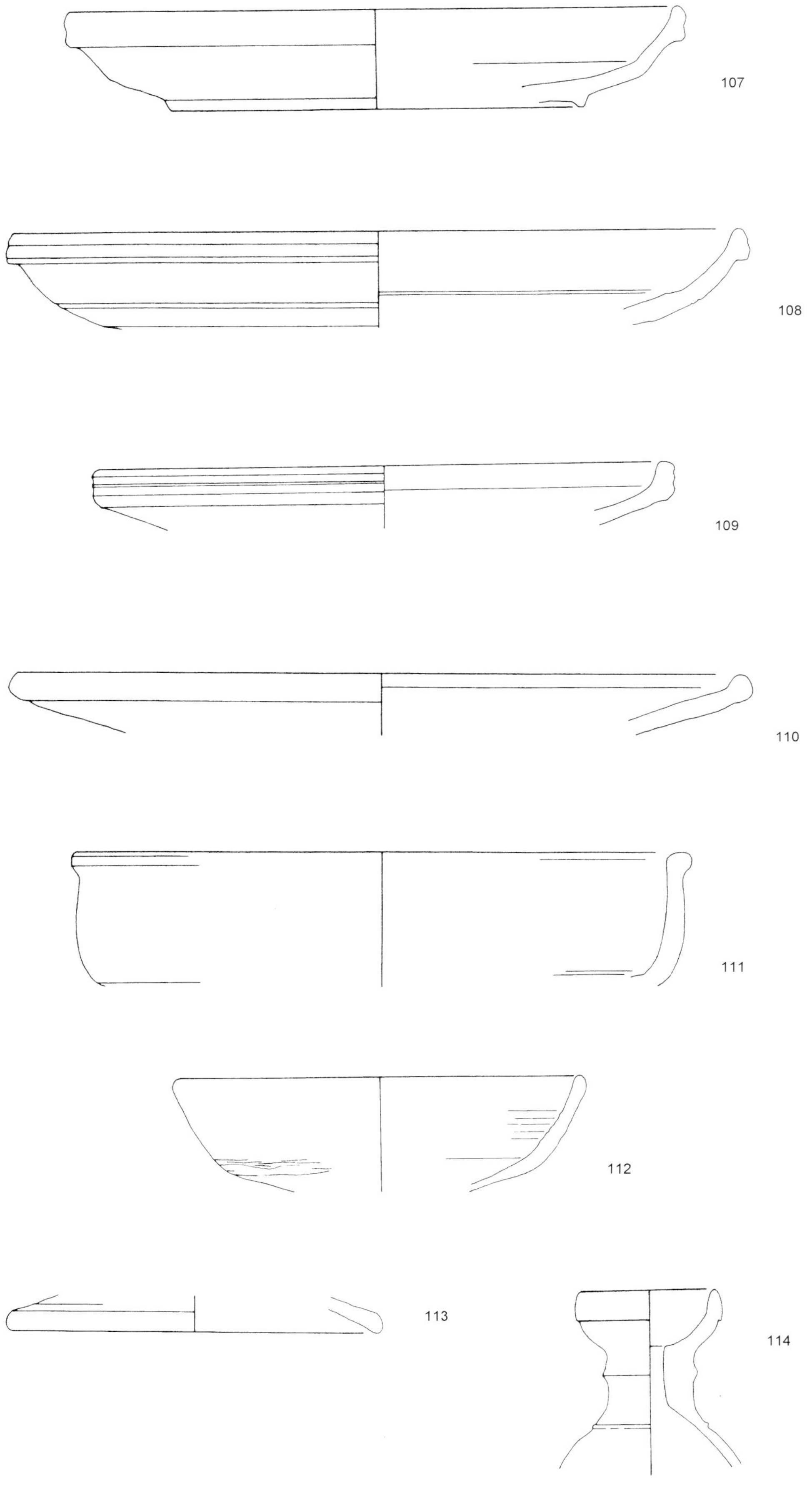


*Figure 2.14 Catalogue 107–114, Egyptian Red Slip 'B' ware. Scale 1:3*

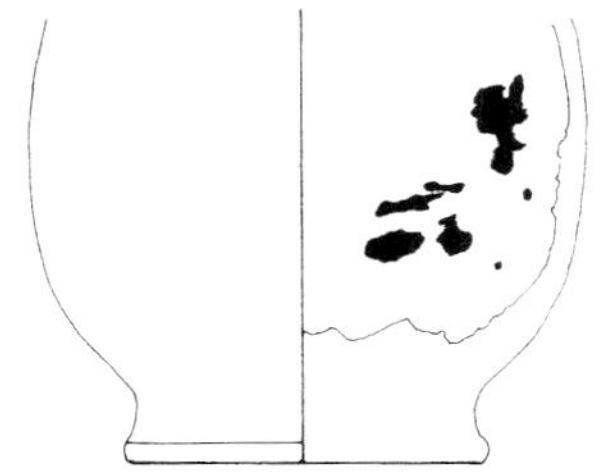

115

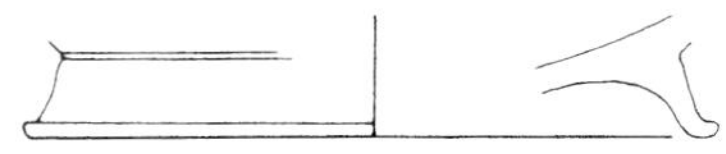

116

117

118

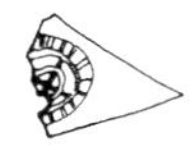

119

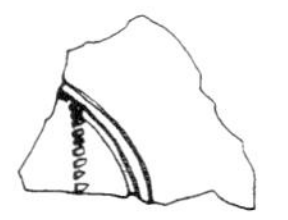

120

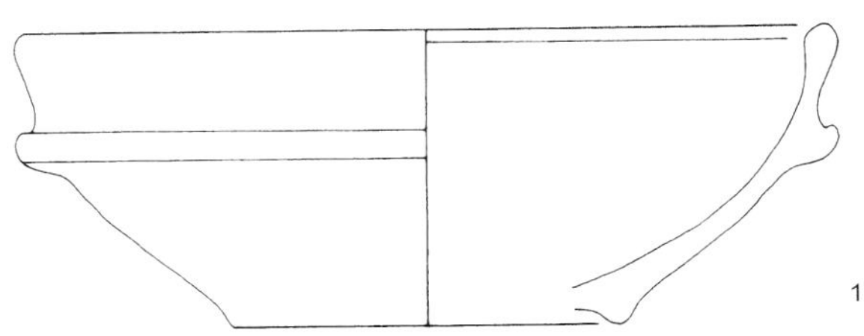

121

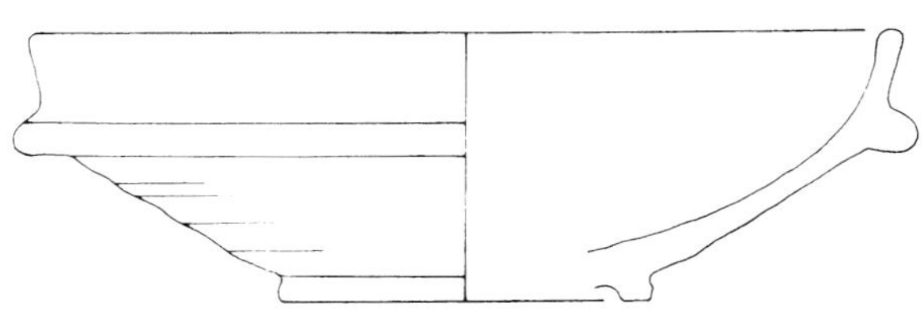

122

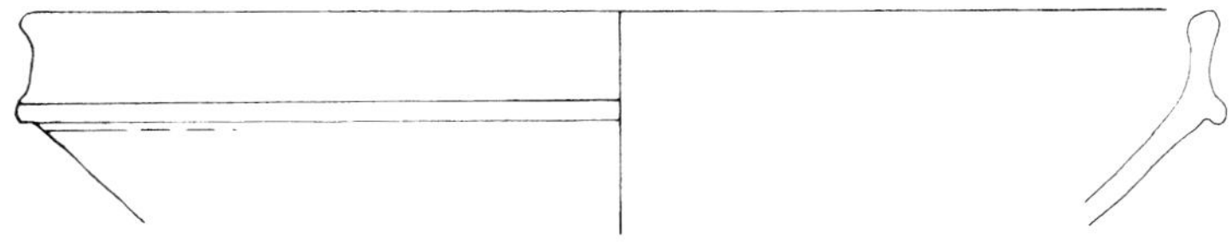

123

*Figure 2.15 Catalogue 115–123, Egyptian Red Slip 'H' ware. Scale 1:3*

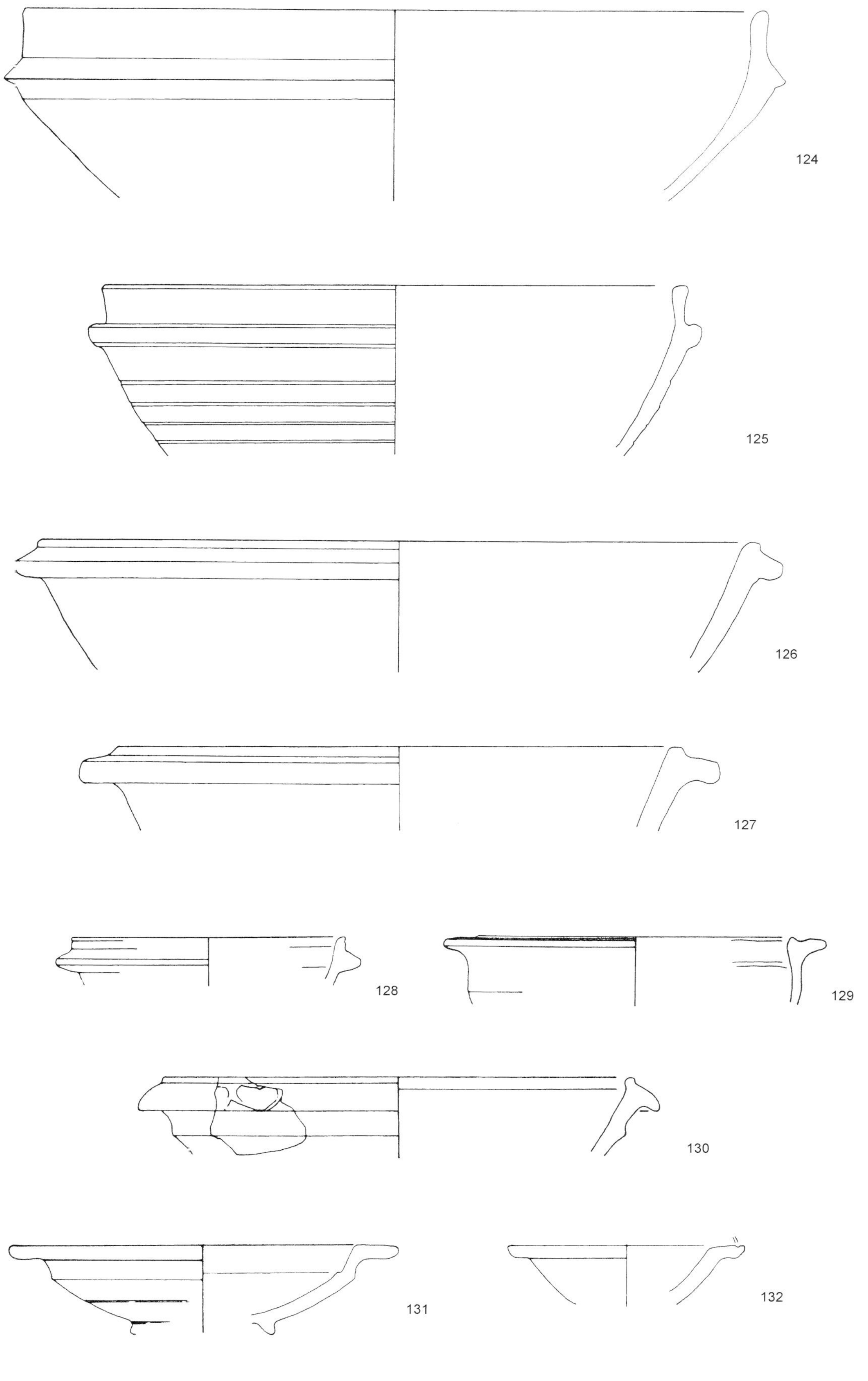


*Figure 2.16 Catalogue 124–132, Egyptian Red Slip 'H' ware. Scale 1:3*

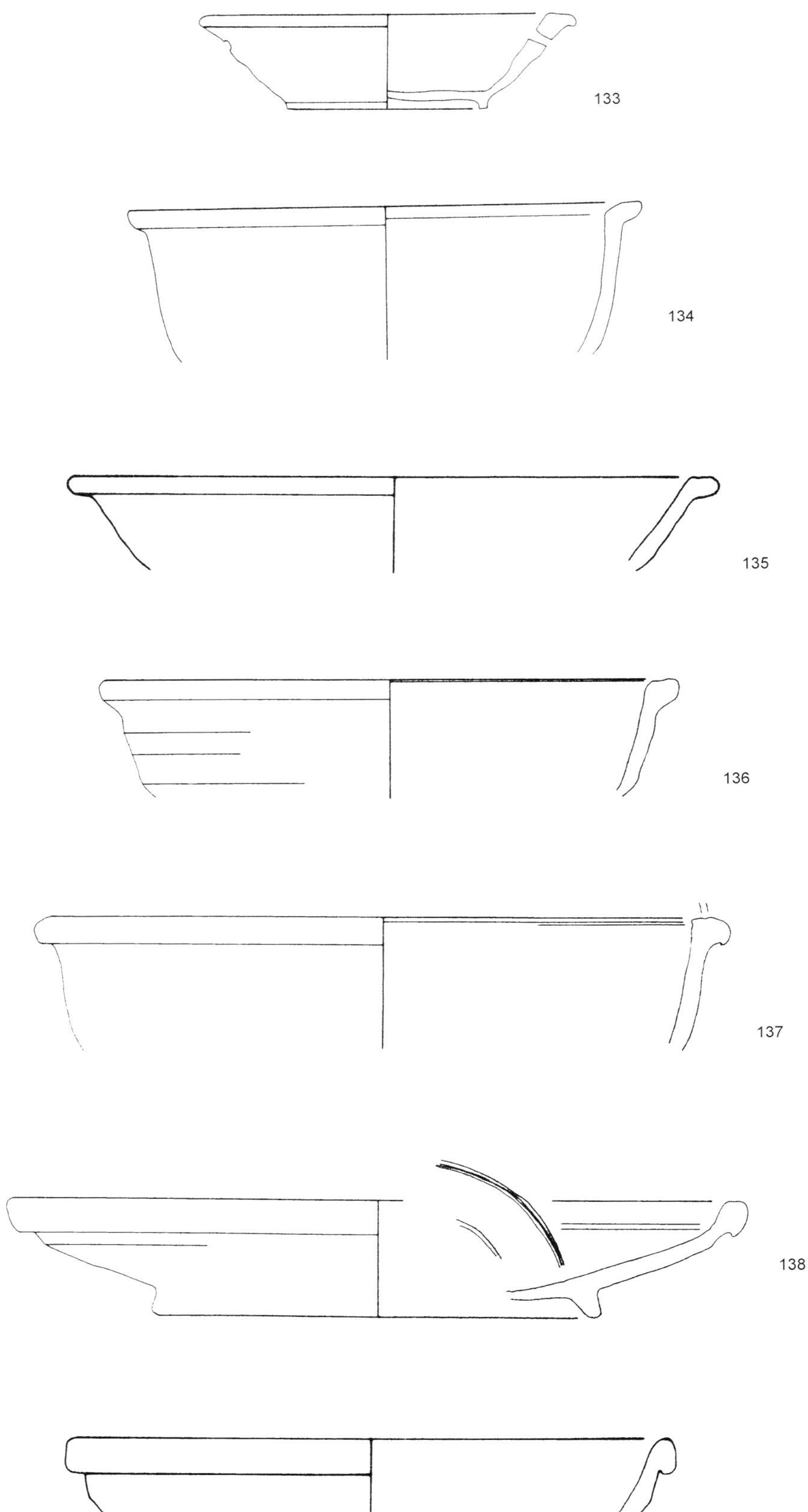


*Figure 2.17 Catalogue 133–139, Egyptian Red Slip 'H' ware. Scale 1:3*

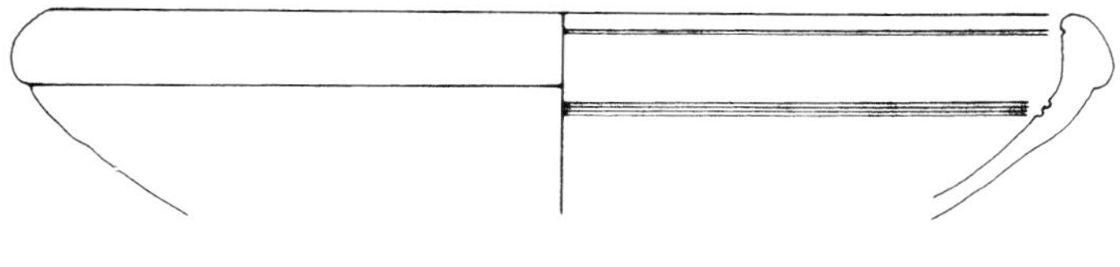
140

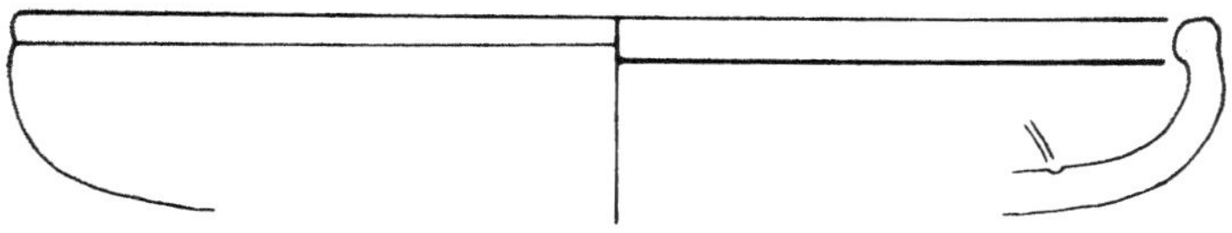
141

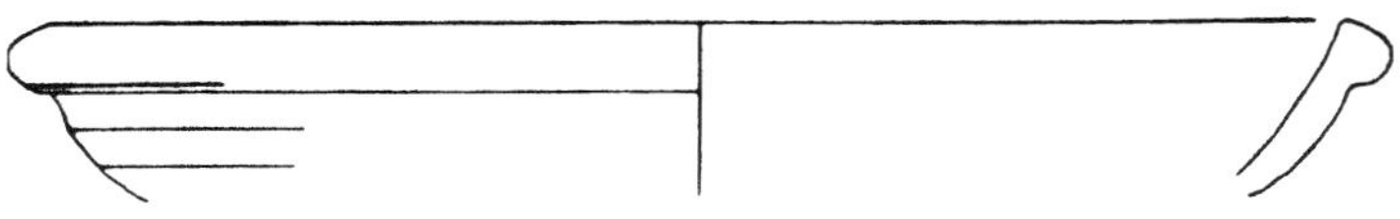
142

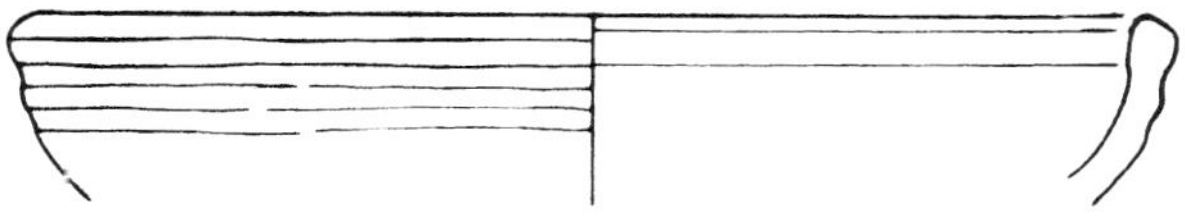
143

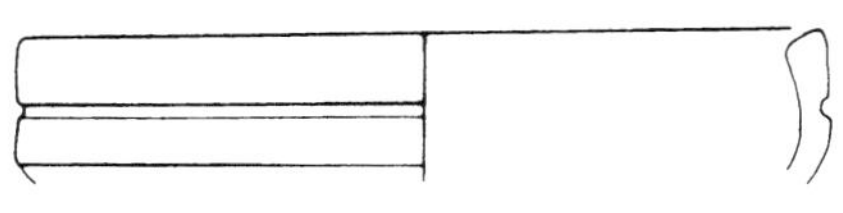
144

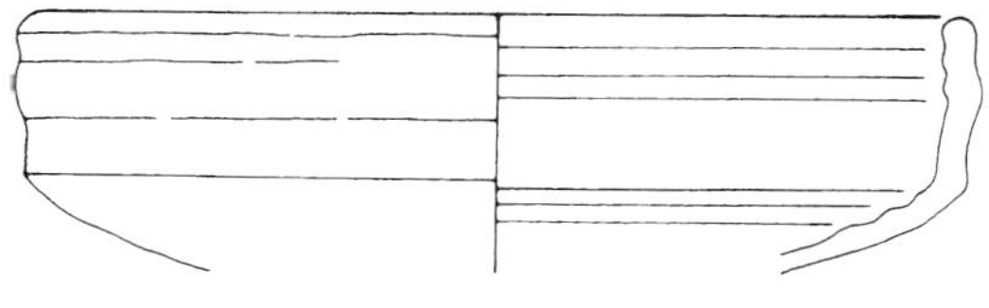
145

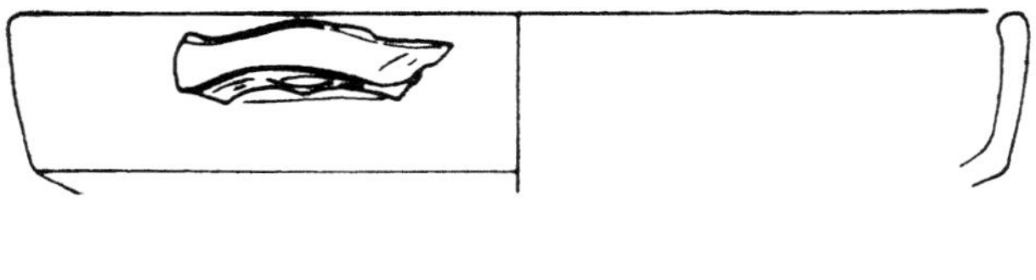
146

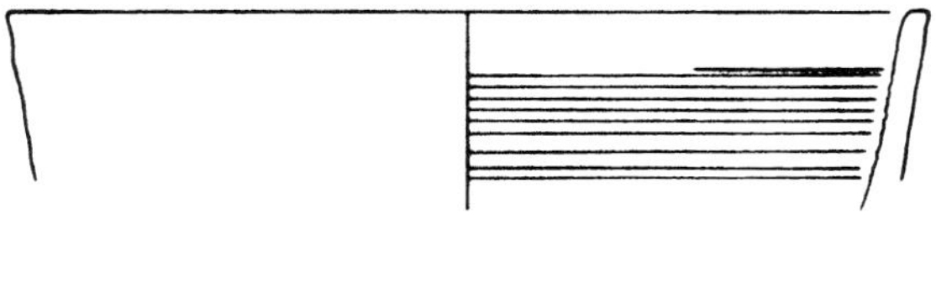
147

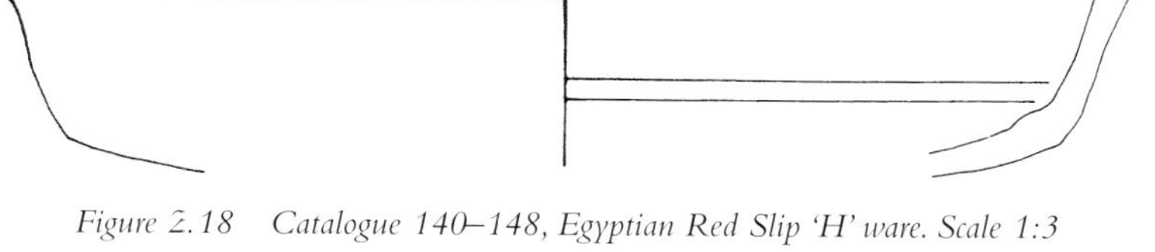
148

*Figure 2.18 Catalogue 140–148, Egyptian Red Slip 'H' ware. Scale 1:3*

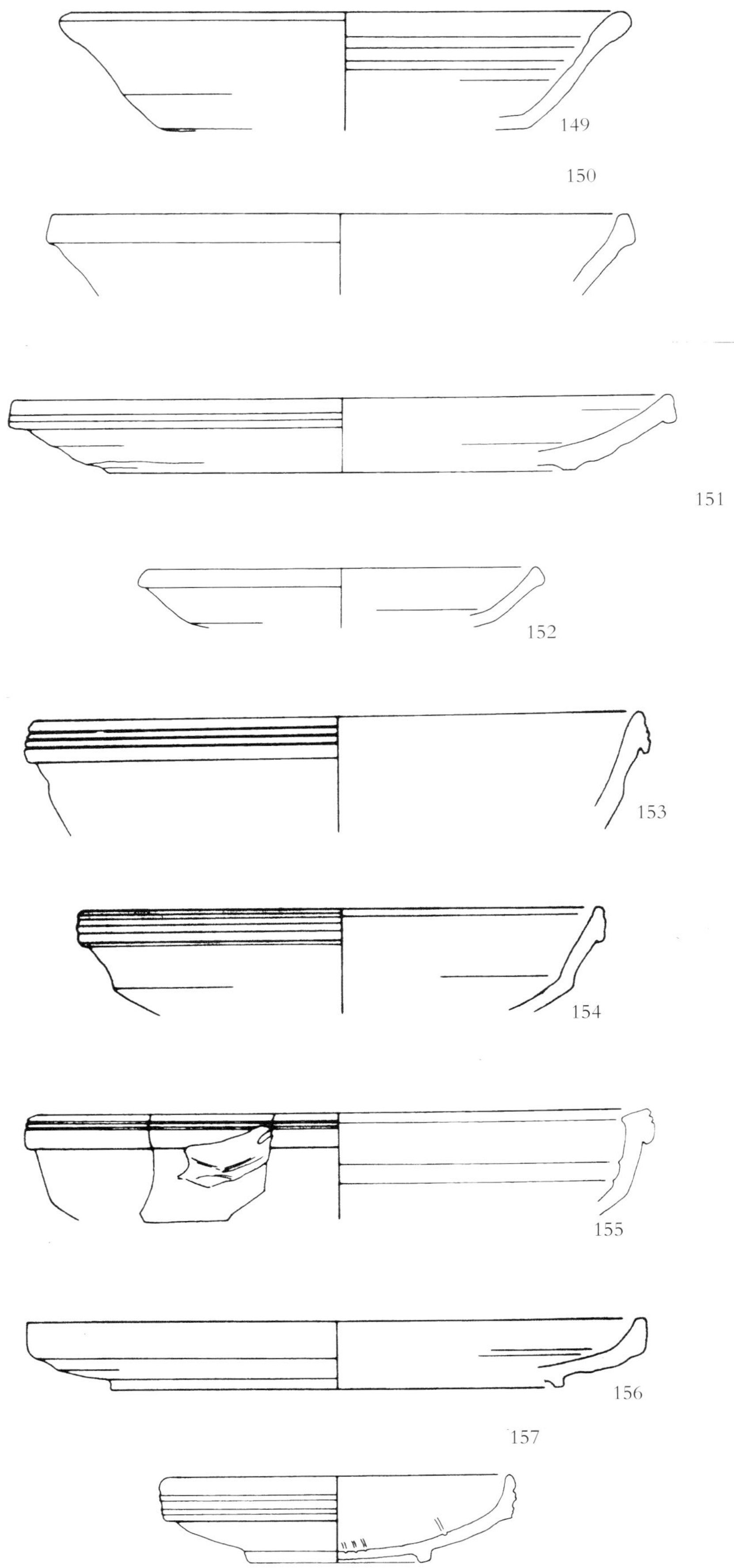


*Figure 2.19 Catalogue 149–157, Egyptian Red Slip 'H' ware. Scale 1:3*

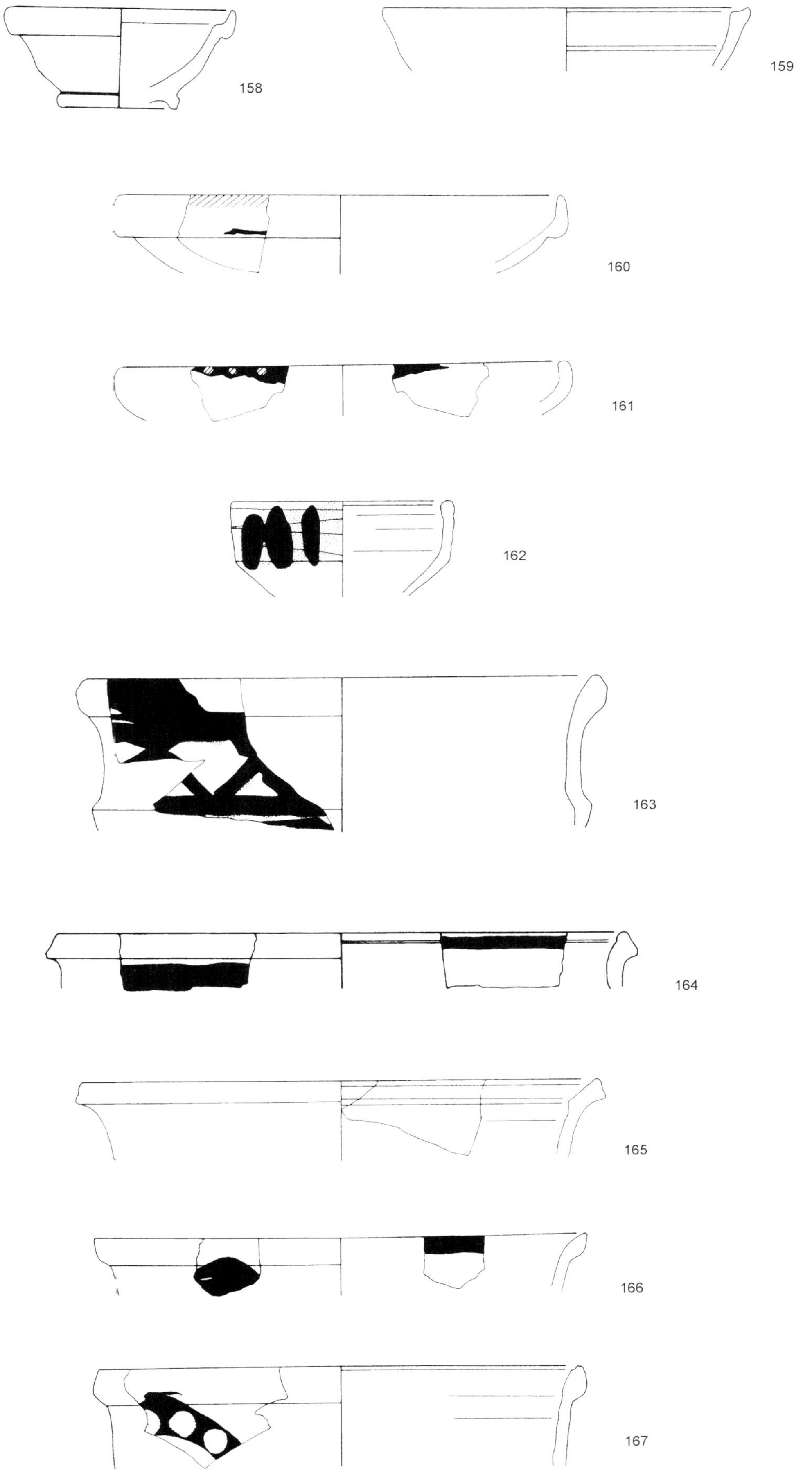


*Figure 2.20 Catalogue 158–167, Egyptian Red Slip 'H' ware. Scale 1:3*

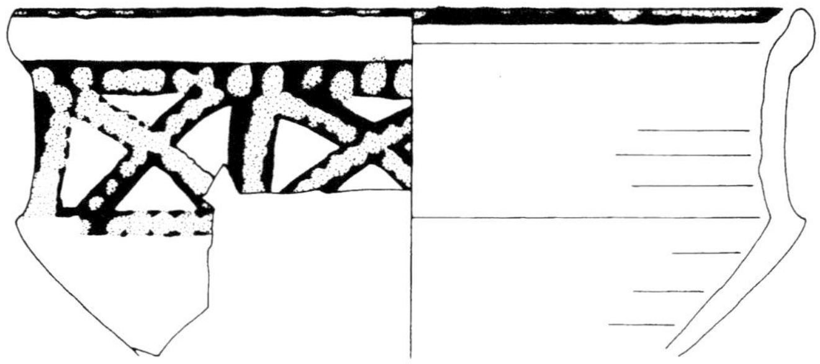
168

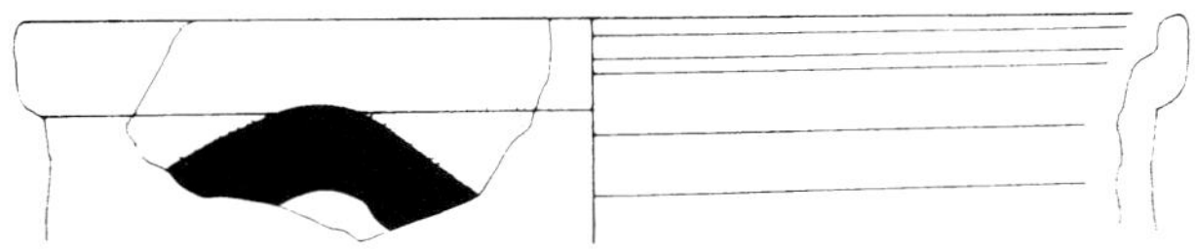
169

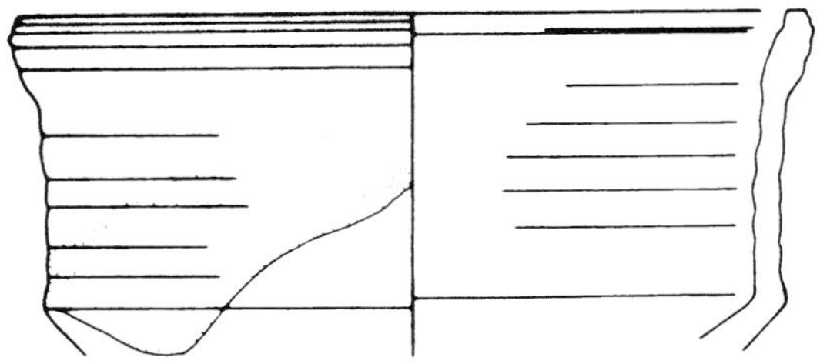
170

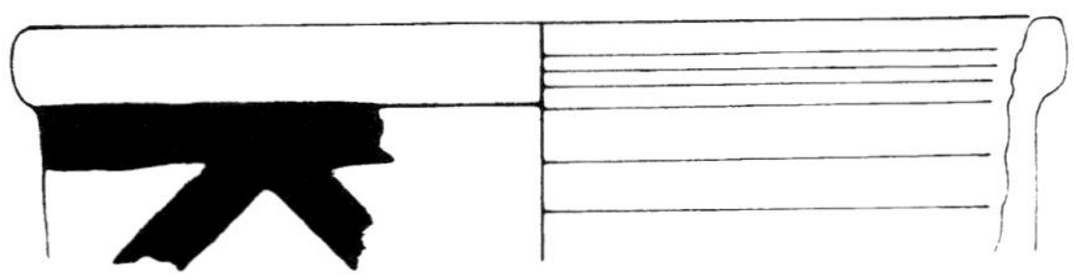
171

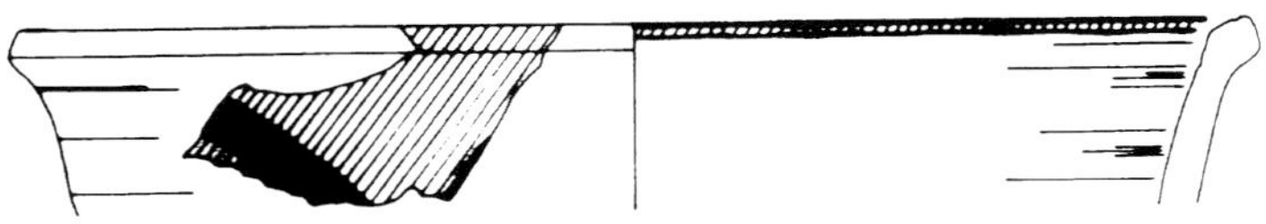
172

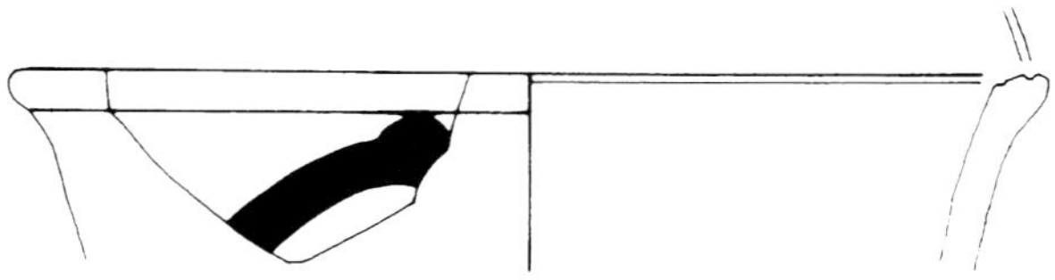
173

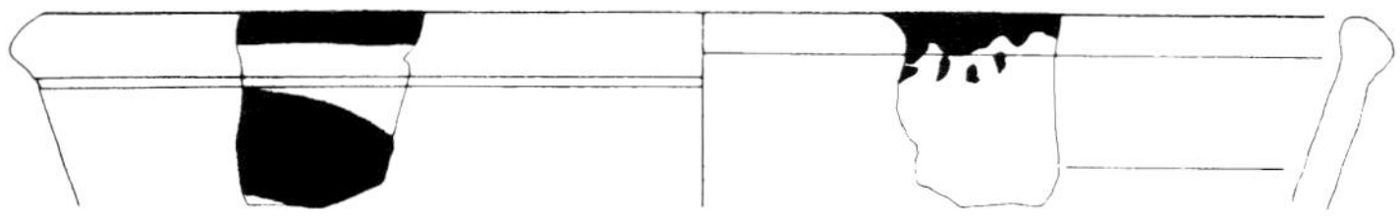
174

*Figure 2.21 Catalogue 158–167, Egyptian Red Slip 'H' ware. Scale 1:3*

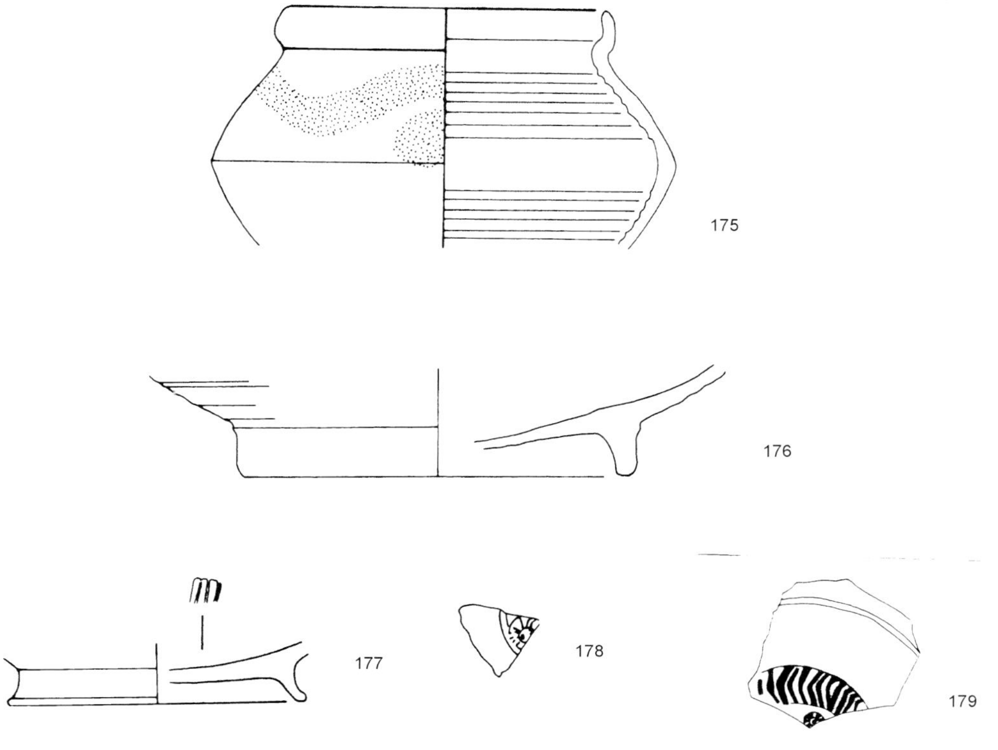


*Figure 2.22 Catalogue 175–179, Egyptian Red Slip 'H' ware. Scale 1:3*

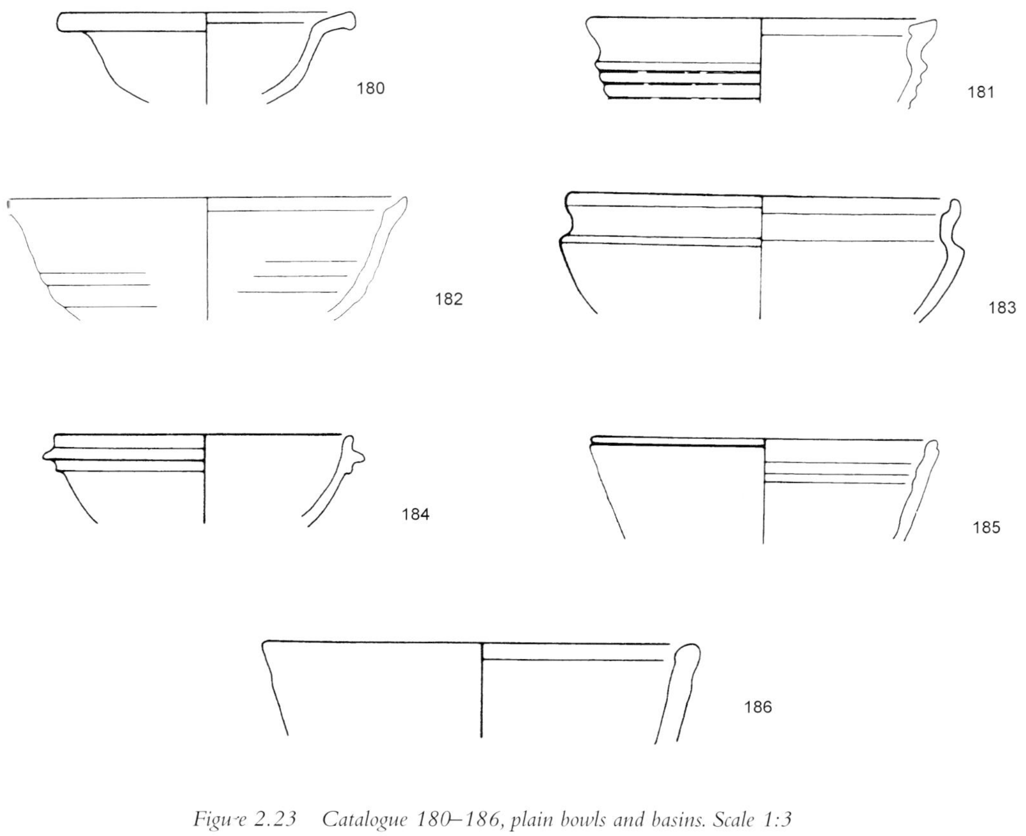


*Figure 2.23 Catalogue 180–186, plain bowls and basins. Scale 1:3*

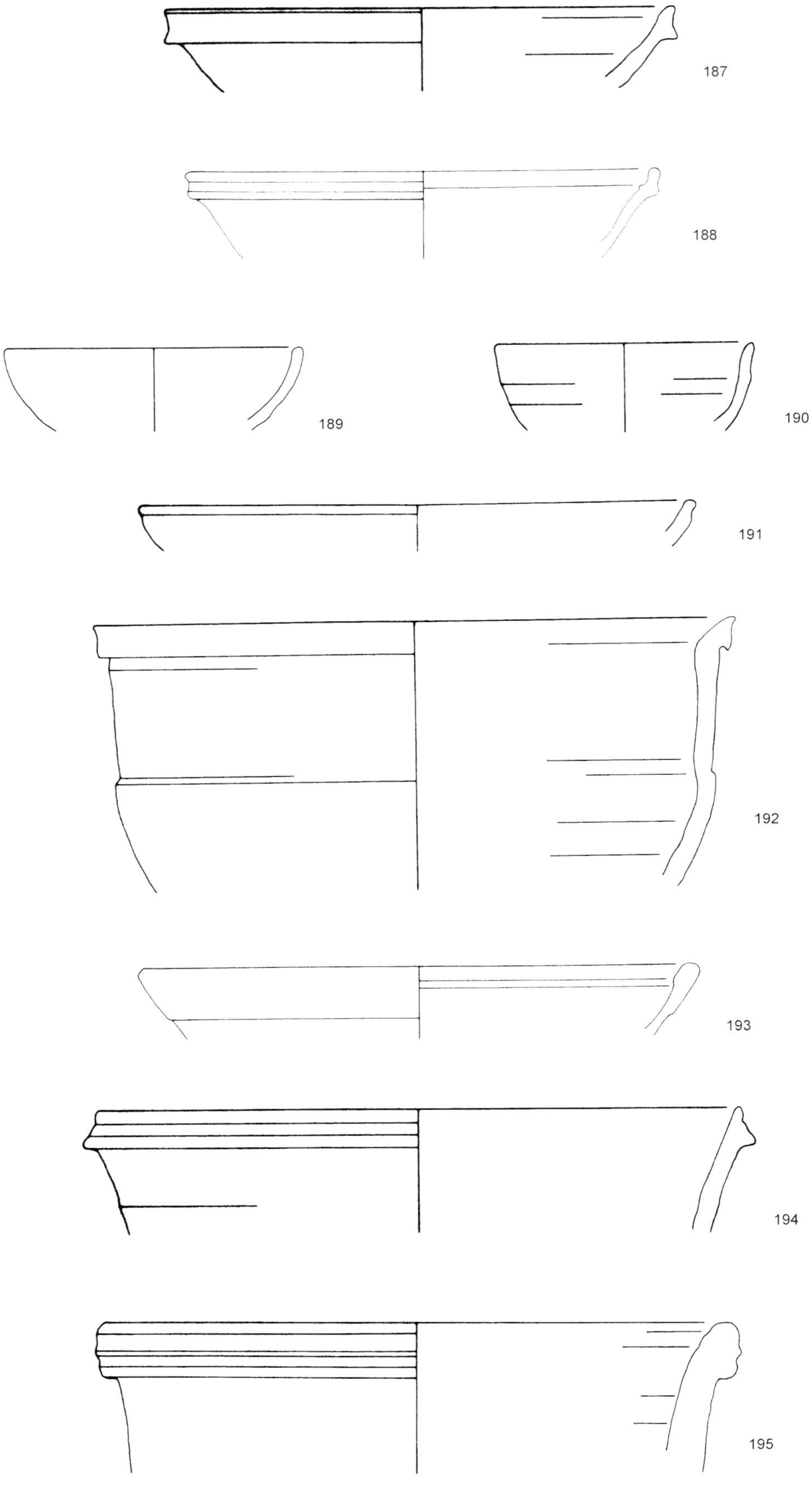


*Figure 2.24 Catalogue 187–195, plain bowls and basins. Scale 1:3*

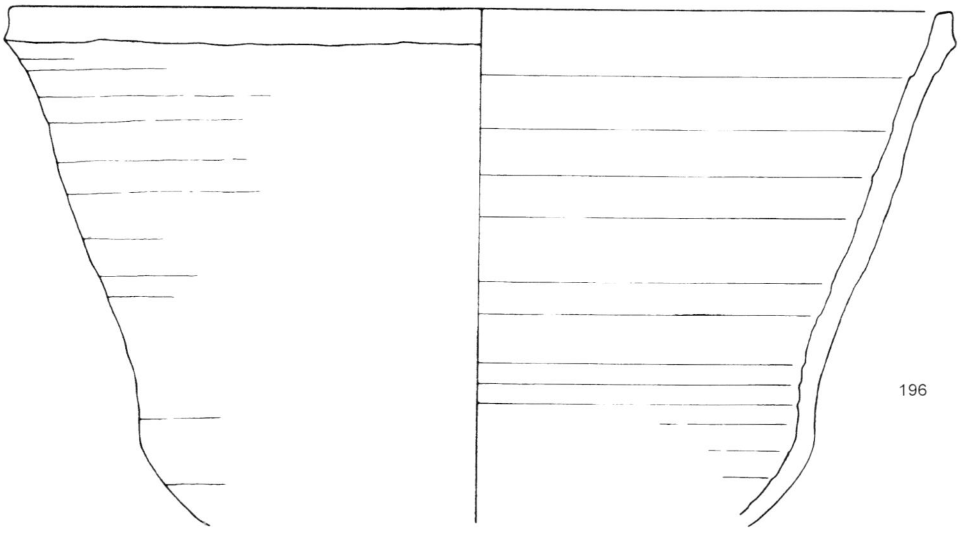

196

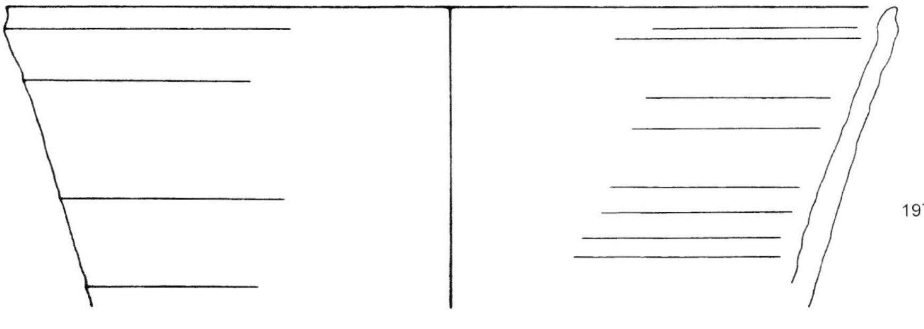

197

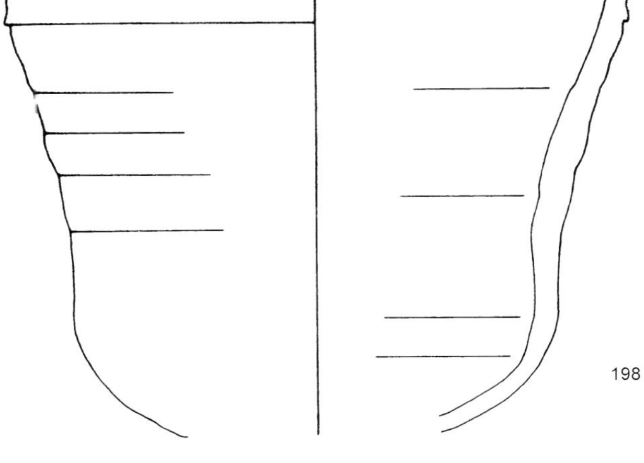

198

*Figure 2.25 Catalogue 196–198, plain bowls and basins. Scale 1:3*

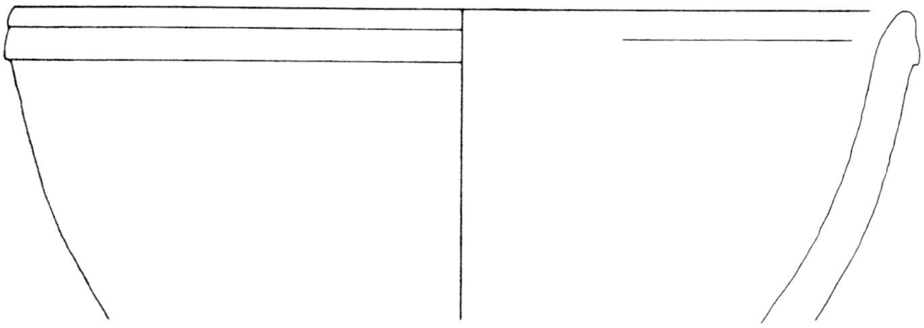
199

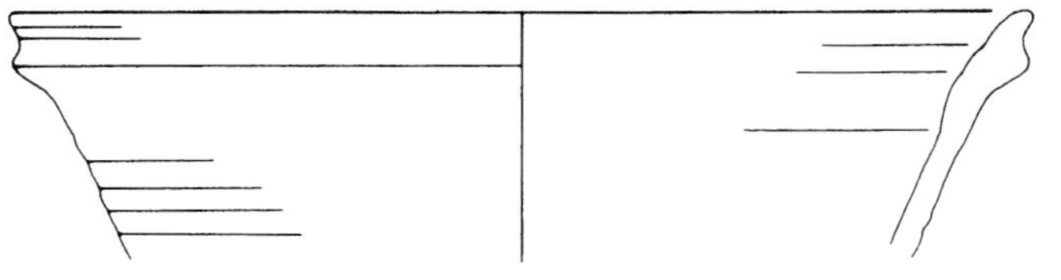
200

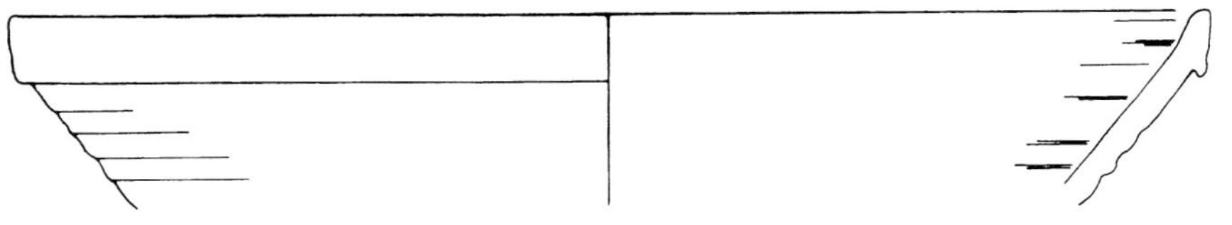
201

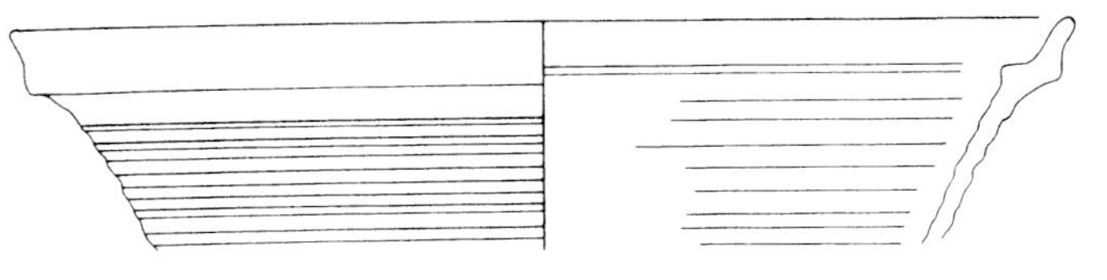
202

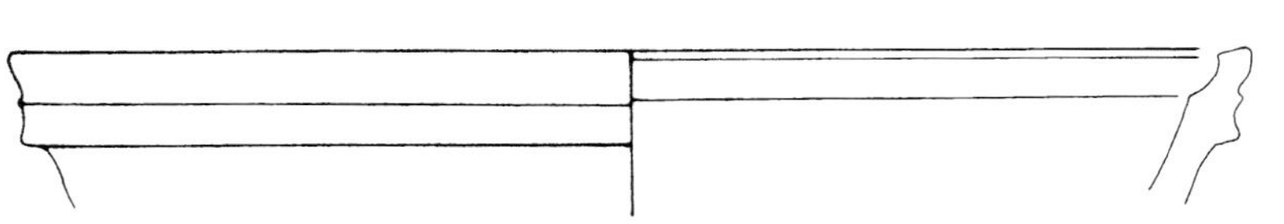
203

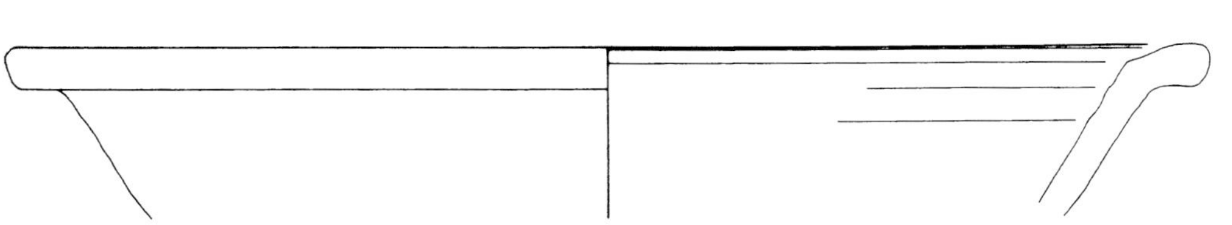
204

*Figure 2.26 Catalogue 199–204, plain bowls and basins. Scale 1:3*

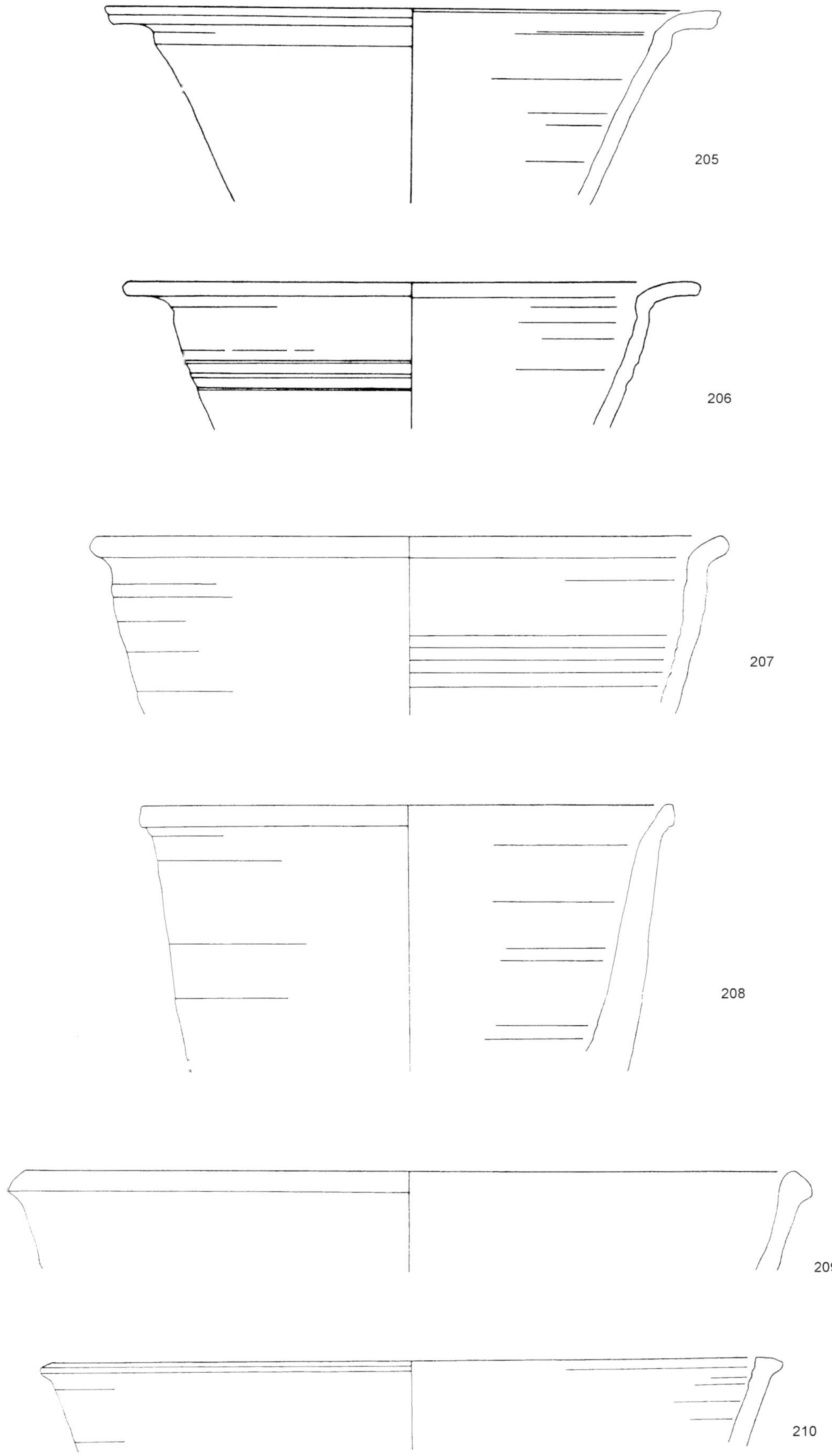


*Figure 2.27 Catalogue 205–210, plain bowls and basins. Scale 1:3*

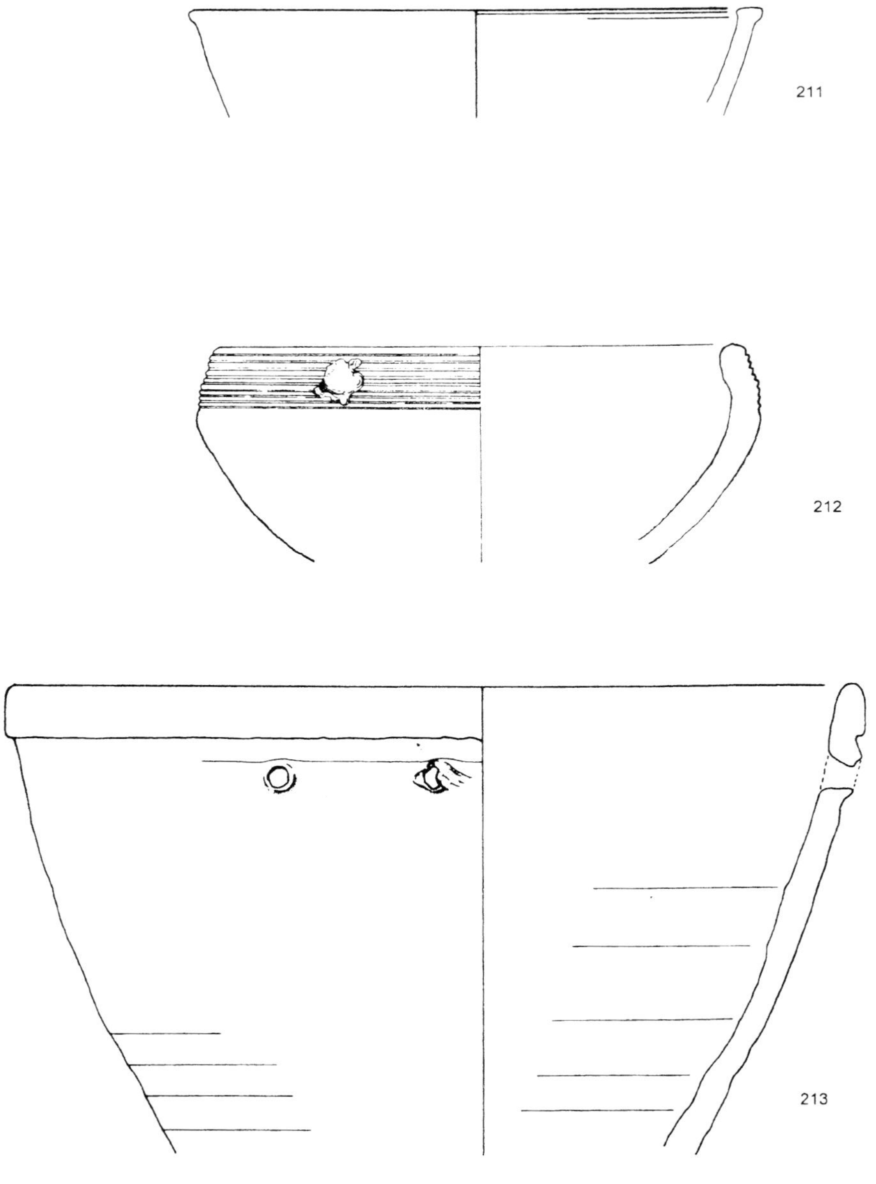


*Figure 2.28 Catalogue 211–213, plain bowls and basins. Scale 1:3*

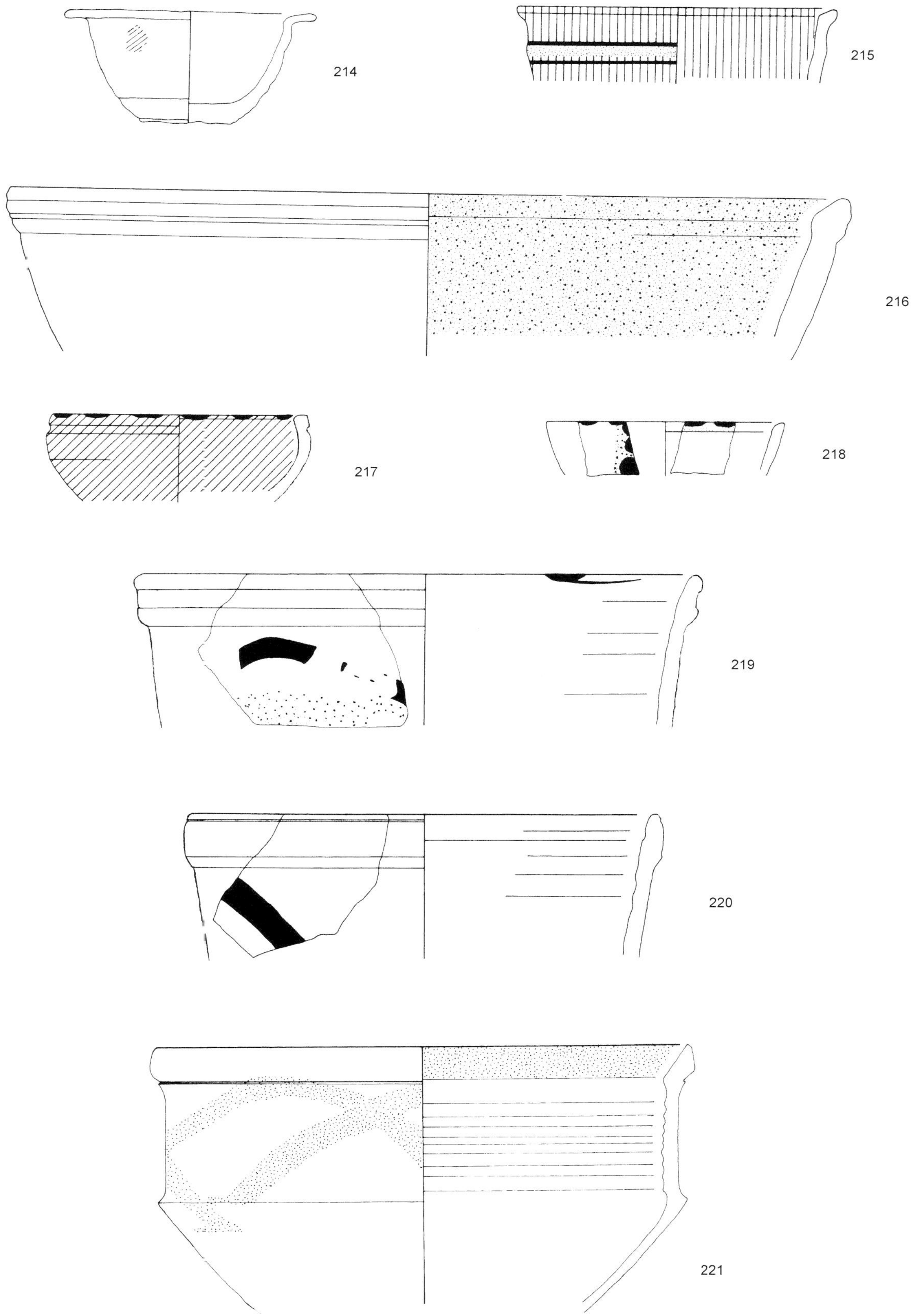


*Figure 2.29 Catalogue 214–221, painted bowls and basins. Scale 1:3*

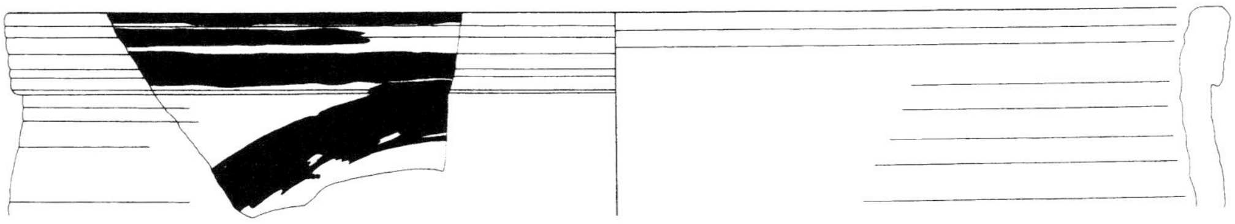

222

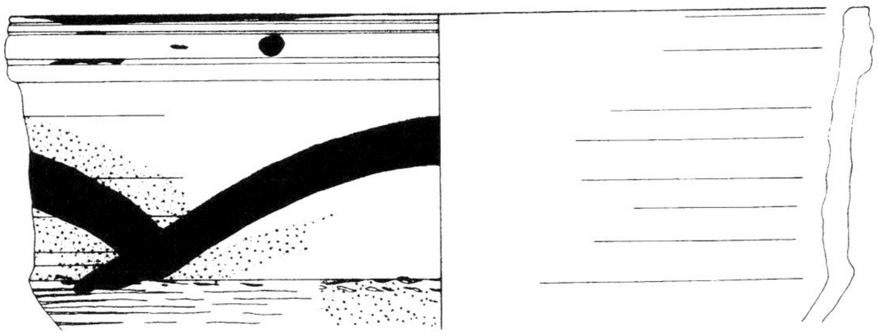

223

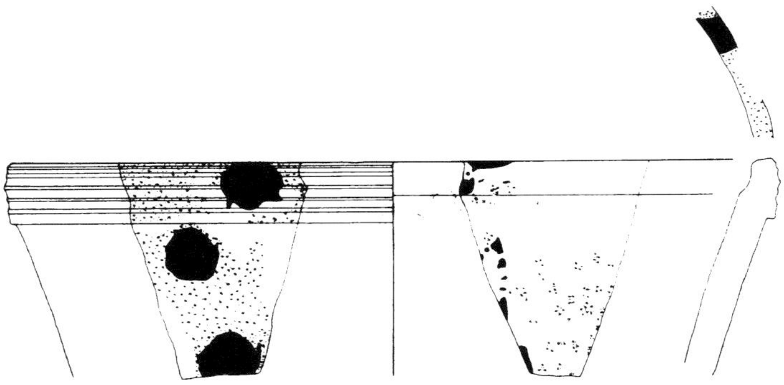

224

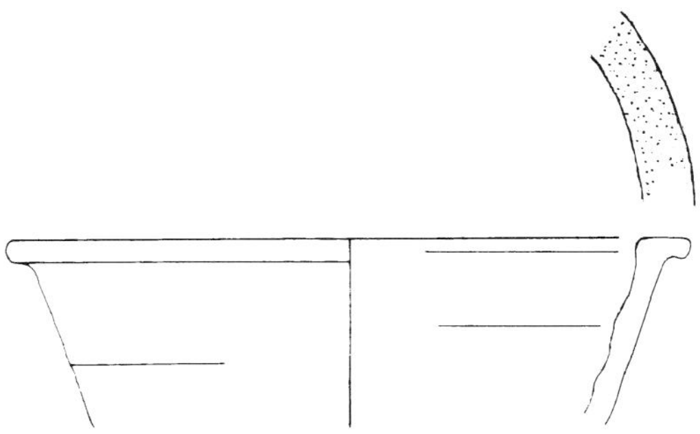

225

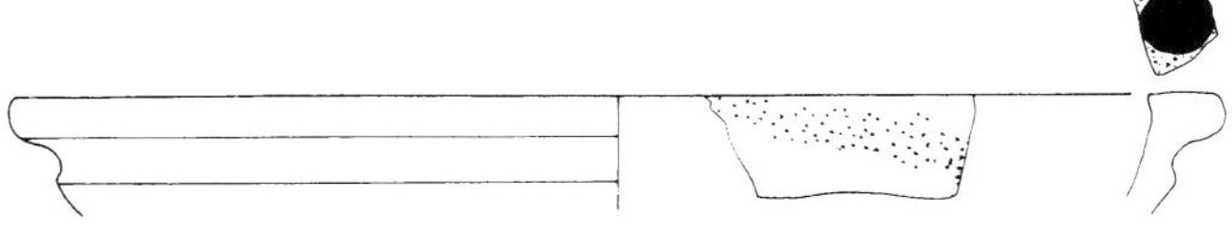

226

*Figure 2.30 Catalogue 222–226, painted bowls and basins. Scale 1:3*

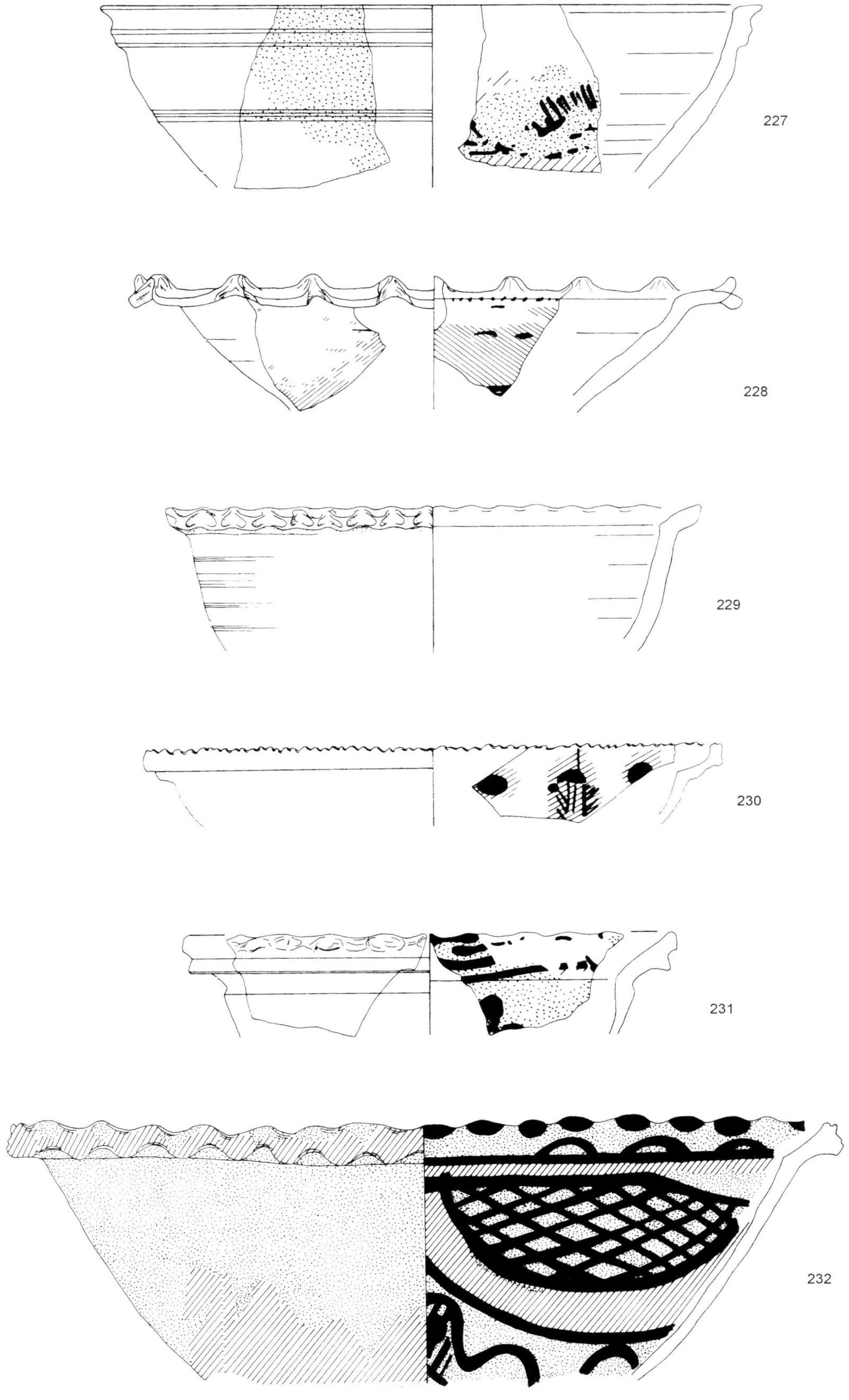


*Figure 2.31 Catalogue 227–232, painted bowls and basins. Scale 1:3*

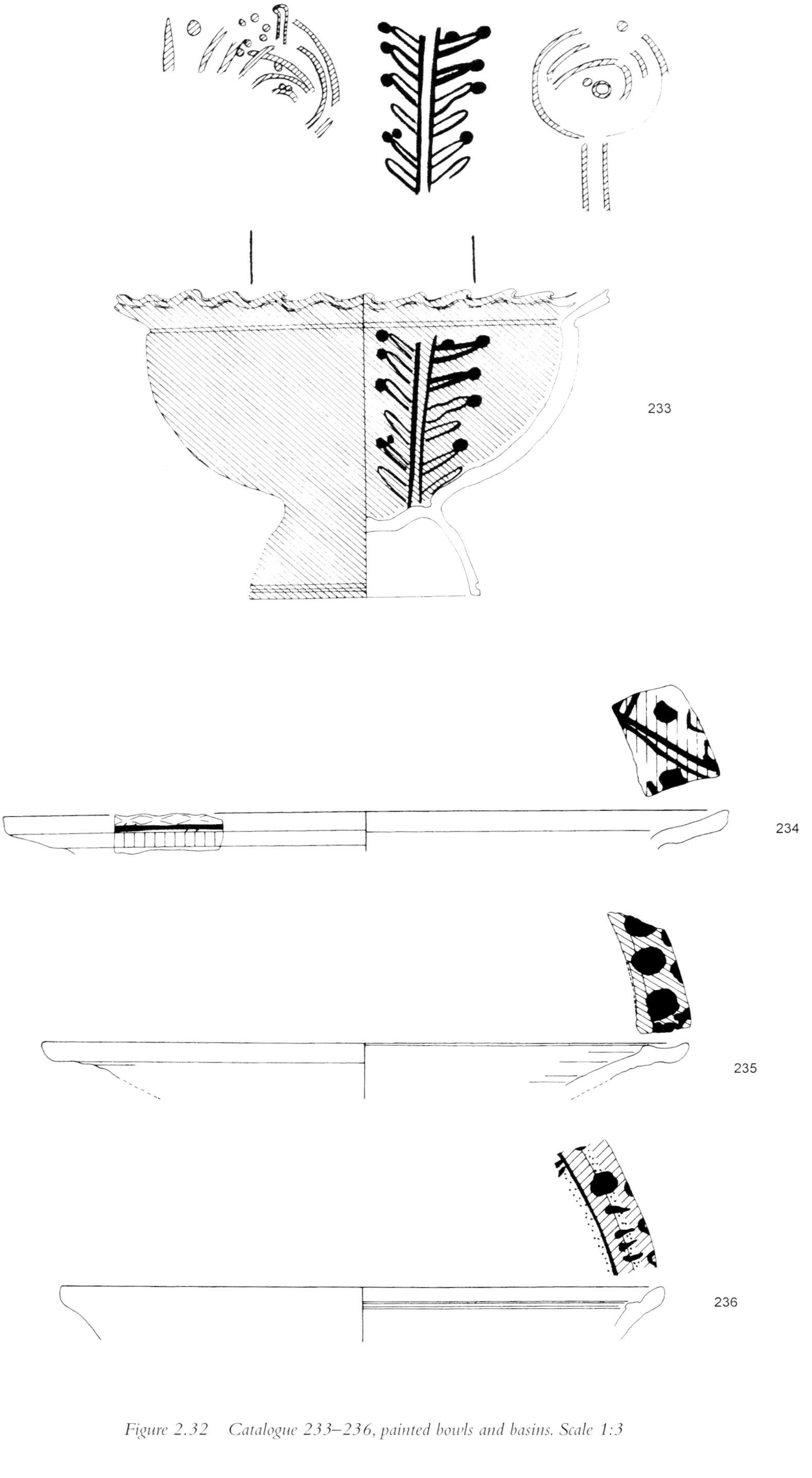


*Figure 2.32 Catalogue 233–236, painted bowls and basins. Scale 1:3*

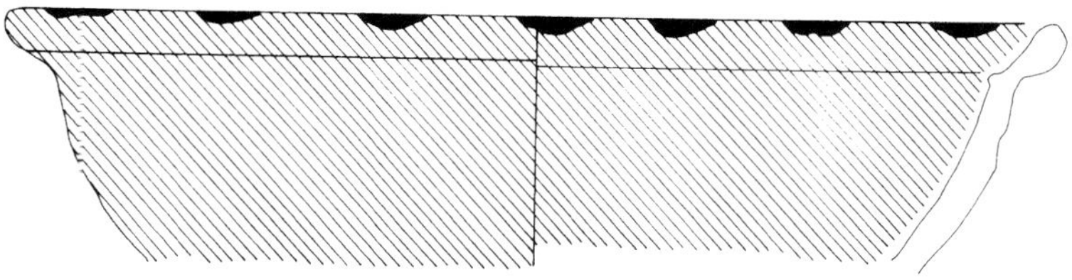

237

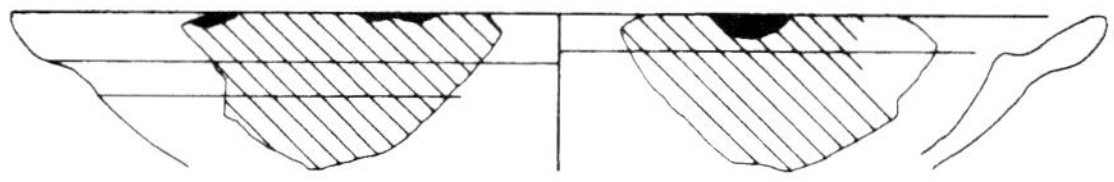

238

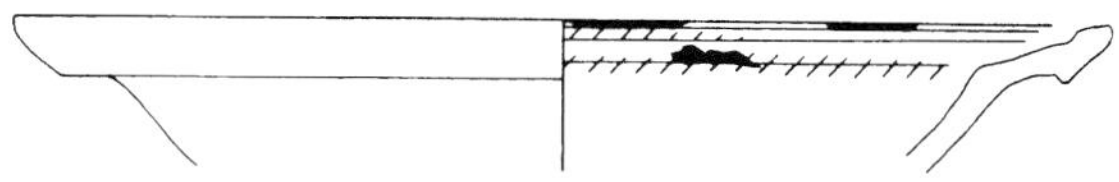

239

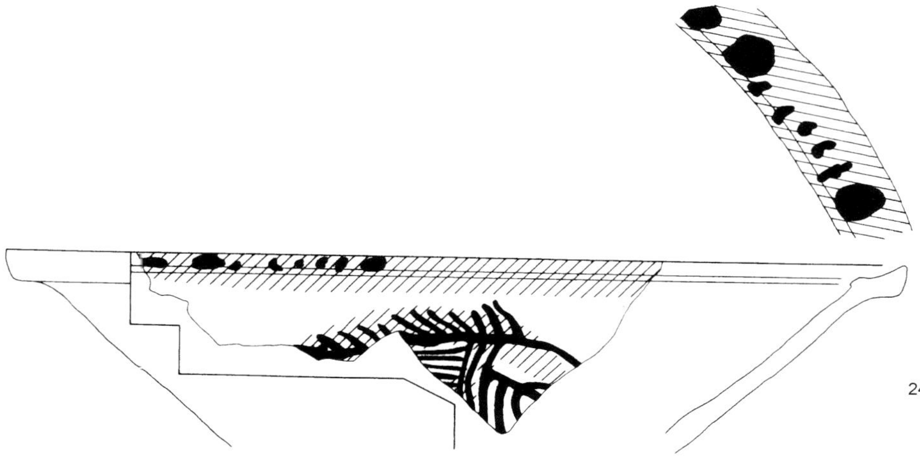

240

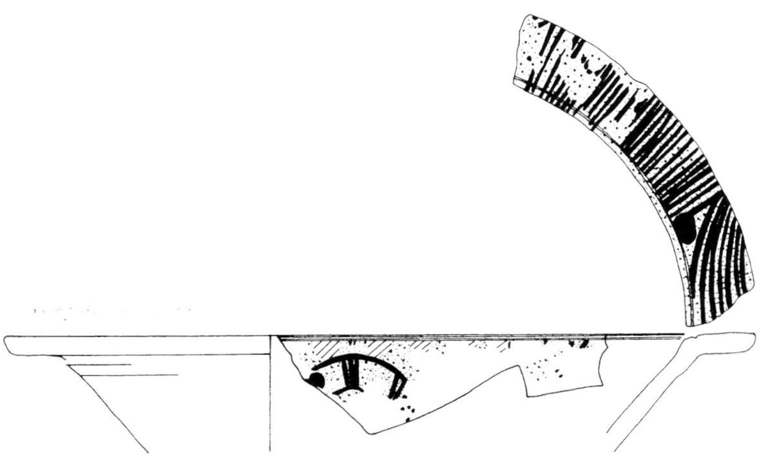

241

*Figure 2.33 Catalogue 237–241, painted bowls and basins. Scale 1:3*

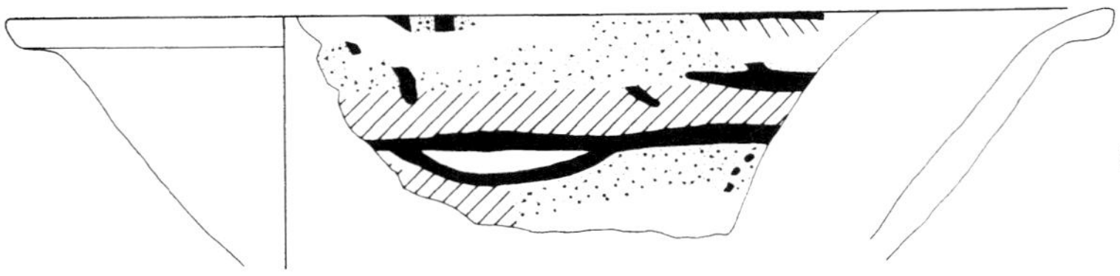

242

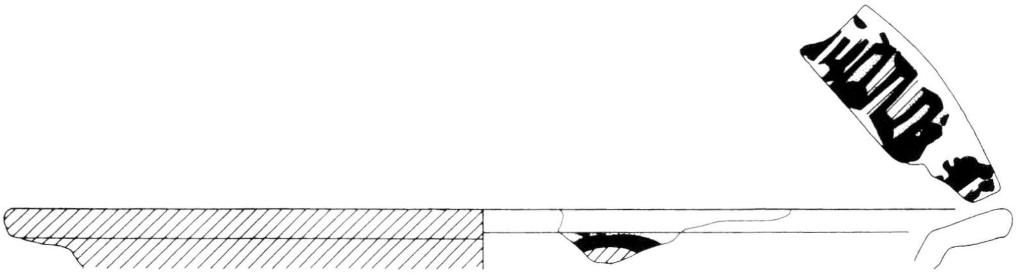

243

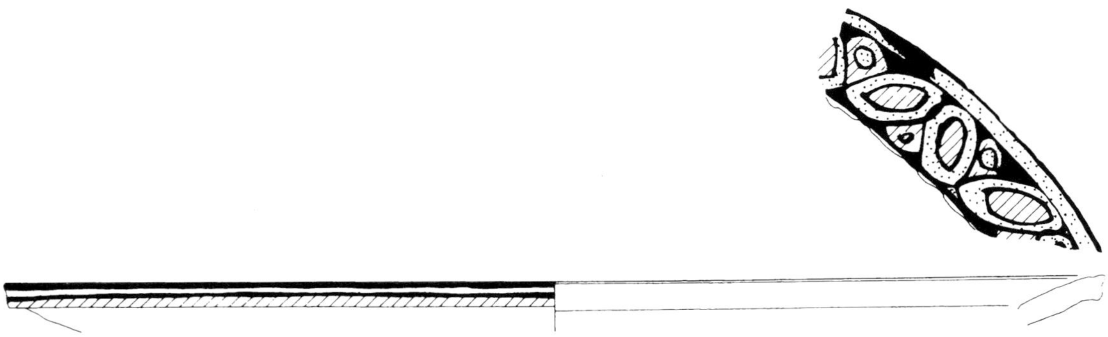

244

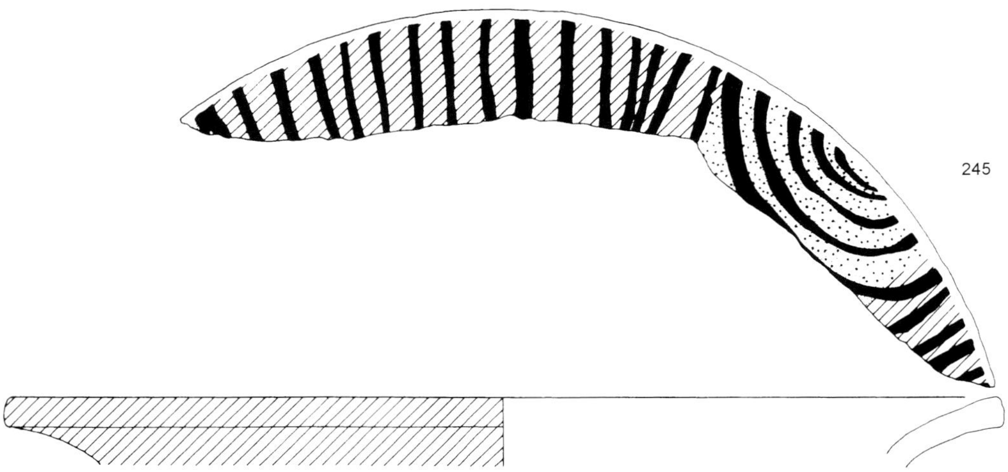

245

*Figure 2.34 Catalogue 242–245, painted bowls and basins. Scale 1:3*

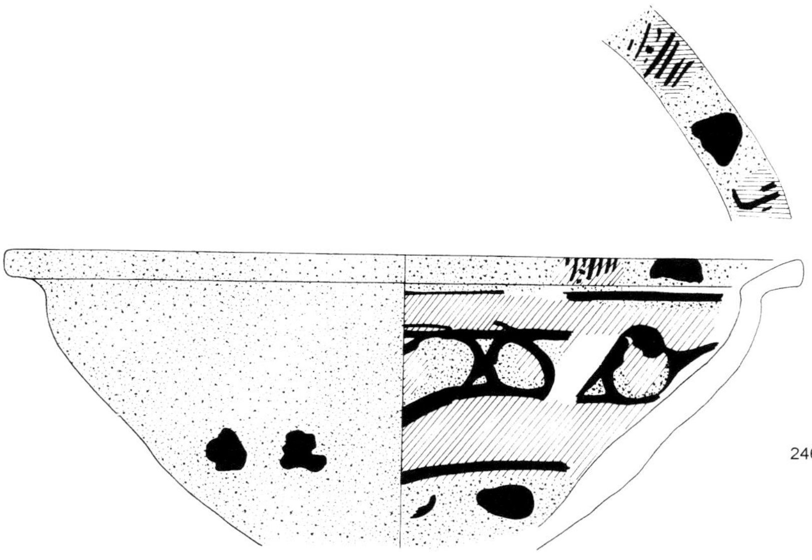

246

247

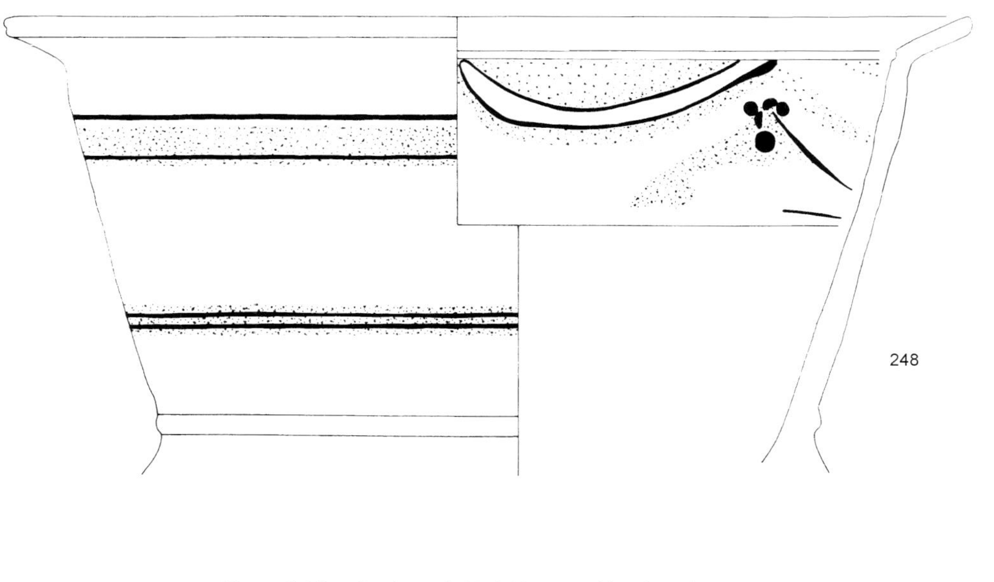

248

*Figure 2.35 Catalogue 246–248, painted bowls and basins. Scale 1:3*

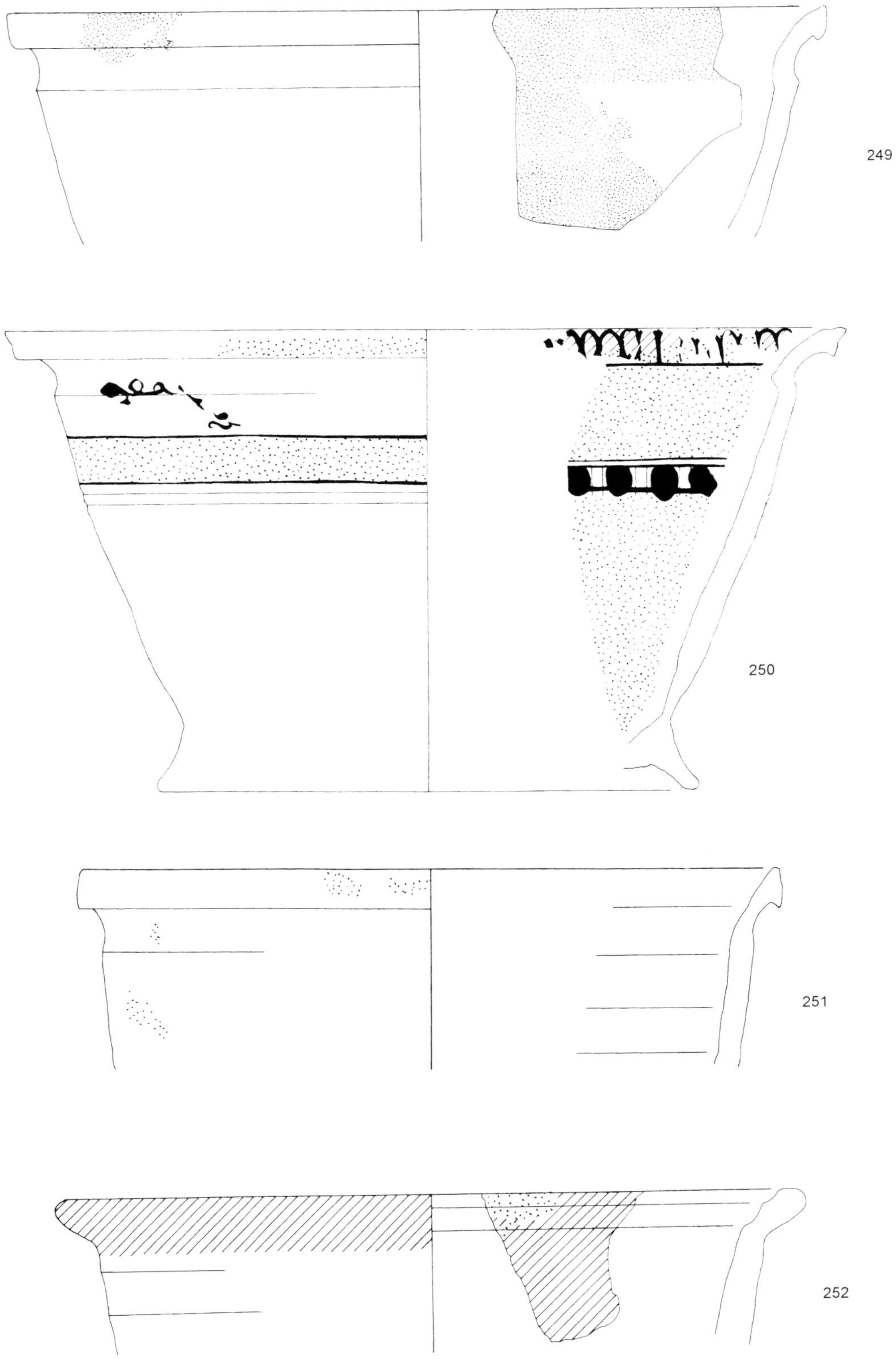


*Figure 2.36 Catalogue 249–252, painted bowls and basins. Scale 1:3*

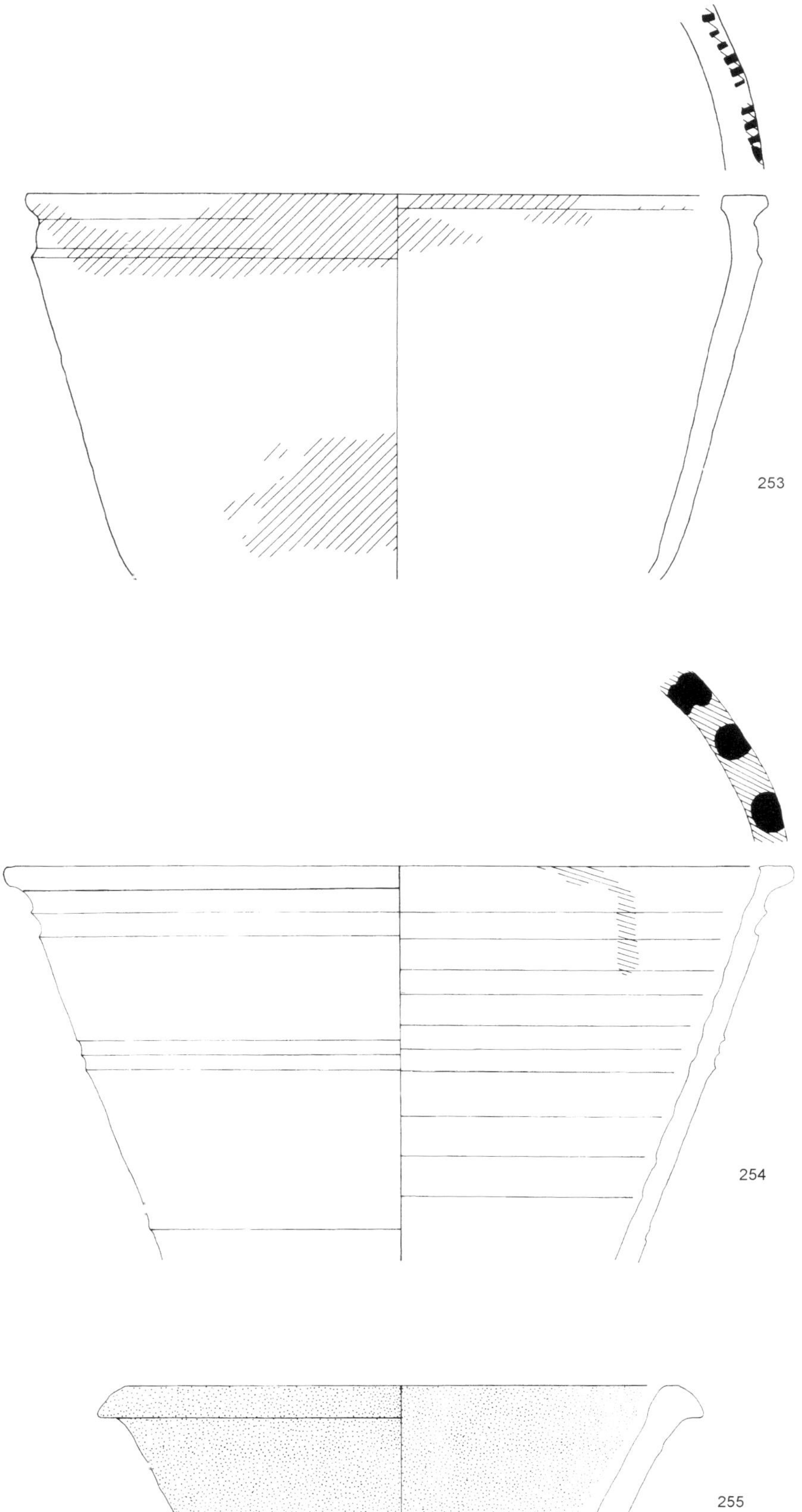


*Figure 2.37 Catalogue 253–255, painted bowls and basins. Scale 1:3*

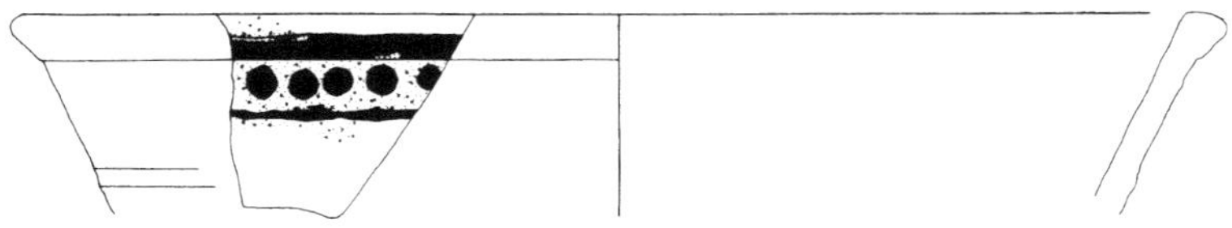

256

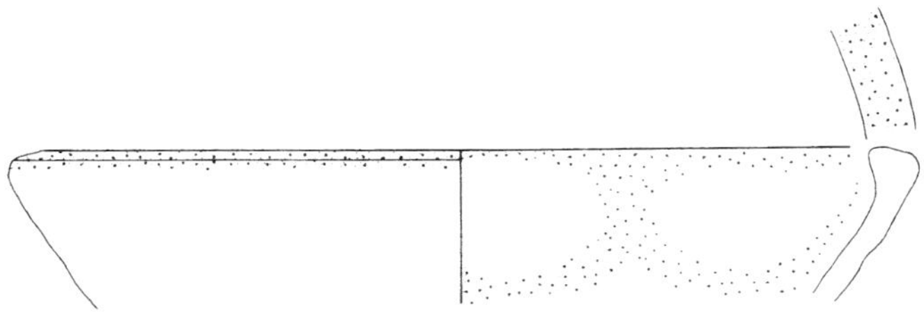

257

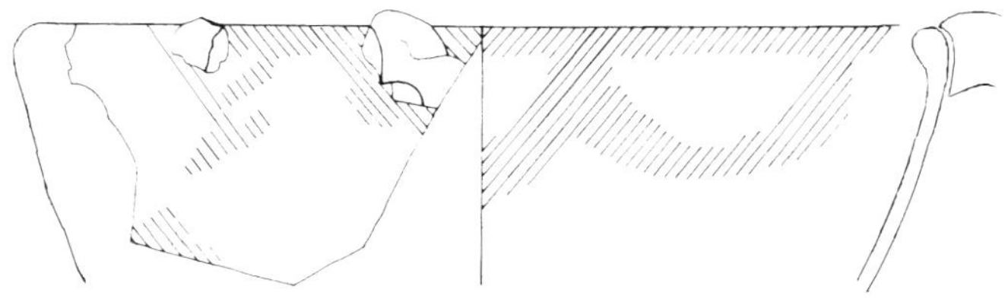

258

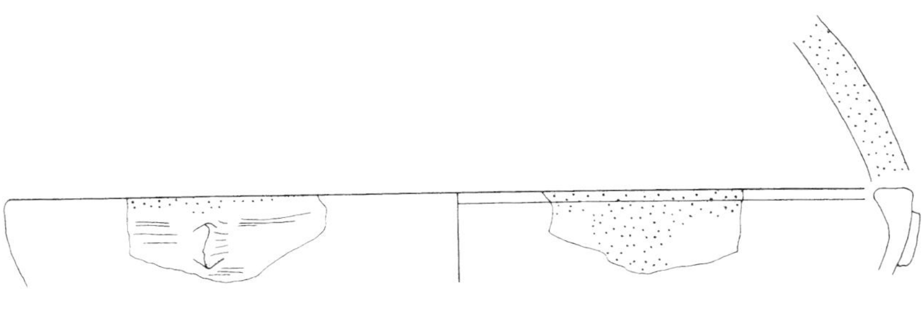

259

260

*Figure 2.38 Catalogue 256–260, painted bowls and basins. Scale 1:3*

*Figure 2.39 Catalogue 261–262, tubs, storage bins and large basins. Scales 1:3*

*Figure 2.40 Catalogue 263–264, tubs, storage bins and large basins. Scales 1:3*

265

266

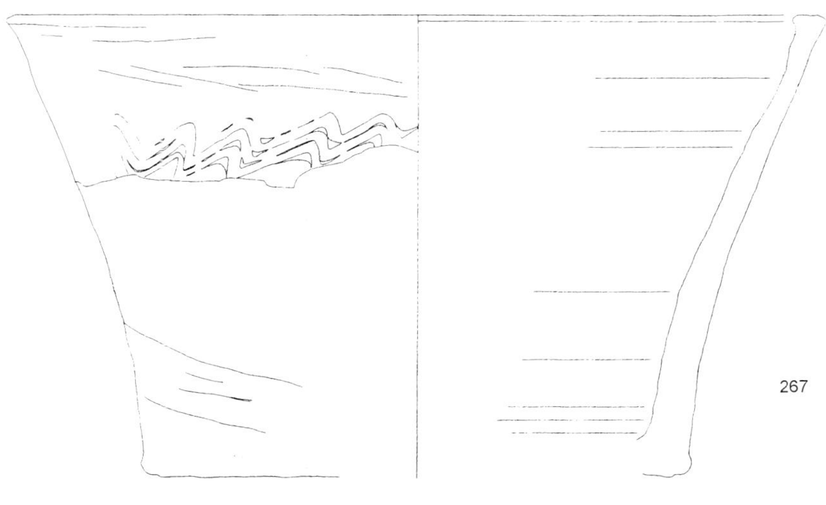

267

*Figure 2.41 Catalogue 265–267, tubs, storage bins and large basins. Scales 1:3*

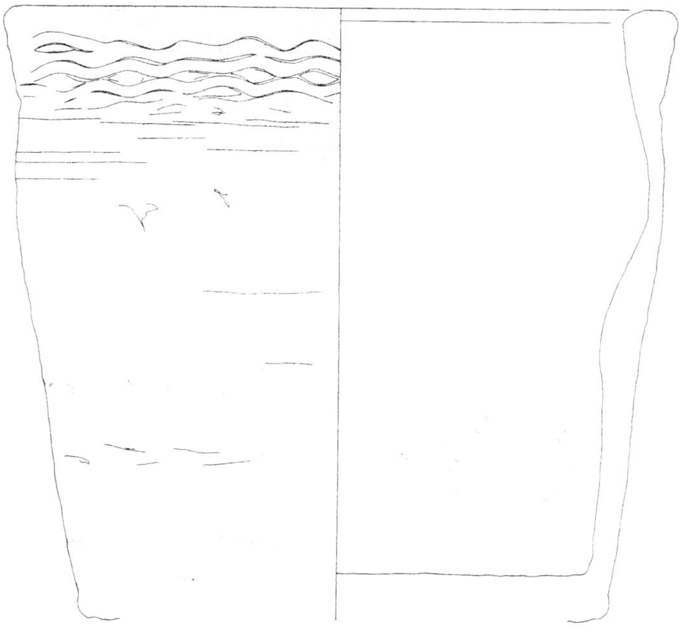

268

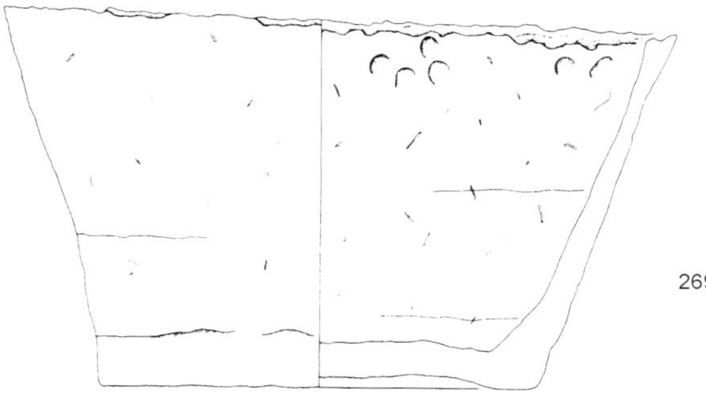

269

*Figure 2.42 Catalogue 268–269, tubs, storage bins and large basins. Scales 1:3*

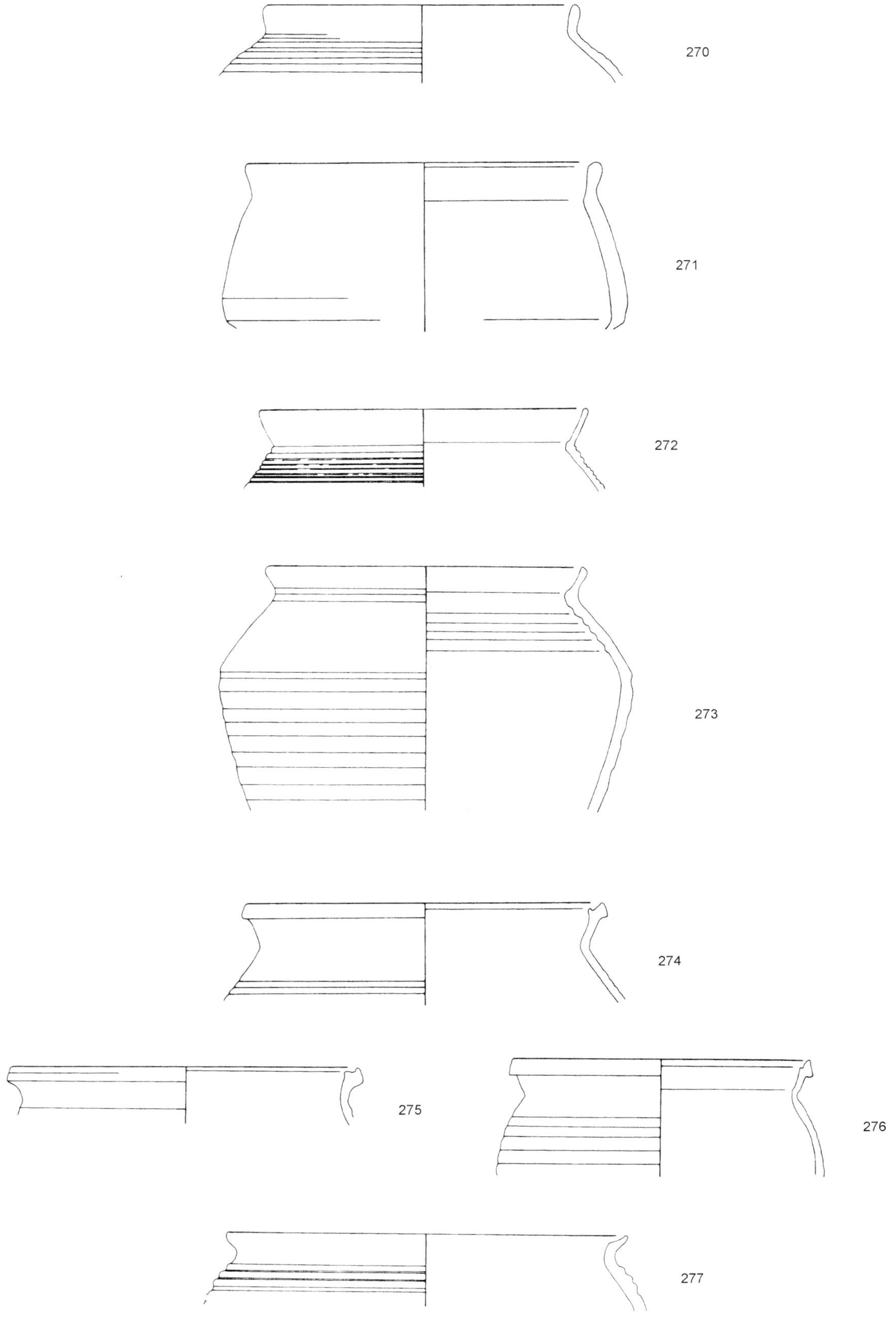


*Figure 2.43 Catalogue 270–277, cooking wares. Scales 1:3*

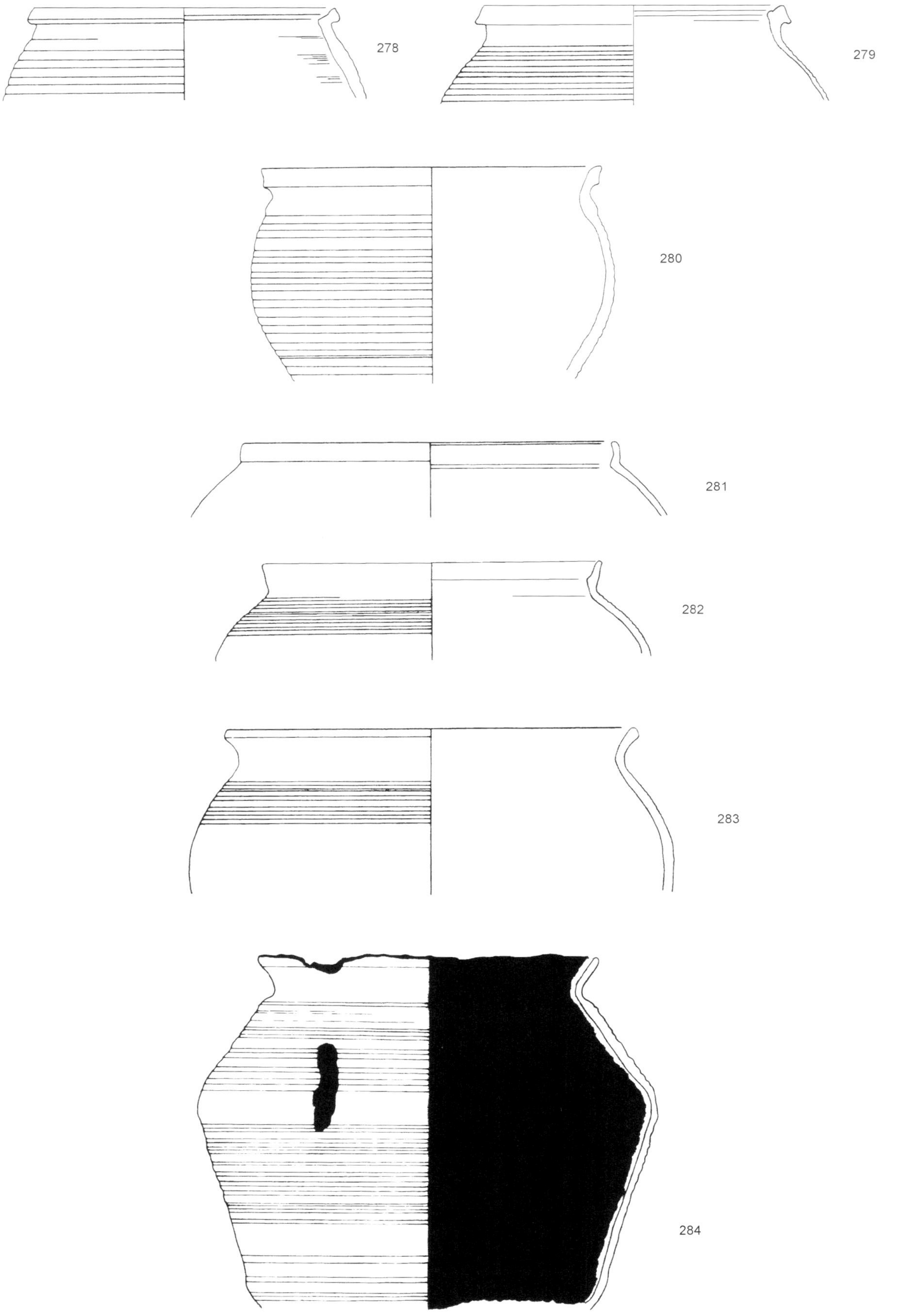


*Figure 2.44 Catalogue 278-284, cooking wares. Scales 1:3*

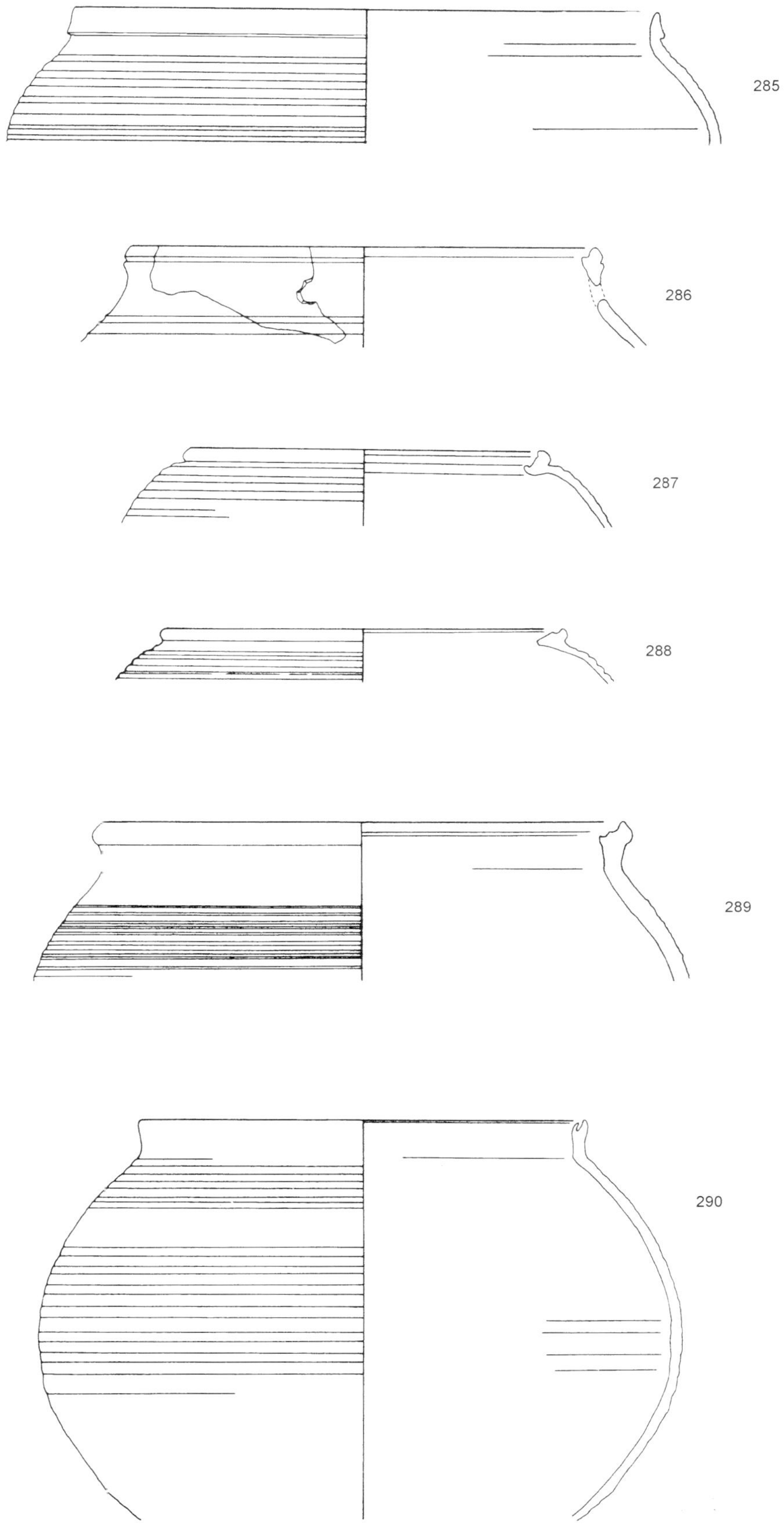


*Figure 2.45 Catalogue 285–290, cooking wares. Scales 1:3*

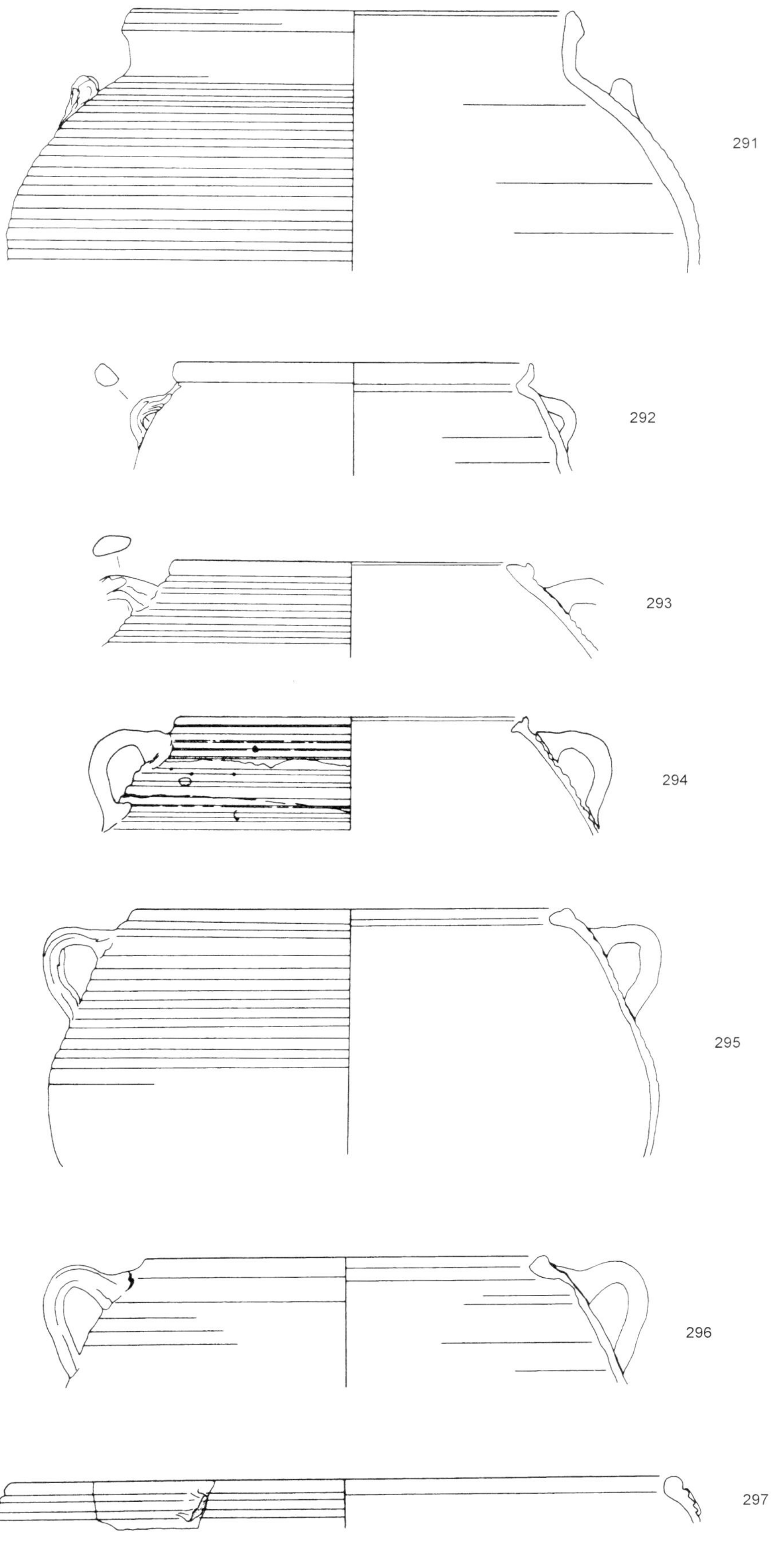


*Figure 2.46 Catalogue 291–297, cooking wares. Scales 1:3*

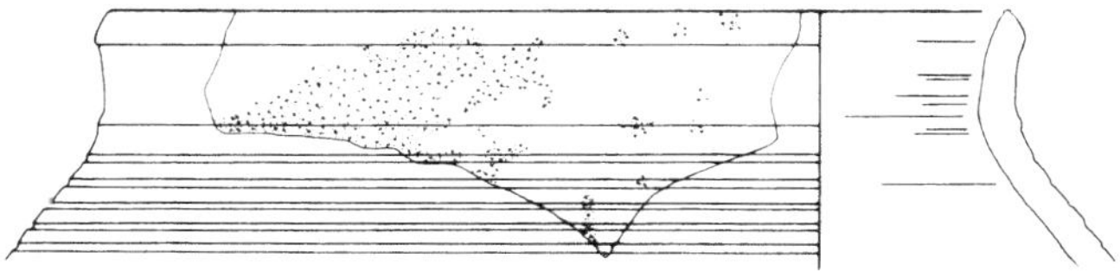

298

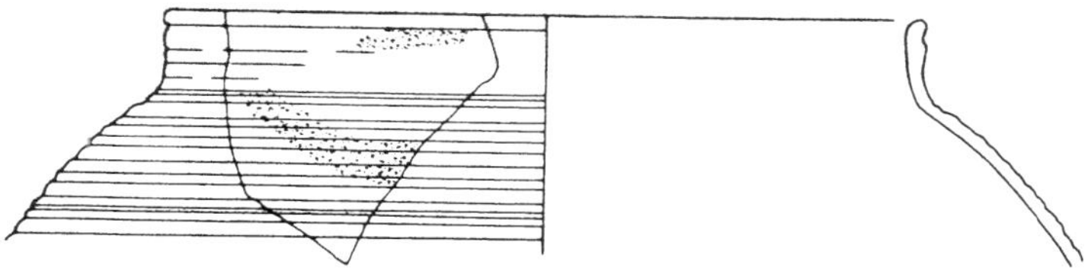

299

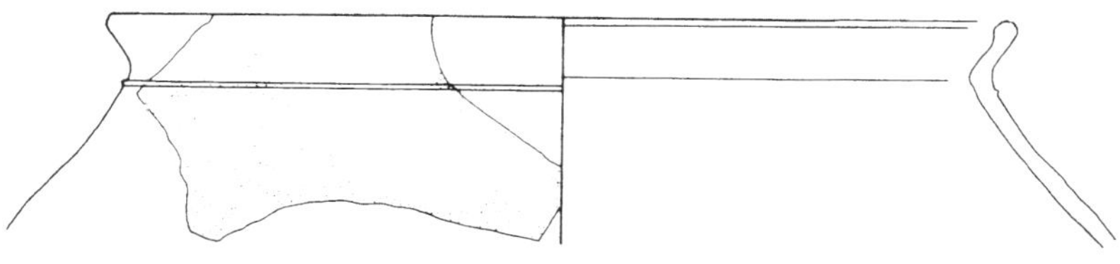

300

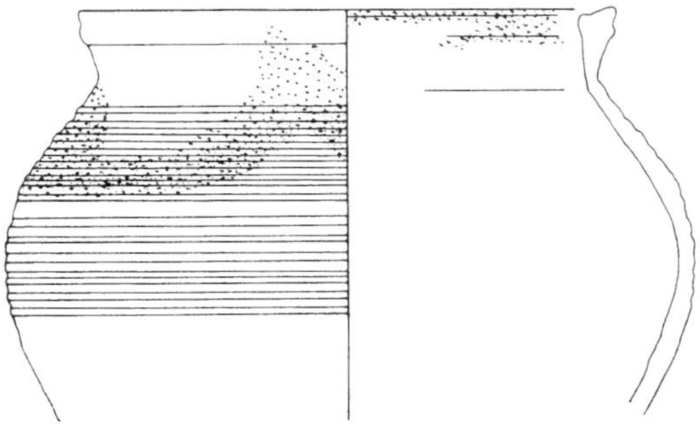

301

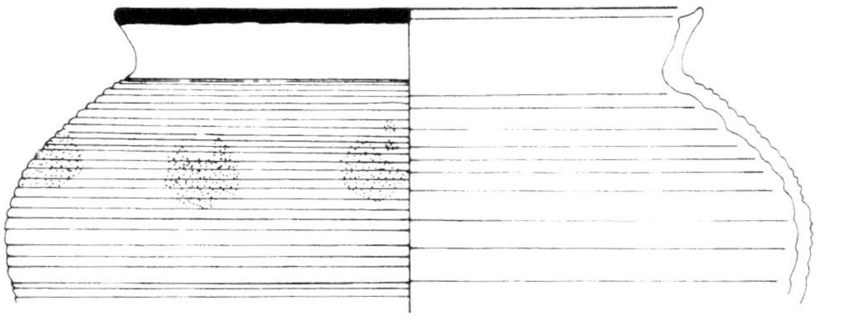

302

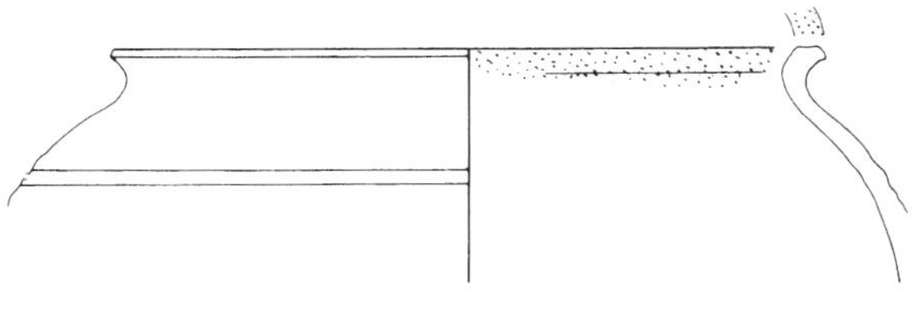

303

*Figure 2.47 Catalogue 298–303, cooking wares. Scales 1:3*

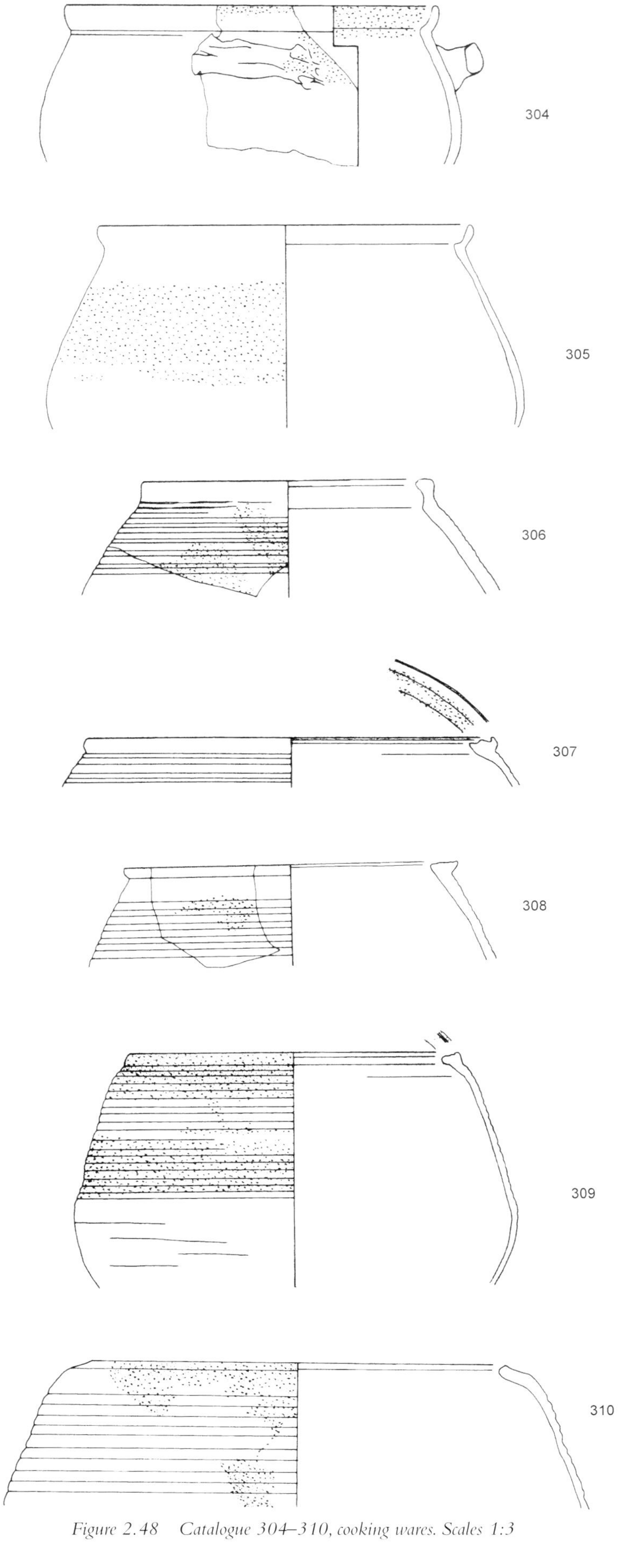


*Figure 2.48 Catalogue 304–310, cooking wares. Scales 1:3*

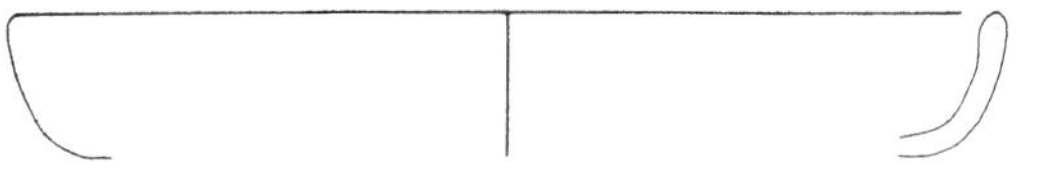
311

312

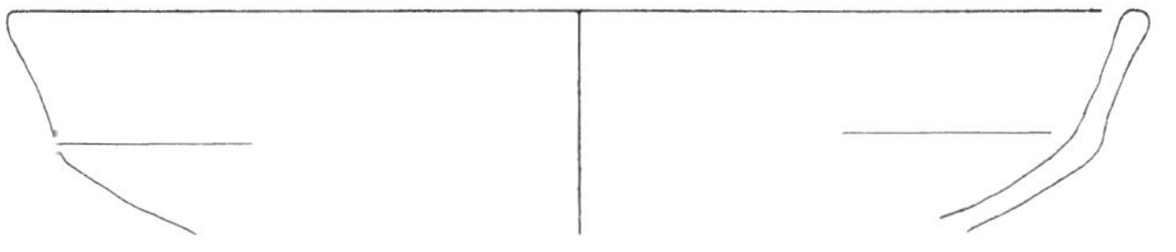
313

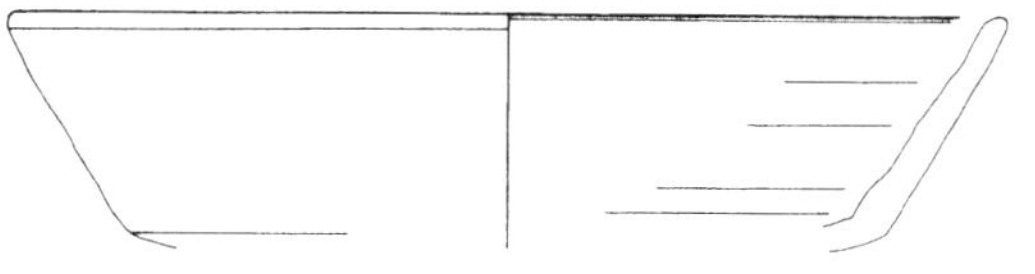
314

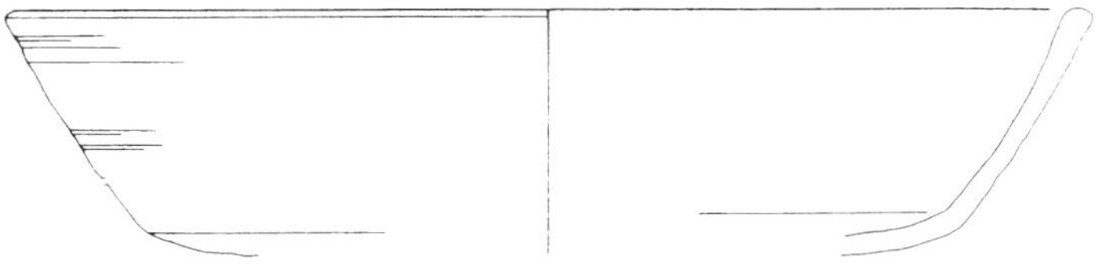
315

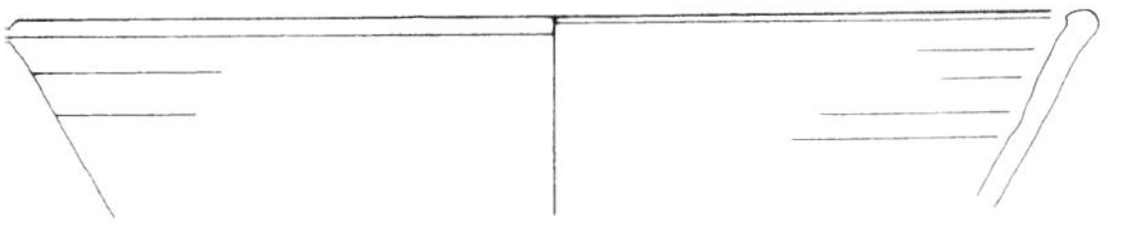
316

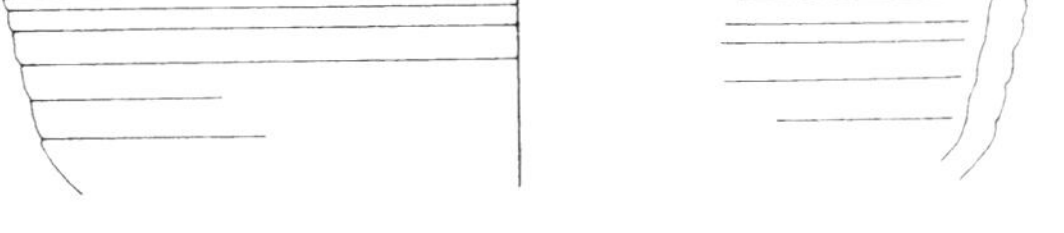
317

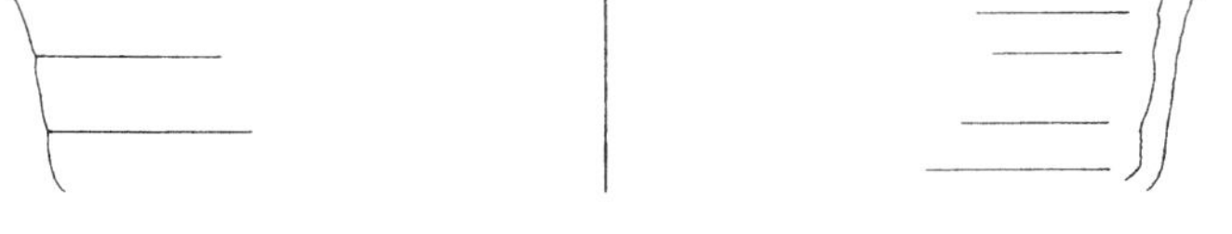
318

*Figure 2.49 Catalogue 311–318, cooking wares. Scales 1:3*

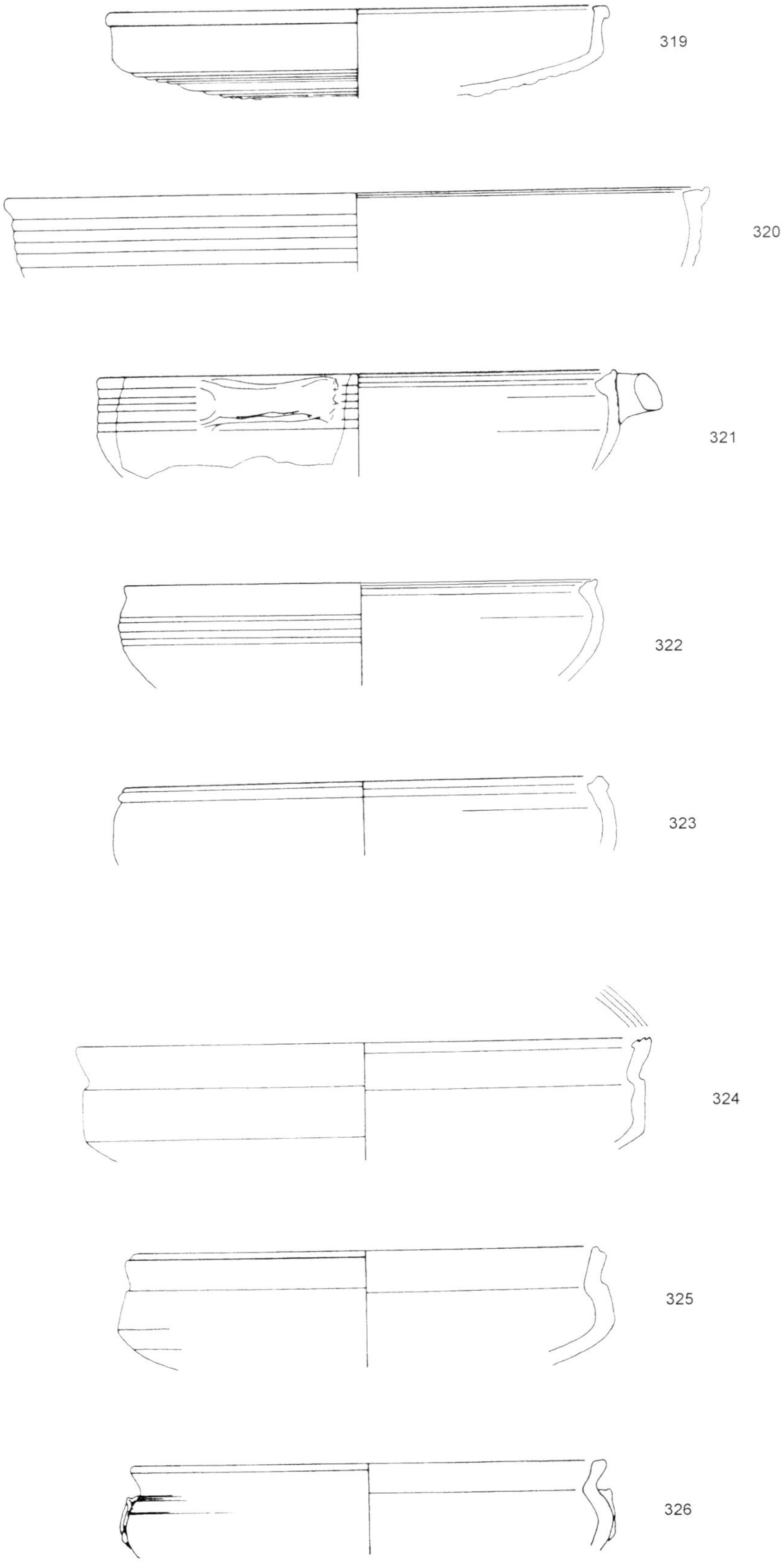


*Figure 2.50 Catalogue 319–326, cooking wares. Scales 1:3*

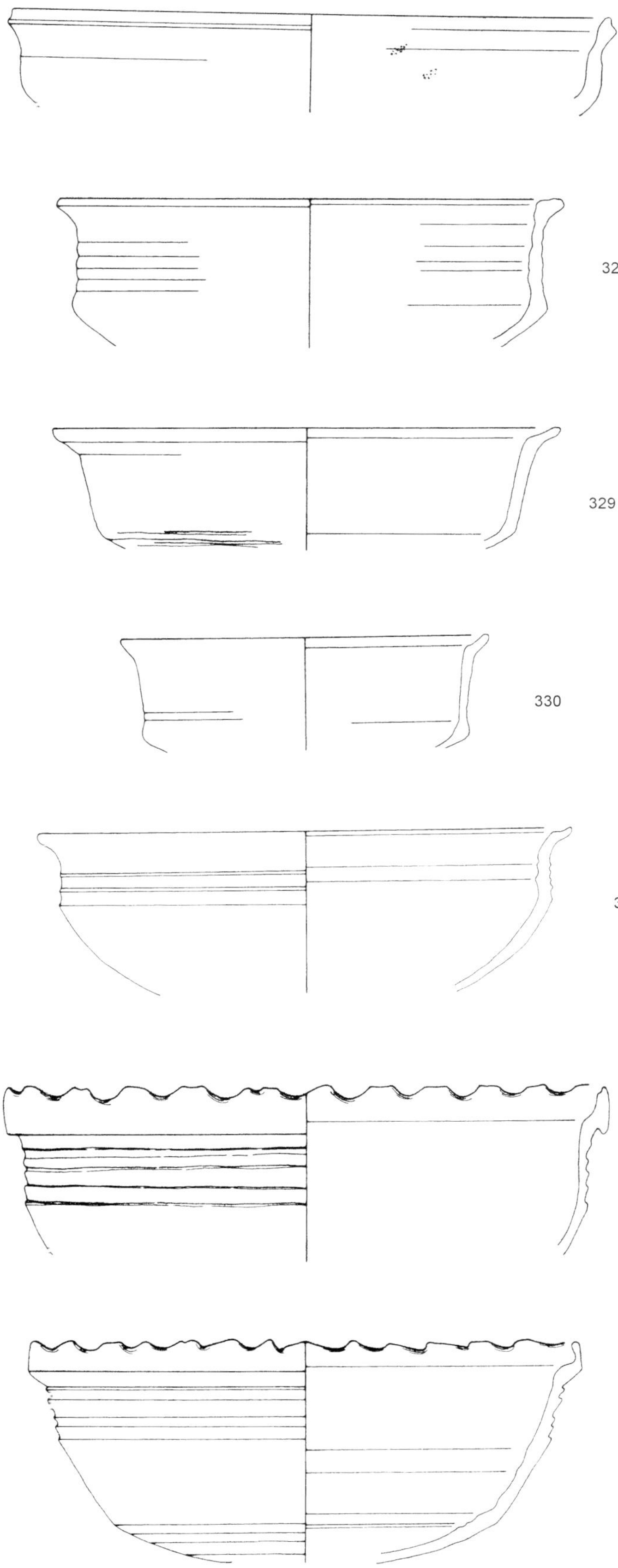

327

328

329

330

331

332

333

*Figure 2.51 Catalogue 327–333, cooking wares. Scales 1:3*

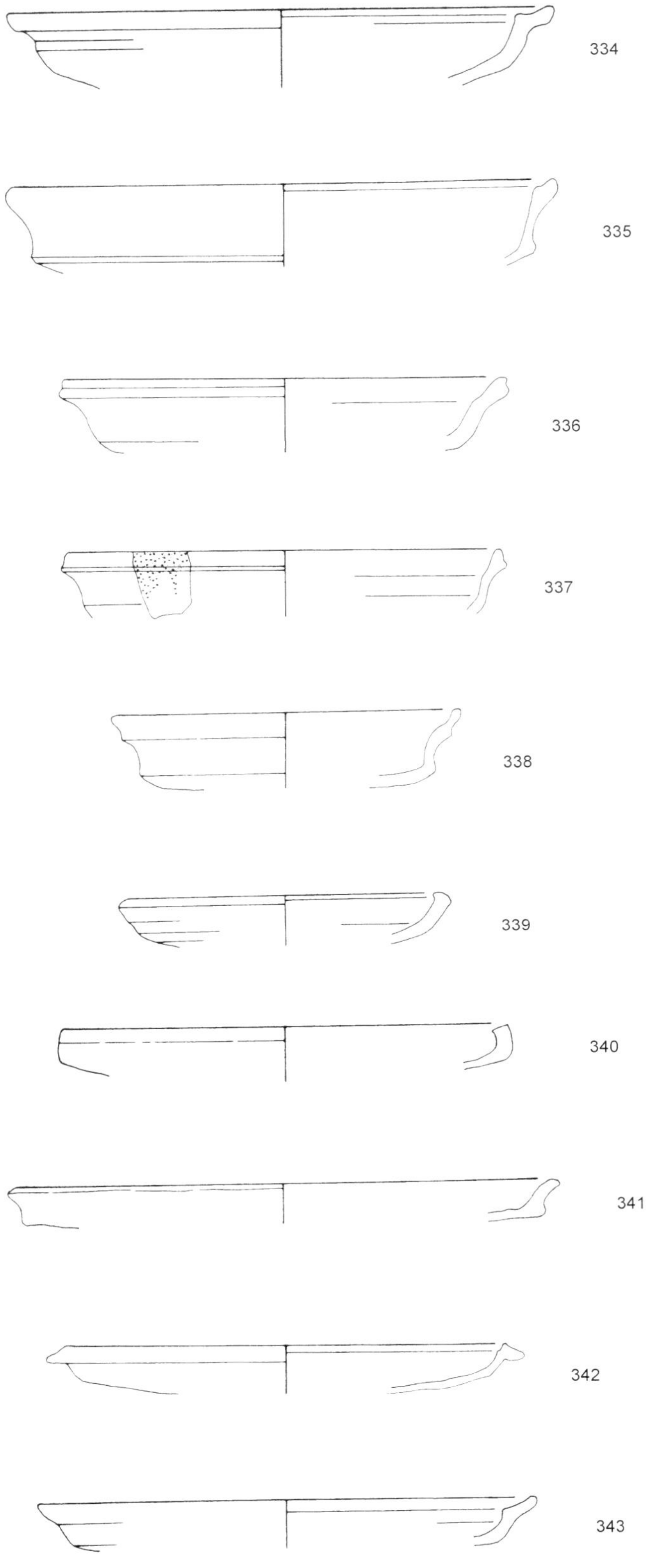


*Figure 2.52 Catalogue 334–343, cooking wares. Scales 1:3*

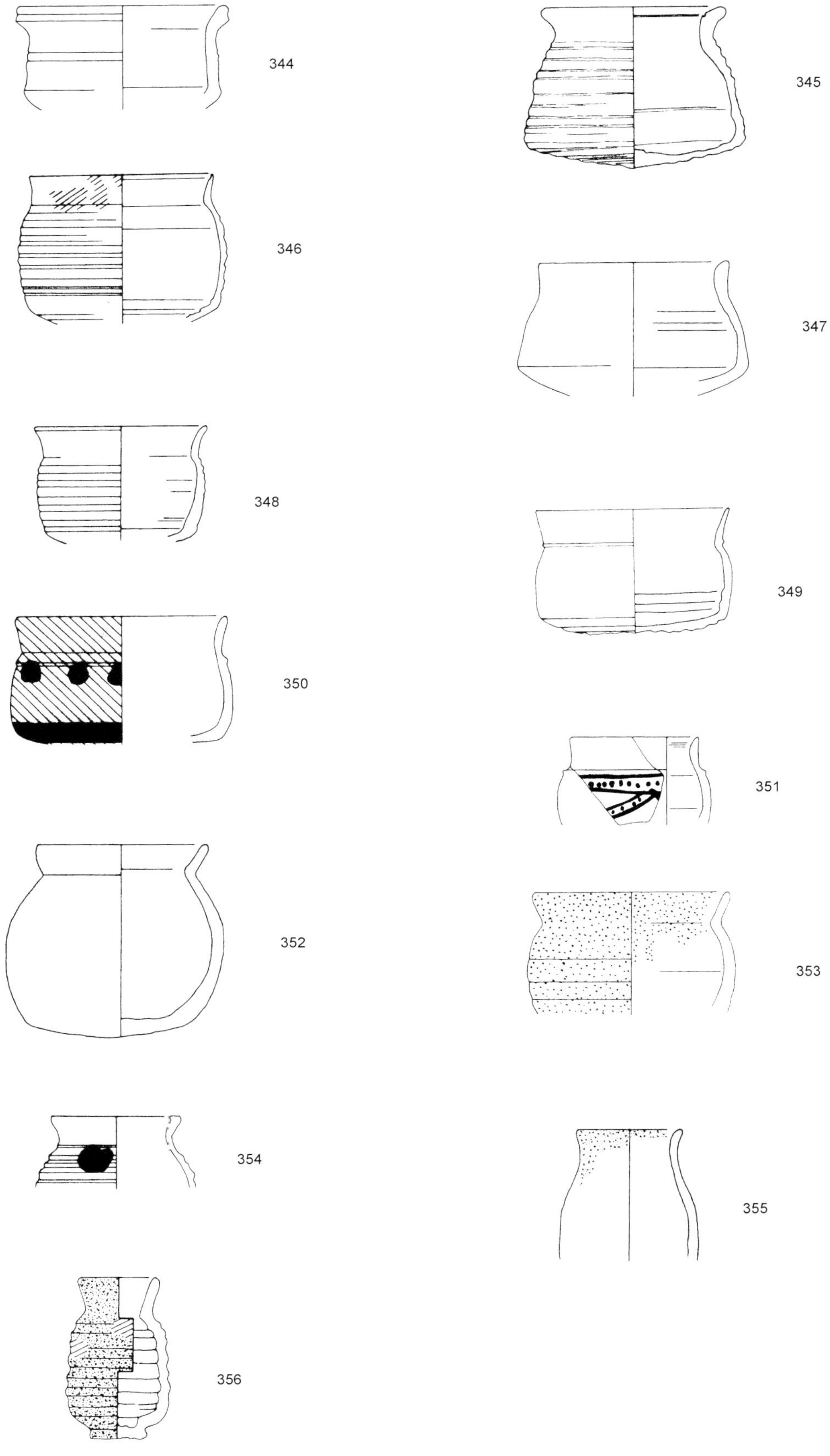


*Figure 2.53 Catalogue 344–356, miniature cooking pots and jars. Scale 1:3*

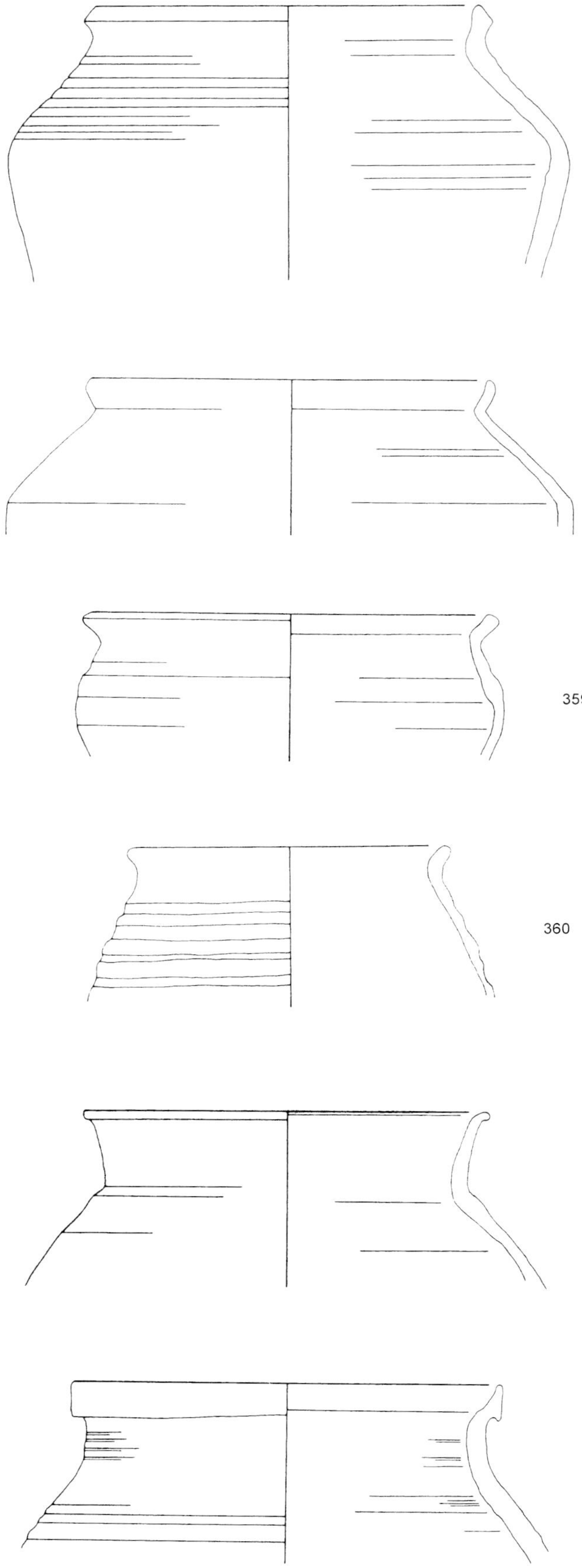

357

358

359

360

361

362

*Figure 2.54 Catalogue 357–362, plain jars. Scale 1:3*

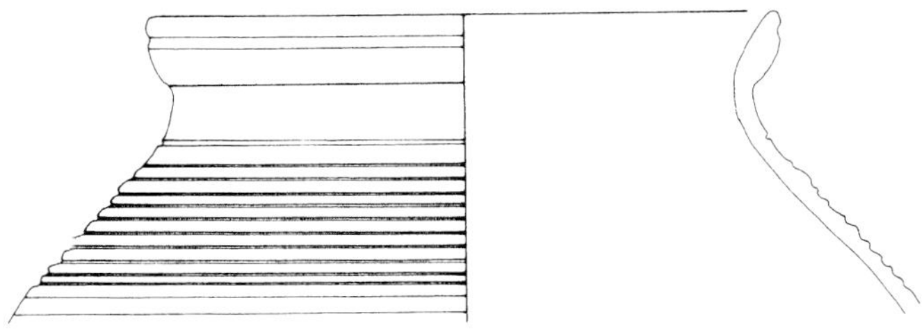

363

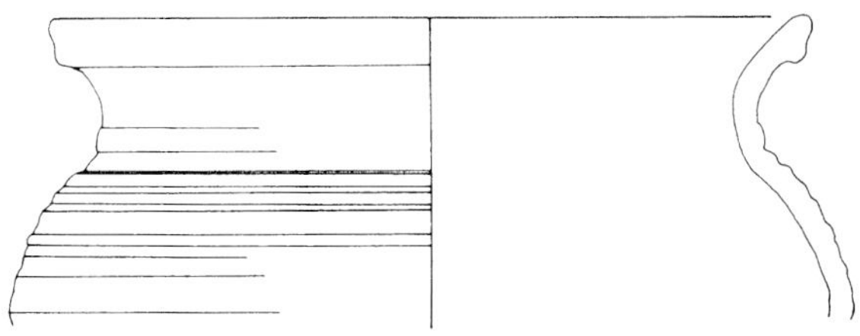

364

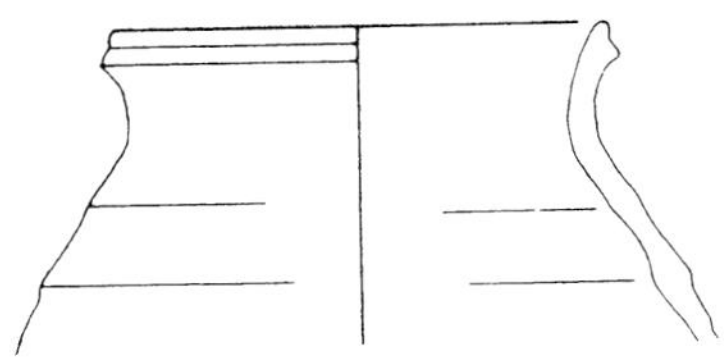

365

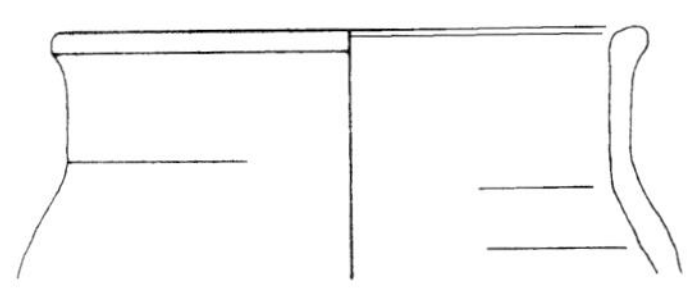

366

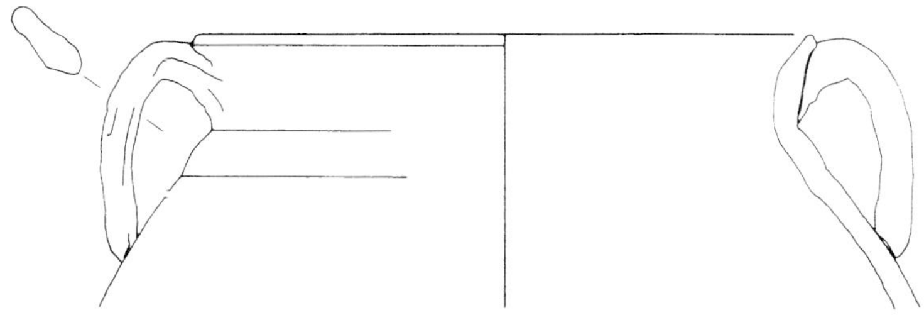

367

*Figure 2.55 Catalogue 363–367, plain jars. Scale 1:3*

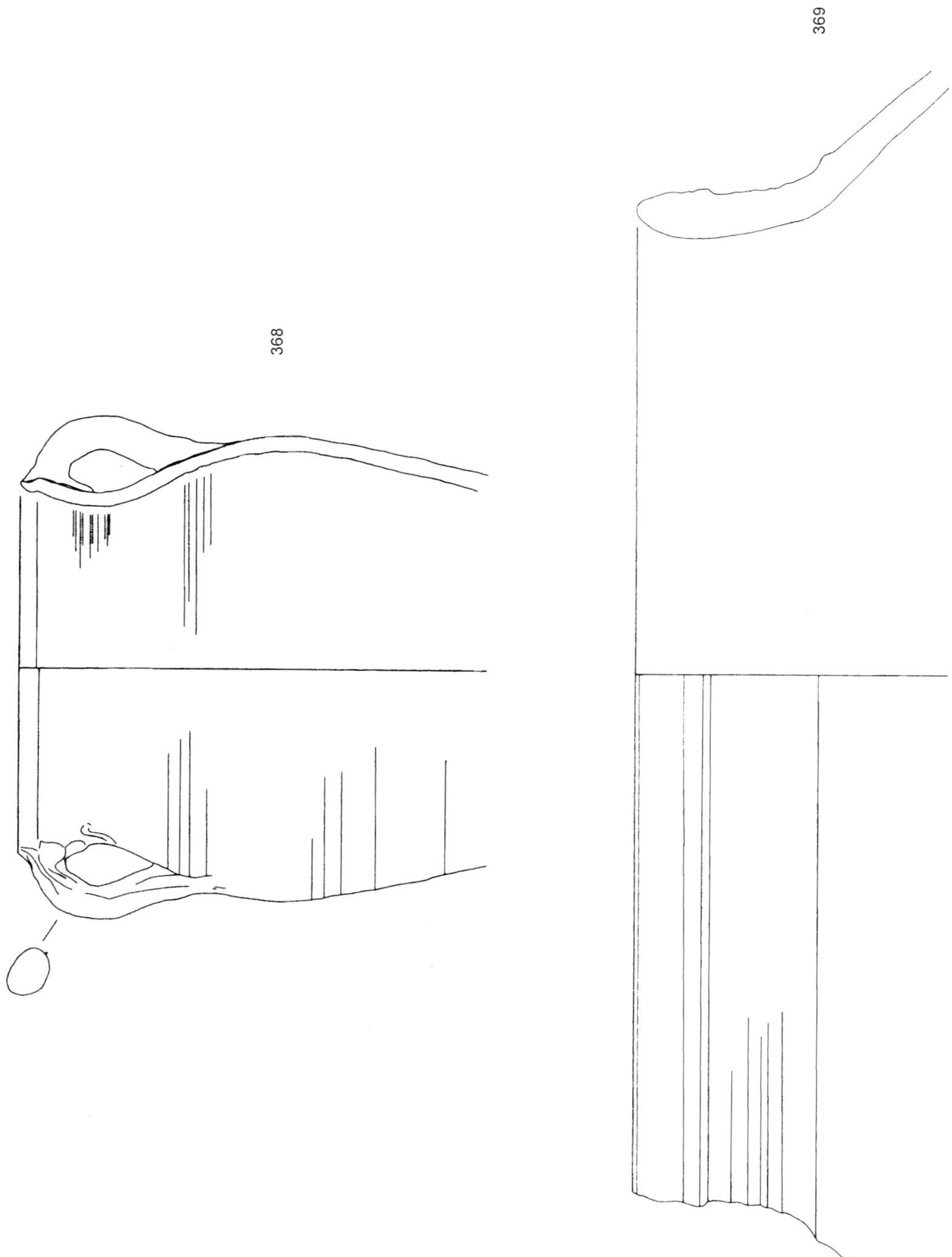


*Figure 2.56 Catalogue 368–369, plain jars. Scale 1:3*

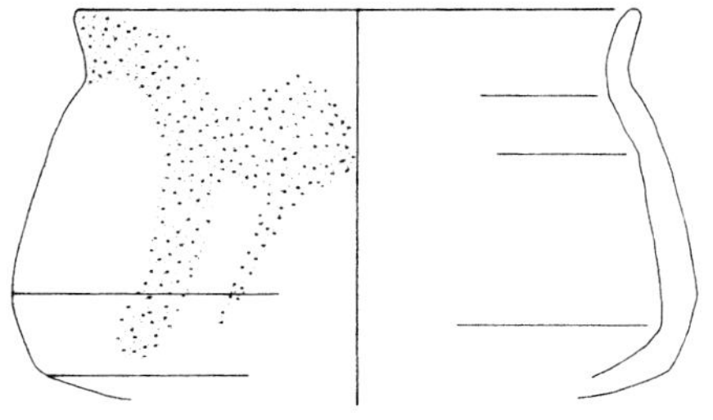

370

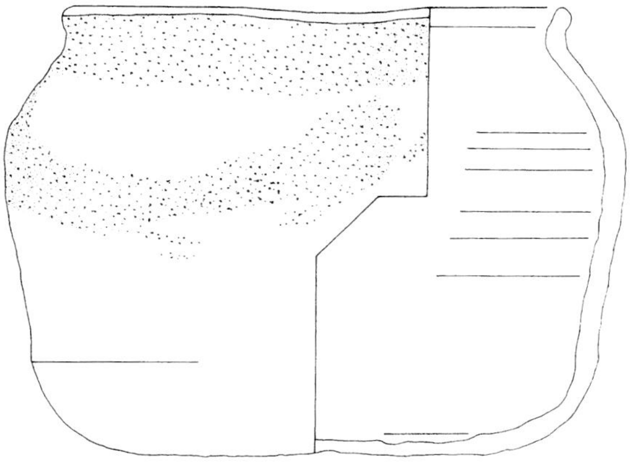

371

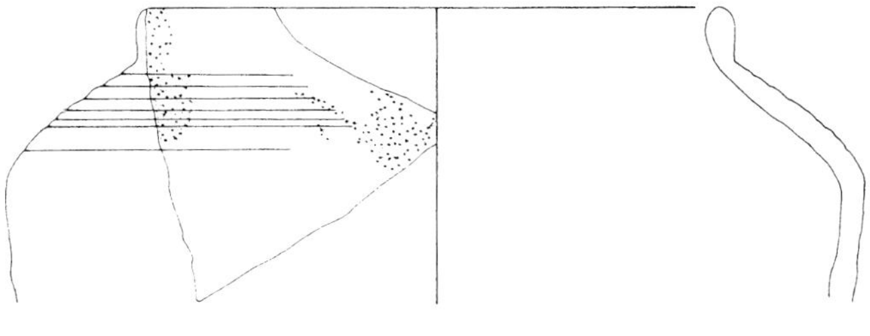

372

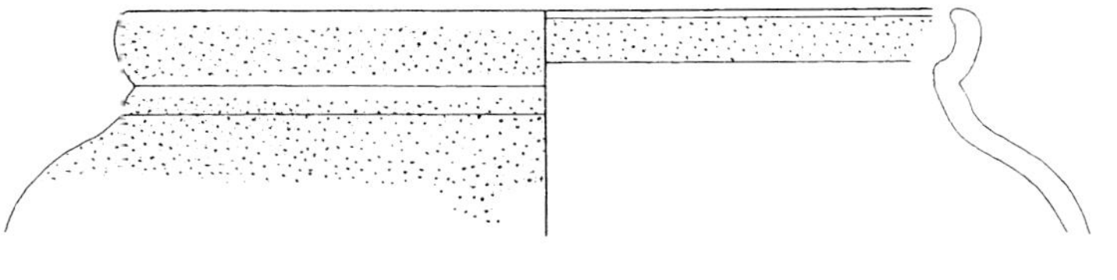

373

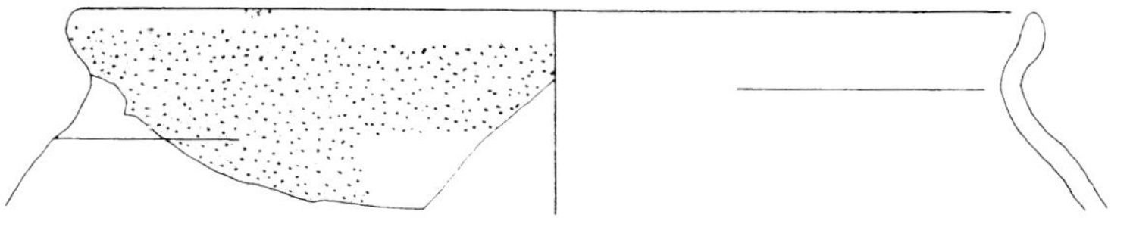

374

*Figure 2.57 Catalogue 370–374, painted and decorated jars. Scale 1:3*

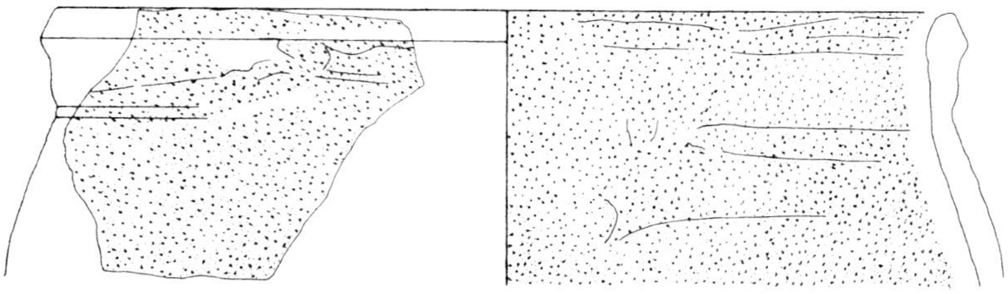

375

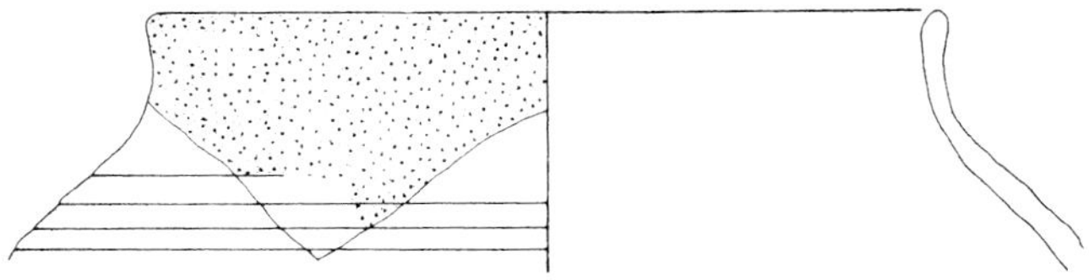

376

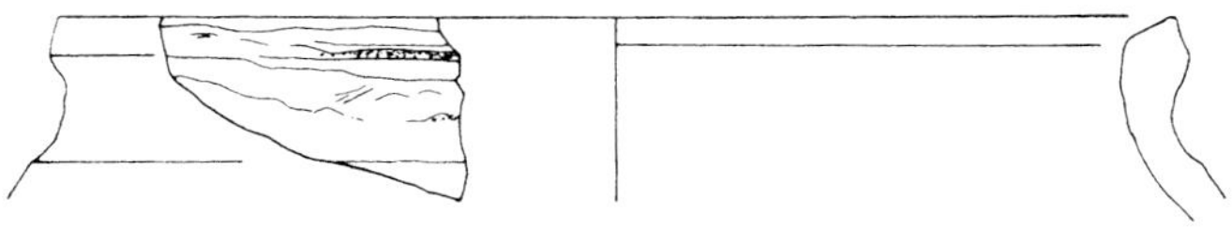

377

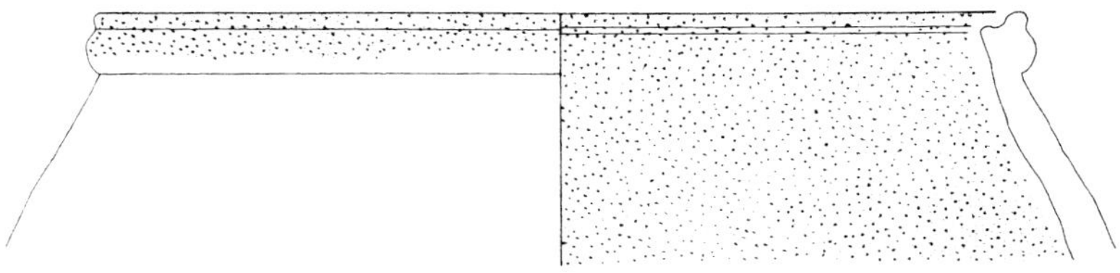

378

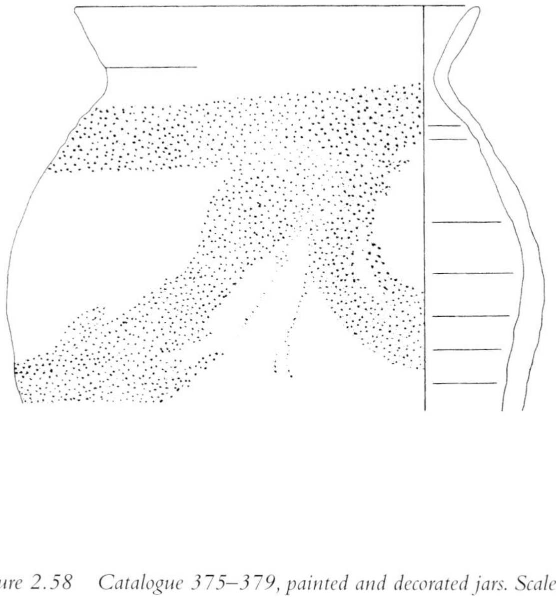

379

*Figure 2.58 Catalogue 375–379, painted and decorated jars. Scale 1:3*

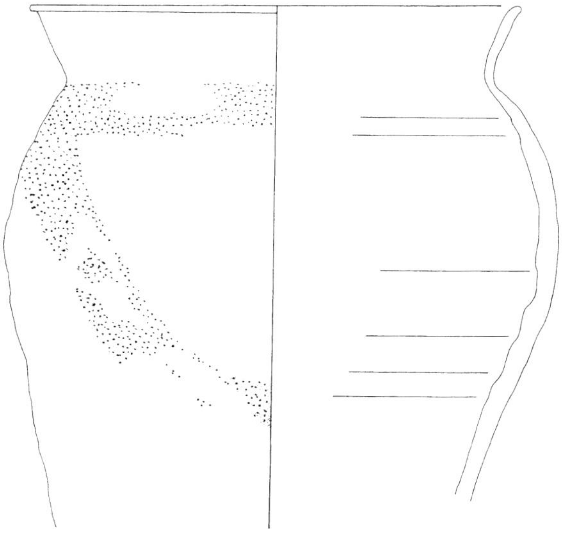

380

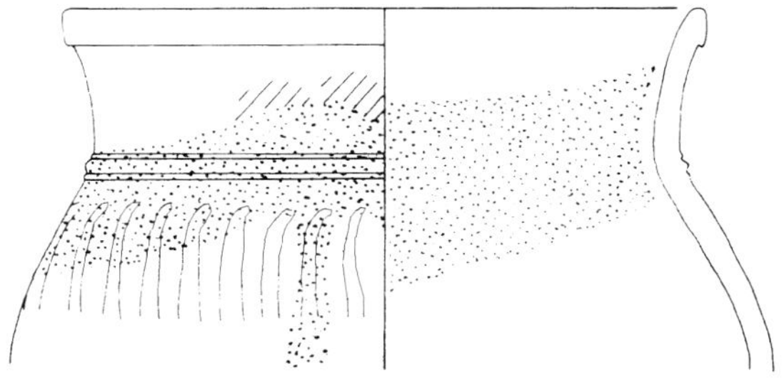

381

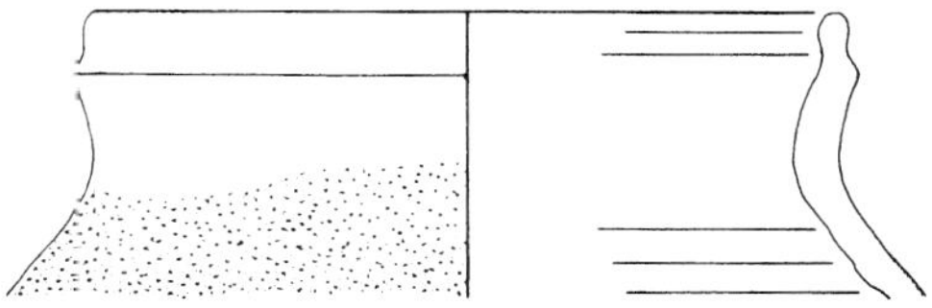

382

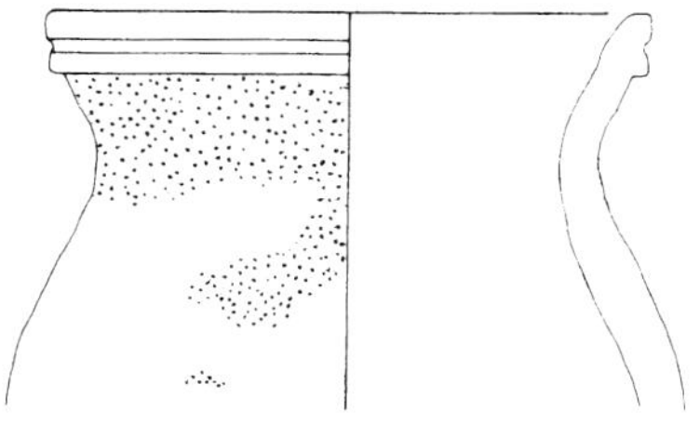

383

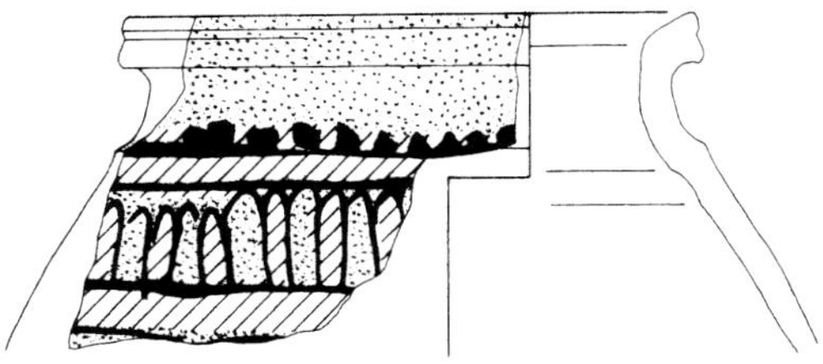

384

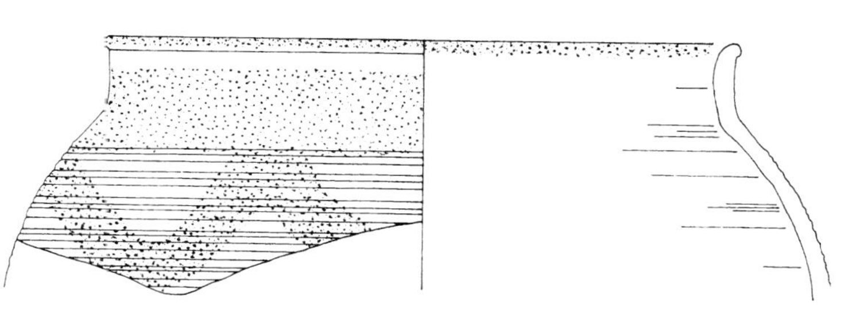

385

*Figure 2.59 Catalogue 380–385, painted and decorated jars. Scale 1:3*

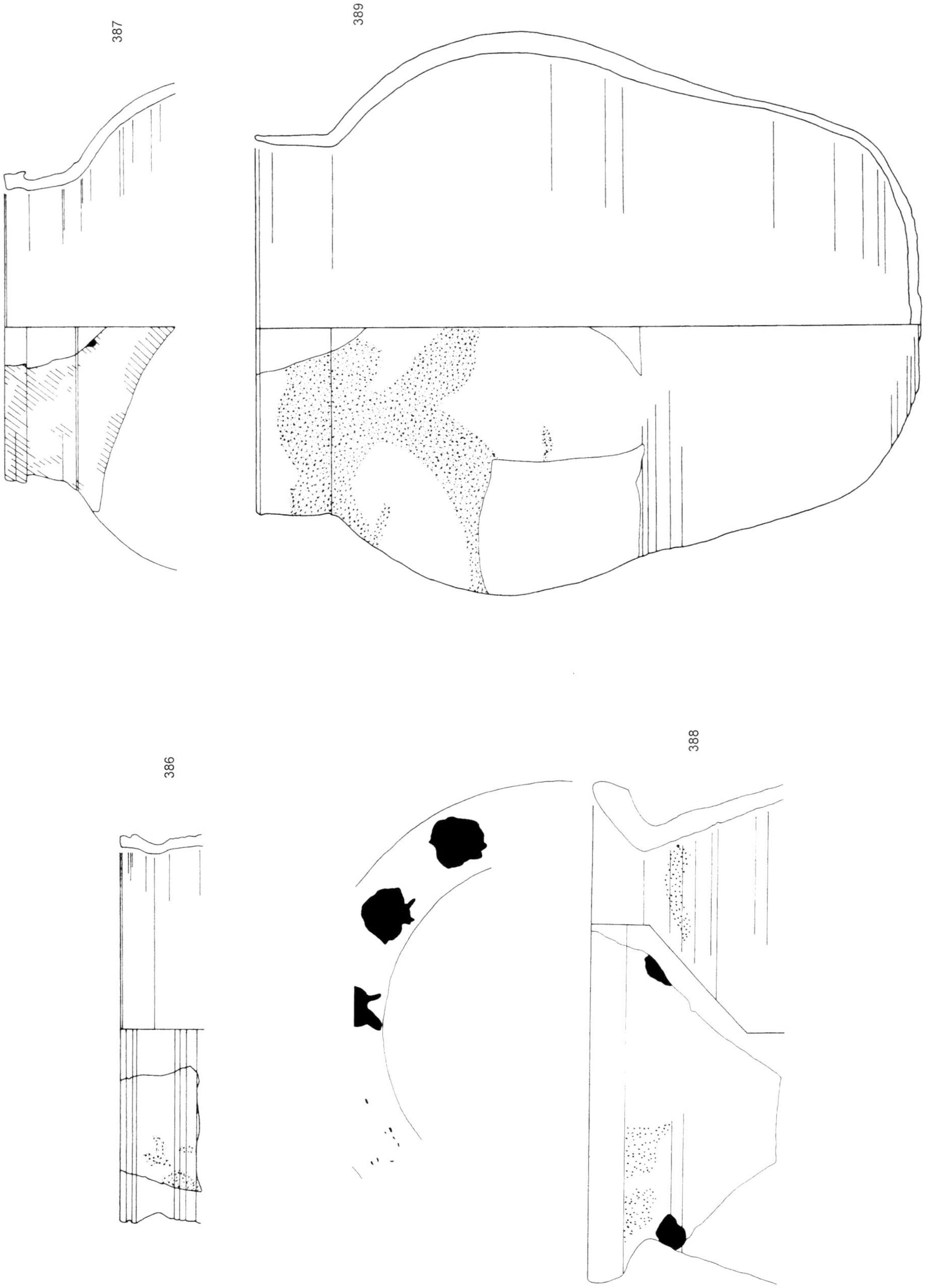


*Figure 2.60 Catalogue 386–389, painted and decorated jars. Scale 1:3*

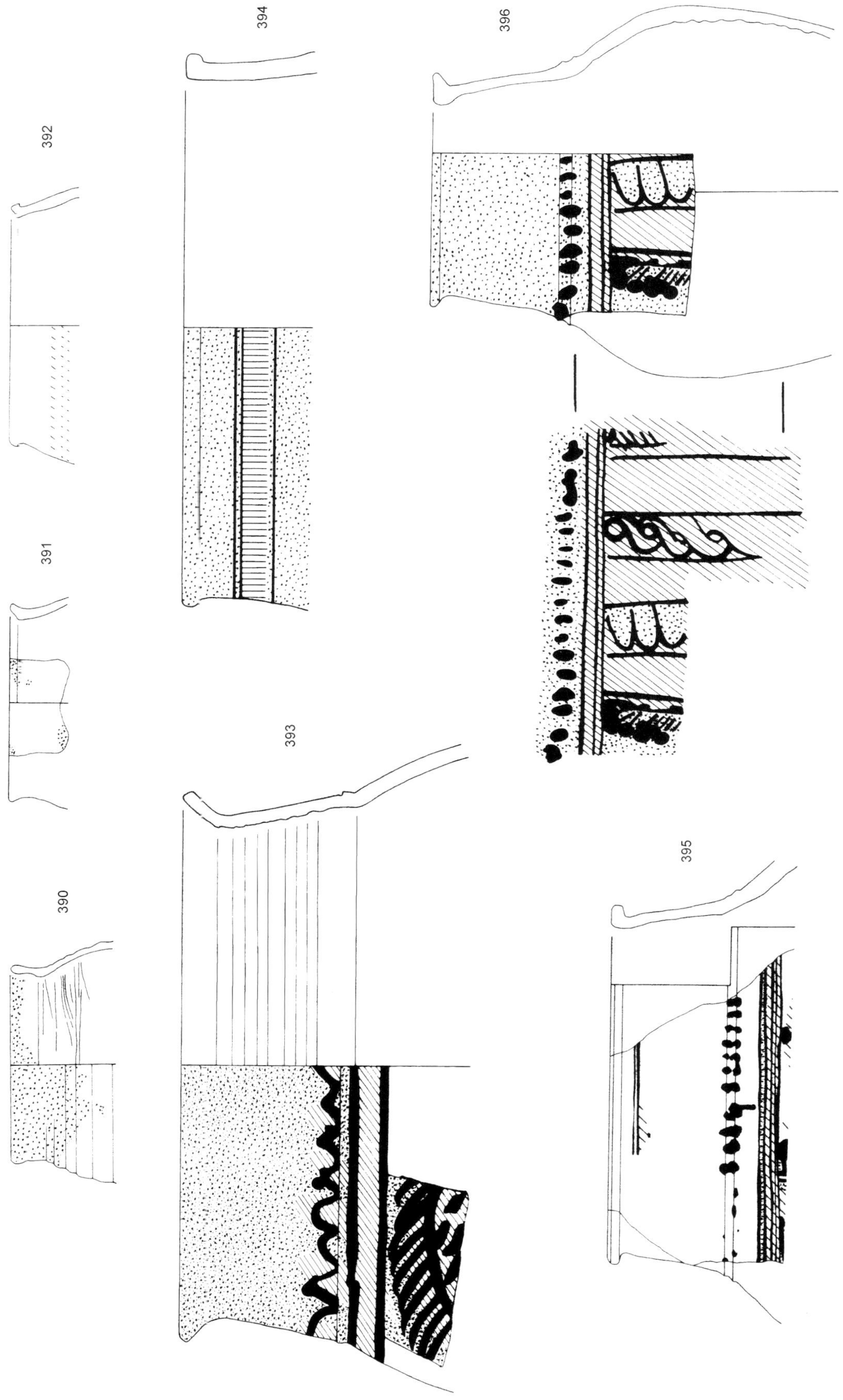


*Figure 2.61 Catalogue 390–396, painted and decorated jars. Scale 1:3*

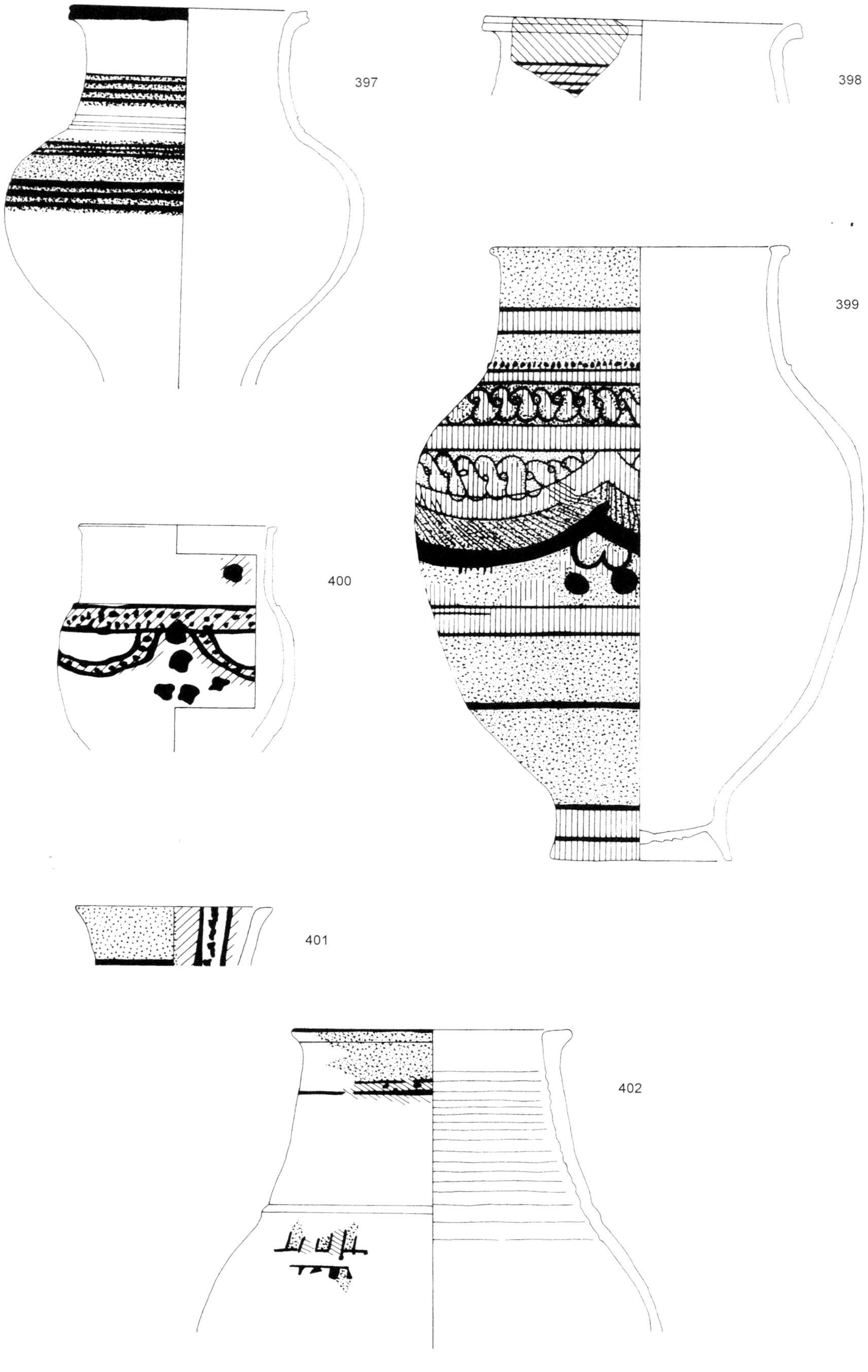


*Figure 2.62 Catalogue 397–402, painted and decorated jars. Scale 1:3*

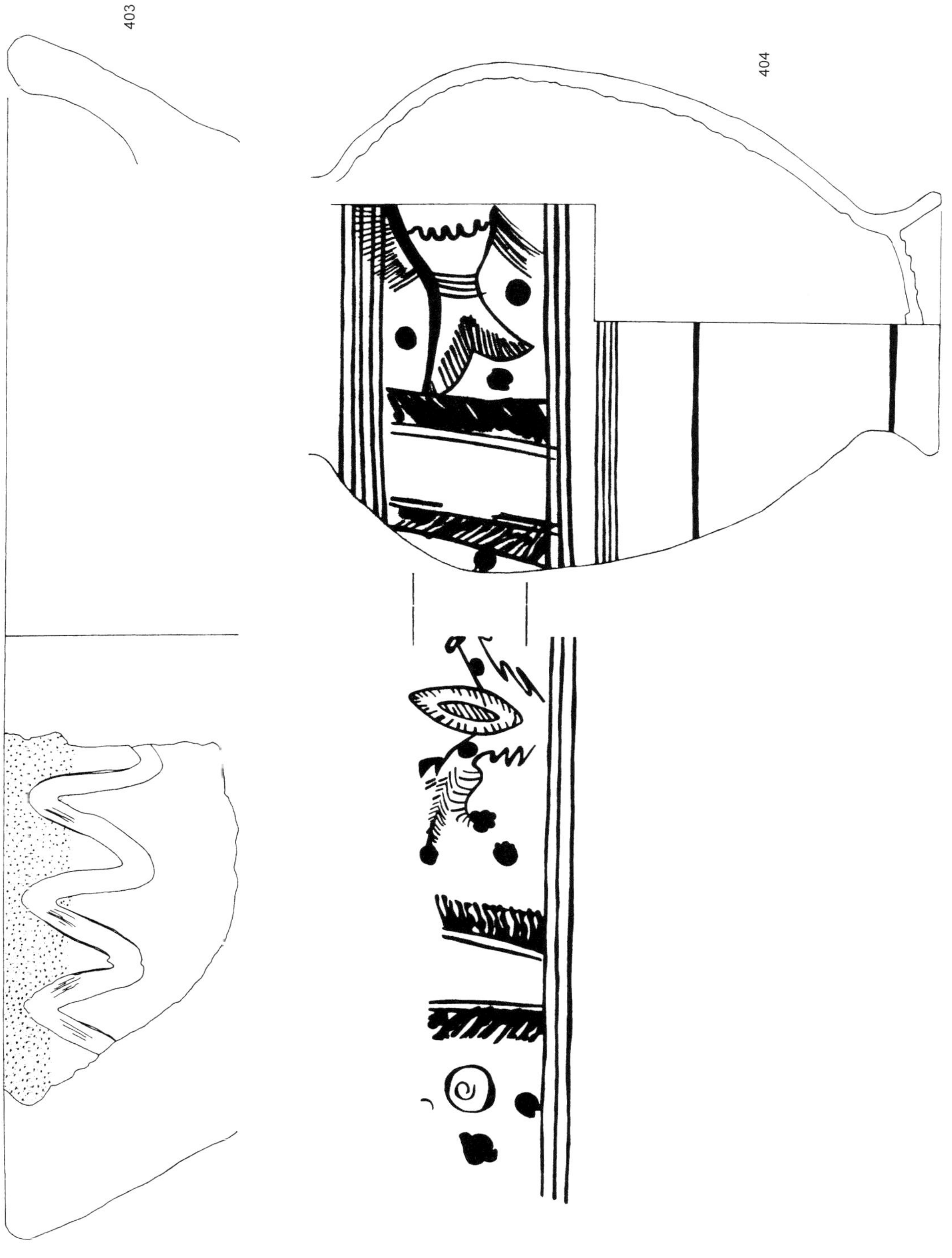


*Figure 2.63* Catalogue 403–404, painted and decorated jars. Scale 1:6 (403) and 1:3 (404)

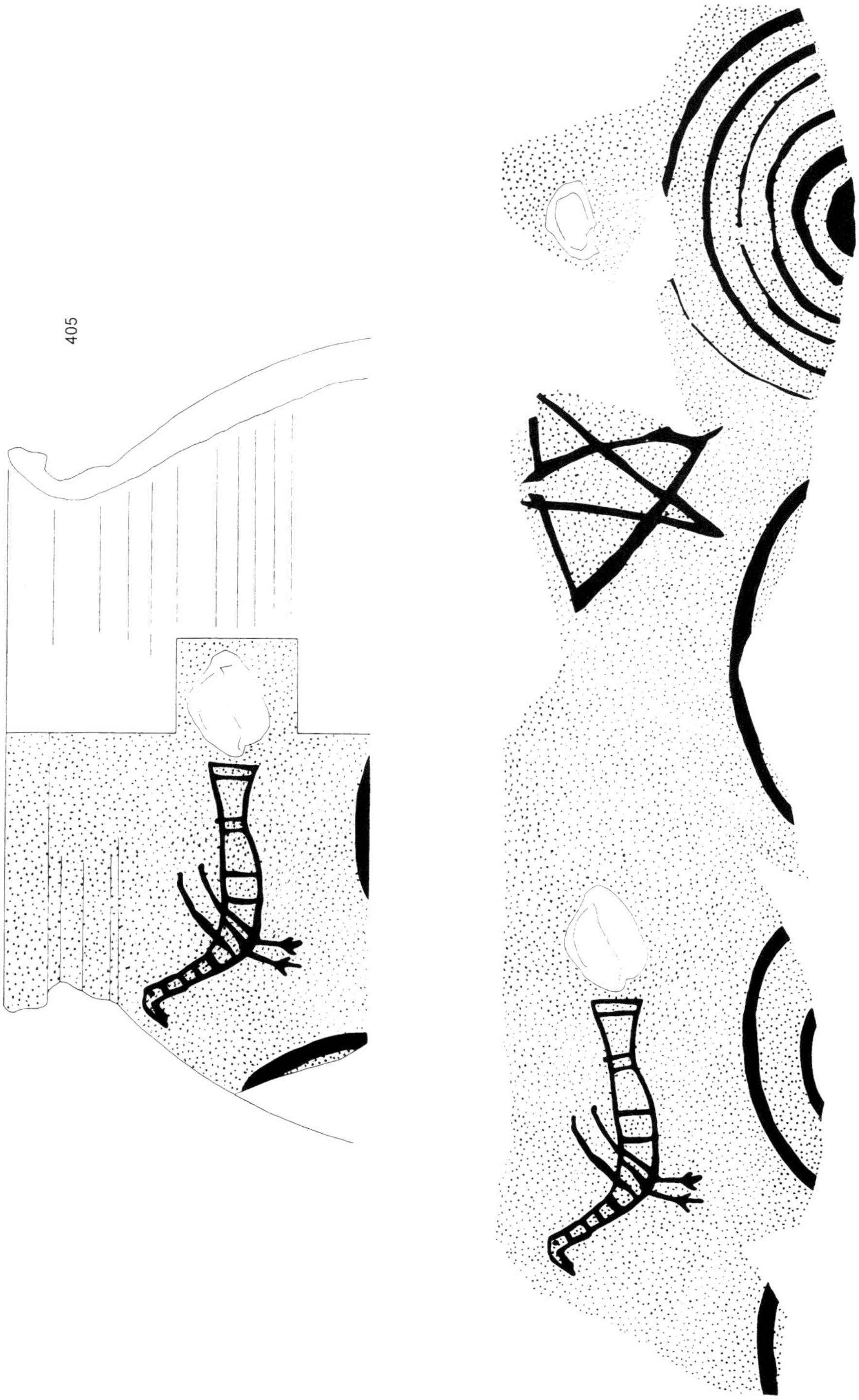


*Figure 2.64 Catalogue 405, painted and decorated jars. Scale 1:3*

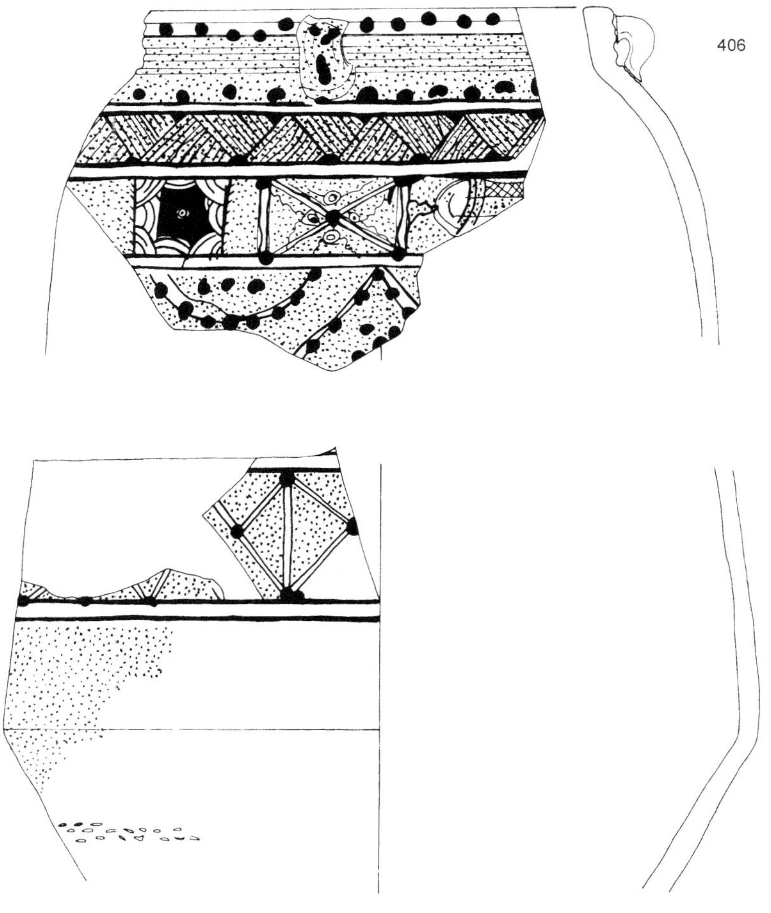


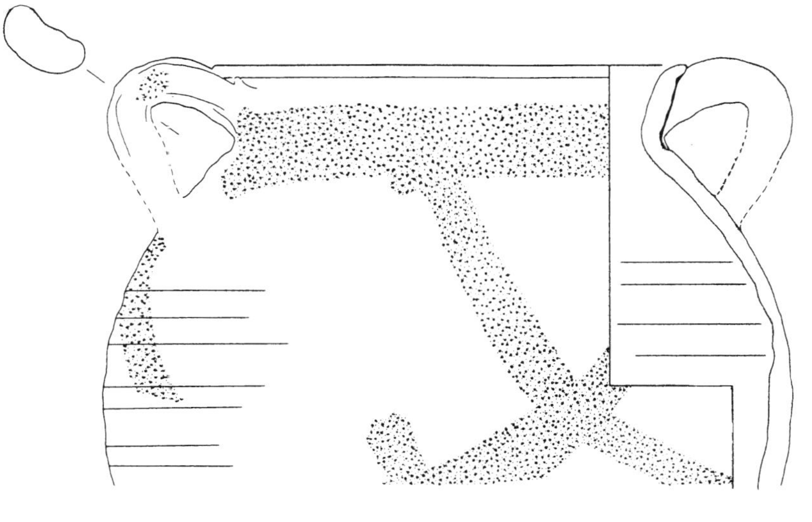


*Figure 2.65 Catalogue 406–407, painted and decorated jars. Scale 1:6 (406) and 1:3 (407)*

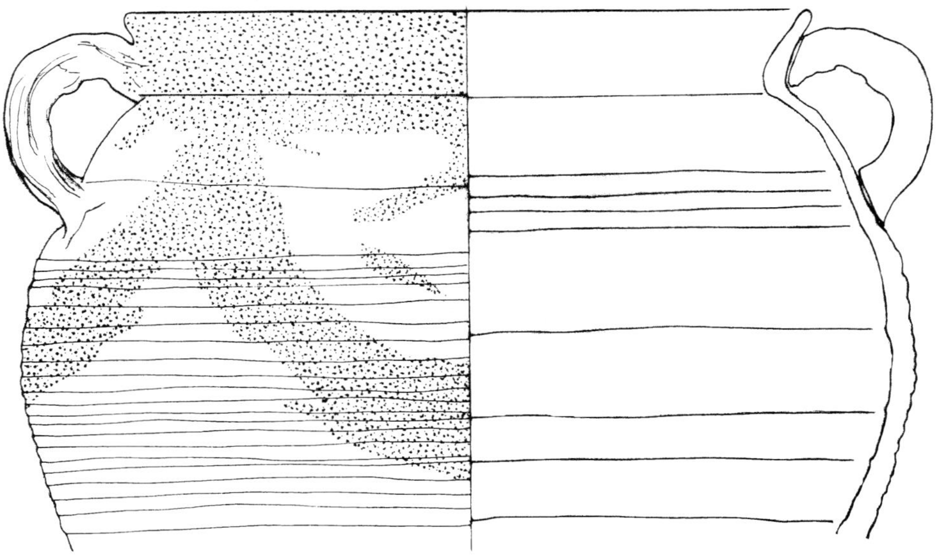

408

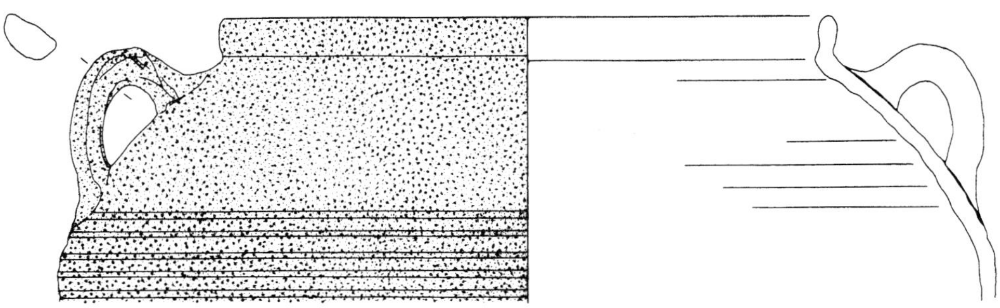

409

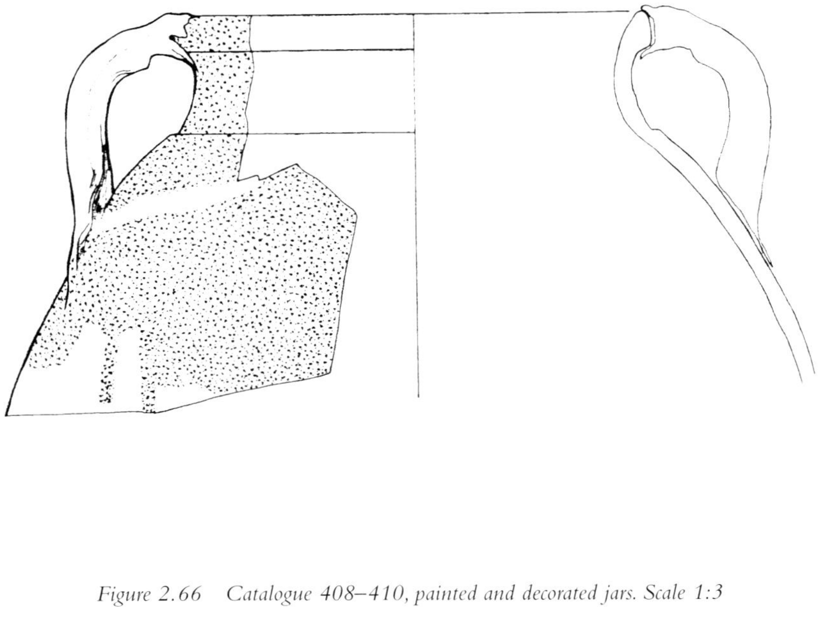

410

*Figure 2.66 Catalogue 408–410, painted and decorated jars. Scale 1:3*

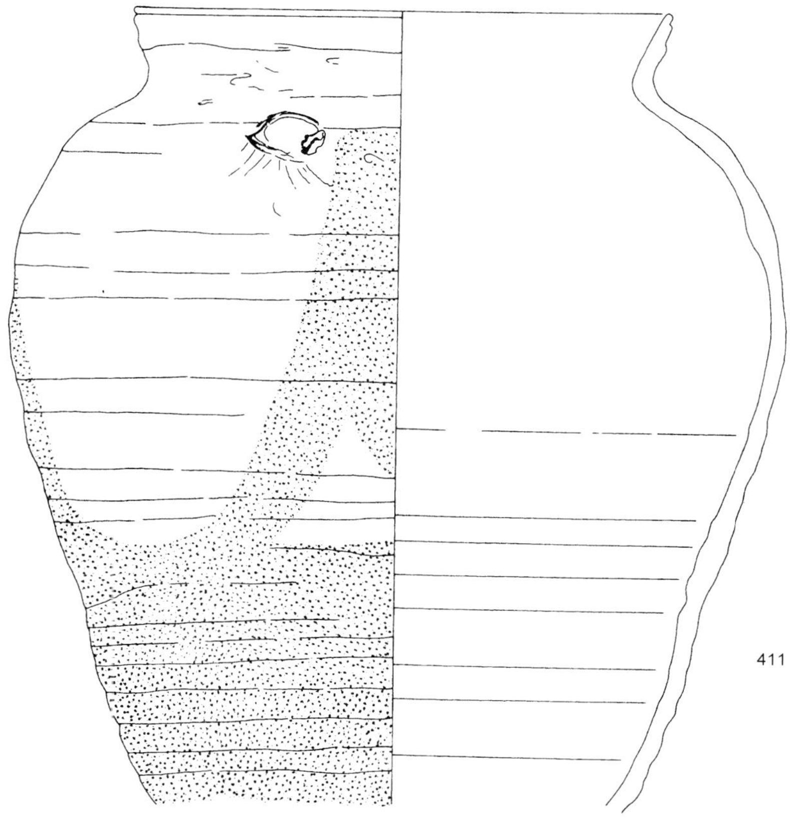

411

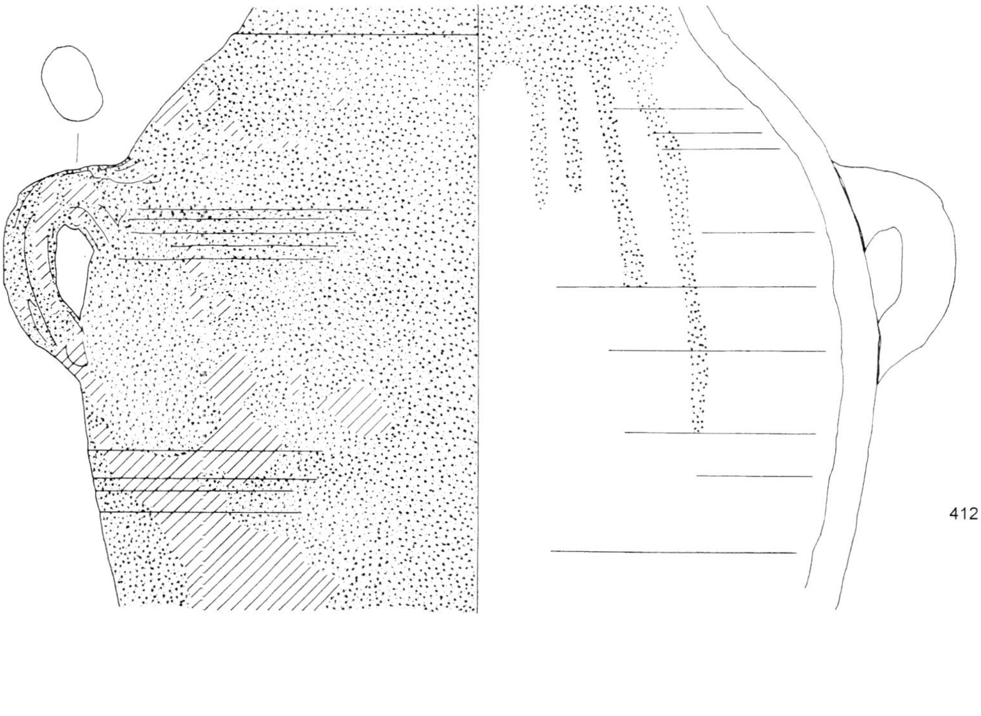

412

*Figure 2.67 Catalogue 411–412, painted and decorated jars. Scale 1:6 (411) and 1:3 (412)*

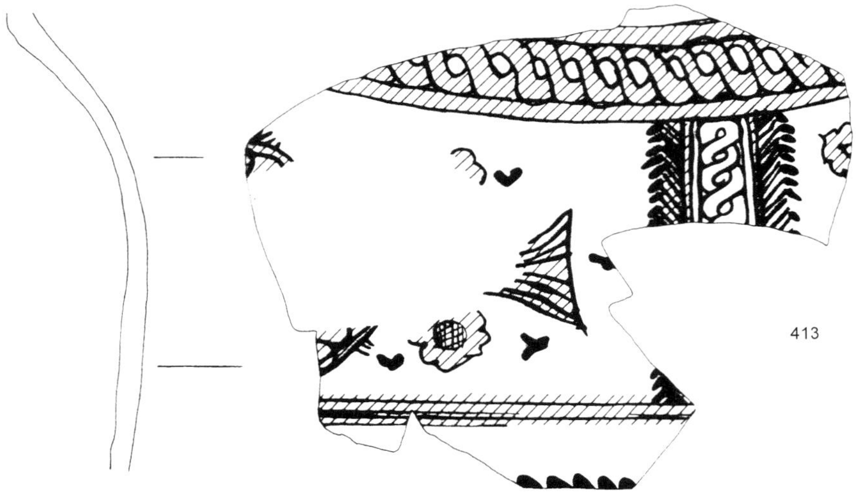

413

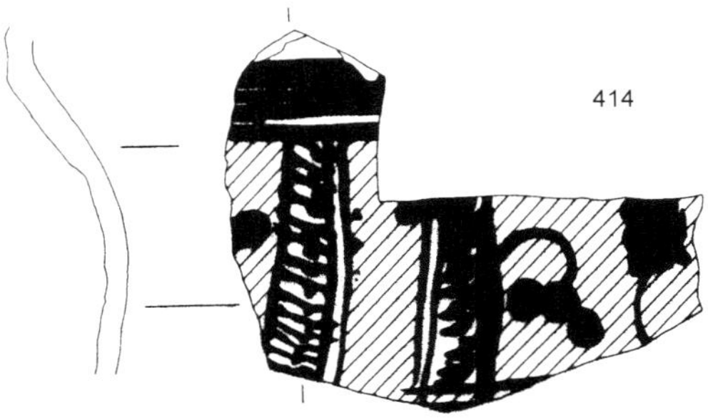

414

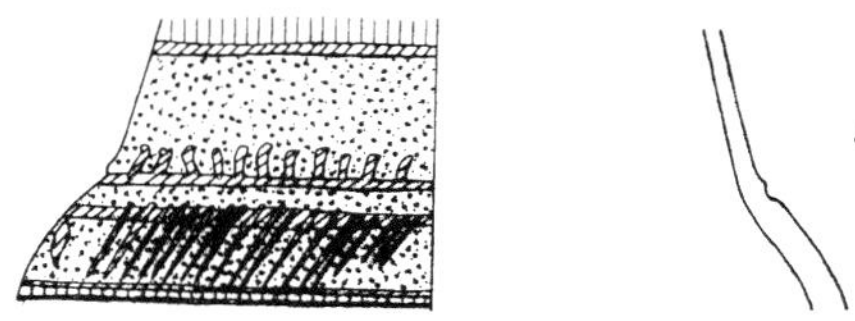

415

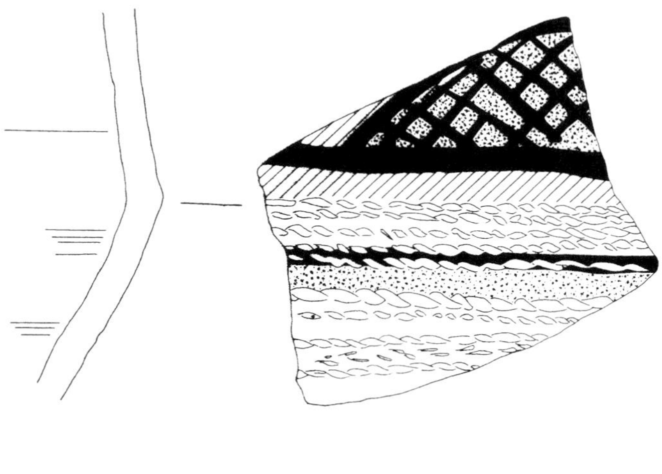

416

*Figure 2.68 Catalogue 413–416, painted body sherds. Scale 1:3*

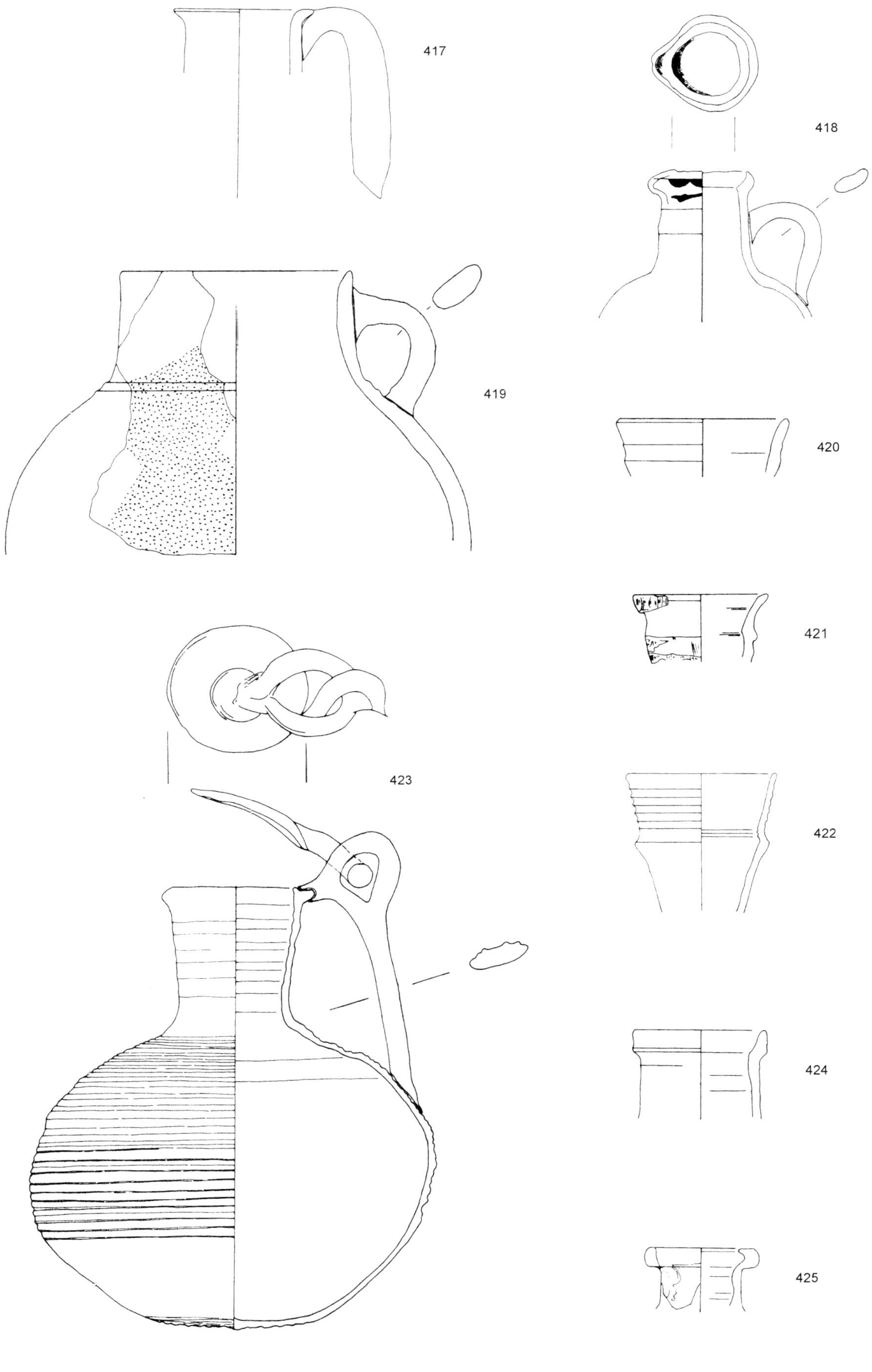


*Figure 2.69 Catalogue 417–419, jugs or pitchers, and 420–425, plain flagons. Scale 1:3*

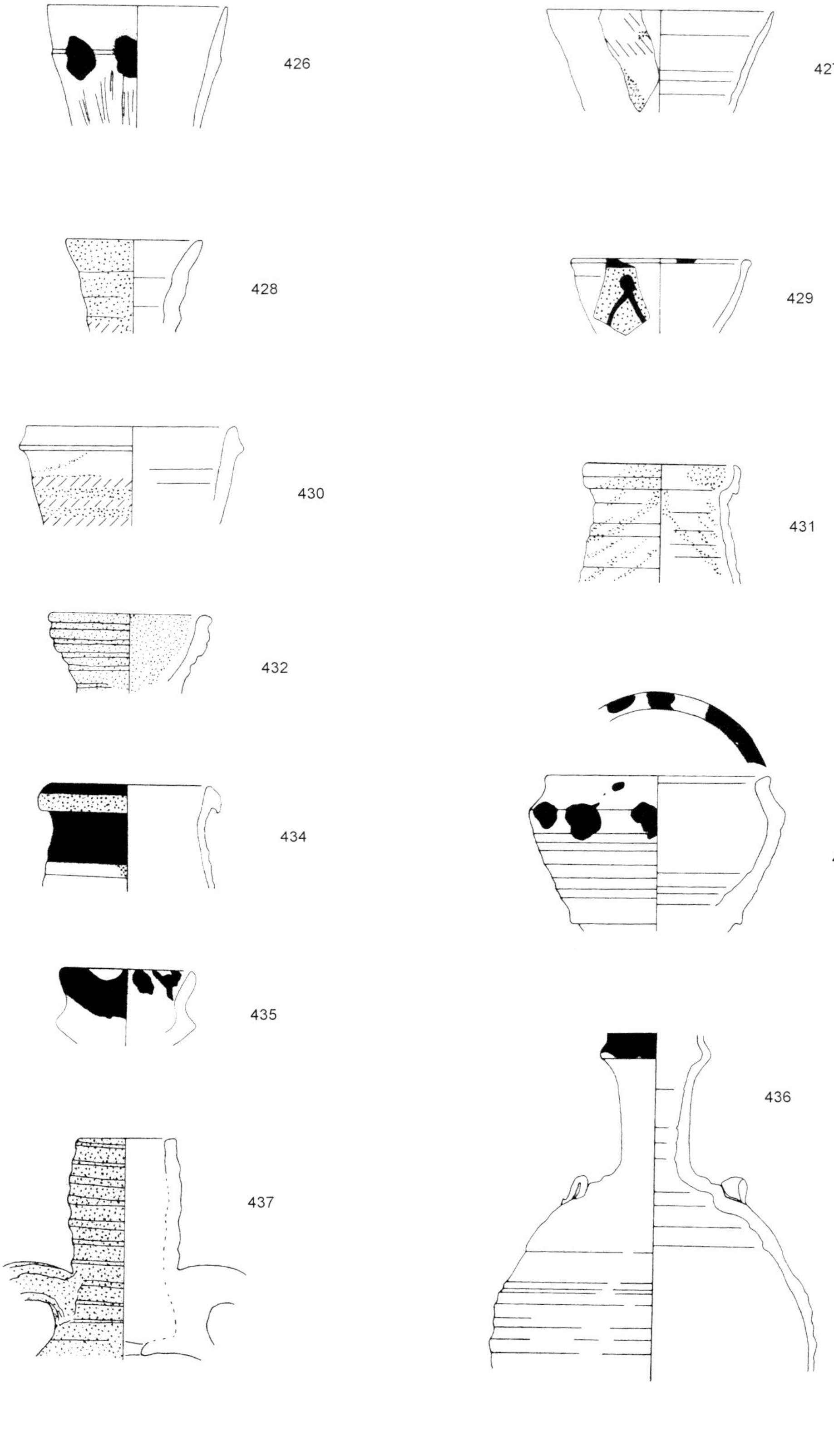


*Figure 2.70 Catalogue 426–437, painted or decorated flagons. Scale 1:3*

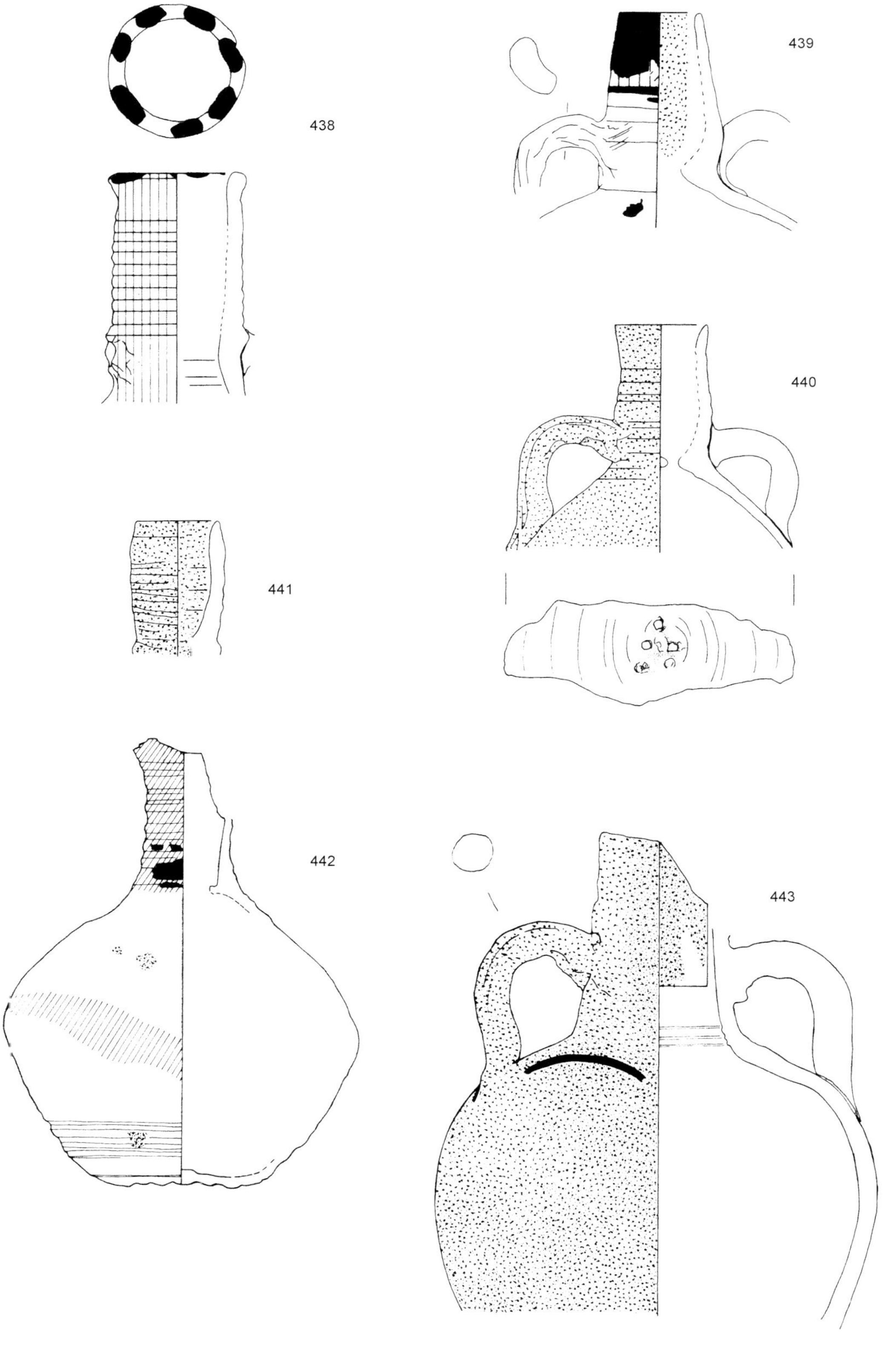


*Figure 2.71 Catalogue 438–443, painted or decorated flagons. Scale 1:3*

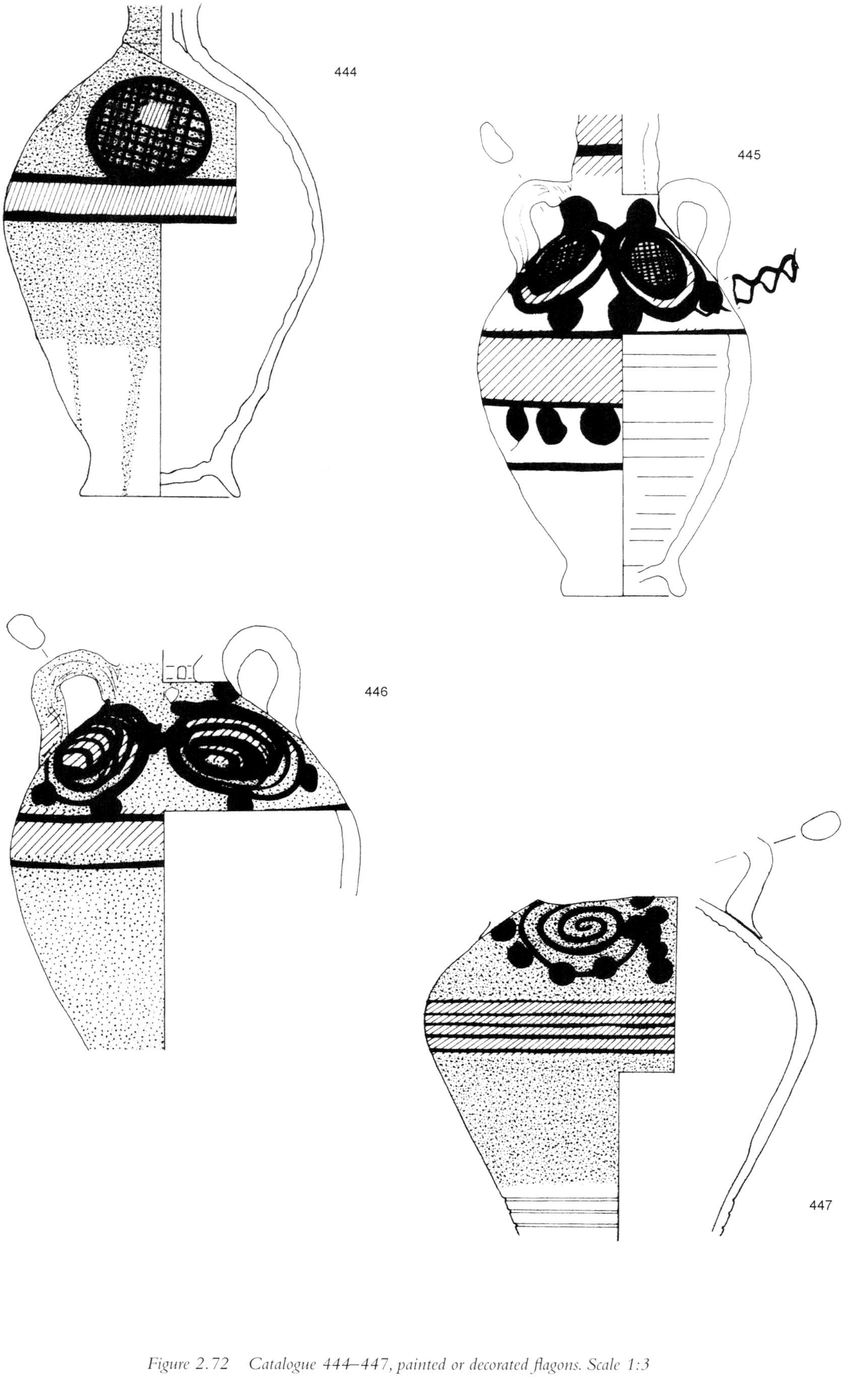


*Figure 2.72 Catalogue 444–447, painted or decorated flagons. Scale 1:3*

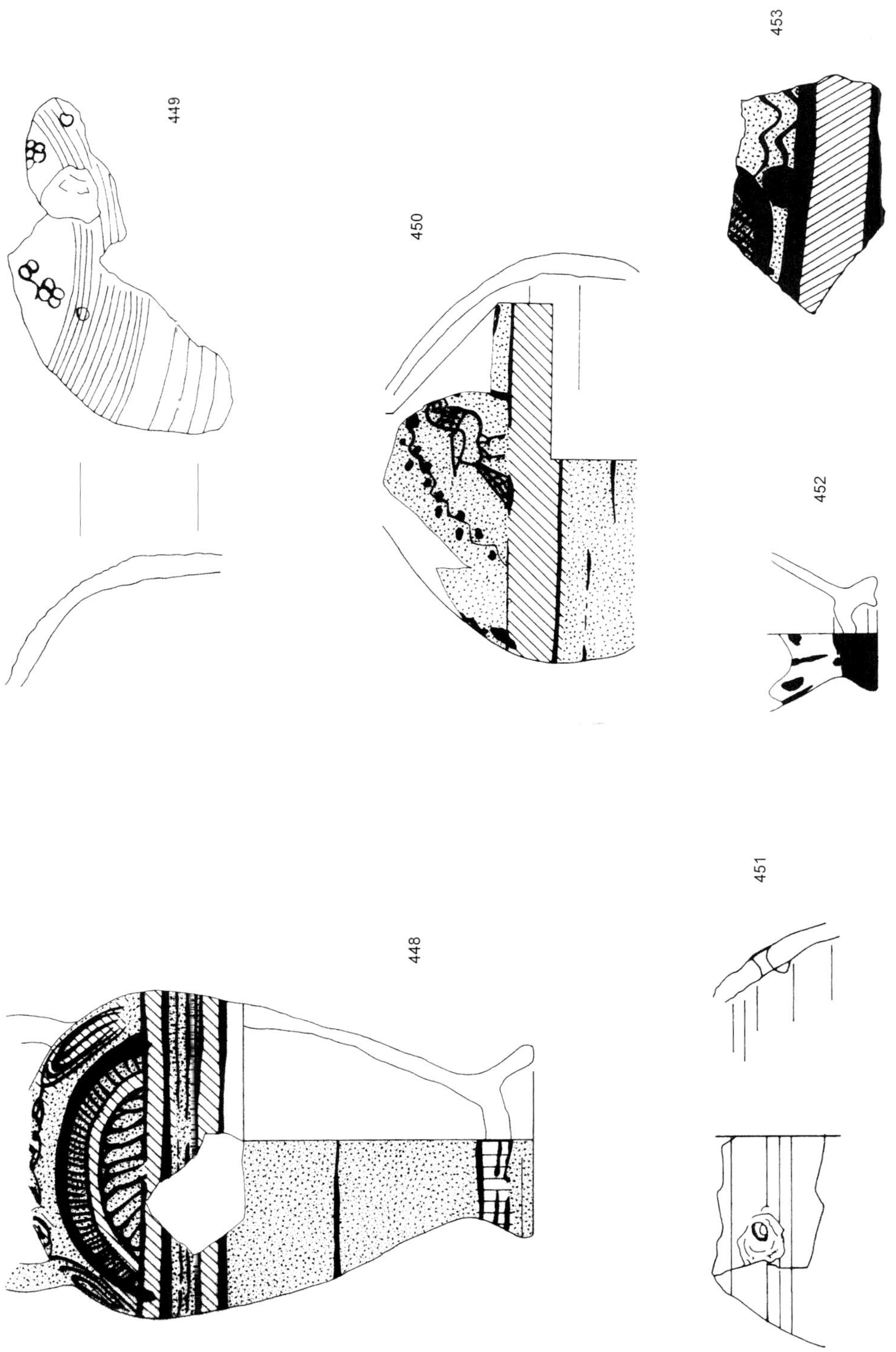


*Figure 2.73 Catalogue 448, painted or decorated flagons, and 449–453, flagon body sherds and base Scale 1:3*

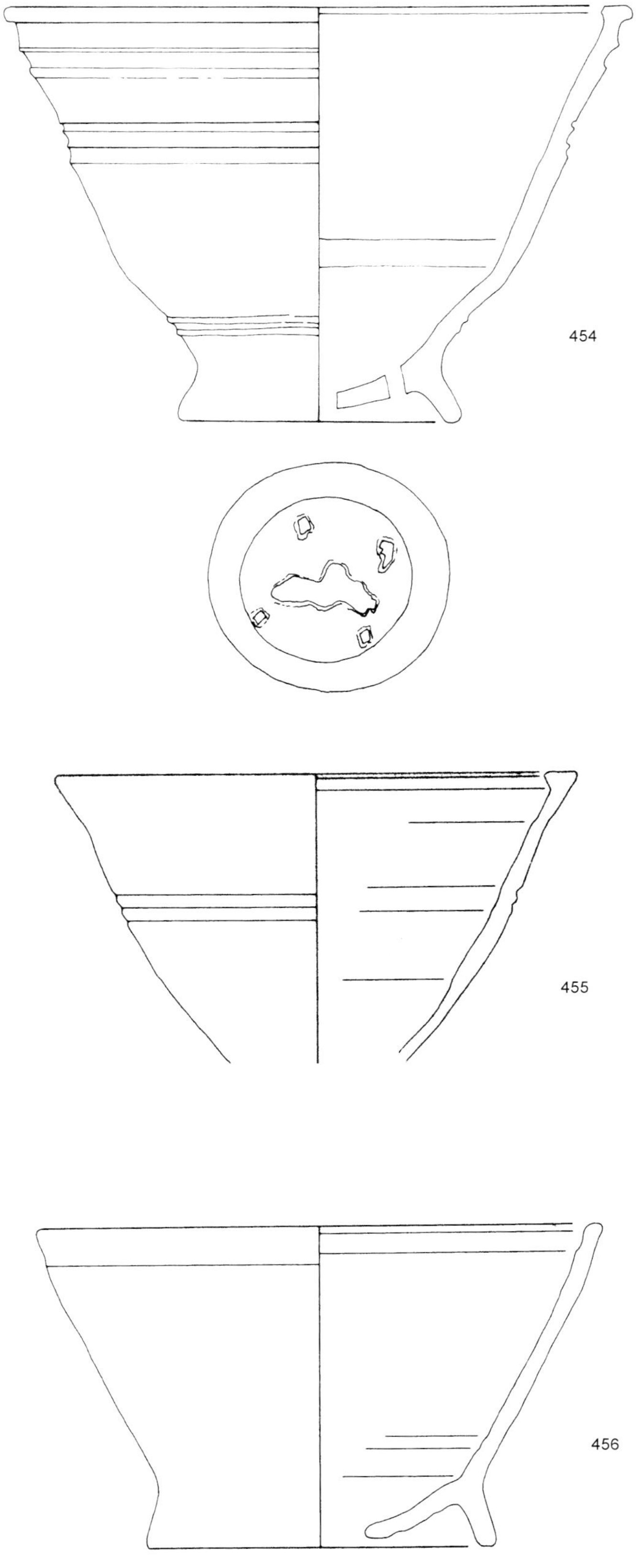


*Figure 2.74 Catalogue 454–456, plain colanders. Scale 1:3*

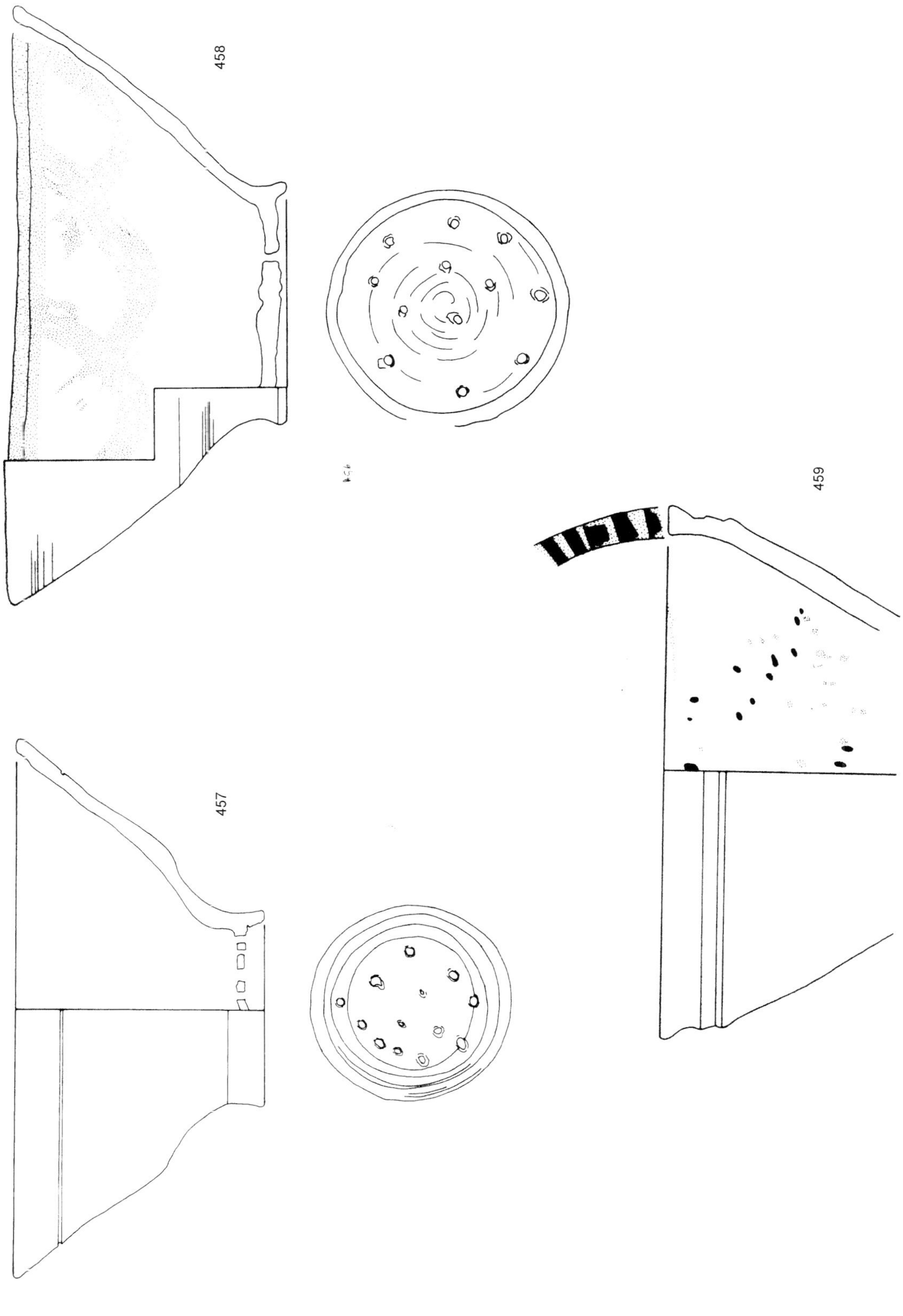


*Figure 2.75* *Catalogue 457, plain colanders, and 458–459, painted colanders. Scale 1:3*

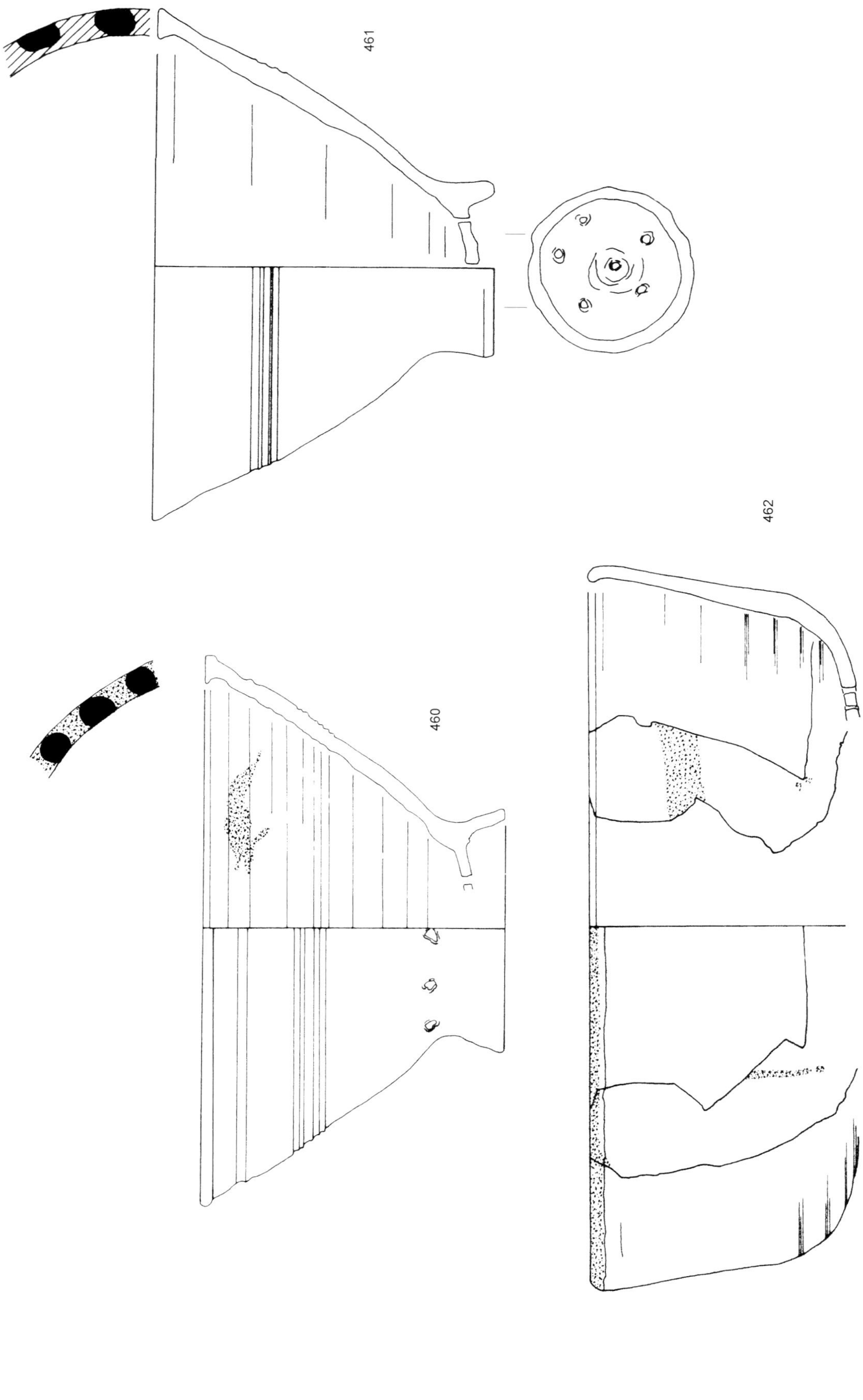


*Figure 2.76 Catalogue 460–462, painted colanders. Scale 1:3*

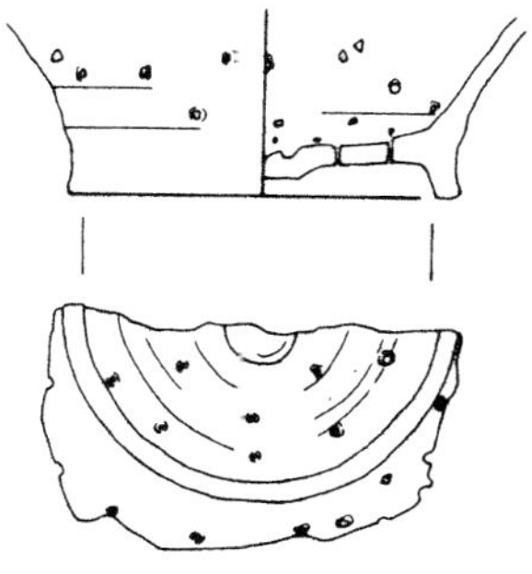

463

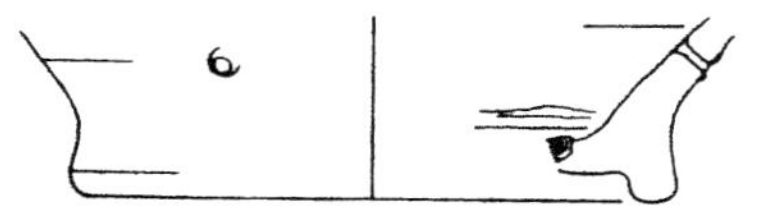

464

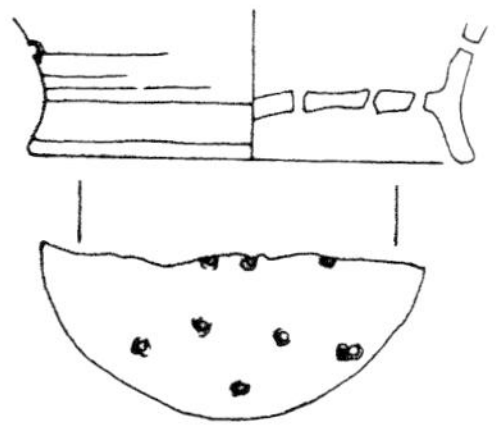

465

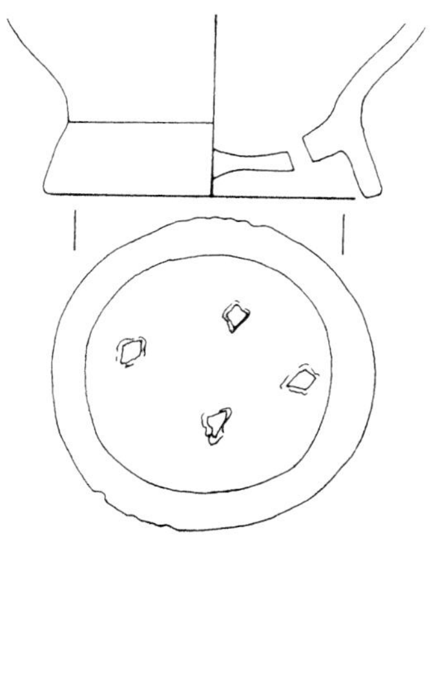

466

*Figure 2.77 Catalogue 463–466, colander bases. Scale 1:3*

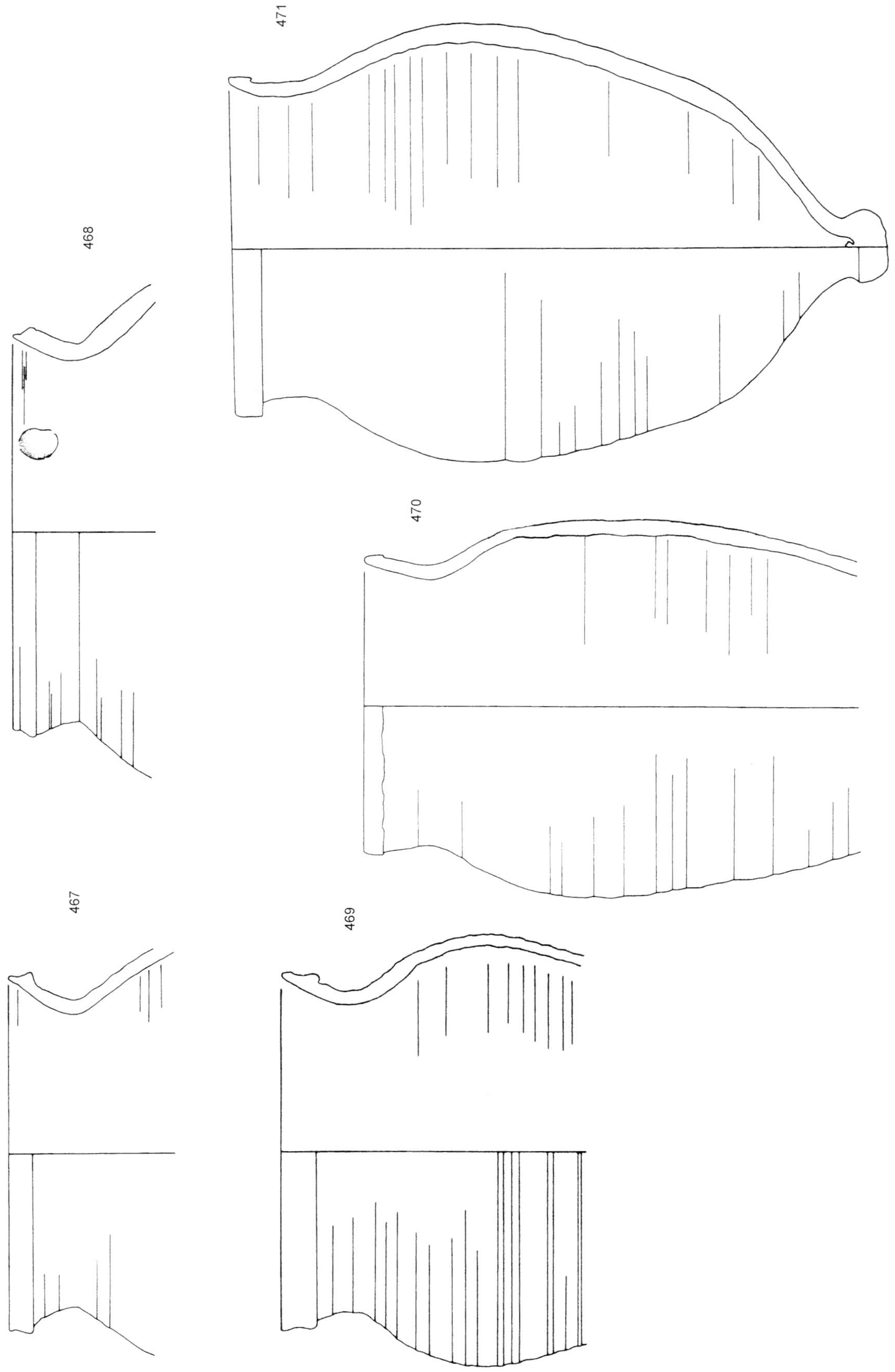


*Figure 2.78 Catalogue 467–471, water pots. Scale 1:3*

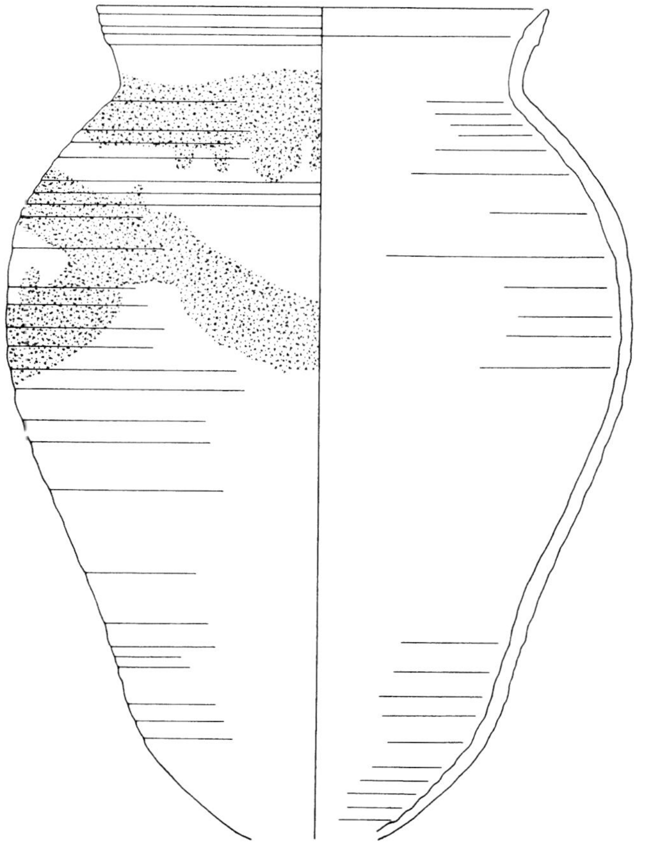

472

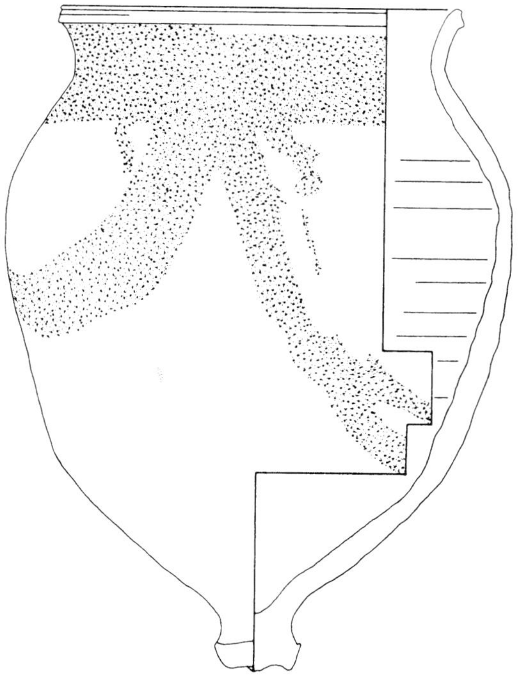

473

*Figure 2.79 Catalogue 472–473, painted water pots. Scale 1:3*

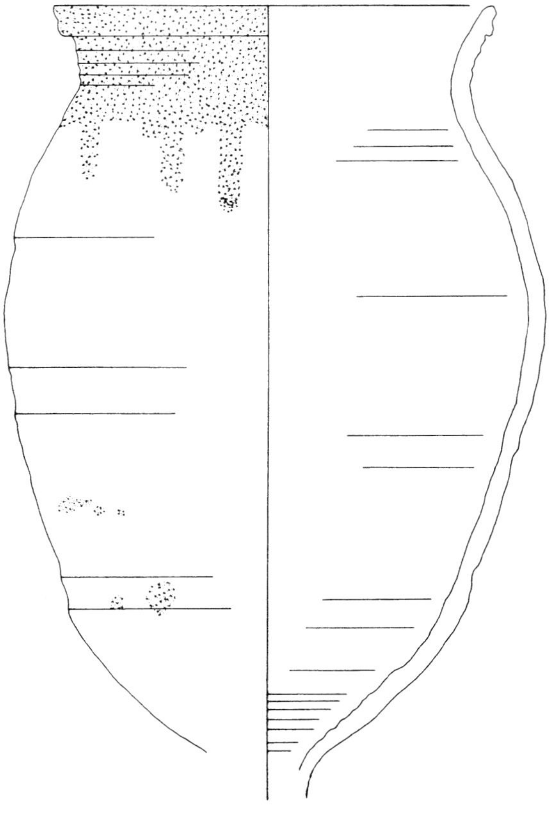

474

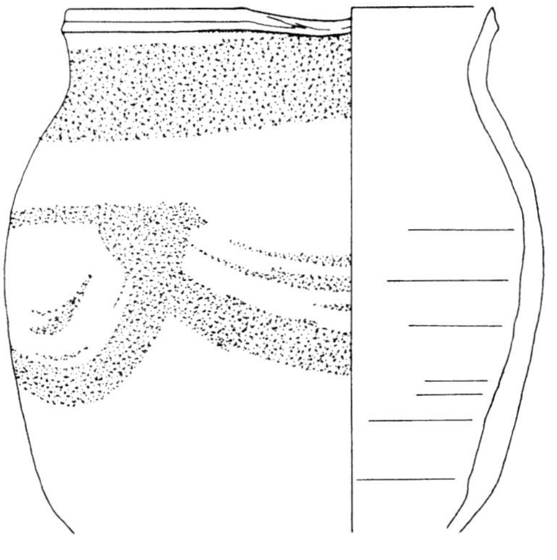

475

*Figure 2.80 Catalogue 474–475, painted water pots. Scale 1:3*

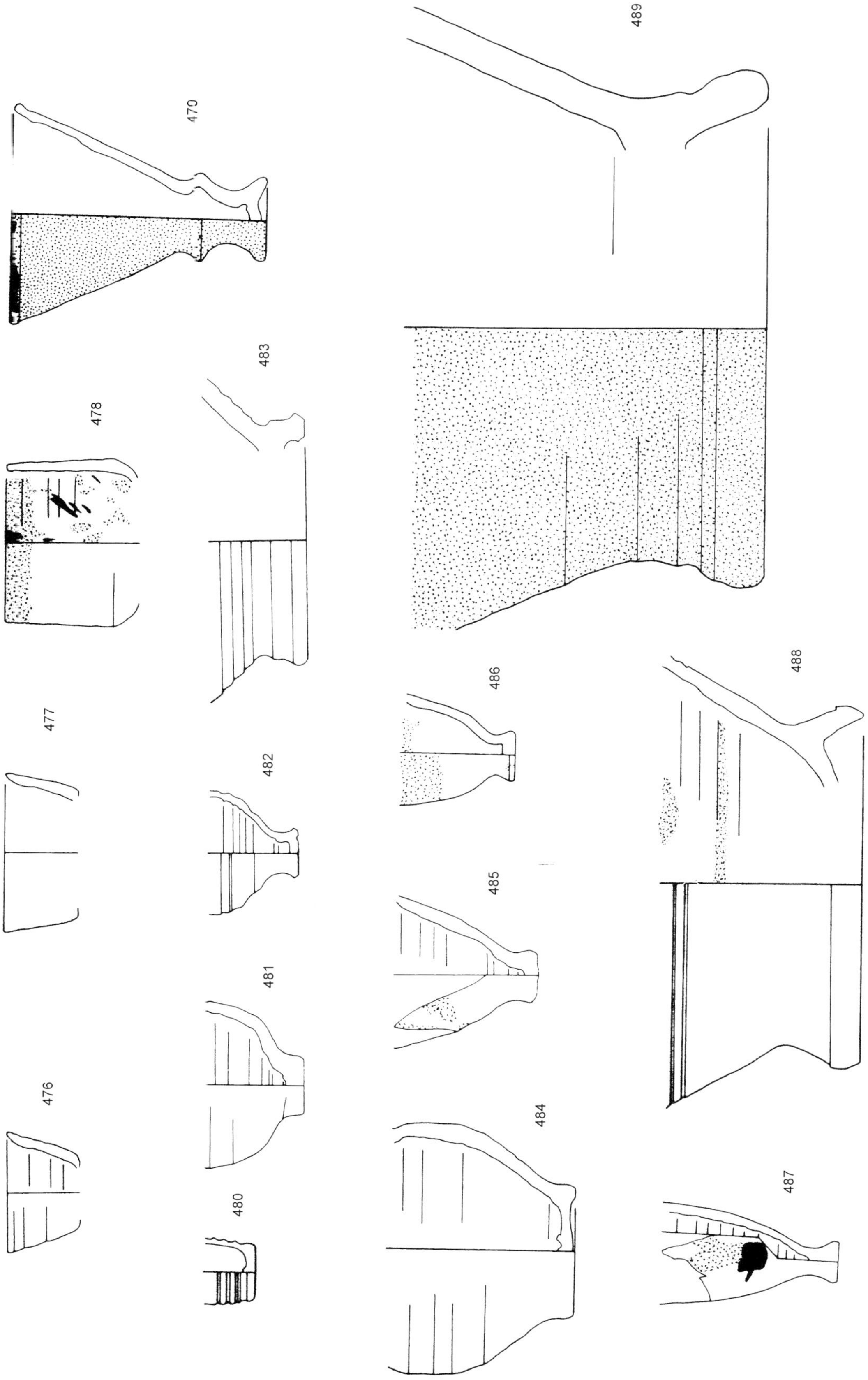


*Figure 2.81 Catalogue 476–477, plain cups, and 478–479, painted cups and goblets and, 480–484, plain bases, and 485–189, painted bases. Scale 1:3*

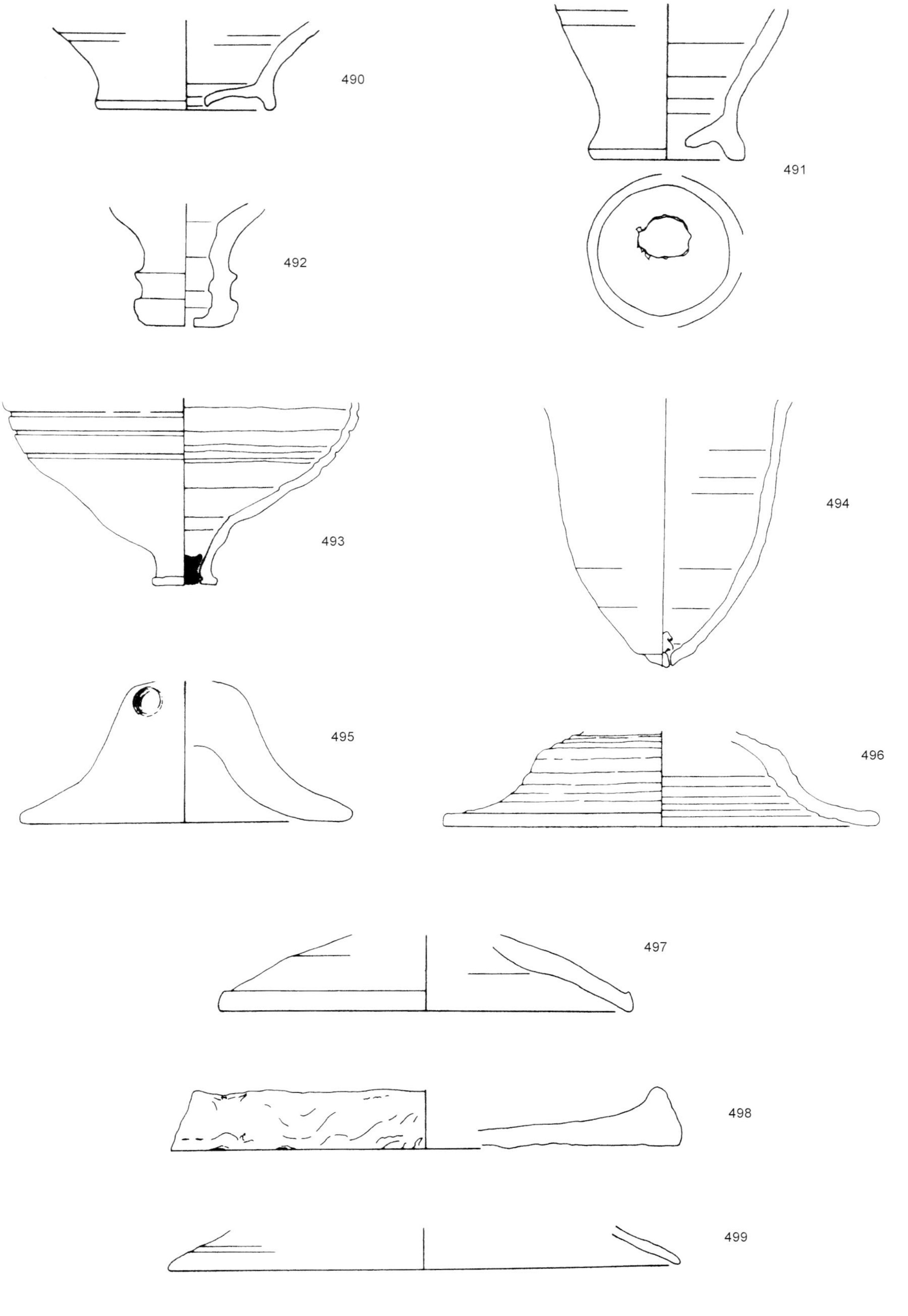


*Figure 2.82 Catalogue 490–494, bases with holes, and 495–499, plain lids. Scale 1:3*

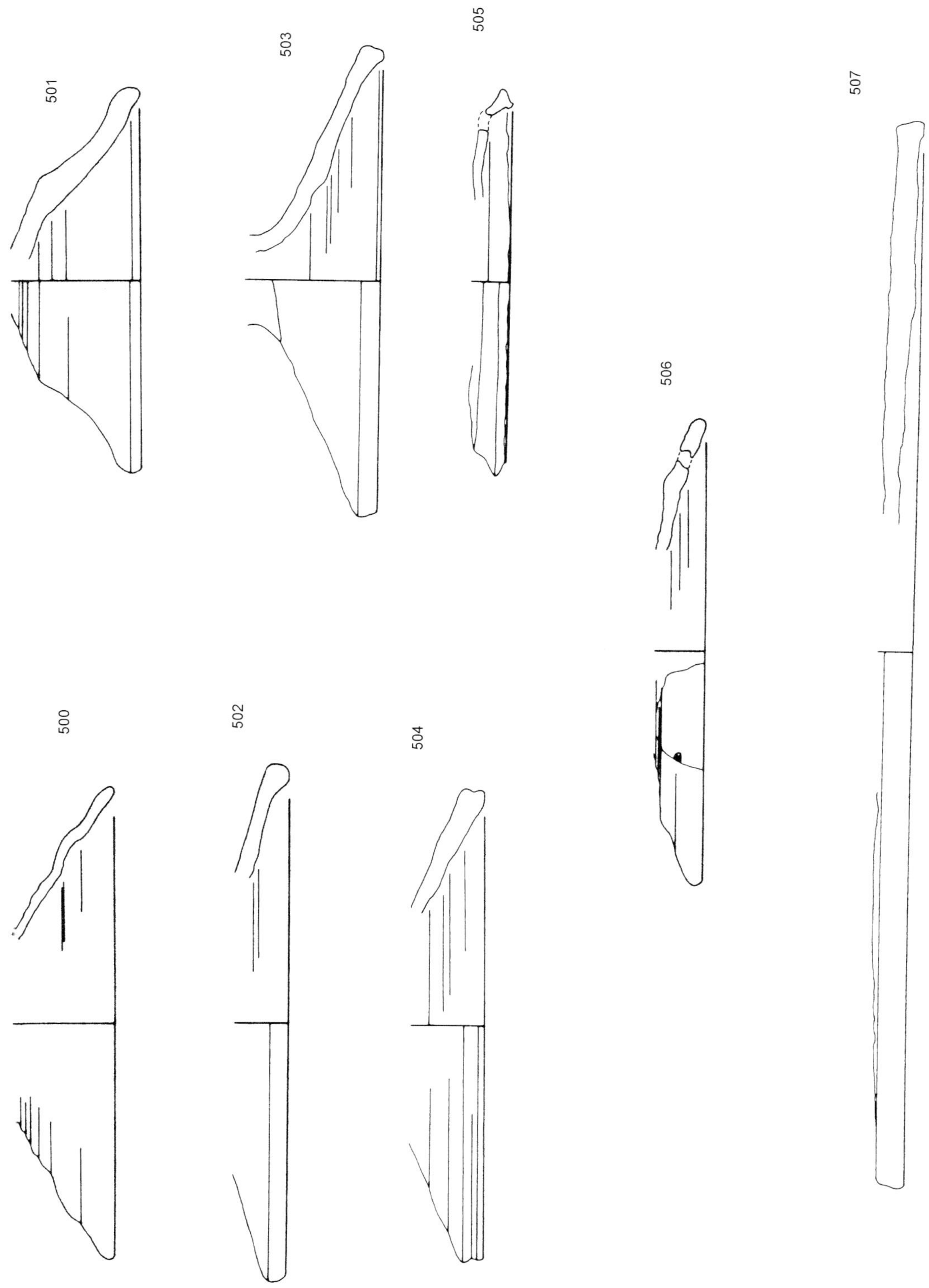


*Figure 2.83 Catalogue 500–507, plain lids. Scale 1:3*

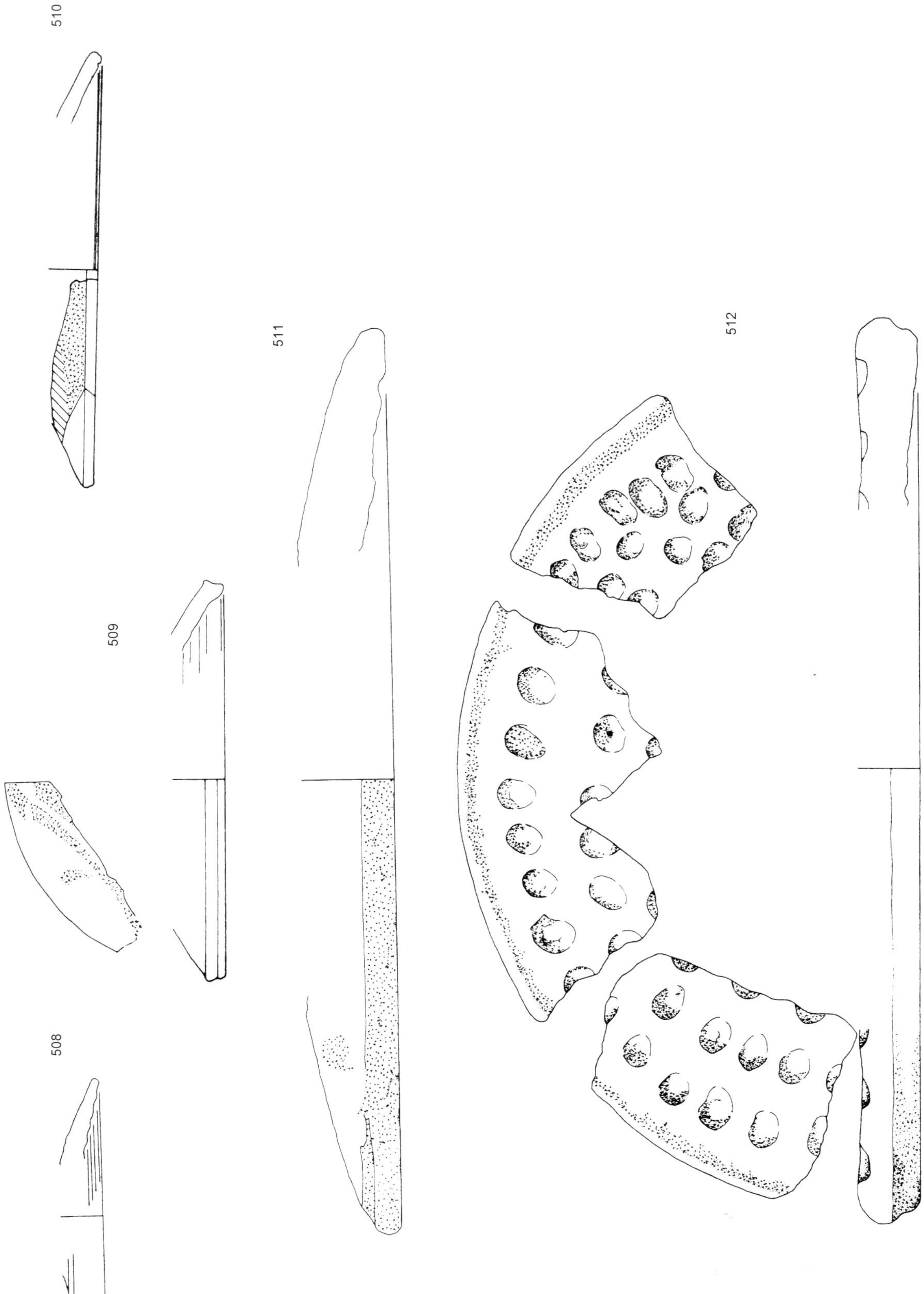


*Figure 2.84 Catalogue 508–512, painted or decorated lids. Scale 1:3*

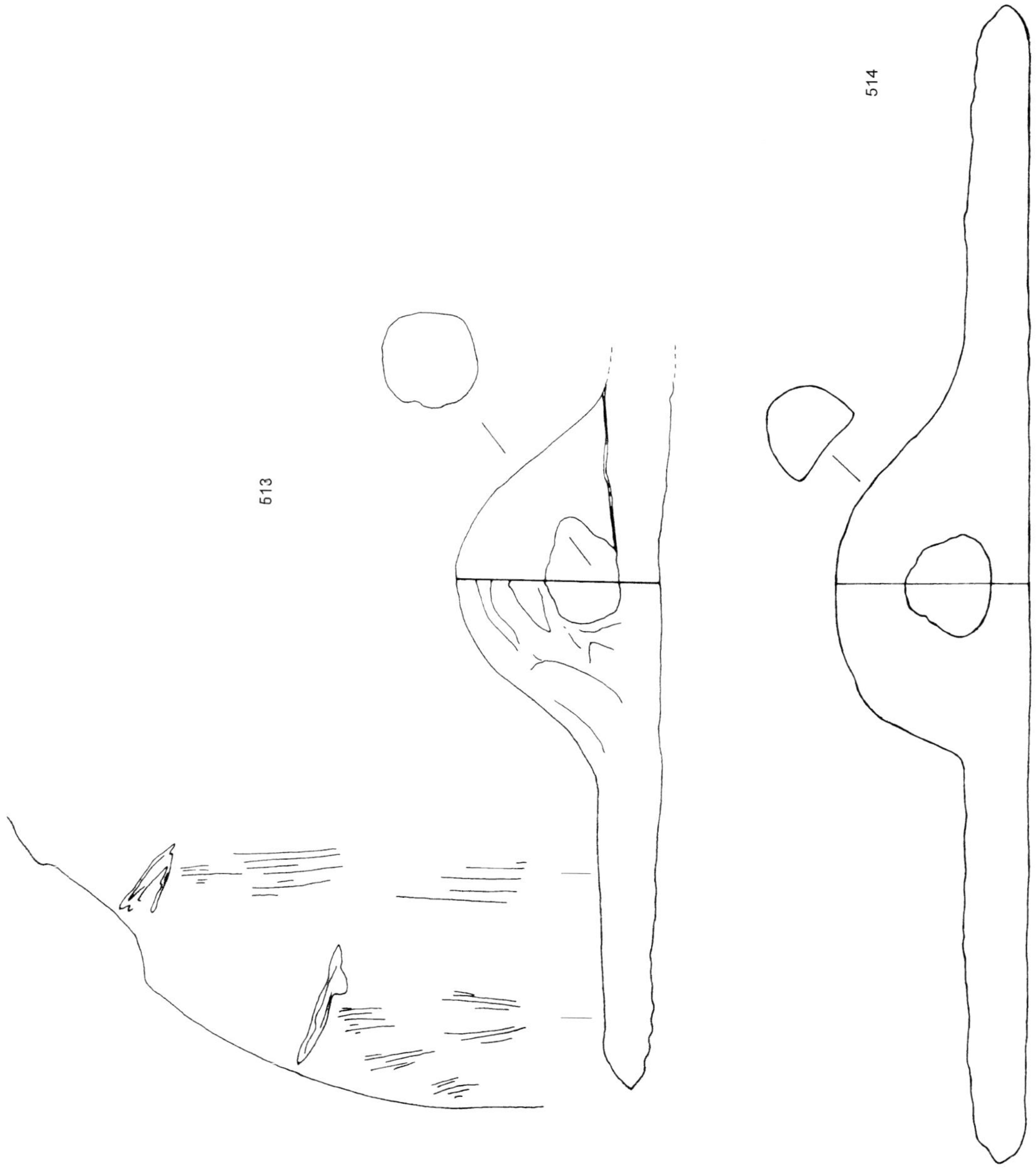


*Figure 2.85 Catalogue 513–514, painted or decorated lids. Scale 1:3*

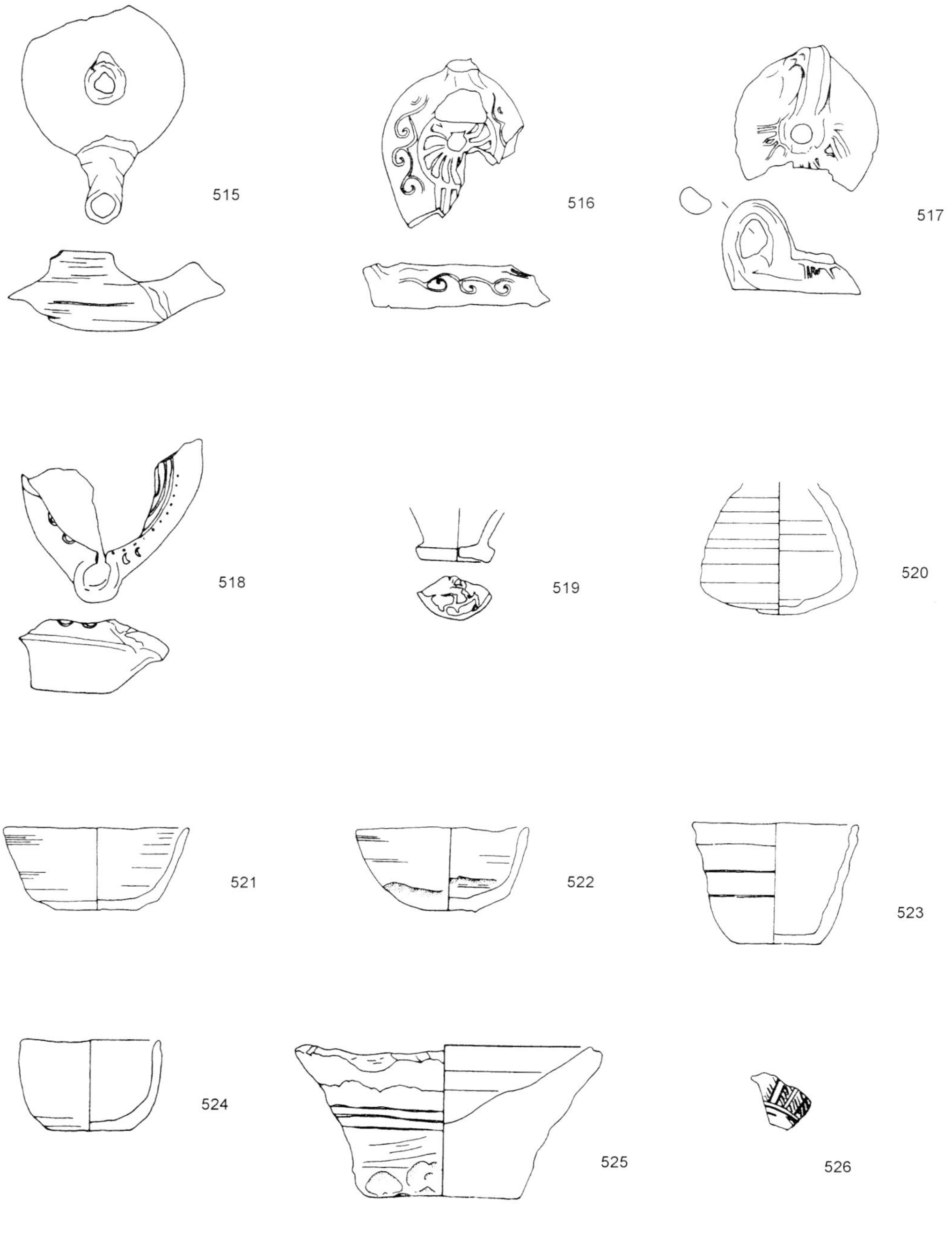


*Figure 2.86 Catalogue 515–526, lamps. Scale 1:3*

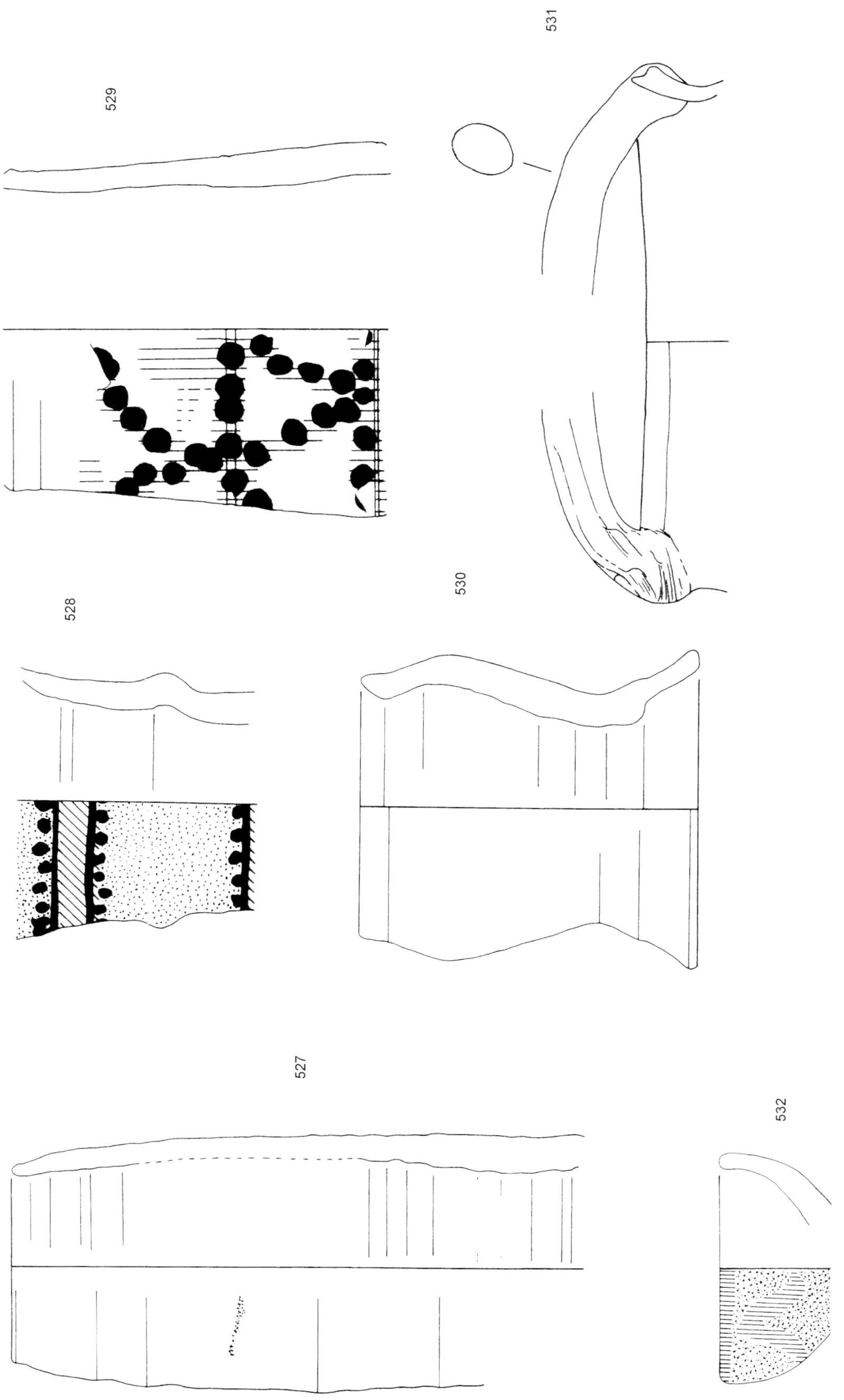


*Figure 2.87 Catalogue 527–532, miscellaneous vessels. Scale 1:3*

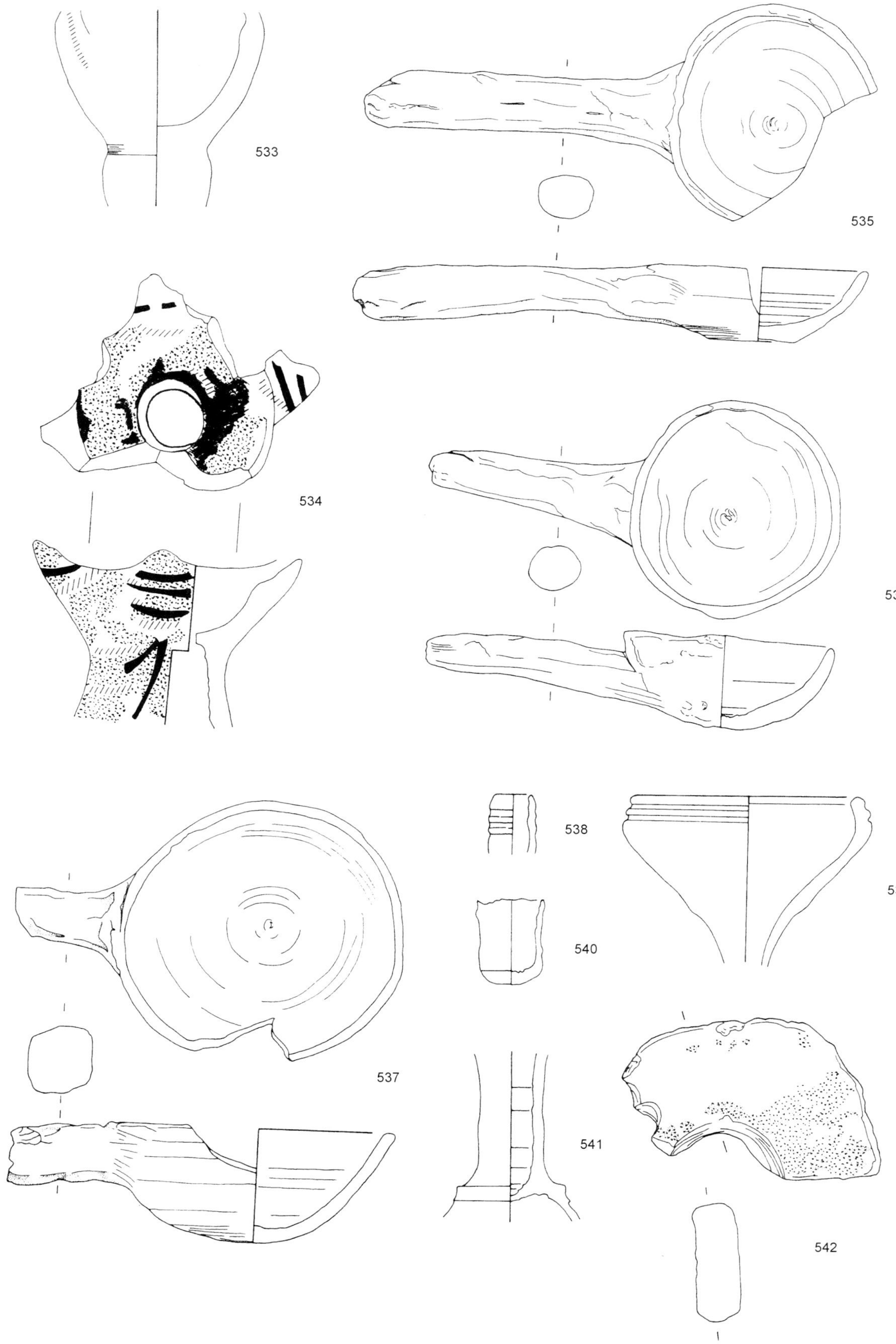


*Figure 2.88 Catalogue 533–542, miscellaneous vessels. Scale 1:3*

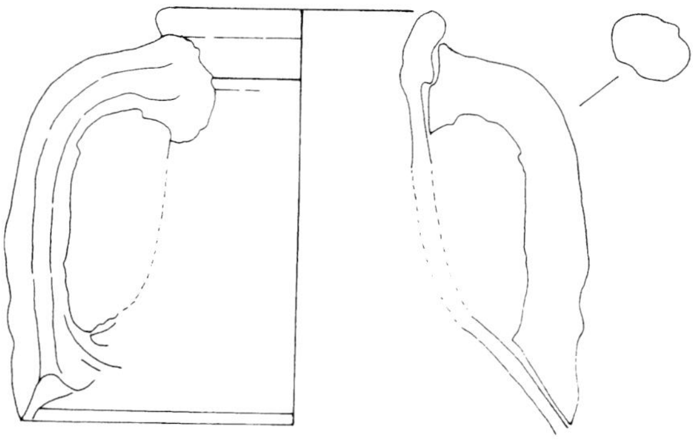

543

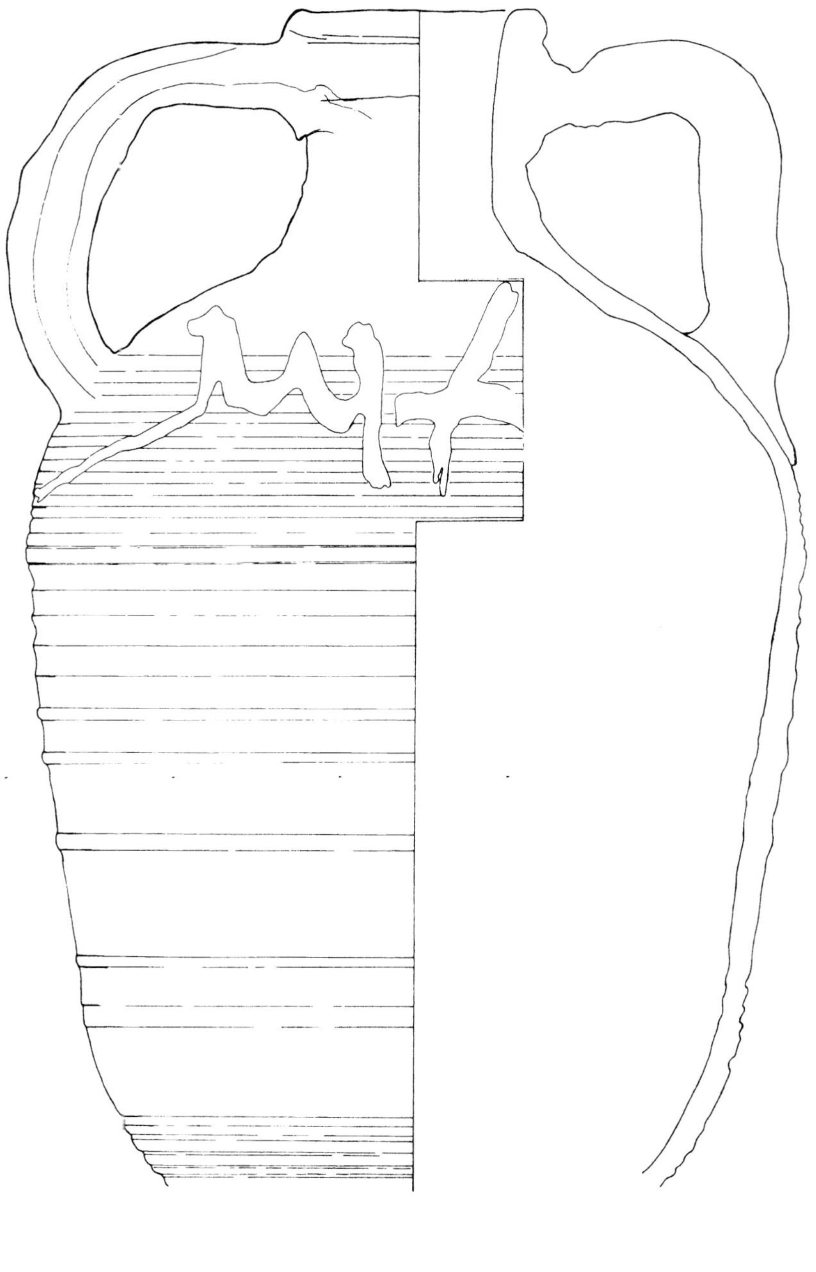

544

*Figure 2.89 Catalogue 543–544, amphorae. Scale 1:3 (543) and 1:6 (544)*

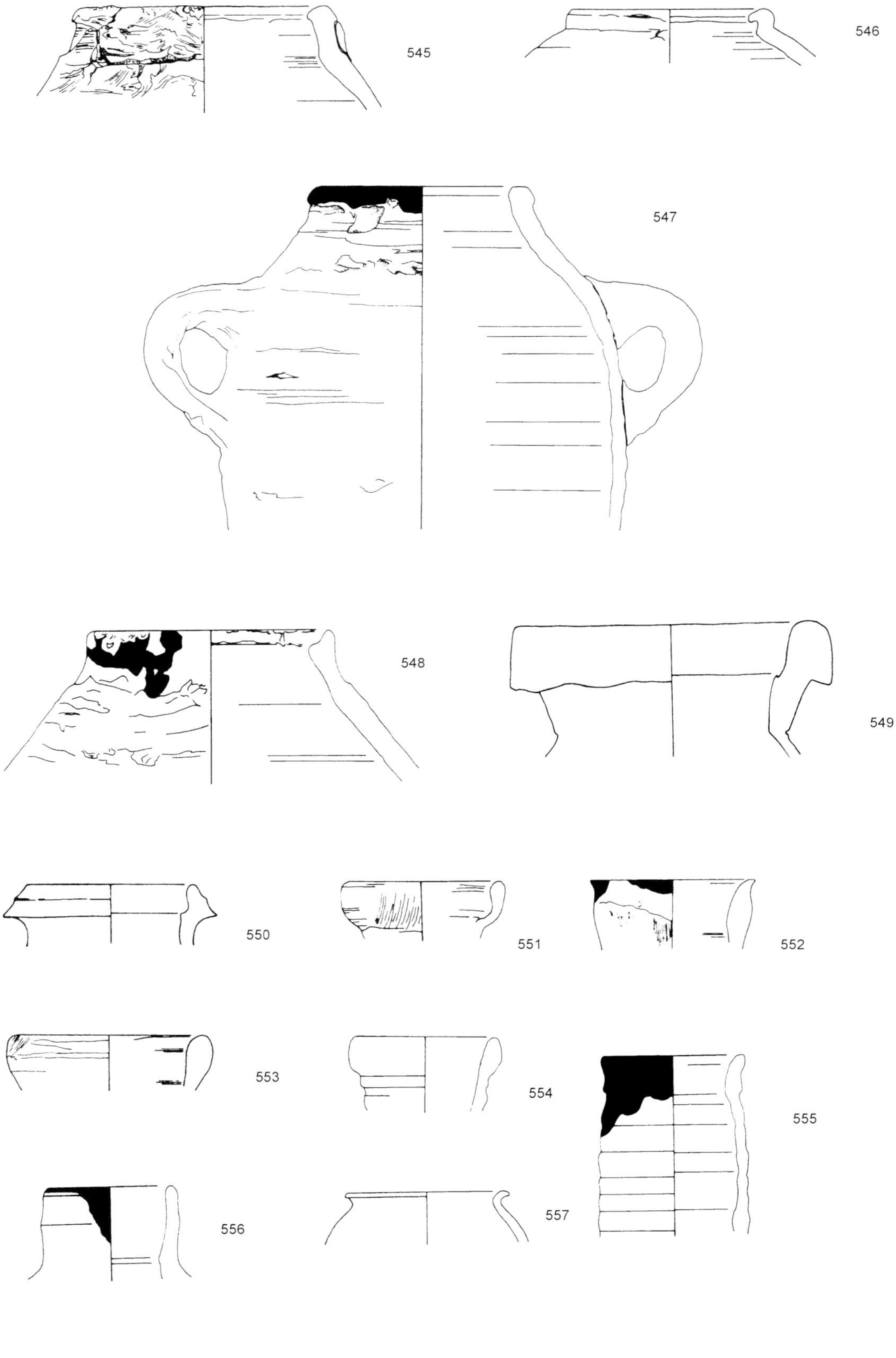


*Figure 2.90 Catalogue 545–555, amphorae. Scale 1:3*

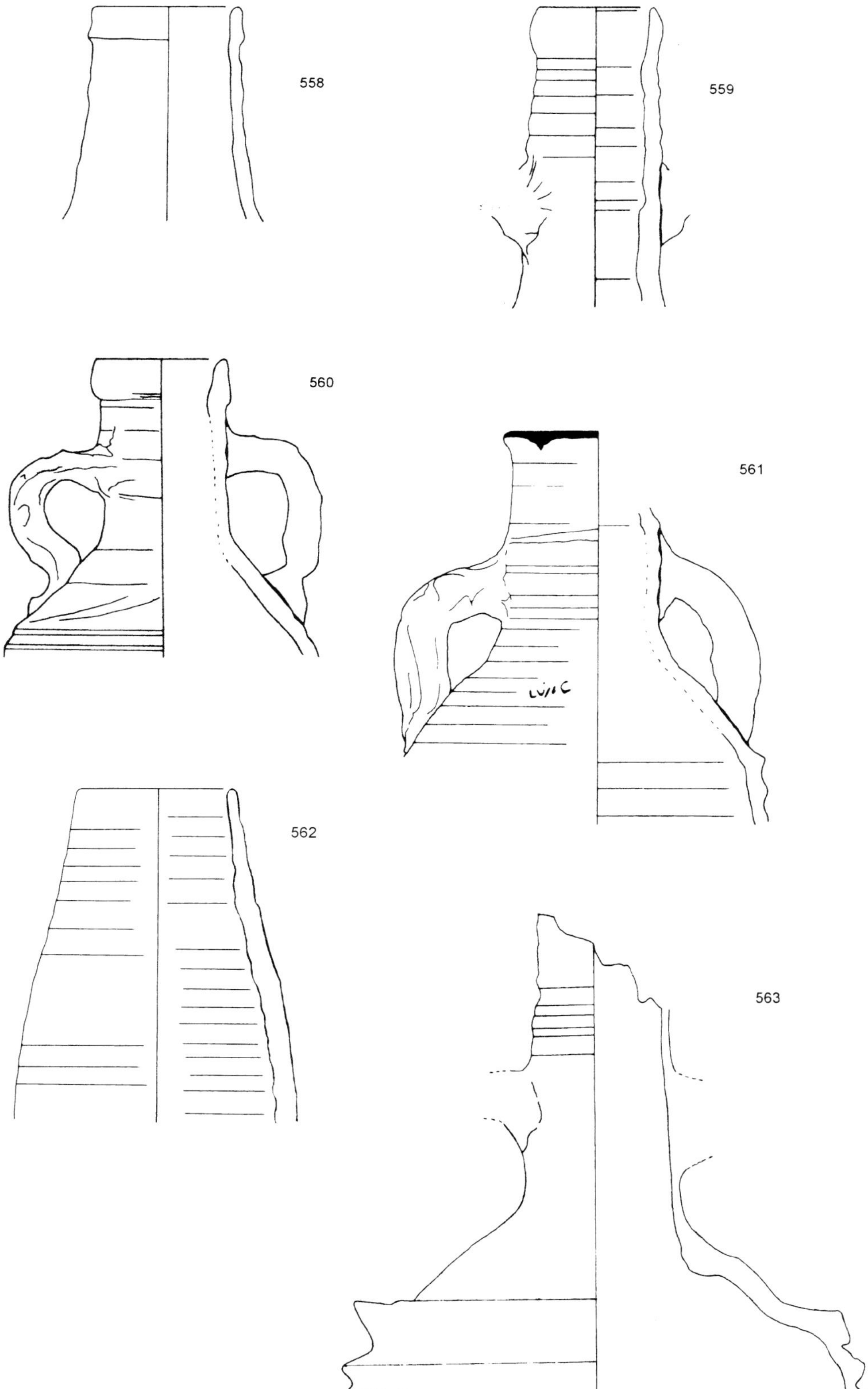


*Figure 2.91 Catalogue 558–563, amphorae. Scale 1:3*

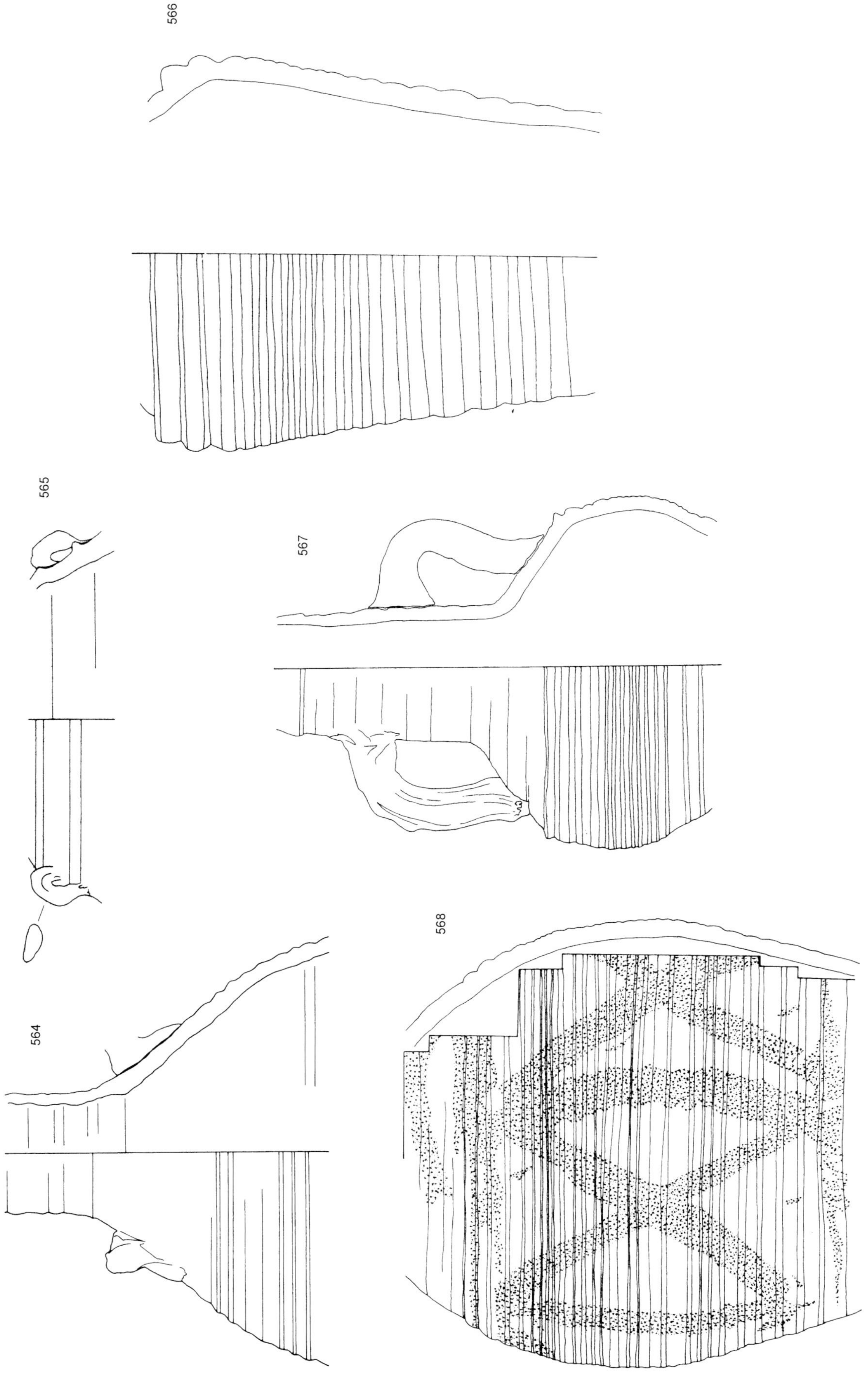


*Figure 2.92 Catalogue 564–568, amphorae. Scale 1:3*

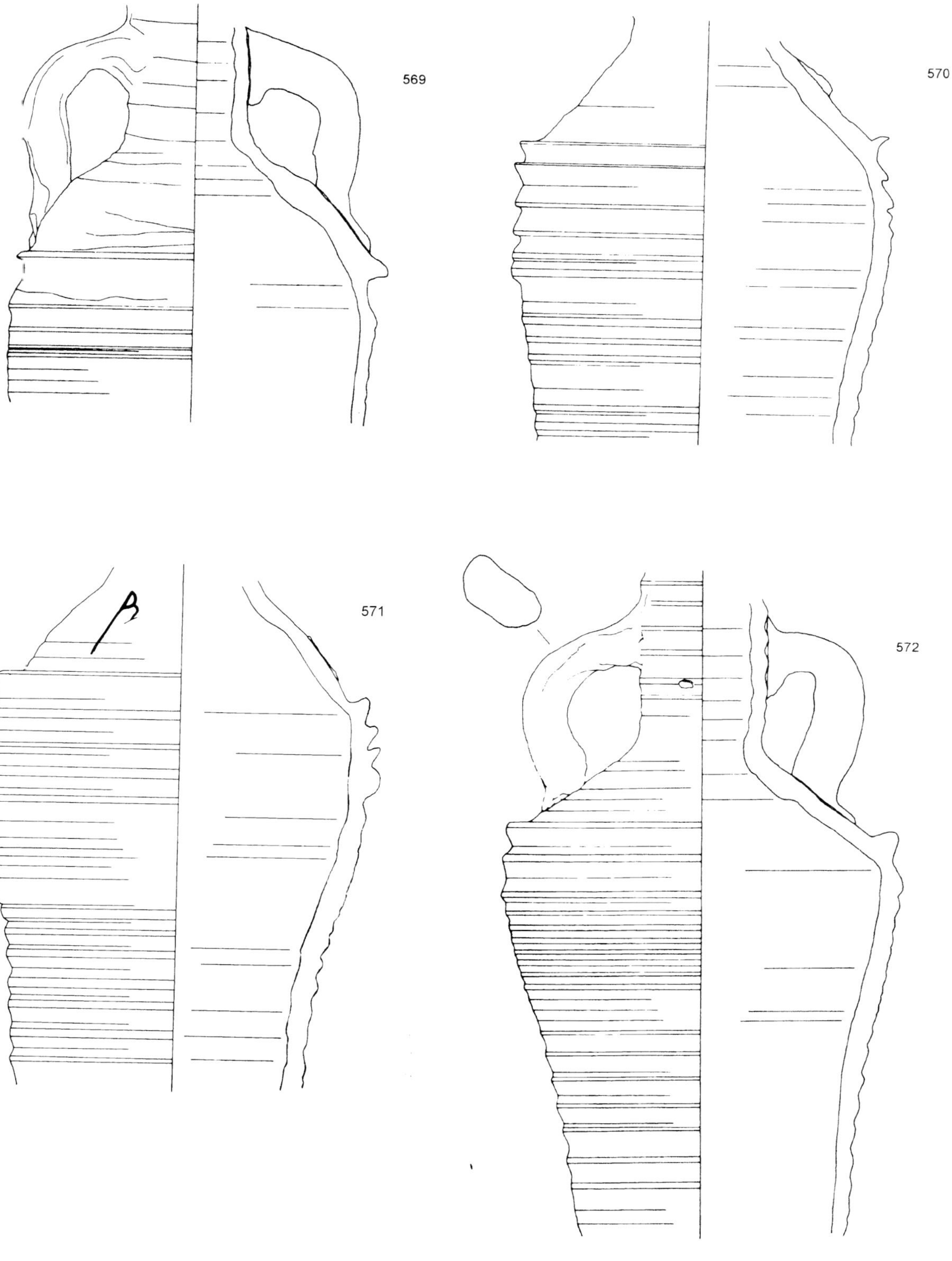


*Figure 2.93 Catalogue 569–572, amphorae. Scale 1:3*

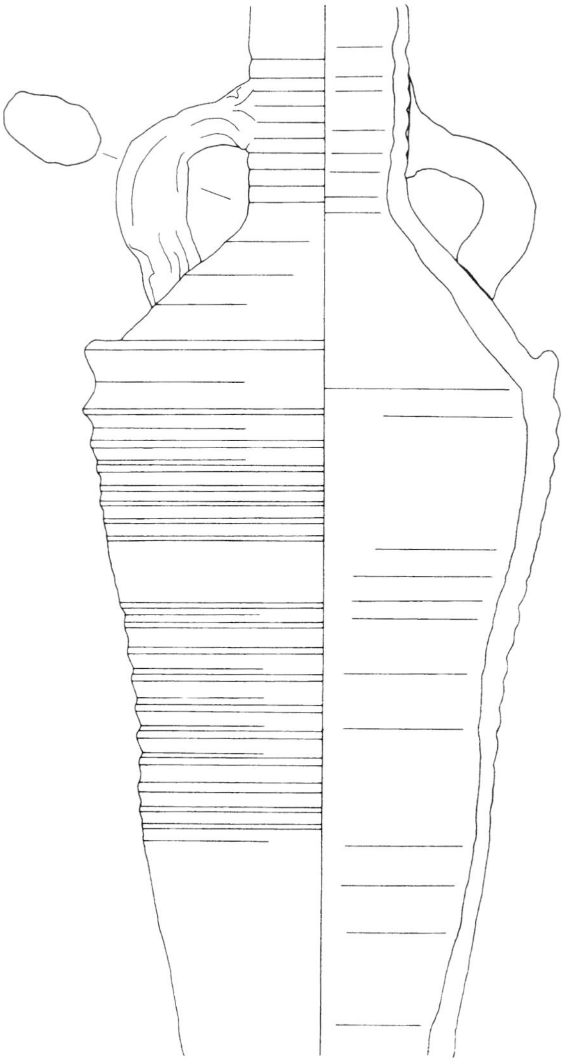

573

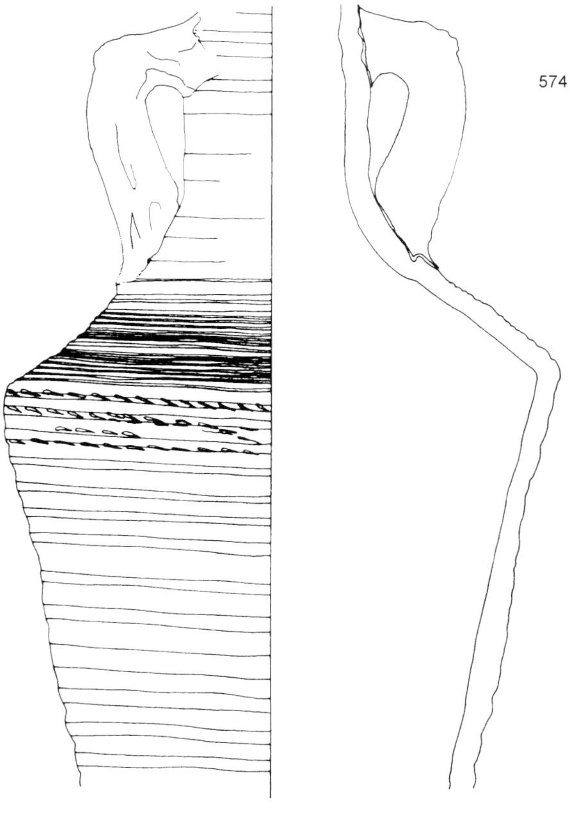

574

*Figure 2.94 Catalogue 573–574, amphorae. Scale 1:3*

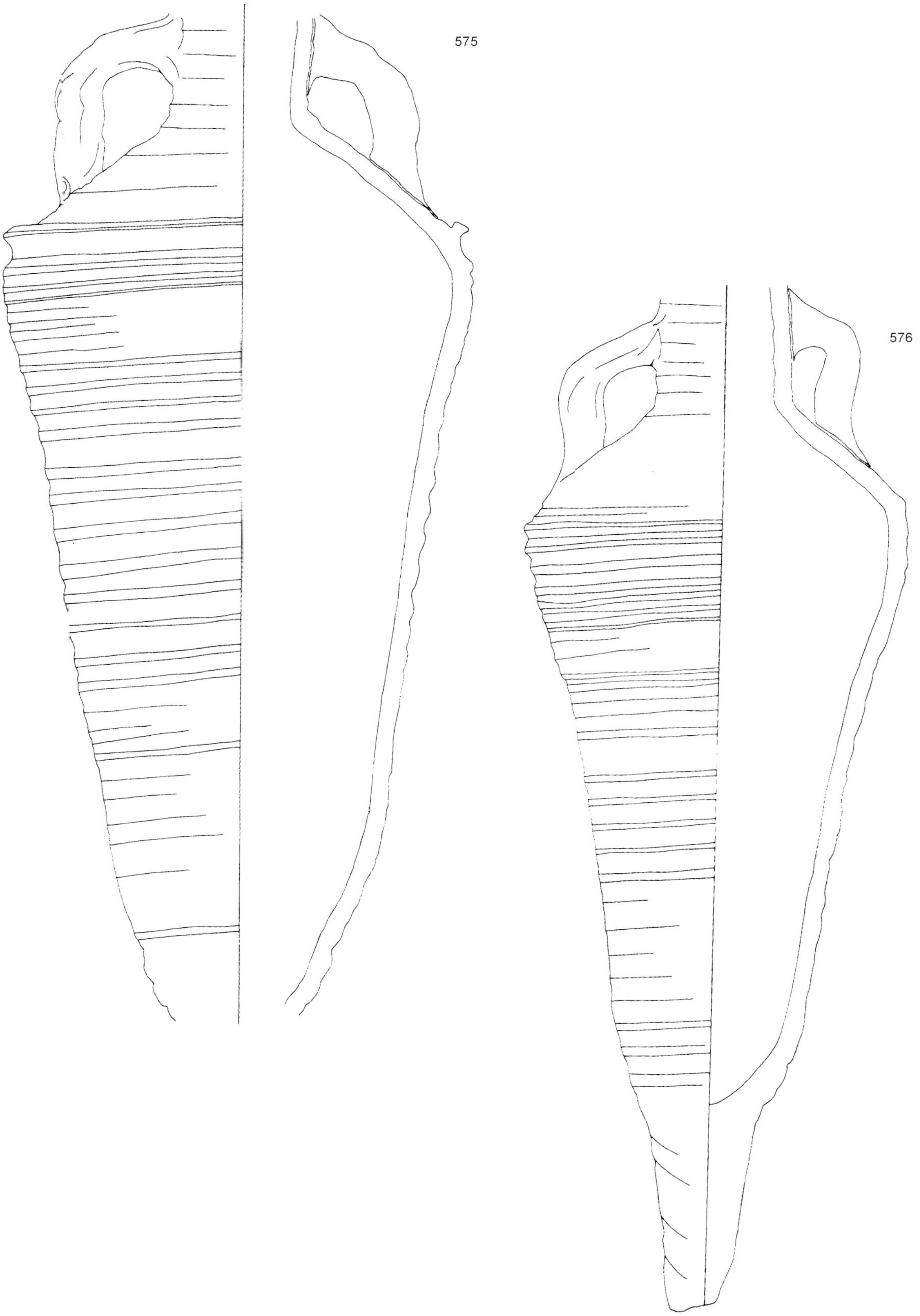


*Figure 2.95 Catalogue 575–576, amphorae. Scale 1:3*

577

578

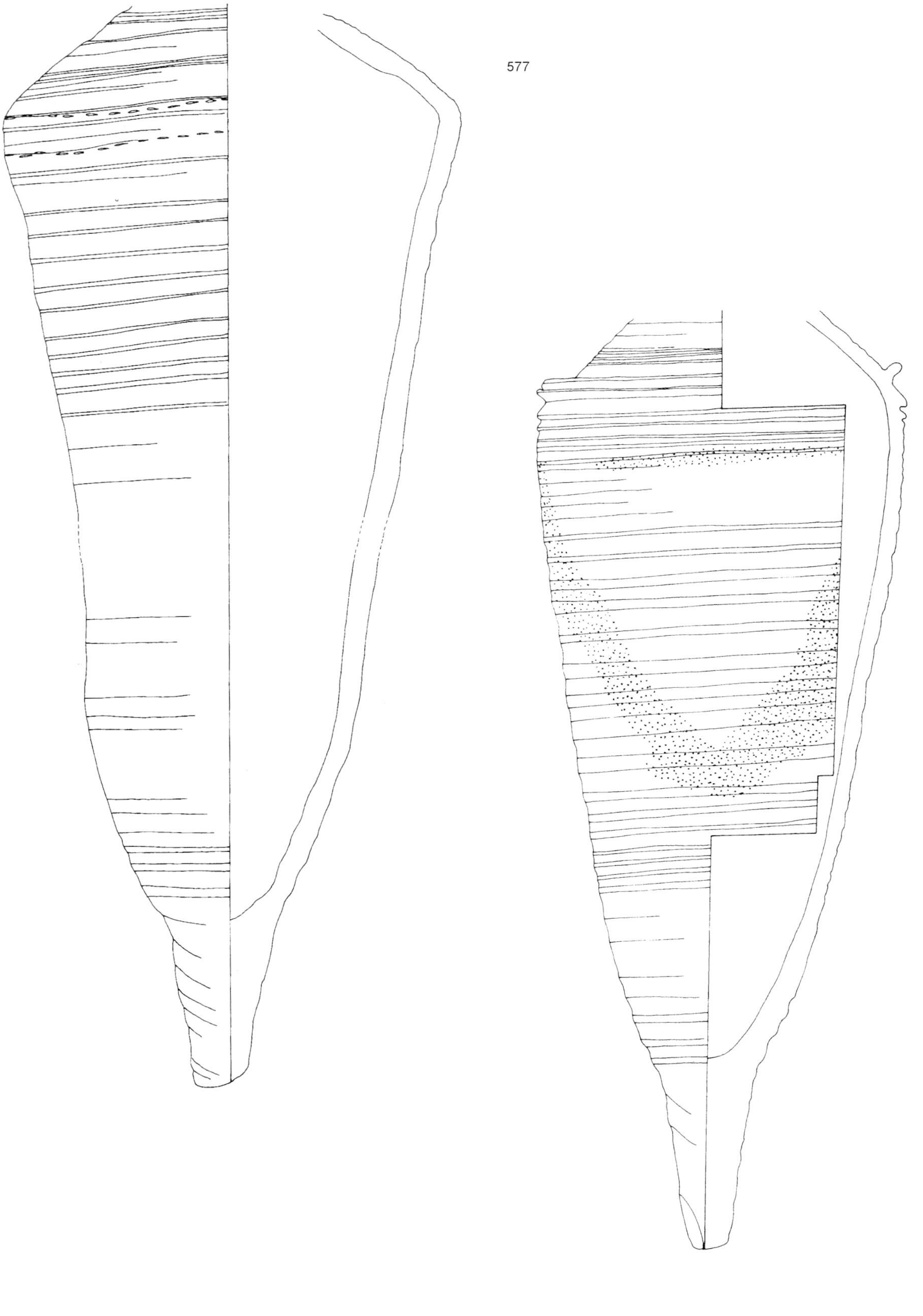

*Figure 2.96 Catalogue 577–578, amphorae. Scale 1:3*

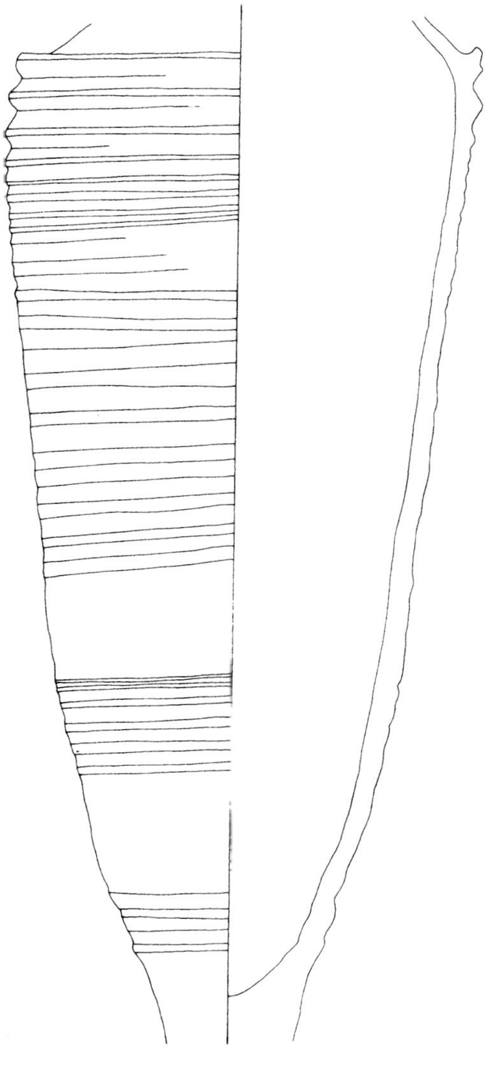

579

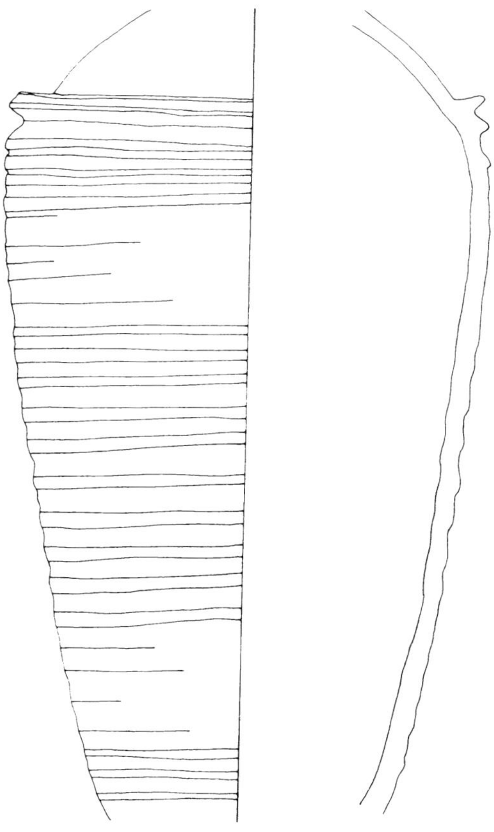

580

*Figure 2.97 Catalogue 579–580, amphorae. Scale 1:3*

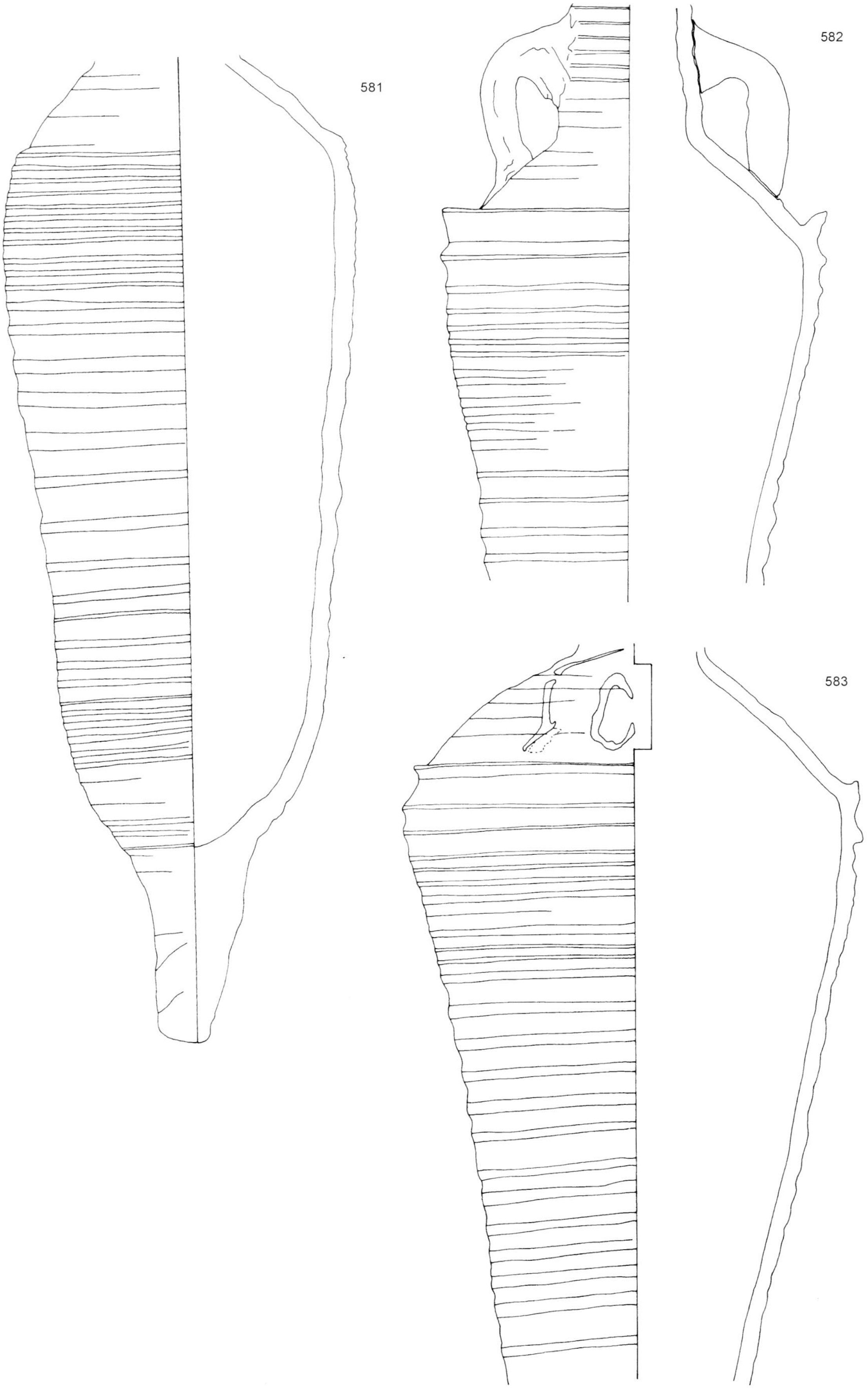


*Figure 2.98 Catalogue 581–583, amphorae. Scale 1:3*

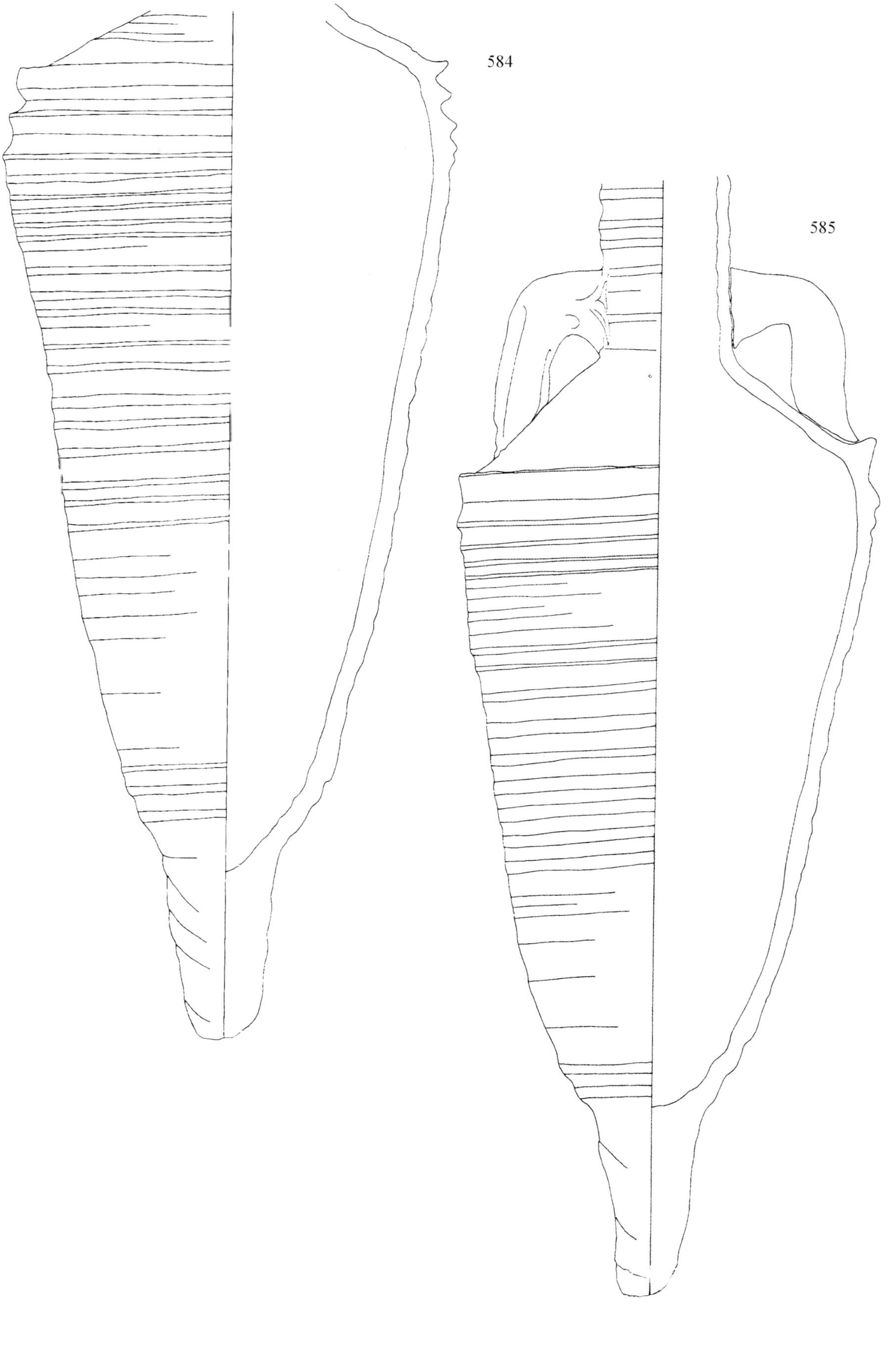


*Figure 2.99 Catalogue 584–585, amphorae. Scale 1:3*

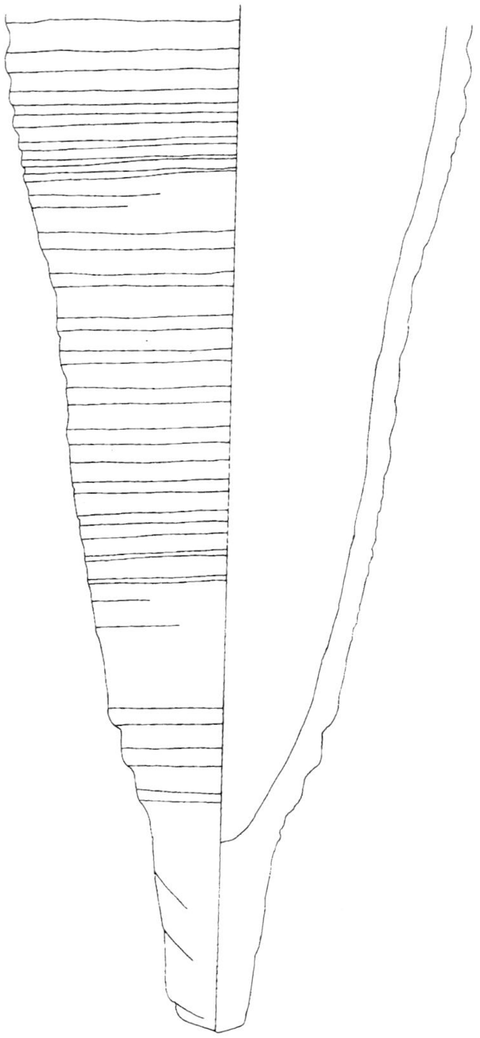

586

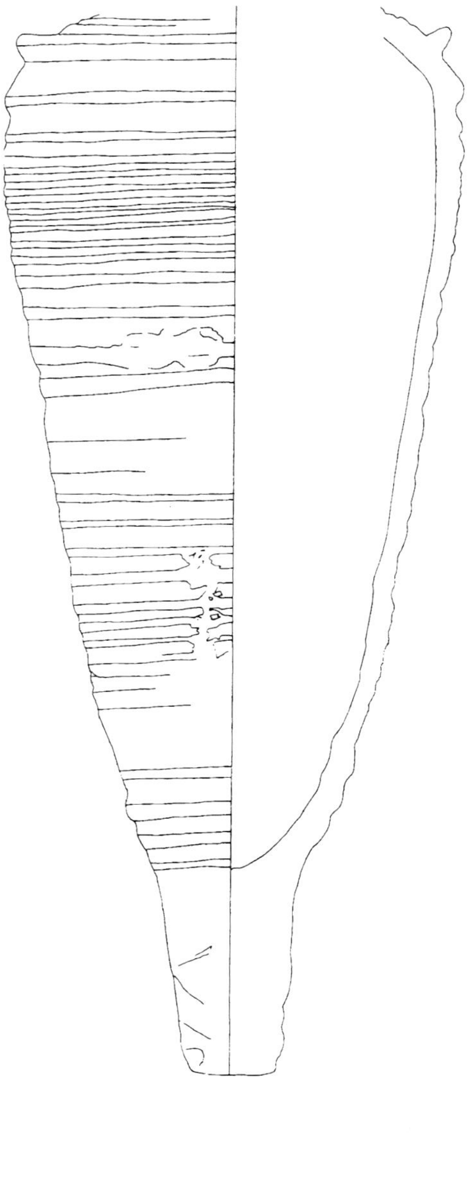

587

588

*Figure 2.100 Catalogue 586–588, amphorae. Scale 1:3*

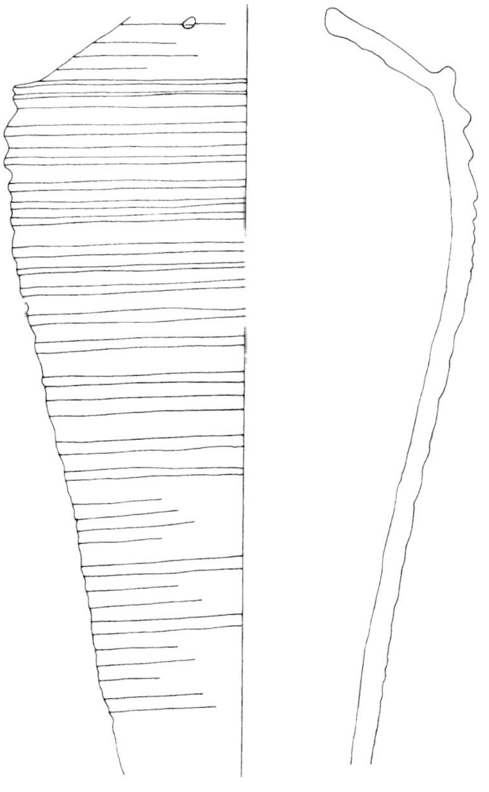

589

590

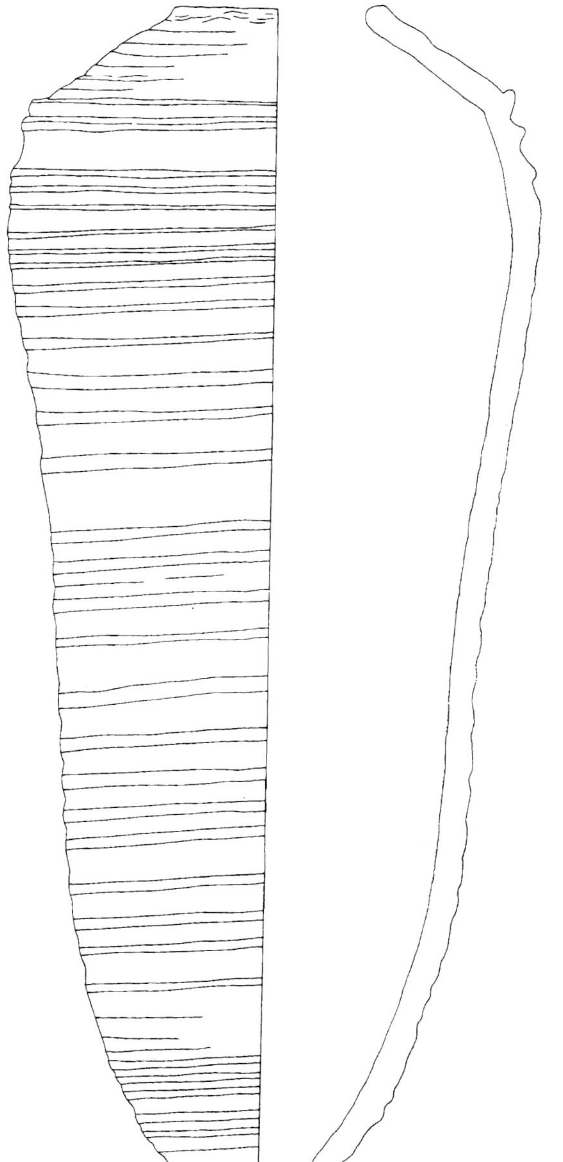

*Figure 2.101 Catalogue 589–590, amphorae. Scale 1:3*

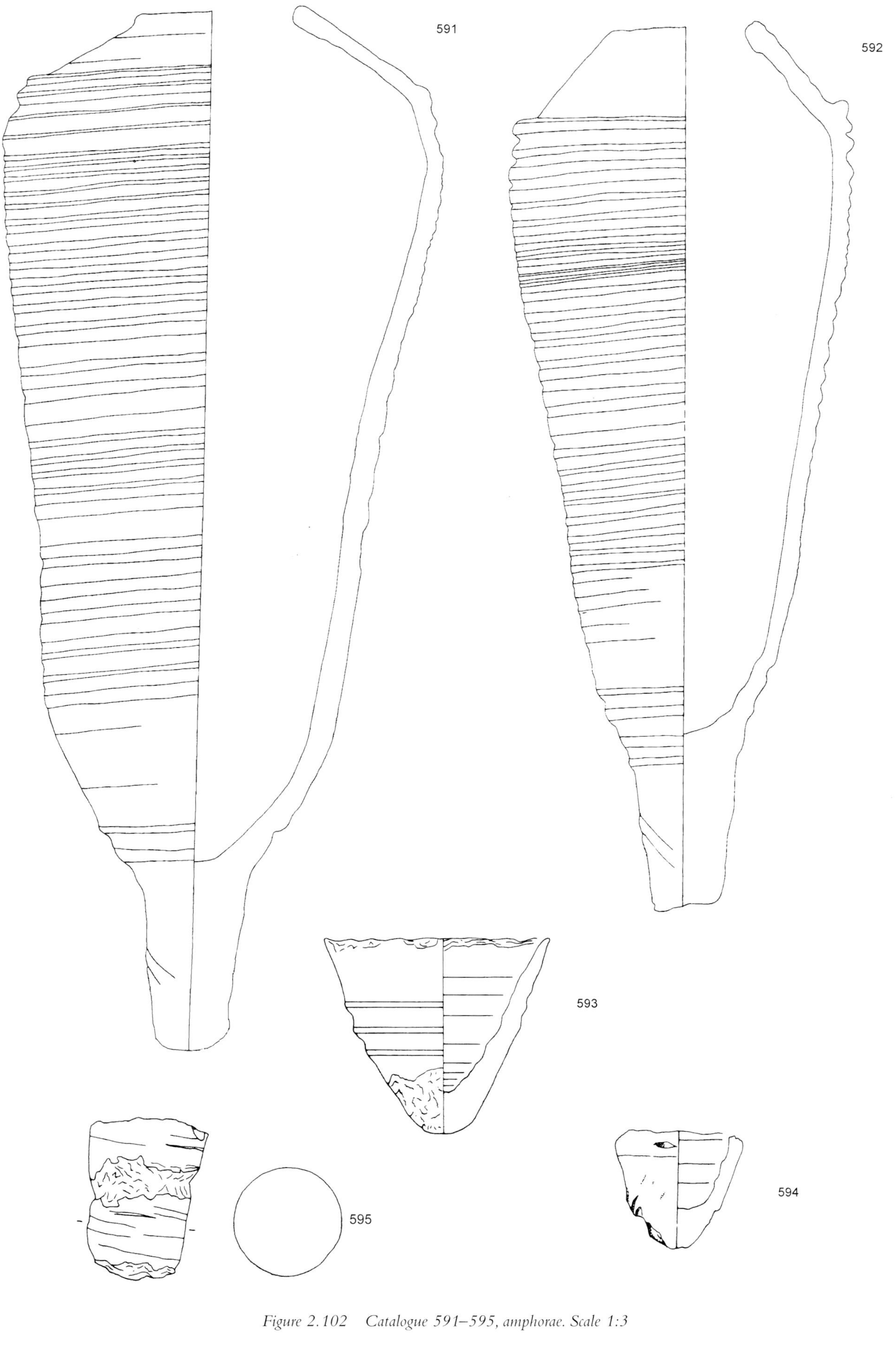


*Figure 2.102 Catalogue 591–595, amphorae. Scale 1:3*

# CHAPTER 3

# Distribution of Pottery and Glass at the Monastic Site of Kom el-Nana

by Jane Faiers and Gillian Pyke

This chapter investigates whether the pottery and glass finds can provide insights into the function or use of the various parts of the monastery. Statistical data was used to determine the frequency and proportion of different wares, both in general terms, following the artificial unit of excavation square, and in specific areas of the site, the function of which can be suggested by the preserved architectural remains and archaeological deposits.

This is, of necessity, a preliminary discussion, as the function of particular areas cannot always be identified with certainty and the site has not been fully excavated.

Excavation has shown that, in the 1,400 years or so since its abandonment, the structures comprising the monastery gradually filled with sand, and roofs and walls collapsed. Stone architectural elements and bricks were removed for reuse, the site repeatedly being pitted in search of building materials, and perhaps in the hope of finding more valuable treasures. The long post-occupation history of natural decline and human activity at the site has resulted in the movement of materials that presumably must include both pottery and glass. The question of how far these finds can be assumed to be in their original place of deposition has been addressed to some extent through the tracking of joining sherds of individual vessels. This has shown that some dispersal through unknown taphonomic agents can be expected (site map at fig. b).

## The monastic setting

The study of Egyptian monasticism is a dynamic discipline, the scope of which is extremely broad. For the purposes of this investigation, two considerations can be highlighted as particularly pertinent: the population of the monastery and their activities.

Documentary evidence suggested that thousands of monastics lived in Egypt during the period that Kom el-Nana was in use — that is, between approximately the mid fifth and mid seventh centuries AD (Faiers, 2005, 267).

St Jerome (*c.* AD 347–419/420) spoke of 50,000 monks at the annual meeting of Pachomian monks in around AD 400 (Jerome, 23.64) while Severus of el-Ashmunein in his *History of the Patriarchs* asserts that during the reign of Peter IV (AD 567–579) in the area of Alexandria "there were six hundred flourishing monasteries like beehives in their populousness" (Severus of el-Ashmunein, trans. Evetts, Ch.XIV). About 5,000 monks are said to have lived in and near Bawit during the sixth century AD (Clugnet, 1901, XVII). A population of male and female monastics lived under Shenoute's leadership during the late fourth to mid fifth centuries, according to Amélineau's manuscript of the Arabic *Life of St Shenoute* (Amélineau, 1889, 331, see also Bell, 1983, 5 and Layton, 2002, note 12). Similarly high numbers of monks offered in the fourth century *Historia Monachorum in Aegypto*, are discussed by Ward (1981, 20) who concludes that "all that can be counted on in this is that there were many monks and nuns to be seen in the places visited". Unfortunately, the fact that the Kom el-Nana monastery has not been completely excavated means that it is not possible to estimate the number of its inhabitants. However, the impression of a well-populated monastic landscape, as seen in the *Historia Monachorum* (Ward, 1981, 20), can be seen in the immediate vicinity of Kom el-Nana during its lifetime, perhaps extending as far north as the monastery of Deir el-Dik near the ancient city of Antinoopolis (Martin, 1971).

The structures within the excavated area at Kom el-Nana indicate that it was a walled monastery containing a number of architectural elements and activity areas including towers, a church, sleeping/living accommodation, refectories, associated kitchen and storage areas and bakeries. Other structures, such as housing for guests, workshops, mills and hospital facilities have not been identified among the excavated architectural remains at Kom el-Nana. Details of the social organisation of the Kom el-Nana monastery are uncertain, for example, whether the inhabitants followed the Rule of Pachomius (Amélineau, 1889), Shenoute (Layton, 2007; Goering, 2008), or another model entirely.

Many activities, and therefore by extension their architectural/spatial setting, were charged with meaning within a monastery. A significant example is food consumption, which was regulated both through the rules of the monastery and the ascetic agenda of each individual monastic (Layton, 2002, 25). Monastics following the Rule of Shenoute enjoyed a formal meal only at midday, with an optional evening meal of bread and condiments (Layton, 2008, 76, fig. 7.2).

Anderson's (1999, 79) examination of the rule of Pachomius and early Greek sources from Egypt shows that elsewhere there were two formal mealtimes: one at midday and the other at or about the ninth hour, and not all monks chose to attend both meals. Therefore, there may have been more monks present on site than that proposed by the numbers of vessels present, or the amount of space provided by the refectory, if there were in fact two 'sittings'. This may well have changed when the later refectory was built in the south-east sector later in the monastery's life.

The ceramic data suggests that the most popular sizes of cooking pots were 18 cm, 20 cm and 16 cm, in that order. These are the same sizes, in the same order, as were found in the numbers of cooking pots in the midden deposits (Faiers, 2005, 114). These also coincide with the most popular sizes made by Royal Worcester pottery today, i.e. 17 cm and 21.5 cm, that are intended to cater for up to four persons and may well have been the sizes most easily handled when cooking in a reasonably small space.

## The architectural setting

In order to contribute anything to the understanding of the monastery, the distribution of the pottery and glass at Kom el-Nana must be understood within its architectural and archaeological context. While it is not the intention of this discussion to present the archaeological findings of the project, a brief overview is needed.

A number of architectural elements were identified during the course of the excavations (Kemp, 2000, 12–13), all of which are comparable to examples at other published monasteries. There are, however, a number of architectural idiosyncrasies that seem to be peculiar to Kom el-Nana, highlighting the danger of assuming too much conformity between monasteries, particularly given the small number that have been scientifically excavated.

The primary example of this is the three towers, one of which is not yet excavated, located within the walled enclosure of the Kom el-Nana monastery. Single towers are a well-attested feature of walled monasteries, often accessed, as in the case of the south-east tower at Kom el-Nana, via a separate staircase tower (Grossman, 1991, 1395–6). While the function of these multi-storey buildings is thought to have been primarily defensive (Grossman, 1991, 1395–6), it seems unlikely that they would not be used for other purposes, such as storage or accommodation. The significance of the presence of multiple towers at Kom el-Nana is not easily explained, but might relate to the combination of defensive and non-defensive functions, perhaps providing a method of accommodating additional monks or visitors.

A small area of ovens or kilns (**Area 5**, squares **Z52** and **Y52**) to the north of the north-east tower could be industrial or for small-scale food production (Anonymous, 1994, viii (G9); Smith, 2003, figs 3.5, 3.8, 3.23 and 3.36). There are also hearths in various places over the site, presumably needed for heating, i.e. **Area 2** in the south-east sector and **Areas 2, 3, 5, 8** and **9** in the north-east sector.

The presence of the three towers might appear to indicate a need for defence against attack but this is negated by the significantly less substantial enclosure wall (fig. 3.1) which delimits the area of the monastery without either the thickness or probable height that would characterise a defensive construction. The wall perhaps is there merely to emphasise the separation between the monks and the outside world and the towers provide extra accommodation and storage.

Immediately to the south and east of the north-east tower is an open courtyard with benches along its walls for seating and informal inscriptions (Pyke et al., in preparation) on the walls indicating that the area was perhaps a public space. This space separates the church, to its south west, from the north-east sector, which seems to be concerned with food preparation, amongst other functions.

Leading off the north-east corner of this space is an east–west covered corridor giving access to the north-east sector of the monastery. The north-east sector includes a refectory, kitchen (**Area 2**), and storage areas (**Area 3**, for the ceramic under-floor component, for which see Chapter 4) and **Area 4,** as well as to a niched room that might have acted as a reception room for visitors (**Area 6**). A second corridor, this one running north–south, is located to the east of this complex of rooms, separating it from the animal pens and possible gatehouse and/or lookout point adjacent to the east wall of the monastery. This corridor is also host to numerous inscriptions (Pyke et al., in preparation).

Two possible refectories have been identified, one of which is located immediately adjacent to the cooking and storage area in the north-east sector of the monastery (north-east sector, **Area 1**). The other is in the south-east sector of the monastery where it is associated with the south-east tower (south-east sector, **Area 3**). It is not clear whether both refectories were in use at the same time or if one superseded the other. The north-east refectory room would be able to seat around 20 monks. Possible correlations between size of refectory, size of monastery and number of monks, therefore, cannot easily be addressed.

In addition to rooms for the storage needs of the population of the monastery during the year, there might have been storerooms set aside for the produce to be bartered, as at Wadi Sarga (Crum and Bell, 1922) where a carpenter is to be paid in wine, fodder, corn, barley, a sack-cloth (garment) and a pair of sandals (Crum and Bell, 1922, text 161) or alternatively, given away, a small *lahe* of wine to Irene the nun (Crum and Bell, 1922, text 168). Taxes such as *demosion* payments on agricultural land were required to be paid in gold (Clackson, 2005, 245–6, Ostracon 1). Money is rarely mentioned in the Wadi Sarga texts and is sometimes paid back 'in kind', as with a certain Brother Germanus who needs a *solidus* (a coin struck at the rate of 72 from a Roman pound of pure gold, each coin weighing 24 Roman/Greek carats, or about 4.5 grams of gold per coin), for which he will repay the loan with cheese instead of gold (Crum and Bell, 1922, text 166).

Such large amounts of produce would need a great deal of storage space as shown at the Monastery of St. Simeon at Aswan (Bagnall, 1993, pl. 11). Ostraca at Bawit show large amounts of cereals (Boud'hors, 2004, 27–45), grain (Boud'hors, 2004, 16–24) and wine (Boud'hors, 2004, 27–45) arriving, together with other goods including fish in brine and palm fibres (Boud'hors, 2004, 46–49).

The monastery, and indeed the monks personally, may have been an integrated part of the nearby population, having ownership and cultivation of land in the vicinity, and perhaps friends and relations in the surrounding area and elsewhere.

Monastics do not appear to have had to relinquish ownership of property on entering a monastery. Bagnall (2003, 298) cites a text showing a *coenobitic* nun lending funds for repayment with 2,400 wine jars. There was a continual flow of goods to and from any monastery. Visitors, or at least large numbers of visitors, appear to have presented a problem at times (Bagnall, 1993, 299) or may have provided an opportunity for the miraculous, such as the provision of bread during a famine (Besa, *Life of Shenoute* (trans. D.N. Bell), 27–8).

At harvest time, some monks hired themselves out as labourers in the fields (Rousseau, 1985, 155). They also carried out work in the monastery for both the upkeep of the monastery itself and for supply to the outside world. Palladius mentions that monks included tailors, metalworkers, carpenters, camel drivers, fullers, gardeners, smiths, bakers, basket makers, shoemakers and copyists (Rousseau, 1985, 82). This is certainly borne out by the texts from Wadi Sarga which mentions Cyriacus, a monk, as a camel-herd (Crum and Bell, 1922, text 373), Brother Germanus a carpenter (Crum and Bell, 1922, text 166) and lists objects of iron, including a large bar and a measure of iron (Crum and Bell, 1922, text 143), and an account of a vegetable garden for the large part of a month (Crum and Bell, 1922, text 124).

Documentary evidence from the White Monastery shows that within Shenoute's Federation at least, professional medical care was provided for both the monastic and non-monastic communities (Crislip, 2008, 21–30). At Kom el-Nana there is also archaeobotanical evidence for the presence of plants that might have been grown for medicinal use, including the opium poppy (Smith, 2003, 80). Another somewhat dubious cure of goat gall and honey is also mentioned at Wadi Sarga (Crum and Bell, 1922, text 21).

Excavation at Kom el-Nana also revealed animal bones of beef, pork, sheep and goat, much of which was heavily fragmented and thus not identifiable (Luff, 2007, 165). Of the 166 identifiable samples, 43.4 per cent belonged to sheep/goat, 34.3 per cent to pig and 22.3 per cent cattle (Luff, 2007, 165). Much of the mammal remains were found in alley and floor deposits, whilst the middens contained most of the bird and fish bone. If the bones of identifiable mammal, fish, bird and molluscs are added together the mammal bone only manages 5.1 per cent against 91.5 per cent fish, with birds and molluscs coming a poor third and fourth at 1.8 per cent and 1.6 per cent respectively, out of a sample of 3,284 items (Luff, 2007,165). This may indicate the keeping of some animals for food, and if not actively engaging in fishing expeditions, the monks were acquiring fish from the local population (possible fishing weights were among finds, A. Cornwell, 2001, personal communication).

There is also the interesting proposition that the fish

remains found at Kom el-Nana (Luff and Bailey, 2003, 103) may be the residue of production or storage of pickled fish (*salsamenta*), as at the monastery of Bawit (Van Neer et al., 2007, 153; Luff, 2007, 161–174). See Chapter 2, nos 589–592 for amphorae which may have been reused for this purpose.

## Distribution of pottery and glass

This analysis used several methods in order to investigate various aspects of the distribution of the pottery and glass. The main questions to be addressed are spatial and functional in nature. Where is the pottery and/or glass concentrated (or absent) and how can this be explained? Can a functional explanation be suggested, such as the use of sherds as fill of a casemate or the presence of a pottery fill deposit? More specific functional questions were examined typologically, investigating the distribution of the different vessel types. Can concentrations of specific vessel types be distinguished? Are these types associated with particular activities, such as cooking or storage? Finally, the findings were drawn together to give an overview of what the distribution of the pottery and glass can tell us about activities at the monastery.

Two methods were used to quantify the ceramic and glass material. The first combines the number of rims, bases and handles (RBH), essentially giving a total number of diagnostic sherds. This can be used for gross quantification, for example giving the total RBH for a square or deposit, or more sensitively to compare the quantity of specific types within a deposit. Some caution must be exercised in this type of comparison as it does not take into account whether specific types habitually have no handles, or have a rim likely to break into many pieces and cannot be used to estimate the number of examples of each vessel type present. Pottery numbers have been represented by rims, bases and handles in the tables, but only rims and bases in calculating the estimated numbers of vessels present.

Quantification of the frequency of each vessel type used the Estimated Vessel Equivalent (EVE), based on the calculation of *rim per cent + base per cent, divided by two* (Orton, 1980, 166). This simple method is a useful tool for comparing the number of vessels of each type present in each area. It is, however, problematic in that it does not take account of the relative fragility of vessels, nor the fact that, especially in the case of M3 amphorae, they might remain in use long after the rim had been lost and the handles which do remain are not counted. Numbers can also be skewed by condition and find site of the pottery, whether abraded or worn, or in situ and undisturbed. EVE at least gives an idea of the amounts of the various forms in each area so that these can be compared. The 'Other' category at the end of the tables also has an EVE value reflecting the number of different types present.

In order to examine the distribution of pottery and glass within specific structures and complexes, the excavated area of the site was divided into five 'sectors': south-east (comprising the south tower and adjacent area), north-west, north-east tower (including the paved courtyard), the north-east (comprising the complex of rooms, corridors and activity areas) and the church. Within the sectors, 'areas' were distinguished based on the architectural elements and archaeological deposits. These areas are numbered sequentially within each sector.

## Square-by-square analysis

The analysis began with a square-by-square examination of the total number of RBH. The data were divided into numerical groups, and spatially by sector, to gain a sense of the overall distribution of ceramic material and areas of concentration that should be investigated in detail. The majority of squares contained between 100 and 200 RBH, which can be taken as the average for the concentration of sherds across the site. This interpretation is supported by the fact that this level of concentration is seen in all the excavated sectors. The concentration of RBH is quite high throughout the north-east sector, which might mean that it is the focus of activities related to the use of ceramics. The variable concentrations in different parts of this sector can be seen as a gross indicator that different activities are associated with specific areas, as suggested by the architectural remains.

The similarly high concentration of sherds in two squares of the north-east tower sector might also indicate an activity in which ceramics were used, but could also represent the discarding of sherds. The extremely high concentration of RBH in square **Z36** is significantly greater than both the average quantity which is present in the other squares in this area, and that probably relating to the use of ceramics in the north-east sectors. The quantity of sherds in this square initially suggested that this should be interpreted as a midden deposit, but further investigation showed that an architectural use is indicated (see below).

The square-by-square analysis of the glass shows that glass RBH is significantly less frequent than pottery RBH, the average glass RBH over the whole site can be proposed to be only 1–5 RBH. The pattern of concentrations generally follows that of the pottery, with the greatest overall quantity found in the north-east and north-east tower sectors, where they are presumably again associated with specific activities, which need not be the same as those for which the pottery was used.

## Detailed sector-by-sector analysis

The division of the excavated areas of the site into sectors allows the more detailed examination of the distribution of the pottery and glass, which may indicate areas of similar use and perhaps suggest what function that particular part of the site served.

### The south-east sector

This sector comprises the south-east tower and associated structures, including the main tower, **Area 1 (Z36)**; a smaller tower, **Area 2** (**AB36**), probably acting as the staircase tower giving access to the main tower; a long rectangular room that was possibly a refectory, **Area 3** (**AB24** and **AB35**); and a room north of the staircase tower, **Area 4** (**AA37**).

The total pottery RBH of 2,033 for this sector gives it 17 per cent of the site total, while the total glass RBH is 62, which is 11.7 per cent of the site total.

*South-east sector, main tower (Area 1)*

The largest concentration of pottery within this sector, accounting for 78.8 per cent of the total sector RBH, was found within the large square tower, **Area 1** (**Z36**). The lower-most deposits within the tower consist of a considerable quantity of pottery used as a casemate fill for construction of the base of the tower, comprising 34.3 per cent of the pottery in **Z36** and 55 EVE, the latter being the fifth largest number of vessels recorded on site. The casemate fill also contained 39 per cent of the total amphorae from this sector and nearly nine per cent of the site amphora total.

Three vessels in this deposit can be dated: an African Red Slipware (ARS) sherd of Hayes, Form 76.3, AD 425–475; no. 53 in this volume (Chapter 2), AD 400–500; and no. 110 in this volume (Chapter 2), AD 550–625. Sherds from the upper part of the casemate fill include types of slightly later date (no. 113, dated fifth to eighth century AD, and no. 55 (Chapter 2), sixth to seventh century AD). The latest of these sherds gives a *terminus post quem* for the deposition of the casemate fill that suggests that this part of the site

*Figure 3.1 Plan of the south-east sector*

was constructed when the monastery was already functioning, possibly towards the later part of its life.

The other significant feature of the south-east sector is a post-abandonment pit cut through the collapsed mudbrick structure of the tower and into the casemate fill. This pit accounted for 18 per cent of the sector pottery RBH and 4.9 per cent of the site total RBH, while the collapse deposits contained 8.2 per cent of the sector total RBH and 1.2 per cent of the site total RBH.

A wide range of forms is represented in the **Z36** deposits, but interestingly these forms do not include any colanders. They are dominated by the locally produced M3 amphorae and these are accompanied by a much smaller quantity of imported N1, N9 and N10 amphorae. The finewares include African Red Slipware (ARS) imported from Tunisia, wares from Aswan and those that are locally produced. The coarsewares comprise a variety of vessel types for food preparation, consumption and storage. Other noteworthy forms include possible strainers (Faiers, 2005, nos 424–426) and vessels intended for lighting and heating.

The glass from the large square tower comprises 53 per cent of the glass RBH for this sector. The upper part of the casemate deposit contained seven glass RBH which included two lamp bases, a jar, flagon and goblet rim and two platter rims.

*South-east sector, staircase tower (Area 2)— 5.6 per cent of the sector total RBH and 0.8 per cent of the site total RBH*

The second, smaller keep located to the south-east of the main structure is probably a staircase tower giving access to the main keep. The architectural association between the two towers argues that they were in use at the same time. The deep, ashy deposit on the ground floor of the staircase tower was probably a hearth or fireplace. It contained sizeable sherds, only seven of which were diagnostics, and these were all M3 amphora RBH: three bases and four handles. Relatively little pottery was found in this area, the total of 97 RBH represents five per cent of the total pottery RBH for this sector. Only 27 of these RBH were from occupation deposits with the other 70 RBH being from mudbrick collapse and sandy debris from post abandonment and windblown sand.

Two datable sherds were found in this area, one (no. 21, Chapter 2) giving a date of the late fifth to early sixth century AD and the other (no. 548, Chapter 2) dating to the mid fifth to the end of the sixth century AD. These dates are similar to those suggested by vessels from the casemate fill of the main tower of the south-east sector (**Area 1**) and should perhaps be taken as a *terminus post quem* for construction here.

The range of pottery types here is more restricted than that in the neighbouring main tower, but is again dominated by the M3 amphora, accompanied by N1, N9 and Aswan amphorae. The same finewares are present, along with coarsewares for the preparation, cooking, serving and storage of food, except colanders which were also absent in the main tower. No vessels associated with lighting or heating were found here. The glass RBH—five goblet rims and one bowl base—represent 10 per cent of the RBH for this sector.

*South refectory (Area 3)— 15 per cent of the sector total RBH and 2.5 per cent of the site total RBH*

This long rectangular room (**AB35** and **AB34**) leads off to the south of the staircase tower. There is a mastaba in the north-east corner of the room and the room itself is of the same orientation and a similar size to the north refectory in the north-east sector. The room was filled with a large amount of mudbrick rubble, some of which was from the collapsed roof vault which accounted for 188 RBH of the total 304 for this area.

Only half of **Area 3** was excavated, but it contained the second largest number of pottery RBH (304) for this sector. An occupation deposit accounted for 13 RBH and a pit for nine RBH. The remainder were windblown sand and mudbrick rubble.

Dating evidence for this area comes from a vessel type African Red Slipware (no. 18, Chapter 2) dated AD 550–625 and a fifth to sixth century AD coin in the same layer, which is consistent with finds throughout the monastery. The range of vessels found is consistent with the storage of food and drink, including large vessels with diameters of 72 cm, 66 cm, 54 cm, 46 cm, and 36 cm, a lid measuring 42 cm, and four of the unidentified vessels (Faiers, 2005, 161–163). Amphora RBH are common, especially the local M3 type, and the range of fine- and coarsewares is similar to that seen in the other parts of the south-east sector.

Twelve glass RBH were found in this area, representing 32 per cent of the total glass RBH for this sector. These included a number of open and closed serving wares, such as bowls, bottles, jars and beakers, as well as a lamp. This is a wide range of types for this sector and seems quite consistent with the use of this room as a dining area.

*Room north of staircase tower (Area 4)— 6.8 per cent of the sector total RBH and one per cent of the site total RBH.*

Only limited evidence was found for a room in the area (**AA37**) immediately to the north of the open space between the main tower and staircase tower. There was a wall and possible doorway on the east side at the edge of the excavation area terminating against the north wall of the staircase tower. Against this wall was a brick bin or bench and remains of a vaulted roof. The archaeological deposits in this area are characterised by several episodes of mudbrick collapse, presumably from the adjacent structures, associated with windblown sand accumulation. The only possible occupation deposit (called a secondary occupation by the excavator) contained 13 RBH out of the 117 recorded for this area.

The only datable vessels, nos 78 and 126 in this volume (Chapter 2) indicate dates of AD 400–550 and mid-to-late fifth century AD. The same amphora types were found here as throughout this sector, with a number of Egyptian finewares.

This area, however, had an interesting collection of coarseware forms, including an incense burner or *tazza*, a candlestick and part of the brazier found in the main tower in this sector. A total of eight glass RBH were found, 13 per cent of the total glass RBH for this sector, including a lamp and drinking vessels.

*South-east corner of monastery enclosure (Area 5)—Table 3.8 above—9.1 per cent of the sector total RBH and 1.3 per cent of the site total RBH.*

Excavation of squares **AF33** and **AF34** revealed the south-east corner of the monastery enclosure, which appears to have been an open area containing no structures other than the enclosure wall itself. Although this area might form part of the activity area of the south-east quadrant, it lies at a considerable distance from the three main structures. The pottery RBH from this area is quite low—only 157—which is eight per cent of the total RBH for the south-east sector. The datable pottery from this area, nos 15 (AD 400–500) and 135 (AD 650–800, Chapter 2), possibly span the life of the monastery, although the latter appears rather late.

Approximately the same assemblage was found here as in the other parts of the south-east sector: the amphorae, comprising the local M3 and imported N1, and the coarsewares, including cooking, storage and food preparation vessels. Two examples of the unidentified vessels found in the main tower were also found here, as well as part of a drainpipe and a hanging bowl. The significance of the unusually high proportion of Aswan finewares is not clear. The fact that one of the bowl sherds was found to join another from **AE52** in the north-east sector shows the sherds' capacity for travel either immediately at the moment of discard, or as a result of taphonomic forces during the life of the monastery or after its abandonment.

The six glass RBH, represent 10 per cent of the total glass RBH for this sector and include a jar, goblet and platter.

*Overview of the south-east sector*

The ceramic evidence from the main tower, staircase tower and the refectory suggests that these related structures were built at the same time, possibly in the sixth century. The casemates of the tower were probably filled with ceramics gathered from local middens associated with the monastery. It is possible that this construction was intended to cater for larger numbers of monks, or possibly visitors, combining the provision of additional accommodation with a defensive structure in case of attack. The area seems to have continued in use to the end of the life of the monastery.

## The north-west sector

Kemp (2005, 225) describes this sector as follows:

> "The rooms exposed by the excavation are a small and arbitrary sample of what was probably an extensive built-up area which can be followed also for some distance to the south, from the tops of walls visible at the surface. To judge from the wall alignments and the sizes of the bricks used, the Byzantine builders had dug out a series of Eighteenth Dynasty rooms, which might have been magazines, and had then added additional brickwork both to support new vaulted brick roofs and to create further subdivisions."

*Accommodation complex (Area 1, V50, V51, V51/52 and V52)—55 per cent of the sector total RBH and 3.4 per cent of the total site RBH*

Part of **Area 1, V50** and part of **V51** were not fully excavated but amphora sherds accounted for 39 per cent of the 419 pottery RBH found in this area, 55 per cent of the RBH for the sector and 10.5 per cent of the site total.

Of note was the rim of a storage jar measuring 42 cm. There were also three large basins, two measuring 40 cm and one of 44 cm, together with two large lids of 40 and 56 cm. There was also a piece of a glass bracelet which was of Islamic date, along with only two other glass RBH: a platter and jar. The pottery found in part of this area (**V52**) was described as very worn and abraded. Other than the large amphora sherds there were 63 fineware RBH and a coarseware ladle handle in this area.

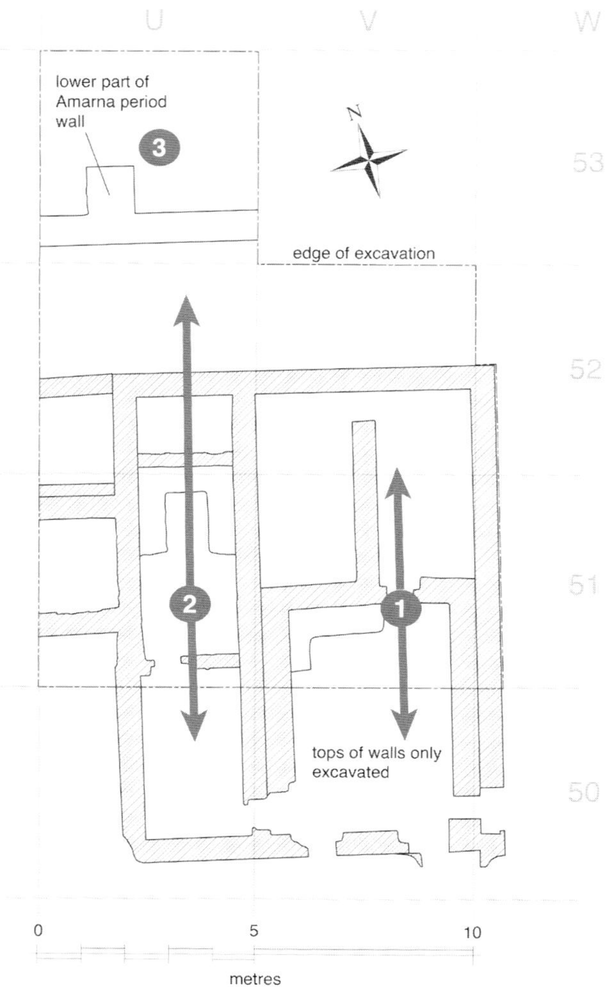


*Fig. 3.2 Plan of the north-west sector*

The architectural elements of this sector comprise what might be a section of the monastic living quarters. The main component (**Area 1**) of the sector is the complex of five rooms focussing on a large rectangular room in the south-east corner, possibly a communal space, with a smaller two-room suite leading off to the north. An L-shaped brick bench (mastaba) for sitting or sleeping is located in the north-west corner of the large room. As the area was not fully excavated, it is possible that these living quarters extended further to the south, as suggested by the doorway in the south wall of the complex as excavated. Two worn and abraded African Red Slipware sherds of LRP Form 74 (74.1 and 74c) dating to AD 450–475 were found in one of the northern rooms (**V52 [8683]**). The early date of these sherds coincides with the proposed founding of the monastery in AD 425–450, but their condition indicates that they cannot be used to date the context or area in which they were found. The half-drachma coin found in the same area (Reece, 2005, 265) should probably be seen as an intrusion or keepsake due to its very early date of AD 200–250, significantly before the foundation of the monastery. A variety of vessel types were found in the accommodation complex, dominated by amphora sherds, as is common throughout the monastery. There are no particularly common types that could be associated with any specific activity.

*Storage rooms (Area 2, U51 and U52)— 19.7 per cent of the sector total RBH and 1.2 per cent of the total site RBH*

This area comprised the partly excavated 'suite' of two rooms leading off the south-west corner of the large room, and includes a U-shaped brick mastaba at the north end of the north room. These rooms were probably included in the living quarters during the early part of the life of the monastery, but appear to have been used to store amphorae by the time the building was abandoned (Pyke, 2005, 212–243). The reason for this abandonment is unclear; whether it was because the number of monks had declined so that the living quarters were no longer needed, because the monks were living elsewhere on site, or that the building was by then in disrepair. It must be borne in mind, however, that this area was probably only part of the extensive built up area (Kemp, 2005, 255). Amphora RBH accounted for 49 per cent of the pottery RBH found here, the balance of the RBH comprising a range of types represented by infrequent sherds. Five glass RBH were also found.

*Activity area (Area 3, U52/53 and U53)— 25 per cent of the sector total RBH and 1.6 per cent of the total site RBH*

The exact identification of the two rooms to the west of the storage rooms is not clear, nor is their relationship with the accommodation complex and storerooms, as they have no access from these structures but seem instead to have a western focus. The pottery from these rooms is of little help in determining either their function or associations. The vessel types chiefly comprise amphorae and general kitchen and household wares, including a bucket handle, bottle, flowerpot and a large lid (44 cm), with few fineware sherds (eight per cent). No glass RBH were recorded (Table 3.8 above).

*Overall conclusions for the north-west sector*

Although a wide range of vessel types were found in the accommodation complex, none was sufficiently frequent to suggest an association with a particular function, as would be expected in private rooms primarily for sleeping. At some point towards the end of the life of the accommodation complex, two of its rooms were used for the storage of amphorae, perhaps suggesting that the number of monastics had declined by this time, or that this particular complex underwent a change of use. The architectural and functional relationship between the accommodation complex and the two rooms on its west side remains unclear. The pottery unfortunately offers no insights, being dominated by general kitchen and household wares, with an unspectacular number of amphorae.

**The north-east tower sector**

This sector comprises the main tower structure with an internal staircase, activity area and three-room 'suite'; an activity area between the north side of the tower and the enclosure wall; and the stone-flagged courtyard lying to the east. Only the lower part of the tower, filled with the tumbled remains of the upper storey(s), is preserved, in which a number of architectural features can be distinguished. These include the staircase tower at the south-west corner, the adjacent utility space to the west and the series of three interconnected rooms to the north.

*Tower Staircase (Area 1, Z50)— 9.45 per cent of the sector total RBH and 1.1 per cent of the total site RBH*

The heavily robbed-out remains of a staircase platform to the upper floor (or floors) of the tower are located in the south-east corner of the structure. Eighty per cent of the pottery RBH derives from two specific contexts: one a patch of *in situ* mudbrick collapse, the other a compacted mix of sand and mudbrick tumble. The other 20 per cent comes from mudbrick debris. Only one glass RBH was found here, suggesting that glass was not used in this area (Tables 3.11 and 3.12). For dating purposes there were two African Red Slipware (ARS) sherds of *c.*AD 450–530 (Chapter 2, no. 8) and no. 4 in Faiers, 2005, which was mid-to-late fifth century AD; these offer a *terminus post quem* for the abandonment of the tower. This area also contained sherds of Pharaonic pottery that were probably used as chinking in the mud brick construction.

*Tower activity area (Area 2, Y50)— 13 per cent of the sector total RBH and 1.6 per cent of the total site RBH*

This room comprises the south-west corner of the tower. A doorway leads into the room and thence to the three rooms to the north. Access to the three-room 'suite' comprising the northern part of the tower is via a doorway at the east end of the north wall of the room. Immediately to the west of the doorway is a rectangular mud structure of unknown function which contained 15 sherds of pottery, of which eight were burnt and badly eroded. One of the pottery sherds in the upper fill within this structure could be dated to *c.*AD 500/525–600+ (?) (Faiers, 2005, no. 153).

The pottery of this area included ARS sherds of forms dating to *c.*AD 570–600 and *c.*AD 501–540, offering a possible *terminus post quem* for at least the abandonment of the tower. The presence of nine storage vessels, ranging in size from 34 to 50 cm, suggests that one of the functions of this space was for storage, and the three lamps found indicate that the preferred form of lighting was portable. Thirty-seven per cent of the RBH came from structural collapse within this area.

*Three-room suite (Area 3, Y5l and Z51)— 19 per cent of the sector total RBH and 2.3 per cent of the site total RBH*

This area comprises three rooms in the north part of the tower, accessed from the activity area immediately

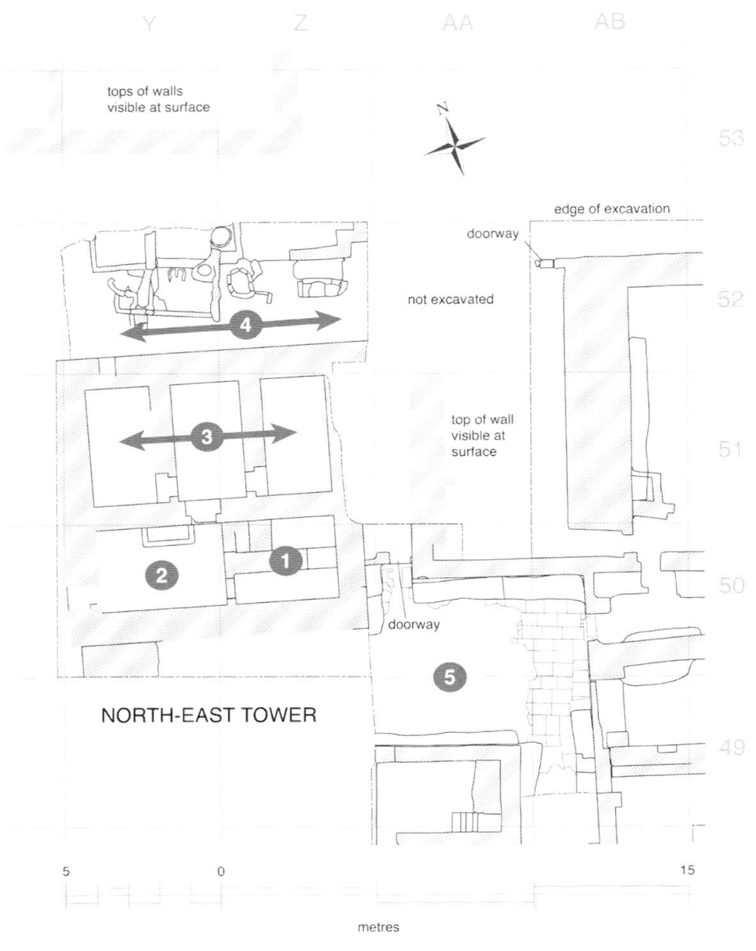


*Figure 3.3 Plan of the north-east tower sector*

to the south. The identical sequence of upper floor, makeup layer and collapsed vaulted ceiling that forms the fill of these rooms has confirmed their treatment as a single unit in the discussion of the pottery distribution. A single distinguishing feature is that the excavator noted that a pit in the north-west corner of the western room was found to contain a large amphora on its side, but the exact relationship, if any, between the vessel and the pit could not be determined. This room also contained a large decorated storage jar published in Volume 1 (nos 277–282). Adjoining sherds from this vessel came from Y50 [8254] (surface sand) and Y50 [8259] (collapsed wall rubble).

The only deposits which may have proved of use in dating were a mudbrick surface covering two of the rooms (29 pottery RBH); a possible floor surface (six RBH); makeup for foundations (10 RBH) and the makeup to the upper-storey floor under mudbrick collapse (two RBH). None of these had datable finewares included in their composition. The overall quantity and frequency of individual types of pottery is consistent with that in the other areas of the north-east tower, suggesting a shared function for all the areas. The only exception in the case of the three-room 'suite' is a slightly higher occurrence of amphorae—nearly 21 per cent of the sector total—suggesting that these rooms might have been particularly associated with storage commodities stored in this vessel type. Four diagnostic sherds of glass were found.

*Industrial/kitchen area (Area 4, Y52 and Z52)—43 per cent of the sector total RBH and five per cent of the total site RBH*

Situated to the north of the tower, the layout of **Area 4** seems to have undergone remodelling during its life, with ovens replacing pits—the function of which is uncertain—and numerous re-laid floor surfaces.

This seems to be an open 'industrial' or kitchen area with four ovens, one of which was possibly a kiln (although the absence of pottery 'wasters' or glass dross from either process makes this unlikely). There was also a comprehensive selection of pottery forms, including 13 large vessels ranging in size from 36 cm to 60 cm, and a lid of the same diameter as the latter vessel. This area had more pottery RBH than other areas in this sector, with fragments of jars, bowls/basins, *qawadiis,* cooking pots, colanders, flasks and storage vessels particularly common. The estimated number of amphorae is the fourth largest concentration on the whole site (five per cent) which, taken with the other vessel types present, suggests a function of food preparation for this area. Interestingly, this area also has the highest quantity of glass RBH in the north-east tower sector.

The nature of the architectural features and concentration of vessel types associated with food preparation suggests that this is an open-air area for bread production; an interpretation that is also consistent with its close proximity to both the refectory and the church. Large-scale bread production would certainly not be possible in the confines of the proposed kitchen at **Area 2** and **3** of the north-east sector of the monastery, which lacks the necessary oven capacity. Bread was a staple monastic food, prepared within the monastery and consumed in the refectory and infirmary, used in the church liturgy and given out to visitors (Layton, 2002, 38–9, 44–6, table 3). Architectural evidence from other monasteries shows that bread ovens, usually made of ceramic, can be included in a more general cooking area or can form a separate architectural feature in a different location, either singly or in a group (for overview see Pyke and Brooks Hedstrom, in press). Textual evidence from the White Monastery indicates that at the time of Shenoute (late fourth to mid fifth century) bread was prepared in a special installation (Layton, 2002, 46).

Dating evidence found within this area, although resting on several dates for the Aswan wares (there being no African Red Slipware of dateable size), appears to give a timescale well into the sixth century AD (nos 19 and 57, Chapter 2 in this volume).

*Paved courtyard (Area 5, AA50, AA49, AA48 and AA47)— 15.3 per cent of the sector total RBH and 1.8 per cent of the total site RBH*

The L-shaped courtyard lies to the north and east of the church, with the north-east tower and adjacent room on the north side, and rooms of the north-east sector to the east. It probably also extended to the west, between the tower and church. It was paved with stone flagging (most of which had been robbed out), with two mastabas against the north-west and south side walls of the courtyard. Graffiti and *dipinti* were found on various sections of the remaining wall plaster. Brick tumble in the middle of the courtyard might have been a stand for a large jar, possibly for water. Body sherds of a large jar were found in this area and there was a jar rim measuring 38 cm found in AA50 [9834]. This deposit also contained an ARS sherd with fairly vague dating, i.e. mid-to-late fifth century AD, but possibly fourth to seventh century AD (pottery catalogue Chapter 2, no. 4). There were two other ARS sherds, also with a fairly vague dating of AD 350–400+ (pottery catalogue Chapter 2, no. 3) and AD 570–600 (Chapter 2, no. 9).

Almost all the deposits in this area comprised mixed wall collapse, mudbrick wall collapse or windblown sand deposit.

*Observations on the north-east tower sector*

The internal organisation of the north-east tower and its associated pottery suggests that the ground floor element of the tower was used predominantly for storage. No evidence remains for the day-to-day use of the upper storey(s), which can be supposed to have had a function beyond that of 'refuge' (for summary of this use see Grossmann, 1991, 1395), which would have been the exception rather than the rule for this building.

In **Area 4**, to the north of the tower, there was probably a bake-house facility with several ovens. Of special note here are the large storage vessels and the elevated numbers of amphora and other types associated with food production.

In **Area 5** of this sector there were benches against the two north-west and south side walls with a paved courtyard and possible emplacement for a large storage vessel, which might have contained water. This outdoor space appears to have been in use throughout the life of the monastery, the walls providing a focus for resident and visiting monastics to record their prayers (Pyke et al., in preparation).

This sector, particularly the proposed bakery in **Area 4**, has a high quantity of pottery accounting for 12 per cent of the total site pottery RBH and 4.4 per cent of the glass RBH. The usefulness of the dating evidence offered by fragments of finewares is, unfortunately, limited by the fact that none was found within *in situ* deposits, and therefore may have come from a deposit elsewhere. They do, however, provide broad dating evidence for the monastery as a whole.

## The church

The Church is located to the south-west of the north-east sector, bordered on its north and east sides by the paved courtyard (north-east tower sector, **Area 5**). It was discovered in the final season, and was excavated to the floor level in the staircase room only (**Area 4**).

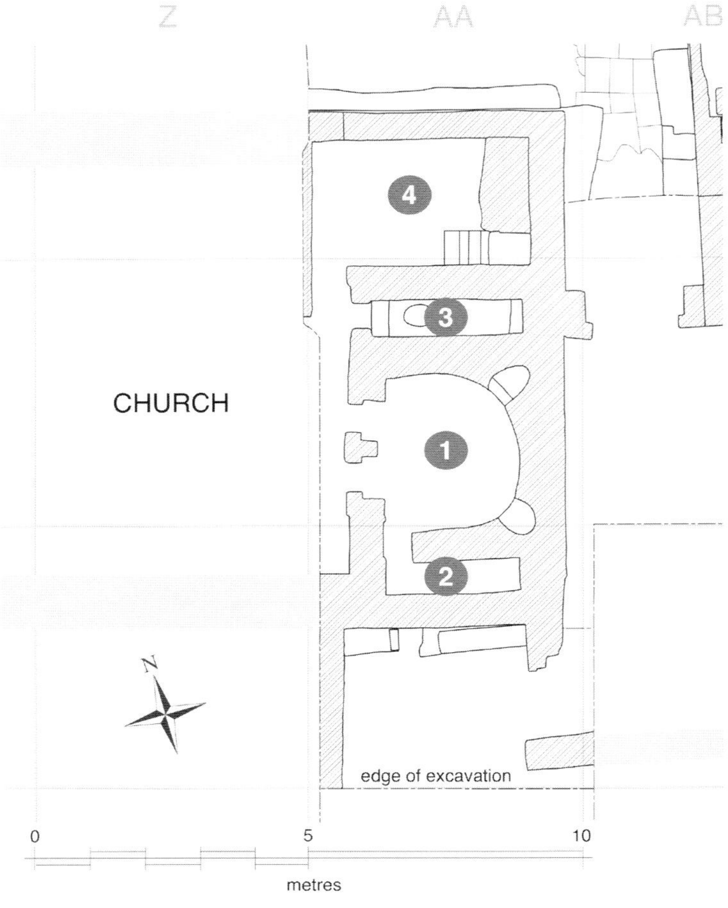


*Figure 3.4 Plan of the church, as excavated*

The east end of the church consists of a semi-circular apse (**Area 1**), flanked by long narrow *pastophoria* on the south (**Area 2**) and north (**Area 3**) sides, with an additional room containing a staircase (**Area 4**) located to the north of the north *pastophorium*.

The pottery found in the apse (**Area 1**) came from the surface (52 RBH); sandy debris and rubble (115 RBH); a robber pit (six RBH); and a sandy debris and painted plaster context (79 RBH). The five tub sherds belonging to a vessel 62 cm in diameter were all found in the rubble and sand context. The glass RBH included flagons, a jar, a bottle and a lamp, all of which were found in sandy debris and rubble except for a jar found in the sandy debris and painted plaster context. This area contained 38 per cent of the sector pottery RBH and two per cent of the total site pottery RBH.

In the south *pastophorium* (**Area 2**), surface and windblown sand deposits accounted for 102 pottery RBH; architectural debris, rubble, and collapse of mudbrick and sand, 40 RBH; and yellow coarse sand, 18 RBH. A lamp sherd was found in the windblown sand deposit. Glass RBH forms were platters found in the yellow coarse sand deposit, bottles and a cup in surface and windblown sand and a bowl from the collapse of mudbrick. This made up 24 per cent of the sector RBH and 1.3 per cent of the site total RBH.

Sandy mudbrick rubble and architectural debris in the north *pastophorium* (**Area 3**) yielded 50 pottery RBH; a thin layer of yellow sand (possibly windblown), 10 RBH; and only three RBH were found in sand above the white plastered floor. The two glass lamp RBH were both found in the sandy mudbrick rubble. This made up 9.5 per cent of the sector total RBH and 0.5 per cent of the site total RBH.

A total of 33 pottery RBH was found in the surface and windblown sand deposits in the staircase room (Area 4), while mudbrick debris and sand and rubble layers accounted for 154 RBH. The glass RBH consist of jug, bowl, jar and two goblet glass fragments, all found in the mudbrick debris. This makes up 28 per cent of the sector total RBH and 1.5 per cent of the total site RBH.

None of the pottery or glass found in the church came from *in situ* deposits associated with its function. The composition of the ceramic material from these areas is consistent with the general range of types

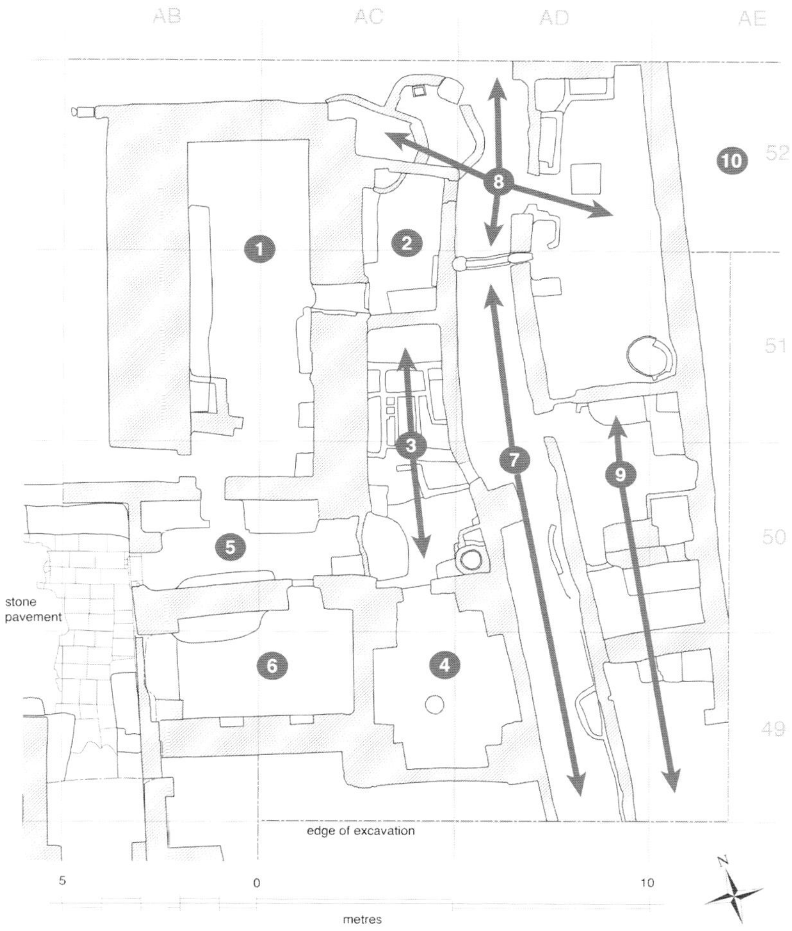


*Figure 3.5 Plan of the north-east sector*

found in surface, tumble and windblown sand deposits throughout the monastery.

### The north-east sector

The north-east sector, which is now to be considered, is the most complex and includes several rooms, open spaces and thoroughfares (numbered 1–10 on fig. 3.5) and contained 40 per cent of the site pottery RBH, 35 per cent of the site amphora and 50 per cent of the glass RBH.

*The refectory (Area 1, AB AC 51 and AB AC 52)— 12.9 per cent of the sector total pottery RBH and five per cent of the total site pottery RBH*

The long, barrel-vaulted room (9 m x 3 m) with a north–south axis, located in the north-west corner of the north-east sector, is tentatively identified as the main refectory due to its architectural features, and its proximity to the food preparation area (**Area 2**, see below). These include a bench (mastaba) along its western wall, with traces of a further bench along the south wall and two niches in the east wall. The organisation of these features suggests a linear seating arrangement, comparable to that at, for example, Deir el-Baramous in the Wadi Natrun. The complex sequence of floors laid in this room suggest it was in use for a significant period, with the benches eventually going out of use and a water installation built in the south-west corner of the room. It is not clear exactly who used the refectory, which can be estimated to have seated about 20 people, allowing half a metre for each person sitting at a table six metres by one metre, with 10 on each side. However, this is only guesswork and we do not know just how many were catered for at each meal. Were there several sittings for each meal? Was it for a group of monks housed in this area? Unfortunately the ceramic and glass evidence offers no insights into these questions.

A coin found in the southern part of the refectory dated AD 425–450 would seem to indicate an early date for this part of the monastery. However, later in its existence the north-east corner of Area 1 contained a midden or dump which implies that the room was now redundant as an eating area.

The fill of this room, which consisted of periods of mudbrick collapse and sand, contained 608 pottery

RBH (five per cent of whole site) and 58 glass RBH (nine per cent of the glass RBH site total), the forms and distribution of which can be seen on Table 3.17.

The composition of the pottery mirrors that of most areas on site, dominated by amphorae but including vessels for food storage, preparation and consumption. The number of vessels for the service and consumption of food is not particularly high. This might suggest that while food may have been eaten here, the vessels associated with this activity were either kept elsewhere, or removed when the monks quit the monastery.

*Kitchen(?) Area (Area 2, AC51 and AC52)— 2.65 per cent of the sector total pottery RBH and one per cent of the site pottery RBH*

A doorway in the centre of the east wall of the refectory leads to a possible kitchen (**Area 2**), which was provided with an adjacent storeroom/larder (**Area 3**). **Area 2** contained two mastabas which could have served, among other usages, as surfaces for food preparation. There was a simple hearth in the north-west corner. No trace of a mudbrick vault was found in the tumble of this room, suggesting that the roof may have been of a different type. There were two rough, rounded structures to the north of this room and it seems that the northern-most one is of a slightly later date than the southern. The northern structure is provided with a small, shallow mud-plastered trough that might have been for animal feed. This contained weed/wild plant and fruit remains (Smith, 2003, figs 3.23 and 3.36). Similar ad hoc structures are still in use in Egypt today for feeding animals (Pyke, 1993–2011, personal observations). These possible animal-keeping areas are included in **Area 8** (see below).

A substantial drain made from reused amphorae, including a Gaza Jar (LRA 4), connects **Area 2** with **Area 8** (animal-keeping area) across the alleyway (**Area 7**) between them. The presence of this drain suggests that water was used in **Area 2**; an interpretation that is supported by the presence of a low brick sill across the doorway connecting **Area 2** with **Area 1** which would have prevented water getting into the refectory. Organic remains found within the drain included fruit (Smith, 2003, 50), which support a link with food processing in **Area 2**.

The most frequent pottery form is again the LRA 7 amphora, with the usual range of other types, each represented by one vessel, which is surprising in the case of the cooking wares, given the proposed function of this room. An exception to this is the *qadus,* which is slightly more numerous. The slightly elevated frequency of this type, which has the specific function of being used for the collection of water in a water wheel, cannot be easily explained, but this may be due to the same rim form being used for jars and *qadus*, making it difficult to determine which is which in the absence of a base. In the course of collecting data, any indeterminate vessels were judged as both jars and *qadus* (J/Q), the figures being divided in two when allocating to vessel types. Only two glass RBH were found here, one of which was a bead, suggesting that glass vessels were not used in the preparation of food.

*Storeroom/larder (Area 3, AC 51)— 11.7 per cent of the sector total RBH and 5.3 per cent of the site total RBH*

The organisation of the room immediately to the south of the kitchen changed considerably throughout its lifetime. It seems that the northern part of this room (see Chapter 4) was originally a storeroom, but during its life had been reorganised as a cool room or larder for the storage of perishable foods needing a more stable atmosphere, such as bread or cheese (Bagnall, 1993, 297).

At some time, the southern end of **Area 3** had been partitioned off from the northern (larder/cool room) end. There was an oven at the south-east end that appears to have become a fireplace at the end of its life. Abundant charred organic remains were found in the oven and desiccated remains from this general area are consistent with the storage and preparation of food (Smith, 2003, 44 and 50). A cooking pot set into the floor in the southern part of the room was found to be filled with dates and complete fish skeletons.

During the earlier part of the history of this space, it could be accessed from the south-west via the corridor (**Area 5**), which was later blocked and the southern end of **Area 3** seems likely to have become another kitchen. For a full discussion of the development of this area, see Chapter 4. Briefly, low-level mudbrick wall partitions were constructed in **Area 3**, forming a number of small bays or 'slots' across the room. In the next phase of construction, three of the 'slots' were apparently intentionally filled with broken and/or nearly complete pots. Three of the other 'slots' contained fragmentary or smashed vessels, which were recovered in a jumbled state, and another two slots were empty apart from brick spacers, perhaps to accommodate standing vessels. A hard mud/plaster floor was then laid over and surrounding the three 'slots' containing the most complete vessels with the other slots sealed over to form shelves or mastabas.

Analysis of the arrangement of the sherds (broken and complete vessels within the slots forming the under-floor installation) shows that considerable care was taken in both the selection and utilisation of all the materials (Faiers and Smith, 2009, 91, 93 and 98). Many of the vessels were not broken beyond all hope of reuse before being included in the deposit, and the general pattern of the selection of large-sized sherds from closed coarse- and transport-ware forms suggests that this was an important factor in their being chosen to fill the area, thought to be to aid in maintaining a cool, dry atmosphere (Faiers and Smith, 2009, 98). These ceramics were clearly not derived from a midden deposit, but the significance of the selected types is not clear. As throughout the Kom el-Nana material, Egyptian M3 amphorae (17 individual vessels) are dominant, some showing signs of having been reworked for a secondary use before inclusion in the slots. The composition of the coarseware forms in this assemblage is interesting, as seven of the 10 are moderately to highly decorated jars, flasks and goblets, which are in the minority in the main assemblage (the goblets being particularly rare), while only one is for cooking and two probably for storage. Were these used/stored nearby before inclusion in this deposit?

The dates of the pottery underneath the floor in **Area 3** were in the fifth to the early sixth century AD for the amphorae, AD 460–560 for a decorated jar and *c.* AD 450–550 for a flagon. If the reorganisation of the whole of **Area 3** took place at the same time, then it is likely to be in the time scale given by the pottery, which although not very narrow possibly indicates a rise in the population of monks being catered for at this time. This may coincide with the evidence in the south-east sector where the casemate fill contained later pottery suggesting that this structure was a later addition to the site. Therefore, it is suggested that the monastery was undergoing reorganisation to allow for this rise in residents.

Just inside the doorway, between this room and the alleyway, a coarseware tall-necked jar (fig. 3.6) was found sunk into the floor. It is comparable to the

*Figure 3.6 Coarseware jar at doorway between the storeroom/larder and alleyway.*

decorated jar type included in the assemblage within the sub-floor slots.

The composition of the other deposits within this room is consistent with that seen throughout the site, with a slightly elevated number of cooking pots probably associated with the function of the room. No functional explanation could be found for the high number of *qadus*, although this vessel type also includes medium storage-type jars with a similar rim shape.

*Storeroom with sub-floor installation (Area 4, AC AD 50 and AD 49)— 14 per cent of the sector total RBH and 5.5 per cent of the site total RBH*

The pottery RBH (659 RBH) was mainly derived from deposits of rubble, robber-pit fill and sand (618 RBH), whilst the remainder came from three deposits of cistern fills (17 RBH), a brown floor deposit (five RBH) and a deposit beneath the floor deposit (19 RBH). None of the remainder contained datable pottery.

This room was originally furnished simply with a plastered brick mastaba, but in its second phase, a large, internally plastered storage installation (possibly used to store grain) occupied part of the space. Similar installations have been found at other monasteries, including the Monastery of Epiphanius (Winlock and Crum, 1926, pl. III), Saqqara (Quibell, 1912, 2) and Naqlun (Urbaniak-Walczak, 1999, 93–136; Godlewski, 1997, 123–45). Quibell (1912, 2) describes storage pits in the floor as part of the organisation of the monastic dwellings at Saqqara.

The fact that in its final phase this room could only be accessed from the kitchen suggests that its function was associated with that area. There were 34 glass RBH found here, which is the third highest in the sector. High quantities of EVE and glass RBH make this area similar to that noted in the proposed bakery in the north-east tower sector, where the most common ceramic types are also comparable.

It is tempting to see the modifications to the room's structure as linked to the changes made to the adjacent room to the north (**Area 3**). It is possible that the modifications to **Area 4** were made in order to improve storage conditions; a domed roof helping to keep the room cool and the sealed plaster floor and storage installation discouraging vermin and termites.

*Corridor (Area 5, AB AC 50)— 3.4 per cent of the sector RBH and 1.3 per cent of the site total RBH*

**Area 5** was originally a corridor leading through to the southern part of the storeroom/larder (**Area 3**).

Mastaba benches were later added against the north wall, either side of the doorway to the north refectory and access to the storeroom/larder blocked off. As one might expect of an interior thoroughfare and possible waiting area, the corridor had a low estimated number of vessels at 17, and only two vessels in glass: a beaker and a bowl. All deposits were of rubble or cleaning. Subsequent to its modification, this area may well have been made into an anteroom or waiting room associated with the room immediately to the south (**Area 6**).

*Possible reception room (Area 6, AB AC 50 and AB AC 49)— 13.6 per cent of the sector total RBH and 5.3 of the site total RBH*

This room is accessed from the corridor (**Area 5**) to the north, is furnished with a mastaba along its north wall adjacent to the doorway, and has two niches in the opposite south wall. Similar vessel types are well represented in this room as in the adjacent corridor, albeit occurring in higher numbers. Local and Aswan tablewares are, however, considerably more common in this room, which might be significant given its proposed function as a reception room, based on its architectural arrangement. Of the 642 recorded pottery RBH, 398 came from sand and mudbrick debris, with the other 244 RBH from a deposit described by the excavator as "silt and sand with a high organic content, charcoal and lenses of grey (?) ash and mudbrick", which she attributed to 'squatter activities' post-dating the abandonment of the monastery.

*The alleyway or passage (Area 7, AD 49, 50, 51 and 52)— 20 per cent of the sector total RBH and eight per cent of the site total.*

The alleyway or passage (**Area 7**) runs north to south with the kitchen and storage rooms (**Areas 2–4**) on its west side and utility rooms, including one with a staircase (**Areas 9** and **10**), on its east side. An area probably for keeping animals is located at the north end of the alleyway; this is included with **Area 8** (Table 3.24). The alleyway probably provided access to the rooms on either side and from north to south. Doorways led from **Areas 2**, **3**, **8**, and **9** to the alleyway at various phases in the monastery's history, and a drain made of a Gazan amphorae ran across the passage, east to west, from the kitchen (**Area 2**) into the possible stable area (**Area 8**). There was what appeared to be a 'mounting block' about halfway down the alleyway/passage to the south outside the southern end of the storeroom/larder (**Area 3**). Deposits in the same part of the alleyway contained a significant ceramic component (211 RBH), the date range of which spans the proposed fifth to seventh century lifetime of the monastery.

On what was presumed to be the final floor surface in the southern half of the alleyway, as far north as the mounting block, only four pottery RBH were recorded, including an Aswan bowl of sixth century AD date. Other pottery in the alleyway included an Aswan compartmented dish consistent with a sixth to seventh century AD date, although the type lasts until the ninth century. Joining fragments of this vessel were found in **Areas 4**, **9** and **8** of the north-east sector and **Area 5** of the south-east sector, which indicates a fair degree of dispersal which might be expected, due to the busy nature of the thoroughfare, not only at the time of disposal, but also in the intervening years between the abandonment of the monastery and now.

As would be expected in a thoroughfare, the pottery found in the alleyway does not reflect a function associated with the use of ceramic vessels. The range and frequency of vessels is consistent with the general assemblage across the site.

*Animal-keeping area (Area 8)—animal pens, 0.02 per cent of the sector RBH and 0.01 per cent of the total site RBH; midden (north part of alleyway), 2.01 per cent of sector total RBH and 0.8 per cent of the site total RBH; north-east activity area, 6.53 per cent of the sector total RBH and 2.5 per cent of the site total RBH*

The north-east utility area comprises the structures immediately north of the kitchen (**Area 2**), the north part of the alleyway as far south as the east–west drain and the large rectangular room in the north–east corner of the monastery. During its life the area underwent numerous modifications such as the replacement of mud floors and the rearrangement of various installations.

The western element of this area, at the north end of the alleyway, comprises a pair of mud-built elliptical structures against the north wall of the kitchen (**Area 2**) and the north-east corner of the refectory (**Area 1**), the function of which has been proposed as animal pens. There is no specific evidence as to the type of animals kept here; a text from Wadi Sarga (Crum et al., 1922, 98–9, text 107) indicates that pigs were kept at that monastery; domestic fowl are another possibility. Only one pottery jar rim was found in these structures, indicating that pottery vessels were not required for activities in this location, and that the area was probably cleaned regularly and kept free of debris.

The northernmost part of the alleyway is attributed

to this area because it gives access to both areas that are apparently linked with animal husbandry, and it includes a sherd-free dung heap or midden that seems more likely to derive from activities in this area than the alleyway (**Area 7**), adjacent to the south.

In its earliest phase, architectural features in the eastern part of the area included a possible fireplace or hearth and pot stand, with evidence of structures against the west wall. In later phases, the north and south parts of this area seem to have had separate functions. The architecture of the south part contains at least one cooking installation, judging by the presence of charred cereal grain, chaff, pulses and fruit inside the circular feature in the south-east corner (Smith, 2003, figs 3.5, 3.8, 3.11 and 3.24). The architecture in the north includes a series of troughs possibly for feeding stabled animals, the contents of which included desiccated chaff, oil crops and fruit (Smith, 2003, figs 3.8, 3.15, and 3.24). The deposits in this area were noted by the excavator to contain abundant organic material including dung (not identified), beetles, fly pupae, straw and chaff.

It is possible that this part of **Area 8** was where beasts of burden belonging to the monastery were stabled. These animals would have included donkeys, the main land transport of the day for moving both passengers and produce (Bagnall, 1993, 38–9). Husbandman and camel-driver are listed among the specialisations of the monks that Palladius (Lausiac History, 32.12; Meyer, 1965, 95) observed at Panopolis, and Gascou (1991, 1640) proposes that animal husbandry was probably one of the 'tasks' performed by monks. Rousseau (1985, 82–3) asserts that agriculture, including looking after animals, was one area in which specialisation occurred, with only those skilled in husbandry being allowed to look after the monastery's animals, which were kept in a specific stable area, known as the *villa*. A total of 49 pottery RBH can be attributed to organic layers (one of which, AD51 [7634], contained an ostracon), but the remainder was found in mudbrick rubble and sand.

Two-thirds of the bowls/basins found in this area are finewares, the ARS sherd dating to AD 425–475, and the dates of the Aswan vessels included the third quarter of the fifth century AD, the early sixth, and sixth to seventh centuries. Other vessels are possibly associated with food preparation and storage, including several cooking pots, a storage vessel, bucket tub and ladle. Some of these vessels could equally have been used for storing and presenting animal feed. The inclusion of a cooking pot reused as a paint pot brings to mind the equivalent of a modern day garden shed, storing useful odds and ends, or even 'throw outs' which might also have formed part of the function of this space in its later existence. A pottery disc with a hole in the middle was found in **Area 8**; this was identified as a possible spindle whorl or loom weight, though probably the former (Faiers, 2005, 163, no. 423).

*Lookout point (Area 9)—north room, 5.47 per cent of the sector total RBH and 2.1 per cent of the site total RBH; south room, 2.7 per cent of the sector RBH and 1.07 per cent of the site RBH*

The southern two rooms (**Area 9**) to the east of the alleyway (**Area 7**) are tentatively identified as a lookout point on the basis of the pair of staircases that gave access to the upper part of the enclosure wall, an interpretation proposed by the excavator. The space below both of the staircases was open and functioned as both a support for the stairs and a cupboard. The presence of a number of mastabas in this room suggest that it was also used for seating or, more likely, sleeping, presumably by those sharing watch duty. This area underwent some reorganisation during its lifetime, one of the latest additions being a hearth constructed above one of the mastabas.

The coin from this part of the site is broadly dated from the fourth to the sixth century. The three datable Aswan vessels in the pottery assemblage, on the other hand, give a broad *terminus post quem* of the sixth to the seventh century.

The consistency of the vessel types supports a shared function for the two rooms comprising this area. The composition of the assemblage suggests that they might have been used for limited storage and perhaps even cooking, with neither of these activities being particularly large scale. Fineware vessels were slightly more common in the north than the south room, perhaps indicating that if food was consumed in this area, it was more likely in the north than the south room.

*Midden/garden (Area 10)—cultivated area, 0.78 per cent of the sector total RBH and 0.3 per cent of the site total RBH; midden, 1.19 per cent of the sector total RBH and 0.46 per cent of the site total RBH; pottery layer beneath midden running along wall, 1.17 per cent of the sector total RBH and 0.41 per cent of the site total RBH; path, 1.8 of the sector total RBH and 0.7 per cent of the site total RBH*

**Area 10** lies outside the monastery walls to the east of the animal pens (**Area 8**) and lookout point (**Area 9**). It comprises an area apparently used for cultivation, a midden and a pathway between the wall of the settlement and the cultivation. One hundred and thirty-nine of the 367 RBH were associated with windblown sand deposits and collapsed walls. Most of the pottery was badly shattered and eroded, consistent with having been exposed to the elements and trampled by humans and animals. The pathway was perhaps originally part of the midden, but provided a shortcut between it and the wall. The midden, comprising 14 per cent of the RBH for **Area 10**, was built up against the exterior face of the enclosure wall and lapping up against the cultivated area. A collection of 50 pottery RBH was found beneath the midden and against the wall. This would have been a convenient place to dump rubbish if there was a door into the monastery at the lookout point at **Area 9**.

The cultivated area is characterised by a series of linear criss-cross markings on the ancient surface and remains of the root balls of plants, which was covered by mudbrick tumble, presumably from the enclosure wall, mixed with sand. The cultivation accounts for 12 per cent of the total RBH in **Area 10**. Pharaonic sherds were present in the cultivated soil, possibly left when the others had been sifted out for use as spacers in vaulted roofs within the monastery. This area had a coin of the fourth to fifth century AD.

It seems likely that all the late Roman pottery in **Area 10** derives from the midden, which was trampled over and dispersed to form the pathway, and perhaps also crept into the cultivation. Alternatively, the organic midden material (with associated sherds) might have been deliberately added to the cultivation to improve the fertility of the soil.

*Observations on the north-east sector*

This part of the monastery seems to have undergone radical refurbishment involving the reconfiguration of a number of areas, in some cases suggesting a change of function, often relating to food preparation and storage. Access between the areas, especially around the kitchen/larder was also modified.

A detailed examination of the ceramic material from the north-east sector has offered limited insights into the function of specific areas. No elevated quantity of tablewares that might be associated with food consumption was noted in the refectory (**Area 1**), the composition of the ceramics instead being quite consistent with that seen throughout the monastery. Were tablewares kept elsewhere, such as in **Area 4**, or were they taken with the monks when they left?

The small size of the kitchen space (**Area 2**) might argue for keeping vessels elsewhere while not in use, and indeed these vessels do not form a significant component of the ceramic material. A slightly elevated frequency of cooking wares was, however, observed in the adjacent storeroom/larder. The inclusion of ceramics in the architecture of these two rooms indicates that particular conditions were desired here. The drain in the kitchen suggests that the floor was regularly sluiced with water, while the under-floor installation in **Area 3** promoted a cool, dry atmosphere for storage purposes. The source of the vessels used in the latter context is uncertain, but selection favoured closed forms, (almost) complete vessels — especially amphorae — and decorated jars. The vessel types found in the rooms with the sub-floor installation (**Area 4**) suggest an association with the kitchen/storage areas (**Areas 2** and **3**) and the refectory (**Area 1**), all in close proximity. The very high RBH in this room (**Area 4**) might be indicative of its function for the storing of vessels for use in these areas, and possibly also of foodstuffs. Alternatively, the sherds could have come from elsewhere on site during the period between abandonment and the present day.

The frequency of sherds in both the alleyway **(Area 7)** and the animal-keeping area (**Area 8**) is quite low, as might be expected in areas with a function that is not associated with the use of pottery. The extremely low number of sherds in the proposed animal pens further suggests that this area was kept clean and probably cleaned regularly.

The consistency of vessel types in the two rooms comprising the proposed lookout point (**Area 9**) suggests that they might have been used for limited storage and possibly cooking by the watchmen, whose watch duties might have prevented them from attending the daily meal. The slightly higher occurrence of the tablewares in the northern rooms suggests that food was more likely to have been consumed here than in the southern room.

## Joins between pottery sherds

Joining sherds belonging to the same vessel generally derived from a single deposit, albeit one that occurred over several of the artificial excavation squares. This is not, however, the case for a small number of vessels, sherds of which were much more dispersed across the site.

In the south-east sector, two joins were found between **Area 1** south-east sector and the north-east tower, **Areas 3** and **4**, comprising an O1 bowl and an unidentified vessel. The single join between **Area 5** in the south-east sector and **Area 10** in the north-east sector was a hanging bowl.

There were two joins between the north-east sector and the church (**Area 5** north-east sector and **Area 1** church; **Area 8** north-east sector and **Area 2** church), one of which was a bowl and the other was not identified.

The north-east tower had one join between its **Area 4** and an area of windblown sand surface in AB27 outside the monastery.

The north-west sector only had joins between its own areas and their layers, which is interesting as it may indicate that this part of the monastery does not seem to have been in use for a period of time before the abandonment, allowing a build-up of debris and thus avoiding dispersal of any sherds left there.

It would seem, therefore, that the main bulk of the broken pottery from the site remained on the site, not travelling too far from its point of origin, after the building fell into disuse, with anything useable and visible being removed shortly after this event took place.

## Discussion and conclusions

The extent to which the pottery and glass can actually give a true indication of the activity carried out in a particular area, or indeed provide an insight into the changes that took place in the monastery, is open to conjecture. In this chapter we have tried to tie the pottery and glass into what the architectural information indicates may have existed on the site, whilst not attempting to prejudge what might be found. However, Rowley-Conwy's (1994, 31) observation that "If contemporary assemblages from different contexts preserved snapshots of different behavioural events one might expect the pot proportions to reflect this and vary widely between assemblages. They rarely do so; the ceramics…have been blended and homogenised by the dumping process" demands careful consideration. At Kom el-Nana, a large proportion of the pottery RBH comes from deposits characterised by mudbrick rubble and windblown sand, and comprises a similar assemblage (albeit in differing amounts), which fits with Rowley-Conwy's statement.

It is unreasonable therefore, to expect, after a period of 1,600 years, that pottery and glass will remain in the position they occupied in the past in the manner of Pompeii (Binford, 1981, 195–208), or the Marie Celeste (Rowley-Conwy, 1994, 31). There are, however, exceptions (sometimes quite small exceptions) which have been sealed by later deposits and do offer an indication of what was happening in that particular place at that particular time. Fortunately, there are some of these at Kom el-Nana.

A straightforward example of the use of an architectural space to store ceramic vessels is found in the north-west sector (Pyke, 2005, 213–245), where amphorae comprised nearly 55 per cent of the sector's pottery and 4.5 per cent of the total site amphora RBH. Whether the building had fallen into disuse when the monastery was abandoned and the amphorae stored there were not seen as of any use or value to the people leaving (or in the years after) is open to conjecture. The sector was only partially excavated and further work may throw light on whether amphorae were habitually stored here or whether it was because the building was no longer in use.

Ceramic vessels are used in a specific architectural context in a very small number of locations within the monastery, each giving an insight into the activity conducted here. These include the drain made from a Gaza amphora (LRA 4) that crossed the alleyway (**Area 7**) from the kitchen (**Area 2**) to the animal-keeping area (**Area 8**) in the north-east sector. The fact that this drain contained organic remains including fruit supports the interpretation of **Area 2** as having an association with food processing. It is also likely that a kitchen would have needed the floor washed down regularly, thus the need for the drain. In the same area, ceramic vessels and large sherds incorporated in the 'Pot Slots' in **Area 3** form part of a sophisticated architectural installation that is thought to have been used to maintain a controlled, cool atmosphere for the storage of perishable foodstuffs.

The architectural use of sherds is attested in the small midden in the north-east sector at the top of the alleyway (**Area 7**), outside the kitchen (**Area 2**) and animal-keeping area (**Area 8**). This might have been filling a runnel or dip in the surface of the alley caused by water seepage from the drain crossing this area.

Sherds are also a significant component of the casemate fill of the south-east tower (**Area 1**, south-east sector). The uppermost sherds in this deposit give a *terminus post quem* for the deposition of the casemate fill, which would suggest that this part of the site was constructed when the monastery was functioning, towards the end of its life in the sixth century AD. Why was this new tower needed? Might it have been to accommodate visitors to the monastery? Perhaps an influx of individuals wishing to become monastics had swelled the ranks of the monastery. In the unsettled times of the mid sixth century, with outbreaks of plague in various areas of the Mediterranean, religious fervour may well have brought new recruits wishing either to thank God for their survival, or in hopes of averting disease.

Entomological deposits do not show evidence of plague at Kom el-Nana (Eva Pangiokopoulous, personal communication, 3.11.2011), but this does not mean the area around may not have been affected. The residue of communities of smaller monastic sites nearby may have joined the community. Site S.1 at Hawara, el-Ar'bein (Faiers, 2005, 270), possibly also monastic, seems to have been occupied from a slightly earlier date (according to the coin evidence) but overlapping with (according to the pottery evidence) Kom el-Nana. Christian influence can be found in the pottery at this site: a jar sherd decorated with a fish and a lamp with a cross on the upper surface behind the nozzle. The S.19 area south of el-Hawara (Faiers, 2005, 54 and 273) shows signs of being quite a large community utilising the caves above the valley floor.

The North Tombs settlement at the north end of the Amarna region was perhaps occupied in the mid-to-late fifth century, judging by the datable ARS vessels (Pyke, 2010, 24). The survey of the site found that it comprised individual self-contained dwellings, the ceramic material associated with which was chiefly concentrated in midden deposits lying outside, but immediately adjacent to, the dwellings (Pyke, 2010, 24). The midden assemblages were homogeneous across the site and comprised domestic wares for food storage, preparation and consumption. The relationship between this monastic foundation and the one at Kom el-Nana is not clear, but dating evidence from the two sites suggests that they were in use at the same time. It is not known why the North Tombs settlement was abandoned, or whether its inhabitants joined the monastery at Kom el-Nana.

In conclusion, analysis of the distribution of pottery and glass finds at Kom el-Nana has had to take into account not only the various phases of occupation of the monastery, but also the approximately 1,600 years of human activity in the area following its abandonment. The main finding has been that, apart from a few specific cases, it is likely that the pottery and glass is no longer in its original place of use, discard or abandonment. The ceramic and glass assemblages can therefore only offer a broad repertoire of types and date range for activity. The architectural use of vessels and/or sherds is in keeping with examples at other monasteries, and attests both its significance as a building material and, in the case of the cooling installation, the ingenuity of the inhabitants of the monastery. The *terminus post quem* offered by the casemate fill suggests that the monastery was expanded towards the end of its lifetime, but the circumstances of the addition of new buildings and the reconfiguration of existing ones remains obscure.

| Pottery RBH | Sector | | | | |
|---|---|---|---|---|---|
| | **SE** | **NW** | **NE Tower** | **NE** | **Church** |
| Less than 100 | AF33<br>AB36<br>AB34 | | | | |
| 100-200 | AC39<br>AF34<br>AA37 | V52<br>U53<br>U51 | Y50<br>AA50<br>Z51<br>Z50<br>Y51 | AB51<br>AB52<br>AE51<br>AE49 | |
| 201-300 | AB35 | V51 | | AB49<br>AC50<br>AB48<br>AC51<br>AB49/50<br>AB50 | AA49<br>AA47 |
| 301-400 | | | Y52<br>Z52 | AD51<br>AE52<br>AC52 | AA48 |
| 401-500 | | | | AD52<br>AC49<br>AD50 | |
| 501-1000 | | | | AD49 | |
| 1000+ | Z36 | | | | |

*Table 3.1 Number of pottery RBH by sector and square*

| Glass RBH | Sector | | | | |
|---|---|---|---|---|---|
| | **SE** | **NW** | **NE tower** | **NE** | **Church** |
| 0 | AC39 | U51<br>U53<br>V52 | Y50 | | |
| 1 to 5 | AF34 | V51 | Z51<br>Z50<br>Y51<br>AA49 | AE52<br>AB48<br>AE51<br>AE49<br>AF51 | AA49 |
| 6 to 10 | AA37 | | Y52<br>AA50 | AB49/50<br>AB51<br>AC49<br>AD52 | AA47<br>AA48 |
| 11 to 15 | AB35 | | Z52 | AB50<br>AC51 | |
| 16 to 20 | | | | AC50<br>AC51 | |
| 21 to 30 | Z36 | | | AC52<br>AB49 | |
| 31 to 50 | | | | AD49 | |

*Table 3.2 Number of glass RBH by sector and square*

| Pottery RBH | Amphora RBH | Finewares | Forms found | Forms in this volume | Forms in Volume 1 or coins | Glass RBH | Forms found |
|---|---|---|---|---|---|---|---|
| 1,358 | M3 574<br>N1 32<br>N9 18<br>N10 1 | ARS 1<br>O1 55<br>O1W 1<br>M5 64<br>M6 56 | Jar, bowl/basin, dish, qadus, pitcher/jug, cooking pot, flask/flagon, storage vessel, lamp, brazier, funnel, bucket | ARS not illustrated AD51 [7575] nos. 24, 25, 53, 85, 94, 110, 113, 124, 138, 143, 159, 212 | nos. 76 and 83 | 30 | Jar, dish, platter, flask/ flagon, goblet, bowl, lamp, beaker |

*Table 3.3 Distribution of forms of pottery and glass RBH in the main tower (Area 1) of the south-east sector*

| Pottery Form | Casemate Fill | | Pit | | Collapse | | Tower Overall Total | |
|---|---|---|---|---|---|---|---|---|
| | RBH | EVE | RBH | EVE | RBH | EVE | RBH | EVE |
| Amphora | 340 | 20 | 165 | 2 | 73 | 2 | 625 | 51 |
| Jar | 41 | 5 | 35 | 3 | 8 | 1 | 131 | 9 |
| Bowl/basin | 93 | 7 | 47 | 2 | 23 | 1 | 263 | 12 |
| Dish | 22 | 2 | 14 | 1 | 5 | 1 | 59 | 3 |
| Qadus | 13 | 8 | 20 | 1 | 11 | 1 | 101 | 11 |
| Pitcher/jug | 1 | 1 | 0 | 0 | 1 | 1 | 5 | 1 |
| Cooking pot | 52 | 3 | 15 | 1 | 9 | 1 | 84 | 5 |
| Lid | 4 | 2 | 0 | 0 | 0 | 0 | 12 | 1 |
| Colander | 0 | 0 | 0 | 0 | 0 | 0 | 0 | 0 |
| Flask | 24 | 5 | 17 | 1 | 6 | 1 | 70 | 6 |
| Cup | 0 | 0 | 1 | 1 | 0 | 0 | 1 | 1 |
| Storage vessels | 1 | 1 | 2 | 1 | 4 | 1 | 3 | 1 |
| Other* | 0 | 0 | 0 | 0 | 1 | 1 | 4 | 4 |
| Total | 591 | 55 | 316 | 13 | 141 | 11 | 1358 | 104 |
| *Other includes bucket, funnel, lamp and brazier | | | | | | | | |

*Table 3.4 Pottery forms RBH and EVE in the main tower casemate fill, pit and collapse (Area 1) in the south-east sector*

| Area | Pottery RBH | Amphora RBH | Finewares | Forms found | Forms in this volume | Forms in Volume 1 or coins | Glass RBH | Forms found |
|---|---|---|---|---|---|---|---|---|
| 2 | 97 | M3 53<br>N1 1<br>N9 1 | O1 13<br>M5 2<br>M6 2 | Jar, bowl/basin, dish, qadus, cooking pot, lid, flask/flagon | nos. 21 and 548 | Nil | 6 | Goblet, bowl |
| 3 | 304 | M3 124<br>N1 8<br>N9 1 | ARS 1<br>O1 13<br>O1W 1<br>M5 5<br>M6 10 | Jar, bowl/basin, dish, qadus, pitcher/jug, lid, flask/flagon, cup, storage vessel, funnel (?), vessel | nos.18, 89, 209, 217, 293, 328, 334, 353, 365, 398, 440, 485, 492 | Nil<br>Coin: 5th–6th century AD | 12 | Jar, bowl/ bottle, lamp, jug, goblet, beaker |

*Table 3.5 Distribution of forms of pottery and glass RBH in the staircase tower (Area 2) and south refectory (Area 3) of the south-east sector*

| Pottery Form | Staircase tower Area 2 | | South refectory Area 3 | |
|---|---|---|---|---|
| | RBH | EVE | RBH | EVE |
| Amphora | 55 | 4 | 133 | 19 |
| Jar | 10 | 1 | 43 | 7 |
| Bowl/basin | 12 | 1 | 38 | 3 |
| Dish | 3 | 1 | 8 | 1 |
| Qadus | 7 | 2 | 32 | 9 |
| Pitcher/jug | 0 | 0 | 3 | 1 |
| Cooking pot | 5 | 1 | 14 | 2 |
| Lid | 2 | 1 | 11 | 1 |
| Colander | 0 | 0 | 0 | 0 |
| Flask | 3 | 1 | 8 | 2 |
| Cup | 0 | 0 | 2 | 1 |
| Storage vessel | 0 | 0 | 8 | 1 |
| Other* | 0 | 0 | 4 | 4 |
| Total | 97 | 12 | 304 | 51 |
| *Other includes funnel, mini beaker, tiny pot, unidentified vessel | | | | |

*Table 3.6 Pottery forms RBH and EVE in the staircase tower (Area 2) and south refectory (Area 3) of the south-east sector*

| Pottery Form | Staircase tower Area 2 | | South refectory Area 3 | |
|---|---|---|---|---|
| | RBH | EVE | RBH | EVE |
| Amphora | 55 | 4 | 133 | 19 |
| Jar | 10 | 1 | 43 | 7 |
| Bowl/basin | 12 | 1 | 38 | 3 |
| Dish | 3 | 1 | 8 | 1 |
| Qadus | 7 | 2 | 32 | 9 |
| Pitcher/jug | 0 | 0 | 3 | 1 |
| Cooking pot | 5 | 1 | 14 | 2 |
| Lid | 2 | 1 | 11 | 1 |
| Colander | 0 | 0 | 0 | 0 |
| Flask | 3 | 1 | 8 | 2 |
| Cup | 0 | 0 | 2 | 1 |
| Storage vessel | 0 | 0 | 8 | 1 |
| Other* | 0 | 0 | 4 | 4 |
| Total | 97 | 12 | 304 | 51 |
| *Other includes funnel, mini beaker, tiny pot, unidentified vessel | | | | |

*Table 3.7 Distribution of forms of pottery and glass RBH in the room north of the staircase tower (Area 4) and south-east corner of monastery enclosure (Area 5) in the south-east sector*

| Form | Area 4 | | Area 5 | |
|---|---|---|---|---|
| | RBH | EVE | RBH | EVE |
| Amphora | 48 | 3 | 40 | 4 |
| Jar | 21 | 1 | 17 | 1 |
| Bowl/basin | 15 | 1 | 35 | 2 |
| Dish | 1 | 1 | 7 | 1 |
| Qadus | 7 | 1 | 11 | 2 |
| Pitcher/jug | 0 | 0 | 0 | 0 |
| Cooking pot | 7 | 1 | 22 | 1 |
| Lid | 3 | 1 | 10 | 1 |
| Colander | 0 | 0 | 5 | 0 |
| Flask/flagon | 5 | 1 | 1 | 1 |
| Cup | 0 | 0 | 1 | 1 |
| Storage vessel | 0 | 0 | 1 | 1 |
| Other* | 3 | 3 | 7 | 7 |
| Total RBH | 117 | 13 | 157 | 22 |
| *Other includes candlestick, brazier, tazza, lamp, tiny pot, unidentified vessel, drainpipe | | | | |

*Table 3.8 Pottery forms RBH and EVE in the room north of the staircase tower (Area 4) and south-east corner of monastery enclosure (Area 5) in the south-east sector*

| Area | Pottery RBH | Amphora | Finewares | Forms found | Forms in this volume | Forms in Volume 1 or coins | Glass RBH | Forms found |
|---|---|---|---|---|---|---|---|---|
| **1** | 419 | M3 171<br>N1 5<br>N7 1 | ARS 2<br>O1 17<br>M5 10<br>M6 34 | Jar, bowl/basin, dish, lid, flask/flag, cooking pot, *qadus*, pitcher/jug, cup, ladle, storage vessel | nos. 27, 101,133, 280, 301 and 568 | nos. 18, 23, 42, 50, 99, 121, 127, 171 | 3 | Platter, jar, bracelet |
| **2** | 149 | M3 70<br>N1 2 | O1 3<br>M5 2<br>M6 6 | Jar, bowl/basin, dish, *qadus*, cooking pot, lid, flask/flagon | Nil | no.72 | 5 | Platter, goblet, bowl |
| **3** | 190 | M3 71<br>N1 2<br>N9 2 | O1 8<br>M5 3<br>M6 5 | Jar, bowl/basin, dish, *qadus*, pitcher/jug, cooking pot, flask/flagon, cup | nos. 11, 73, 445 | nos. 43, 72, 82, 119, 184, 187 | Nil | Nil |

*Table 3.9 Distribution of forms of pottery and glass RBH in the north-west sector*

| Pottery Form | Accommodation Complex Area 1 | | Storage Rooms Area 2 | | Activity Area Area 3 | |
|---|---|---|---|---|---|---|
| | RBH | EVE | RBH | EVE | RBH | EVE |
| Amphora | 177 | 33 | 72 | 17 | 75 | 11 |
| Jar | 58 | 9 | 17 | 1 | 37 | 5 |
| Bowl/basin | 91 | 5 | 22 | 2 | 14 | 3 |
| Dish | 13 | 1 | 1 | 1 | 3 | 1 |
| Qadus | 14 | 3 | 11 | 2 | 9 | 3 |
| Pitcher/jug | 4 | 1 | 0 | 0 | 5 | 1 |
| Cooking pot | 39 | 1 | 18 | 1 | 27 | 3 |
| Lid | 7 | 1 | 2 | 1 | 7 | 1 |
| Colander | 0 | 0 | 0 | 0 | 0 | 0 |
| Flask/flagon | 14 | 1 | 5 | 1 | 7 | 1 |
| Cup | 1 | 1 | 0 | 0 | 2 | 1 |
| Storage vessel | 1 | 1 | 0 | 0 | 0 | 0 |
| Other* | 1 | 1 | 0 | 0 | 4 | 4 |
| Total RBH | 419 | | 149 | | 190 | |
| Total number of vessels | | 67 | 26 | 26 | 32 | 32 |
| *Other includes bottle, flowerpot, bucket and ladle | | | | | | |

*Table 3.10 Pottery forms RBH and EVE in the north-west sector*

| Area | Pottery RBH | Amphora | Finewares | Forms represented | Forms in this volume | Forms in Volume 1 or coins | Glass RBH | Forms represented |
|---|---|---|---|---|---|---|---|---|
| 1 | 138 | M3 43<br>N1 4<br>N9 1 | ARS 2<br>O1 5<br>O1W 1<br>M5 5<br>M6 9 | Jar, bowl/basin, dish, qadus, pitcher/jug, cooking pot, flask/flagon, storage vessel, bottle | nos. 8, 102, 186 | no. 4 | 1 | Jar |
| 2 | 191 | M3 36<br>N8 1<br>Unid. 2 | ARS 3<br>O1 5<br>M5 14<br>M6 4 | Jar, bowl/basin, dish, cooking pot, lid, colander, flask/flagon, storage vessel, lamp, bottle | nos. 93, 512 | nos. 8, 11, 118, 130, 150, 277 | Nil | Nil |
| 3 | 277 | M3 86<br>N1 4<br>N7 1 | ARS 1<br>O1 6<br>O1W 1<br>M5 9<br>M6 15 | Jar, bowl/basin, dish, qadus, cooking pot, lid, flask/flagon, cup, storage vessel | nos. 7, 52, 98, 152, 163, 278 | Nil | 4 | Goblet, flask/flagon |

*Table 3.11 Distribution of forms of pottery and glass RBH in the north-east tower (Areas 1–3) in the north-east tower sector*

| Form | Area 1 Tower Staircase | | Area 2 Activity Area | | Area 3 Three-Room Suite | |
|---|---|---|---|---|---|---|
| | RBH | EVE | RBH | EVE | RBH | EVE |
| Amphora | 48 | 5 | 39 | 4 | 91 | 10 |
| Jar | 20 | 1 | 33 | 2 | 31 | 2 |
| Bowl/basin | 33 | 2 | 60 | 2 | 65 | 4 |
| Dish | 5 | 1 | 11 | 1 | 24 | 1 |
| Qadus | 5 | 2 | 4 | 1 | 15 | 1 |
| Pitcher/jug | 1 | 1 | 0 | 0 | 0 | 0 |
| Cooking pot | 13 | 1 | 25 | 1 | 26 | 5 |
| Lid | 1 | 1 | 3 | 1 | 12 | 1 |
| Colander | 0 | 0 | 1 | 1 | 0 | 0 |
| Flask/flagon | 9 | 1 | 3 | 1 | 9 | 1 |
| Cup | 0 | 0 | 0 | 0 | 0 | 0 |
| Storage vessel | 1 | 1 | 9 | 1 | 3 | 1 |
| Other* | 2 | 2 | 3 | 3 | 1 | 1 |
| Total RBH | 138 | | 191 | | 277 | |
| Total number of vessels | | 18 | | 18 | | 26 |
| *Other includes lamp, ladle, bottle, goblet, candlestick | | | | | | |

*Table 3.12 Pottery forms RBH and EVE in the north-east tower (Areas 1–3) in the north-east tower sector*

| Area | Pottery RBH | Amphora | Finewares | Forms found | Forms in this volume | Forms in Volume 1 or coins | Glass RBH | Forms found |
|---|---|---|---|---|---|---|---|---|
| 4 | 632 | M3 184<br>N1 7<br>N9 4 | ARS 2<br>O1 51<br>O1W 2<br>M5 20<br>M6 28 | Jar, bowl/ basin, dish, qadus, pitcher/jug, cooking pot, colander, flask/flagon, cup, ladle, storage vessel | nos. 13, 19, 31, 57, 61, 69, 86, 574 | nos. 29 and 403 | 16 | Bowl, jar, flask/ flagon, beaker, platter, goblet |
| 5 | 226 | M3 59<br>N1 2<br>N7 1<br>N9 1<br>Unid. 1 | ARS 4<br>O1 9<br>M5 15<br>M6 10 | Jar, bowl/ basin, dish, qadus, cooking pot, lid, colander, flask/flagon, cup, storage vessel, ladle, candlestick | nos. 3, 4, 9, 403 | Nil | 6 | Bowl, goblet, jar, beaker |

*Table 3.13 Distribution of forms of pottery and glass RBH in the industrial kitchen (Area 4) and courtyard (Area 5) of the north-east tower sector*

| Form | Area 4 Industrial/ Kitchen Area | | Area 5 Courtyard | |
|---|---|---|---|---|
| | RBH | EVE | RBH | EVE |
| Amphora | 195 | 3 | 64 | 5 |
| Jar | 88 | 5 | 33 | 2 |
| Bowl/basin | 131 | 8 | 52 | 3 |
| Dish | 17 | 1 | 11 | 1 |
| Qadus | 45 | 8 | 13 | 1 |
| Pitcher/jug | 3 | 1 | 0 | 0 |
| Cooking pot | 54 | 2 | 13 | 1 |
| Lid | 24 | 1 | 9 | 1 |
| Colander | 11 | 2 | 7 | 1 |
| Flask/flagon | 39 | 4 | 12 | 1 |
| Cup | 8 | 2 | 3 | 1 |
| Storage vessel | 13 | 1 | 3 | 1 |
| *Other | 4 | 4 | 3 | 3 |
| Total | 632 | 42 | 223 | 21 |
| *Other includes lamp, ladle, bottle, goblet, candlestick | | | | |

*Table 3.14 Pottery forms RBH and EVE in the industrial kitchen (Area 4) and courtyard (Area 5) of the north-east tower sector*

| Area | Pottery RBH | Amphora | Finewares | Forms represented | Vessels in this volume | Vessels in Volume 1 or coins | Glass | Forms represented |
|---|---|---|---|---|---|---|---|---|
| 1 | 252 | M3 36<br>N9 3<br>Unid. 1 | O1 11<br>O2 1<br>M5 19<br>M6 22 | Jar, bowl/basin, dish, qadus, cooking pot, lid, colander, flask/ flagon, cup, storage vessel, tub | nos. 28, 35, 37, 39, 90, 92, 104, 109, 112, 128, 150, 166, 176, 262, 387, 390, 545, 546, 551, 588 | Nil | 7 | Jar, flagon, lamp, bottle |
| 2 | 160 | M3 29<br>N1 2 | ARS 1<br>O1 10<br>O1W 1<br>M5 4<br>M6 14 | Jar, bowl/basin, dish, qadus, cooking pot, lid, colander, flask/flagon, storage vessel, lamp | nos. 5, 14, 29, 164, 226, 228, 386, 553 | Nil | 8 | Platter, bottle, cup, bowl |
| 3 | 63 | M3 9<br>O1 1 | O1 2<br>M5 1<br>M6 9 | Jar, bowl/basin, dish, qadus, cooking pot, lid | nos. 122, 168, 377, 385 | Nil | 2 | Lamp |
| 4 | 187 | M3 23<br>N1 1<br>N9 2 | ARS 1<br>O1 9<br>M5 11<br>M6 13 | Jar, bowl/basin, dish, qadus, pitcher/ jug, cooking pot, lid, colander, flask/ flagon, cup, storage vessel | nos. 6, 38, 43, 46, 91, 105, 119, 129, 151, 168, 172, 191, 235, 241, 385, 441, 464, 467, 509, 510, 545, 552 | Nil | 5 | Jug, bowl, goblet, jar |

*Table 3.15 Distribution of forms of pottery and glass RBH in the church*

| Form | Area 1 The Apse | | Area 2 South Pastophorium | | Area 3 North Pastophorium | | Area 4 Staircase Room | |
|---|---|---|---|---|---|---|---|---|
| | RBH | EVE | RBH | EVE | RBH | EVE | RBH | EVE |
| Amphora | 40 | 6 | 31 | 7 | 10 | 3 | 26 | 7 |
| Jar | 46 | 2 | 27 | 9 | 20 | 2 | 39 | 3 |
| Bowl/basin | 80 | 3 | 43 | 2 | 10 | 1 | 48 | 2 |
| Dish | 25 | 1 | 14 | 1 | 1 | 1 | 9 | 1 |
| Qadus | 16 | 1 | 16 | 1 | 13 | 1 | 21 | 2 |
| Pitcher/jug | 0 | 0 | 0 | 0 | 0 | 0 | 1 | 1 |
| Cooking pot | 31 | 2 | 18 | 1 | 8 | 1 | 27 | 1 |
| Lid | 1 | 1 | 1 | 1 | 1 | 1 | 4 | 1 |
| Colander | 1 | 1 | 1 | 1 | 0 | 0 | 2 | 1 |
| Flask/flagon | 1 | 1 | 1 | 1 | 0 | 0 | 6 | 1 |
| Cup | 2 | 1 | 0 | 0 | 0 | 0 | 1 | 1 |
| Storage vessel | 4 | 1 | 3 | 1 | 0 | 0 | 3 | 1 |
| Other* | 5 | 1 | 1 | 1 | 0 | 0 | 0 | 0 |
| Total RBH | 252 | | 160 | | 63 | | 187 | |
| Total number of vessels | | 21 | | 26 | | 10 | | 22 |
| *Other includes lamp, tub | | | | | | | | |

*Table 3.16 Pottery forms RBH and EVE in the church*

| Area | Pottery RBH | Amphora | Finewares | Forms represented | Vessels in this volume | Vessels in Vol. 1 or coins | Glass RBH | Forms represented |
|---|---|---|---|---|---|---|---|---|
| 1 | 608 | M3 249<br>N1 10<br>N7 1 | ARS 3<br>O1 26<br>O1W 1<br>O2 1<br>M5 17<br>M6 23 | Jar, bowl/basin, dish, qadus, cooking pot, lid, flask/flagon, cup, storage vessel, tub, tazza/lamp | nos. 1, 68, 73, 107, 175, 184 and 254 | nos. 48, 98, 186, 432<br>Coins: 40<br>AD 425–450<br>AD 541–552<br>22 x 4th–6th century<br>3 x AD 527–565<br>5 x 5th century<br>6 x 5th–6th century | 58 | Platter, dish, jar, beaker, goblet, lamp, jug |
| 2 | 125 | M3 79<br>N1 1<br>N10 1 | O1 6<br>O1W 1<br>M5 3<br>M6 5 | Jar, bowl/basin, dish, qadus, cooking pot, lid, flask/flagon, ladle | nos. 75 and 592 | nos. 136 and 395<br>Coins: 11<br>2 x 4th–5th century<br>5 x 4th–6th century<br>1 x AD 527–565<br>1 x AD 539–565<br>1 x AD 565–578<br>1 x 578–582 | 21 | Goblet, bead |
| 3 | 558 | M3 208<br>N1 5<br>N7 1<br>N9 2 | ARS 1<br>O1 36<br>O2 4<br>M5 6<br>M6 17 | Compartmented dish, jar, bowl/basin, dish, qadus, cooking pot, lid, colander, flask/flagon, storage, vessel, ladle, bucket, lamp, goblet | nos. 17, 23, 40, 48, 66, 71, 84, 157, 284, 329, 349, 366, 399, 404, 431, 478, 527, 531, 576, 589, 591 | nos. 55, 172, 285, 429<br>Coins: 2<br>1 x 4th–5th century<br>1 x 5th–6th century | 5 | Beaker, goblet, bottle, flask, lamp |
| 4 | 629 | M3 149<br>N1 3<br>N7 2 | O1 42<br>M5 8<br>M6 17 | Jar, bowl/basin, dish, qadus, cooking pot, lid, flask/flagon, cup, colander, storage, vessel, ladle, tazza, bucket, funnel, lamp | nos. 40, 41, 42, 47, 48, 49, 63, 71, 76, 158, 395, 429 | nos. 191, 243<br>Coins: 24<br>AD 527–565<br>AD 530–534<br>4th to 5th century<br>3 x 5th–6th century<br>16 x 4th–6th century<br>2 x 4th–7th century | 34 | Beaker, goblet, platter, bottle, flask, jar, lamp, bowl |

*Table 3.17 Distribution of forms of pottery and glass RBH in the refectory (Area 1), kitchen (Area 2), storeroom/larder (Area 3) and large storeroom (Area 4) of the north-east sector*

| Form | Area 1 Refectory | | Area 2 Kitchen | | Area 3 Storeroom Larder/Kitchen 2 | | Area 4 Large Storeroom | |
|---|---|---|---|---|---|---|---|---|
| | RBH | EVE | RBH | EVE | RBH | EVE | RBH | EVE |
| Amphora | 260 | 33 | 81 | 25 | 230 | 31 | 154 | 29 |
| Jar | 70 | 5 | 5 | 1 | 79 | 4 | 135 | 9 |
| Bowl/basin | 110 | 6 | 10 | 1 | 27 | 5 | 92 | 8 |
| Dish | 22 | 2 | 8 | 1 | 22 | 1 | 22 | 2 |
| Qadus | 35 | 7 | 3 | 3 | 44 | 5 | 38 | 5 |
| Pitcher/jug | 0 | 0 | 0 | 0 | 0 | 0 | 3 | 1 |
| Cooking pot | 40 | 3 | 8 | 1 | 93 | 4 | 109 | 6 |
| Lid | 25 | 2 | 3 | 1 | 13 | 1 | 16 | 1 |
| Colander | 8 | 1 | 0 | 0 | 8 | 1 | 17 | 2 |
| Flask/flagon | 28 | 2 | 4 | 2 | 11 | 1 | 27 | 4 |
| Cup | 4 | 1 | 0 | 0 | 12 | 1 | 2 | 1 |
| Storage vessel | 3 | 1 | 0 | 0 | 6 | 1 | 8 | 1 |
| Other* | 3 | 3 | 3 | 3 | 13 | 13 | 6 | 6 |
| Total RBH | 608 | | 125 | | 558 | | 629 | |
| Total number of vessels | | 66 | | 38 | | 68 | | 75 |
| *Other includes funnel, bucket, tazza, ladle, lamp | | | | | | | | |

*Table 3.18 Pottery forms RBH and EVE in the refectory (Area 1), kitchen (Area 2), storeroom/larder (Area 3) and large storeroom (Area 4) of the north-east sector*

| Pottery Form | Kitchen (Area 2) | | Storeroom/larder (Area 3) | | | | Storeroom with sub-floor installation (Area 4) | |
|---|---|---|---|---|---|---|---|---|
| | | | Pots in Slots | | Other | | | |
| | RBH Total | EVE Total | RBH Total | EVE Total | RBH Total | EVE Total | RBH Total | EVE Total |
| Amphora | 81 | 25 | 55 | 8 | 175 | 18 | 154 | 29 |
| Jar | 5 | 1 | 23 | 2 | 56 | 2 | 135 | 9 |
| Bowl/basin | 10 | 1 | 5 | 1 | 22 | 3 | 92 | 8 |
| Dish | 8 | 1 | 3 | 1 | 19 | 1 | 22 | 2 |
| Qadus | 3 | 3 | 4 | 1 | 40 | 4 | 38 | 5 |
| Pitcher/jug | 0 | 0 | 0 | 0 | 0 | 0 | 3 | 1 |
| Cooking pot | 8 | 1 | 27 | 2 | 66 | 3 | 109 | 6 |
| Lid | 3 | 1 | 1 | 1 | 12 | 1 | 16 | 1 |
| Colander | 0 | 0 | 1 | 1 | 7 | 1 | 17 | 2 |
| Flask/flagon | 4 | 2 | 6 | 1 | 5 | 2 | 27 | 4 |
| Cup | 0 | 0 | 0 | 0 | 12 | 1 | 2 | 1 |
| Storage vessel | 0 | 0 | 6 | 1 | 0 | 0 | 8 | 1 |
| Other* | 3 | 3 | 7 | 7 | 6 | 6 | 6 | 6 |
| Total RBH | 125 | | 138 | | 420 | | 629 | |
| Total number of vessels | | 38 | | 26 | | 42 | | 75 |
| *Other includes funnel, ladle, bucket ,lamp, goblet, tazza | | | | | | | | |

*Table 3.19 Pottery forms RBH and EVE in the kitchen (Area 2), storeroom/larder (Area 3) and storeroom with sub-floor installation (Area 4) in the north-east sector*

| Area | Pottery RBH | Amphora | Finewares | Forms represented | Vessels in this volume | Vessels in Volume 1 or coins | Glass RBH | Forms represented |
|---|---|---|---|---|---|---|---|---|
| 5 | 160 | M3 46<br>N9 1<br>N1 3 | O1 10<br>M5 5<br>M6 2 | Jar, bowl/basin, dish, qadus, cooking pot, lid, flask/flagon, cup, colander, storage vessel | nos. 157, 314, 366, 453, 461, 478, 527 | Nil | 2 | Beaker, bowl |
| 6 | 642 | M3 119<br>N9 6<br>N1 4<br>N10 1 | O1 17<br>O1W 3<br>M5 25<br>M6 22 | Jar, bowl/basin, dish, qadus, cooking pot, lid, flask/flagon, cup, colander, bucket, goblet, storage vessel | nos. 54, 206, 219, 257, 405, 434 | no. 58 | 32 | Beaker, bowl, goblet, platter, jar, lamp |

*Table 3.20 Distribution of forms of pottery and glass RBH in the anteroom/corridor (Area 5) and reception room (Area 6) of the north-east sector*

| Form | Area 5 Ante-room to Area 6 | | Area 6 Reception Room | |
|---|---|---|---|---|
| | RBH | EVE | RBH | EVE |
| Amphora | 50 | 4 | 130 | 14 |
| Jar | 19 | 1 | 120 | 6 |
| Bowl/basin | 30 | 2 | 133 | 5 |
| Dish | 3 | 1 | 16 | 1 |
| Qadus | 12 | 1 | 75 | 7 |
| Pitcher/jug | 0 | 0 | 1 | 1 |
| Cooking pot | 13 | 1 | 98 | 4 |
| Lid | 4 | 1 | 19 | 1 |
| Colander | 17 | 2 | 18 | 1 |
| Flask/flagon | 4 | 1 | 9 | 1 |
| Cup | 2 | 1 | 14 | 1 |
| Storage vessel | 5 | 1 | 7 | 1 |
| Other | 1 | 1 | 2 | 2 |
| Total RBH | 160 | | 642 | |
| Total number of vessels | | 17 | | 45 |

*Other includes bucket, goblet, flower pot, lamp, pot stand

*Table 3.21 Pottery forms RBH and EVE in the anteroom/corridor (Area 5) and reception room (Area 6) of the north-east sector*

| Area | Pottery RBH | Amphora | Finewares | Forms represented | Vessels in this volume | Vessels in Volume 1 or coins | Glass RBH | Forms represented |
|---|---|---|---|---|---|---|---|---|
| Area 7 | 872 | M3 232<br>N1 4<br>N9 3 | ARS 4<br>O1 94<br>O2 1<br>O1W 1<br>M5 27<br>M6 24 | Jar, bowl/basin, qadus, dish, cooking pot, lid, flask/flagon, cup, colander, storage vessel, lamp, tub, bucket | nos. 2, 23, 30, 77, 114, 125, 145, 146, 196, 198, 250, 260, 285, 302, 399, 402, 405, 413, 432, 454, 457, 476, 477, 515, 526 | nos. 32, 35, 36, 63, 64, 116, 122, 432<br>Coins:<br>1 x AD 538–565<br>2 x 4th–6th AD<br>3 x 5th century AD<br>1 x 5th–6th century AD | 76 | Beaker, bowl, goblet, platter, flagon, jar, lamp |

*Table 3.22 Distribution of forms of pottery and glass RBH in the alleyway (Area 7) of the north-east sector*

| Form | Area 7 | |
|---|---|---|
| | RBH | EVE |
| Amphora | 239 | 16 |
| Jar | 156 | 3 |
| Bowl/basin | 166 | 18 |
| dish | 38 | 2 |
| Qadus | 59 | 4 |
| Pitcher/jug | 2 | 1 |
| Cooking pot | 133 | 6 |
| Lid | 22 | 1 |
| Colander | 35 | 4 |
| Flask/flagon | 13 | 1 |
| Cup | 2 | 1 |
| Storage vessel | 4 | 2 |
| Other* | 3 | 3 |
| Total RBH | 872 | |
| Total number of vessels | | 62 |
| *Other includes bucket, tub, lamp | | |

*Table 3.23 Pottery forms RBH and EVE in the alleyway (Area 7) of the north-east sector*

| Area | Pottery RBH | Amphora | Finewares | Forms represented | Vessels in this volume | Vessels in Volume 1 or coins | Glass RBH | Forms represented |
|---|---|---|---|---|---|---|---|---|
| Area 8 | 409 | M3 92<br>N9 3<br>N11 1 | ARS 1<br>O1 35<br>O2 1<br>M5 11<br>M6 14 | Jar, bowl/ basin, qadus, dish, cooking pot, flask/ flagon, cup, colander, storage vessel, tub, ladle, bucket | nos. 20, 26, 58, 83, 111, 139, 263, 281, 282, 285, 330, 333, 350, 361, 400, 530, 542, 595 | nos. 30, 33, 137, 212, 250<br>Coin: AD 565–578 | 19 | Beaker, goblet, platter, jar |

*Table 3.24 Distribution of pottery and glass RBH in the animal-keeping area (Area 8), in the north-east sector*

| Pottery Form | Animal Pens | | Midden in North Part of Alleyway | | North-East Activity Area | |
|---|---|---|---|---|---|---|
| | RBH | EVE | RBH | EVE | RBH | EVE |
| Amphora | 0 | 0 | 11 | 2 | 85 | 8 |
| Jar | 1 | 1 | 10 | 1 | 29 | 3 |
| Bowl/basin | 0 | 0 | 17 | 1 | 73 | 4 |
| Dish | 0 | 0 | 0 | 0 | 13 | 1 |
| Qadus | 0 | 0 | 2 | 1 | 23 | 2 |
| Pitcher/jug | 0 | 0 | 1 | 1 | 2 | 1 |
| Cooking pot | 0 | 0 | 47 | 2 | 50 | 2 |
| Lid | 0 | 0 | 2 | 1 | 10 | 1 |
| Colander | 0 | 0 | 0 | 0 | 3 | 1 |
| Flask/flagon | 0 | 0 | 5 | 1 | 4 | 1 |
| Cup | 0 | 0 | 0 | 0 | 5 | 1 |
| Storage vessel | 0 | 0 | 0 | 0 | 7 | 1 |
| Other* | 0 | 0 | 4 | 1 | 5 | 2 |
| Total RBH | 1 | | 99 | | 309 | |
| Total number of vessels | | 1 | | 11 | | 28 |
| *Other includes bucket, tub, ladle | | | | | | |

*Table 3.25 Pottery forms RBH and EVE in the animal-keeping area (Area 8), in the north-east sector*

| Area | Pottery RBH | Amphora | Finewares | Forms represented | Vessels in this volume | Vessels in Vol. 1 or coins | Glass RBH | Forms represented |
|---|---|---|---|---|---|---|---|---|
| 9 | 388 | M3 73<br>N1 8<br>O1 1 | O1 20<br>O1W 2<br>M5 5<br>M6 11 | Jar, bowl/ basin, qadus, dish, cooking pot, lid, flask/ flagon, cup, colander, storage, vessel | nos. 51, 74, 118, 197, 322, 332, 357, 374, 488 | nos. 31, 132<br>Coin: 4th–6th AD | 7 | Beaker, goblet, platter, bottle |
| 10 | 367 | M3 49<br>N1 3<br>N9 2<br>O1 2 | O1 48<br>M5 25<br>M6 34 | Jar, bowl/ basin, qadus, dish, cooking pot, lid, flask/flagon, colander | nos. 59, 75, 80, 100, 103, 132, 153, 162, 170, 213, 215, 220, 258, 310, 401, 427, 449, 459 | no. 54<br>Coins: 2 x 4th–6th AD<br>1 x 5th–6th AD | 12 | Beaker, goblet, bowl, platter, jar, bottle |

*Table 3.26 Distribution of forms of pottery and glass RBH in the lookout point (Area 9) and midden/garden (Area 10), in the north-east sector*

| Form | North Room | | South Room | |
|---|---|---|---|---|
| | RBH | EVE | RBH | EVE |
| Amphora | 54 | 8 | 28 | 6 |
| Jar | 33 | 3 | 33 | 2 |
| Bowl/basin | 62 | 3 | 18 | 1 |
| Dish | 14 | 1 | 2 | 1 |
| Qadus | 19 | 2 | 8 | 1 |
| Pitcher/jug | 0 | 0 | 0 | 0 |
| Cooking pot | 60 | 4 | 18 | 1 |
| Lid | 3 | 1 | 9 | 1 |
| Colander | 1 | 1 | 6 | 1 |
| Flask/flagon | 9 | 1 | 7 | 1 |
| Cup | 3 | 1 | 0 | 0 |
| Storage vessel | 0 | 0 | 1 | 1 |
| Other | 0 | 0 | 0 | 0 |
| Total RBH | 258 | | 130 | |
| Total number of vessels | | 25 | | 16 |

*Table 3.27 Pottery forms RBH and EVE in the look-out point (Area 9), in the north-east sector*

| Form | Midden | | Pottery layer beneath midden | | Pathway | | Cultivation | |
|---|---|---|---|---|---|---|---|---|
| | RBH | EVE | RBH | EVE | RBH | EVE | RBH | EVE |
| Amphora | 15 | 2 | 12 | 10 | 9 | 2 | 5 | 1 |
| Jar | 2 | 1 | 4 | 1 | 8 | 1 | 3 | 1 |
| Bowl/basin | 18 | 1 | 10 | 2 | 36 | 2 | 17 | 1 |
| Dish | 4 | 1 | 1 | 1 | 7 | 1 | 5 | 1 |
| Qadus | 5 | 1 | 10 | 2 | 4 | 1 | 2 | 1 |
| Pitcher/jug | 0 | 0 | 0 | 0 | 0 | 0 | 0 | 0 |
| Cooking pot | 5 | 1 | 12 | 2 | 20 | 1 | 3 | 1 |
| Lid | 0 | 0 | 1 | 1 | 0 | 0 | 0 | 0 |
| Colander | 1 | 1 | 0 | 0 | 1 | 1 | 0 | 0 |
| Flask/flagon | 3 | 1 | 0 | 0 | 0 | 0 | 0 | 0 |
| Cup | 3 | 1 | 0 | 0 | 0 | 0 | 2 | 1 |
| Storage vessel | 0 | 0 | 0 | 0 | 0 | 0 | 0 | 0 |
| Total RBH | 56 | | 50 | | 85 | | 37 | |
| Total number of vessels | | 10 | | 19 | | 9 | | 7 |

*Table 3.28 Pottery forms RBH and EVE in the midden/garden (Area 10) in the north-east sector*

# CHAPTER 4

# Plant Macrofossils and Pottery from Area 3, Room C

by Jane Faiers and Wendy Smith

This chapter focuses on one particular result from the Late Roman excavations at Kom el-Nana. During the 1994 season a portion of a room that may have formed part of the domestic catering arrangements for the monastery was revealed (fig. 4.2). This room (Chapter 3, north-east sector, Area 3, Room C) contained several hearths at its southern end, suggesting a cooking area, but the rest of the room appears to have been constructed as a store or larder.

As can be seen from the sketch plans (figs 4.3a, b and c) and the elevated photograph of this general area of the site (fig. 4.2), low-level mudbrick wall partitions were constructed, forming a number of small bays, or 'slots', across the room. In the next phase of construction, slots D, E and F were apparently intentionally infilled with broken and/or nearly complete pots (figs 4.4 and 5).

Pots or parts of pots had been deliberately laid on their sides, upside down, inside and/or underneath other pots within these low-level mudbrick bins, which hereafter are termed 'pot slots' or 'slots'. For example, vessel no. 2 was placed under vessel no. 6 and vessel no. 20 was placed intentionally inside vessel no. 21 (see figs 4.3b and 4.14). Slots H and G were empty, but these slots were of a smaller size than the other slots and had brick spacers, possibly to facilitate access to larger vessels standing in these slots. Slots A, B and J contained the most fragmentary vessels, all of which were smashed, largely incomplete and recovered in a jumbled state within these slots. A hard mud-plaster floor was then laid over and surrounding the pots in slots D, E and F. Slots I and C then appear to have been sealed over to form shelves or 'mastabas', with slot J either being made up to the same level or possibly higher (fig. 4c).

Out of the 29 vessels recovered from Area 3, Room C, 17 were Egyptian wine amphorae, (Egloff 177, Late Roman 7, Kom el-Nana M3), approximately 58% of the total. Four of these clearly had been reused prior to being deposited in the slots. Two pots (Pot Slot Vessel 3 and Pot Slot Vessel 20 (not drawn), see Table 1 and fig. 4.7, no. 3) contained plant remains (see below).

The pots were planned and numbered *in situ* and their vessel number in the plan of Area 3, Room C (figs 4.3 and 4.14) appears after the entry of each pot in the catalogue (Tables 1–2). Pot Slot Vessels 7, 20 and 21 were not drawn. Vessels 7 and 21 were body sherds of Egyptian amphorae and no. 20 a badly misshapen *qadus* (a water-wheel pot). Archaeobotanical remains associated with the *qadus* (Pot Slot Vessel 20, not listed in Table 2) and the shoulder and body of an amphora (Pot Slot Vessel 3, see Table 1 and fig. 4.6, no. 3) are commented on below, together with general archaeobotanical remains recovered from the fill of several of the Pot Slot low-level mudbrick bins.

The pottery recovered included Egyptian amphorae (Egloff 177, Late Roman 7, Peacock and Williams Class 52, Kom el-Nana M3 (Table 1, figs 4.6–11)). These amphorae were primarily used as wine containers and are dated from the late fourth century AD to the sixth and seventh centuries AD (for a more detailed discussion of this form see Bailey, 1998, 129–32). Coarsewares recovered from the slots included several pedestal jars and flagons, a cooking pot and a goblet (Table 2, figs 10–11). Several vessels could be reasonably closely dated to AD 450–550; however, the slightly later date of the amphorae (Table 1) from these contexts suggests the coarseware may have continued to be used at Kom el-Nana long after these vessel forms ceased to be produced locally. Alternatively, the two could well have been in existence at the same time to be buried together. Four of the amphorae found in Area 3 had been reused before being put into the Pot Slots (Pot Slot 1, 2, 3A and 15, which appear as nos 589–592 in Chapter 2).

## The plant remains

Excavation of the pot-slot area within Area 3 included detailed recording of the layout of the low-level mudbrick walls forming the pot-slot system, as well as numbering of individual pottery vessels—albeit that in some cases, sherds proved to come from more than one vessel. Soil samples were collected from the fill within vessels, as well as from the general fill of the mudbrick bins within the pot-slot area. Figures

4.14a–c show the general location of the pot-slot area in a 25-square-metre area of the excavation; the specific location of six bulk soil samples fully analysed from the pot-slot feature within Room C; and the location of vessels which had the entirety of their contents sampled for archaeobotanical remains, other environmental evidence and/or artefacts. A list of all pot-slot vessels sampled is presented in Table 3.

Each vessel was visually examined for residues; however, only Vessel 2 (TAKN94 AC50/51 8412) had an obvious residue. An orange-coloured accretion was found on two fragments of a thick-walled M3-fabric amphora and sub-samples of this material were collected for future analysis. Several of the vessels had resin on the inner or outer surface, and this was also sampled and is indicated in Table 3.

The volume of sediment within all sampled vessels was relatively small, ranging from 7.5 l (TAKN94 AC51 8412, Vessel 9) to 0.022 l (TAKN94 AC51 8571, Vessel 14). In all cases, the sediment collected from complete and near-complete vessels was processed by bucket flotation. The precise volumes of sediment, the sieve sizes used, observations regarding photography and other finds (e.g. resin, bones, plant remains, etc.) for the flots[1] and heavy residues are recorded in Table 3. In general, most of the pot-slot vessel fills were fairly poor with only a few plant remains noted in rapid scanning of flots and, therefore, were unlikely to contain primarily fills. However, two vessels did contain plant remains which are likely to be stored plant products.

An M3-fabric amphora (see Pot Slot Vessel 3, Tables 1 and 3) produced a congealed and charred conglomeration of pure Nile acacia (Acacia nilotica L.) pods (see figs 15 and 16). This vessel was located at the southern end of Room C, which later contained several cooking hearths and it is possible that the residual heat from these cooking installations may have gradually charred the contents of this vessel. In addition to this find, a saqiya or qadus water-wheel pot was also recovered from this area with primary contents (Pot Slot Vessel 20, not drawn but picture at fig. 4.17 and Table 3). The contents of this vessel have yet to be fully identified, but strips of bark cut to even lengths have been preliminarily identified as comparing quite favourably with Nile Acacia (cf. Acacia nilotica L.) bark (see fig. 4.17). Further work was not completed on this sample and initial collection of bark samples from native and/or commonly cultivated tree taxa in Minya province was curtailed by changes in the security situation post 1994.

1 The light, organic material that floats when an archaeobotanical sample is immersed in water. This light fraction is usually retained on a 0.3 mm mesh. The remainder is known as the residue.

*Acacia nilotica,* or *sant* in Arabic, is indigenous to Egypt. Nile Acacia wood is a hard wood that has been used in building and boat making since Pharaonic times (Hepper, 1990, 22–23). Nile Acacia leaves, pods and beans also make a highly nutritious animal fodder (El-Hadidi and Boulos, 1988, 32). Acacia gum, leaf and flowers are used in medicines, the bark is high in tannin and is used for the preparation of leather and hides, and the pods produce a blue dye (Hepper, 1990, 23; Manniche, 1993, 65–67). Other species of Acacia have also been found in Egypt (Barakat and Baum, 1992; Germer, 1985; Newberry, 1889). Although there is no report devoted to the plant remains from the monastery at Esna, a brief reference to a find of Acacia nilotica pods within a pot in a kitchen in Hermitage 5 was published in the pottery report (Sauneron and Jacquet, 1972, Vol. III, 7). However, human culinary use of Nile Acacia pods seems unlikely; more likely, it was some kind of medicinal, textile dye or leather tanning use, which would have required heating (most likely boiling or infusing) the Nile Acacia pods (or other plant parts).

In addition to sampling contents of individual vessels (see fig. 4.14c), bulk soil samples were collected from the general fill within separate mudbrick bins of the pot-slot area (see fig. 4.14b). The full results of these samples, as well as other bulk soil samples collected in excavations from the 1989, 1993 and 1994 seasons at Kom el-Nana, are presented in full elsewhere (see Smith 2003). Table 4 presents a summary of the number of identifications and their relative proportions for each type of plant remain category for both the desiccated and charred components of each sample. In general, these samples were highly mixed, but were mostly made up of a combination of cereal chaff, fruit (primarily the seeds from the common fig, *Ficus carica L.*, and sycamore fig, *Ficus sycomorus L.*, galls) and weed/wild taxa (especially purslane, *Portulaca oleracea L.*), which accounted for 283 identifications (or 58% of all identifications) from the desiccated component of samples 94–182s' flot, and 234 identifications (or 46.9% of all identifications) from the desiccated component of samples 94–183s' flot. Both types of fig (common and sycamore) and purslane are prolific seed producers, and are likely to be superabundant. In each case, thousands of seeds (or galls in the case of sycamore fig) are possible from a single fig or a single purslane plant. The general pattern in this data is typical of results from many 'mixed' deposits on site, such as middens, mudbricks and mudbrick rubble, and house floors (most likely reflecting detritus building up in open and abandoned buildings). Most of the archaeobotanical evidence from the bulk soil samples and pot-slot vessels suggests that this assemblage is probably made up of rubbish and/or packing materials intentionally placed in and around disused pottery vessels to infill these mudbrick bins, prior to sealing them off with a hardened mud/plaster floor.

## Discussion

At first, a straightforward interpretation of this area of the monastery as a storeroom, which was later reorganised, possibly for catering purposes seemed the most obvious for the 'pot slot' feature in Area 3, north-east sector, Room C. The layout of this area and the specific disposition of the pottery, however, is strikingly similar to another under-floor arrangement, or *vide sanitaire*, dating to the first and second centuries AD from St. Romain-en-Gal, (present day Vienne) in France (figs 4.18a and b), and may well equate to the "cool rooms for the storage of dry bread" mentioned by Husson (1979) and cited in Bagnall (1993, 297).

The example from St. Romain-en-Gal is constructed using the amphorae most common in the area at the time (second century AD), which is also the case at Kom el-Nana in the sixth century AD. The St. Romain-en-Gal example uses upturned Dressel 20 amphorae in the floor of what is thought to be a storage room for dry goods (see fig. 4.18a). The large number of amphorae used in the Kom el-Nana example—58% of the 29 vessels—is higher than the average amount of Egloff 177/M3 amphorae found in the whole assemblage at Kom el-Nana (1989–2000), which was 30%. This indicates a deliberate choice of material to put into the slots.

The precise construction of the 'cool rooms' mentioned in Bagnall (1993, 297) is not outlined, but it appears that the examples at St. Romain-en-Gal and Kom el-Nana relied on condensation in the pottery below the floor to keep the room above cooler than it would otherwise have been, given outdoor temperatures in both the south of France and middle Egypt. The room is situated in the centre of the monastic site (i.e. most shaded by surrounding buildings) and contains hearths at one end, which were presumably used for cooking and as a source of heat in cold weather.

Storehouses/rooms of various sorts must have existed elsewhere within the monastery to supply both the food for the monks, not gathered on a daily basis, and other goods and articles to be used in the monastery or sent and bartered elsewhere. The Wadi Sarga texts contain references to a pickle store (Crum et al., 1922, no. 87) and to the distribution of various commodities in differing amounts to the people mentioned, i.e. sacks of onions, (Crum et al., 1922, no. 88); salt, wine and a cloak (Crum et al., 1922, no. 164); bread (Crum et al., 1922, 186); and cheese (Crum et al., 1922, no. 166), the last two items requiring a cool, shaded environment. The room at Kom el-Nana may well have been a larder for food and/or other items that would easily spoil without cooler temperatures. Certainly, it is our opinion that the arrangement and layout of the vessels within mudbrick bins and their intentional packing underneath a hardened mud/plaster floor was not mere remodelling (i.e. a storage room falling out of use), but was likely to be the intentional construction of a cool room for improved longevity of perishable goods at the Kom el-Nana monastery.

Note: The content of this chapter was first published as part of the Festschrift for Barry Kemp in 2009 (S. Ikram and A. Dodson, 2009, V1, 89).

| Item | Description | Type/Date | Context | Drawing Number | Pot Slot Vessel Number | Figure Number |
|---|---|---|---|---|---|---|
| 1 | Amphora shoulder and most of body. Rim, neck and handles removed to the base of the neck which has then been carefully smoothed | | AC50 [8579] | GP129 | 1 | 4.6 |
| 2 | Amphora shoulder and most of the body. Rim, neck and handles removed to the base of neck which has then been carefully smoothed | Bailey, 1998: V28, dated fifth to early sixth century AD | AC50/51 [8412] | GP 142 | 2 | 4.6 |
| 3 | Amphora shoulder and body. Rim, neck and handles removed to the base of the neck which has been carefully smoothed | Date as no.2 | AC51 [8412] | GP 123 | 3 | 4.7 |
| 4 | Amphora body sherd | | AC51 [8412] | GP 126 | 4 | 4.7 |
| 5 | Amphora neck, toe and handles missing. *Dipinto* on shoulder | Date as nos. 2 and 3 | AC51 [8412] | GP 153 | 5 | 4.7 |
| 6 | Amphora. Rim missing | Bailey, 1998: V29, AD 500–650 | AC51 [8412] | GP 131 | 12 | 4.8 |
| 7 | Amphora. Neck and handles removed or missing | | AC51 [8412] | GP 133 | 9 | 4.8 |
| 8 | Amphora shoulder and most of body. Red spot on slope of shoulder. Rim, neck and handles removed to the base of the neck which has then been carefully smoothed | Date as nos. 2, 3 and 5 | AC50 [8579] | GP 134 | 15 | 4.9 |
| 9 | Amphora neck and shoulder | | AC51 [8579] | JF 712 | 18 | 4.9 |
| 10 | Amphora body sherd. Exterior burning and oily residue | | AC51 [8412] | GP 127 | 8 | 4.9 |
| 11 | Amphora. Rim missing | | AC50 [8580] | GP 130 | 17 | 4.9 |
| 12 | Amphora. Neck and handles missing. Rope marks on shoulder | | AC51 [8579] | GP 136 | 24 | 4.10 |
| 13 | Amphora. Rim and toe missing | Date as nos. 2, 3, 5 and 8 | AC51 [8579] | GP 135 | 22 | 4.10 |
| 14 | Amphora. Part of body, neck and two handles | Date as nos. 2, 3, 5, 8 and 13 | AC51 [8580] | GP 132 | 19 | 4.11 |
| 15 | Amphora shoulder | | AC51 [8579] | GP 151 | 26 | 4.11 |
| 16 | Amphora. Neck, shoulder, part of body and two handles | | AC51 [8588] | GP 150 | 27 | 4.11 |

*Table 4.1 Amphorae identified in pot slots from Room C (figs 6–11)*

| Item | Description | Type/Date | Context | Drawing Number | Pot Slot Vessel Number | Figure Number |
|---|---|---|---|---|---|---|
| 17 | Cooking pot with out-turned rim and rilled body. Rim chipped. Pitch covering the whole of the interior and splashed onto the exterior. Hard, medium-fine red-brown Nile-silt fabric, well and evenly fired with a thin red core in section. D = 18 cms | | AC51 [8588] | JF 698 | 25 | 4.12 |
| 18 | Jar with pedestal foot. Painted decoration in black and cream. Hard, red-brown Nile-silt fabric, with thin red core in section. D = 14 cms.<br><br>Elements of this design are quite common in Coptic pottery (Egloff, 1977, pl.96, no.61, and Jacquet-Gordon, 1972, pl.CCXXXII, item 1X and 1Z). Also similar to Bailey, 1996, pl.XXV, no 1 from the South Church site at Ashmunein | The Ashmunein jar post dated the destruction of the church (seventh century AD or even earlier). See also Faiers, 2005, p136, nos. 283–289. There was coin evidence of AD 460–560 for no.286 in this group | AC51 [8580] | JF 615 | 16 | 4.12 |
| 19 | Jar with pedestal foot. Missing rim and most of neck. Red-slipped overall with black painted decoration which includes a fish. Hard, medium-brown Nile-silt fabric with a thin red core in section | Probably to be equated with nos. 18 and 21 for dating | AC50 [8579] | JF 710 | 13 | 4.12 |
| 20 | Jar with pedestal foot and high neck. Black painted decoration. Hard, medium-brown Nile-silt fabric with a thin red core in section. D = 16 cms | See no.18 for dating. | AC51 [8588] | JF 614 | 26B | 4.12 |
| 21 | Jar with pedestal foot and high neck. Black painted decoration. Hard, medium-brown Nile-silt fabric with a thin red core in section. D = 16 cms | See no.18 for dating | AC50/51 [8412] | JF 750 | 11 | 4.12 |
| 22 | Jar with lid seating and two handles. Cream-slipped on exterior and dribbled beneath handles. Hard, medium-brown Nile-silt fabric with a thin red core in section. D = 24 cms | | AC51 [8579] | JF 708 | 23 | 4.13 |
| 23 | Flagon body and neck. Base and rim missing. Two handles. Cream slipped with a black arc painted on exterior. Dribbles of cream slip inside neck. Hard, slightly 'corky' fabric with numerous voids where organic matter has fired out. Limestone and other inclusions visible, wide carbon streak in section | | AC51 [8588] | JF 716 | 26A | 4.13 |

*Table 4.2 Coarseware pottery identified in pot slots from Room C (figs 12 and 13)*

| Item | Description | Type/Date | Context | Drawing Number | Pot Slot Vessel Number | Figure Number |
|---|---|---|---|---|---|---|
| 24 | Flagon body and base with foot and part of neck. Two handle scars. Cream-slipped exterior with two black bands enclosing a red band on body and black 'grille' design with a central red spot just below neck. Neck strainer. Hard, slightly 'corky' fabric with limestone and other inclusions visible, wide carbon streak in section | Egloff, 1977, pl. 103: type 204, *c.* AD 450–550 | AC51 [8412] | JF 709 | 10 | 4.13 |
| 25 | Flagon body with ribbed base and most of the ribbed neck. Neck strainer. No handles evident. Red, black and cream decoration on exterior. Hard, slightly 'corky' fabric with limestone and other inclusions visible, wide carbon streak in section | | AC51 [8579] | JF 711 | 14 | 4.13 |
| 26 | Goblet. Cream slipped with resin/pitch on interior and over rim. Hard, slightly 'corky' fabric with limestone and other inclusions visible, carbon streak in section. D = 11 cms | Godlewski et al., 1989–1993, 247, figs. 19.12–15. | AC50/51 [8412] | JF 696 | 6 | 4.13 |

*Table 4.2 cont. Coarseware pottery identified in pot slots from Room C (figs 12 and 13)*

| Season | Square | Unit No. | Pot Fill from Pottery Vessel Type (S) | Pot Slot Vessel | Flotation Method & Sieves Used | Volume (L) | Sorted Hr? | Other Observations |
|---|---|---|---|---|---|---|---|---|
| TAKN94 | AC50 | 8579 | Long-necked pedestalled jar, M2 fabric | Vessel 13 | BUCKET FLOTATION 0.5mm & HR TO 1mm | 6.35 | | Mudbrick fragments removed before sieving and retained |
| TAKN94 | AC51 | 8412 | M3 Amphora | Vessel 8 | BUCKET FLOTATION 0.5mm & HR TO 1mm | 1.75 | Yes | Inside and outside sampled for resin work 1998 |
| TAKN94 | AC51 | 8142 | M3 Amphora | Vessel 9 | BUCKET FLOTATION 0.5mm & HR TO 1mm | 7.5 | Yes | Mudbrick fragments removed before sieving and retained |
| TAKN94 | AC51 | 8412 | M1 flagon (?) | Vessel 10 | BUCKET FLOTATION 0.5mm & HR TO 1mm | 2 | Yes | |
| TAKN94 | AC51 | 8579 | Cooking pot, pedestal jar (no rim), pie-crust bowl, cooking pot, M3 rim | Vessel 23 | BUCKET FLOTATION 0.5mm & HR TO 1mm | 5.75 | Yes | |
| TAKN94 | AC51 | 8580 | M3 amphora and a few sherds of other vessels | Vessel 19 | BUCKET FLOTATION 0.5mm & HR TO 1mm | 2.75 | Yes | |
| TAKN94 | AC51 | 8588 | M2 cooking pot with resin inside | Vessel 25 | BUCKET FLOTATION 0.5mm & HR TO 1mm | 1.75 | Yes | |
| TAKN94 | AC51 | 8588 | M1 flagon | Vessel 26A | BUCKET FLOTATION 0.5mm & HR TO 1mm | 1.75 | Yes | Vessel renumbered by Gillian Pyke |
| TAKN94 | AC51 | 8412 | M3 amphora | Vessel 12 | BUCKET FLOTATION 0.5mm & HR TO 1mm | 5.5 | Yes | |
| TAKN94 | AC51 | 8579 | M3 amphora | Vessel 24 | BUCKET FLOTATION 0.5mm & HR TO 1mm | 4.5 | Yes | |
| TAKN94 | AC50 | 8580 | M3 amphora | Vessel 17 | BUCKET FLOTATION 0.5mm & HR TO 1mm | 2.75 | Yes | Large globule of resin in base—sampled in 1998 |
| TAKN94 | AC51 | 8412 | M3 amphora | Vessel 4 | BUCKET FLOTATION 0.5mm & HR TO 1mm | 3 | Yes | |

*Table 4.3 Summary of archaeobotanical samples collected from vessels in the pot slots (TAKN 94 AC50/51 Room C) (shaded rows indicated those vessels with clearly stored plant remains)*

| Season | Square | Unit No. | Pot Fill from Pottery Vessel Type (S) | Pot Slot Vessel | Flotation Method & Sieves Used | Volume (L) | Sorted Hr? | Other Observations |
|---|---|---|---|---|---|---|---|---|
| TAKN94 | AC50 | 8579 | M3 amphora | Vessel 15 | BUCKET FLOTATION 0.5mm & HR TO 1mm | 3 | Yes | |
| TAKN94 | AC50 | 8579 | M3 amphora | Vessel 1 | BUCKET FLOTATION 0.5mm & HR TO 1mm | 2 | Yes | |
| TAKN94 | AC51 | 8579 | M3 amphora | Vessel 22 | BUCKET FLOTATION 0.5mm & HR TO 1mm | 6 | Yes | |
| TAKN94 | AC51 | 8412 | M3 amphora—reused broken pot, floor & wall | Vessel 3 | BUCKET FLOTATION 0.5mm & HR TO 1mm<br><br>NB *Acacia nilotica* pods (carb) from base of M3 vessel kept separate and not exposed to water | 1.75 | Yes | Photo of vessel taken by W. Smith & J. Faiers |
| TAKN94 | AC51 | 8579 | *Saqiya* | Vessel 20 | BUCKET FLOTATION 0.5mm & HR TO 1mm | 2.75 | Yes | Full of tree bark—kept some back (not exposed to water)—stored in separate plastic box |
| TAKN94 | AC50 | 8579 | *Saqiya*—identified by G. Pyke, 1998 | Vessel 7 | BUCKET FLOTATION 0.5mm & HR TO 1mm | 3 | Yes | |
| TAKN94 | AC51 | 8579 | M3 amphora | Vessel 18 | BUCKET FLOTATION 0.5mm & HR TO 1mm | 1.75 | Yes | |
| TAKN94 | AC51 | 8412 | M3 amphora | Vessel 5 | BUCKET FLOTATION 0.5mm & HR TO 1mm | 0.6 | Yes | |

*Table 4.3 cont. Summary of archaeobotanical samples collected from vessels in the pot slots (TAKN 94 AC50/51 Room C) (shaded rows indicated those vessels with clearly stored plant remains)*

| Season | Square | Unit No. | Pot Fill from Pottery Vessel Type (S) | Pot Slot Vessel | Flotation Method & Sieves Used | Volume (L) | Sorted Hr? | Other Observations |
|---|---|---|---|---|---|---|---|---|
| TAKN94 | AC51 | 8579 | M1 jug, M1 dimpled vessel, M4 cooking pot, M3 fragments (bagged sherds with resin attached from this vessel separately within the bag), M1 jug with drips down the outside. All five vessels bagged separately. | Vessel 21 (actually five vessels) | BUCKET FLOTATION 0.5mm & HR TO 1mm | 2.5 | Yes | |
| TAKN94 | AC51 | 8579 | M3 amphora | Vessel 26 (originally labelled Vessel 25) | BUCKET FLOTATION 0.5mm & HR TO 1mm | 0.9 | Yes | |
| TAKN94 | AC51 | 8588 | M1 flagon | Vessel 26A | BUCKET FLOTATION 0.5mm & HR TO 1mm | 0.052 | No HR produced | |
| TAKN94 | AC51 | 8588 | M3 amphora—fill of neck | Assumed to be part of pot slots, but no vessel number | BUCKET FLOTATION 0.5mm & HR TO 1mm | 0.162 | No HR produced | |
| TAKN94 | AC51 | 8579 | Water flagon or goula with sieves | Vessel 14 | BUCKET FLOTATION 0.5mm & HR TO 1mm | 0.022 | No HR produced | |
| TAKN94 | AC50/51 | 8412 | Thick-walled M3 amphora | Vessel 2 | BUCKET FLOTATION 0.5mm & HR TO 1mm | 1.1 | Yes | Orange patch on left side of longest fragment; not sure if anything. Some more observed on second fragment. Made note and bagged separately with rest of vessel. |

*Table 4.3 cont. Summary of archaeobotanical samples collected from vessels in the pot slots (TAKN 94 AC50/51 Room C) (shaded rows indicated those vessels with clearly stored plant remains)*

| **Season** | **Square** | **Unit No.** | **Pot Fill from Pottery Vessel Type (S)** | **Pot Slot Vessel** | **Flotation Method & Sieves Used** | **Volume (L)** | **Sorted Hr?** | **Other Observations** |
|---|---|---|---|---|---|---|---|---|
| TAKN94 | AC51 | 8588 | Fill of N1 amphora | From pot slot area, but no vessel number | BUCKET FLOTATION 0.5mm & HR TO 1mm | 0.4 | No HR produced | |
| TAKN94 | AC 50/51 | 8412 | Goblet | Vessel 6 | BUCKET FLOTATION 0.5mm & HR TO 1mm | 0.08 | No HR produced | |
| TAKN94 | AC51 | 8412 | M2 wide-mouthed cooking pot with two handles | Vessel 11 is part of Vessel 21's five vessels | BUCKET FLOTATION 0.5mm & HR TO 1mm | 0.046 | Yes | |

*Table 4.3 cont. Summary of archaeobotanical samples collected from vessels in the pot slots (TAKN 94 AC50/51 Room C) (shaded rows indicated those vessels with clearly stored plant remains)*

| **Pot Slot Sample Number** | **94–178** | | **94–180** | | **94–182** | | **94–183** | | **94–184** | | **94–186** | |
|---|---|---|---|---|---|---|---|---|---|---|---|---|
| Trench | AC51 | | AC51 | | AC51 | | AC51 | | AC51 | | AC51 | |
| Context | 8581 | | 8580 | | 8579 | | 8579 | | 8588 | | 8587 | |
| Sample volume (litres) | 3 | | 8 | | 16 | | 16 | | 18 | | 17 | |
| Proportion of flot sorted | ½ | | ¼ | | ¼ | | ¼ | | ¼ | | ⅛ | |
| **Flot** | **Desc** | **Carb** | **Desc** | **Carb** | **Desc** | **Carb** | **Desc** | **Carb** | **Desc** | **Carb** | **Desc** | **Carb** |
| Cereal grain | 0 | 0 | 0 | 0 | 0 | 0 | 0 | 0 | 1 | 0 | 1 | 0 |
| Cereal chaff | 65 | 0 | 17 | 1 | 18 | 2 | 74 | 5 | 55 | 12 | 48 | 1 |
| Fruit | 35 | 0 | 36 | 0 | 124 | 0 | 98 | 1 | 48 | 1 | 61 | 0 |
| Other crops | 31 | 0 | 12 | 0 | 9 | 0 | 6 | 0 | 27 | 0 | 5 | 0 |
| Weed/wild plants | 23 | 1 | 57 | 0 | 296 | 2 | 285 | 3 | 28 | 9 | 104 | 1 |
| Unidentified/indeterminate | 10 | 0 | 9 | 1 | 22 | 0 | 14 | 0 | 1 | 0 | 14 | 0 |
| Total identifications flot | 164 | 0 | 131 | 0 | 469 | 0 | 477 | 0 | 160 | 0 | 233 | 0 |
| **Heavy Residue** | **Desc** | **Carb** | **Desc** | **Carb** | **Desc** | **Carb** | **Desc** | **Carb** | **Desc** | **Carb** | **Desc** | **Carb** |
| Cereal grain | 0 | 0 | 0 | 0 | 0 | 0 | 0 | 0 | 0 | 0 | 0 | 0 |
| Cereal chaff | 3 | 0 | 0 | 0 | 0 | 0 | 0 | 0 | 0 | 0 | 1 | 1 |
| Fruit | 8 | 0 | 5 | 0 | 15 | 0 | 14 | 0 | 17 | 0 | 5 | 0 |
| Other crops | 1 | 0 | 2 | 0 | 3 | 0 | 2 | 0 | 4 | 0 | 1 | 0 |
| Weed/wild plants | 2 | 0 | 1 | 0 | 1 | 0 | 3 | 0 | 0 | 0 | 1 | 0 |
| Unidentified/indeterminate | 1 | 0 | 0 | 0 | 0 | 0 | 3 | 1 | 1 | 0 | 0 | 0 |
| Total identifications heavy residue | 15 | 0 | 8 | 0 | 19 | 0 | 22 | 0 | 22 | 0 | 8 | 0 |
| Combined flot and heavy residue total identifications | 179 | 1 | 139 | 2 | 488 | 4 | 499 | 10 | 182 | 22 | 241 | 3 |

*Table 4.4a Summary of archaeobotanical results of six samples collected from the general fill of individual pot slots*

| **Pot Slot Sample Number** | **94–178** | | **94–180** | | **94–182** | | **94–183** | | **94–184** | | **94–186** | |
|---|---|---|---|---|---|---|---|---|---|---|---|---|
| Trench | AC51 | | AC51 | | AC51 | | AC51 | | AC51 | | AC51 | |
| Context | 8581 | | 8580 | | 8579 | | 8579 | | 8588 | | 8587 | |
| Sample volume (litres) | 3 | | 8 | | 16 | | 16 | | 18 | | 17 | |
| Proportion of flot sorted | 1/2 | | 1/4 | | 1/4 | | 1/4 | | 1/4 | | 1/8 | |
| **Proportion of Desiccated Flot** | **Desc** | **Carb** | **Desc** | **Carb** | **Desc** | **Carb** | **Desc** | **Carb** | **Desc** | **Carb** | **Desc** | **Carb** |
| Cereal grain | 0.0% | 0.0% | 0.0% | 0.0% | 0.0% | 0.0% | 0.0% | 0.0% | 0.5% | 0.0% | 0.3% | 0.0% |
| Cereal chaff | 28.3% | 0.0% | 8.3% | 50.0% | 3.1% | 50.0% | 11.7% | 50.0% | 25.5% | 54.5% | 15.9% | 33.3% |
| Fruit | 15.2% | 0.0% | 17.5% | 0.0% | 21.5% | 0.0% | 15.6% | 10.0% | 22.2% | 4.5% | 20.3% | 0.0% |
| Other crops | 13.5% | 0.0% | 5.8% | 0.0% | 1.6% | 0.0% | 1.0% | 0.0% | 12.5% | 0.0% | 1.7% | 0.0% |
| Weed/wild plants | 10.0% | 100.0% | 27.7% | 0.0% | 51.3% | 50.0% | 45.2% | 30.0% | 13.0% | 40.9% | 34.6% | 33.3% |
| Unidentified/indeterminate | 4.3% | 0.0% | 4.4% | 50.0% | 3.8% | 0.0% | 2.2% | 0.0% | 0.5% | 0.0% | 4.7% | 0.0% |
| **Proportion of Desiccated Heavy Residue** | **Desc** | **Carb** | **Desc** | **Carb** | **Desc** | **Carb** | **Desc** | **Carb** | **Desc** | **Carb** | **Desc** | **Carb** |
| Cereal grain | 0.0% | 0.0% | 0.0% | 0.0% | 0.0% | 0.0% | 0.0% | 0.0% | 0.0% | 0.0% | 0.0% | 0.0% |
| Cereal chaff | 1.3% | 0.0% | 0.0% | 0.0% | 0.0% | 0.0% | 0.0% | 0.0% | 0.0% | 0.0% | 0.3% | 33.3% |
| Fruit | 3.5% | 0.0% | 2.4% | 0.0% | 2.6% | 0.0% | 2.2% | 0.0% | 7.9% | 0.0% | 1.7% | 0.0% |
| Other crops | 0.4% | 0.0% | 1.0% | 0.0% | 0.5% | 0.0% | 0.3% | 0.0% | 1.9% | 0.0% | 0.3% | 0.0% |
| Weed/wild plants | 0.9% | 0.0% | 0.5% | 0.0% | 0.2% | 0.0% | 0.5% | 0.0% | 0.0% | 0.0% | 0.3% | 0.0% |
| Unidentified/indeterminate | 0.4% | 0.0% | 0.0% | 0.0% | 0.0% | 0.0% | 0.5% | 10.0% | 0.5% | 0.0% | 0.0% | 0.0% |
| Combine flot and heavy residue total proportions | 99.4% | 0.6% | 98.6% | 1.4% | 99.2% | 0.8% | 98.0% | 2.0% | 89.2% | 10.8% | 98.8% | 1.2% |

*Table 4.4b Relative proportions of plant-remain categories for the pot-slot samples (NB, all proportions calculated from combined total of all desiccated and carbonised flot and heavy residue identifications)*

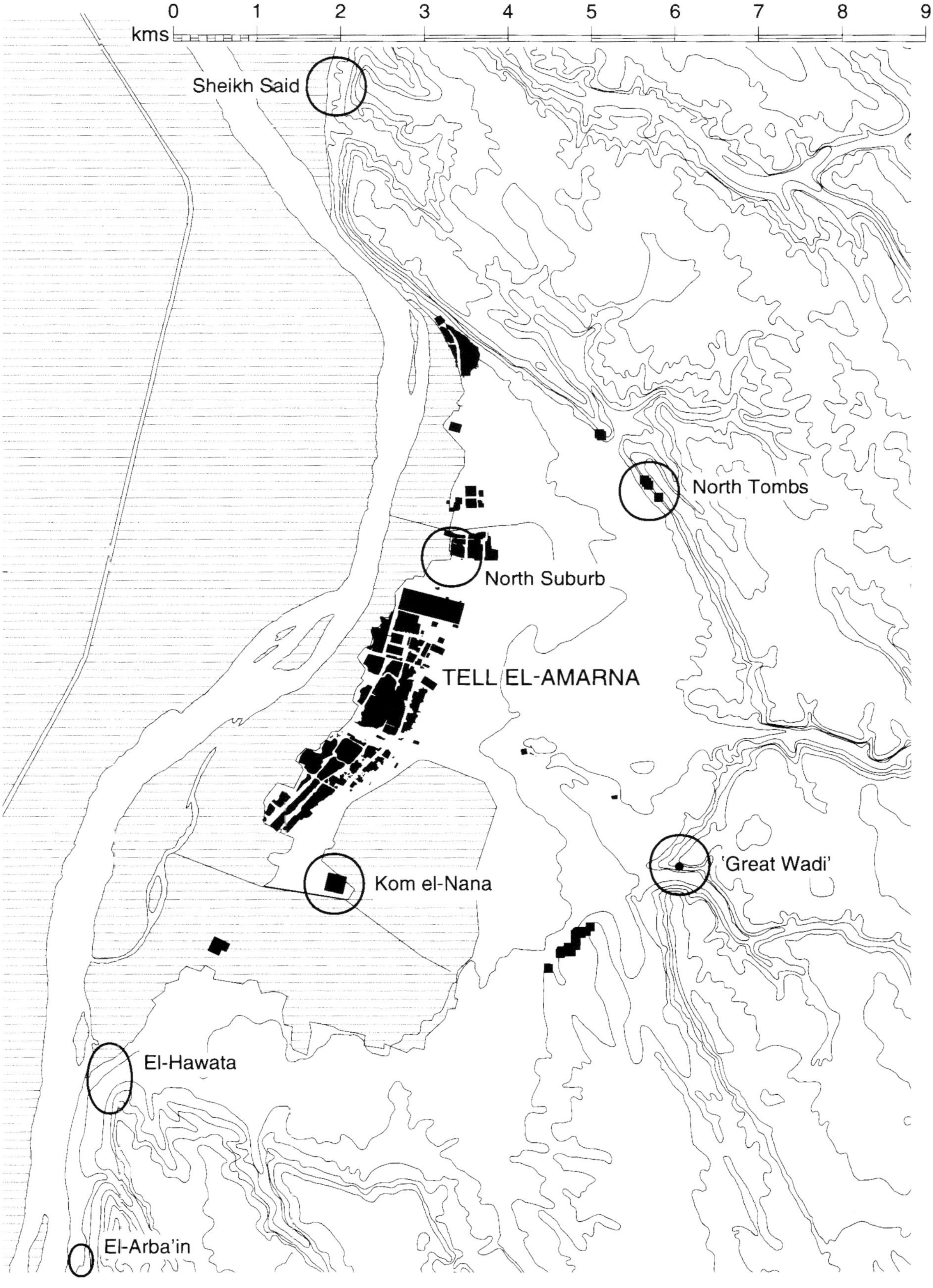


*Figure 4.1 Location of Kom el-Nana at Tel el-Amarna and surrounding sites with Late Roman remains*

*Figure 4.2 An aerial view of the 1994 excavations. The subject of this chapter can be seen towards the top centre of this figures (the arrow indicates area discussed)*

a.

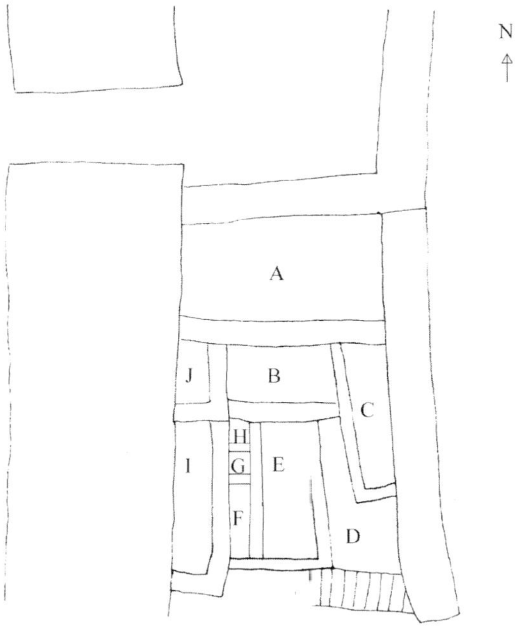


b.

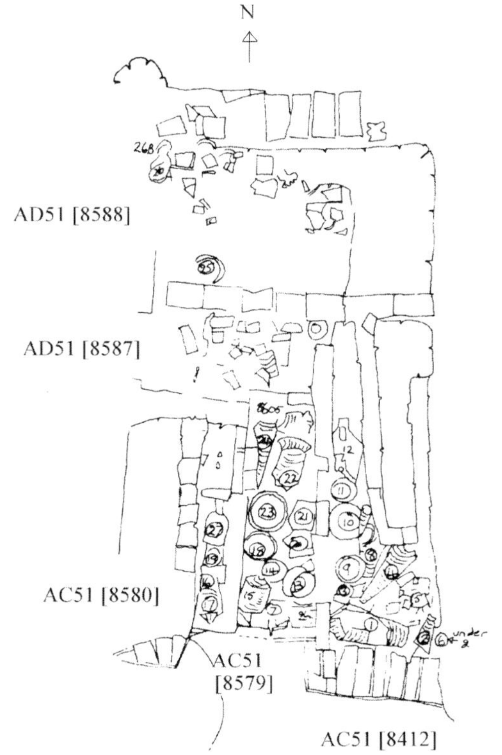


c.

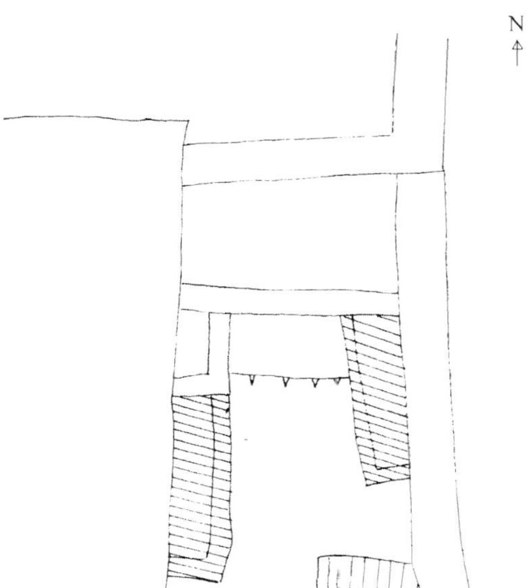


Fig. 4.3 a,b,c

a. Sketch-plan of Room C, showing all mud-brick partitions or 'slots', before modification (not to scale)
b. Plan of Room C, showing the position of whole and partial vessels within slots (not to scale)
c. Sketch plan of Room C, showing the proposed layout after the mud/plaster floor was laid over the 'pots in slots' and 'shelves' were constructed over slots V and I (not to scale).

*Figures 4.3a, b and c.*

*Figure 4.4 Personal snapshot of unexcavated pot-slot area, 1994 field season (trowel at top of photograph pointing north)*

*Figure 4.5 Personal snapshot of unexcavated pot slot mudbrick bin, showing compacted pottery vessels in situ*

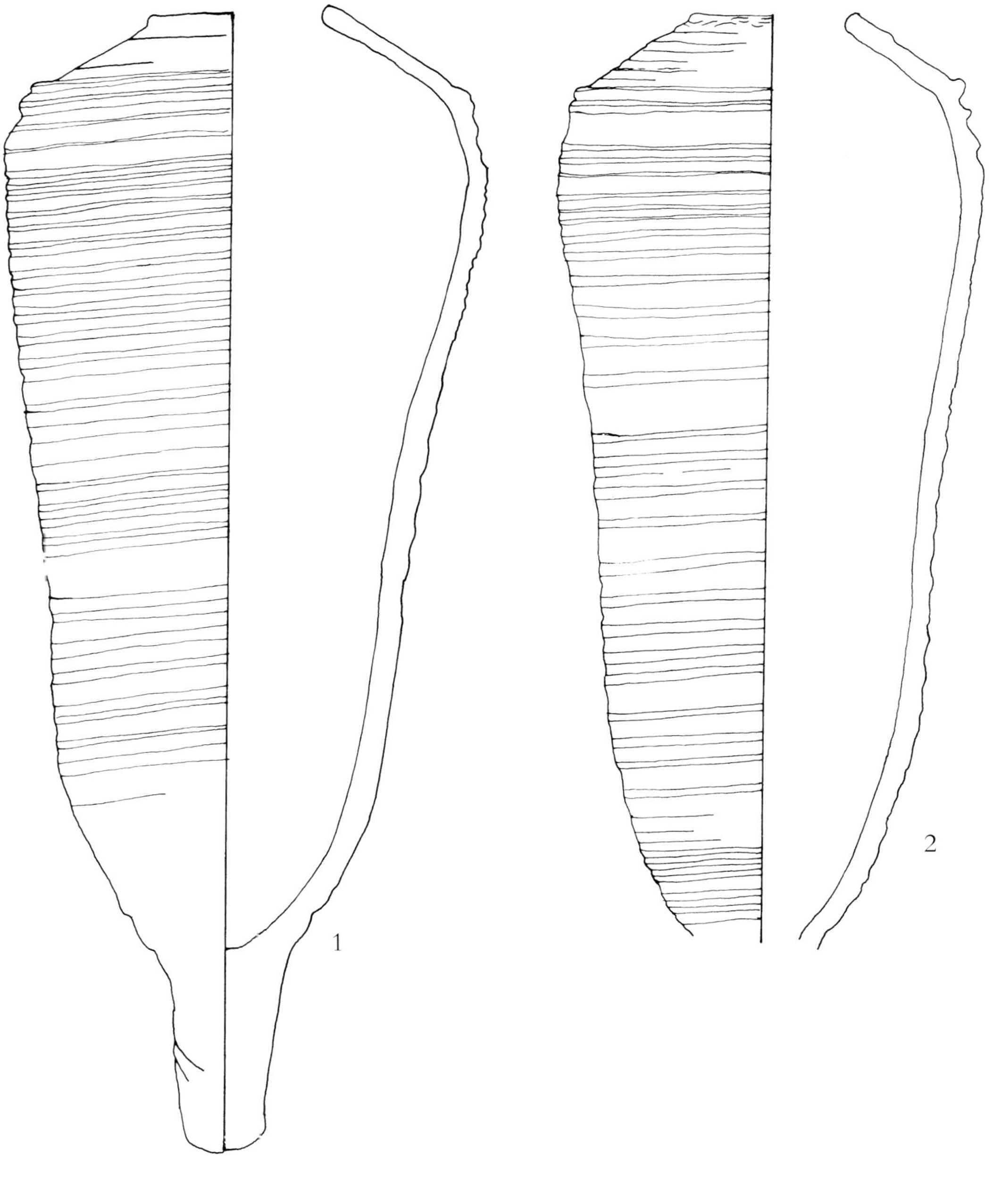

*Figure 4.6 Catalogue 1–2, amphorae. Scale 1:3*

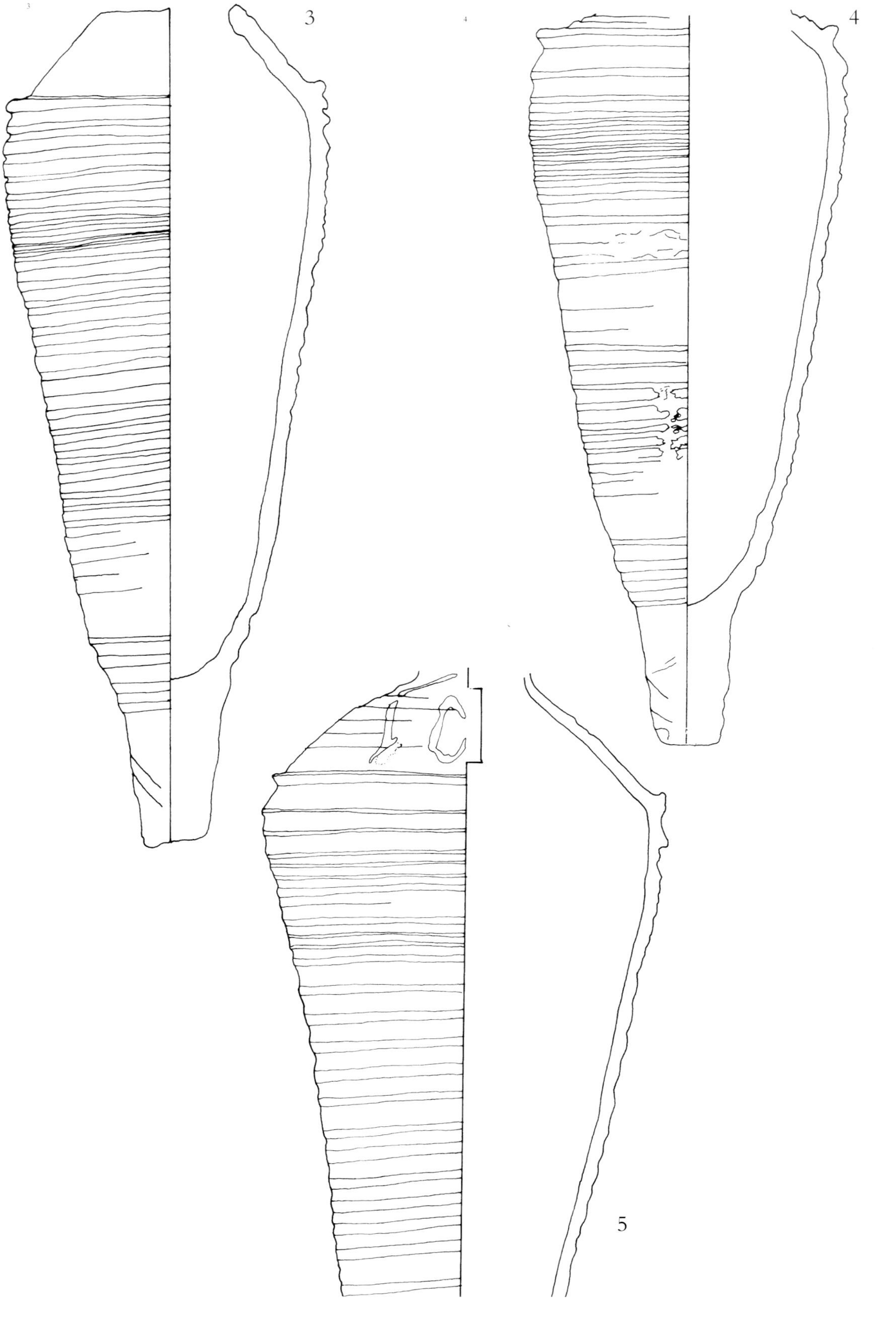


Figure 4.7 Catalogue 3–5, amphorae. Scale 1:3

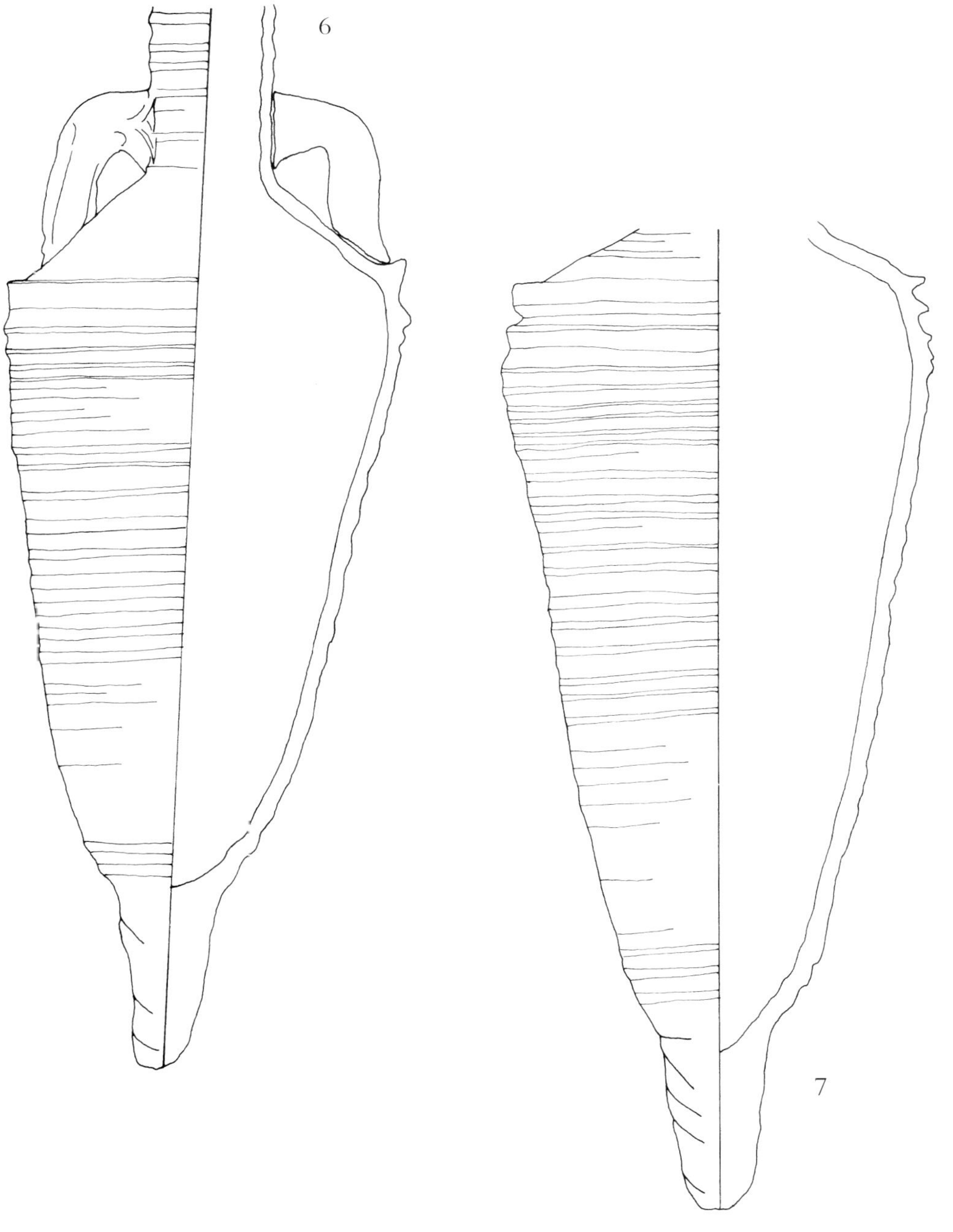


*Figure 4.8 Catalogue 6–7, amphorae. Scale 1:3*

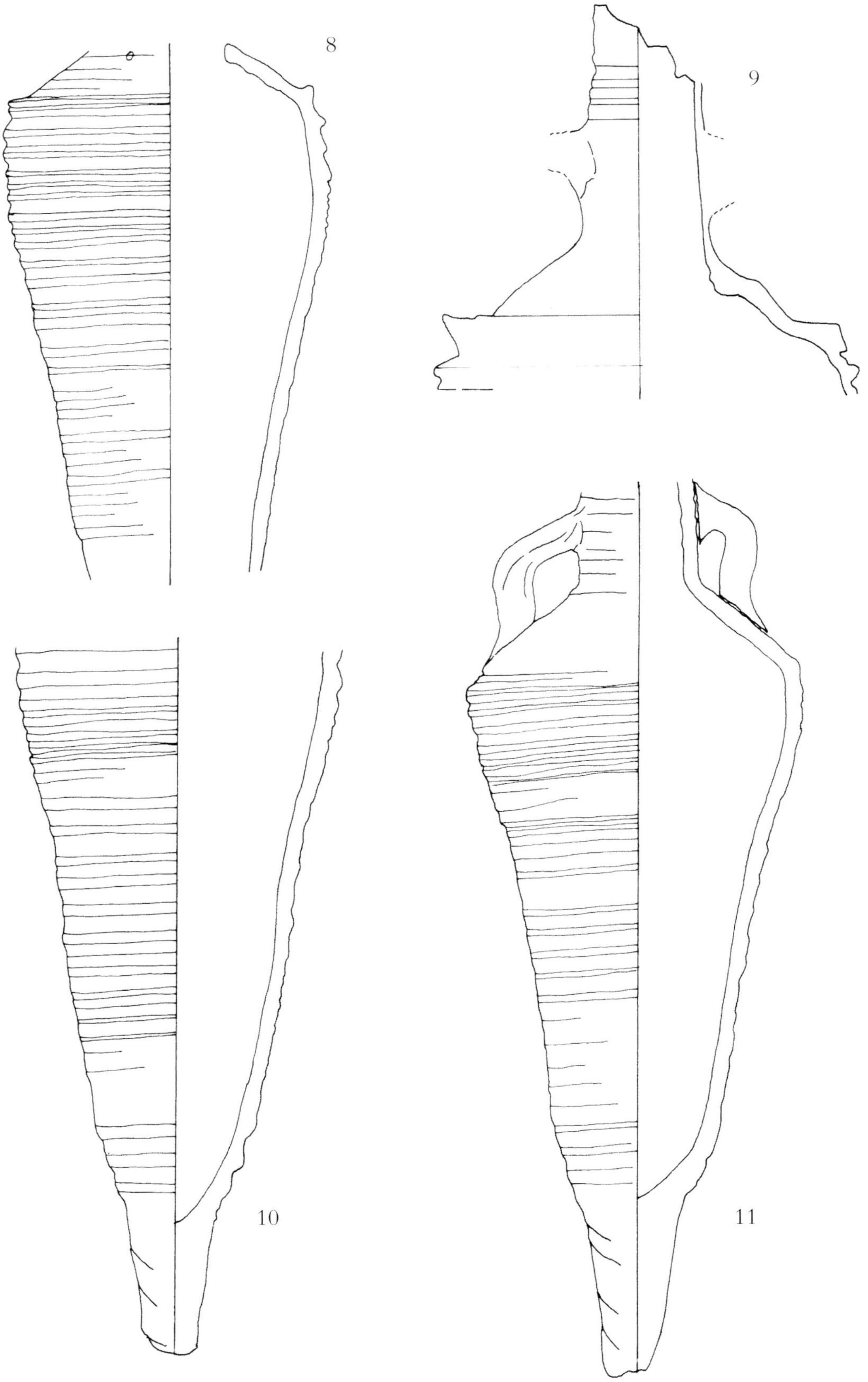


*Figure 4.9 Catalogue 8–11, amphorae. Scale 1:3*

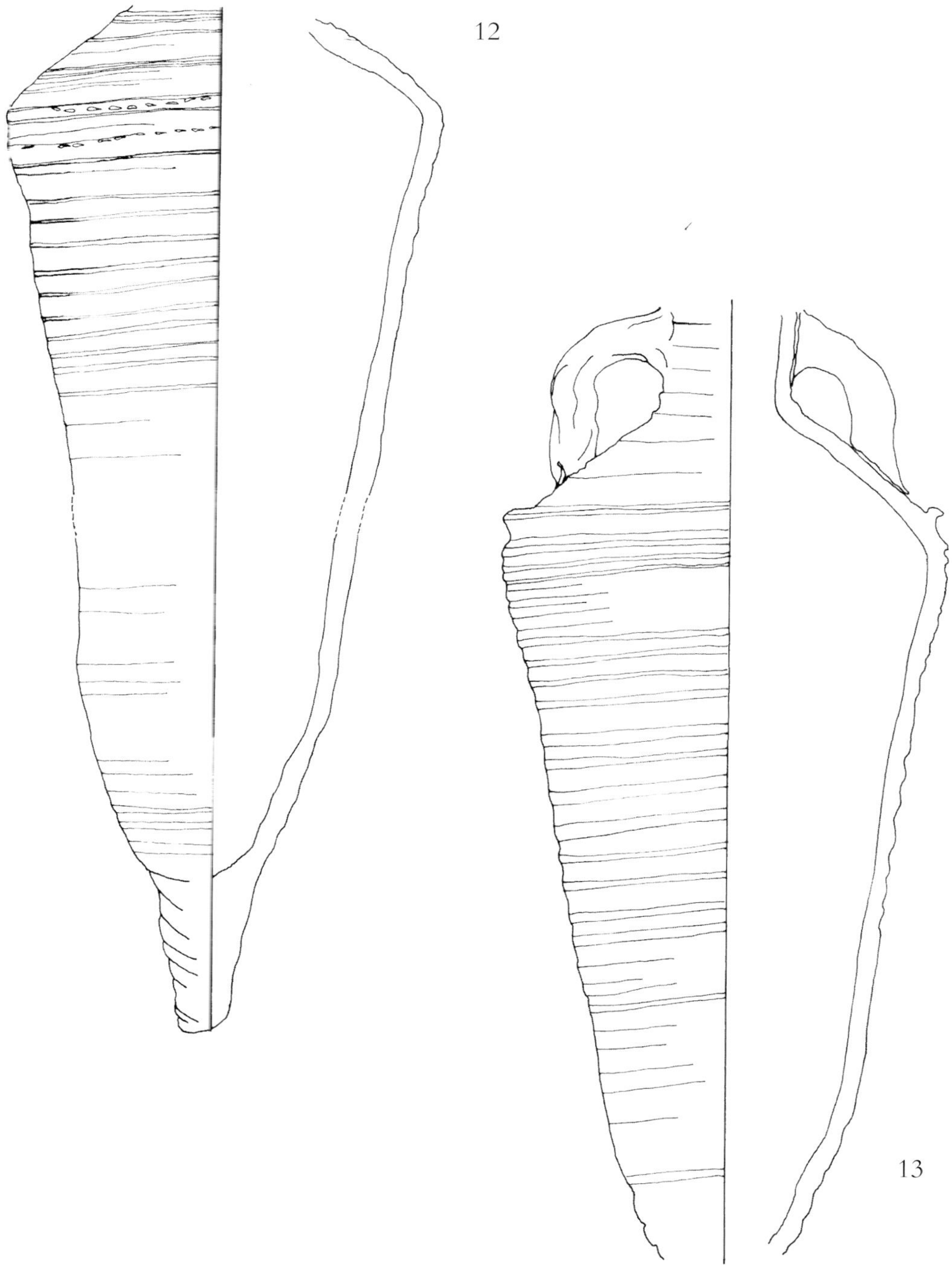


*Figure 4.10 Catalogue 12–13, amphorae. Scale 1:3*

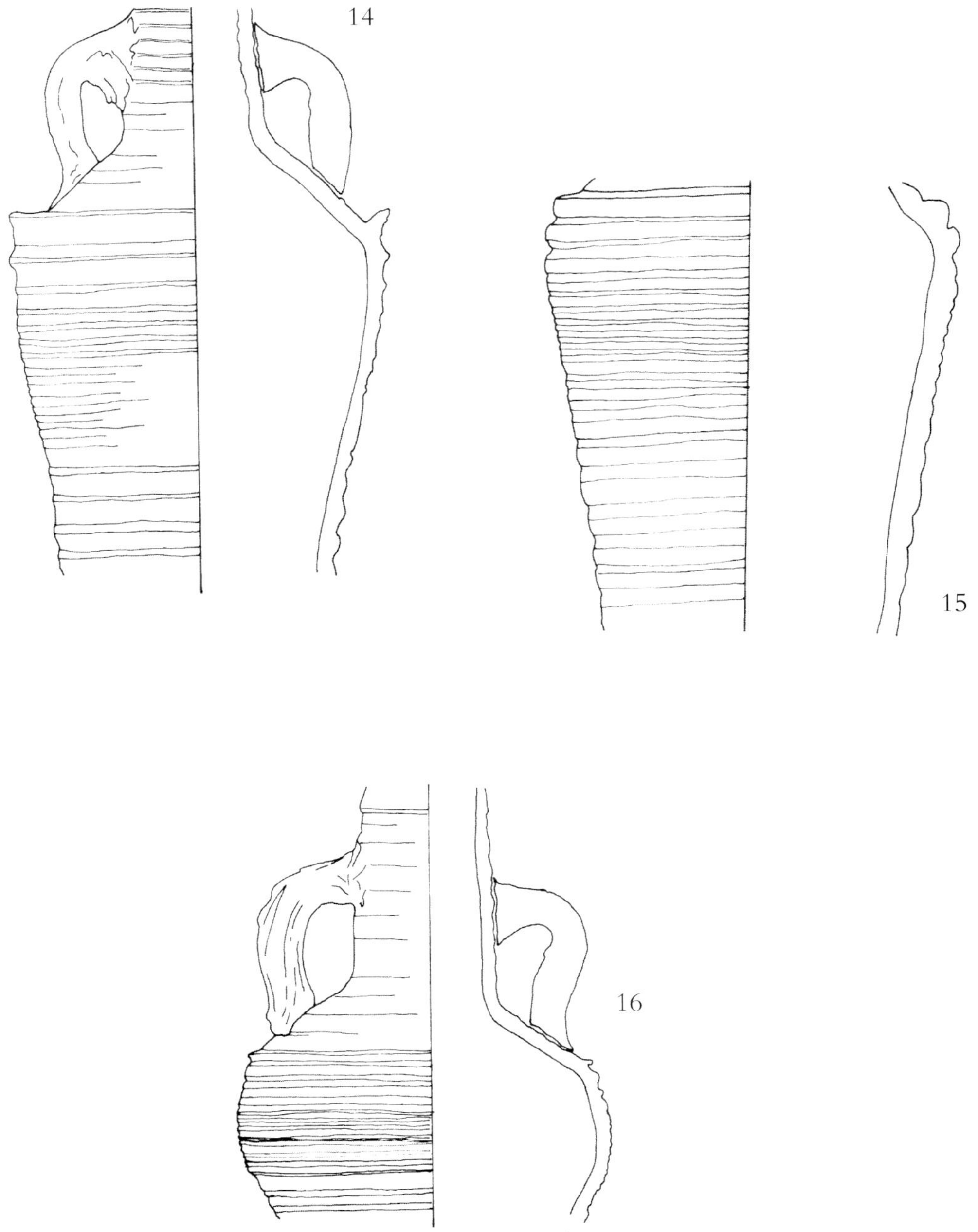


*Figure 4.11 Catalogue 14–16, amphorae. Scale 1:3*

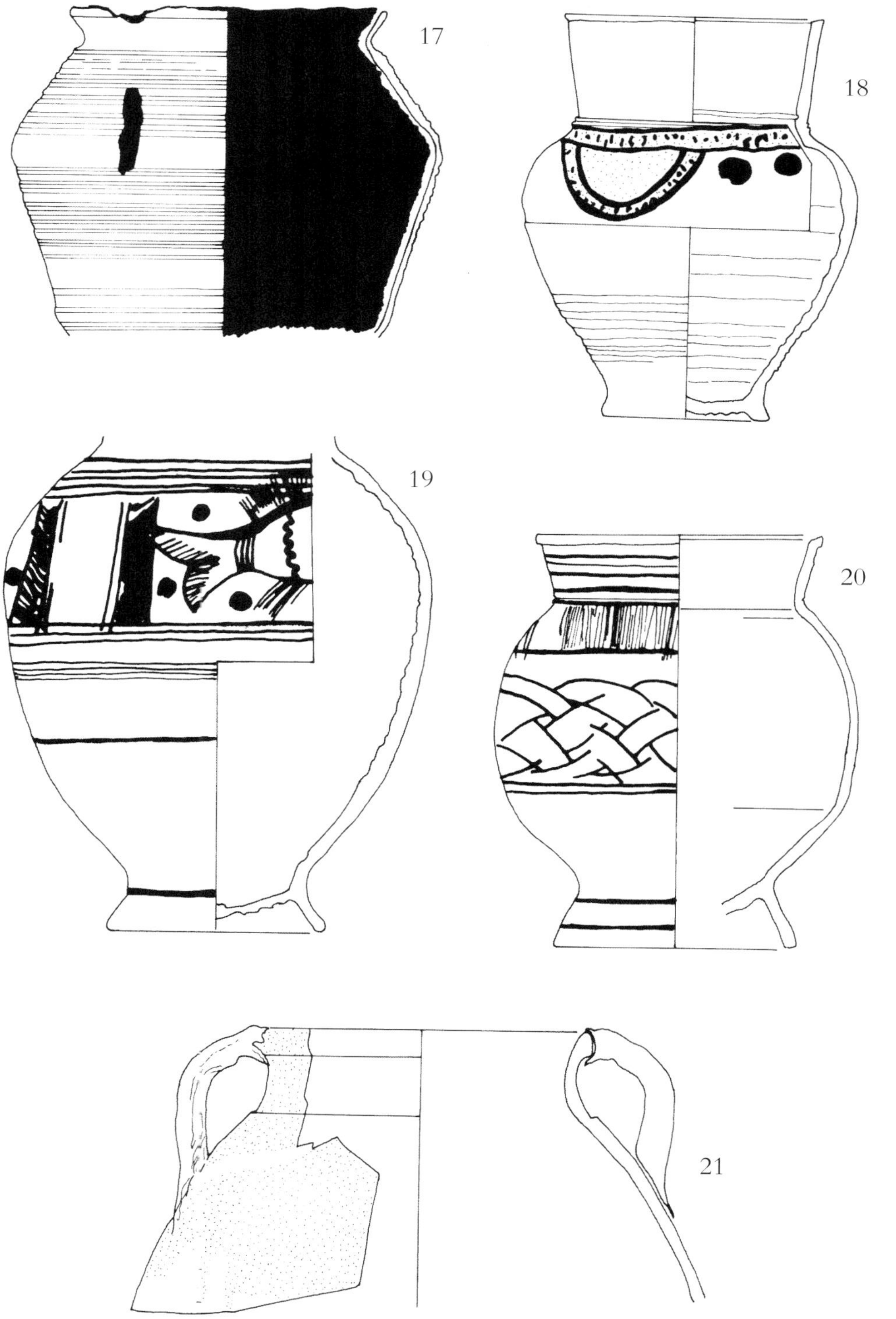


*Figure 4.12 Catalogue 17–21, coarse pottery. Scale 1:3*

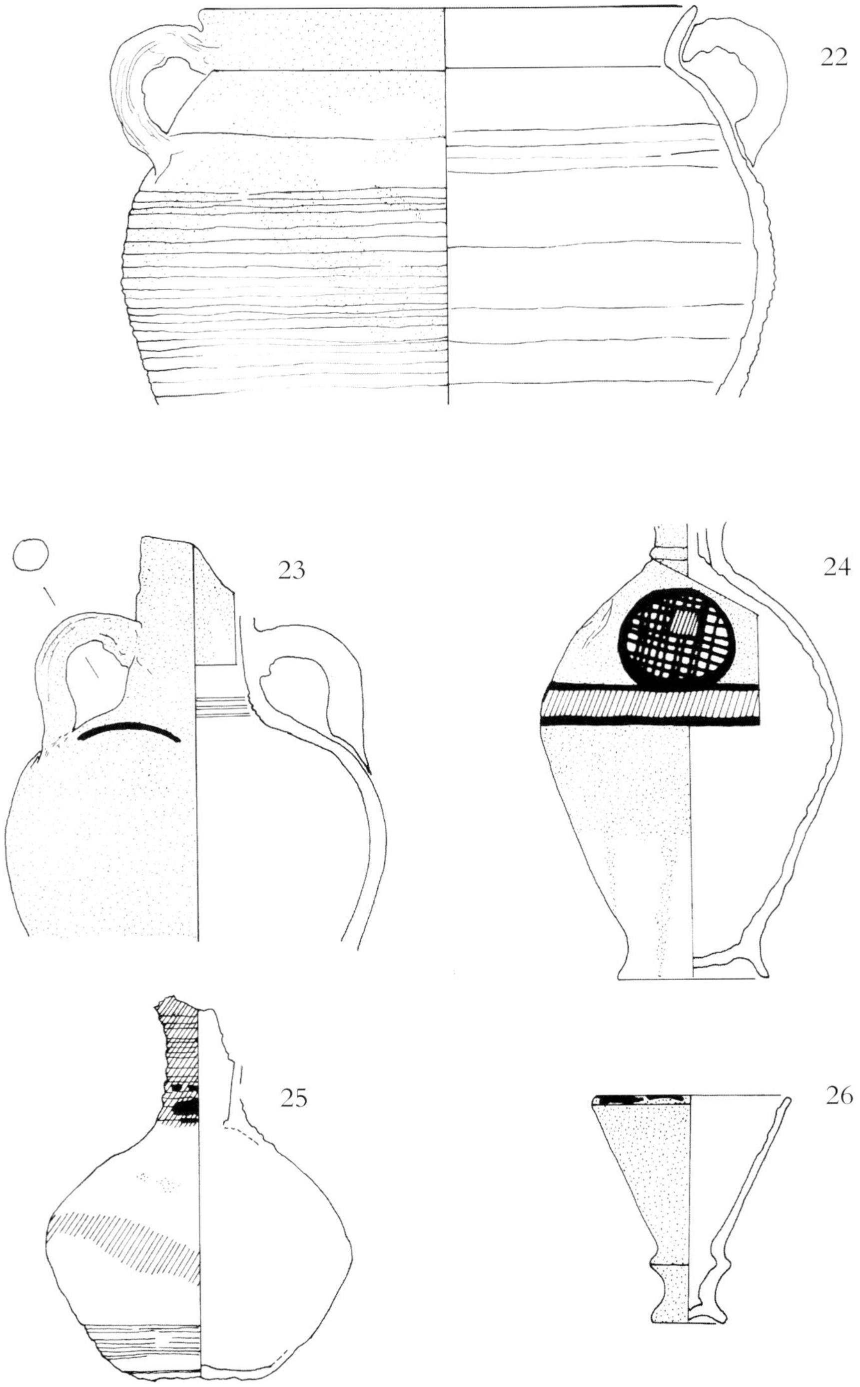


*Figure 4.13 Catalogue 22–26, coarse pottery. Scale 1:3*

*Figure 4.14*

*a) general plan of 25 square metre area of site—pot-slot area (Room C) within box*

*b) location of bulk soil samples collected from mudbrick pot slots*

*c) plan of vessels within pot slots—black diamond indicates those vessels with fills, which were sampled for environmental remains and artefacts*

*Figure 4.15 Pot Slot Vessel 3 (M3-fabric amphora) with charred Nile Acacia pods at base*

*Figure 4.16 Close-up of charred, concerted Nile Acacia pods*

*Figure 4.17 Unidentified bark (believed to compare favourably with Nile Acacia), found within Pot Slot Vessel 20 (a water-wheel pot or* qadus*)*

*Figure 4.18a and b St Romain-en-Gal vide sanitaire:*
*a) upturned amphorae under floor*
*b) upturned amphorae covered by floor*

# CHAPTER 5

# Other Sites with Late Roman Pottery in the Area Around Kom el-Nana

by Jane Faiers

In 1988 Dr Robert Miller took borings and made surface pottery collections from a number of sites in the area around Kom el-Nana. This was noted by Kemp in Chapter 1 of the previous volume on Kom el-Nana (Faiers, 2005, 25). The sherds found by Miller ranged in date from the Pharaonic period to the present day. The pottery catalogue in this chapter only includes Late Roman pottery found by Dr Miller at the five sites listed below. There are also sherds of a slightly later date which have been included as they are in keeping with the fabrics of the Late Roman period, showing a continuation in supply over time. What is interesting is that there are only three vessels which can be paralleled at Kom el-Nana and these are of fifth to seventh century AD (nos 13, 15 and 64). This may indicate that Kom el-Nana had ceased to function after the seventh century, or even the late sixth century AD (See Chapter 6).

Also included is the surface collection of pot sherds from Ezbet Milik, (Ezbet el-Malik) made by Professor Barry Kemp in 1995. These are distinguished by the initials BJK in brackets after his drawing number, i.e. JF/ELM/*X* (BJK).

There were five sites, other than those below, where pottery collected by Dr Miller could be identified as Late Roman. These were:

- Tanda
- Sheikh Azab (or Kom el-Azab)
- Nazlet Sirgir/Jahrud
- Ma'asara
- Umm Qummus

As the sherds collected were very small and connected with borings they are not illustrated here.

Dr Sarah Parcak also undertook a survey of sites in this area for her doctoral thesis (Parcak, 2005) and this included some of the sites visited by Miller. These were:

- Abu el-Hidr
- Ezbet el-Malik
- Ismu (or Esmu) el-Arus
- Kafr Kuzam
- El Nisariya
- Kom el-Rikab
- Tell Sheikh Masara
- Singirg
- Tanda
- Tanuf
- Umm Qummus

Only one parallel was found between the catalogue of pottery contained in Parcak's thesis and the sites in the catalogue below, although there were 42 illustrated Late Roman sherds in the Parcak thesis which could be dated. Twenty-four of these were from Ismu el-Arus. The other sherds came from Kom el-Ahmar (four), Ezbet Milik (four), Singirg (six), Kom el-Rikab (three). All these vessels, but for two, (no. 54 from Kom el-Rikab, dated *c.* AD 400, and no. 201 from Ismu el-Arus, dated *c.* AD 375–450), would have been in use during the period of Kom el-Nana's existence (*c.* AD 425–650). This demonstrates not only the scope of vessels available to the local population, but also the degree of settlement during the Late Roman period.

The fact that so many of the vessels found by Parcak do not appear at Kom el-Nana appears to indicate a difference in supply between monasteries and the surrounding centres of population. Certainly, there are no painted vessels evident in the Parcak thesis, which may point to a desire on the part of the local population for purely functional pottery, possibly through lack of means, or indeed lack of supply, as the larger centres such as el-Ashmunein or Antinoe do have painted vessels in their pottery collections. Another explanation is that the pottery found at Kom el-Nana was from excavated areas and the pottery found by Parcak was a random collection at a particular site.

Only one of the sites mentioned in the pottery catalogue below was not visited by Parcak, (Sheikh Ali Ghindi).

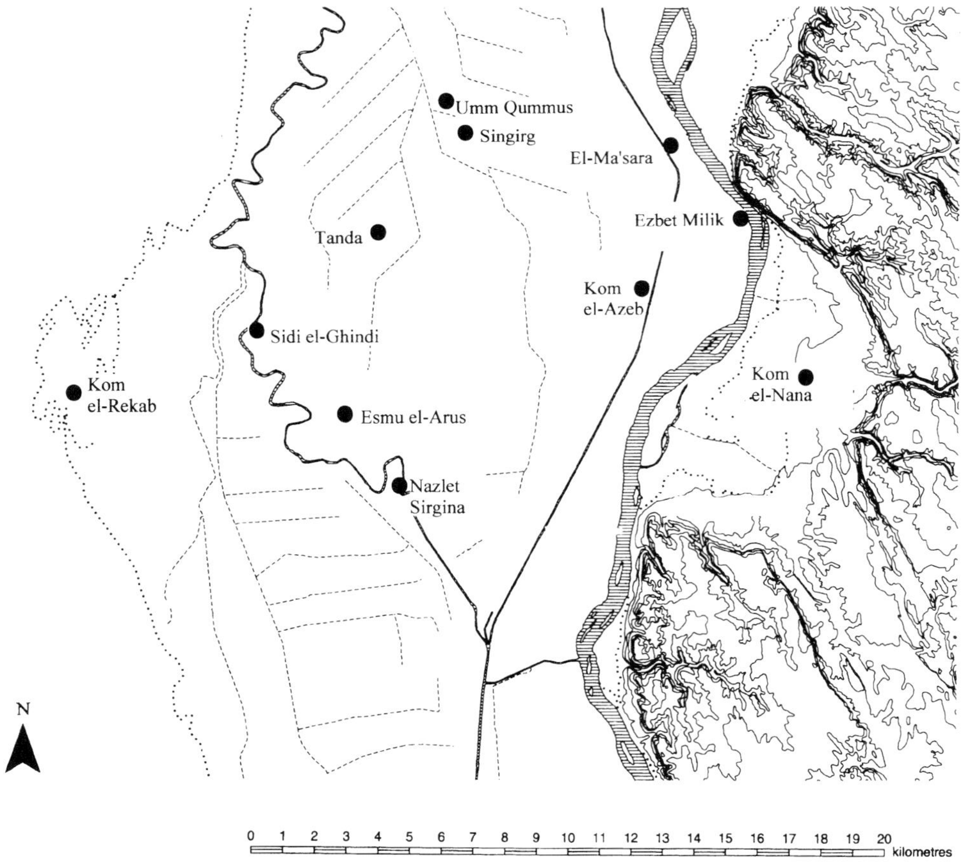


*Figure 5.1 Map to show five sites with Late Roman pottery visited by Dr Miller and the five sites with Late Roman pottery listed in this chapter (after Kemp, 2005)*

## Pottery catalogue

### Sheikh Ali Ghindi

*Finewares: Egyptian Red Slip 'A' wares (O1)*

1. Flagon. Badly eroded. Traces of rouletting on rim. O1. D = 8 cm.
JF/SAG/12.
Near Elephantine X, Abb.77, 24, T727, which is 5 cm in diameter, second half of the fifth (?) to the sixth century AD.

2. Base of small bowl? O1. D = 12 cm.
JF/SAG/16.
Near Elephantine X, Abb.75, 15, T641 (but without decoration), last quarter of the sixth to the seventh/eighth century AD.

*Coarsewares*

3. Cooking pot with ribbed body. M2. D = 18 cm.
JF/SAG/11.
A selection of these, plus a discussion on this form, can be found in the cooking pot section of this volume and in Volume 1 (Faiers, 2005, 118–123). See also Ashmunein, 1998, pls 35–40.

4. Cooking pot with ribbed body. M2. D = 16 cm.
JF/SAG/10.
See comments for no. 3.

5. Cooking pot with ribbed body. M2. D = 16 cm.
JF/SAG/15.
See comments for no. 3.

6. Jar with out-turned rim and ribbed body. M1. D = 22 cm.
JF/SAG/2.
Ashmunein, 1998, E150, AD 650–800+.

7. Base of a *qadus*. M1.
JF/SAG/12.

*Amphorae*

8. Shoulder of an Egyptian amphora (Egloff, 177/Late Roman 7). M3.

JF/SAG/9.
Ashmunein, 1998, V92, eighth/ninth century AD.

**Ezbet Milik**

*Finewares: Egyptian Red Slip 'A' wares, ERS 'A' (01) and ERS 'A' Variant with cream/yellow slip (01W)*

9. Flanged bowl with high rim and downturned flange. Red/orange slip over rim and flange. Possibly rouletted on rim but eroded. O1. D = 16 cm.
JF/ELM/15.
*MDAIK*, 1975, 78, 15b, late sixth to the start of the seventh century AD.

10. Bowl or dish with gently sloping sides. Orange-slipped over rim. O1W. D = 20 cm.
Elephantine X, Abb.20, 3, T233, first half of the sixth to the second quarter of the seventh century AD. See also *MDAIK*, 1975, 78, 14a, second half of the sixth century AD. The *MDAIK* vessel is decorated.

11. Dish with knobbed rim. O1W. D = 24 cm.
JF/ELM/2.
Elephantine X, Abb.24, 6, T253, third quarter of the sixth to the middle of the second half of the seventh century AD. Gurna, 1028, AD 395–640. Also in O1W.

12. Bowl with knobbed rim. Traces of rouletting on body with small half-circle/triangular indents. O1. D = 20 cm.
JF/ELM/14.
Ashmunein, 1998, C214, fifth to eighth century AD.

13. Dish with double groove on knobbed rim. Orange-slipped overall and darker orange slip over rim. O1. D = 26 cm.
JF/ELM/BJK2.
Elephantine X, Abb. 13, T219, closest to no. 6, second quarter of the fifth to the last quarter of the sixth century AD. See also Chapter 2, no. 49, from Kom el-Nana.

14. Dish with double groove on knobbed rim. Traces of rouletting on body. Orange-slipped overall but with darker orange slip over rim. O1. D = 28 cm.
JF/ELM/12.
Near Elephantine X, Abb.18.6, T230a, around the middle of the sixth to the seventh century AD. See also Ashmunein, 1998, C145, AD 600–700.

15. Dish with single groove on knobbed, incurving rim. Orange-slipped overall and darker orange slip over rim. Ol. D = 22 cm.
JF/ELM/BJK1.
Elephantine X, Abb.43, T344b, sixth to the seventh/eighth century AD. Close to Ashmunein, 1998, C273, fifth to seventh century AD. Parcak, 2005, no. 49. See also Chapter 2, no. 47 from Kom el-Nana.

16. Dish with single groove on knobbed rim. Red-slipped over rim. O1W. D = 36 cm.
JF/ELM/1.
Ashmunein, 1998, C293, around the late fourth to eighth century AD. Nazlet Tuna, 133, 2. Kellia, pl. 40, 3.

17. Dish with knobbed rim and internal groove in rim. O1. D = 32 cm.
JF/ELM/5.
Probably to be equated with no. 16 above.

18. Base of dish or bowl with high foot and two grooves on body near base. Orange-slipped overall. Badly abraded inside. O1. D = 11 cm.
JF/ELM/BJK4.
Possibly an O1 (Aswan) copy of Hayes LRP Form 96. See Kom el-Rekab below for an example in ARS. If it is this form, the dating is late fifth to early sixth century AD for the ARS example, but probably sixth century or later for this O1 vessel.

19. Base of small bowl with high foot. Orange-slipped overall. O1. D = 3.5 cm.
JF/ELM/6.
Ashmunein, 1998, C624, which is compared to Elephantine X, T349–53, of around the sixth to seventh century AD.

*Finewares: Egyptian Red Slip 'B' wares (M5)*

20. Bowl with knobbed rim and two grooves in rim. Red/brown-slipped overall. ERS. D = 24 cm.
JF/ELM/18.
No clear parallel, but close to Ashmunein, 1998, D113 or 131, AD 400–500.

*Coarsewares*

21. Basin with sloping sides. Painted decoration in cream and black. M1. D = 40 cm.
JF/ELM/11.
Gurna, 1529.

22. Basin. M1. D = 50 cm.
JF/ELM/13.

23. Jar, medium high neck and out-turned rim. M4. D = 22 cm.

JF/ELM/8.
Esna, pl. CCXXIII, 9–11. Also similar to Chapter 2, no. 361.

24. Large jar with 'pie crust' rim. Decoration in black overlaid with white blobs. M1. D = 38 cm.
JF/ELM/21.
Esna, pl. CCXXIII, 10.

25. Jug with one handle and lid seating. M2. D = 14 cm.
JF/ELM/10.
Similar to Esna, pl. CCXXVII, 1, but this does not have a lid seating.

26. Base of *qadus*. M1.
JF/ELM/BJK6.

27. Lid with part of a cream painted swag on outside. M1. D = 22 cm.
JF/ELM/19.
See Chapter 2, no. 509.

*Amphorae*

28. Amphora shoulder and upper body. No pitch/resin evident (Egloff, 177, Late Roman 7). M3.
JF/ELM/BJK7.
Ashmunein, 1998, V47, around the fifth to seventh century AD.

29. Amphora shoulder and upper body. No pitch/resin evident (Egloff, 177, Late Roman 7). M3.
JF/ELM/BJK8.
Resembles Kellia, 177, AD 330–550, but certainly no later than the sixth century AD. Also found at this site was a body sherd of Gazan amphora.

**Kom el-Rekab**

*Finewares: African Red Slipwares (ARS)*

30. Dish with knobbed rim, two grooves on outer rim. Feather rouletting on body under rim. Two grooves towards base on inside. D = 36 cm.
JF/KER/7.
Hayes LRP, Form 82.2, Type A, AD 430–475.

31. Base of dish with high foot. Two grooves on outer body towards base and two grooves towards base on inside. D = 26 cm.
JF/KER/8.
Hayes LRP, Form 93.23, Type B, after AD 500.

*Egyptian Red Slip 'A' wares, ERS 'A' (01)*

32. Dish with knobbed rim. Orange-slipped overall. Dark red slip over rim. D = 26 cm.
JF/KER/12
Elephantine X, Abb.14, 1–7 (closest to 7), Form T220, second quarter of the fifth to the start of the seventh century AD and later.

33. Dish with knobbed rim. Orange-slipped overall. Dark red slip over rim. D = 18 cm.
JF/KER/14
Elephantine X, Abb.39, 7–14, Form T324a, second quarter to the middle of the fifth to the end (?) of the seventh century AD. Nazlet Tuna, 131, 3.

34. Dish with knobbed rim. Orange-slipped overall. Dark red slip over rim. D = 22 cm.
JF/KER/13.
Elephantine X, Abb.19, closest to 2, Form T230b, first half of the sixth to the seventh century AD.

35. Dish with knobbed rim. Orange-slipped overall with darker orange slip over rim. D = 28 cm.
JF/KER/11.
Elephantine X, Abb.43, Form T344b. This form was very frequently found at Elephantine and is dated sixth to seventh/eighth century AD. See also Nazlet Tuna, 135, 1.

36. Dish with knobbed rim. Orange-slipped overall with darker orange slip over rim. D = 24 cm.
JF/KER/15.
Elephantine X, Abb.43, Form T344c, not frequently found at Elephantine. Date as no. 35.

37. Small bowl with slight flange and high rim. Rouletting on rim. Orange-slipped overall. D = 14 cm.
JF/KER/1.
Nazlet Tuna, 137, 2. Ashmunein, C361, from *sebakh* sievings. Elephantine X, Abb.39, T323b, AD 550–630.

38. Bowl with flat rim. Orange-slipped overall but slip very worn from five centimetres down on inside of bowl. Possibly used as a mixing bowl. D = 24 cm.
JF/KER/16.
Nazlet Tuna, 121, 2. Elephantine X, Abb.37, Form T319b is a bowl, which has a decorated rim and is given a probable fourth century AD date.

39. Base of bowl with rouletting on outer surface. Dark orange slip outside with lighter orange slip on inside and base. D = 18 cm.
JF/KER/10.

This vessel is closest to that shown at Elephantine X, Abb.75, Form T643, unsafe dating, but probably eighth century AD.

40. Base of dish. Band of rouletting inside groove on inner surface at base. Orange slipped. D = 10 cm.
JF/KER/3.
Possibly as Elephantine X, Abb.18, Form T228, 1–4, last quarter of the fifth to the third quarter of the sixth century AD. See also *MDAIK*, 76, 13d.

41. Base of dish with stamped 'target' intersecting a groove. Orange slipped. D = 14 cm.
JF/KER/2.
Ashmunein, 1998, C530, AD 650–800+. See also Chapter 2, no. 54.

*Egyptian Red Slipped 'H' wares, ERS 'H' (M6)*

42. 'Frying pan'. Red-slipped inside. Worn. D = 30 cm.
JF/KER/25
As Chapter 2, no. 148 from Kom el-Nana. Ashmunein, 1998, D5, late fourth to eighth century AD.

43. Flanged bowl. Dark orange slipped overall.
D = 20 cm.
JF/KER/17.
Ashmunein, 1998, D299, around AD 400–550.

44. Base of bowl with small foot. Red slipped.
D = 12 cm.
JF/KER/5.

*Coarsewares: Bowls*

45. Bowl with flat, reeded rim. M2. D = 22 cm.
JF/KER/6.
Bailey, CC4, 1996, pl. V, fig. 8, 34, from below the South Church at el-Ashmunein and dated about AD 390–460.

46. Bowl with knobbed, flattened rim. One groove towards edge of rim. Black blob on rim and band of black paint on inner rim. M2. D = 20 cm.
JF/KER/31.
Close to Gurna, 1523.

47. Flanged bowl. 'Pie crust' wavy edge to flange. M1.
D = 20 cm.
JF/KER/18.

*Coarsewares: Cooking pots*

48. Cooking pot with ribbed body. M1. D = 18 cm.
JF/KER/20.
Faiers, 2005, no. 215. Ashmunein, 1998, E150, fifth to eighth century AD. Nazlet Tuna, 37, 1.

49. Cooking pot. Lid seating. M2. D = 18 cm.
JF/KER/32.
Faiers, 2005, no. 237.

50. Cooking pot with ribbed body. M4. D = 16 cm.
JF/KER/19.
Close to Ashmunein, 1998, E274, *c.* AD 400–550.

*Coarsewares:* Qadus

51. *Qadus*. M1. D = 18 cm.
JF/KER/30.

52. *Qadus* base. M1.
JF/KER/9

*Coarsewares: Lid*

53. Small lid with tall knob. No steam hole. M1.
D = 10 cm.
JF/KER/21.

*Amphorae: Imported*

54. Rim, neck and handle (Late Roman 1, Peacock and Williams, 44A). N1. D = 12 cm.
JF/KER/33.
See notes on these amphorae in Chapter 2. Fifth to eighth century AD.

*Amphorae: Egyptian*

55. Neck, part of upper body and two handles (Egloff 177, Late Roman 7). M3.
JF/KER/34.
Faiers, 2005, 218, GP Type 3a. See also Ashmunein, 1998, V14, 15, 21, 22 and 24, around sixth to seventh century AD.

56. Part of neck and upper body (Egloff 177, Late Roman 7). M3.
JF/KER/35.
Ashmunein, 1998, V86, AD 650–800+.

57. Part of upper body (Egloff 177, Late Roman 7). M3.
JF/KER/28.
Ashmunein, 1998, V61, AD 650–800+.

**Sheikh el-Habse/Ismu el-Arus**

*Finewares: Egyptian Red Slip 'A' wares, ERS 'A' (01), and variant with cream/yellow slip (01W)*

58. Vertical rim of bowl with high-placed internal step. Cream/yellow-slipped inside rim with dark orange slip on outside of rim. O1W. D = 36 cm.
JF/EEA/11.
Close to Ashmunein, 1998, C582, undated, but likened to Elephantine X, Abb.46, T353b, dated second quarter of the sixth to the first quarter of the seventh century AD, or perhaps later.

59. Vertical rim of bowl with high-placed internal step and groove internally near top of rim. Red-slipped over rim. O1. D = 26 cm.
JF/EEA/7.
Close to Elephantine X, Abb.46, T353a, dated as no. 58.

60. Small bowl with incurved rim, slipped red on outside of rim. O1. D = 16 cm.
JF/EEA/5.
Elephantine X, Abb.39, 11, T324a, second quarter/middle of the fifth to the end (?) of the seventh century AD. See also Nazlet Tuna, 131, 3, which is close.

61. Base of bowl with rouletting on inside of base. Red-orange slipped overall. O1. Base D = 10 cm.
JF/EEA/6.
Possibly from a flanged bowl such as Elephantine X, Abb.51, T359b, sixth century AD.

*Finewares: Egyptian Red Slip 'H' wares, ERS 'H' (M6)*

62. Bowl with knobbed, overhanging rim. Red-slipped overall. M6. D = 24 cm.
JF/EEA/6.
Close to Ashmunein, 1998, D259, *c.* AD 600–700.

63. Small bowl with flat rim. Groove near edge of rim. M6. D = 18 cm.
JF/EEA/10.
Probably to be likened to Kom el-Rekab no. 62, above, which was close to Bailey CC4, 1996, pl. 5, 34, AD 390–460.

*Coarsewares*

64. Jar with pulley rim, short neck and ribbed body. M1. D = 20 cm.
JF/EEA/4.
See Chapter 2, no. 364. Also Nazlet Tuna, 41, 5.

*Amphorae*

65. Rim and neck of Egyptian amphora (Egloff, 177, Late Roman 7). M3. D = 8 cm.
JF/EEA/1.
Fifth to sixth century AD.

66. Shoulder sherd of Egyptian amphora (Egloff, 177, Late Roman 7). M3.
JF/EEA/2.
Ashmunein, 1998, V28, fifth to early sixth century AD.

67. Shoulder sherd of Egyptian amphora (Egloff, 177, Late Roman 7). M3.
JF/EEA/3.
See Chapter 2, no. 574. Close to Ashmunein, 1998, V53, AD 400–550.

**Singirg**

*Finewares: Egyptian Red Slip 'A' wares, ERS 'A' (01)*

68. Dish with knobbed rim. O1. Orange-slipped overall. D = 20 cm.
JF/SIN/3.
Elephantine X, Abb.39, T324a, second quarter/middle of the fifth to the end (?) of the seventh century AD. Similar vessels at Kom el-Rekab, no. 4, and Sheikh el-Habse/Esmu el-Aris, no. 3.

69. Dish with knobbed rim, slightly in-turned. Orange-slipped overall. O1. D = 16 cm.
JF/SIN/2.
Comments and dating as for no. 1 above.

*Finwares: Egyptian Red Slip 'H' wares, ERS 'H' (M6).*

70. Bowl with out-turned knobbed rim.

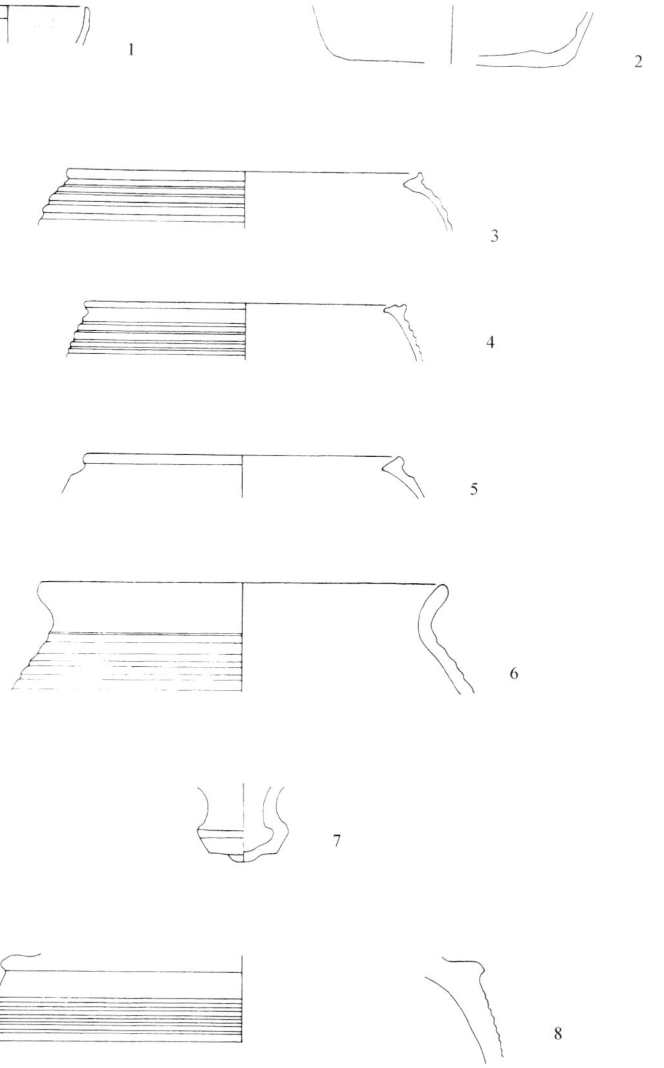


*Figure 5.2 Sheikh Ali Ghindi, nos 1–8. Scale 1:3*

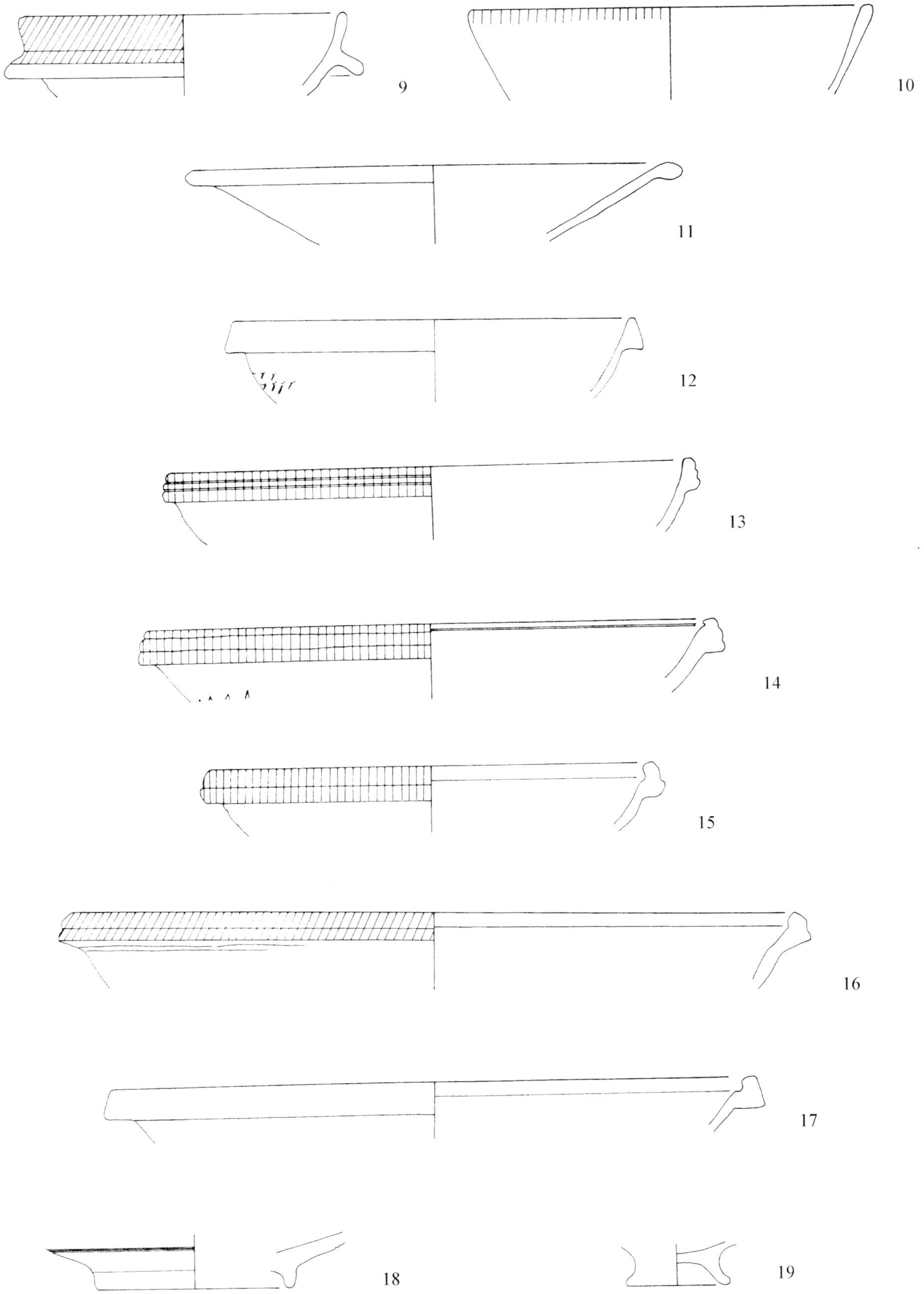


*Figure 5.3 Ezbet Milik, nos 9–19. Scale 1:3*

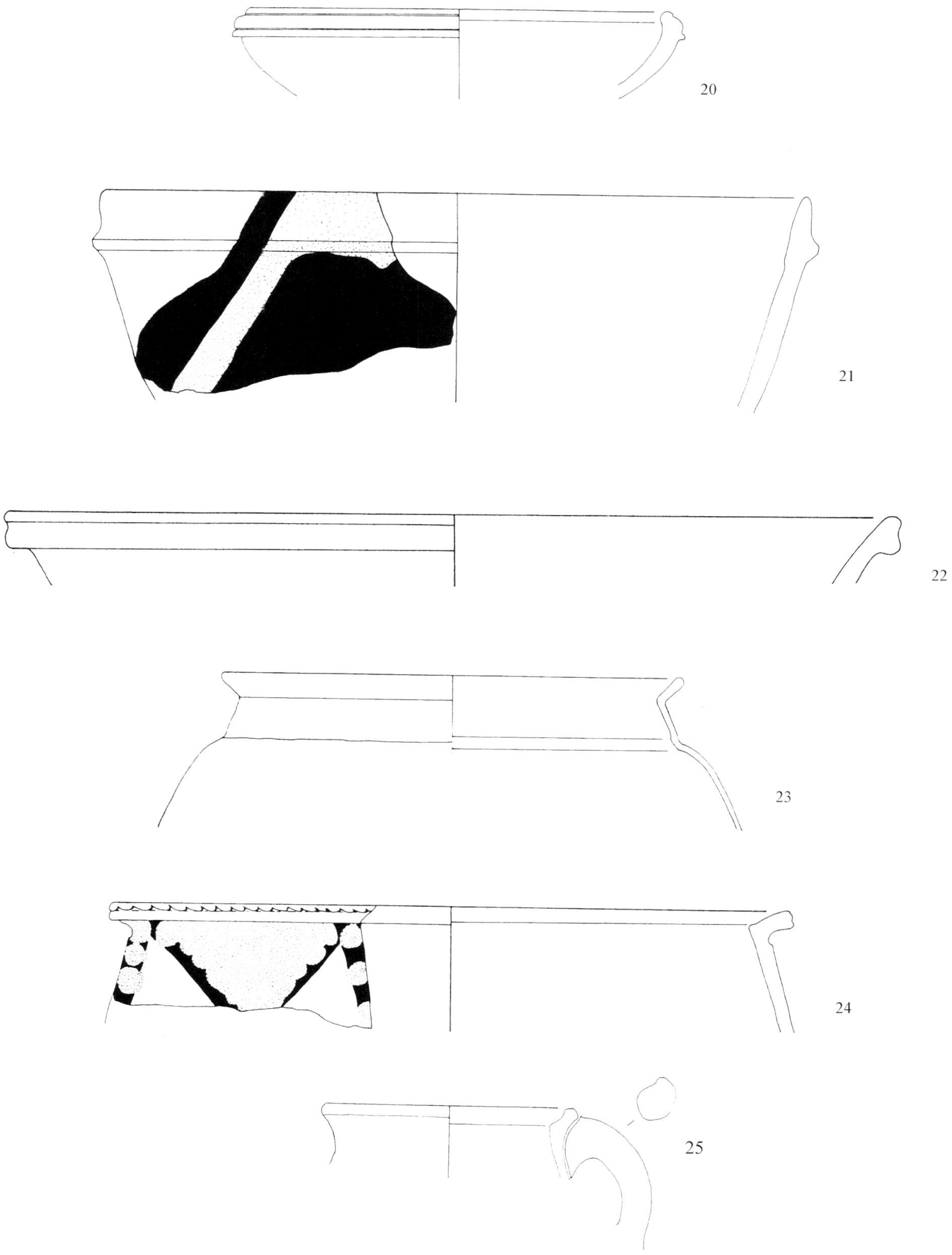


*Figure 5.4 Ezbet Milik, nos 20–25. Scale 1:3*

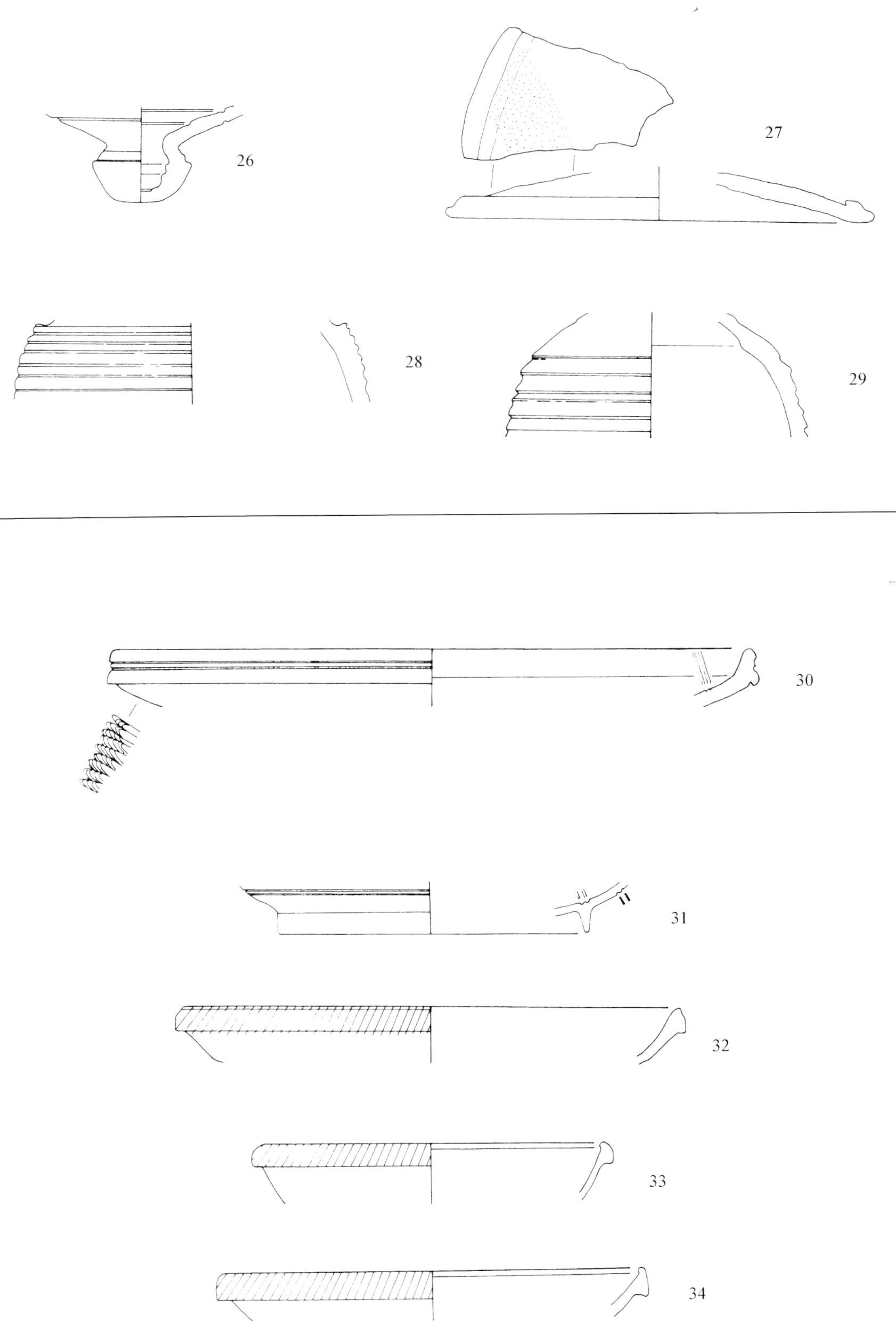


*Figure 5.5 Ezbet Milik, nos 26–29, and Kom el-Rekab, nos 30–34. Scale 1:3*

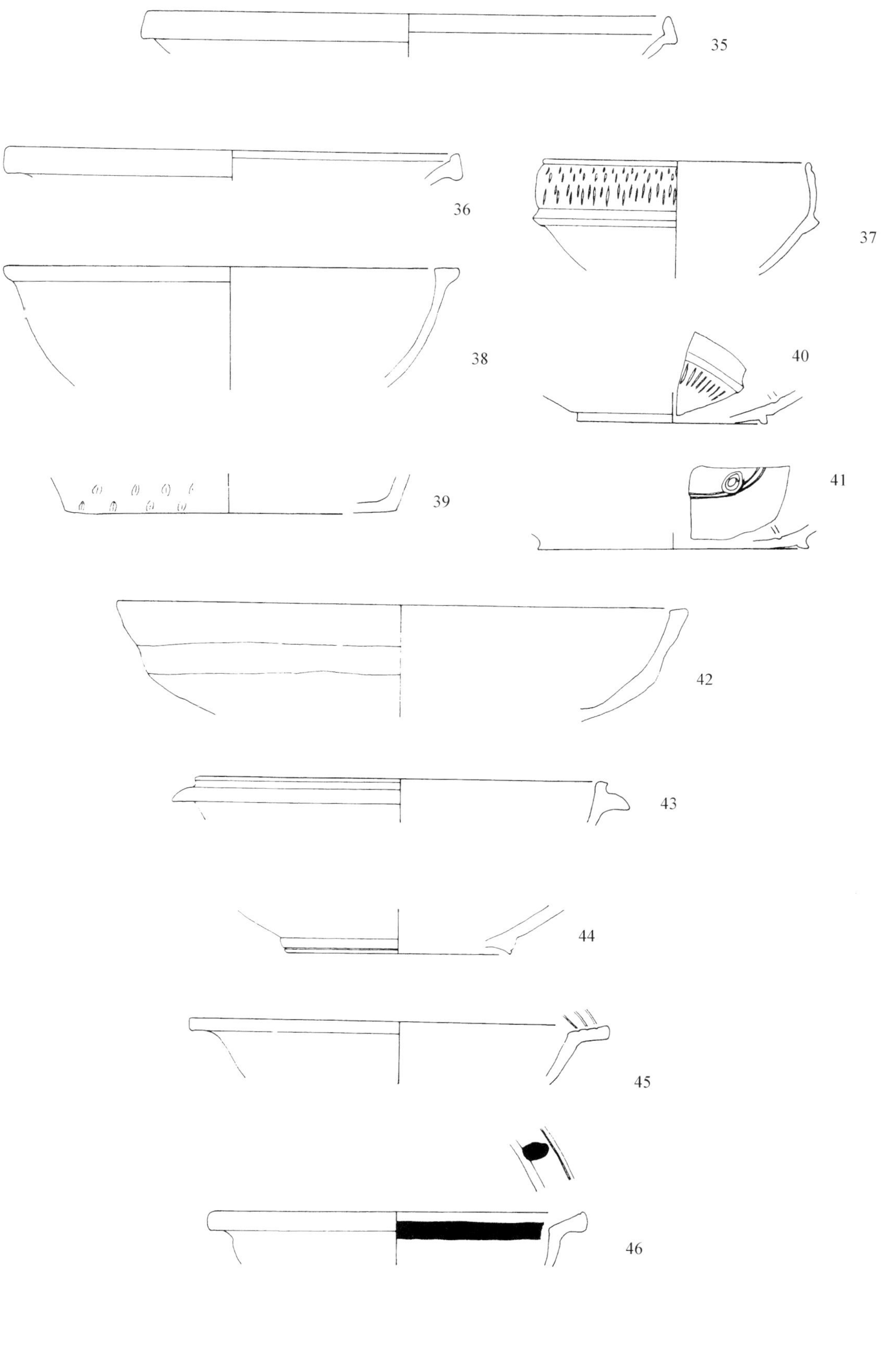


*Figure 5.6 Kom el-Rekab, nos 35–46. Scale 1:3*

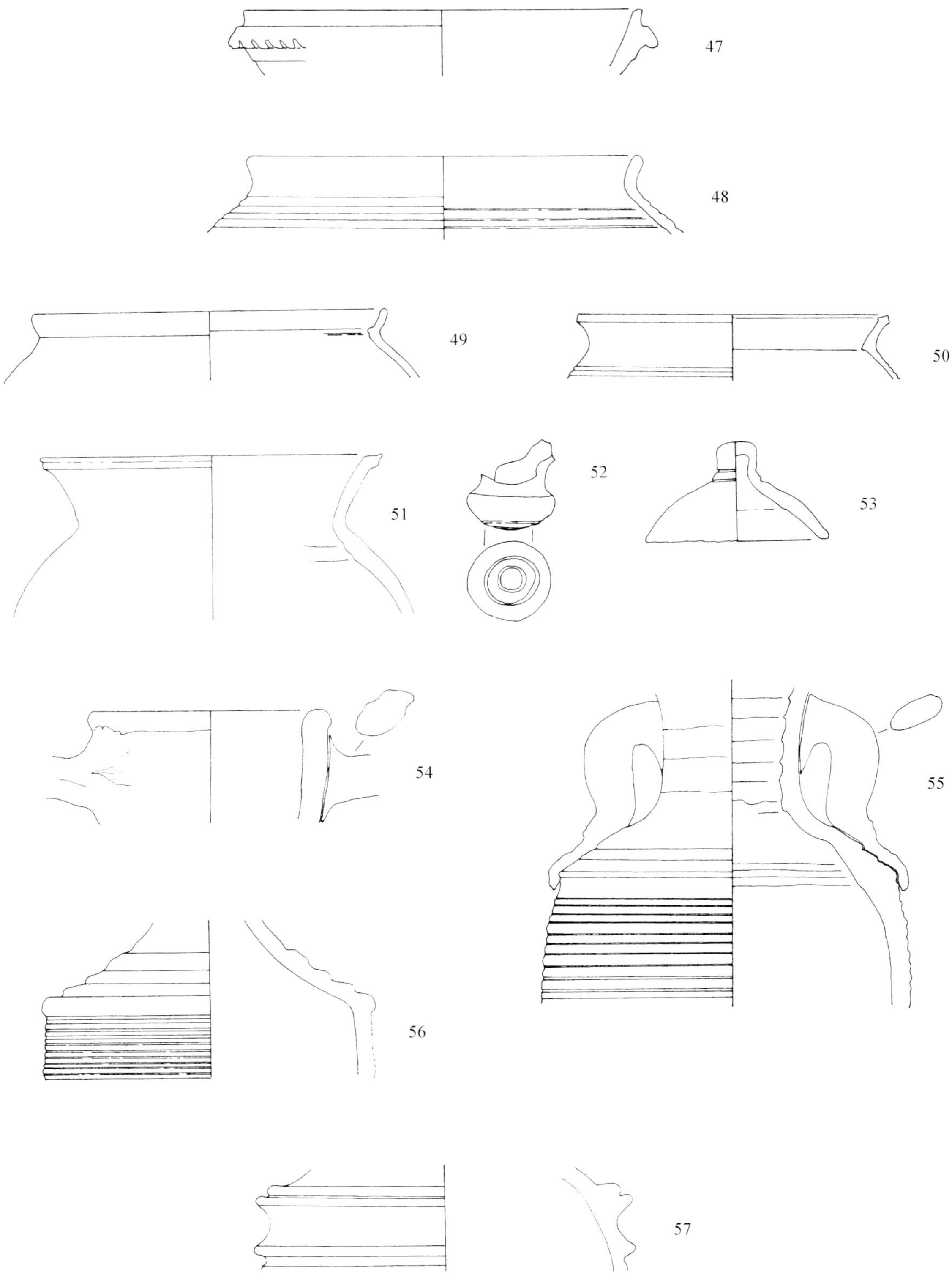


*Figure 5.7 Kom el-Rekab, nos 47–57. Scale 1:3*

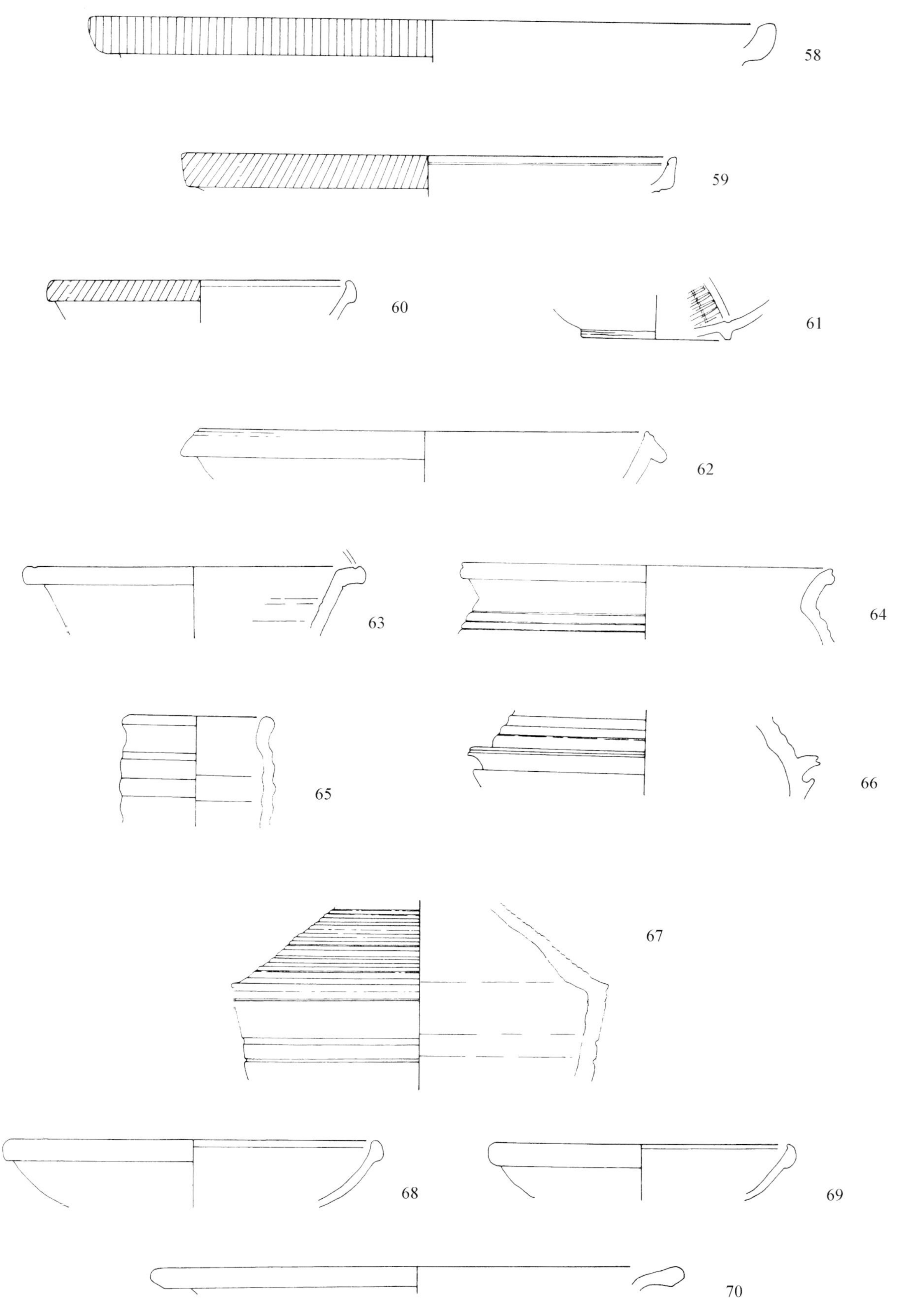


*Figure 5.8 Ismu el-Arus, nos 58–67, and Singirg, nos 68–70. Scale 1:3*

# CHAPTER 6

## End Game

by Jane Faiers

In the previous volume, a dating for Kom el-Nana was proposed as *c.* AD 425/450–650. In light of the evidence provided by the excavations, is this still the case, or is the later date of AD 650 optimistic? The monastery, as such, may have ceased to function well before this date.

The previous volume included the dating of pottery and coins from ten sites close to Kom el-Nana on the same side of the Nile (Faiers, 2005, 181–213 and Faiers and Kemp, 2005, 267–275). (Two of Kemp's diagrams for these are reproduced here at figs 6.1 and 6.2.) The evidence provided by the coins (fig. 6.1) shows that the latest coin from all the sites, including Kom el-Nana, dates from before AD 600. No legible coin from Kom el-Nana need be dated later than AD 582 and it was surmised by Richard Reece that "…there was no reason why the coins of Phocas and Haeraclius (early seventh century) which reached other North African sites should fail to reach this area…their absence might suggest the end of the occupation" (Reece, 2005, 263).

At el-Ashmunein about 20 miles away there are five coins minted at Alexandria between AD 527 and 668 which appears to show that coins are getting to this part of Middle Egypt (Spencer, 1989, 52, 141–145). So, coin supply in the area was still present. Did the community at Kom el-Nana simply stop using coins? This would be difficult to understand given that it had used them in the past, but would be possible, as a community could exist without coins, or was the monastery simply no longer there?

If we move on to the pottery evidence, fig. 6.2 shows a general date range for the pottery from the other ten sites around Amarna listed in the first volume. The conclusions drawn from the evidence was that the spread of dates across the sites was closely comparable to Kom el-Nana (Faiers and Kemp, 2005, fig. 7.1); particularly true of the later limits, which suggested a time of general abandonment that was common to all of the sites. This demonstrates evidence for a major change, and it was thought when Volume 1 was written that this change could have taken place early in the seventh century AD, but could it have happened at the end of the sixth century instead?

The 'Other Sites' chapter (Chapter 5) of this volume deals with more of the sites around Kom el-Nana which were investigated by Barry Kemp, Robert Miller and Sarah Parcak, who all made random collections of pottery. A few of the vessels collected by Miller were of a later date than those found at Kom el-Nana, nos 6, 8, 39, 41, 56, and 57, and none of these was present at Kom el-Nana, which seems to suggest that pottery supply was still functioning at a later date than the vessels recorded at the monastery.

At nearby Hermopolis Magna (el-Ashmunein), the occurrence of African Red Slipwares (a ware considered to be the most securely dated) seems to be the same as at Kom el-Nana, with the majority of the few sherds found dating from the fifth century AD to the last quarter of the sixth century AD, but with no later forms.

At Kom el-Nana, the archaeological excavations which have taken place on site have revealed pottery, coins and ostraca and also paintings on the church walls. Using pottery as a measure of dating is problematic in that the coarsewares can only be dated fairly vaguely, and of the so-called finewares, Aswan wares usually have a tighter date, but notice must be taken as to where the parallel given was found and in what context, as dates differ. The imported wares, such as African Red Slipware, are the only means of suggesting a more exact date. Even then the pottery may well have continued in use well after its given dates due to its rarity or intrinsic value to the owner, or indeed other factors.

An Aswan (ERS 'A') vessel which copies an imported fineware, such as African Red Slipware (ARS), can be dated initially by the start date of the ARS vessel. The vessel would have to be seen to be copied and, given the dominance of Nile transport, consignments of ARS pottery could have reached Upper Egypt within a short time of manufacture.

In Volume 1, two examples of Aswan wares which have ARS as their prototype, and are also dated by coins from the same layer, show the time lapse before copying. No. 63, an ERS 'A' vessel based on LRP 109 (*c.* AD 580/600 to mid seventh century AD), was found in the same layer as a coin of Justinian dated AD 538–565, and no. 98, in Egyptian Red Slipware (ERS 'B') (a copy of LRP 61, AD 400–500), was found in the same layer as fifth to sixth century coins which would probably have dropped out of use by the mid sixth century AD. In the first instance, the coin date for no. 63 is earlier than the suggested start of LRP 109, although the coin could well have still been in circulation by the suggested date of '*c*.580/600'. On the other hand, no. 98 could be dated a hundred years after the LRP end date of AD 450, if the coin was at the end of its life, but could just as well be mid-to-late fifth century AD, which would be concurrent with its ARS counterpart. Bailey suggests that an Aswan vessel copying LRP Form 84 (no. 58, Volume 1) could still have been in production up to a century-and-a-half after the end date of the ARS vessel (Bailey, 1996, 56). This could give the ERS vessel a date of *c*.AD 440–650 instead of *c*. AD 440–500.

Four of the eleven ARS sherds in the first volume (Faiers, 2005) were from stratified contexts, but unfortunately not *in situ* deposits: no. 4, Z50 [8510], dated mid-to-late fifth or second half of the fifth century AD; no. 5, AE49 [8589], cleaning, *c*.AD 560/580–620; no. 8, Y50 [8274], a large sand dump, AD 500 to the third quarter of the sixth century AD; and no. 11, Y50 [8254], windblown sand and demolition debris, AD 575–600.

In this volume, 11 ARS sherds are listed (ten illustrated), only two of which are from deposits not associated with mudbrick rubble and sand. These are:

1. AC52 [7655] (north-east sector), organic buildup on the latest surface (?), out of use, dated AD 550–625

2. AD51 [7575], not illustrated. Ash below big pit [7573], *c*. AD 425–475

These appear to span the life of the monastery.

There are three vessels in Faiers 2005 which can be dated to the late sixth to mid seventh century: no. 48, an Aswan bowl with black and red painted lines and rouletting, which came from sand and rubble north of the sill and in a doorway of the refectory (north-east sector, Area 1, Chapter 3); no. 410, which was found in the covering debris/midden; and no. 421, which came from the alleyway in the north-east sector, in a sandy layer containing pottery above floor levels but prior to the collapse of walls (see Chapter 3, Area 7). Both 420 and 421 were decorated with an impressed herringbone pattern. All three came from layers associated with the abandonment of the monastery.

The pottery appears to have a longer date span than the coins, mainly due to the vagueness of dating any wares other than the fine ones. In addition, coins do not break and could, therefore, have been in use for longer than the pottery.

Although certain pottery and coin evidence seem to indicate a lack of evidence for continuous occupation at Kom el-Nana after AD 600, there would need to be more information on coins and pottery from other sites in the area in order to make an informed judgement. What is evident is that there appears to have been a remodelling of the monastery in the sixth century AD to cater for more inhabitants (see Chapter 3, south-east sector). Admittedly, Kom el-Nana may have acquired monks from nearby, smaller, failed houses, thus increasing the monastic community.

By all accounts, the last 65 years of the sixth century AD appear to have been a difficult place in which to survive and the question must be asked whether the events during this time had an effect on Kom el-Nana. There are no signs of vandalism or destruction of the monastery and it seems to have been just abandoned with certain parts then being occupied by squatters.

Climate change has been suggested during the past few years to account for events happening on a global level during the sixth century. Keys suggests that it was an eruption of Krakatoa (or a volcano in the Sunda Straits between Java and Sumatra) in AD 535, whose resulting dust cloud blocked sunlight in AD 535/6 (Keys, 1999, 307). There is evidence for a volcanic eruption at this time which is substantiated by a correlation between tree ring minimal growth width and volcanic signals reported in Greenland and Antarctican ice cores of AD 536 (Salzer and Hughes, 2007, 62; Baillie, 2008; Larson et al., 2008) but Keys' theory is not generally accepted.

Adverse weather conditions apparently prevailed during the second half of the sixth century with a dust-veil, wetter- and colder-than-usual weather, or droughts causing harvests to fail. This is supported by historical evidence either from those living at the time or taking their information at a later date from those who did.

Several contemporary writers described the darkening of the sun. Procopius, employed at the court of the emperor Justinian, wrote, "and it came about during this year that a most dread portent took place. For the sun gave forth its light without brightness, like the moon, during this whole year, and it seemed exceedingly like the sun in eclipse, for the beams it shed were not clear not such as it is accustomed to shed…and it was the time that Justinian was in the tenth year of his reign [AD 536–537]" (Procopius, *History of the Wars*, IV, 15.4); John of Ephesus wrote, "the sun became dark and its darkness lasted eighteen months. Each day it shone for about four hours and still this light was only a feeble shadow", text as recorded in the Chronicle of Michael the Syrian, 9.296, which incorporates much of John's Chronicle in a manuscript dated to the eighth century AD, now in the Vatican Library (see A. Harrak, 1999). Admittedly, the evidence may have been overstated.

Recurring bouts of bubonic plague from AD 542 onwards devastated populations around the world. On balance it seems unlikely that Kom el-Nana would have escaped unscathed, but there is no entomological evidence that it suffered from plague (E. Panagiotakopulu, personal communication), and no burials dating to the fifth or sixth century AD have been found at Kom el-Nana which might give more evidence of diet and disease.

Writers at the time state that the plague started in Pelusium in Egypt (Procopius, *Wars II*, 461) or Ethiopia (Evragius, *Book IV*, 29, 229). Eva Panagiotakopulu, a paleoentomologist, has shown that plague affected those at the workmen's village at Amarna some 3,500 years ago and puts forward the hypothesis that plague originated in Africa, not Asia (Panagiotakopulu, 2004, 269–275). This is corroborated by Sarris (2007, 121–123) who argues that of the three ancient *foci* of plague activity — the foothills of the Himalayas, the vicinity of the Great Lakes of Africa and, lastly, scattered across the Manchurian Steppe to the Ukraine — Africa is the most probable.

What is certain is that elsewhere in the Mediterranean, the effects of the plague were disastrous. Procopius records that in Constantinople during the years AD 541/2 the plague was killing 10,000 people a day, rich and poor (Procopius, *Wars II*, 464). Both Emperor Justinian and Evragius, the historian and hagiographer, suffered and survived, whilst John of Ephesus, travelling from Palestine and Syria to Constantinople, wrote of sheep, goats, oxen and pigs wandering about with no one to tend them and unharvested fields of wheat, fruit crops and vineyards, due no doubt to the mortality in the countryside (Morony, 81). The effects of plague on high concentrations of populations would no doubt be greater due to crowded and perhaps unsanitary living conditions which would allow rats and their fleas to survive. Monasteries may have been harder hit than most, being close-knit communities.

In the area of Constantinople, records list over 80 monasteries before AD 542, most of which seem to disappear after this date (Evans, 164). The total population of the religious houses in England shortly before the Black Death of AD 1346 was approximately 17,500, and not far short of half of these appear to have perished in the two years of the epidemic (Knowles, 256–257).

All this, though, was happening hundreds of miles away in the Mediterranean, and whilst there is papyrological evidence for Egypt, it is not forthcoming on population demographics for the sixth century which would enable a picture to be built up of how certain communities either suffered or survived. Papyri exist with census returns datable to the first to third centuries AD, but this is three hundred years too early (Bagnall and Frier, 75–91). So, in the light of a lack of written evidence and burials of the monks who lived at Kom el-Nana, reliance must be placed elsewhere, and at the moment the coins and pottery are the only tools available.

In conclusion therefore, it is suggested that, on the evidence as stated in the preceding pages, the monastery at Kom el-Nana had ceased to function as such by AD 600. This may well be revised in the light of further excavation or knowledge obtained from written sources in the future (both at Kom el-Nana and at sites nearby), but at the time of writing this seems to be the best estimate.

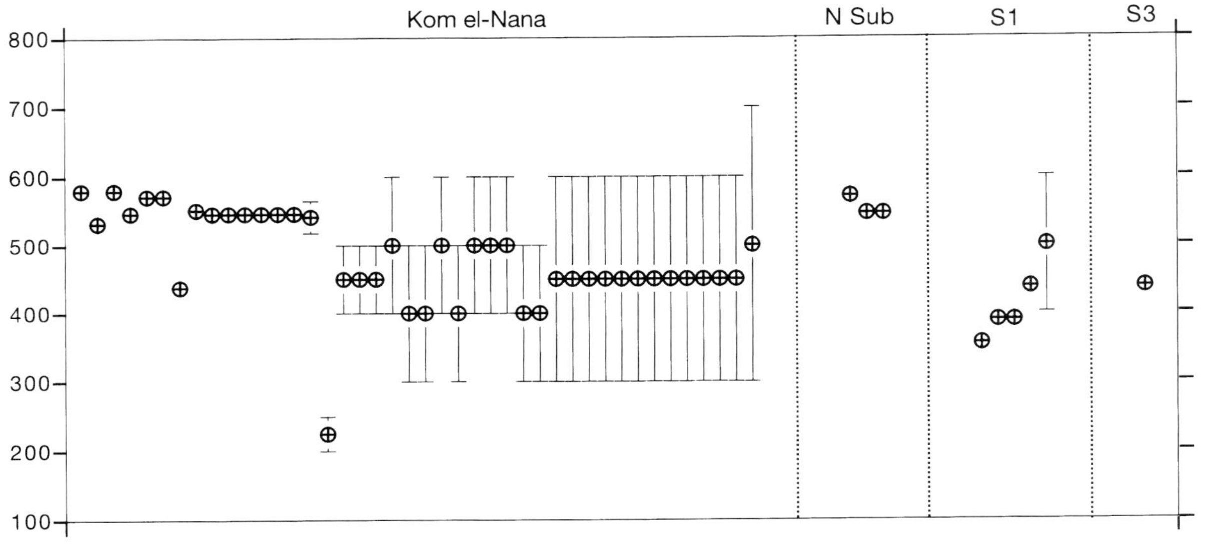


*Figure 6.1 Amarna region: date ranges for coins, sorted by duration of range*

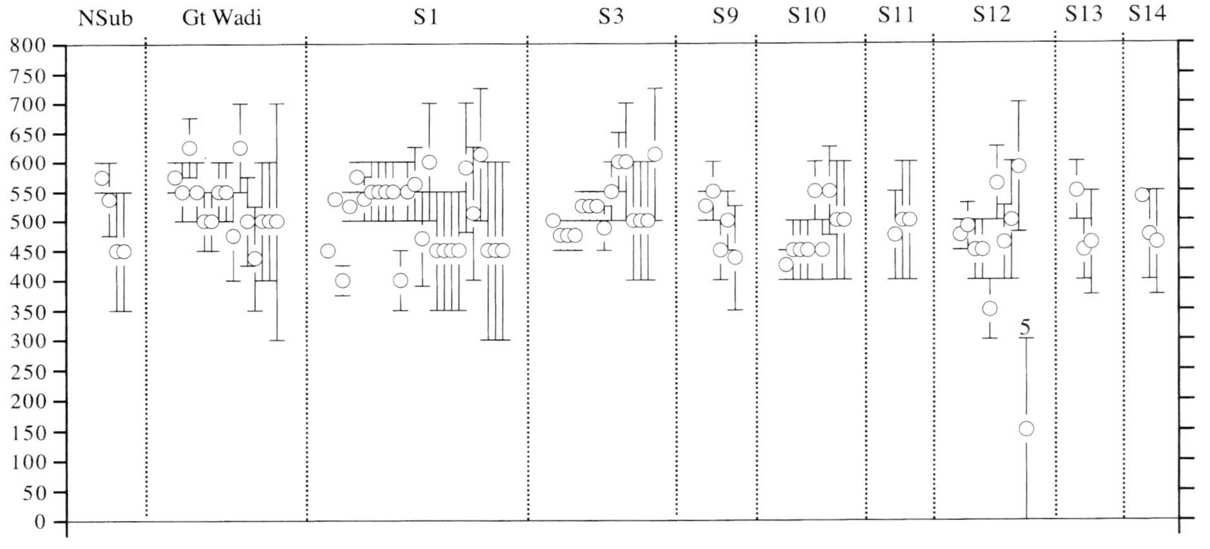


*Figure 6.2 Other Late Roman sites: date ranges for pots, sorted by duration of range*

# Bibliography

### Abbreviations

*AI*: *Annales islamologiques, Institut Francais d'Archéologie Orientale due Caire*, Cairo
BAR: British Archaeological Reports, Oxford
*BASOR*: *Bulletin of the American Schools of Oriental Research*
*CCE*: *Cahiers de la céramique égyptienne*, Cairo
*JARCE*: *Journal of the American Research Centre in Egypt*, American Research Centre in Egypt
*BASP*: *Bulletin of the American Society of Papyrologists*, New Haven, CT.
*JJP*: *Journal of Juristic Papyrology*, Warsaw
*JRS*: *Journal of Roman Studies*, London.
*MDAIK*: *Mitteilungen des Deutschen Archäologischen Instituts, Abteilung Kairo*, Cairo
*JEA*: *Journal of Egyptian Archaeology*, London
*ZAS*: *Zeitschrift fur Agyptische Sprache und Altertumskunde*, Leipzig/Berlin


Alston, R., *Soldier and society in Roman Egypt* (London, 1995)

Amélineau, E. C., *Monuments pour servir a l'histoire de l'Egypte chrétienne au IV au V siecle. Histoire de saint Pakhôme et de ses communautes* (Annales du Musée Guimet 17, Paris, 1889)

Anderson, J., 'Monastic Lifestyles of the Nubian Desert: Seeking the Mysterious Monks of Makuria', *Sudan and Nubica Bulletin No. 3* (The Sudan Archaeological Research Society, 1999), 71–83

Bagnall, R. S., 'Archaeology and papyrology,' *Journal of Roman Archaeology* 1 (1988), 197–202

Bagnall, R. S., *Egypt in Late Antiquity* (Princeton, 1993)

Bagnall, R. S. and Frier, B. W., *The Demography of Roman Egypt: Studies in Population, Economy and Society in Past Time 23* (Cambridge, 1994)

Bailey, D. M., *A Catalogue of the Lamps in the British Museum iii, Roman Provincial Lamps* (London, 1988)

Bailey, D. M., 'The local Late Roman red slip ware of Hermopolis Magna' in W. Godlewski (ed.), *Coptic and Nubian Pottery* 1 (Warsaw, 1990)

Bailey, D. M., 'The pottery from the south church at el-Ashmunein' (*CCE* 4, Cairo, 1996), 78–9

Bailey, D. M., *Excavations at El-Ashmunein V: Pottery, lamps and glass of the Late Roman and Early Arab Periods* (London, 1998)

Bailey, D. M., *The Rathbone-Polemon Survey* (forthcoming)

Bailey, D. M., 'The glass vessels of Mons Porphyrites and Badia', in D. P. S. Peacock and V. Maxfield (eds), *The Roman Imperial Quarries Survey and Excavation at Mons Porphyrites. Volume 2: The Excavations* (London, 2007), 234–266

Bailey, D. M., W.V. Davies and A. J. Spencer, *Ashmunein (1980)* (London, 1982)

Baillie, M. G. L., 'Proposed re-dating of the European ice-core chronology by seven years prior to the 7th century AD', *Geophysical Research Letters*, 35 (4) (2008)

Ballet, P. and Picon, M. 'Recherches préliminaires sur les origines de la céramique des Kellia (Egypte). Importations et productions égyptiennes', in P. Ballet (ed.), *CCE* 1 (Cairo, 1987), 17–48

Ballet, P., Mahoud, F., Vichy. N. and Picon, M., 'Artisanat de la céramique dans l'Égypte romaine tardive et byzantine. Prospections d'ateliers de potiers de Minia á Assouan', in P. Ballet (ed.), *CCE* 2 (Cairo, 1991), 129–143

Barakat, H. N. and Baum, N., *La Végétation Antique de Douch (Oasis de Kharga): Une Approche Macrobotanique.* (Documents de Fouilles, Vol. XXVII, Cairo, 1992)

Bell, D. N. 'Introduction', in Besa, *The Life of Shenoute*, D. N. Bell (tr.) (Kalamazoo Cistercian Publications, 1986), 1–35

Binford, L., 'Behavioural archaeology and the "Pompeii Premise"', *Journal of Anthropological Research* 37, (1981), 195–208

Boud'hors, A., *Ostraka grecs et coptes de Baouit.* (Cairo, 2004)

Bourriau, J., *Umm El-Ga`ab: Pottery from the Nile Valley before the Arab Conquest* (Cambridge, 1981)

Bowman, A. K., *Egypt after the Pharaohs: 332 BC–AD 642 from Alexander to the Arab Conquest* (London, 1986)

Brooks Hedstrom, D. L., 'Divine architects: Designing the monastic dwelling place', in R. S. Bagnall (ed.), *Egypt in the Byzantine World, 300–700* (Cambridge, 2007)

Campbell-Thompson, R., 'Byzantine Research Fund: Excavations at Wadi Sarga', *JEA* 1 (1914), 187–188

Chitty, D. J., *The Desert a City* (New York, 1966)

Clackson, S. J., 'Fish and chits', *ZAS* 129 (2002), 6–11.

Clackson, S. J., 'Coptic and Greek ostraca from Kom el-Nana', in J. E. Faiers, *Late Roman pottery at Amarna and related studies* (Egypt Exploration Society 72, London, 2005)

Clédat, J. 'Le monastère el la nécropole de Baouît (Mémoires de l'Institut français d'Archéologie du Caire XII)', in Bachatly, D. (ed.), *Le Monastere de Phoebammon dans la Thebaide* (Publications de la Societe d'Archeologie copte. Rapports de Fouilles 3, Cairo, 1904), 55–6

Clugnet, L., *Vie et Récits de l'Abbé Daniel le Scétiote (VI siècle)* (Bibliothèque Hagiographique Orientale, Paris, 1901)

Crislip, A., 'Care for the sick in Shenoute's monasteries', in G. Gabra and H. Takla, *Christianity and Monasticism in Upper Egypt, Volume 1 Akmin and Sohag* (Cairo, 2008), 21–30.

Crum, W. E., Bell, H. and Campbell-Thompson, R., *Wadi Sarga: Coptic and Greek Texts* (Coptica III, Hauniae, 1922)

Dodson, A., and Ikram S. (eds), *Beyond the Horizon: Studies in Egyptian Art, Archaeology and History in Honour of Barry J. Kemp* I and II (Cairo, 2009)

Donadoni, S. et al., *Antinoe (1965–68)* (Rome, 1974)

Drew-Bear, M., *Le nome Hermopolite: toponymes et sites* (American Studies in Papyrology 21, Missoula, 1979)

Egloff, M, *La Poterie Copte (*Kellia III, Geneva, 1977)

El-Duweini, A., 'Identifications botaniques, zoologiques et chimiques', in Bachatly, C. (ed.), *Le Monastere de Phoebammon dans la Thébaïde* (Publications de la Société d'Archéologie copte. Rapports de Fouilles 3, Cairo, 1961), 55–6

El-Hadidi, M. N. and Boulos, L., *Street Trees of Cairo* (2nd edn, Cairo, 1988)

Evans, J. A. S., *The Age of Justinian: The Circumstances of Imperial Power* (London and New York, 1996)

Evetts, B., *History of the Patriarchs of the Coptic Church of Alexandria* attributed to *Severus of Al'Ashmunein (Hermopolis)* (Oxford, 1904)

Faiers, J. E., *Late Roman pottery at Amarna and related studies* (Egypt Exploration Society 72, London, 2005)

Faiers J. E. and Smith W., 'Plant Macrofossils and Pottery from Room C, Kom el-Nana: a preserved 'vide sanitaire' at a Late Antique monastery' in S. Ikram and A. Dodson (eds), *Beyond the Horizon: Studies in Egyptian Art, Archaeology and History in Honour of Barry J. Kemp* (Cairo, 2009)

Frankfort, H. and Pendlebury, J. D. S., *The City of Akhenaten – Part II: The North Suburb and the Desert Altars – the Excavations at Tell El Amarna during the Seasons 1926–1932* (Egypt Exploration Society, London, 1933)

Foy, D., 'Secteur nord de Tebtynis (Fayyoum), le verre bysantin et islamique' *AI* 35, 465–89

Godlewski, W., Derda, T. and Gorecki, T. *1988–1989, Deir el Naqlun (Nekloni)* (Second Preliminary Report, Nubica III/I 1989–93, 2001)

Foy D, Picon M., Vichy M and Thirion-Merle, V., 'Charactérisation des verres de la fin de l'Antiquité en Méditerranée occidentale: l'émergence de nouveaux courants commerciaux', in Foy, D. and Nenna, M-D., *Échanges et commerce du verre dans le monde antique* (Montagnac, 2003)

Fulford, M. and Tomber, R. (eds), *Excavations at Sabratha 1948–1951. Volume II. The Finds Part 2. The Finewares and Lamps* (Society for Libyan Studies Monograph 3, London, 1994)

Gabra, G., *Coptic Monasteries* (Cairo, 2002)

Gascou, J., 'Monasteries, Economic Activities of', in *The Coptic Encyclopedia* Volume 5 (New York, 1991), CE: 1639–1645

Gazda, E. K. (ed.), *Karanis: An Egyptian Town in Roman Times: Discoveries of the University of Michigan Expedition to Egypt 1924-1935* (Michigan, 2004)

Gempeler, R., *Elephantine X, Die Keramik romanischer bis früharabischer Zeit* (Mainz, 1992)

Germer, R., *Flora des pharaonischen Ägypten* (Abteilung Kairo, Sonderschrift 14, Mainz, 1985)

Guidotti, M. C. and Pesi, L, *La Ceramica Da Antinoe* (Florence, 2004)

Gill, M. A. V., *Amorium Reports, Finds* I: *The Glass (1987–1997)* (BAR IS 1070, 2002)

Godlewski, W., 'Deir el-Naqlun: Topography and Tentative History' in A. D. Natale and C. Basile, *Archeologia e Papiri nel Fayyum* (Atti del Convegno Internazionale, Siracusa, 24–25, Maggio 1996, Siracusa, 1997), 123–125

Godlewski, W., Derda, T. and Gorecki, T., 'Deir el Naqlun (Nekloni), 1988–1989, Second Preliminary Report', in *Nubica III/I* (Cologne, 1993)

Guerrini, L., 'Materiali ceramici', in S. Donadoni et al., *Antinoe (1965-8)* (Rome, 1974), 93–5, pl. 37 [3]

Guidotti, M. C. and Pesi, L., *La Ceramica da Antinoe* (Florence, 2004)

Harden D. B., *Roman Glass from Karanis* (Michigan, 1936)

Harden D. B., 'The Glass', in R. Mond, *Temples of Armant: The Text and Plates*, (Egypt Exploration Society 47 and 48, London, 1940), 117–23

Harper, R. P., 'The Glass', in *Upper Zohar An Early Byzantine Fort in Palaestina Tertia Final Report of Excavations in 1985–1986* (Oxford, 1995), 39–43

Harrak, A., *The Chronicle of Zuquin Parts III and IV* (Toronto, 1999)

Hayes, J. W., *Late Roman Pottery*. (London, 1972)

Hayes, J. W., 'Pottery: Stratified Groups and typology', in J. H. Humphrey (ed.), *Excavations at Carthage Conducted by the University of Michgan 1975*, 1 (Tunis, 1976), 47–124

Hayes, J. W., *Supplement to Late roman pottery* (London, 1980)

Hayes, J. W., *Ancient Lamps in the Royal Ontario Museum* (Toronto, 1980)

Hayes, J. W., 'The Glass', in P. M. Kenrick, *Excavations at Sabratha 1948–1951* (Gloucester, 1986), 297–311

Hepper. F. N., *Pharaoh's Flowers: The Botanical Treasures of Tutankhamun*. (London, 1990)

Hirschfeld, Y., *The Judean Desert Monasteries in the Byzantine Period* (New Haven and London, 1992)

Humphrey, J. H., *Excavations at Carthage Conducted by the University of Michgan 1975*, 1 (Tunis, 1976

Husson, G., 'L'habitat monastique en Égypte à la lumière des papyrus grecs, des textes chrétiens et de l'archéolcgie', in *Hommages à la mémoire de Serge Sauneron II* (Bulletin d'Egypte 82, Cairo, 1979), 191–207

Isings, C., *Romen Glass from Dated Finds (*Archaeologica Traiectine Edita ab Academiae Rheno-Traectinae Instituto Archaeologico 2, Djakarta, 1957)

Jacquet-Gordon, H., *Les ermitages chrétiens du désert d'Esna III, céramique et objets* (Cairo, 1972)

Jaritz, H. and Rodziewicz, M., 'Syene – Investigation of the Urban Remains in the Vicinity of the Temple of Isis (II)', *MDAIK* 52 (1996)

Jerome, *Regulae Sancti Pachomi: Praefatio7*, in J. P. Migne, (ed.), *Patrogia Latina*, 23.64. (Paris, 1841–64)

Jeuté, P., 'Monasteries in Nubia – an open issue' in *Nubica III/I, 1989–1993* (Warsaw, 1994), 59–97

Johnson, B., *Pottery from Karanis* (Michigan, 1981)

Jones, M., 'The Early Christian sites at Tell el-Amarna and Sheikh Said', *JEA* 77 (1991), 129–44

Kawanishi, H., *Akoris. Report of the excavation at Akoris in Middle Egypt 1981–1992* (Kyoto, 1995)

Kemp, B., 'Amarna's other period' in *Egyptian Archaeology* 3 (London, 1993), 13–14

Kemp, B. (ed.), *Amarna Reports VI* (Egypt Exploration Society Occasional Publications 10, London, 1995a

Kemp, B., 'The Kom el-Nana enclosure at Amarna' in *Egyptian Archaeology* 6 (London, 1995b), 12–17.

Kemp, B., 'Tell el-Amarna, 2000' *JEA* 86 (London, 2000), 12–17

Kemp, B., 'Settlement and landscape in the Amarna area in the Byzantine period', in J. Faiers, *Late Roman Pottery at Amarna and Related Studies* (Egypt Exploration Society, London, 2005), 11–57

Kenrick, P. M., *Excavations at Sabratha 1948–1951*. (Gloucester, 1986)

Keys, D., *Catastrophe. An Investigation into the Origins of the Modern World* (London, 1999)

Knowles, D., *The Religious Orders in England* II (Cambridge, 1955)

Larson, L. B., Vinther, R. M., Briffa, K. R., Mervin, T. M., Clausen, H. B., Jones, P. D., Siggaard-Anderson, M-L., Hammer, C. U. et al., 'New ice core evidence for a volcanic cause of the AD 536 dust-veil', *Geophysical Research Letters 35* (2008)

Layton, B., 'Social Structure and Food Consumption in an early Christian Monastery: The Evidence of Shenoute's Canons and the White Monastery Federation A.D. 385–465', *Le Muséon* 115 (2002), 25–55

Layton, B., 'Rules and the exercise of power in Shenoute's monastery; the problem of world replacement and Identity maintenance', in *Journal of Early Christian Studies* 15 (2007), 45–73

Layton, B., 'The ancient rules of Shenoute's monastic federation', in G. Gabra and H. N. Takla *Christianity and Monasticism in Upper Egypt,* 1 (Cairo, 2008), 73–90

Lecuyot, G. and Pierrat, G. 'Corpus de la céramique de Tôd. Fouilles 1980-1983 et 1990', in *CCE* 7 (2004), 145–203

Little, L. K. (ed.), *Plague and the End of Antiquity*, (New York, 2007)

Luff, R. and Bailey, G., 'The aquatic basis for ancient civilisations: the case of Synodontis schall and the Nile Valley', in Bailey, G., Charles, R., Winder, N. (eds), *Human Ecodynamics. Proceedings of the Association for Environmental Archaeology Conference 1998 held at the University of Newcastle upon Tyne. Symposia of the Association for Environmental archaeology* 19 (Oxford, 2000), 100–113

Luff, R. M., 'Monastic diet in Late Antique Egypt: zooarchaeological finds from Kom el-Nana and Tell el-Amarna, Middle Egypt', *Environmental Archaeology* 12 (2) (2007), 161–174

Luff, R. M. and Rowley-Conwy, P. (eds) *Whither Environmental Archaeology?* (Oxbow Monograph 38, Oxford, 1994)

Majcherek, G., 'Gazan amphorae: typology reconsidered',. in H. Meyza and J. Mlynarczyk (eds), *Hellenistic and Roman pottery in the Eastern Mediterranean – advances in scientific studies* (Warsaw, 1995), 163–79

Manniche, L., *An Ancient Egyptian Herbal* (2nd edn, London, 1993)

Martin, M, *La Laure de Dêr al Dîk à Antinoe* (Bibliothèque d'études coptes 8, Cairo, 1971)

Maspero, J. and Drioton, E., *Fouilles Exécutées a Baouît* (Mémoires Publiés par les Membres de l'Institut

Français d'Archéologie Orientale 59, Cairo, 1931

Meyer, C., *Glass from Quseir al-Qadim* (Chicago, 1992)

Monneret de Villard, U., *Description générale du monastére S. Simeon à Asouan* (Milan, 1927)

Mond, R. and Myers, O. H., *Temples of Armant* (London, 1940)

Montserrat, D., 'Early Byzantine Church Lighting: A New Text', *Orientalia* V64, fasc. 4 (Rome, 1995)

Morony M. G., 'For Whom Does the Writer Write?', in L. D. Little (ed.), *Plague and the End of Antiquity* (New York, 2007), 59–86

Michelucci, M., *La collezione de lucerne del Museo Egiziodi Firenze* (Florence, 1975)

Mysliwiec, K., *Keramik und Kleinfunde aus der Grabung im Tempel Sethos' I. in Gurna* (AVDAIK 57, Mainz, 1987)

Newberry, P., 'On the vegetable remains discovered in the cemetery of Hawara', in W. M. Flinders-Petrie, (ed.), *Hawara, Biahmu and Arsinoe* (London, 1889), 46–53

Orton, C., *Mathematics in archaeology* (London, 1980)

Palladius, *Historia Lausiaca*, ed. G. J. M. Bartelink,

Panagiotakopulu, E., 'Pharaonic Egypt and the origins of Plague', *Journal of Biogeography* 31, (2) (2004)

Parcak, S. H. 'Settlement pattern studies in the Nile's floodplain: satellite imagery analysis and ground survey in Middle Egypt and the Delta', (unpublished thesis, University of Cambridge, 2005)

Peacock, D. P. S. and Williams, D. F., *Amphorae and the Roman economy* (Harlow, 1986)

Peacock, D. P. S. and Blue, L. (eds), *Myos Hormos – Quseir al-Qaudim: Roman and Islamic ports on the Red Sea. Volume 1: Survey and excavations 1999–2003* (Oxford, 2006)

Peacock, D. P. S. and Maxfield, V. A. (eds),. *Mons Claudianus: Survey and Excavation, 1987–1993. Volume 1. Topography and Quarries.* (Fouilles de l'Institut français d'archéologie orientale due Caire 37, Cairo, 1997)

Peacock, D. P. S and Maxfield, V. A. (eds), *Mond Claudianus: survey and excavation 1987–1993. Volume II. Excavations: Part I* (Fouilles de Institut français d'archéologie orientale due Caire 43, Cairo, 2001)

Peña, J. Theodore, *Roman Pottery in the Archaeological Record* (New York, 2011)

Pierrat, G. 'Essai de Classification de la Céramique de Tôd', in *CCE* 2 (1991), 145–204

Pyke, G., 'Late Roman Egyptian amphora from squares U and V at Kom el-Nana', in J. Faiers, *Late Roman Pottery from Amarna and Related Studies* (London, 2005), 213–244

Petrie, W. M. F., *Tell El Amarna* (London, 1894)

Petrie, W. M.F., *Roman Ehnasya (Herakleopolis Magna) 1904* (London, 1905)

Procopius, *The Secret History*, G. A. Williamson, and P. Sarris (trs) (London, 2007)

Procopius, *History of the Wars Books I and II (The Persian War)*, H.B.Dewing (tr.), 1 (Cambridge, 1954)

Procopius, *History of the Wars III and IV*, H.B. Dewing (tr.) (London, 1989)

Quibell, J. E., *The Monastery of Apa Jeremias* (Excavations at Saqqara IV, Cairo, 1912)

Read, C. H. (ed.), *British Museum, A guide to the Early Christian and Byzantine antiquities in the department of British and Mediaeval Antiquities* (London, 1921)

Reece, R., 'Coins from Kom el-Nana', in J. Faiers, *Late Roman Pottery at Amarna and Related Studies* (London, 2005), 263–266

Riley, J. A., 'Pottery from the first session of excavation in the Caesarea hippodrome', *BASOR* 218 (1975), 25–63

Riley, J. A., 'The classification and quantification of the pottery', in A. J. Lloyd (ed.), *Excavations at Sidi Khrebish, Benghazi (Berenice),* 2 (Tripoli, 1979)

Riley, J. A, 'The pottery in fieldwork on the Red Sea coast: the 1987 season', *JARCE* 25 (1989), 149–61

Rodziewiec, M., *Alexandrie I, La céramique romaine tardive d'Alexandrie* (Warsaw, 1976)

Roeder, G., *Hermopolis 1929–1939. Vorläufiger Bericht über die Ausgrabunden in Hermopolis* (Hildesheim, 1959)

Rosen, W., *Justinian's Flea* (New York, 2007)

Rousseau, P., *Pachomius: the Making of a Community in Fourth-Century Egypt* (Berkeley, 1985)

Rowley-Conwy, R., 'Dung, Dirt and Deposits: site formation under conditions of near-perfect preservation at Qasr Ibrim, Egyptian Nubia', in *Whither Environmental Archaeology?* (Oxbow Monograph 38, Oxford, 1994), 33–38

Salzer, M. W., and Hughes, M. K., 'Bristlecone pine tree rings and volcanic eruptions over the last 5000 years', *Quaternary Research* 67 (1), (2007), 57–68

Sarris, P., 'Bubonic Plague in Byzantium. The Evidence of Non-Literary Sources',. in P. Little, *Plague and The End of Antiquity* (New York, 2007), 119–132

Sauneron, S. and Jacquet, J., *Les Hermitages Chrétiens du Désert D'Esna,* I (Cairo, 1972)

Sauneron, S. and Jacquet, J., *Les Hermitages Chrétiens du Désert D'Esna,* II (Cairo, 1972)

Shier, L. A., *Terracotta lamps from Karanis, Egypt* (Michigan, 1978)

Sidebotham, S. E. and Wendrich, W. Z. (eds), *Berenike 1994: Report of the 1994 excavations at Berenike (Egyptian Red Sea Coast) and the Survey of the Eastern Desert* (Leiden, 1995)

Sidebotham, S. E. and Wendrich, W. Z. (eds), *Berenike 1995: Report of the 1995 excavations at Berenike*

*(Egyptian Red Sea Coast) and the Survey of the Eastern Desert* (Leiden, 1996)

Sidebotham, S. E. and Wendrich, W. Z. (eds), *Berenike 1996: Report of the 1996 excavations at Berenike (Egyptian Red Sea Coast) and the Survey of the Eastern Desert* (Leiden, 1998)

Sidebotham, S. E. and Wendrich, W. Z. (eds), *Berenike 1997: Report of the 1997 excavations at Berenike (Egyptian Red Sea Coast) and the Survey of the Eastern Desert, including Excavations at Shenshef* (Leiden, 1999)

Sidebotham, S. E. and Wendrich, W. Z. (eds), *Berenike 1998: Report of the 1998 excavations at Berenike and the survey of the Egyptian eastern desert, including excavations at Wadi Kalalat* (Leiden, 2000)

Smith, C. A., 'Plague in the Ancient World: A Study from Thucydides to Justinian', *The Student Historical Journal* XXVIII, 1996–1997 (New Orleans, 1997), 43–58

Smith, W., *Archaeobotanical Investigations of Agriculture at Late Antique Kom el-Nana (Tell el-Amarna* (Egypt Exploration Society Excavation Memoir 70, London, 2003)

Spencer, J., *Excavations at El-Ashmunein II: The Temple Area* (London, 1989)

Tatton-Brown, V.A. 'The Glass', in H. R. Hurst and S. P. Roskams, *Excavations at Carthage: The British Mission I, pt. 1,* (Sheffield, 1984), 194–212

Timby, J. R., 'Red Slipped Wares', in M. Fulford and R. Tomber (eds), *Excavations at Sabratha 1948–1951. Volume II, The Finds Part 2. The Finewares and Lamps* (Society for Libyan Studies Monograph 3, London, 1994), 67–144

Tyldesley, J. A. and Snape, S. R., *Nazlet Tuna* (BAR IS 414, Oxford, 1988)

Urbaniak-Walczak, K., 'Deir el-Naqlun: die koptischen Texte aus der Ermitage nr.25', *JJP* 29 (1999), 93–136

Van Neer, W., Wouters, W., Rutschowscaya, M.-H., Delattre, A., Dixneuf, D., Desender, K., and Pablome J., 'Salted fish products from the Coptic monastery at Bawit, Egypt: evidence from the bones and texts', in H. H. Plogmann (ed.), *The role of fish in ancient time* (Leuven, 2007), 147–159

Waddell, H., *The Desert Fathers* (London, 1936)

Walters, C., *Monastic Archaeology in Egypt* (Warminster, 1974)

Wenke, R. J. and Pyne, N., 'The ceramics', in R. J. Wenke, *Archaeological Investigations at El-Hibeh 1980: Preliminary report* (*JARCE*, 9 (London, 1984), Appendix 199-121

Winlock, H. E. and Crum, W. E., *The Monastery of Epiphanius at Thebes* I (New York, 1926)

Whitby, M., *The Ecclesiastical History of Evagrius Scholasticus* (Liverpool, 2000)